THE NIXON PRESIDENCY

Also by Deborah Hart Strober and Gerald S. Strober

The Kennedy Presidency: An Oral History of the Era
The Reagan Presidency: An Oral History of the Era
The Monarchy: An Oral Biography of Elizabeth II

Also by Gerald S. Strober

American Jews: Community in Crisis
Billy Graham: His Life and Faith
Graham: A Day in Billy's Life
Religion and the New Majority

THE NIXON PRESIDENCY

An Oral History
of the Era

DEBORAH HART STROBER
AND
GERALD S. STROBER

Brassey's, Inc.
Washington, D.C.

Library of Congress Cataloging-in-Publication Data

Strober, Deborah H. (Deborah Hart), 1940–
    The Nixon presidency : an oral history of the era / Deborah Hart Strober and Gerald S. Strober.— 1st ed.
        p.   cm.
    Rev. ed. of: Nixon : an oral history of his presidency / Gerald S. and Deborah H. Strober. c1994.
    Includes index.
    ISBN 1-57488-582-0 (acid-free paper)
    1. Nixon, Richard M. (Richard Milhous), 1913–   2. United States—Politics and government—1969–1974.   3. Nixon, Richard M. (Richard Milhous), 1913—Friends and associates—Interviews.   4. Oral history.   I. Strober, Deborah H. (Deborah Hart), 1940–   II. Strober, Gerald S. Nixon. c1994.   III. Title.
    E856.S76   2003
    973.924′092—dc21   2003004963

Softcover ISBN 1-57488-582-0
(alk. paper)

Printed in the United States of America on acid-free paper that meets the American National Standards Institute Z39-48 Standard.

Brassey's, Inc.
22841 Quicksilver Drive
Dulles, Virginia 20166

First Edition

10   9   8   7   6   5   4   3   2   1

In loving memory of our late parents,
Leah Greenhouse Hochstein,
Faye Cogert Strober, and Philip Strober.

You are constantly in our thoughts.
Oh, how we wish you were still among us.

Contents

Foreword

It is now almost twenty years since Richard Milhous Nixon became the first president in American history forced to resign that office.

Our decision to undertake this project was based on our belief that by virtue of the passage of two decades since 1974 an opportunity has been created for an objective approach to the events of the Nixon presidency.

In the intervening years since his resignation as the thirty-seventh president of the United States, Mr. Nixon sought and received an injunction against the release of over 2,900 hours of tapes and thousands of pages of documents that make up a significant portion of the primary source material of his presidency.

In light of this situation, we determined that the most effective way to chronicle the Nixon presidency would be through the medium of oral history, in which the views and recollections of a wide cross-section of Mr. Nixon's associates and contemporaries could be utilized as the depictions of those who were insiders during the tumultuous years.

In compiling this project we were constantly reminded of the challenge of dealing with a person, who at that time was still alive and—our research tells us—was in contact with many of our interviewees.

Our first hurdle was to obtain interviews: Would our subjects be reluctant to speak with us? Or, if they agreed to be interviewed, would certain subjects be off-limits? Or, would they be less than candid, seeking to bolster in print their relationship with the former president? Or, the opposite: Would his detractors seek to vent their hostility in our book?

In order to chronicle the major aspects of the Nixon presidency, we developed a list of potential interviewees among Mr. Nixon's associates and contemporaries.

We then wrote to these individuals, apprising them of our project and requesting interviews. Many of them replied by return mail, while the remainder were reached by telephone.

While most of the approximately ninety interviews—each lasting from one to three-and-a-half hours—were conducted in person, throughout the United States and in Israel and Egypt, some of them were done by telephone, in order to accommodate individual interviewees' needs.

As far as we know, we are the only writers to have interviewed, during the past five years, more than 200 of the most prominent political figures of the 1960s and 1970s. As we had experienced with *"Let Us Begin Anew,"* our oral history of the presidency of John F. Kennedy, most of the Nixon insiders and contemporaries with whom we sought interviews were willing to cooperate, and with no preconditions regarding subjects of discussion.

With regard to Mr. Nixon, on January 6, 1994, we sent a fax to Kathy O'Connor, an aide to the former president, noting that we had not received an answer to an interview request letter sent to Mr. Nixon in late 1992, and again requesting an interview, stating that, "We would like to have his reactions to statements made by our interviewees."

We never received a response to our January 6 fax, but on the following day, we did receive a fax from John H. Taylor, the director of the Richard Nixon Library and Birthplace, which reads as follows:

Dear Ms. and Mr. Strober:

The Library & Birthplace being something of a watering hole for the Nixon faithful, a number of eminences have contacted us in the past few months to ask if we know anything about your oral history project. We have had to plead ignorance enough times that I thought it might be useful for both our sakes if I was to get in touch and see what you might be willing to tell me about it. I would greatly appreciate any information you may be able and willing to share. My numbers and addresses are below.

With best wishes

We reached Mr. Taylor by telephone two days later and in a twenty-minute conversation we briefed him on the project.

In our research, we were struck by the parallels in the political careers of Presidents Kennedy and Nixon: Kennedy and Nixon were of

the same generation; they both emerged from World War II military service as staunch "cold warriors" and political conservatives; they began
their respective political careers in 1947, as members of the first postwar
Congress, and both were later elected to the Senate; Mr. Nixon went on
to be nominated and elected vice-president of the United States, while
Mr. Kennedy sought, but failed to win, his party's vice-presidential nomination; they were the presidential nominees of their respective parties in
1960; television reduced the fortunes of one while elevating those of the
other candidate; and sadly for the nation—and perhaps, the world—neither man would serve out his elected term of office, albeit for very different reasons.

But whereas in death President Kennedy became a mythological figure whose reputation later suffered through the revelations of negative
material concerning his personal life, President Nixon, who resigned in
disgrace due to his involvement in a series of events that fall under the
rubric of Watergate, enjoyed a rehabilitation of sorts prior to his recent
death.

Our research of the Nixon presidency, as in our earlier efforts concerning the Kennedy administration, recalled to us those events that had
impacted upon our young adulthood. At that time, we were observers
from afar; now, twenty years later, through our interview process, we
have had the good fortune to be propelled toward a closer examination
of the central events of that era.

We have faithfully attempted to recount these events, and in doing
so we believe that we have explicated much information on the Nixon
years. Yet, we realize that only in future generations will all of the outstanding questions concerning the Nixon presidency be answered.

Deborah Hart Strober
Gerald S. Strober
April 1994

Acknowledgments

Nixon: An Oral History of His Presidency could not have been undertaken without the cooperation of our interviewees, all of whom responded to our requests for interviews with courtesy, and gave of their time and best efforts at recollection of the complex and sometimes perplexing events of President Nixon's two administrations.

We also appreciate the cooperation of Scott Parham, supervisory archivist of the Nixon Presidential Materials Project of the National Archives and Records Administration.

As we sought to illuminate some of the dark paths of the Nixon presidency, we received support from our professional colleagues, personal friends, and family. Among our colleagues in the creation and preparation of this book, we are especially indebted to Carol Shookhoff, who as in the case of our oral history of the Kennedy presidency, *"Let Us Begin Anew,"* patiently coped with reams of manuscript and revisions as she transformed our typescript into a neatly word-processed finished project; our editor at HarperCollins, Buz Wyeth, whose calm assurance was most welcome as we sought the most effective context for our material; and our agent, Mitchell Rose, whose counsel we freely sought and received at all stages of our endeavor.

It goes without saying that our siblings and their children are most deserving of our gratitude for their faith in our project, and their oft-repeated assurances regarding its outcome. To them and to our children, Jeremy Benjamin and his precious Gaby; and Lori, Jonathan, and Robin Strober, we say: thank you for your interest in the Nixon era; thank you for your critical opinions; and most important, thank you for being *you*—caring and thoughtful individuals.

Part One

The 1968 Election and Beyond

1

Nixon is Elected President

THE 1968 PRESIDENTIAL CAMPAIGN

The Prelude

On November 5, 1968, Richard Milhous Nixon narrowly defeated the Democratic candidate, Vice-President Hubert H. Humphrey, for the presidency of the United States in a comeback unprecedented in the annals of U.S. political history.

Mr. Nixon's victory, by only 550,000 votes (43.4 percent of the popular vote), followed both his disputed loss to John F. Kennedy in the 1960 presidential race—vote counts in Illinois, Missouri, and Texas had been questioned—and to Edmund (Pat) Brown, Sr., in the 1962 California gubernatorial race, following which Mr. Nixon bitterly denounced the press and, seemingly, sealed his political fate.

Upon losing the California race in 1962, Mr. Nixon moved to New York, where he joined the law firm, Mudge, Rose* and began to think ahead to future political activity.

Leonard Garment, assistant to the president There had been discussion about Nixon's joining Mudge, Rose; the firm didn't have what most large firms should have—a public partner. Although Nixon had been an automatic bête noire to me, a New York Jewish liberal, he seemed to be

---

* Which became known as Nixon, Mudge, Rose, Guthrie, Alexander, and Mitchell.

what the doctor ordered for the firm. There were disputes about this: He was discredited; damaged goods. But the dispute was academic, because Elmer Bobst—the head of Warner Lambert,* one of our major clients—wanted him in the firm. I also wanted him; he was a man of real size and significance—a major figure in American history. I also thought he would make things more interesting for us. Shortly after he joined the firm, I went in to see him. It was a visit of some duration, in which he made a more or less complete psychological inventory of me. He mentioned that he believed in hard work, and that it wasn't necessary for all lawyers to come from Harvard or Yale. I fell under the mysterious, charismatic charm of this less than handsome man, because the quality about Nixon that immediately struck one was that he looked like Nixon. The nature of our discussion showed me that he was not out of politics, by any means; the subtext of the conversation was the political future of Richard Nixon, so with Rose Mary Woods, I was almost the first person he worked with as he looked five years ahead.

Marshall Green, assistant secretary of state for Far Eastern and East Asian affairs; U.S. ambassador to Australia He came out to Indonesia and stayed with us for two nights when I was ambassador,† and he met with President Suharto and other officials. I gave a dinner party, with Mr. Nixon as the honored guest, and after dinner, we sat down and talked for two or three hours. He took out a tape recorder, which surprised me. We talked about China and Far Eastern policy, in general. It was a good conversation. I had thought of Nixon, as vice-president, as having been ultra-right wing—a China-firster. But he was very different: he was open-minded, with a very clear understanding of the interrelationships between the great powers. He seemed to be remarkably enlightened, not only about the world in general, but with particular reference to China and the Soviet Union.

I found him very easy to talk to. We had a lot of shared opinions and values—a man I had been prepared to dislike because of his connections with [Senator Joseph R.] McCarthy [R-Wis.], who had done such disservice to the Foreign Service. When we met with President Suharto, he took out a yellow foolscap [legal pad] and took down notes on what they were saying—he explained to Suharto that what he was saying was of such importance to history that he wanted to make sure he had it down correctly. When my wife and I drove him to the airport, I said, "You were taking notes of what the president said, and you tape-recorded our conversation. What do you do with all this material?" He said, "When I get back to New

---

* The pharmaceuticals company.
† In 1967.

York, my secretary transcribes it, files it, and cross-files it; and I have it there for the future."

Backward Glances

Kenneth Rush, U. S. ambassador to West Germany; deputy secretary of defense; deputy secretary of state One of my students at the Duke [University] Law School was Richard Nixon. He was very thoughtful, he had qualities of statesmanship, and I thought he would have a great political future. When the time came for him to go to work, I recommended that he go to California, and go into politics, rather than going to New York. He went to California, but not because of me; he didn't get a job in New York.

Herbert Klein, director of communications for the White House and the executive branch I got to know him in 1946, when he first ran for Congress. I was just out of the Navy, as he was, and was the news editor of a small paper in Alhambra [California] and also covered politics. He ran, basically, on domestic issues: housing, jobs, price controls—the bread-and-butter issues. After the election [to Congress], he would come back to the district and have breakfast with the local publishers. He would come by and we would have coffee. He went to Europe with the Herter Committee° and then made a separate trip to Greece and Turkey, and I remember his talking of the dangers of Tito;† I got the feeling that he had an above-average understanding of things. He had the ability to attract a lot of young people—a lot of us who were "Junior Chamber" types.‡ The Hiss°° case got him a lot of publicity, but there were basic issues: the Whittier Narrows Dam—a flood-control dam—was a real bread-and-butter issue in that district.

THE 1952 PRESIDENTIAL CAMPAIGN

Herbert Brownell, attorney general, Eisenhower administration; Republican leader I was with Eisenhower the night before Nixon's

---

° Headed by state department official Christian Herter during the Eisenhower administration, to assess the post-World War II threat posed by the Soviet Union to European nations.

† Josef Broz, the postwar leader of Yugoslavia, who although communist, defied Moscow.

‡ The Junior Chamber of Commerce, a series of local organizations comprised largely of young, up-and-coming professionals.

°° Nixon was a prominent member of the House Un-American Activities Committee (HUAC) of the U.S. House of Representatives, before which Hiss, a state department official, was brought when he was named by Whittaker Chambers, a former communist, as a member of the party.

["Checkers"] speech.* I got a call from General Eisenhower to come out to Cincinnati and join him in his railroad car. We met for a considerable length of time—it was after midnight; his stops were over for the day. He asked what I thought of the Nixon episode. He was undecided as to what to do. He said that he had received a lot of conflicting advice. I told him my political opinion: "If you find out that there was anything shady about the fund, then you must get a replacement; but if it's as it appears to be—perfectly on the level, and used to supplement political expenses—then I can advise you that if you throw him off the ticket, you will be defeated. The campaign will become chaotic and so disorganized that you won't recover." Eisenhower had asked accountants to go in and see if everything was in order. He did not tell me that night what he planned to do, but it was clear to me that if the accountants found that Nixon had not spent any of that fund for favors to constituents—or things of that sort—he would keep Nixon on the ticket. I would be surprised if he had anyone else in mind, at that point; he felt Nixon was entitled to his day in court.

NIXON AS VICE-PRESIDENT

Rocco Siciliano, undersecretary of commerce He is very intense, very decent and courteous, not revealing of what he really thought of whatever substance you were there to discuss. I once made a presentation to the Cabinet on the federal pay system. When I finished, Secretary [of State John Foster] Dulles immediately objected. He said, "You don't mean to include those covered by the Foreign Service Act?" I was very young, but I had to meet him head-on, so I said, "Yes, we mean to include this group." Dulles was outraged. I didn't know what to do. I watched the president's [Eisenhower's] face. Then Nixon winked at me and nodded his head, indicating that I should stay with it. And the president said, "Fine. We'll talk about that." Nixon's support meant a lot to me, because he knew that Dulles walked on water.

Robert Hartmann, aide to Gerald R. Ford, majority leader, U.S. House of Representatives, vice-president and president of the United States One of the drivers on the Hill took sick, and Nixon went out to the hospital to see him. He asked the fellow, John, if he needed anything. John

---

* A nationally televised address in which Mr. Nixon defended his use of a special fund established by contributors. Named the "Checkers" speech in reference to the Nixon family's pet dog, the address was credited with saving Mr. Nixon's candidacy as General Eisenhower's vice-presidential running mate.

says, "Mr. Vice-President, they don't let us have any beer. Do you think you could sneak me a few bottles?" Nixon replied, "Never mind. I am going to send you a whole case." Nixon did, and never told anybody. I remember this when people say he can't have a human side.

Herbert Brownell He was pretty young in those days, but he had an enthusiasm about him. He made lots of friends for the administration. Eisenhower sent him on quite a few missions, and he performed ably. I was quite close to him in those years, and our relationship was harmonious.

Maurice Stans, campaign aide, 1968; secretary of commerce; chairman, Finance Committee to Reelect the President, 1972 Nixon came in to see me during the summer.* I was then director of the budget in the Eisenhower administration. He asked me what my views were on the idea of a tax cut; he had suggested it and it hadn't gotten into the public eye. Eisenhower was against it; he didn't think the budget could afford it. I think Nixon was looking for support, but I couldn't support him under those circumstances. I told him that my job was to balance the budget. Since then, I have thought about that many times. If I had had any good reason to go along with him on the idea, it might very well have meant that he would have been elected president; I think that was one issue that might have made the difference in that very close election.

Vice-President Nixon's Relationship with President Eisenhower

Robert Finch, counselor to the president; secretary of Health, Education and Welfare (HEW) At the outset, it was arm's-length. Nixon worked on that with some intensity, in terms of doing the chores he was given and playing the good soldier, particularly in the diplomatic field. When I came to work with him in 1958, his stock—internationally and nationally—was well down, because the Republicans had taken a real beating in 1958; he had been the leading campaigner. Rockefeller was the only successful Republican, and he was way ahead in the polls, in terms of people who wanted to see him as the nominee of the Republican Party. But when Sherman Adams† and some of the others who had been personally hostile

---

* Of 1960.
† Appointments secretary to President Eisenhower, who resigned in the wake of an influence-peddling scandal, after having accepted an expensive vicuña coat from industrialist Bernard Goldfine.

to Nixon were out, and as Rockefeller began to attack Eisenhower's proposals on armaments and other issues, the president's attitude began to change dramatically, and then, when Nixon began to win the primaries, he came solidly on board. So what had been a limited and tentative relationship at the start, developed considerably. The family ties came together with Julie [Julie Nixon, Richard Nixon's younger daughter] and David [David Eisenhower, grandson of President Dwight David Eisenhower, who would marry Ms. Nixon in 1968]. By the time of the 1960 campaign, it [the relationship between Eisenhower and Nixon] was in pretty good shape, and Nixon—even though we all wanted Eisenhower to do more—had said to me, "Don't push him too hard," because he was worried about him, physically.

Herbert Brownell They never were pals; they were of such different ages and backgrounds. Eisenhower was quite formal in all of his relationships with political associates.

Maurice Stans I observed them working together in Cabinet meetings, and it was what I considered to be a normal relationship between a president and a vice-president; Eisenhower was definitely in charge. Nixon was not afraid to make recommendations or suggestions, so it appeared to me they were both doing a darn good job. I saw no evidence of any friction, no evidence of any closeness, in their relationship.

President Eisenhower's response when asked by the press about Vice-President Nixon's qualifications as the 1960 presidential candidate. *

Herbert Brownell Eisenhower told me that the question had come at the end of the news conference. As far as he was concerned, the conference had ended, so he didn't think the thing through. He didn't want to reopen the press conference; he was annoyed at the reporters shouting at him. He just didn't foresee the public reaction to his answer. He did not mean to brush Nixon off; he thought if he were going to make a statement on the serious issue as to whether Nixon would stay on the ticket, he would need time to collect his thoughts. Nixon was angry when he saw how the media treated it: that it was a deliberate slap by the president. This was exacerbated by the fact that, at that time, there was talk of other candidates: Harold Stassen†

---

* During a White House press conference on August 24, 1960, when asked by *Time* magazine correspondent Charles Mohr to give an example of a major idea of Nixon's "that you have adopted," the president responded, "If you give me a week, I might think of one. I don't remember."
† A Republican leader.

had announced that he wanted to be vice-president. Eisenhower was not deliberately snubbing Nixon, but I don't think that Nixon was ever convinced of that. Those around Nixon resented the way Eisenhower spoke; they didn't realize the circumstances under which the statement had been made. It encouraged those around Nixon to say, "We have to fight all the harder for this."

THE 1960 PRESIDENTIAL RACE

On November 8, 1960, Mr. Nixon was defeated by John F. Kennedy by a margin of approximately 118,000 votes. There was much speculation at the time— and there continues to be—as to why Mr. Nixon did not contest the result.

Herbert Klein Nixon had to decide whether to contest the results. Some people had gone to Chicago and found a lot of preliminary evidence that some votes had been stolen. We talked about it, and Nixon decided that it would disrupt the country too much were he to contest, and that it would take a long time, and leave the country in turmoil. I felt that he should not contest, but there were others who strongly felt that he should, including his campaign manager, Len [Leonard] Hall. Bob [Robert] Finch agreed with me. But he made up his own mind.

Robert Finch Many of the ballots had disappeared in Cook County [Illinois]. [Senator Everett] Dirksen told us about that. He said, "You won't get a recount; they [the ballots] are already gone." In Missouri, the only way to get a recount is to have the state legislature pass a law that allows for a recount to be taken—which would have taken three or four months. I can go on and on: Texas, et cetera. In each case, there was a whole series of problems, all of which would have resulted in there being a complete stalemate and our being without a president for six months on; it would have gone on and on. Nixon felt very strongly that the United States couldn't afford to be leaderless; that was why he basically made a quick decision, against a lot of people who wanted to challenge it, simply because it wasn't really workable.

Herbert Brownell He felt that to have a period of several months of a recount would be very divisive. He was always very meticulous in thinking out the reactions of foreign nations to what happened in Washington, and he foresaw a lot of chaos if the recount were to proceed. He didn't have a clear mandate at the polls, so it would have been seen as a political dog-fight—grabbing for power—and the public would not be on his side; he would look like a sore loser. I think he felt that if there had been a recount in Texas and Cook County, Illinois, he probably would have won. I think so, too. Election fraud in Texas and Cook County was more or less a way of life.

After Nixon's Loss to Kennedy

Herbert Klein Herbert Hoover* had a call from [Ambassador Joseph P.] Joe Kennedy to explore the possibility of a Nixon-Kennedy meeting on how to deal with the postelection period. I went over to the vice-president and told him about the call, and he immediately brightened up. We went out to a phone booth in a restaurant lobby and he put in a call to [President Dwight D.] Eisenhower, who was at Augusta [Georgia], to tell him about it. The maître d' says, "There is a call from Jack Kennedy," so while Nixon is talking to Eisenhower in the phone booth, I'm talking to Jack Kennedy on the maître d's phone. It was a nice conversation; he commended me on my job as press secretary;† he said he had waited to make his announcement until he saw me on television. I told him that I expected the vice-president to arrive soon, and if I could have his number, I was sure that Nixon would want to call him; I didn't want to tell him that Nixon was talking to Eisenhower. When the two calls were finished, we talked about what Eisenhower said, and then Nixon went back to the phone booth, put a dime in,‡ and called Jack Kennedy. That's how they got together to settle their differences in the postelection period.

Following his defeat in the 1960 presidential election, Mr. Nixon returned to California, where he ran for governor in 1962 against Edmund [Pat] Brown, Sr.

Maurice Stans He came to see me, among others, before he decided to run. I was one of those who took the attitude that he'd be better off if he did run than if he didn't. First of all, the party needed him—or somebody like him; secondly, it didn't appear that [Edmund P.] Brown would be difficult to beat; and thirdly, if he didn't run, it might appear as though he was shying

---

* A Republican, and the thirty-first president of the United States.
† During the 1960 campaign.
‡ In 1960, it cost ten cents to make a local telephone call from a public booth.

away from an obligation to his party. It was a close decision for me, and for other people, but I said, "I would go for running to keep you active; to keep you in the public eye. And as a governor, you would have a much better platform to run for president."

Gerald Warren, deputy press secretary After losing by a close, if not questionable, margin in 1960, he felt the need to redeem himself. This was a decision made in haste, which he later wished he hadn't taken. He also needed a base and a challenge, so this was a target of opportunity.

ON THE CAMPAIGN TRAIL

Richard Bergholz, political editor, the *Los Angeles Times* Nixon was hard to like. We'd gone on a campaign tour—a typical Nixon tour. It was organized right to the nines. We arrived at a hotel near the Oakland airport. This was their first stop. They worked in some time in their structured schedule for social time, which meant that after we had checked into our rooms and were down at the bar having a drink, Nixon and Pat would come down and chat with us. Well, we thought that was just great: we'll get a chance to talk about something other than why you hate the press. He comes down, and Pat disappears into the woodwork, and we suddenly realize: What can we talk to Nixon about? The only subject we could find to talk to him about was football. The season was starting and he professed some knowledge because—as he's said so many times—he was a third-stringer benchwarmer on the Whittier football team—that qualified him as an expert. After we exhausted the football subject, there wasn't anything left for us to talk to him about. It was very stiff. I could sense that someone had said to him: Go down and charm those guys; be nice to them; show them what a warm human being you are. So there was a lot of what seemed to be forced conviviality at the beginning, and when that ran out, there wasn't anything left. In a relatively short time he turned around and went back to the room.

James Wrightson, editor, the *Sacramento Bee* When he started his campaign for governor, they wanted to give him a California glow. There is a highway here called the Forty-Nine—that's where the Forty-Niners* went,

* People who came from the East to seek their fortunes in 1849 in what became known as the "Gold Rush."

up in northern California. So we started out in the morning on a bus with him and stopped at all these little towns. And as they used to do with Eisenhower, they let these kids out of school in these towns, and it made quite a crowd. We had a lunch, and the Republican county chairman introduced him and he went on and on about Nixon. As we walked back to the bus, I happened to find myself beside Nixon, so to make small talk, I said, "Gee, a lot of people saw you at breakfast"—he had met a Brownie Scout troop there—and Nixon said, "Those goddamn Brownies! It took a half an hour just to meet those goddamn Brownies." I said, "Well, the chairman of the Republican Party must have read *Six Crises*° a couple of times," and Nixon said, "Yeah. That son-of-a-bitch went on and on; I had to cut the nuts out of my speech because of that." He could have said to me: It was a nice day, but he had to express his resentments. He was an angry man.

When he would go to the local areas, you would ask him about farm labor, and his people resented that. One of his aides was griping to me. He said, "You know, we come to some of these towns and they ask him how many black swans should be on the lake?" That is what the local paper wanted to know; that's the only thing they had. He was very impatient about that. First, he didn't know; and second, he didn't think it was important, and he let them know he didn't think it was important. The man didn't take advice very well. I knew someone who was in the campaign who told me of the time Nixon was in a cab and this fellow said, "Why don't you go by the McClatchey newspaper and talk to them?" Nixon said, "I wouldn't give them the sweat off my balls." This is a local paper, so instead of Nixon asking him: What should I tell them? he says this. This kind of thing turned people down [off].

Robert Finch It's very hard to sustain a political base from Washington, and he recognized this. I was very much opposed to his running for governor; I knew he wasn't physically ready; he wasn't emotionally ready. In a statewide race, there are many nitty-gritty issues. But he had run for president in 1960, and after the Bay of Pigs, he couldn't have a press conference without having to go into international issues, and everybody would just say, "He's running for president, again." Kennedy was very popular, and Nixon may have felt he didn't want to go against him again. Once he had been defeated in California, he was pretty well written off, and once he decided to go back to New York to practice law, he was not actively thinking about running for president.

° Richard Nixon, *Six Crises* (Doubleday, 1962).

Charles Wiggins, member, U.S. House of Representatives (R-Calif.); member, House Judiciary Committee His loss to John Kennedy was a major blow, but he still aspired to be president and understood that his political base was California, and by running for governor he could maintain the exposure that the position would afford him, and springboard that into a later presidential candidacy. So he went back to California, joined a law firm, bought a lovely home in the Trusdale Estates section of Los Angeles, and promptly ran for governor. He ran a good race, but he didn't have his heart in it. After he lost the election, he bugged out of California. I thought that, politically, it was very sensible to move to New York and get himself away from the isolation of California and into the mainstream of finance, law, politics, and government that is afforded to a resident of New York City.

"YOU WON'T HAVE NIXON TO KICK AROUND ANYMORE . . . "

On the morning after his defeat by Mr. Brown, Nixon uttered these bitter words concerning the press treatment of him during the campaign, which seemingly put an end to his political career.

Herbert Brownell The majority of his advisers had wanted him to run in 1962 [for governor of California] as preparation for the next presidential election [in 1964], so at the time he definitely expected to run again, and beat Kennedy. At the press conference, he did not think through his comments; he was furious at losing, and furious at the way the media handled the campaign. He had been bitterly attacked, and responded humanly, without regard to political consequences: he lost his temper, and the media loved that. It proved what they had been saying about him: that he wasn't mature enough to be president. So, it was a political mistake of the first magnitude, and they have never let up on it, to this day.

Richard Bergholz When he came out here to run for governor, he thought that he was going to get the same treatment he had received from the press in the presidential campaign. He suddenly discovered that there were reporters out here who probably knew a hell of a lot more about what was happening in California than he did; it was our bailiwick. He discovered that he couldn't finesse it anymore; he couldn't just get by with generalities, because someone would nail him as to details. As we went along, this made him madder and madder. This had a lot to do with his frustration the day after he lost. Maybe someone on his staff had said: "You can't go out there and talk about water problems in California unless you know what you are talking about." He would have said, "Oh sure, I know California. I've been a congressman here. I know the problems." Well, he didn't know. And furthermore, Pat Brown was in large measure the father of many of the water improvements; he had the advantage of knowledge and he had a good record; Nixon wasn't running against somebody who had botched it.

Nixon did appear to be inadequately informed on some issues. Running for governor is a little different from running for king of the U.S.A. He can talk about the wonderful achievements of the Eisenhower years, the Cold War, and communism. But that's not a terribly effective selling point in California.

James Wrightson Someone close to Nixon told me the candidate had been drinking all election night, and taking sleeping pills, and sometimes those pills go the other way—they keep you awake, and that is the way that person explained the speech. By ten in the morning, Nixon had been up all night; he had been brooding, been drinking, and that is how the outburst was explained. It was not a planned thing.

Herbert Klein He was exhausted—out on his feet, mentally and physically—so we left him alone in his suite.* Early in the morning, Bob Finch, Bob Haldeman, and I went into the suite. The first thing Nixon said to me was, "Goddamn it, Herb; don't talk me into going down to see the press." I said, "We don't intend to; our intent is to do it just like we did in 1960; we think you need to send a concession wire to Pat Brown and thank the workers, and then I'll go down at the set time and have a press conference and announce your concession, and give our analysis as to why we think you lost."

We left him. I went down, and at about this time, he came out of his suite and started to thank the various workers for what they had done. Then two things occurred: he went to thank an assistant television producer—who was Italian, and very emotional—and as he was thanking him, this fellow broke into tears. At about that time, two close friends of his came up and said, "Goddamn it, Dick. You can't let the press chase you out; you ought to go down and tell them what you think."

We had set it up that while I was doing the press conference, he would go out through the lobby and into a car and drive home. One of the people who was at the car, to let him in, was then-campaign aide Pete Wilson. Suddenly—I am having this press conference—I hear applause across the lobby, and I think that people have spotted Nixon leaving, and I announce that he's

* At the Century Plaza Hotel, in Los Angeles.

left. But I see Bob Haldeman rushing across, waving at me, and the next thing I know, Nixon is tapping me on the shoulder, and he has started his comments. He felt good that he had gotten it off his chest. I took him to the car, and he apologized for doing something he knew I didn't like. Then he went home and I went off with a friend and got a drink.

Raymond Price, assistant to the president I remember reading the wire copy on his statement. I thought it made a lot of sense; he had been kicked around pretty mercilessly by the media, and I thought his was a rather restrained commentary. I guess that this was the first time anyone in my profession had been talked back to by a politician; it has since become a little less uncommon for politicians not to pander to the press. In the 1968 campaign, a lot of people were saying that he had to worry that one of the Democrats was bound to play that tape and destroy him for it, so we looked at that television clip—and others—to help us find some means of presenting Nixon on television in a way that would let the public see the Nixon we knew—who was so much more impressive than the one they perceived. This led, among other things, to the *Man in the Arena* format that Roger Ailes produced for us. When I saw the clip, I knew that the opposition was not going to play it, because the actual clip was so much milder than the myth about it was.

Robert Finch My sense of it then was that he was certainly through for the short haul, but that he would probably emerge in some subsequent Cabinet, or in some public role. But I didn't regard him as a finished political property at that point.

Ronald Ziegler, press secretary, White House I was twenty-three at the time of the 1962 campaign. I had become very involved in political public relations. Certainly, there was a first impression that Nixon's political career was over with that "You won't have me to kick around anymore"; it sort of brought closure to the campaign. But it became old news pretty quickly, if one knew Richard Nixon; he got heavily involved in the 1964 campaign, and you could foresee political possibilities at that time.

RUN-UP TO THE 1968 CAMPAIGN

Upon resuming his career as an attorney in New York, Mr. Nixon maintained his keen interest in politics, working on behalf of Barry Goldwater's presidential candidacy in 1964.

Building his own constituency through the fostering of relationships with grassroots Republicans, Mr. Nixon by late 1966 had begun to seriously consider a bid for the presidency in 1968.

Maurice Stans When he decided to go to New York, I observed that nobody seemed to be giving him a farewell party, so I invited him to a farewell party at my home. I had about fifty people who had been active in California politics as guests, and it made a distinct impression on him—and on me—because I didn't understand why he didn't have more friends seeing him off. It was the only farewell party that was given for him. By coincidence, I moved to New York within a year after he did; by coincidence, I took an apartment two blocks from his; I had a position with a company on Wall Street, and by coincidence, his office was two blocks from mine. And we began to see each other from time to time. I was in on some of the earliest discussions—there were three or four at the Plaza—as to whether Nixon should be a candidate and, of course, he was always noncommittal.

The first step in getting him support was to get him around the country in 1966. I raised some of the money; Peter Flanigan* raised some of the money. We raised enough money to get him around the country and make a lot of speeches on behalf of candidates. That brought him back into the forefront and created a lot of obligations on the part of local politicians to think about Nixon if he ran for president. Our meetings continued into '67, and in the early part of the year, somebody said: "We have to have a committee." And Nixon and Haldeman, and a few others, got together and—lo and behold—I became chairman of the first Nixon for President Committee in 1967. I took the year 1968 off from my business on Wall Street and set out first as chairman of the committee, and then much more logically, as chairman of the Finance Committee, to raise the money to get him elected. From then on, I had very little contact with the Campaign Committee.

Raymond Price On Washington's birthday [February 22], 1967, I woke up with one of the worst hangovers of my life. I got a call from my old friend, Walter Thayer, who had been president of the *New York Herald Tribune*. He said that he had received a call the night before from Dick Nixon, wondering if I might have an interest in joining him for what might be a campaign for the presidency in 1968. This was about six months after the *Trib* had folded; I had not even thought of who my candidates for 1968 would

---

* White House aide.

be—I had led the *Tribune* in supporting LBJ [Lyndon B. Johnson] over Goldwater in 1964. I had never been anti-Nixon; I had supported him over Rockefeller in 1960. I told Walter, "I will talk to Nixon, but as long as he understands that I probably won't do this." Ten minutes later, the phone rang again, and a deep voice said, "This is Dick Nixon. Can you come to lunch?" I dug through my hangover remedies, traveled across the park, and had lunch at his apartment on Fifth Avenue. I spent three of the most fascinating hours I had ever spent—talking about life, literature, philosophy, politics, and personalities. I found—as I would later discover with people who had only known him through the media—that he was vastly more impressive than I had expected.

In anticipation of seeking the Republican nomination, Mr. Nixon invited a select group of conservatives within the Republican Party to his apartment at 812 Fifth Avenue in 1967.

William Rusher, a leader of the Conservative movement; publisher, *National Review* Nixon was quite relaxed and, as near as he can, was enjoying himself. To me, the most interesting and substantive part of the afternoon was that whenever Nixon discussed any subject, he did so in terms of alternative ways of looking at it; he seemed to be captivated by this polar nature of the universe. He would say, "Well, on the one hand . . . " Then he would flip his hands and say, "Well, on the other hand . . . " This went on all afternoon. I remember that, at one point, there was a telephone message for Bill [William F.] Buckley [Jr., a conservative Republican and editor of the *National Review*], and the butler, Manolo Sanchez, came in—in a white jacket—and gave Buckley the message, in broken English. Buckley shifted to Spanish, as did Manolo, and Nixon was listening, fascinated. At the end, Buckley said, "Gracias," and Nixon said, "Well, at least I got through that."

Gearing Up for the Campaign

Dwight Chapin, appointments secretary to the president In June 1967 [H. R.—Harry Robbins] Haldeman came to New York and we had dinner. He told me to expect a call from Rose Woods, and that I should think about whether I would like to go to work for Nixon. I was so excited, I could hardly stand it. I got called down to the law firm and went in to see Nixon. He said, "Dwight, it looks like I'm going to take a stab at this presidential thing; you will start work in a month." He never said, "Would you like the job?" He just assumed it, which I found fascinating. My dad thought I had lost my mind, since who would want to work for Nixon at this juncture, because he was pretty dead.

Donald Rumsfeld, director, Office of Economic Opportunity; counselor to the president; director, Cost of Living Council; U. S. ambassador to the North Atlantic Treaty Organization (NATO) In 1967, John Mitchell and Bob [Robert] Ellsworth* asked me to help actively with the Nixon campaign. I had been impressed with Nixon as a very thoughtful, intelligent, dedicated, and energetic person. I was somewhat concerned that he had not been engaged in much, other than politics—that is to say, he'd gotten out of the Navy and gone into politics: he had been very briefly a congressman, then very briefly a senator, then a vice-president—which is a very different kind of a position; the buck doesn't stop with you. Then as vice-president he had been getting ready to be president—as former vice-president he had been getting ready to be president. I've always believed that you develop most when you're actually physically doing something— when you are engaged in activity—whether it's business, or governing, and that through happenstance, Mr. Nixon's life during much of that period was *preparing* to do something, as opposed to doing something. I really wanted Nixon to run around the track a little bit to see how he handled himself prior to my committing to supporting him for president. Not long after that, I did agree to support him and ended up being an assistant floor manager at the convention.

Raymond Price In 1967, we had a very small group of people trying to figure out how to organize what might be a campaign; Nixon really didn't make the decision to run until New Year's weekend. No one really knows his mind—even he, probably, at times; he is always looking at everything from many angles. I think that he had to settle, in his mind, that he had a reasonable chance of winning both the nomination and the election. He likely felt that he was the best person for it. The most difficult thing was whether he would put his family through all the strain that a campaign entailed. We talked a lot about the defeats in 1960 and 1962 because, in terms of getting the nomination, the one thing, above all, that he had to overcome was the conventional wisdom in the party that he was a loser: in the eastern wing of the party, the wisdom was that George Romney was a big winner, so he

---

* Republican activist.

should be nominated, because he could win. It was precisely because of that loser perception that Nixon knew he had to get the nomination through the primary route in major states—which he did. And he took them all, including of course, New Hampshire, where Romney dropped out because his polls—like ours—showed him losing to Nixon, nine to one.

President Johnson Announces He Will Not Be a Candidate in 1968

On March 31, 1968, President Lyndon Baines Johnson, who had succeeded to the presidency upon the assassination of John F. Kennedy on November 22, 1963, announced that he would not seek reelection, stating that the situation in Vietnam was a major consideration in his decision not to run.

William Westmoreland, chief of staff, U.S. Army President Johnson chose not to run for another term not because of the Vietnam War, but because of his health. During the time I talked with him, he was taking nitroglycerine pills about every ten minutes. He said, "I am a sick man. It is unfair to the American people to have anything but a healthy person as president." And so he told me he was not going to run. It was not the Vietnam War; it was his health, and although the written histories have ignored this, I can tell you, categorically, that this was the reason he did not run again.

Bobby Baker, former chief Senate staff aide to Lyndon B. Johnson Lyndon Johnson invited me and my wife down to the ranch in late September 1972. Very few people know this, but when Johnson was president, he went to the Bethesda Naval Hospital and they operated on his throat for polyps. They turned out to be cancerous, which was never told to the American people. This is why Lyndon Johnson, in my opinion, did not run for a second, elected term. Had he run, he would have defeated Nixon. After his second heart attack, he was examined by Dr. Michael DeBakey,* who told him that he could keep him alive, heartwise, for a few years more, but he asked Johnson to have an examination at the Mayo Clinic, so that before he operated on Johnson's heart, he would know his general physical condition. Johnson went to Minnesota [where the Mayo Clinic is located], and the doctors there ascertained that the polyps that were cancerous when he was

---

* A pioneer in heart transplant surgery.

president had spread, and that he would be dead in six months. Johnson was a master at keeping secrets; I'm sure he had all the Navy doctors petrified to tell anybody about his condition.

THE REPUBLICAN NATIONAL CONVENTION, MIAMI BEACH, FLORIDA, AUGUST 1968

Defeating last-minute challenges on August 7 by both Ronald Reagan and Nelson Rockefeller, Mr. Nixon was nominated on the first ballot to be the presidential candidate of the Republican Party, receiving 692 votes—25 more than needed.

Mr. Nixon selected Spiro T. (Theodore) Agnew, governor of Maryland, as his running mate. In the face of a last-minute challenge by George Romney, governor of Michigan, Governor Agnew won handily on the first ballot.

Selecting a Running Mate

Mr. Nixon's announcement of the selection of Governor Agnew took many political pundits and the press corps by surprise, witness the reaction of one journalist: "Spiro T. Who . . . ?"

Herbert Brownell There were two leading candidates for vice-president: Governor [John] Volpe, of Massachusetts, and Agnew. I was concerned that something unfavorable would turn up during the campaign on Volpe, who was a contractor. Agnew was the governor of a border state, successful, as far as we knew; a good speaker. He made a very pleasing impression. He was helpful in the campaign. Today, you would say, "Didn't they know he was a crook?" But that is hindsight. At the time, Agnew had a good reputation.

Howard Phillips, deputy director, executive director, President's Council on Youth Opportunity; associate director, director, Office of Economic Opportunity Agnew's nomination came out of a virtual toss-up between him and Volpe. I helped Agnew to get picked—even though he didn't know it at the time—because of some feuds I had with Volpe. When I was chairman of the Republican Party in Boston, I was able to call on some of my national Republican connections to warn people about some of the problems I had had with the Volpe people, and to suggest that they move toward Agnew.

Herbert Klein When you selected a vice-presidential nominee, there was not a lot of research, or FBI checks; it's a political decision, and you look at someone who has a political reputation. Agnew had a good reputation. He brought in the elements of being a kind of Southerner, someone who would speak, and would take the role assigned to him. The selection was never made on the basis of a person being the one Nixon would feel most comfortable with being the next president of the United States; I suspect that's rarely true.

Robert Finch It was an effort, without playing directly to the South, to take someone who was looked at as a mainstream governor. [John] Mitchell was pushing very hard for it; Thruston Morton* and Rogers Morton† were pushing very hard for it, as was John Tower.‡ It was felt to be the best way to attack then what we knew was going to be a tough ticket, and that would play against [Governor George] Wallace [of Alabama] and other factors, without deliberately getting into integration-segregation disputes.

Gerald R. Ford, member, U.S. House of Representatives (R-Mich.); vice-president of the United States; president of the United States I had nothing to do with the Agnew nomination. At that meeting in Miami, I suggested John Lindsay.** I made no headway with that name. I gathered that Lindsay was unacceptable, because their chemistry didn't mix; Dick Nixon always wanted somebody who would be totally compatible with him. I don't think that the Lindsay personality and record fitted in.

H. R. (Harry Robbins) Haldeman, assistant to the president I've often wondered [why Agnew was selected]; I was there, and I still don't know why. It came about after an incredibly painstaking process of evaluation, elimination, reinstitution, and reelimination—and pulling and tugging, in Nixon's mind, as to who would be his running mate. He talked to just about everybody. My guess is that he saw Agnew as the least of evils. He really thought there was not much a running mate could do to help; there was a substantial amount he could to do to hurt. He needed a tie to the Rockefeller†† wing of the party: Nixon was a Westerner; he needed an Easterner

---

* Member, U.S. Senate (R-Ky.).
† Member, U.S. House of Representatives (R-Md.)
‡ Member, U.S. Senate (R-Tex.)
** Former member, U.S. House of Representatives (R-N.Y.); former mayor of New York City.
†† Nelson A. Rockefeller, former Republican governor of the state of New York, a liberal Republican, had sought the party's presidential nomination in 1964, losing to the ultraconservative senator from Arizona, Barry Goldwater.

for balance. He had been impressed by what he had seen of Agnew, but he did not know him well. But I really don't know why he picked him. We had a midnight meeting at the convention. The story that he offered it [the vice-presidential nomination] to Bob [Robert] Finch is true; Finch didn't want it, so it ended up being Agnew.

Raymond Price Nixon called me in at about 6:30 the night before he made the selection. We talked privately, and he told me that Agnew was going to be his choice. My guess is that, in the long series of meetings he subsequently held into the small hours of the morning—supposedly to help him make a decision—he was actually trying to bring people aboard on Agnew. Agnew was regarded as an effective governor—a progressive, who handled racial and urban affairs competently. Nixon had met with him in his apartment in New York, and told me afterward how impressed he had been.

Richard Kleindienst, deputy attorney general; attorney general I was walking by. Nixon saw me and said, "In a couple of minutes, Governor Agnew is going to be here, and I'm going to tell him he is going to be the vice-presidential candidate." In 1968, Agnew had started out as head of the draft Rockefeller movement. Then in March, Agnew had all of his committee chairmen in his governor's office in Annapolis, waiting for Rockefeller to say he was going to run, and without informing Agnew, Rockefeller announced he was not a candidate. This was very embarrassing to Agnew, and a couple of days later, John Mitchell got into a car and drove to Annapolis to talk to Agnew and got him immediately involved in Nixon's campaign.

Richard Moore, special counsel to the president Nixon had what we later called the stroking session: he invited about twenty Republican leaders to the top floor of the Hilton. Earlier that night, I got a call from Bob Finch—a secret call: Can you come over to room such-and-such right away? And don't tell anybody. I went to see him, and he said, "Nixon wants me to go on the ticket, but I don't want to do it." I said, "Bob, how can you say no?" At two o'clock in the morning, there was another meeting with very close staff. I felt at the meeting that Nixon had still not made up his mind. Finch's name came up, and Nixon said, "That would be fine, but it would look like nepotism," using the same word Bob had used with me earlier, as a reason for his not wanting to go on the ticket. I had mentioned John Volpe; then someone said Governor Agnew would be very good. The discussion went on, and there were two more meetings that night, as the group (of candidates) narrowed. I have the feeling that Bob Finch probably misunderstood the candidate; I don't think he was thinking about Finch for the ticket. If the candidate smiles at you, you think: that's a job offer.

Robert Finch The job I wanted at that time was being in the Senate, where you could affect long-term policy. I had run Nixon's vice-presidential office; I was not interested in foreign policy, but I loved domestic politics. When it was clear Nixon was going to be nominated, he said, "Would you be interested" [in the vice-presidential spot]? There were many factors to be considered: a lot of the Reagan partisans would have been very unhappy if I had been on the ticket; there was the question of whether you would have two Californians running, even though Nixon was then a legal resident of New York; or, that I was the "younger brother"; we had been very close. For all of those reasons, I said that I was not going to do it, and I said so early on. Then, he came back that night and again pushed me, with a pretty good power group around him. I took him outside and said, "No. I meant it. I will be happy to serve in the Cabinet, if I can focus on domestic matters that are within my orbit." I was convinced at that time that Nixon would find a way to end the Vietnam War, and that we would have a peace dividend and be able to focus on domestic problems.

Donald Rumsfeld I was in the room that evening—from about one in the morning until about 5 A.M.—when he made the decision on Agnew. It was fascinating. I had received a note on the floor of the convention at eight or nine o'clock saying that Nixon wanted to have a group of people meet with him. As I recall, he had two or three meetings that night. Ours started at about one o'clock. I was amazed when I walked in the room. Haldeman and Mitchell were there; I believe Finch was there; Billy Graham was there; I think Barry Goldwater and Herb Brownell were there; and some others. My recollection is that we came up there and a number of people were seated; some were standing, or leaning against bookcases. Nixon, in effect, said, "Look, I want to pull this party together; I don't want to select somebody for vice-president who will have the effect of dividing the party." So he set aside the Goldwaters, Towers, Lindsays, and Rockefellers of the left and right, and forced the people in attendance to focus on the center. He then turned in a swivel chair and said, "Let's go around the room." And somebody started and said who they felt was appropriate, and before it was over, he went all around the room, probing and asking questions.

When it was over, I drove to my hotel after five in the morning, and my wife said, "Who is it?" I said, "Well, you won't believe it; it's either Agnew or Volpe, with an outside chance at Mark Hatfield." That was my assessment in listening not so much to the other people, but to Mr. Nixon. I think, basically, he decided he wanted somebody whom nobody would be against; it was pretty clear to me when Mr. Nixon came into the room that he had in his mind John Volpe and Spiro Agnew.

The concept was flawed—the idea that you want to pick someone that no one is against. When you are in politics, almost of necessity you are driven to someone no one knows. It wasn't that everyone else had flaws, or enemies, or weaknesses—except for those two people; it was basically that people didn't know what Mr. Agnew's flaws and weaknesses were. At that time, he had probably been in government a total of thirty months, from county executive to governor. I think it wasn't that the process was flawed; I think the concept behind inviting those people up and beginning with that conclusion was possibly not a great idea. On the other hand, all of us in there had a chance to say: Wait a minute; we don't think that's a good idea.

THE CAMPAIGN

Mr. Nixon's opponents were the Democratic Party's candidate, Vice President Hubert H. Humphrey, and Governor George Wallace of Alabama, who was running as a third-party candidate.

Frederick C. LaRue, campaign aide, 1968; White House consultant; campaign aide, 1972 I worked in New York to devise and operate a campaign in the South. The war was an issue, but the basic problem we had in the South was the Wallace candidacy, so the main thrust of the campaign there was to counter him, but not to get involved in the civil rights issues, which were the thrust of the Wallace campaign.

George McGovern, member, U.S. Senate (D-S.Dak.); Democratic candidate for president, 1972 The Southern Strategy was very cynical; that was the worst part of their civil rights stance. Nixon, who grew up in California, in a multicultural setting, had to know better than to feel he was serving the best interests of the country by placing as much credence as he did in the Southern Strategy, which had certain racial undertones to it. But it was more than that; it also had to do with maintaining a strong posture on national defense. I've always felt that a certain amount of cynicism about politics, and about the American public, was Nixon's biggest weakness. I don't say that he is the only president who had paid more attention to domestic political pressure, but I think that whenever you do that, you are flirting with a very dangerous situation.

Stephen Bull, special assistant to the president I worked in the campaign as an advance man in the summer of 1968. The Nixon campaign had sort of an old man's image. I think, quite frankly, that they wanted some young faces around. An advance man goes out; works with the local people, crowd raising, putting together the program; all of the details that go into putting together a campaign staff.

Dwight Chapin There was a certain quietness that allowed for thinking time. In retrospect, there was a lack of spontaneity; on the other hand, we won. Keep in mind that he's lost to Kennedy and to Pat [Edmund] Brown, and he probably has only one shot left. So he figured out what worked best for him. Some of the arguments between Haldeman and Ehrlichman would be over that sacred time—or that sacred way of managing him—which was dictated by Nixon, and enforced by Haldeman, with others always trying to grab it. The system that we set up in the campaign was carried into the White House.

Richard Bergholz In the 1968 campaign, he came out to speak at San Jose State University—this was at the very height of the student unrest. When he finished his speech—to a very carefully selected audience—he walked outside, and here were all these screaming kids. He was in no great physical danger at that moment, but it was possible. He jumped up on the hood of his limousine and waved his arms and gave them a V sign. And then he got down and said, "These kids hate this."

James Wrightson They could have gotten him out of that auditorium easily and nobody would have known where he was. The way he came out and everybody saw him, there is reason to believe he was trying to confront that crowd; it looked like he deliberately provoked that crowd—like in Detroit, where he chose to visit CIO districts* of the city. He knew he wasn't going to get his votes in Detroit. It was like Caracas,† which he liked to brag about.

Maurice Stans I had very little contact with Nixon, except on a few occasions that we talked about some meeting he was attending that I could tie into, and I really didn't see him then until the campaign was over. He decided that he wanted nothing to do with handling money, under any cir-

---

* Heavily Democratic areas of Detroit, Michigan.
  † On May 13, 1957, while vice-president, Mr. Nixon was set upon by an angry, anti-U.S. mob while riding in a motorcade with Venezuelan officials.

cumstances, as a matter of policy, not for any other reason. I think, even at that point, he was bedeviled a little bit by the loan somebody had made to his brother.* Also in 1960, he had been bedeviled by that small fund that had been created in Pasadena, and he determined not to have anything to do with money. I went through the 1968 and 1972 campaigns without any discussion that I can recall on the subject of money, in either year—about whom to collect money from, or who gave money. Just before he took office in 1969, I sat down with him and said, "Mr. President, here is the list of people who have given the largest amounts to your campaign. I know you are not interested in how much money people give, but you ought to know these names, so that at least you can recognize them when you see them." So he went over the list; that was the only time that I ever discussed money with Nixon, believe it or not. He just didn't want to know about it.

Leonard Garment We had campaign managers who were good, but were not what he needed. What he needed was John Mitchell; he was a very experienced bond lawyer who knew his way around politics, because he had worked with state officials for years. I liked Mitchell from the beginning to the end. A real study in loyalty, he made a lot of mistakes, got in over his head, and had a lot of problems, but very few people have the almost primitive type of loyalty that he had to Nixon; he took it on the nose in the end: on the one hand, he fought; on the other hand, he did not squeal to hurt Nixon.

Raymond Price Mitchell did not have campaign experience, but he had just about the best network of contacts with state and county and local officials around the country. He had devised many of the new financing plans states and counties were using; he was probably the top municipal finance lawyer in the country. He and Nixon became quite close friends, and he was a very good influence on Nixon, who really trusted John's judgment. I happened to like John Mitchell very much, and I think he got a bum rap on a lot of things.

Agnew's Campaign Performance

Herbert Klein Agnew was really green; his biggest trip had been to Annapolis from Baltimore. We had some of our people working in the

---

* $205,000 advanced by industrialist Howard Hughes to Donald Nixon, the then vice-president's younger brother, in 1956.

Agnew campaign, so we knew what he was doing all the time. We had learned with [Henry] Cabot Lodge;* we didn't know that he was sleeping all the time. Agnew made a speech in Harlem, saying that there was going to be a black in the Cabinet, and he made it to Puerto Ricans. That caused us to break off the campaign and have a hurried meeting in Hartford, Connecticut; the discussion was on strategy, and what Agnew should say—not on philosophy.

ELECTION CONCERNS

In late October, President Lyndon B. Johnson announced a halt in the bombing of North Vietnam and a round of negotiations with the North Vietnamese in Paris, a move that greatly troubled the Nixon campaign. But the bombing halt's political effect was muted when, on November 2, South Vietnam's president, Nguyen Van Thieu, announced that he would refuse to participate in the negotiations.

Robert Finch All the dynamics of the campaign were so uncertain: we were pretty badly torn asunder as a nation; the Wallace thing was unpredictable; Humphrey was a very tough campaigner. He knew that things would turn on any last-minute developments in the Vietnam War. At the Waldorf† on election night, I was reasonably confident; Nixon was, maybe, less so.

Raymond Price The assumption was that Johnson used the bombing halt for political purposes and that it might very well work—and it almost did. Our sense, at the time, was that if the election had been one day earlier, we would have lost; one day later and we would have won—by a much more substantial margin.

H. R. Haldeman We thought it would be close. It was tough to figure, because of the unknown of Vietnam. In the last ten days, Johnson was moving on the bombing halt to bring Humphrey on, and we were fully aware of the potential of Johnson's making of a dramatic move that could shift things very rapidly; he tried, and almost did. On election night, Nixon went to bed, and we stayed up all night in a room just down the hall from his. At about

---

* Nixon's vice-presidential running mate in the 1960 race against John F. Kennedy.
† The Waldorf-Astoria Hotel, in New York City.

6:30 A.M., he came into our room just as the networks were giving him the election. He was not elated; he did not leap up with joy. But he was obviously very pleased. He is a strongly self-disciplined man, and it is at a moment of victory like this that he will say: "What can we now do about this; how can we consolidate the victory?" rather than celebrate.

Richard Moore In the last thirty-six hours, we were all very concerned. We were in the Century Plaza Hotel, in Los Angeles, on the Saturday before the election, and at two o'clock in the morning, Haldeman—who had been with the candidate—came into the room where several of us had gathered. Someone asked, "How does he feel, Bob?" He answered, "Consider the following: the Scripps Howard papers have predicted a Humphrey victory; there will be a story tomorrow about campaign finance; a new poll has shown us in a virtual tie—so how do you think he feels?"

Ronald Ziegler He was getting a little shaky and concerned toward the end, but I believe that he felt it would be tight, but that he could win. I have a general impression that there wasn't pessimism. Of course, I was very young [twenty-nine] and tended to be optimistic; I never thought of Nixon losing the election.

ELECTION DAY ON NIXON'S AIRCRAFT: RETURNING TO NEW YORK FROM CALIFORNIA

Richard Moore Nixon did very well that Sunday on "Meet the Press." Herb Kaplow asked a question that knocked over the fence: "How can I tell my eleven-year-old son that the president of the United States is smarter than his father?" Coming back to New York on the airplane on Election Day, the candidate was very reflective and low-key. He made it a point to have every one of us who had been on the plane come up for a chat. He was ready for whatever happened. I said to him while we were sitting there, talking—we were over Kansas—"Down below, levers are being pulled all across the country." He kind of grinned and said, "This is a very memorable trip."

Raymond Price On the airplane coming back to New York on Election Day, he brought groups of three or four of us in, to try to prepare us for defeat—to ease the blow if the election went against us. It was a relaxed trip; there was nothing more we could do. We were looking down from

35,000 feet, knowing people were voting down there, and wondering what they were doing.

ELECTION NIGHT IN NEW YORK WITH MR. NIXON

Stephen Bull On election night, I was in New York City. Most of the advance people were brought in; that was kind of a reward for the months—and in some cases, years—of campaign activity. We were at the Waldorf, the election night headquarters. We were a bit apprehensive. It was an all-nighter; Illinois didn't come in until six the next morning. I recall Walter Cronkite on CBS being the first to call the election for Nixon.

Raymond Price Election night was eerie for us; we recalled 1960, when two states, Texas and Illinois, were pretty clearly stolen; [Mayor Richard] Daley [of Chicago] was pretty brazen about it, and Mitchell—knowing that Daley would repeat what he had done in 1960, which was to hold back many precincts he controlled so that when he knew how many votes he had to steal, he could alter the numbers and present the state to the Democratic ticket—held back some suburban votes. At about 3 A.M., I got a call—along with a few others—to join Nixon in his suite. The election had started see-sawing. Every so often, Nixon would send Mitchell out to make a phone call. What made it so scary was that the three states we were mainly waiting for were Illinois, Missouri, and Texas; there were accounts of voting machines breaking down in Texas, and things being delayed in Illinois and Missouri. Nixon, remembering 1960, was getting very impatient; he couldn't get things moving—couldn't get the count going. Finally, at about 6 A.M., Mitchell went into the other room, called CBS in Chicago, and got through to Mike Wallace on the set. He asked Mike to challenge Daley to release his precincts. Mike contacted Daley, who complied. We then released ours, and we carried Illinois, but we wouldn't have if we hadn't been able to dislodge Daley's little hoard.

Leonard Garment I felt that he was destined to win—a mystical sense that had propelled me from the start. On the other side was a fear that he would not win; it was a great fear, almost like a fear of dying. But on the day-to-day level, it looked like he was in a very good position: the Democratic convention had been a total mess, while our convention was orderly; the polls looked good, but I didn't know then that these numbers are will-o'-the-wisp—they are puffed up by abnormal events, and in 1968, there was the riot in Chicago; the disaffection with Humphrey because of his ties to Johnson's Vietnam policy. But people like Murray Chotiner,* who was very smart—and whom Nixon would never let go—were saying, "A lot of this is puffed up; people will start coming home to the Democrats." Chotiner was like Mitchell—they didn't mind accepting the fact that politics is shabby most of the time, filled with lies and deceptions. So we allowed for a slide, and one did take place when Johnson let Humphrey go free on the war issue, and the labor people realized that they were going to end up with the Republicans, and Nixon. The slide was a strange sensation; there was nothing you could do about it. We threw in everything: Frank Shakespeare† and I spent $50,000 on a documentary that the Nixons hated; it was an intimate portrait of Nixon. He talked about his childhood and family experiences. We spent millions of dollars on TV time; we ran the film all day. It was like a soap opera aimed at women—a constituency we were having trouble with. Then, he squeaked through.

REACTION TO NIXON'S ELECTION

Yuri Barsukov, Washington correspondent, *Izvestia* Nixon's election in 1968 was unwelcome news for Moscow. He had a very strong reputation as an anticommunist; he was seen as a close friend of Senator Joseph McCarthy, and he had been active as a member of the [U.S.] House of Representatives—on the Un-American Activities Committee. Also, his very hot debate‡ with Khrushchev in 1959 was still remembered by the Soviet leadership, so when Nixon was elected, they believed that they would have to deal with a very stubborn president.

---

* A longtime political associate of Richard Nixon, from California.
† Campaign aide; later director, U.S. Information Agency.
‡ The "Kitchen Debate," which took place at an American exhibition in Moscow featuring a model of a middle-class house.

2

Nixon's Character and Personality

FIRST IMPRESSIONS

Robert Finch He wasn't nearly as attractive, physically, as some of the other candidates, but he was so intense; he was a strong personality. You regarded him as a comer, someone who would be effective and successful in political activity. I was impressed by his obvious political skills, his intelligence, and his drive.

Stephen Bull I had been an advance man for a couple of months. John Ehrlichman was our contact; he was the "tour director." I remember saying to him, "It would be great if I could meet Mr. Nixon, just so that when I am out on the road and dealing with the local representatives, I can at least say that I have met the candidate." So he brought me onto the airplane and did the introduction. Mr. Nixon was very friendly, very warm, although it was a very brief meeting.

Dwight Chapin This was not a position of friendship—camaraderie—but one of servitude, a certain separation. I went on to be his personal aide, and my career with him worked out the way it did because I had in perspective the way he wanted the relationship to work; my job was to carry out the orders that were given to me, so my first impressions were of servitude and respect.

Aharon Yariv, chief of military intelligence, state of Israel Nixon came to Israel in 1967, after the Six Day War. I was called by a military officer, saying, "Will you come to dinner at my home tonight, because Nixon will be there and nobody is coming." So Haim Bar Lev [general, Israel Defense Forces] and I came. Nixon had just been on the Golan Heights, and I recall him saying, "Whatever anyone tells you, don't move an inch on the Golan Heights." He made a very favorable impression on me.

A. M. Rosenthal, executive editor, the *New York Times* The first time I met him was when I was the *Times* correspondent [in India] and he came out to Karachi as vice-president. I was looking at him there, thinking: Hmm, Tricky Dick. Then, when I was in the receiving line, the ambassador said to him, "You know Abe Rosenthal, the India correspondent of the *New York Times*." And Nixon replied, "Well, yes, A. M. Rosenthal." So I thought, well, he's not such a bad guy.

OBSERVATIONS

Robert Odle, Jr., administrator, Committee to Reelect the President (CRP) There was the nickname he got at Duke [University Law School], "Iron Butt," the ability to stick it out—to persist—and to study and think. Working for Richard Nixon was like an intensive course in Latin: it taught you English; it taught you how to think; it taught you logic; it taught you persistence.

Alexander Butterfield, special assistant to the president How are we going to get the president visible [during a public appearance]? Well, let's boost him up on a car. But he's so awkward that he can't stand on top of a car very well; he's likely to lose his balance up there. So there would be a picture of Richard Nixon on top of a car, but it would be awkward. He doesn't even wave gracefully.

David Packard, deputy secretary of defense He was a very hard person to really get acquainted with. He was very supportive of what I was doing, but I always had the feeling that I never really knew what he was thinking about. That was one of his problems.

H. R. Haldeman He didn't like the idea of going out to church, because it caused such a stir: the security arrangements; the Secret Service would flood the place. But he was also uncomfortable, symbolically, with the thought that the president did not regularly go to church, so he thought it would be good for the church to come to the White House. He came up with the idea of a monthly service in the White House, which we would invite ministers, rabbis, priests, evangelists, and laypeople to conduct. These services were wonderful. White House staff and their families were invited, on a rotating basis, all the way down to waiters, and those working in the Mess.

SOCIAL INSECURITY

Alexander Butterfield He does not know how to make small talk. We used to have six or seven Cabinet members at every social function. He once asked me who was best [in social situations]. I said, "Well, I think George Bush is probably best." He said, "Yeah. Bush would be." Then, he said, "Who's worst?" and I said, "Probably [John] Mitchell"; he was so shy. Then Nixon said, "God knows, I couldn't do that; I hate it, but Bush has the facility for that." Bush would say, "Hi, there. I'm George Bush, your U.N. ambassador." At a state dinner, Nixon timed it to when were we going to get the hell out of there.

Herbert Klein I think that small talk does come hard to him; he doesn't think in terms of small talk, unless you are talking sports; his interest in it prevails even today.

Stephen Bull He was a very formal guy—not a back-slapping type. He was a hand-shaker but he was not an embracer—a Jimmy Carter type. I don't recall much physical interaction; he was relatively uncomfortable with some of the more routine interpersonal dealings.

Robert Odle, Jr. I would often bring groups of young people into the Oval Office. Initially, the president would be uncomfortable. Then, as the conversation progressed, he would sit on his desk and develop a theme relevant to the meeting; then he was very much at home. Once, I brought in a delegation from Young Americans for Freedom, who were having a convention in Washington. They reviewed their agenda, and by the end of the session, Nixon had completely changed it, sending Kissinger and Ehrlichman over to address them.

William Ruckelshaus, assistant attorney general, Civil Division; administrator, Environmental Protection Agency (EPA); acting director, FBI; deputy attorney general Nixon was very uncomfortable around people; in my experience with him, he had very little use for small talk. He was not good at putting people at ease, unlike almost every major politician I had ever met. I don't think he genuinely liked people; I think he was fascinated by them, and interested in them, and tried to understand them, but I don't think he liked them. I marveled at how much he had to control himself—how desirous he was of possessing power—because he overcame this unease.

John Dean, associate deputy attorney general; counsel to the president After the mantle wore off a little bit and I started seeing the man rather than the president, I saw somebody who operated on lots of levels; there are many Richard Nixons. There is somebody who is caring—who worries about when your wife has the flu; who cares about the impact of his decisions on other people—and hurting people; and there is somebody who is mean-spirited at the other extreme; who will do anything that he has to do to accomplish what he wants to accomplish; he was all those people—a very complex person. He took himself very seriously. He seemed almost to be playing the role of being president. As I got to know him more, he would become more relaxed. He got kind of announcerish and pronouncing at times, and at times he was very conversational. By March 21, 1973, we had a rapport, and in that meeting, he wasn't terribly presidential; he was trying to learn what the hell to do with this mess that his counsel brought in.

Robert Odle, Jr. He is an enormously complicated, complex man; what you read is all there—and isn't there: a man who is uncomfortable with small talk and cocktail chatter; a man who is enormously interested in the long view. It's too bad that he never studied chess; he certainly would have been a champion. One point that perhaps wouldn't come out from reading about him is the small acts of kindness toward domestic staff that served the White House, toward family members of his own staff, and enormous dedication to his family. Until the Bushes, I don't know if there was a more normal, loving, and closer family in the White House.

NIXON THE FAMILY MAN

H. R. Haldeman He would spend a fair amount of time with the family [at Camp David] bowling, swimming, sledding, or walking. In the evenings, he would watch a movie. Nine out of ten times, it would be *Around the World in Eighty Days*. For some strange reason, he loved that movie.

Alexander Butterfield The president didn't eat at home with Mrs. Nixon most nights; Manolo [Sanchez, the president's valet] would serve him dinner over in his EOB (Executive Office Building) office. He'd be working on his yellow pad, about ideas he had for the presidency; always with the yellow pad and always about the presidency and image.

Mrs. Nixon

Stephen Bull Mrs. Nixon appeared to be extremely supportive. She played the role of active first lady. I don't recall a complaint ever—and we put them through some arduous trips. But she was always right there, always in good humor—a marvelous woman.

Dwight Chapin The campaign was very, very hard for her. He spent a great deal of his time getting ready—thinking of what he was going to say; therefore, the amount of time they spent together was minimal. In many cases, she would have her own schedule. While I don't think she relished it, she did a spectacular job of putting up with it all; she didn't want to be there. Later, when we got into the White House, it took her a while to find her niche. The public loved her, and she took on a whole new personality.

Susan Porter Rose, appointments secretary to the first lady She was not very thick-skinned about criticism. It was very hurtful, but it was so much a part of their lives—Vietnam, and all the things he was attacked for. It was tough on all of them.

The "Plastic Pat" Label

Susan Porter Rose She was tall, erect, and sort of linear, and therefore, if she was quiet and off to one side—as spouses tended to be in those days—someone who wants to give it a negative twist is going to call her "Plastic Pat." But she certainly wasn't like that at all. She would instantly put people at ease. You would be surprised at how many people who visit the White House are nervous; even grown-up, sophisticated people are terrified. She would walk into a room, and people would relax. There was a wonderful aura about her.

Bobby Baker It was not a fifty-fifty marriage; she gave eighty and he gave twenty [percent]. She was a good wife and mother; she had had a tough life and she was a tough lady. She was a good political wife, but she didn't like all of it, and she wasn't a plastic lady. I think that history will be very kind to her.

The Nixon Marriage

Ben [Benjamin C.] Bradlee, vice-president and executive editor, the *Washington Post* He had that sort of dingy marriage; I have a feeling they never touched each other in any way—physically, or any other way.

Alexander Butterfield I was responsible for the smooth running of the president's official day. I also did a great many other little things. I was the liaison with the first lady's staff, the reason being that everyone else on the staff had been in that role before. I didn't know this, but Haldeman said, "Butterfield is the new guy; let's try him on for size," because Mrs. Nixon could never trust anybody who did it; she had come not to trust whoever was working with her from Nixon's staff. They sent Dwight Chapin over to work with her. He was a nice person, obviously well raised by his parents, and mannerly, but even he struck out with Mrs. Nixon over a period of time. Now I'm the new guy; I'm the only person in the Nixon White House who had not been part of the campaign, but I had worked in the Johnson White House;[*] I was fairly close to Johnson himself, so there were reasons that Haldeman wanted me there. Bob had been the principal intermediary, and I think that he felt she had learned not to trust him—that he was trying to pull the wool over her eyes, because oftentimes, she didn't see things as the president did.

You see, the president didn't speak to her much. For example, [with] the president's official photograph—this is the picture that is going to hang in all the post offices, all the ships at sea. I think we changed it three or four times during his first four years [in office]. Most men would find out what the office staff thought—what the secretaries thought—and would go home and say to his wife, "These are the ones that everyone seems to like. What do you think?" Richard Nixon was not built that way; he could not, or would

* As White House liaison and military assistant to Secretary of Defense Robert McNamara.

not, do that. . . . She [Mrs. Nixon] would talk, maybe, about going up to Camp David, or which secretary should go up there. The president couldn't talk that over with her, or the White House menu. . . . He decided who would play at the [state] dinner. He thought it should be "the jazz guy from New Orleans." Mrs. Nixon thought it should be "The Strolling Strings." Well, he didn't argue with her about that. At dinner that night, I would have to go over and settle that with her—and I am representing the president. He would say, "Don't come back unless you have her sign off on Dizzy Gillespie" or whoever. . . . They would never speak in the helicopter, ever. And here you are, going up to Camp David at night. The only people there are the president and Mrs. Nixon—he in a chair right next to her. I was beside them, and in the back, two Secret Service men, one of the military aides, and the doctor. There was no comment. They lived in separate houses down in Florida.

Richard Bergholz In my limited contact with Nixon, what I saw was a cold, calculating man who treated Pat like just a piece of furniture in the room. She was there—she would have the adoring smile, trot out the kids— but he had a hard time showing affection. If you read the transcript of what he really said in the "Checkers" speech, that was a hell of a tour de force; he did a great job. That was a tremendous ad lib presentation. Sure, it was a case when he talked about Checkers, and Pat's cloth coat, and he's really a poor guy. It wasn't the real Nixon. But it was right on the button.

Susan Porter Rose I don't think that there is any question that he was con-sumed with what he was doing. From time to time, we would wish that he would be overtly more beckoning to her—with more of a public display of affection. But having gone out to her funeral and to the Library,* and seeing some of the letters he wrote before they were married, I know how close they were. There may have been some periods when they were out of phase, but there is no question about the depth of that relationship.

Alexander Haig, member, NSC staff; vice-chief of staff, U.S. Army; assistant to the president He was accused of being gay. My God! He wor-shiped Pat. I knew this when I worked for him. Their relationship was not ostentatious, or phony. They weren't out there holding hands and gaga-ing each other, like Reagan and Nancy; that was all Hollywood bullshit.

---

* The Nixon Presidential Library, in Yorba Linda, California.

Robert Odle, Jr. At the time of the phlebitis operation, he said, "I'm not going to make it," and Mrs. Nixon said, "Yes, you can." He would say later that the only two times in his life when he gave up were the Checkers speech—where she said, "Yes, you can," and during the phlebitis surgery—where she said the same thing. One time she saved him politically, and one time physically.

Nixon and His Parents

H. R. Haldeman The kind of person he intensely disliked would be the young, Ivy League college kid who comes in [to the Oval Office] for some reason with his grizzled, shopworker father, and the kid is clearly embarrassed—the father says something, and the kid corrects him. Nixon just detests the kid and thinks the father is great, and he talks about this for days afterward. He is infuriated: this kid, who got to college because his father made it possible for him, looking down on the father as an inferior.

Howard Phillips To understand Nixon, you have to understand his relationship to his father, Frank: the dominant factor in his psyche was rejection by his father, and his love-hate relationship with his father was mostly hate, with exaggerated exaltation of his mother, Hannah. In many ways, Frank Nixon was the personification of the American establishment. On the one hand, Nixon resented—and was angry with—the American establishment; on the other hand, he yearned for its approval, so even as he denounced the *Washington Post*, he wanted it to write nice editorials about him. He spent most of his life trying to win the approval of the American establishment through his activities in foreign policy. There is a real analogy between Nixon and Lincoln: there is that same hatred between Abraham Lincoln and his father, Thomas Lincoln, and the exaltation of Lincoln's stepmother. Lincoln's hatred was no more clearly demonstrated than when he refused to attend his father's funeral. Nixon never worked out his hatred, which was reflected in his approach to public policy.

Richard Bergholz When he came home, one of the features was a reunion with his mother, Hannah. I couldn't help positioning myself so I could see the precise moment when Nixon and his mother met. He came in with a whole entourage, and she came in from a side door. I just couldn't believe my eyes. When he saw her walking in, he walked over and shook her hand. And here is a guy who hadn't seen his mother in—I don't know how long—

and all he could do was shake her hand; he couldn't kiss her or hug her; he couldn't show any form of affection. It troubled me, in the sense that even a reasonably hardened politician would know better than to react that way— even if he had to put on an act.

Richard Kleindienst He is one of the brightest, broad-gauged, able men who ever held that office. He was able to conceptualize foreign affairs and domestic problems. One of the problems he had—and it might have been his great, limiting factor—was that he carried around within him grudges; he permitted himself to develop thoughts of retribution and revenge. I think it was the small, dark side of his character that might have led to his downfall. You have to go back and look at Richard Nixon, starting in 1946. I don't know what happened to him as a teenager, with his mother or his father— whether somebody caught him masturbating, or something that scarred his character. It's now popular for people to say it's not my fault. Starting back in 1946, when he ran against Jerry Voorhis,* that was a highly controversial election; then he takes on Helen Gahagan Douglas,† and then when he was vice-president, everybody was kicking the hell out of him.

He was an embattled person from the beginning of his political career, in great part due to some of the very strong positions he was taking, and his ability to articulate those very strong positions. I remember in 1968, there was a Herblock cartoon showing Nixon pouring dirt on the graves of Romney and Rockefeller. I thought it was funny as hell. I said, "Hey, boss. Take a look at this," and he looked at it, and his face just went stone cold. Compare that to a guy like Barry Goldwater—in his home he's got a whole wall of cartoons about him, most of which are a lot more severe than any that anyone ever cartooned about Nixon. And Barry gets a kick out of it. He has never had any feelings of bitterness, or hate, toward anyone, particularly anybody in the press.

VARIOUS FACETS OF THE NIXON PERSONALITY

Donald Segretti, campaign worker Nixon is basically a good person with a black, dark side—and the dark side has to do with politics and how you play it. I don't know whether he realizes that now, but that is his problem— his negative.

---

  * The incumbent Democratic candidate from the Twelfth Congressional District of California in the 1946 congressional race.
  † Nixon's Democratic opponent in the 1950 California race for the United States Senate.

Walter Hickel, secretary of the interior Of all the presidents I have known, I would rate Eisenhower the great convener and middle-of-the-roader; Johnson the brilliant political person; and Dick Nixon the most brilliant of all. He was bright, and decent, but there were two sides to Richard Nixon—the dark and the light side. I always played to his light side; if you did, he would just light up. If you played to his dark side, he would turn inward. Kissinger played to his dark side; he did it more than anyone else.

Alexander Butterfield He was a nice man, but as Haldeman once said, after Watergate was over, "He's the strangest man I ever met." I loved it when Haldeman said this; it made me know I wasn't crazy, because I always thought, deep down, that this was the strangest man—a great man in many ways, with all of these attributes, but he does have a dark side for sure; he is complicated.

Vernon Walters, deputy director, Central Intelligence Agency (CIA) I sat with that man in a car [in Caracas, Venezuela] with people beating on the windows with steel pipes and baseball bats to get at him and kill him. That man was cool as a cucumber. A Secret Service agent pulled out his gun and said, "Let's kill some of these sons-of-bitches and get out of here." Nixon said, "Put away that gun. If they open one of these doors and pull me into the street—and only if I tell you—do you use it." And I am supposed to believe that he was crawling on the floors of the White House, talking to the pictures on the walls [during the Watergate crisis].

INTERACTION WITH STAFF
AND CLOSE ASSOCIATES

Alexander Butterfield [H. R.] Haldeman told me once, "You know, Jo [Mrs. Haldeman] and I have only been to one dinner with Pat [Mrs. Nixon]." And only once did they go over to his house—and it wasn't the White House; he was never close to Richard Nixon, socially. At Camp David, the president would have Bob [Robert Abplanalp]° and [Charles Bebe] Rebozo and sometimes Hobart Lewis† at Aspen Cabin, but Bob would be with me, at Laurel Cabin.

° A wealthy businessman who lent the president the money to buy land adjacent to his San Clemente property in order to ensure security and privacy.

† Editor, *Reader's Digest*.

Stephen Bull Abplanalp and Rebozo were his closest friends; if they wanted to talk to him, they would call me, and say, "I'd like to talk to the president when he has a chance." If they wanted to get through directly, they could, but they didn't. As staff members, we had concerns about the influence the president's friends might have.

Robert Hartmann I expect that Bebe Rebozo was working for the CIA all those years. I never did understand what he and Nixon saw in each other. I don't say that there was anything queer about Nixon—or Bebe, for that matter. If they were, it would have come out.

Gerald R. Ford Shortly after I was sworn into the House of Representatives for my first term, in January 1949, Congressman Nixon came up and congratulated me, and I thought this was a very nice gesture from someone I had never known before. My first real opportunity to get acquainted was when a group of us in the House organized the Chowder and Marching Society, in 1949; it was a permanent social, political, legislative gathering that would meet every Wednesday night.

Alexander Butterfield [President George] Bush would say, "How is your wife or child?" Nixon wouldn't do that. But when my little girl had a terrible automobile accident and was very badly hurt, they got the White House chopper out to take her to Bethesda.° When she got out of the hospital, he insisted that I take time off. I didn't want to, but he said, "You are going to take a week off." And he sent a note and some flowers.

G. Gordon Liddy, general counsel, CRP The only time I had direct contact with the president was when I drafted the Explosives Control Act. I was present when he signed the bill, and I had a direct conversation with him. I was quite impressed that, although there were other people in the room, he spoke directly to me. It was a one-on-one conversation, in which he was very knowledgeable about what I had done—and very complimentary. He looked wonderful—hale and hearty. I went home and said, "You should have seen the boss today; he looks great." Then, we turned on the television and he looked like he was going to die. He looked great in person, but on the screen he looked terrible.

° A naval hospital in neighboring Maryland.

William Rusher [Vice-President Spiro T.] Agnew told me that Nixon hates like hell to ask anybody for anything. One time, Nixon was asked to speak to the annual Gridiron Dinner.° He didn't want to do it, so he said to an aide, "Ask Agnew if he will do it." Agnew replied, "Yes, if the president himself will ask me." This ran against some deep bone in Nixon's throat, so he sent Bryce Harlow† to try to convince Agnew. Agnew told him, "I'll be glad to do it, but I must have a request from the president, personally." Finally—and very grudgingly—he got a short, scribbled note from Nixon, saying, "Please do this." So he did.

Charles Wiggins When I was running for Congress in 1966, I made a strong effort to induce him to come to my district. I did so because he was a former member of Congress, because he was a predecessor of mine from that district, and because I was running on the twentieth anniversary of his first election to Congress from that district. But I wasn't successful. I couldn't talk him into coming back to his old home district to campaign for me until the day before the election. I got a call from New York City; it was Richard Nixon. He said he was going to be flying out to the West Coast and wanted to know if he could come by my district. I thought it was much too late to affect the election and, frankly, I thought that I had the election won anyway, and I turned him down.

Alexander Butterfield The president had these Saturday morning calls, which he hated to make. Usually, he would take off for Camp David at about noon; he could hardly wait to get there. But he had to make these calls, and he'd make them like a little boy—maybe he would be calling some congressman who was opposing a piece of legislation we were trying to pass, or a little schoolteacher in Ottumwa, Iowa, because that makes big news there—and he's saying, "I don't want to call the goddamn teacher"; he's complaining just like a little boy, and we're saying, "Make the call." And we hand him the phone. It was like pulling teeth. I got to see how fake everything is; it's all for image. It's what's outside that counts in politics.

Ben Bradlee For a period when he was president, he started calling me up on Saturday mornings. By God, one morning the operator said that the president was on the phone. I thought it was Art Buchwald or somebody pulling my leg—and it was Nixon! It was most uncomfortable, awkward;

° Held by journalists and featuring self-inflicted "roasts" of speakers.
† Congressional liaison, Nixon administration.

there was no way to explain the call, except that somebody had said: "You know, you ought to try to get to know Bradlee." He talked about OPA* and tire prices; I didn't give a shit. He tried it two more times and then realized it was a bad, bad idea.

George P. Shultz, secretary of labor; secretary of the treasury; director, OMB He has a flair for doing things dramatically. He wanted to announce his whole Cabinet at once. This had never been done before. He was always looking for a first, so he didn't make an announcement that he had invited me to become secretary of labor. I asked to see him and he said, "The day after tomorrow I will be at the Century Plaza Hotel [in Los Angeles]. Why don't you come over?" I worked very hard getting ready for the appointment; I was determined that he would know what I thought about labor relations and collective bargaining, and civil rights. We were in a room by ourselves, and he talked about how, as a university professor, I could be comfortable in his Cabinet. I couldn't get a word in edgewise. I thought to myself: this man has just been elected president, and he is selling himself to me; it was his insecurity in talking to a university person. I was a supporter of his—and a Republican—and he had no reason to question whether I would support him.

Kenneth Rush Nixon was very emotional on some things: I recall that when someone in the State Department had gone before Congress and said, "Eisenhower would have turned over in his grave if he knew Nixon had done . . . ," Nixon called me that night in a rage. He said, "I want that man fired—in one hour." I remember that when the large invasion from the North [Vietnam] occurred, in April 1973, he called me at the Defense Department; he was mad as hell at [Melvin] Laird, who, he thought, had known the invasion was coming but hadn't told him. Actually, Mel didn't know it was coming.

William H. Sullivan, deputy assistant secretary of state for Far Eastern affairs; U. S. ambassador to the Philippines He was a man without emotion. He had always been totally, pragmatically rational. I think he found a certain value of political support by associating himself with certain groups. When circumstances changed, it was not difficult for him to follow a path of rationalization because he had no emotional commitments to impede him, so he could make these changes far more rapidly than those

* The World War II Office of Price Administration.

who—like Ronald Reagan—were affiliated more for emotional and senti-mental reasons than for intellectual reasons. He's probably always had a more dedicated attachment to internationalism. The politics of getting elected, particularly in California, may have dictated to him to affiliate him-self with things that he didn't entirely share. The changes in the world, par-ticularly the China overture, were things that he perceived through reason and through changes in events and circumstances that he was quick to exploit.

Stephen Bull Interestingly enough, he was not a profane man. One would get the sense that he was, as a result of the transcripts of some of the tapes, in which there are expletives deleted.

Ben Bradlee I understand he was resolutely foul-mouthed. Somebody told me, "He talks even worse than you do, Bradlee." So I suspect there is at least that reason why he wants to keep the remaining tapes under wraps. And he probably says some terrible things about his buddies. But there are other reasons; there are other crimes, other things that would prevent him from rehabilitating himself.

Dwight Chapin I don't believe that Richard Nixon is profane. Does he salt his language? Yes. Was I surprised when I listened to any of the tapes? No, because I had known all that. Perhaps there is something in the dichotomy of where the public puts the president on a pedestal—and that includes the language he uses—and the public never stops to think that a president may swear, so when the public is exposed to this, its outrageousness is multiplied by the height of the pedestal. I can remember Nixon popping off about something, and you would walk out and laugh, because it was not meant in the harshness that appears when you read it—it took on a whole different perspective when one wasn't there.

Alexander Butterfield I liked the president's profanity, because he is sort of pedantic and straitlaced. It made him more of a man's man. He didn't say horrible things. He'd just say, "What about that son-of-a-bitch? Bob and I think we ought to get rid of that son-of-a-bitch." One day, Bob came into the office and said, "Mr. President, here is a list of journalists that are going on the China trip." And I'll never forget this; this is typical of Richard Nixon—why doesn't he just relax? He is the president of the United States—but he carried these resentments. Do you think it was Haldeman who made up the "Enemies List"? No. It was the president, who said, "No. I don't ever want this guy to set foot in the White House." He takes his pencil and reads the press list and sees some guy's name, and goes, "Bob, what is this?" And he puts the pencil right through the paper, he's pressing so hard. He doesn't just cross him off. "What is this son-of-a-bitch doing here?" Bob comes over and looks, and says, "Well, he *is* the bureau chief." Nixon says, "Don't you remember those articles he wrote back there in the gubernatorials?" meaning 1962. And Bob mentions again that now he is a biggie. I don't think people really know how deep these resentments were. He hated with a passion, and I don't know if anyone has quite captured it yet.

THE RESENTMENTS

The Press Corps

At the beginning of his political career in 1946, Nixon enjoyed the support of the influential Los Angeles Times *and other major news outlets in California. As he emerged on the national scene, the future president continued to maintain positive relations with the media for a time.*

Gerald Warren Early on, relations with the press were quite good; a camaraderie had developed between the press and the staff during the 1968 campaign. There were stories about the "new" Nixon. As time went on, and Vietnam became a problem and the demonstrations against the war grew in number and intensity, that affected relationships between the press corps and the administration. The president decided that he had to speak directly to the American people. He couldn't rely on the press to be friendly to him because of the history of his relations with them over the years. But the real poisoner of the well was Vietnam. The Ellsberg case, wiretapping, all of the things done in the name of national security because of leaks and concern about getting our troops out of Vietnam in an honorable way, added to the division—the enmity, if you will—between the president and the press.

Ronald Ziegler Relations with the press were good during the 1968 campaign, and well into the first term, despite the turmoil the nation was in, and the polarization that had taken place relevant to the Vietnam War. There was a real sense of hope on the part of every segment of society for a healing to take place, and an ending of the division. I know that President Nixon desired that to happen; he worked extensively to try to make it happen. He did not fully succeed—as history shows—and I think that is probably more an indication of the depth of the division than of his trying and having the desire to see a healing and a new spirit in coming together.

Herbert Klein He thought that the press corps was against him, and it was him against them. The basis of his dislike of the press was that he felt that it was liberal and would never give him a fair break. At his press conferences in the 1960 campaign, or in 1968, he felt that questions were directed to trap him, or were being planted by our opponent. In 1960, I think, a lot of them were; the press was extremely biased in 1960. I don't think it was in 1968. Nixon would go for three or four days without talking to the press, and then he would talk to someone he considered a friend, like William Edwards of the *Chicago Tribune*.

Alexander Butterfield As he read the news summary, he would write in the margin: "Who the hell does this guy think he is; get on this son-of-a-bitch!" So I would dictate a memo to Henry [Kissinger]: "The president saw this in the news summary and he wants you to follow up with [William] Rogers," or whoever.

Herbert Klein The person in the press who really antagonized him to a tremendous degree was Dick Bergholz; in a conversation, he is a very congenial guy; he likes to play tennis. The other person he mentioned was Carl Greenberg,* who was a very good reporter.

The Eastern Establishment

H. R. Haldeman There was always an "us against them" attitude—just as there is with every president: "If you are not with us, you are against us." When you get into a political campaign, you are in a battle, a battle for survival—administrative survival, in the case of 1972. So you plan it on an "us against them" basis. The jump that the Teddy Whitest and Woodwards attempt to make, from that almost universal fact, or axiom, is to say that Nixon was paranoid. I don't believe that at all. He had strong opinions, but opinions based on reality: that he had a battle to fight with his opponent; with a good segment of the press; with a lot of the Washington and Eastern establishment. And he was ready to fight those battles. He saw the example

* *Los Angeles Times* reporter.
† T. E. White, chronicler of presidential campaigns.

of a president who wasn't ready to fight, who was now retired to private life.

Robert Mardian, general counsel, Department of Health, Education and Welfare (HEW); assistant attorney general in charge of the Internal Security Division I always thought he was a brilliant man. There was an insecurity because of his background, his beginnings; he was a poor young boy. He was successful in making friends with some very wealthy people, but, by the same token, I don't think he liked rich people. He solicited them, but he was basically for the underdog—the common man type.

Herbert Brownell Nixon and Justice [William O.] Douglas were very much alike, in that they both were very suspicious of Easterners: Wall Street, New York, the Eastern establishment. Whenever things went wrong for them, they had a scapegoat. It served both of them very well in their political careers. He had that bias, and the more conservative he became in his views, the more noticeable this became. It developed into "All the liberals are against me."

Herbert Klein I don't think that Nixon had a hatred of the Eastern establishment; in some ways he was, perhaps, jealous of it, and that influenced some of the decisions in the White House: early on, Ehrlichman was going to set up some kind of royal police force with funny uniforms; that was part of trying to recapture the glamour that had surrounded Kennedy. Nixon always made a political point of saying that he was not among the intellectuals, but I never had any question that, in his own mind, he thought he was an intellectual. If you look at the people he was close to, a lot of them were in the Eastern establishment; when he chose to move back [to New York] from California, he went to the heart of the Eastern establishment, so I don't think that there was ever any hatred. It was t¹ e feeling of a poor boy from a small store in a small town* who kind of wished he had some of the trappings that go with being a Yale graduate, although he went to Duke [University] Law School, which is very establishment.

John Ehrlichman, assistant to the president for domestic affairs Nixon used to talk about the Eastern establishment, but a lot of good people

---

* Nixon's father, Frank, was the proprietor of both a grocery store in Whittier and of a gas station for a time.

came from Harvard and similar places. He took them on, muttering and chirping all the time, about how deplorable it was, but he took them on, and confided in them.

Robert Bork, solicitor general; acting attorney general I was teaching at Yale* and was at home watching "The Avengers" with my kids when a phone call came saying I would get a call from [Attorney General Richard] Dick Kleindienst. So he called and said, "If you were offered the post of solicitor general, would you accept?" I answered, "I certainly would." Then John Ehrlichman called and asked if I could come down to Camp David the next day. Then John Dean called and asked if I had any skeletons in my closet—in retrospect, I find this an interesting question. I went down to Camp David and spent about forty-five minutes with Nixon, discussing the job and legal philosophy, which he was very good at. I had met Nixon once before. At that time, I had a red beard. He came around the table and someone said, "This is Professor Bork, from Yale." He hated the Ivy League; he looked up, and saw my beard, and recoiled two steps. It was like someone had blundered—how did they let this guy in the room? At Camp David, Nixon and I were, for the most part, alone. He gave me a twenty-minute lecture on the proper role of a judge; how he should act and behave. I was pretty impressed, because I thought I could have been given a slightly better lecture on the topic, but then I had been working at it for years—and this was a guy who was running all kinds of issues in the world. He was enormously knowledgeable, enormously intelligent—from the details of local politics, to foreign policy, to judicial philosophy.

Raymond Price He has always had individuals within the Eastern establishment with whom he has good rapport. [The resentment] has been more not of his resentment of them, but their resentment of him. A lot of what developed traces back to the Hiss case and Helen Gahagan Douglas; I have often thought that my liberal friends in the Eastern establishment—of which I have been a part—could never forgive him for being right about Alger Hiss. Nixon likes to think of himself as a practical idealist; he believes in the morality of consequences. He inherited an office which, in the hands of his celebrated predecessors—like Roosevelt, Truman, Kennedy, and Johnson—had been much more manipulative than his own, and had cut many more legal corners than he had, and had been celebrated for having done so. He was always acutely sensitive to being on the short side of a dou-

---

* In 1973.

ble standard which was operated by the Eastern establishment. After being beaten up on—and being beaten up on over the years—you get a little defensive.

Robert Finch He was very conscious of his hard-scrabble background, and that marked him in certain aspects of his political life, where it was "me against the world." I think that there were some overtones of that in the fight against Kennedy.* He was proud of the fact that he had earned his spurs.

Robert Odle, Jr. Running through Nixon's whole life is a problem with people like the Rockefellers, the Lodges, the Kennedys, who had advantages he did not have: the Palm Beaches to escape to in the winter; the Fifth Avenue apartments; never having to worry about putting the kids through college; having parents who gave them much when they were children; having Joe [Kennedy] to help them in West Virginia. This was juxtaposed to his own situation: the mother who had to take the son to Arizona; finding oil after Frank Nixon sold the property. I don't think you can possibly overestimate the importance of all that; it's the thread you see all through his career—in his books, his speeches; it's at the heart of the concept of the silent majority; it explains the selection of Spiro Agnew; it's what he saw in John Connally; it's at the core of understanding Nixon.

Howard Phillips The contrast between Nixon and Kennedy is striking: Kennedy had lifetime friends who played a key role in all that he did—if you got on the boat, you stayed on the boat until the end of the trip; Nixon was not close to almost anyone—he spoke of his admiration for [French president Charles] de Gaulle, who always spoke of the need to have reserve, mystery, distance from others. Nixon, in trying to construct himself as a heroic figure—and because of his own lack of confidence and self-esteem, which comes from a father's approbation—found it difficult to get close; perhaps he was afraid that if people got too close, they would discover how little of him was really there.

John Ehrlichman I remember when Bobby Kennedy announced for president, sitting with Nixon in Portland, Oregon, and hearing his reaction. He felt that, somehow or other, his life and the Kennedys' lives were intertwined. He had met Jack in Florida when they were both congressmen, so

---

* The 1960 presidential campaign against then-Senator John F. Kennedy.

when someone like [E. Howard] Hunt or [Anthony] Ulasewicz* was given a trick to do with relation to Kennedy, you can be sure it always emanated from Richard Nixon; it was not anybody else's preoccupation but his. He was the driver about the concern with the Bay of Pigs. He had me try to get hold of the CIA files on the Bay of Pigs; to find out what, in fact, Kennedy's orders were. Richard Helms displayed his ambivalence in being very reluctant to give up those files. I don't think he ever did; I don't think Nixon ever got his hands on those files, but he certainly wanted them.

Alexander Butterfield He called me in once, furious. It was in 1971 or 1972. He heard the president of Harvard† was on the White House grounds: "What is that son-of-a-bitch, Bok, doing here?" I found out that he was a member of the Committee for Preservation of the White House; Harvard is a big donor of these lovely paintings. So I said, "He is meeting with Mrs. Nixon; he's a member of her committee and she is entertaining all those people in the East Room." Well: "Never again! How did he get in, in the first place?" He asked me once—in very profane language—"Did one of those dirty bastards ever invite me to his f–ing men's club or his goddamn country club? Not once." He was shaking. He was a guy from Whittier [California]; he didn't have the social graces, the education. The hatred was very deep-seated. He didn't just not like them; he hated them. Why doesn't he mellow? He's the president now; he's got it all over them.

Herbert Brownell To be so divisive is bound to fail in the long run. It's too big a country. Nixon had eight years of bipartisanship under Eisenhower, so I was surprised by his attitude, which led, of course, to his downfall.

Marshall Green He came to office having more of an instinct for foreign policy than any other president before him—with the possible exception of Thomas Jefferson. But there were fatal flaws: suspicion, secrecy, and friends who were not really friends.

William Rusher Nixon is a deeply flawed personality. There is probably a terrible story he could tell on the psychoanalyst's couch of things that happened to him as a boy that left him permanently insecure and resentful. Nixon has the soul of an alley cat; he travels alone at night, stealthfully. He is a conniver. I say that without any pejorative connotation. That's just the way he is.

---

* A retired New York City policeman engaged by John Ehrlichman to do political undercover work for the White House.
† Derek Bok.

Stephen Bull He didn't like to criticize people. If he had a problem with me, for example, he would have been more comfortable saying to Haldeman, "Bull is really messing up," rather than saying to me, "You really messed up." He wouldn't chew people out, nor praise them; it wasn't his style. With his close staff—the key people—he was informal. He wasn't a joke teller, but he enjoyed a good joke.

NIXON'S HUMOR

Charles Colson, special counsel to the president He had a wry sense of humor. Sometimes he would laugh hysterically. There was a time when Kissinger would walk into the Oval Office unannounced. It was something we tolerated because he played such a key role. But Nixon tried to break him of that [habit] but in subtle ways. One day, Kissinger came in, and without any rehearsing between us, Nixon said, "I don't know, Chuck, about that idea you had about dropping a nuclear weapon on Hanoi. I'm not sure the time is quite ready. But if we try to do it, let's not tell Henry." He could see Kissinger out of the corner of his eye. Kissinger froze in his tracks.

George P. Shultz Sometime in 1973, Nixon decided that he wanted to reimpose wage and price controls, and a wage-price freeze. The freeze had been a political winner, even though the policy, in the long run, had been a catastrophe. He decided to reimpose them over my objections. I told him that while I would support him, I wanted to resign, because I didn't agree with him at all. He asked me to stay for [Soviet General Secretary Leonid] Brezhnev's visit, to handle the economic issues, which I did. This was the occasion for one of the few flashes of humor that I recall with Nixon. Herb Stein,* who agreed with me and opposed the controls, said to Nixon, "Mr. President, you can't walk on water twice." Nixon replied, "Herb, you can, if it's frozen."

Daniel Ellsberg, defendant, the Pentagon Papers trial I was in Vietnam with retired Brigadier General Edward Lansdale. We were working with the South Vietnamese to run elections for a constituent assembly in 1966—Lansdale thought that if we could make these the first really honest elections in Vietnam's history, it would show people that they had a way to get rid of a district chief other than by having the Vietcong kill him. In 1966,

---

* Chairman, Council of Economic Advisers.

Nixon came to Vietnam to visit his old running mate, Henry Cabot Lodge, who was then the U.S. ambassador. He was going to spend an evening with his old friend, Ed Lansdale—when Nixon was vice-president, he had had a lot of dealings with Lansdale in covert operations—so he dropped in on Lansdale. There were about a dozen of us at the house, in Saigon. Lansdale introduced all of us to Nixon. It was about five in the afternoon, so he had his five o'clock shadow—which looked a little like Yasser Arafat's. He seemed intelligent. When we were about to sit down, he said, "Ed, what are you up to?" Lansdale said, "Well, Mr. President, we are trying to help make the coming elections the most honest they have ever had in Vietnam." We then sat down, and Nixon, who was sitting next to Lansdale, said, "Well, yes. Honest, yes, as long as you win!" And he slammed his elbow into Lansdale's elbow and slapped his knee in the same motion. It was clear we didn't have a kindred spirit as our guest.

3

Administrative Style

PUTTING THE ADMINISTRATION TOGETHER

In planning his campaign for the Republican Party's presidential nomination in 1968, Mr. Nixon had worked with a small circle of assistants and advisers, including Patrick Buchanan, Dwight Chapin, Leonard Garment, Raymond Price, and his longtime secretary, Rose Mary Woods.

Following his nomination at the Republican National Convention—which took place in Miami Beach, Florida, in August 1968—Mr. Nixon drew longtime California aides John Ehrlichman, H. R. Haldeman, Murray Chotiner, and Ronald Ziegler into his expanding inner circle.

As Mr. Nixon organized his first administration, he developed a close-knit system in which a very small group of key staff had the greatest access, including Haldeman, as chief of staff; Ehrlichman, as counsel and later head of the Domestic Policy Council; his national security adviser, Dr. Henry Kissinger; attorney general John Mitchell; and his press secretary, Ronald Ziegler. This group was later supplemented by George Shultz, who served as secretary of labor, secretary of the treasury, and director of the Office of Management and Budget (OMB); and special assistant Charles Colson.

Some longtime Republican Party leaders were not, however, invited to join the administration.

Herbert Brownell I am puzzled about this. My own experience was that when Nixon was elected president, I saw him once or twice, and got the distinct impression that I was persona non grata to the group around him. There was a definite move on their part to displace anybody who had been close to Nixon before, in an advisory capacity. The same thing happened to

[Robert] Finch and some of those men who had been loyal on Nixon's behalf in earlier years. Also, at that time, Nixon was changing from a middle-of-the-road Republican to a conservative Republican. It's easy to blame Ehrlichman and Haldeman for those changes but, perhaps, they were taking orders.

Dwight Chapin Nixon was always bringing in new people: Len Garment, Pat Moynihan,* Frank Shakespeare, George Shultz, and on and on; this was one of the keys to his success. Some of the best political minds of the past twenty years have been Nixon's finds. He understood that people can perform up to a certain level; then they may lose interest, or may get bored. He's got this incredible sense: if I want to continue to rise, I must continue to bring in people who are knowledgeable and bright—perhaps smarter than I am. In Labor, for example, he brought in George Shultz, who was much brighter than Nixon would ever be in that area—the only place where this didn't happen is State, because Nixon intended to run the State Department—or when he brought in John Mitchell to run the campaign. Mitchell is imperative in understanding Nixon's success in later years: forgetting Watergate, what Mitchell accomplished in 1968 was incredible.

Donald Rumsfeld There is no question that a major portion of it was Nixon. He was the leader, the president, the person who was deciding who he would bring in, and he was very bold. He reached out and brought in Kissinger—who had been with Rockefeller; he brought in [Daniel Patrick] Moynihan, who had been with Kennedy and Johnson; he brought me out of Congress; he brought George Shultz out of the University of Chicago; he had a very talented group of people connected with that administration. I can remember Nixon, when he was trying to get me to come into the Cabinet in 1969, mentioning George Shultz and how pleased he was with the quality of the people. Maurice Stans had been a star performer in the Eisenhower administration; Bill Rogers had been attorney general under Eisenhower.

There were really two kinds of people in the Nixon administration. There were people who had roots that were both professional and political—they had been in and around administrations for a long time. Kissinger had been at Harvard and involved in the Johnson administration; Bryce Harlow had been in the Eisenhower administration. None of those people's principal relationships with Nixon or the government of the United States was related to the 1968 campaign. Then there were people whose principal relationship

---

* Assistant to the president for urban affairs; counselor to the president.

with Nixon and the government of the United States was that they had been involved with the campaign, and developed very close, intimate relationships with the president. And Nixon mixed those; the campaign becomes a continuity, to a certain extent, and they are the ones who plan the day, the travel, the schedule, the issues, the whole campaign apparatus. If you lose, it's disbanded; if you win, it moves right into the transition and then into the administration.

Alexander Butterfield When Finch had his little breakdown, it was all pretty hush-hush. He had a tremendously stressful time and wasn't hacking it; he was coming apart at the seams. Nixon brought him immediately over [to the White House], gave him a title [counselor to the president], and gave him an office at the EOB [Executive Office Building]. I don't know what the hell he did; I never saw him around very much.

Bobby Baker The biggest, dumbest mistake Richard Nixon ever made was not making Bob Finch his chief of staff in the White House. The Washington media didn't like Nixon, but they liked Finch; he would have kept Nixon from those silly, dictatorial things. It just seemed natural to me—and to other politicians—for Nixon, who was an introvert, to have a warm, friendly guy named Bob Finch. But he put him in the worst department in town— HEW [Department of Health, Education and Welfare].

William Saxbe, attorney general One of Nixon's problems was that he surrounded himself with guys that had no involvement in a political campaign. I referred to Haldeman and Ehrlichman as Nazis when I was in the Senate; that is the way they operated.

Alexander Butterfield Haldeman was invaluable; he was a very good staff chief. He was not well liked by the staff. People like Ehrlichman, even though he had a little arrogance—people thought he was arrogant when he testified [before the Senate Select Committee on Watergate]. But people forget that we—the White House staff—hated the committee; they were trying to harm our man. But Haldeman was very abrupt with everyone—he was all business; he did exactly what Richard Nixon wanted him to do.

Ronald Ziegler In assessing a very good—and complex—leader like Richard Nixon, you must realize that in order to lead in thought and action, you have to constantly reach out for new ideas, new thinking, new people, to contribute to the process. If you look at the contemporary scene, this is one of Clinton's shortcomings. By keeping around you only those people who have been around you, you may get good thinking and have good people, and it does not indicate that they are not good enough because you add new thought and dimension to your leadership. That was what Nixon did. Some people interpret that as shunting Finch or Klein aside. If you look at President Nixon's formation of his government, he brought a great variety of thought into it: Arthur Burns,° Paul McCracken,† George Shultz, [James] Schlesinger, [Daniel Patrick] Moynihan, Kissinger—a wide range of thought. And because of this, his administration generated and stimulated a lot of new ideas and creative thought, both on the socioeconomic side and on the domestic side, and certainly on foreign policy. And I don't have to say this as a partisan, because history shows it. People who get involved in the petty argument that Nixon came in and shunted aside people who had been loyal to him for all of those years have a very shallow and narrow-minded approach; it is far off the mark in assessing his leadership.

Robert Hartmann The old friends, like [Bryce] Harlow, were fine, but the Californians were a bunch of jerks; they didn't need to be told anything— not by me, or even by the Republican congressional leadership.

Leonard Garment Over the years, Nixon observed politics very closely; it's not a tea party or a love match, but a form of combat. Part of what fueled him to be effective was anger, ambition, and the appetite for revenge—the knowledge that unless you made yourself fearful to your enemies, they would savage you. He had a tendency to pursue these instincts with self-damaging consequences. People would say he's tricky, and he was; he could be awful at times, so he became, in a sense, the most hated man in modern politics. He learned from this that he had to be nicer—the new Nixon. He also had to be very careful about having people near him who would say "no" when he was being carried by those tides of fury into dangerous waters. Most important, he developed a keen sense of compartmentalization: he saw that in campaigns the worst thing was for too many people to do too many things without a sense of limitation and restraint. So you learn to avoid having people in the wrong areas; you minimize leaks; and—most important—you maintain control. He needed this, and he needed a ringmaster to keep the lions on their separate stools. That man was Haldeman. In the first year, Nixon had these things working effectively: he had Kissinger, the best

---

° Chairman, Board of Governors, Federal Reserve System.
† Chairman, council of ecomonic advisers.

foreign policy brain in the country; he had in Haldeman one of the most organized, disciplined, loyal, self-denying ringmasters; in Ehrlichman, he had a very smart, tough, lawyer-politician, policy manager.

James R. Schlesinger, staff, Bureau of the Budget; chairman, Atomic Energy Commission; director of Central Intelligence; secretary of defense Richard Nixon had a very high respect for governance—for the art of government. Peculiarly enough, he divided that very sharply from politics—and perhaps he did so far more sharply than was beneficial to his career in the long run. He had a very high regard for government officials. He was influenced by Charles de Gaulle, who said one had to go out and recruit the very best people one could find for government service, and then to provide those people with a high degree of authority within their confined areas of responsibility. So government was separated in Nixon's style and mind from politics. As a result, he recruited some excellent people, but they were not to intrude, by and large, into the special area of politics. He was also prepared to move them around, probably thinking it was not a good thing to have anybody stay in a particular slot for too long.

Frederic V. Malek, deputy undersecretary, Department of Health, Education and Welfare (HEW); special assistant to the president for personnel; deputy director, Committee to Reelect the President (CRP); deputy director, Office of Management and Budget (OMB) He was looking for philosophical compatibility, but competence was number one; he really wanted competence. I often made the case: don't make political loyalty or philosophical compatibility a given, because the bulk of America doesn't live or think in those terms; look for people of great ability who can accept your leadership. If you say: This is where we are going, philosophically, they will accept that, and go in that direction. We will bring them on and convert them to your philosophy. So look primarily for people of intellectual capacity and managerial competence.

Richard Kleindienst After the election was over, I was back in Arizona. Mitchell called me and said the president-elect wanted him to be the attorney general. Mitchell told him he would accept only if I became his deputy attorney general. I said, "John, I don't want the job." The next thing I knew Nixon was on the phone. I tried to explain to him that I had to think of my family, but he said, "Dick, I need John to be attorney general, and he says he won't do it unless you're his deputy. So I'm asking you to change your mind," and I said yes.

Maurice Stans It didn't come up until after the election. It was strange in the way in which it happened. John Mitchell called me one day when I was visiting a friend in New York, and it was one of John's usual, short conversations. He said, "Maury, the president would like you to be the postmaster general." I said, "John, I'd like to do almost anything for the president, but that's one position I don't think I want. I was deputy postmaster general for two years; I know the workings of the department. I don't think it's a viable operation in which to make any kind of a record. Tell the president I'm sorry—that is one I just have to say no to." He said, "Are there any other positions you feel that your ability and background would fit?" I said, "Yes. There are just two: I think I could do a good job in Treasury or in Commerce." He called me back a week later: "Maury? John Mitchell. That Commerce job is available if you'd like to have it." I said, "John, nothing would please me better." He said, "Okay, I'll tell the boss."

Roy Ash, director, Office of Management and Budget (OMB) My first meeting with him was in 1968, at the time of the presidential campaign, when I and Tex Thornton—with whom I worked at the time at Litton Industries—wanted to make a financial contribution. Since it was going to be a significant contribution, we did so by visiting him at home and delivering it to him there.

After the election, I got a telephone call saying that the president-elect wanted to see me. I went to the Pierre Hotel and he recalled the meeting we had had at his house—he's got a great memory; he must have a thousand names, pictures, events in mind. He said very simply, "Now that I have this job, and having been vice-president, I know what it is. I have a big management job ahead of me. I understand you know something about management. Do you want to help?" I didn't know what he was talking about exactly, but I said, "Okay. I will." The president asked me to put together a group to study the question of the structure of the executive branch. A good deal of work on this question had been done in previous administrations, so it was not so much a matter of conducting research, but determining what conclusions reached before could be applied.

We started to work in 1969 to put together a staff. The first thing to do was to strip out of the White House functions that had been put there in earlier times, but were no longer appropriate for the White House. We also recommended the creation of the Office of Management and Budget (OMB). The Environmental Protection Agency (EPA) also came out of our work, as did the Drug Enforcement Agency (DEA). John Connally was on our committee, and he was always thinking Texas-style. He led us in proposing four major departments to replace the existing Cabinet structure. This blew all the fuses in town; people in the Congress wanted to know how this would affect the relationship between the Congress and the executive branch. They had in mind the fact that the congressional committee structure parallels the executive branch structure. If there is a Department of Energy, there is going to be an energy committee; therefore, every time you change or reduce the executive branch, there will be committee chairmen and subchairmen who don't have jobs anymore. So nothing came of this idea.

Walter Hickel John Mitchell called me on Thanksgiving Day, 1968, and said that the president was considering me for [the post of] secretary of the interior. I said, "John, I don't want to go to Washington; I have much to do up here [in Alaska]." John replied, "Can I tell the president-elect that you will keep an open mind?" I said, "Sure." The next day, [Vice-President-elect] Spiro Agnew calls for no real reason and wishes me a happy holiday. Then, on Sunday, Nixon called—he had obviously been briefed by Mitchell and Agnew—and said, "Wally, we have chosen you as secretary of the interior." I hung up the phone and cried.

James Farmer, assistant secretary for administration, Department of Health, Education and Welfare (HEW) Bob Finch called and asked me to have breakfast at the Waldorf. He asked if I would consider a high-level appointment at HEW. I told him that for me to take such an appointment would be the kiss of death, politically; I would be painting a bull's-eye on my chest, my back, and both my sides, because 96 percent of the registered blacks were Democrats, and Nixon was one of the most unpopular of the Republican politicians among blacks. However, I would not turn it down out-of-hand; I would want to know what job was being offered, what responsibilities I would have, and what authority I would have.

He indicated he would have to talk to the president-elect about that. He offered me three jobs; the one I favored was assistant secretary of administration. I consulted with black civil rights leaders, who said I should take the offer. The black students—including militants, such as the Black Panthers—said, "Yes it is your duty to take it; we have to have somebody who knows where the bodies are buried—somebody who knows where the pots of money are that the organizations can go to, to get funding for community projects. We have to have somebody we can trust there."

So I took the assistant secretary position. Bob Finch told me that when he informed Nixon that he was considering me for a high-level position, the president-elect replied, "James Farmer? He's a TV cowboy; he shoots from the hip. What makes you think the first time he fails to get his way, he won't call a press conference and blast us to hell?"

Finch said, "I don't know, of course, but I have confidence in Jim's integrity. I think he will play by the rules as long as he can."

Vernon Walters When I came to the CIA, I had just come from running an operation about which the agency knew nothing. [Richard] Helms, who had wanted someone else, said, "I've heard about you; what do you know about intelligence?" I said, "Well, I've been negotiating with the Chinese and Vietnamese for three years, and smuggled Henry Kissinger into Paris fifteen times without you or anybody in the agency knowing anything about it."

William Ruckelshaus My coming over to EPA [Environmental Protection Agency] was the result of my name having been floated by a friend to *Newsweek* in the spring of 1970, without any authorization from me—or even knowledge from me; I didn't even know what EPA was when my name appeared in the magazine. The administration was having trouble in filling the position. I went to see the attorney general and told him that while I hadn't floated my name as potential EPA administrator, if they were looking for somebody, I was interested.

Leonard Garment I did not start at the White House right away. After the election, Nixon suggested that I go to work in the Washington office of our law firm. I don't think they knew how to fit me in at the White House; it was sort of like the music stopped. Nixon said to me, "You'll be like Clark Clifford;* you'll make money, entertain, be in demand. I'll see to it that you receive messages from me—back-channeling."

So there I was, at the firm at 1701 Pennsylvania Avenue, looking right down at the White House, and there were all those guys I had hired, having the time of their lives, running the world, and I was sitting in the office, having coffee and danish. So I finally said to Peter Flanigan, "Tell the president that either I am going into the White House or I am going back to New York." Peter called back and said, "The president says welcome aboard." They gave me the royal treatment: I had the perks and status of Kissinger, Haldeman, and Ehrlichman, but I was kept separate from the inner circle; I think that Nixon knew that I didn't have the temperament to kick heads around—that was what Nixon wanted, at the time, to get things done. I got involved with

---

* Secretary of Defense in Johnson administration and quintessential Washington insider.

civil rights, school desegregation, the arts, and the National Goals Research Staff; anything that nobody else wanted to do, I did. I never saw Nixon alone during this period—when I first met him, when I really didn't know him, I saw him a lot. Ehrlichman would say, "Why don't you go inside and talk to him? Get on the president's schedule and shoot the breeze with him; it would be good for him." But I thought: if he wants me, he'll call me.

Raymond Price I am not sure that Nixon understood that Len wanted into the White House; he tried to create a nice situation for Len in Washington, so that Len could do well in the law firm and also be available to him. Len was a very valuable part of the team even while he was in the private sector.

Charles Colson Bryce Harlow said, "The president needs you; he needs to be kept in contact with the outside world. Haldeman and Ehrlichman are cutting him off. You're the only guy who can do it."

John Dean I was the associate deputy attorney general, which meant that I worked in the office of the deputy attorney general, and my function was as the Justice Department liaison with the Congress. I had a pleasant working relationship with Mitchell at Justice—not a particularly close relationship; I saw him when I had business with the attorney general. Later, other people categorized me as a Mitchell man. I never felt that; I never felt I was anybody's man—and certainly not John Mitchell's. In fact, Mitchell had recommended that I not go to the White House to work when I had an opportunity to go over there. He said, "You ought to stay at the Department of Justice; there will be more here for you, and you will go up the ladder here."

I was recruited to go to the White House by [deputy counsel to the president and deputy assistant to the president for domestic affairs Egil] Bud Krogh. It was just too good a title, with too good a potential to turn down at that age, and that stage of my career. Had I to do it over again, I am sure I would do the same thing. It was a great position—middle-level staff, but a nice job for a young man. I was a young man on the make and this was a great job. Philosophically, I liked some of what Nixon believed in—and some of it I didn't like. I've never been an ideologue. I was not driven by ideology—a love of Richard Nixon—as much as the fact that I was fascinated by the presidency and the way the city worked. I wanted to really learn how government worked and get some of the best jobs I could get, as a young man, because I was planning to leave government and go out with that experience and do my own thing. That was my agenda, and as the opportunities came along, I just leaped at them—as I wrote in a book called *Blind Ambition*. That is what young men do.

Lawrence Higby, campaign aide, 1968; administrative assistant to H. R. Haldeman Dean came in through Mitchell. Chapin and I interviewed him. He seemed like a good young guy who could handle the day-to-day legal affairs. It was never envisioned that he would become a policy person. We thought he was conducting an investigation. We knew he had been involved in the discussions of Liddy's plan, but we thought the whole thing had been shut down and was ridiculous, which, I think, Haldeman agreed with—the idea that they were going to have a boat at the Democratic convention with prostitutes on it. Anybody who knew anything about the Nixon administration knew that they were the most straitlaced people; Haldeman would get mad if we had a second drink at dinner.

Morton Halperin, staff member, National Security Council (NSC); consultant to the NSC I had known Kissinger; we had taught together at Harvard. I was scheduled, before he got appointed, to go up and speak at the defense policy seminar that he ran—which we had taught together for a number of years. I was then working in the Defense Department. When I went up, he had been appointed, and we talked after class and he asked me to come to work for him.

I spent most of my time writing or reviewing memos that were going to the president, or to the National Security Council—writing memos for Kissinger on issues that he was trying to move forward—and waiting for Kissinger; that was the single largest amount of time, standing outside his office waiting to see him. Sometimes there was a line; sometimes he would call you over; and then there would be a call from the president; or call you over and then decide something else was very urgent. He had a tendency to do that—which he had at Harvard, as well.

He was looking for lots of different things in terms of staff. In my case, I knew him well and we had a good relationship. I also think—from his point of view—he wanted somebody who had a Harvard connection and had a good relation to his Harvard colleagues, who were pressing him to hire a number of people. I think he thought he had to hire one person who came out of that. He also wanted people who knew the bureaucracy. He understood that he had never worked in the government and didn't really know how the bureaucracies worked, and wanted somebody, in particular, who knew the Defense Department. We only hired a couple of people who had worked in the campaign. Kissinger had a free hand to hire his own people, and they were mostly career people, or outside people who didn't seem to have any clear ideology, or—if anything—were probably thought of as being left. There was certainly no sense that Kissinger had a requirement from the president, or anybody else, to hire people with a particular ideological bent.

Helmut Sonnenfeldt, staff member, National Security Council (NSC); counselor to the Department of State He was interested in people he had intellectual respect for—people that he knew something about from his academic life and previous consulting jobs in the government. But there was no kind of litmus test as to substance. He was looking for broad, overall compatibility. The country was divided on Vietnam—whether or not to get out; there were some of each [persuasion] in the NSC staff. There were differences of long standing about how to deal with the Soviet Union.

Winston Lord, staff member, National Security Council; director, State Department policy planning staff I was working on the policy planning staff of the Department of Defense, where my boss was Morton Halperin. He knew Kissinger from Harvard, and he was one of the first people Kissinger asked to join his staff when he was selected as national security adviser. Mort, in turn, asked me to join him at the White House, so about a month after the inauguration, I had an interview with Kissinger, who obviously took me on as a result of Halperin's recommendation. From February 1969 to February 1970, I was in the old Executive Office Building (OEOB), working on option papers for the president within the NSC system and, in addition, working on think pieces. I did not work directly with Kissinger during this period; I only came to the West Wing of the White House in February 1970, when I replaced Anthony Lake as Kissinger's special assistant—primarily for the Vietnam negotiations and the China opening, as well as some speech writing and help on the Russian negotiations.

Stephen Bull About a week before the election, Larry Higby called me and asked if I would be interested in coming to Washington if Nixon won. I had intended to go back to working in New York for Canada Dry* after the election. Then, the Monday after Election Day, I went in to talk to Bob Haldeman at the Pierre Hotel. We had a brief conversation, in which it was assumed that if I had showed up for the appointment, I was ready to take a position. I was told to go downstairs, forthwith, and begin doing things. I worked as an office manager with the transition; it appeared to be a very

---

* A division of the Seagram Corporation.

efficient operation. It was an adventure. I was only twenty-six at the time. I was recently out of the Marine Corps; I returned from Vietnam in 1966, and was generally supportive of Nixon's candidacy. But, I admit it, it [taking the administration post] was half adventure, as much as political commitment.

Ronald Ziegler I was twenty-nine and not thinking in terms of: I wonder what I am going to get out of this; if I had been at a different stage of my career, I would have thought more in those terms. I just assumed there would be something for me to do, but I did not think out a position, nor did I seek the position either of press spokesman or press secretary. It was in Florida—where we went shortly after the election—where I more or less flowed into the spokesman role, just because the transition began. We had our first briefings at the Royal Biscayne Hotel. I gathered the press, which was my role: the basic logistics—travel and dealing with the press—and we had a speaker phone hookup with Herb Klein—who was somewhere else, on business—and Herb and I did the initial briefings. Then, it evolved that I was named transition press spokesman and, in fact, carried on the daily briefings at the Pierre Hotel. It soon became evident that President Nixon would be better served if I became press secretary, so the position of director of communications was formed for Herb Klein—even from the beginning, my initial reporting function, as with all of the White House staff, was through Haldeman.

David Wilson, staff assistant, Office of the Counsel to the President I was hired by John Dean, who was counsel to the president. At that time, there was one other person in the office, Fred Fielding, who was John's deputy. It was one of the few jobs I've ever had where you would walk in in the morning and read the newspaper, and whatever you saw on the front pages, there was a fairly high degree of likelihood that you would be involved in some aspect of it. I spent a fair amount of time on Freedom of Information Act questions—whether the government would have to release certain information, some of which was more sensitive than other information. I remember working on a situation that involved a study done by the Office of Science and Technology on air bags, which the government did not want released; we had to develop a theory to justify not releasing it.

H. R. Haldeman He greatly admired a lot of women: Golda Meir [prime minister, state of Israel]; and—in later years—Margaret Thatcher [prime minister, United Kingdom]. We did have some women in major posts: Virginia Knauer [Consumer Affairs], Anne Armstrong [counselor to the president], and others. The fact that we didn't have more was a reflection of the time, and the nonvisibility of capable women: there weren't many female chairmen of banks, or of corporations, or religious leaders. There was a recognition of the need, but not a driving one. We certainly didn't go way overboard, the way [President Bill] Clinton has.

Frederic V. Malek When I was deputy director of the Office of Management and Budget (OMB), I put together a team of people who are today in major corporate positions: one is the president and CEO of the Brown Group; another is the president of Investor Diversified Services; another is the chairman of Alcoa. That's a pretty strong group. I haven't seen anything like that in the post-Watergate period—and this was just my little group at OMB. This suggests the kinds of people we were able to attract.

SUPREME COURT NOMINATIONS

Two of President Nixon's nominations for the U.S. Supreme Court—Clement F. Haynesworth, Jr., and G. Harold Carswell—were turned down by the Senate. He did, however, appoint four justices who were approved: Warren Burger, who replaced Earl Warren as chief justice; Harry Blackmun; Lewis F. Powell, Jr.; and William Rehnquist.

James Farmer I clearly remembered the reports from CORE [Congress of Racial Equality] staff and attorneys in Florida about Carswell, which indicated that he was hostile to everything that we were working toward—in other words, he was a racist.

The press called me—people who had covered me during the [civil rights] movement days. They asked what I thought of the Carswell nomination. I then had to in my mind go over the things I was working on at HEW, many of which were bringing minority groups into government—all of which would be thrown down the drain if I called a press conference and blasted. So I said, "No comment."

They said "Jim, come on. No comment on Carswell?" It became increasingly difficult for me. How could I have not comment on Carswell?

One evening, a member of the HEW staff who was known as the president's man in the department came into my office. He talked about certain senators who had not made up their minds on Carswell. He said, "We have been thinking—he didn't say who 'we' was—that if you would get on the phone and call the senators on the fence and tell them that Judge Carswell is okay on civil rights, we'd be home free."

I said, "You've got to be kidding. I've been saying 'no comment' for you, and that is the best I can do. Now will you please get out of my office?" And he backed out of the office.

I expected to hear from Haldeman or Ehrlichman, but I didn't. I guess that they knew better than to call me. But that hastened my thinking: I said, "I can't sit here any longer."

I also received a call or letter from Jack Greenberg, who was counsel of the NAACP Legal and Defense Fund. He said, "Jim, don't you think this is the time to get out?" I got a postcard from [former black militant] Eldridge Cleaver filled with four-letter words, ending with, "Get out and come on home, brother." All of this built up the pressure in my mind.

Richard Moore The president knew that I had been a member of the New York Bar, so just before he was to announce his choices for the [Supreme] Court, he called me into his office. He said that a Judge Mulligan, of New York, had been highly recommended to him; what did I think of Judge Mulligan? I knew enough about him to say he would be a perfectly fine appointment—he had been dean of the Fordham [University] Law School. "But," I said, "while he would be easily confirmed, he wouldn't be a spectacular appointment. You haven't mentioned William Rehnquist. Is that because you considered him and then did not select him, or has he not come to your attention?" He said, "Bill Rehnquist is just an assistant attorney general; how can we justify him?" I had known Bill from my year at the Department of Justice. I said, "He is more than just an assistant attorney general; he is the chief interpreter of the Constitution for the president; he is the president's lawyer's lawyer." That impressed Nixon. "Moreover," I said, "he has been to the Court before." Nixon asked, "What do you mean?" I said, "He was a law clerk to Robert Jackson." He said, "Jackson was the only good appointment Roosevelt made. I once wrote an article on an opinion of Jackson's and got a four-page letter from him." I thought: we are getting someplace here.

I got out of there as fast as I could and raced over to the department. There was Rehnquist, looking a little shocked. I said, "What is the matter?" He said, "We have just been going over the short list for the Court"—his job was to evaluate various candidates. Now he was just told he was on the list. At about ten o'clock the next morning, the president decided that he wanted Rehnquist. Years later, in February 1978, I had just been married—I was a widower—and the Bushes gave a lunch for us. Rehnquist and Mr. Nixon were there, and Nixon told the story of the Rehnquist appointment. He was very proud that his appointee became the chief justice. Those two appointments—of Rehnquist and Lewis Powell—were magnificent appointments. If another vacancy had occurred, [Robert] Bork would have been a very likely candidate; he was solicitor general at the time. And he [Nixon] would have gotten him confirmed, too.

John Dean We were involved in the process of helping to do the screening of potential nominees. Again, this was an Ehrlichman project where he called upon myself and David Young—who was then working for him—and we flew around the country and interviewed people to see if they were Supreme Court timber. Some had been suggested by Mitchell, and others by Ehrlichman, or maybe even the president. We would discuss constitutional issues with them and see how they would handle a confirmation hearing, because—by that time—there had been a number of disasters, like Carswell and Haynesworth.

I will tell you a story that I don't know has been told. Richard Moore has always taken credit for the nomination of Bill Rehnquist. It's funny how memories change. It is a lovely memory that he has, but it didn't happen that way. What happened was that we were in trouble finding somebody, and Bill Rehnquist was on a committee that was working on declassification of government documents, so the White House was getting to know him. I'd known Bill Rehnquist and worked with him at the Department of Justice for years. I suggested to Dick Moore, "The perfect person is sitting over at the Department of Justice; he's the one we sent to sift through all of the writings and what have you, as to whether these people are Supreme Court material; he is somebody who clerked the Court; he's somebody who is a true conservative in the law, and believes in it, and knows why he believes in it; he is the perfect candidate. And Dick Moore just kind of twinkled with the idea and then ran with it. That was the genesis of the Bill Rehnquist nomination. I am not looking for the historical credit, but if you want the historical fact, that's where it came from.

STAFF RESPONSIBILITIES

Stephen Bull I was personal assistant to President Nixon; I looked after his schedule on a daily—maybe an hourly—basis. It was a nonsubstantive role; thus, I was not involved in policy. I was about twenty-six or twenty-seven. Three or four of us who were in our twenties were invited to work in the sort of amorphous office of Bob Haldeman, attending to various and sundry tasks. Then, as the duties became better defined, I moved into the position of personal assistant to the president. My job was to get people in and out, to make sure he had the papers in advance, that the right people were there, and to keep the schedule moving. The appointments secretary* was the scheduler; I was the implementor. If he [the president] were going out of town, I would deal with the advance people affecting the president's participation. If there was a campaign stop in 1972, for example, I would not have anything to do with building a crowd, but I would have something to do in talking with the advance man, to ensure that the arrangements being made for the president were in accordance with what I knew the president would want—and not want—to do. Thematic development was an important part of the scheduling process: there was the general philosophy that you could only carry one news story per day, so if you went out to Illinois for a speech to the Chicago Economic Club, the story would have to be economic, and everything would have to relate to it. You might have reinforcing events to that speech, so that he would make good use of his time.

Lawrence Higby My job was to make Haldeman as efficient and as productive as possible. He spent tremendous amounts of time with the president, so his office had to continue running while that was going on. So my day-to-day responsibility was to make sure his office continued to function.

Terrence O'Donnell, staff assistant to H. R. Haldeman; deputy special assistant to the president As assistant to Bob Haldeman, I would help him to perform his chief of staff functions. I would follow up when he came out of meetings with the president; he would always have detailed notes of their conversations, and there would be long lists of things to do. I would sit down at his table—frequently with Larry Higby—and Bob would go over the notes and assign people on the White House staff the responsibliities for performing the various tasks: find someone for this Cabinet job; find someone for the assistant secretary position—a whole host of different items.

David Wilson I got involved in election law—in Nixon's federal and state filings, in part because his campaign was not doing the job fully. We were concerned that the president might be perceived as technically violating the legal requirements unless we rode herd on it. That was the first time I had contact with Gordon Liddy; most of that contact was not very pleasant because I was trying to contact him to see what he was doing about some of the filings and his response was, "We are trying to take care of that, but I am

---

* Dwight Chapin.

very busy—there are more important things to do—so why don't you do it?" I relayed this to John [Dean], who said, "That's right. Gordon is difficult to deal with; he's abrasive. I think you are correct; it's probably falling between the cracks. I want you to get involved." I tried to get Liddy focused on these matters, but—in retrospect—you could understand that he clearly was dealing with other matters: you would call and he would say, "I'm going out of town." I would say, "Where can I reach you?" He would say, "I can't be reached." So I would say, "What do you mean, you can't be reached?" He'd reply, "I can't be reached; it's highly sensitive."

Robert Odle, Jr. I came to the White House in February 1969. I worked with Herb Klein. Nixon and Klein wanted to work with government agencies and bodies so that they would feel they were part of the team; hence Herb Klein's title, director of communications for the executive branch. The idea was that this administration be like the British Cabinet, which speaks with one voice. Our task was to reach out, around the country, to professionals in the media who didn't happen to be attached to the White House—publishers and editors, reporters and columnists.

Alexander Butterfield Nixon didn't have much use for PR guys; he figured they were at the bar all the time. He'd say, "I want to cut the PR people 10 percent at every embassy, out of every staff, every department." In a way, he was right.

Donald E. Santarelli, associate deputy attorney general; administrator, legal enforcement assistance administration Initially, my responsibility was to manage the Nixon crime issue and program response. He was anxious to make sure his campaign promises were translated into a legislative and action program. It was much simpler in those days than it is now, in part because the criminal justice establishment in those days was much smaller than it is now, and the federal government was much less directly involved in the crime issue than it is now. There was greater sensitivity—particularly in Congress, but also from Nixon himself—about the limited role the federal government should play in the crime issue. It was primarily a leadership role, and an assistance-to-state-and-local-governments role. We've sort of lost our compass on that subject in the ensuing twenty years; there is a careless federalization of the law enforcement issue currently.

Frederick C. LaRue I was carried on the White House staff as a special consultant to the president. I basically reported to John Mitchell. I was involved in troubleshooting—we had a lot of civil rights legislation that had to be attended to. The number one priority was school desegregation.

David Wilson In early 1970, when the Democratic Policy Council was set up, John Ehrlichman—who had been counsel to the president—was to head it, and he took with him most of the people who had been involved—to the extent that the council's office was involved—in substantive matters, so that when John Dean was brought on as counsel, he was left with the rudimentary issues of the counsel's office such as clearance of personnel, presidential pardons, legal questions involving presidential gifts, and matters of that sort. We became involved in issues of presidential records: What do you do with them after the presidency is over? And the issue of presidential libraries. There were a lot of personal matters that ended up gravitating toward the counsel's office: the president had his own tax lawyer, but there is an awful lot that is difficult to separate—what is connected with the president—as president—and what is purely personal. As time went on, because there are so many issues dealt with at the presidential level—and because it's a matter of how various personalities interact on the staff level—John became more and more involved in diverse issues and carved out different niches of responsibility.

Donald E. Santarelli I was appointed as LEAA (Law Enforcement Assistance Administration) administrator. My job was to make sure that the federal money went to state and local governments, and also to make sure that the federal establishment didn't take over law enforcement. [FBI Director] J. Edgar Hoover used to rail on the subject when he was alive and well. There was a very limited function then for the law enforcement authorities; we have really lost that issue in the political debate. Feds now just step up to the plate at every swing, and federalization of law enforcement is carelessly engaged in.

A DAY IN THE WHITE HOUSE

Stephen Bull He'd normally come into the office between seven-thirty and eight. In the early morning, he would normally see Kissinger, Haldeman, sometimes Rose Woods. He might have something as early as nine, but generally, the formal schedule would run between nine-thirty and noon. Normally, the main event of the day would be a ten o'clock function; that might be a Cabinet meeting, or something of that magnitude. There would normally be a couple of press events. Normally, nothing would be scheduled between twelve and two. Then he might have another major appointment at about two or three o'clock. Then he would wind up the day with Kissinger again, or Haldeman, or Ehrlichman. He would go back to the residence at around six. I never followed him to the residence. He would work in the Lincoln Sitting Room; he spent a great deal of time there, reading, thinking, writing. The Oval Office was used as somewhat the ceremonial office. He was more comfortable in the office in the Executive Office Building; it was more informal. He would sit in an easy chair there, with his yellow pad and work, and occasionally meet with in-house people.

Frederic V. Malek We had long days. Mine would run for about twelve hours, beginning at 7:30 A.M. Sometime during the day, we would have a staff meeting with Bob Haldeman and a small group, including John Dean, Ron Ziegler, and perhaps Herb Klein and Chuck Colson. I spent a lot of time recruiting people for the key positions in government and working with agency heads and Cabinet members in planning and determining what vacancies were likely to come about—and which should come about due to a lack of performance.

Roy Ash When I first got to the office, I would read the *Intelligence Report* and a digest of important things out of the newspaper, or the previous night's television. One doesn't realize how important those things are to any administration. The previous night's six o'clock news and the morning newspapers help drive the agenda for the day. At eight in the morning, we had a staff meeting with about ten people. The rest of the day was filled with a tremendous amount of paper coming in and out—most of it internally generated. In my second year at OMB, I would meet with every department and agency head to come to a mutual agreement as to what they saw as their goals and objectives in the period ahead. The first time I went to see Secretary of State Rogers, he said, "Our objective is to keep peace in the world." I said, "Let's detail that a little more," and we worked out some pretty good things.

Another thing that never was resolved cleanly was the relative roles of OMB and John Ehrlichman—the role of OMB in preparing option papers for the president. For each issue in front of us, the job was to accumulate all the existing views from the executive branch, distill them, express them honestly to the president, with recommendations, in no more than two pieces of paper, for each issue. As long as Ehrlichman was there, he was pretty much the last guy to deal with on these option papers before they came to the president.

John Ehrlichman My day began at 6:30 A.M. with a car picking me up. I would read the daily news summary on the way in. I had a seven o'clock meeting with my deputy and administrative assistant, for breakfast. Then at seven-thirty, George Shultz and I had a joint staff meeting. We adjourned that at eight o'clock, religiously, when Shultz and I moved to Haldeman's office for a senior staff meeting of about five of us. That ran for about an hour, and was to plan the president's day, to anticipate problems. Henry [Kissinger] was in on it most of the time; he was served his breakfast while the rest of us deliberated. From nine until lunchtime, I had meetings with my staff. I generally had a visitor from outside [the White House] for lunch. The afternoon was more of the same, and in the evening, there was always some sort of dinner. Now, that was the way it was supposed to be; I had a red button on my telephone, and when it was lit up, the president wanted to see me. There was a bell on the wall that would ring; the only way I could stop it was to push the red button. An hour of my morning might be taken up with something he had read in the news summary; two hours in the afternoon might be taken up by some ad hoc assignment he would give me during the day. I would also get a copy of his news summary with notations marked "E." Perhaps eight or ten of these would be directed to me with something like: "Why did this man say this?" At about three o'clock, I would have half an hour with the president to run through my agenda, with six to ten items for decision.

John Dean What was interesting about working at the White House was that you knew everything you processed had the potential for disaster. Problems don't come to the White House unless they are serious problems; they get solved elsewhere, out in the government. So you always have that acknowledgment that you are dealing with something that if you do it wrong, it will be a mistake that will be noticed, so there is subtle pressure in your work. But yet, it becomes fairly routine and you're really working in a crisis center all the time. Because everything is pretty much on a crisis basis, it's always needed yesterday, even though there is good planning, and you are trying to project what you need five months down the road. For example, when the Supreme Court would rule on something, the speechwriters, or the president, or anybody, needed to know: What does this mean? It could be in some esoteric area that I had no knowledge of or my staff had no knowledge of, so we were sent scrambling to find out what the Supreme Court decision meant. A typical day is that everything is untypical; you don't know what you will deal with in a given day.

Lawrence Higby We would get to the White House at about ten of eight. Haldeman would have a series of staff meetings: there was a big-four staff meeting—Kissinger, Bryce Harlow, Shultz, and Ehrlichman would get together in Haldeman's office and go through the issues of the day. During that time, I would either be in that meeting or taking care of the stuff he had given me on the way in. I would join him and brief him on what was going on—scheduling issues and such.

Around nine o'clock, the president would call him in. He would finish up with the president at about ten, when the president started his public day; he would have his meetings between ten and eleven-thirty. He would then be called back into the president's office, and I would try to work on all the things he had given me after his first meeting with the president. I would make a telephone call on an action issue, and follow it up with a memo so there was a record in the staff secretary's system of what people wanted done. He would finish up with the president between twelve and twelve-thirty.

At that point in time, he would come back to his office, and he and I would have lunch together. He would always have just about the same thing for lunch—cottage cheese, pineapple, and a hamburger patty, and, occasionally, a hot fudge sundae, if things were going well. Usually, during the course of lunch, Kissinger and Ziegler would come in, and they would discuss how the morning had gone—what the press briefings had been like. The president's habit was to have a quick lunch, and then a half-hour nap, after which he would call Haldeman back into his office.

Haldeman would come back to his office at about two, and we would repeat the morning routine. We had to make sure that all the stuff the president needed to sign and take care of that day had been taken care of. Haldeman would usually be the last person called in to see the president. That would go on from about five until five minutes before the network news would begin. During that point in time, it was my job to get everything cleared up; to get Haldeman's office packed away, so that he could walk out of the office—give me the two or three things that we had to get done before we left the White House. He would review all the material that needed to go to the president the next day. There was this mad rush so we could get out of the White House and into the car before the president called him after viewing the evening news, because if he didn't get out, he would be called over and, inevitably, end up spending the evening with the president. Haldeman wanted to get home to see his family. On the way home, he would go through his paperwork. I would be sitting there, writing notes as fast as I could. We would drop him off at his house at about seven-ten. Quite often, the president would call, upset about the news coverage. I would get home, kiss my wife, and get on the phone for a half hour, getting all the things he had given me in the car going. I would then have dinner with my wife, try to play with my daughter—who was usually in bed by that time—do paperwork, and go to bed.

H. R. Haldeman If there were any information we needed to be aware of—or if Kissinger was planning to bomb London—he'd report to us about that.

The president would usually arrive in the Oval Office between 8:30 and 9 A.M., and would read the overnight news summary, which was a very good summary of what the international and world press were carrying, and included a recap of the last evening's network news, features from the news weeklies, and from other magazines and periodicals. When the president was ready, he would call Kissinger in for the security briefing. I would go in, in case I had to coordinate anything with him. Then Kissinger would leave and I would review the day ahead with the president, who had the opportunity to chew me out for having made all the wrong appointments. He would then begin his normal ten to twelve appointments schedule ranging from ten- and twenty-minute to half-hour meetings. At about noon, he would have a congressional half hour, where members could be booked in—purely "fanny patting" sessions: a turkey brought in from a district, or a constituent who wanted to meet the president. It also gave the congressman the chance to say, later in the day, "When I saw the president this morning, he said . . ." At about twelve-thirty, I would take in the morning's round of decision memoranda. Later, this chore was handled by my assistant, Alexander Butterfield.

Then the president would have lunch in the Oval Office, or in the small passageway to the left of his desk. His lunch, which would be brought up by the White House Mess, consisted every day of a ring of canned Dole pineapple, a scoop of Knudsen's cottage cheese, a couple of Rye Crisp crackers, and a glass of skim milk.

The afternoon schedule would include meetings, appointments, and ceremonial functions. At around 5 P.M., he would call [Secretary of State William] Bill Rogers, or Kissinger, or [Attorney General] John Mitchell, or someone visiting from out of town—like [the Reverend] Billy Graham, or a business leader—and ask them to come over. They would sit back, with their feet up, and chat. This could last until six-thirty, at which time I would go back in to review the activity of the day, and to go over the next day's schedule. He would go back to the residence.

I would get home at about eight, and the phone would start ringing, because after dinner, the president would be working in the Lincoln Sitting Room with information, action, and signing folders. He also used that time to make phone calls to people around the country. He would call me and say, "I was just talking to Donald Kendall [chairman of Pepsi Cola], and he says that the Russians have set up a business, and I want you to check into this"; or Pat Nixon would have said at dinner that, "The helicopter is blowing my hair when we board; you have to do something about it." So I would be asked to look into it—anything from the minutiae to the monumental—depending upon what had happened that day.

We used to keep Wednesday open. It was the president's own day; he would do whatever he wanted: play golf, read, or work in his hideaway office in the EOB [Executive Office Building]. This gave him some opportunity to be proactive rather than reactive. At Camp David, there was a very different pattern. Nixon had been advised by two people he really respected—Billy Graham and Lyndon Johnson—of the importance of pacing himself, of getting enough rest, and of being ready for the big things. We would usually go up on Friday afternoon. He would often take a guest up, like Bebe Rebozo, John Mitchell, J. Edgar Hoover, or [Senator] Mike Mansfield [D-Mont.], someone he would like to chat with on a nonofficial basis. Kissinger, Ehrlichman, and I would go up for valuable staff time between us, and with the president.

ACCESS TO THE PRESIDENT

Stephen Bull Access depended on what the real need was. Everyone says that they need to see the president—whether it's the president of the United States or the president of General Motors. In most cases, they don't. Perhaps people were overly restrictive; that is arguable. But the president's time was protected; we were all cognizant that his time was the most valuable commodity, so we didn't want to squander it. Primarily, he would be in touch with the Cabinet departments through Haldeman, Ehrlichman, Kissinger, or Rose Woods; if you go back to the telephone logs, you see more calls to Kissinger, Ehrlichman, and Haldeman than to people outside the White House. John Mitchell would be one of the exceptions; he had a personal relationship with him [President Nixon] that went way back to the days in New York and the law firm.

Roy Ash I never saw a guy who was more focused, when he wanted to focus on something; he was able to put everything else out of his mind. There was criticism that he wasn't accessible and, therefore, was deprived of the kind of information that a president should have in making decisions. He wasn't accessible to department heads, but it doesn't mean he was deprived of information. Others—whether it be Haldeman, Ehrlichman, or myself, or others—fed him tremendous amounts of information, and he worked it over and asked lots of questions to augment it. We considered ourselves synthesizers; he didn't like to spend a lot of time with people who were purely advocates. He wanted to make it more of an intellectual exercise: "Let's go through the line of reasoning and thinking, and take into account all views. I don't want to just hear a salesman, as virtually every department is head, by definition, a salesman for his internal organization and constituents." He was businesslike and courteous, but not with a lot of chitchat.

Ronald Ziegler As press secretary, I had—from the first day—direct access to President Nixon. A lot of people assume the contrary and that my direct access only came later. The president understood that the press secretary needed direct access; I would see him before the daily briefing. But any press secretary worth his salt knows that part of the function is to interact with the totality of the White House; you don't just go in to the president and ask, "What do you want me to say today?" From the first day, I had general guidance and tone from President Nixon.

Frederic V. Malek My exposure to the president was somewhat limited; I saw him on the average of once a week. Most of my contact was through Haldeman, and in written decision memos. That was the way the president preferred it; he didn't want to get into a lot of the detail on personnel selection, so we had a lot of latitude in developing the alternatives. But in the final analysis, we would submit a decision memo to the president. And on very important selections, he would meet with Haldeman and myself.

Jerry Jones, director, White House Personnel Office; deputy director, CRP; staff secretary to the president The president could bypass the system by picking up the phone and talking to someone. On the foreign policy side, Kissinger, of course, had direct access; but on the domestic side, the chief of staff took all of the decisions in there to the Oval Office. Or, if he didn't, we submitted them in folders; Nixon lived in a very disciplined, decision-making world.

Rocco Siciliano Maurice Stans had a White House phone on his desk. He would jump up from wherever he was in his office to answer it; it didn't matter who was in the room. I said to him, "Why don't you let your secretary answer it?" He replied, "But it's the White House; it might be the president calling." But it almost never was; we dealt primarily with Haldeman and Ehrlichman, and then Colson, because he had his fingers in everything.

Joseph Sisco, assistant secretary of state for Near Eastern and East Asian affairs; undersecretary of state for political affairs The president felt that some area had to be given to the secretary of state and, from his point of view, the Middle East was the most appropriate. Secretary [of State William] Rogers, as a result of his long friendship with the president, was not as concerned about turf as, perhaps, other secretaries of state might be. The question came up during the transitional period. Mr. Kissinger organized the apparatus such that matters funneled through the national security adviser. Therefore, procedurally and structurally, there was no question that the National Security Council would be the overall coordinating mechanism. Mr. Rogers felt he would have full access.

Charles Colson He only gave access to people he was totally confident in. He would see other people, but he would be very careful not to let himself be vulnerable with someone he didn't totally trust. He wouldn't say anything negative about Haldeman or Ehrlichman, but he said lots of negative things about Kissinger. Haldeman generally had the most access. But there were periods of time when it could change. There were times when I had more access; there were times that [Attorney General John] Mitchell's star was ascending and there would be a lot of calls to him. Some staff member would get the president's telephone logs, so you knew what he was doing.

Stephen Bull The presidency was run somewhat like an efficient corporation, in which the chief executive officer—in this case, the president—operated through a few key vice-presidents. The key to the effectiveness was mutual trust. Watergate may have changed that, but that is how I perceived it back then. You had your vice-president for domestic affairs, John Ehrlichman; vice-president for international affairs, Kissinger; vice-president for political and administrative affairs, Haldeman; and then personal affairs, which was Rose Woods. He would deal primarily through those four people; it was the nature of the man. He probably was more comfortable dealing through a few people, and if he could have dealt through one person, that would have been the ideal.

Jerry Jones The president saw Kissinger, Haldeman, Colson, and Ehrlichman; he operated through them, into the larger staff; he did most of his work with a very small group of guys. He was not comfortable on a person-to-person level, and that was reflected in how he used his staff: he worked with the guys he was comfortable with. He did most of his substantive work with a very small group. The junior staff were not, typically, in there when he made decisions.

David Wilson It was not a White House where the president had a lot of direct involvement with his staff; he was pretty aloof, and primarily dealt with his closest staff. I know that before the Watergate started, John Dean had very few dealings with the president; he essentially reported to Haldeman and Ehrlichman. He would see the president on formal occasions when, for example, the president would meet with the president of the American Bar Association, but he was not consulted regularly to come in and advise the president.

John Dean Nobody, other than the senior staff, had access to the president, and I certainly didn't have access. Until Watergate, and the later stages of Watergate, I never had one-on-one meetings with the president. I knew it operated this way before I went to the White House. When I was at the Department of Justice, I had a fair amount of dealing with the White House. Mitchell did not like to deal with the press, and occasionally, he would ask me to go over to the White House press briefings. I knew from talking with the guys at the White House pretty much how it worked. When I was recruited for the job, I was told that I was just an appendage of Bob Haldeman's staff. Ehrlichman had been counsel. He was a senior staff man, and while I would be on Haldeman's staff, there would be things that Ehrlichman would assign; some would be things that Haldeman would assign; they would come through both; I did have a working relationship with both of them.

As a member of Haldeman's staff, there was an enormous amount of paper flow to process in a job like that on a regular basis. The assignments from Ehrlichman were more periodic—like working on the president's estate plan, or something having to do with a demonstration that Ehrlichman got interested in. They were not constant assignments, because Ehrlichman was running his domestic council, of which I was not a part.

Lawrence Higby Two or three nights a week, I had the responsibility of clearing all the president's calls. There were only two or three of us who could do it—myself, Haldeman, Chapin—and after he left, Bull. The president didn't like to be disturbed during the evening, so you had to make the decision whether or not to put the call through. Ehrlichman, Kissinger, and Haldeman had complete access; Colson did not. After a while, you knew who to put through. He wouldn't take calls from Cabinet officers for the most part, or big businessmen. I always had to carry either a radio or a pager; I was tracked down at parties. Once, Bowie Kuhn* had to call the president; he had to step in to settle the baseball strike. It was one o'clock in the morning; the president was in Florida, and I told Kuhn, "The president has already retired for the evening. I will make sure he gets your message."

ADMINISTRATIVE STYLE

Terrence O'Donnell Almost all the paperwork went through the staff secretary's office to the president. There were two exceptions: Colson and Kissinger had separate channels. Meetings with the president were long and exacting, and Haldeman did have limits on how much time he could spend with the president, so Colson would spend a lot of time with him. I can recall Bob's having been frustrated that Chuck had gone off and done some things—apparently at the president's behest—that Bob may have handled differently. The president would come up with lots of ideas, and Bob would filter them back—and either not do them, or go back and discuss them with the president a day later. I think he expected Bob to do that; he knew full well that that was happening: when the president really wanted something done, he made it very clear. But they would talk, and the president would spew out ideas like a volcano. Bob would make detailed notes, and some of the items would be put on a very low priority, while some would be immediate, must-do. A lot of it would be subject to Bob's judgment as to how—or if—it would be done.

John Dean There was selective decision making. I was confronted with this once I started having dealings with the president and he started opening up

---

* Commissioner, major league baseball.

to me. One example of how I tempered him was that during the [1973] inaugural parade some guy burst out of line and rushed at the president's car. I saw the president in the receiving line after the parade, and he was really upset; he wanted this guy prosecuted; he wanted a major case against him. I thought, this is crazy. This guy was a demonstrator; he wasn't a threat to the president. But the president didn't want to hear this. But by sitting on it, and talking to Henry Petersen so I could tell the president, "I'm working on it," I made sure it didn't go anywhere. It was crazy.

On the Brookings,* when Colson's idea comes in through Caulfield, I fly to Ehrlichman, and his bell obviously goes off, and he says, "We've got somebody here who we shouldn't have in the knowledge loop, so we'd better be careful with this." When Ehrlichman told me to deep-six evidence, I didn't do it.

Howard Phillips Nixon was not a hands-on president in terms of domestic policy; he delegated to his Domestic Council. The council had no sense of what I considered to be Nixon's policy goals or commitments. Agnew was extremely supportive of what I was doing as director of OEO [Office of Economic Opportunity]; he intervened personally on my behalf without any prompting from me: he would summon key players at the White House and say, "Why are you doing this? Why aren't you doing that?" Nixon was oblivious to most of these things.

Donald E. Santarelli Nixon was a student of government, a voracious reader of history, and very respectful of systems. He came from a very different era; he had strong beliefs in the structure of things. He was very much of a lawyer—not a modern, adversarial lawyer; not a modern advocate of a lawyer, but an old-fashioned, thoughtful lawyer. He was respectful of the legal system. He was formal, reserved, and lawyerlike; not given to easy, idle conversation. He was very cognizant of the civil rituals, very much a gentle man. I never saw the side of Mr. Nixon that was reflected in the tapes.

Robert Finch He was as obsessed with the office as any president has ever been; he loved it; he gloried in it, night and day. He was obsessed with the

---

* On July 6, 1971, Charles Colson sent a memorandum to John Ehrlichman, advising him that the Brookings Institution, a major Washington think tank, was putting together a study of American involvement in Vietnam. Later, White House aide John J. Caulfield stated that Colson had recommended that a diversionary fire be started at Brookings, so that the study could be stolen. Mr. Caulfield further stated that the plan was discarded after a July 11 meeting between John Dean and Ehrlichman.

media, in the sense that we had begun, chiefly through Haldeman's activities, the monitoring of what the news media were saying. There was a daily sheet on what the criticisms were, and that was the first thing he wanted to see. In the 1962 campaign [the California gubernatorial race against Edmund "Pat" Brown], it was pretty clear that the bias toward Nixon, whether it was justified or not, was a very real fact of life as far as parts of the working press were concerned.

Herbert Klein He enjoyed the power, the thrill, the ability to rally people, to get them excited, to win their applause—their commitment to you.

Stephen Bull He was totally dedicated to the job; the next step would have been to the exclusion of a personal life. I can't imagine a man spending much more time at the presidency than Richard Nixon. I believe that he relished the challenges and the ability to meet the challenges—and there were many, not the least of which was the Vietnam War.

George P. Shultz He loved the job. He wasn't just in, in the morning; he was thinking twenty-four hours a day. There were things he didn't like; he didn't like economics that much. When I was in the process of proposing a whole new monetary system for the world, it was hard to get his attention. I had a speech to make to the International Monetary Fund meetings, and I had to practically force him to sign off on it. He was really interested in foreign affairs. The same was true of Henry [Kissinger], although by now, he is much more alert to the importance of economics than he was then. When Ted Heath [prime minister, United Kingdom] came over to Washington, he met with Nixon in the EOB [Executive Office Building, where the president maintained a "hideaway" office] office. There was an item at the end, dealing with economics. I was there for that item, and when it came up, Henry just got up and left.

Alexander Butterfield He didn't offer opinions in a meeting; there was a body language that Haldeman and Ehrlichman—who are very bright—understood. He got them to kick things around; maybe he has his own opinion—I never heard him go on for more than a sentence about anything. He would say, "Well, ah well"—he has a hard time articulating anything—but you get the drift of what he wants. He never says, "Alex, what do you think?" He says, "Well, of course, if we did this . . . " He'd seem to lead people into it and feed off that, and form his opinions based on that.

Raymond Price By a factor of at least ten, Nixon could absorb more information from reading than he could sitting and yakking with people, most of whom would tell him things he had heard many times before. He is a phenomenally quick and retentive reader, with a superior intellect and an extraordinary memory. He would devour briefing books and send them back filled with scribbled notes. He also restricted physical access for others, because when you are forced to put down recommendations for the president in a memorandum, you think more clearly. Kissinger had a habit of taking a memo—not even reading it—and telling the person who wrote it, "This is not good enough; redo it." They both liked to force staff to think hard about the recommendations they were making.

Dwight Chapin If we were in the car, on the way to a little radio station in Rhinelander, Wisconsin, he would have his pad out and be working on the points he was going to make. He would work; he would never just wing it, or make small talk, in the car. To the degree possible, we were to maximize his thinking time—not B[ull] S[hit] time. That was one of the things I learned from him: to make your scenario work, you "work" it. He once said to me, "As you go along, the most important thing in life is to keep your learning curve vertical."

Thomas Moorer, admiral, U.S. Navy; chairman, Joint Chiefs of Staff We had something called Washington Special Action Group. Nixon never came to it. Neither did [Melvin] Laird, when he was secretary of defense, because Kissinger chaired the meetings; he had been confirmed by the Senate, and Kissinger wasn't. Perhaps there were two or three times when Mr. Nixon would come in. But he'd never sit down; he would stand, and maybe walk around the table, and say something, and leave.

Rocco Siciliano On July 13, 1970, I was asked to come to the White House to meet with the president. When I arrived, [Secretary of Transportation] John Volpe was there. We went into the Oval Office; we sat on either side of the president's desk, and staff, including Colson, Richard Moore, Bryce Harlow, and Peter Flanigan, were seated behind us. The president talked about minorities—about Italian-Americans and other ethnic groups. He wanted to know what we could do to get them more involved, to get them to understand what his administration was all about. It was a strange, strange meeting; he was quite agitated. I don't know if he thought we had the answers, or whether he wanted to infuse us with a mission.

John Ehrlichman He had extraordinary powers of retention; he would remember an assignment he had given me the previous week. If it was particularly bizarre, I might say, "Well, I was hoping you would have a second thought about that." We winnowed out the chaff. As an example of the bizarre, he told Shultz and me that all federal funds to MIT [Massachusetts Institute of Technology] should be stopped; he was mad at Jerome Weisner* for his position on the ABM [antiballistic missile] controversy.† He said, "All money stops by Friday; I don't want a nickel to go to MIT." Shultz, who had taught there, was shell-shocked. He went out into the hall and asked me, "What are we going to do?" I said, "We are not going to do anything." Shultz replied, "Can we get away with that?" I said, "You watch; he'll change his mind in the next twenty-four hours." Sure enough, he did. There were a lot of these kinds of "queens of hearts," old enmities. You had to know the difference between what he really intended and what was his blowing off of steam. Those of us who were handling policy kept our hands over his mouth a lot of the time; we tried to avoid his making snap decisions.

George P. Shultz Sometimes in the budget meetings he would "showboat," even in a small group. He had a love-hate relationship with the CIA— mostly hate. There was a meeting, and he said, "Now, we want to talk about the CIA's budget." Caspar Weinberger‡ was noted as a big budget cutter. Nixon railed against the CIA and their lousy intelligence, and said, "Cap, I want you to cut the CIA's budget to one-third of its present size." Cap would light up like a Christmas tree. Then Nixon said, "No. Make it one-half the present size." Then we'd leave the meeting, and Cap would be very excited, and I would say, "Cap, relax. He's just showboating; you're not going to cut the CIA's budget in half. Be sensible; just don't do anything for a couple of days." It was Nixon's way of venting his ire, but you didn't take it too seriously.

Alexander Butterfield Richard Nixon had a "talker" for absolutely every meeting, even the little, ten-minute ones. On his desk in the morning was not only the news summary, but also, one on top of the other, in order, briefing papers for the day's meetings. They had to be done succinctly and they

---

* President of MIT, 1971–1980.
† President Nixon believed in the effectiveness of an antiballistic missile system as a bargaining chip with the Soviets. Many in the academic community felt that such a system would cause the Soviets to escalate their own missile programs, thus escalating the Cold War arms race.
‡ Director, Office of Management and Budget (OMB).

were, essentially, talking papers. Richard Nixon just glanced [at them]. That's all he needed to do. If he didn't glance, though, he would not be able to perform. You would not believe how totally inept he would be. He couldn't even say hello. He can't spit out a sentence. He is absolutely tongue-tied. And here he is, this wonderful speaker. But, as a speaker, he has gone through the points; he knows them all in his mind. Let's say Golda Meir is coming on a state visit. She is due to arrive at the White House at eleven-thirty. It is a one-minute walk from his office to where he will meet her; he knows he has to be there.

I used to get nervous, because it is eleven-twenty, and he is still at his desk, and he hasn't looked at the material the speechwriters have prepared for him; it's in a little folder. With five minutes to go, he uses the bathroom for a minute, and then looks at the folder. He already knows essentially what he is going to say; he worked on it the night before. He did homework all the time. He has no hobbies; his hobby was the presidency. Now he looks at the folder material. There are some points he likes. He is fitting them in, mentally; he knows right where to slide in this line that [William] Safire* wrote. It takes him about two minutes to do that. Now it is twenty-eight after. He gets up, walks out the French doors, and welcomes her. He gives this nice little talk, and I hear him using some of the lines from the folder. He is very proud that he gives talks without notes.

Vernon Walters He didn't need anyone handing him pieces of paper. In fact, it would have been a brave soul who would have done so during a meeting with a foreign leader. He was one of the few people I ever saw de Gaulle talk to as an equal. I was the interpreter.

Alexander Butterfield I admired the fact that he always wore his coat [jacket] in the Oval Office. I had been around Johnson; I was fairly close to him. He was always in his shirt sleeves. He was crude and rude. He said terrible things—one of the secretaries told me that she liked him; he was so earthy. I never saw Nixon get mad at anyone to his face; he would berate people to the next person in. I am sure that when I walked out, he would say to Haldeman, a lot: What a dumb son-of-a-bitch!, because when Haldeman, his trusted aide, would go out, he would say, "Goddamn Haldeman!" and he would add some not nice things about him—and about Ehrlichman. And he did it about almost everyone; the fact is, he tended to be hypocritical, behind people's backs.

* A speechwriter in the Nixon White House.

H. R. Haldeman He didn't have to suffer fools gladly, because there were not many fools around. And a fool who had been suffered once wouldn't be around much more. We had an outstanding staff, and they knew how to work with him. He worked them hard and expected a lot. He had no qualms about chewing out Kissinger, Ehrlichman, and me—up one side and down the other. With lower-level staff, he was the epitome of kindness and courtesy. If one of these people did something stupid, he would never chew them out. But we would be told to get rid of the person. At the senior level, he was a tough guy and we had to learn how to deal with him. It wasn't easy.

Frederic V. Malek The president was businesslike in meetings; he was crisp, and very impersonal—none of this looking at you with a big smile, how are you doing kind of thing. He would be preoccupied, reading something; you might be ignored for a minute or two, but after all, I was thirty-three years old and he was the president of the United States. The president would generally be decisive, but Haldeman would sometimes counter his directions, because sometimes Nixon's decisions would be questionable. Haldeman would say, "Look, the president wants this, but forget about it; I am going back to him." Or, he would say, "Let's sit on this for a while." Haldeman wouldn't take it upon himself to simply contradict the president without any follow-up, but he would say, "Ignore that; we will take another look." Or I would say to him, "Bob, this directive doesn't make any sense." He might reply, "You're right; let me go back and ask the president."

Alexander Butterfield Once I heard him [H. R. Haldeman] interrupt the president, who was going to say something about John Volpe [secretary of transportation]. The president didn't care much for Volpe, or for [George] Romney [secretary of housing and urban development], even though they were in the Cabinet. Haldeman came down on the desk with his fist and said the "F" word about Volpe, and he would start fanning the flames: "Don't you remember that Volpe is a son-of-a-bitch." "Yeah, Bob, I guess you're right." Bob could control him in many ways like that.

H. R. Haldeman In attention to detail, he falls between Eisenhower and Carter. He did not want to be bothered with details on some issues, but in other areas he got excruciatingly involved—whether soup should be served at state dinners, the reason being, as it turned out, that he had spilled soup on his white tie costume at a previous dinner. But the reasoning was that the soup course delayed the dinner so long that it would be better to eliminate it. The reason he didn't like state dinners was the requirement that the president be seated between the two top-ranking ladies, and his observation was that the wives of great men are always ungreat people—and not pleasant dinner companions.

Alexander Butterfield He would say, "I don't want salad served as a separate course at a state dinner if we have a dinner of eighty people or less." This is the president of the United States. Wouldn't you think he'd forget about the salad course?

Robert Odle, Jr. Nixon took an interest in the office layout of the West Wing. The national security adviser was given the corner office where, before renovation, the press had filed their stories. Next to this, there was a bathroom, and then Bryce Harlow's office. Once, when Bryce was away, Kissinger convinced Haldeman that it was inappropriate for him to have to go to the basement to use the bathroom, so—with typical Haldemanesque efficiency—the entry to the bathroom from Harlow's office was walled up, and the bathroom was opened up to the hall, so that Kissinger, Harlow, and Haldeman could all use it. When Harlow got back, he joked that he had lost his "head" to Henry.

Thomas Moorer At meetings of the National Security Council [NSC], the president would serve as chairman. Dr. Kissinger would give a briefing, and then the president would go around the room, asking each participant his views. He would never make a decision at the meeting, but would go back to the Oval Office and later—at about two in the afternoon—I would get a memorandum, called a presidential decision memo, that would say: the president has decided on option two or three . . .

David Packard Whenever we took action in Vietnam, the president—or Kissinger—would call. They wanted to know, immediately, what was happening. I had to explain to them: "For Christ sakes. These guys are out there fighting. They are not going to stop every day and write you a report."

Charles Colson Nixon was easy to work with. He would sometimes blow off steam, but we enjoyed political conniving. He would talk about how he was going to nail one of his political opponents with some embarrassing disclosures; he would love to talk about that. He would also talk to me about very serious issues, across the board. He was a quick study; you didn't have to walk him through anything.

Thomas Moorer I got along fine with Mr. Nixon; we were very formal with each other. I had briefed him on the Sontay Prison Raid.* The author of a book on the raid tried to reconstruct this conversation and he put in all kinds of profanity from Mr. Nixon. He sent the book to me to approve, and I said, "Mr. Nixon never once used profanity in my presence. Not once."

Stephen Bull When the two of us were alone together in the Oval Office, as far as the president was concerned, he was by himself. It was my job to understand him, to know him, to get him through the day, to a certain extent, to gauge his moods, to know when was the right time for someone to see him, or not to see him. I was one to be taken for granted—to be invisible. We had a sort of master-slave relationship, and there was no question who was the master. We did not have a personal, close relationship. I wouldn't come in there and put my feet on the desk and say, "Let's talk about the Redskins."

George P. Shultz I had a very touchy issue to handle with regard to Larry O'Brien's [Democratic national chairman] tax returns. Nixon was very hard to handle on this matter. Then, there was the effort to get me to use the IRS to investigate his so-called "Enemies List," which I declined, so there was a lot of strain. He never did it directly. He had John Dean go to John Walters [IRS commissioner] and tell Johnny to conduct this investigation. So John comes to me. I had earlier told him I would not get involved in specific cases, and I said, "Johnny, I thought you didn't want me to get involved in any individual cases." He says, "Well, I'm ordered to do this by the president. What should I do?" I answered, "You don't do anything." He said, "What shall I do when John Dean comes around?" I said, "Tell him I'm your boss and I told you not to do it, and if he has any argument, he can come to me, or the president can bring it up to me." So, that is the last we heard of that, although in the tapes, there is a tape of Nixon talking to Dean. He called me "little blue eyes," and said, "What does he think we brought him here for?" But they didn't have the guts to bring it up, or do anything.

Donald E. Santarelli Occasionally, Mr. Nixon would ask that something be done that was either foolish, wasteful, or of too high a risk. One of Haldeman's assets was that he would sometimes bury these projects. I can recall a project that John Dean seemed to authorize: the so-called "Enemies List"

* An attempt to free U.S. prisoners of war held in North Vietnam.

for IRS auditing. It really came from Colson, but Dean promoted and shopped it around to the agencies. I got it when it came to Justice, and I went to see Kleindienst, who was then attorney general, and we just decided to bury it; it was just wrong. Without bringing down the temple and pushing out the columns and destroying the government by making a public issue of it, we just buried it, figuring that John Dean had lost his marbles, or that it was another one of Nixon's bad ideas. Nobody ever tells the president that he has bad ideas; you just don't act on them. Nixon often asked where something was, and it wasn't anywhere, because it wasn't being done—and nobody had the testicular fortitude to tell him that it was a bad idea and wasn't going to be done.

The President's Relationship with the Cabinet

H. R. Haldeman Nixon never intended the Cabinet to be a board of directors. He never took a vote, and would have cared less concerning the result; he didn't make any pretext of seeking a consensus. He saw the Cabinet as a place for discussion and communication, and show and tell. They [the Cabinet] could have access, but only when the president wanted it, and granted it.

Rocco Siciliano I don't think he had the capacity to engender as much independent reaction for his people as Eisenhower did. Eisenhower had the supreme gift of self-confidence; he wasn't trying to prove anything to anybody. With Nixon, you were always wondering: What is the agenda? What is going on in his mind? Eisenhower had the gift of encouraging discussion; that is why Cabinet meetings worked under him. This didn't happen in the Nixon administration. After one year, I didn't have the same feeling of lift about public service that I had had under Eisenhower.

Donald E. Santarelli Nixon considered himself a synthesizer, as opposed to an original thinker, and he was very good at it. He was very good at Cabinet meetings, in that he could sum up; he liked that role. He liked that role in me, and that's why I was often called in to do things that were beyond my original jurisdiction; I guess he saw a younger version of himself in that capacity to synthesize, conclude, and quickly and colorfully describe a phenomenon.

James R. Schlesinger President Nixon had no higher regard for Cabinet government than most presidents; indeed, he tended to regard the Cabinet departments as containing bureaucracies that might be hostile to a new president. Therefore, he ran a high percentage of things right out of the White House. He also had a somewhat bemused and detached attitude toward some of the Cabinet officers. I can remember, on one occasion, during the energy crisis, he said to the Cabinet at large, "I do not know whether the energy crisis will ever end." I leaned over to him and remarked that we were in close negotiations with the Saudis about ending the embargo. He turned to me and whispered, "I know that, Jim, but I'm not going to say that in front of these clowns." They were his appointees, and his creatures, but he did not necessarily regard them all as fully able to deal with the breadth of issues with which the government dealt, or in some cases, not even particularly competent to deal with the issues of their own departments.

The President's Relationship with Congress

Alexander Butterfield He knew he had enemies. He would say, "Now, this isn't going to be easy to get through; old so-and-so—that son-of-a-bitch—he'll fight this thing." And he would talk to Bryce Harlow and the legislative guys about how to get the thing through. He knew how; he'd worked up there.

Robert Hartmann Deep down in his heart, Nixon had a classic case of contempt of Congress. He was a solo player; he didn't understand the power of the Congress—this kind of bonding of the patriarchs. We soon found out that what Nixon wanted from the House minority leader was to do little errands for him, most of them slightly dirty: if he was attacked by [Edward] Teddy Kennedy [D-Mass.], we were supposed to get up and denounce Teddy on the House floor.

THE RELATIONSHIP BETWEEN THE PRESIDENT AND THE VICE-PRESIDENT

David Keene, deputy assistant for national affairs and assistant for national affairs to the vice-president I was the liaison with political people around the country on behalf of the vice-president, and liaison with the White House on political issues affecting the vice-president. And I also advised him on various issues and on their political impact. Agnew did not have much of a role [in the administration]. He fought for access, and for a role in domestic policy, where he felt he knew things—he was defining himself in more of an intellectual than a political way. He read a lot; he would have writers up to talk to him, not to cultivate the author, but because he was trying to come to grips with where he ought to be; he cared where he was, intellectually. Ehrlichman, in particular, didn't like Agnew. Haldeman mostly had disdain for him—but he had disdain for everyone; he was the resident liberal—he didn't like conservatives—and he didn't like Agnew; he didn't like anything about him. Agnew probably began in the Nixon administration in a deeper hole than Dan Quayle did [in the Bush administration], but he dug his way out of it and became very influential, and the odds-on favorite to be the next nominee of the party. He became a hero of the Republican Party, and the president's chief offensive threat in a partisan sense, and defender out in the country.

Robert Finch He did a number of things that had never been done before. When Nixon was vice-president, he would never go down to the White House unless he was invited. The only office he had was the small office he had when he was a senator from California. So he decided he was going to give Agnew an office in the Executive Office Building, so the vice-president had a little more stature.

Herbert Klein Personally, it was not a close relationship. When we left the convention, we came to California, and I arranged for them to go to church together in the Presbyterian church in La Jolla, and then they had dinner at the home of my publisher.* I don't think they ever had a dinner like that, privately, after that.

Gerald Warren I recall the press office receiving an advance copy of one of the vice-president's speeches, and [Press Secretary] Ron Ziegler trying to get some of the inflammatory words out. But he was unsuccessful because, apparently, there was a decision that Agnew would be the point man—that he would be controversial—and that the press, particularly the television networks, would be the focal point of his attack.

David Keene He relished words; that's why he grabbed that stuff and liked it. He was sort of a self-made guy who grew up on the block in Baltimore and went to night school, and people talked about how he'd studied his list of words in *Reader's Digest*. He liked the political impact of words and

---

* Of the *San Diego Union*.

speeches. He took great pleasure in it. Rhetoric intrigued him. In the 1970 campaign,* when he was given an airplane—and Bill Safire and Pat Buchanan and two typewriters—that was like dying and going to heaven. Safire knew his clients and how to write for them, and what attracts them. He knew the alliteration and all that was just the kind of thing this particular client would go for in a big way.

H. R. Haldeman We tried to involve him in issues, but right from the outset, he was not really involved. There was a wide gap in experience and knowledge between Nixon and Agnew—in terms of geopolitics and national politics—that was pretty much insurmountable; Nixon was on one plane, Agnew on another. It was clear, early on, that bringing Agnew up to speed was not a task worth worrying about. He was kept informed—he sat in on Cabinet meetings—but he was not viewed as a major participant in policy development. He was frustrated by this, and there were times that he made decisions that were ill advised. The president would tell me what to do about them, but Agnew did not appreciate my efforts. He saw himself, and rightly so, as an elected official of all the people, and he didn't like to be told by someone like me—who had no elected status—what he could do. Of course, deep down, he realized that it wasn't me, but the president, who was speaking.

John Ehrlichman Their relations were very poor; there was no personal level. On a professional level, Agnew felt underutilized. He was continually badgering Nixon to give him more to do, and Nixon—and frankly, all of us—lacked the confidence in Agnew to give him much substantive stuff to do. We finally did give him health, and space, and some other things, but he botched them badly. Nixon didn't consider Agnew to be loyal to him; he thought he was much more loyal to Ronald Reagan. Agnew was sent to Africa at right about the time Nixon announced that he was going to visit China. Through back channels, the CIA, I think, we learned that Agnew was bad-mouthing the China trip everywhere he went in Africa. He indicated that he thought it was a very poor idea for us to treat with "the Godless Red Chinese." So, midway in the trip, Nixon jerked him out and brought him back home. He never really felt he could confide in Agnew, or rely on him.

David Keene Agnew became the spokesman for the silent majority. In fact, if you ask yourself who made up the silent majority—in the eighties we

* The congressional campaign.

called them Reagan Democrats—they tended to be second- and third-generation ethnic Americans; more Catholic than most voters; living in the inner suburbs, coming from working-class families. If you describe those people, you are describing Agnew, except that he wasn't Catholic. His strengths and weaknesses were all the strengths and weaknesses of that community, and they identified with him.

H. R. Haldeman The vice-president would make the mistake of speaking out on things he didn't know anything about—or in a direction that wasn't the president's. This would get Nixon exasperated. There was never a close relationship between them. It was not as bad as that of Kennedy and Johnson, or as good as that of Clinton and Gore. There is a built-in problem: the relationship between a president and his vice-president; the vice-president has nothing to do but preside over the Senate, which he rarely does, except to wait around for the president to die. That reminder doesn't cheer the president's heart every time he sees the vice-president—particularly in Nixon's case—and that may be why he chose Agnew. Nixon didn't expect to die; he didn't expect to be incapacitated; he was a relatively young man* and he expected to be around for a long time.

TEAM DYNAMICS

Dwight Chapin Chuck [Charles Colson] didn't get into the team concept. A lot of us were team-oriented; there was very little backbiting, or internal rivalries; it wasn't tolerated. People had their noses to the grindstone; they did their jobs, or they were out. All of a sudden, here comes this guy, Colson. He's got the special-interest groups—the unions, the Catholics—and he's building constituencies for the 1972 election—a political operation. One could question the degree to which that operation should have been in the White House. Chuck instinctively knew how to feed meat to Nixon. He would intrigue Nixon, who loved to know what was going on. If there was a *People* magazine† of the political life, Nixon would never subscribe, but he would want to know what was in it.

The president might say, "Chuck, I can't get across to the public that the demonstrators are prolonging the war. I don't know what I am going to do." Chuck would come up with eighteen ideas, right there, on the

---

* Richard M. Nixon was fifty-six years of age in January 1969, when he took office.
† A weekly, celebrity-oriented publication of Time, Inc.

spot, some of which were questionable. Nixon might say, "I don't know if some of them sound right. Let's do them." Thus, it wouldn't be settled in what we normally call an action step. We had a secretariat that kept track of what was supposed to be done, when, and the due date. Invariably, Chuck's stuff ran around the system, so the opportunity to follow up and know what was to be done wasn't in the hopper; Chuck was off doing it. So, it was very confusing, particularly for Haldeman, to know what had been authorized. He would say to the president: "If Chuck is here, I should be here also; or Alexander Butterfield should be here." He would say this so that things wouldn't be done without the opportunity to rethink whether they should be undertaken.

Stephen Bull It was very collegial; there were some very good personal relationships, particularly on my level. Some of my best friends, to this day, are people with whom I worked. The Nixon crowd really hung together. It could have been a period of adversity in the final year or two of the presidency, but that isn't the whole thing: people really got along. A group of us get together annually and take a trip; this year, we are going to the Grand Tetons.

TENSIONS

Walter Hickel The young people I was in touch with were against the war in Vietnam. They asked me, "Can't you tell this to the president?" I tried to warn the White House about the situation. One evening, the president called the Cabinet to the White House at about seven o'clock and told us he was going into Cambodia. When I heard this, I was literally screaming inside, so I tried to get to see the president. Ehrlichman said that this was not possible, so I said, "John, what do I have to do, call a press conference to get in?" I wrote a letter to Nixon, left it on my desk overnight, and completed it the next morning. It was delivered to Ehrlichman, became public, and made almost every newspaper in the country. Nixon needed me to campaign for Republican candidates in the 1970 election, but soon after—on November 23—I was asked to come to the White House, and Nixon told me he would like me to leave his administration.

Frederic V. Malek I had just come over to the White House Personnel Office—at around Thanksgiving, 1970. The day before Thanksgiving, the president had fired Walter Hickel. On the Friday after Thanksgiving, the president called me and said he wanted all of Hickel's people fired, and that he wanted it done that day. He said, "Identify them, and go over there and get their resignations." I called Haldeman and said, "Bob, Jesus. This is really unfair to the people involved, and it will be perceived very badly." So Bob got into the act and we watered down the president's request. We still got the resignations of a select group whom we identified as being personal staff to the secretary. We did get pasted by the press, but at least we got it somewhat contained.

Marshall Green When we got to Manila,* Nixon and Kissinger met with President [Ferdinand] Marcos, whereas Secretary Rogers and I met with [Fidel] Ramos, the foreign minister, so I didn't know what had happened at the summit meeting. Yet I had to face 200 American newsmen who were traveling with the president, to tell them what had gone on in the main meeting. Ron Ziegler told me about the meeting but, of course, everybody could tell that I hadn't been there; it was very difficult—very embarrassing. I blame this on the president; he didn't trust our ambassadors and foreign service officers the way he should have. I do think that the secretary of state should have been in that meeting. I think that Henry Kissinger was imputing too much to his position. This was the beginning of a problem I had to live with during the next three or four years, when I was assistant secretary, that the president was rather distrustful of the State Department, and Kissinger did all he could to play on the president's prejudices to enhance his own position. Bill [William] Rogers, who was devoted to the president— they were old friends—didn't want to bother the president. He knew he was such a busy man, and he didn't want to complicate his life by intruding, so he tended to play along, and that played right into Henry Kissinger's hands.

We in the State Department greatly admired Nixon for what he was trying to do in terms of China and the Soviet Union; he couldn't have found a group of people who were better informed, or more supportive of him than in the Foreign Service. But he distrusted the Foreign Service, and he said as much—not to our faces, but it got back to us. The problems that arose, including our relationship with Japan, could have been averted had the president consulted us. But I will admit this: had he looked to the bureaucracy completely for the opening to China, we never would have done it, because we didn't know it could go that far; I could never believe that the president would be willing to put his reputation on the line in trying to set up a private meeting with the Chinese; and going there, knowing that the

* In 1969.

right wing of his own party was dead set against it—including two members of the Cabinet and the vice-president.

Helmut Sonnenfeldt I don't think Kissinger necessarily recognized, or assumed, that the relationship between Nixon and Rogers would be as complex as it turned out to be, and that, in fact, Nixon was not going to rely very heavily on Rogers—at least for the development of policy and strategy. This only became clear to Kissinger later. I don't think he recognized at the outset that the balance of power in the administration, as far as foreign policy and, more broadly, security policy, was concerned, would shift as much into the White House as it did. As it developed, that was the center of policymaking. Kissinger was obviously ambitious and determined from the outset, but I don't think he could tell what his relationship with Nixon would be at the beginning. The widespread assumption, including his own, was that Rogers and Nixon had had a close relationship in the Eisenhower administration and, therefore, Rogers would carry a great deal of weight. Kissinger couldn't tell what weight Laird would carry, given that his was a longstanding relationship with Nixon as well. But Kissinger realized fairly early that Nixon, in fact, had no intention of giving much of a role to Rogers.

William H. Sullivan Why was Bill Rogers chosen as secretary of state? The president wanted to run his own foreign policy. He wanted an intelligent, affable man who would decently represent the United States as its secretary of state. But he didn't want one who was going to interfere with Nixon's view of the way he wanted things run. So Bill was the ideal choice for that: he doesn't worry where his place is in the pecking order the way Henry [Kissinger] does. So Nixon never took Rogers seriously with the valence of a real player in foreign policy.

Henry was very aggressive; he did cut Bill out. In due course, they had a pretty sustained level of antagonism. I know this well, because I became sort of the intermediary between the two for almost two years when there were occasions when they were not speaking to each other. I think Nixon knew he couldn't send the two of them together to China; it would be like putting two scorpions in a bottle. Henry was the type who loved this kind of intrigue, and he was the obvious emissary to send. While Bill could keep secrets, I think Nixon and Kissinger never thought he could keep secrets as well as Henry did, almost intuitively.

Morton Halperin It was not preordained that that would be the case. It happened over the first few months of the administration. My sense is that

Nixon did not like people who pushed him, and that both Rogers and Laird made the mistake at meetings with him of pushing him to make decisions that they wanted. Nixon, in general, reacted to that by just not seeing the people who did that. Kissinger understood that by instinct, and dealt with the president in a way that didn't make him feel cornered or uncomfortable, and so quickly built up a relationship. But it was only as that was happening that this took place. I do not think that Rogers was appointed with the notion that he would not be influential.

Kenneth Rush Kissinger and Nixon were both very secretive, suspicious men. Kissinger was the big leaker in Washington, but Nixon blamed the State Department for the leaks. I don't know why Nixon was persuaded that Rogers was a leaker, because he wasn't. When it came to foreign affairs, Nixon felt he could not trust the State Department, or the Defense Department; he wanted to keep foreign affairs for himself—this was his consuming interest in life. He didn't trust Melvin Laird, at Defense, because he felt that Laird had let him down on Vietnam. His view was that you couldn't conduct diplomacy from weakness; you had to have a strong military stance.

WIRETAPPING

Almost from the inception of the Nixon administration, the president and Dr. Kissinger had been troubled by what they perceived to be leaks of highly classified information, and their concern led to the wiretapping of certain journalists, members of the National Security Council staff, and other administration officials.

Richard Kleindienst This was the only aspect of my relationship with John Mitchell that I found less than forthright, candid, and direct. He always maintained to me that there was no such thing; he had nothing to do with it, and it turned out, in later years, that he did. When my name first came up as the nominee for attorney general, that kind of question was raised. I called John and said, "Is there anything to this?" and he said no. My relationship with him was such that if he said no, it *was* no. So he was less than forthright with me on that point.

There are rigid controls with respect to non-court-authorized electronic surveillance. While John was attorney general, the key case had not been decided by the Supreme Court. Generally speaking, there were no wiretaps authorized without the approval of the attorney general. There were several, as I understood it, that were instituted without the final procedures that, heretofore, had been followed. When I was the acting attorney general, the Supreme Court decided the issue and said that even in matters of national security you could not institute a wiretap without an order of the Court. When I found out that some of Kissinger's staff were wiretapped, I was not only surprised, I was astonished. I didn't come to the Nixon government as an empty chair; I had been a student of government all my life, and a very strong believer in the Constitution—literally and figuratively. I believe it is one of the most serious forms of invasion of individual liberty that government, without secure safeguards, can institute eavesdropping devices upon our private lives. Most of us were astonished by the wiretaps.

Winston Lord Nixon and Kissinger were genuinely distraught over the leaks which, they felt, undercut our foreign policy; to be detached about it, they were right. You could argue that some of the things that were leaked were on secrets that shouldn't have been kept in the first place. But basically, when sensitive material is leaked, it does, obviously, hamper your conduct of foreign policy, so they had a right to be concerned, and that was, of course, driving them about how to stop the leaks. The first thing you look at is: who would be aware of the material that is being leaked—a lot of the material was so closely held that there weren't many with access. Kissinger would claim that in order to have credibility, he could not protect all his people from being wiretapped. He obviously didn't resist it; he was assured that it was totally legal. Then, you have to figure out who has access to sensitive information. I probably wouldn't have been wiretapped if I had still been working in the EOB; when I became Kissinger's special assistant, I knew just about everything. I really don't think that wiretapping is all that effective. Leaving aside the moral implications, if someone is going to leak, they are not going to do it over the telephone.

Robert Mardian The leak that came out had to come out of Kissinger's office; he was paranoid. I had the job of making sure that everyone who got transcripts still had them in their possession. Kissinger got transcripts, as did Haldeman. I had a list of who had received copies. I went to see Kissinger and asked him if he had the material, and I'll never forget it; as I sat down, he yelled at the secretary, "Alice, you don't have to turn it on. Mr. Mardian's people have a record of everything." So he had his secretary taping; I don't think he was kidding.

William Ruckelshaus Halperin was one of the people who had been wiretapped. This information ended up in Ehrlichman's safe in the White

House. When I was at the FBI, we recovered it; no one ever said to me that the records were incomplete. This was a terrible dilemma for the FBI; it was almost as if someone had taken an organ out of their bodies, not to have records in their possession. When we got them back, it was a great relief.

Morton Halperin Kissinger says that he warned me, but if he did, I missed it. He certainly told me that I was under suspicion, but it didn't register to me that he was telling me I was being wiretapped—that I was the [suspected] source for the leaking of the Cambodian bombing.

Helmut Sonnenfeldt My view on this may be a little different from some of the others. I had been wiretapped repeatedly since I first came into government. First of all, wiretapping was a routine investigative practice for people with relatively high security clearances—even for just getting the initial clearances, wiretaps were used by the State Department security people. In the fifties, if you knew people in the press, you were automatically suspect of leaking; the State Department security people were zealous in their operations, so there were some wiretaps on me in the fifties. This got cleared up in the Kennedy administration, when I demanded a confrontation with the security people. All of this essentially evaporated, but in the Johnson administration, they apparently again resorted to these taps. So when I found out that I had been tapped in the Kissinger period, it was old hat to me.

I didn't like it—and especially because they were tapping my wife; they were cross-tapping; they were tapping another person who was a friend of my wife, so she didn't particularly like it. But I have to confess that I didn't have the sort of moral outrage that a lot of other people had, because I was more or less accustomed to it. I even rationalized it in the sense that I felt people that did have high security clearances had to accept the fact that, from time to time, they were going to be checked as to their reliability, and that the government was entitled to do that.

Now, it was, of course, obviously abused. And as we discovered later, when Kissinger put together the NSC staff, J. Edgar Hoover warned against a whole bunch of people that Kissinger was recruiting, including me. Once the whole thing became public, it had produced the salutary effect of a much stricter regime than had prevailed in the good old days, going back to the Truman administration. I didn't particularly hold it against Kissinger, because it was the normal method. Now I accept his explanation that he thought that very little would come out of these wiretaps and it would be a way to demonstrate that the accusations and suspicions were unwarranted.

In most respects, that turned out to be the case. Now, whether this was an ex-post-facto rationalization on his part, or whether he rolled with the punch when Hoover or somebody else suggested it, there are still people around who were indignant at the time, because they got tapped. But when they were in the position to know about other people being tapped, their indignation was not quite as rampant.

William H. Sullivan I was ambassador in the Philippines and Bill Rogers sent me a message: "You will read in the newspapers tomorrow, or the next day, that you had been wiretapped." I had some suspicions. I said to Bill, "Look, I've always assumed I was being wiretapped." But I didn't think it was being done by the White House. I had been trained in the culture of never saying anything on the telephone, on the assumption that it was the Soviets, or somebody else, who was wiretapping me—not that it was my own government. So I never said anything of any classified value over the telephone. My first adumbrations of being wiretapped came from my teenage kids, who said that they heard strange noises and clicking on the phone. Later, I agreed that out there in Potomoc, where I was living, there seemed to be a greater prevalence of telephone repairmen stopping at the box outside our house than anywhere else in the neighborhood.

My visceral reaction when I learned about the tap was hardly a fluctuation, because I knew that my own telephone habits were such that nothing embarrassing would come up—I was not enraged, outraged, or embarrassed; my thought was that it went with the territory. Henry [Kissinger] had virtually denied to me that he originated the tap. I've never questioned Al Haig, but my assumption is that it probably came from Nixon, personally; he was given to exploding—particularly in the course of the evening—if he had had a few drinks. He would call up Bill Rogers—or somebody else—and say, "Fire this man." I know that at least once, and maybe twice, he told Rogers to fire me. Bill said that Nixon would forget this the next morning. He would tell me a couple of days later, "By the way, the president fired you two days ago." So I assumed that in one of those fits of exasperation with news leaks that he saw in the newspaper, he scanned those who might possibly have that information, and my blip came up on his horizon fairly often, and so he said, "Sack that man." The amusing thing is that Al Haig was then talking to William C. Sullivan* over at the FBI, so there was always a certain amount of confusion between William H. Sullivan and William C. Sullivan in those days. Had those orders he gave been carried out, half of his admin-

---

* Associate director, FBI.

istration would have been fired. These were emotional outbursts that nobody usually paid any attention to.

DOMESTIC DIFFICULTIES

Rocco Siciliano Nixon concentrated the management of all of the executive branch in the White House. He basically had suspicions about all of us—even those of us who were his political appointees. So after one year, I was not happy. I said to my wife, "I guess I have to get out of here." Yet, he was always unfailingly courteous and very friendly to me. What drove me to leave* was the fact that his staff in the White House were of such a nature that I didn't believe in them, or trust them. I felt that Nixon wanted this kind of management. I had no problems with Haldeman or Ehrlichman; they were both very fine to me.

My number one problem was with Chuck Colson; he definitely was trying to inject himself into our management of the Commerce Department. I can recall sending over for White House clearance a list of nominees for an advisory committee for the maritime industry. The list landed on Colson's desk, and he wanted to pick and choose. One of the people he wanted to put on the committee was a notorious person in the labor movement; he was actually frightening. I told Colson so. I said, "Have you ever seen the FBI report on this man?" He answered that this would not be necessary; this man was politically important; he'd come up with money in the next election. I did prevail in this case, and the man was not put on the committee. But after I left the administration, he was put on. Colson's attitude was: you're doing a pedestrian job over there at Commerce; we are concerned with the big picture—the political picture—which is far more important. I had problems with him, but he was speaking with the strength of the president behind him. He was given a full head of steam and he used it. I'm sure that from his point of view, he did want to strengthen the presidency.

Donald Rumsfeld There was tension between Colson, Ehrlichman, and me. You never knew with Colson and Ehrlichman whether they were speaking for the president or themselves; whether they were responding directly from something the president wanted, or said, or whether they were assuming that the president would, or should—if they had bothered to talk to him. From time to time, Mr. Colson, particularly, would call me with suggestions

* In April 1971.

that I found unacceptable, and it would end in heated discussions—with my declining. Mr. Ehrlichman, on the other hand, from time to time would call and not really understand how government worked.

David Keene I had personal difficulties with Colson that made it hard for us to work together. The first that happened when I joined the vice-president's staff is that Colson attempted to recruit me to provide people to do things that I didn't think should be done. And I just refused. Secondly, an event occurred after Agnew gave his speech in Des Moines, which was an attack on the networks. Nixon said he ought to give another on the *New York Times*. Like much of what Nixon said, he later had second thoughts. Pat Buchanan was designated to produce another broadside, and Agnew was ordered to deliver it. He did not want to; he thought it was overkill. I was not in this loop at all; it was held very closely. Eventually, Colson was. Eventually, Nixon decided not do to that—that Agnew was right and that they shouldn't do it. Unfortunately, the speech in fact was in Colson's hands, and part of his job was to get all this stuff out—to get coverage for it. And he had already stuck it into the machinery.

Some time later, a congressman referred in the *Congressional Record* to the speech that Agnew had given—which he had not given. Haldeman's people read it and immediately demanded who the leak was. Colson, in order to protect his person, sent a memo to Haldeman saying he had looked around and tracked it down, and had discovered that I was the leak, and that I should be dealt with harshly for this. Eventually, Buchanan called me and he said, "You should know, you have a problem. A lot of people in any White House end up getting killed and don't know why. It's about to happen to you." So I wrote a memo to Agnew, pointing out that I knew nothing about this and that it was another example of Nixon's people trying to blame their shortcomings on Agnew's staff. He was enraged and went to Nixon, and Haldeman was called on the carpet, and he calls Colson on the carpet. Buchanan called me and congratulated me on surviving and suggested I not go anywhere near that end of the Executive Office Building because, as he put it, "There's a lion in a cave over there, and if you go anywhere near it, he's going to get you."

From that point on, I didn't have any contact with Colson until the 1972 race began and he went to Agnew, because he was in charge of the surrogates. He kept insisting Agnew was a surrogate, and Agnew kept insisting that he was the vice-president. They had a meeting, and Colson said he had to get quick response from the vice-president, and needed to make sure he could reach him at all times. Agnew called me and asked me to come to the meeting, knowing what had happened earlier, and said he was too busy to be dealing with Chuck, and if Chuck had any ideas he should call me, and if I thought they were worthwhile, maybe he would do it. And Chuck and I worked together because he had no choice. When he left that meeting, Agnew said, "Do you think that will solve the problem?" That was his way of getting back at Colson. Colson and I have since become friends.

Charles Colson Nixon recognized that he was not president of the government, nor CEO of the U.S. government, but rather, the president of the country. He did not want to get into intramural battles over policy issues. He would play devil's advocate. He would say to me, "John Ehrlichman wants to do this. What do you think?" Then Ehrlichman and I would meet and order the pizza at night, instead of the president, as Clinton does. Then we would come up with a consensus and report back to Nixon. But this was arrived at by him playing staff against staff, so there was always a lot of tension in the White House.

Alexander Butterfield I lost my temper two times when I was in the White House: once, on the telephone with Ross Perot*—I was out of control; once, with Rose. We had to tiptoe around Rose; we had to treat her with kid gloves. I was awfully nice to her. She didn't want to go up to Camp David on weekends. She hated the idea, but she didn't want anyone else to go; she was jealous of any other secretary who would go up there with her man. I am sure, knowing something about human nature, that she was in love with him. I had some empathy; I understood, also, how she didn't like being shut out.

We excluded Rose in many ways, and that was the president's doing. I think that, to this day, Rose blames Haldeman for keeping her out of the center, where she had always been before—the loyal secretary. But she didn't get sophisticated and big-time, as he did. She'd come in and say, "Oh, your Aunt Millie . . . " during the middle of a postal strike; she didn't have a sense of what was important, and what wasn't, in the grand scheme of things. And the president just said, "Keep her the hell out, Bob." She had very high rank and very good pay, but she was the first secretary to a president who wasn't right there in the outer office; she was down the hall, on the other side of me. She had been with that man since he was a congressman; I understood her feelings. She also did not like the fact that I had access.

* The Texas industrialist.

One day, I finally went in and said, "Rose, goddamn it! This whole staff tiptoes around here, and bends over backward to please you." I was very profane, and said, "You don't have to worry about me"—you see, I had never tried to ingratiate myself with Nixon. Haldeman once said, "Alex, you don't know how to merchandise yourself; when you are talking to a Cabinet member, you should say, 'I was just talking to the president.' You have to keep reminding people all the time." So I told her, "I am just here to do this job, and then I'm out of here."

Part Two

The Issues

4

Domestic Issues

PRESIDENT NIXON'S POLITICAL PHILOSOPHY

Ronald Ziegler I was active in the Republican Party in college in California. In 1960, Nixon and Kennedy visited the USC [University of Southern California] campus and—for a person raised as a Republican—I took a good look at both men and was very impressed by Jack Kennedy, but I chose the roots of my family on the Republican side, and related to what Nixon was saying. I saw Mr. Nixon more as a moderate, pragmatic leader than as a conservative symbol.

James Farmer Mississippi Governor John Bell Williams had vetoed Head Start money coming into Mississippi. The governor had the right to veto federal funds for any program in his state; the secretary of HEW had the authority to override the veto and get the federal funds into the state.

When I learned about the veto, I called Bob Finch, who was secretary of HEW then, and told him I thought it was essential that we override the veto. Finch informed me that this would be a highly sensitive decision politically because of the fact that one of the most powerful members of the Republican National Committee was from Mississippi. So Finch said that the decision would have to be made by the White House.

So I called the White House. Much to my surprise, when I asked for the president, the switchboard connected me to the Oval Office; Richard Nixon took the call. I told him it was essential that I see him within twenty-four to forty-eight hours. He said "How about first thing tomorrow morning in the Oval Office?"

When I arrived at the White House the next morning, he was there, in the Oval Office, waiting. I told him that I was sure he was aware that Governor Williams had vetoed Head Start money going into Mississippi. He nodded very slightly. I told him that I considered it of utmost importance that we override the veto.

He said, "Mr. Secretary, just tell me one thing: Why do you consider this Head Start matter to be so all-fired important?" I told him that if we allowed the veto to stand, it would become contagious—there would be vetoes in Louisiana, Alabama, Georgia, South Carolina, and perhaps several other southern states. We would then lose Head Start where we needed it most.

He nodded very slightly. I said, "Furthermore, if we did not override the veto, I would consider my role at HEW to be completely untenable."

He looked up sharply, frowned, and thought for a moment, and then nodded. I stood and said, "Thank you, Mr. President, for your attention. I'll take my leave now, with your permission."

After lunch that day, Bob Finch called me and said, "Jim, I'm sure you'll be pleased to know that I have just sent a registered letter to John Bell Williams, overriding his veto."

Well, my feeling was that this happened not because the president liked me; it was because he did not want to have a highly publicized resignation of the best-known black in his administration at that particular time; this was in the fall of 1969.

Howard Phillips His rhetoric was very conservative; Colson built the perception. Mitchell said, "Don't worry about what we say; it's what we do," and, unfortunately, the conservatives got the rhetoric and the liberals got the government. It's not so much that Nixon was an active liberal; it's a combination of his not giving a damn, on the one hand, and his desire to win the approbation of the American establishment, on the other hand. Whenever what the *Washington Post* would call "the darker voices" would get his attention, he would usually do the right thing; that's how I got to be director of OEO [Office of Economic Opportunity]. But when conservatives did not have access to him, Nixon would fall back on his split personality.

Nixon was a liberal; there is no question about it. Go back to his career in Congress—his support for the [Senator Arthur] Vandenberg wing of the Republican Party[*] on foreign policy issues—more foreign aid, more support for international organizations. Look at the people he chose in these areas,

---

[*] The Republican senator from Michigan favored more U.S. involvement in foreign affairs.

like Kissinger. If you look at his economic policy, he supported price controls, closing the gold window, the creation of regional governments. He basically institutionalized and expanded the Great Society; he was the one who perpetuated it; he was far more culpable than Lyndon Johnson, because he raised expectations that he would do otherwise. It was not that he really wanted to do this; it was because of his desire to avoid criticism—his desire to win brownie points with the liberals by giving this or that away.

It was his administration that institutionalized the quota system, subsidized forced busing, heavily promoted abortion. I remember one of Nixon's assistant secretaries at HEW [Health, Education and Welfare] saying, "Yes, we have to have the government pay for abortion, because if we don't abort these kids, we are going to have to support them on welfare; this was before *Roe v. Wade.** So, across the board—on all the key issues of the day—even though he gave some conservative rhetoric, the politics of his government were very, very left.

Raymond Price Domestically, he is a relatively conservative pragmatist; he's not a Pat Buchanan ideologue. He is a believer in strong, but limited, government; this was behind most of our battles with Congress; they wanted central control. He was the first president in 120 years to take the office with both houses of Congress controlled by the opposition party. If the Republicans had controlled either house of Congress, he would have completed his [second] term. In some things, we were too far ahead of our time, as in welfare reform, where what we tried to do is now finding favor. In the first two years, we had great creative ferment when we had Pat Moynihan and Arthur Burns—serious people coming from different points of view—thrashing things out until you had something good. The Domestic Policy Council under Ehrlichman worked well; it had some good people, but not the same spark we had with Pat and Arthur.

Howard Phillips There was no principle to which Nixon was really committed. That is one of the reasons why I organized Conservatives for the Removal of the President in 1974; it got to the point where—on the basis of what I had seen domestically—there was nothing he wouldn't give away to purchase additional time in office. The same thing seemed to be happening in foreign policy—in his relationship with Brezhnev. I said, "Folks, this is our guy; we brought him in. It's time to pull the plug before he takes the country down with him."

* The Supreme Court decision legalizing abortion on demand.

James Farmer Nixon was an almost completely political animal: he was neither moral nor immoral, but was amoral; he made decisions based on how they would affect him politically, not based on whether they were right or wrong—I don't think right or wrong entered into it, although he did use those words quite frequently.

I also think that Nixon was well-trained and qualified to be president; his experience in the Congress and as vice-president had equipped him. Looking back on the presidents I had known, he was one of the two best qualified—the other one being Lyndon Johnson.

Nixon would have been recorded as being a very great president had it not been for that fatal character flaw: he did not believe in anything. He was not an idealogue; he was not a Ronald Reagan.

Donald E. Santarelli Nixon was extremely sensitive to what can be called the system of dual federalism, very much a student of government, and philosophically committed to a limited role for the federal government, which was very consistent with the policy attitudes in those days. Nixon's basic philosophy was that the federal government's function had to be very carefully circumscribed. I can remember his often saying that he couldn't stop the IRS from collecting taxes, but he could sure stop the federal government from spending money. This was also the philosophy of his law enforcement program. The Law Enforcement Assistance Administration [LEAA] was key to that; it was a billion-dollar-a-year program, in 1972 dollars.

Frederic V. Malek At HEW, I was associated with the new federalism; this was a strategy to shift a lot of the power of the federal government—to decentralize from Washington to regional offices, and then to state and local governments; to take more authority out of the hands of federal bureaucrats and to put more authority into the hands of the people closest to the problems. The principal policy initiative involved welfare reform. Throughout all of this was the feeling that government was too large and cumbersome, and that decisions needed to be made by those close to the real problems.

James Farmer I met Richard Nixon just before holding a press conference to announce my resignation from HEW. I had shown him the courtesy of allowing him to read the statement which I was going to present to the press.

He said it was very eloquent, and he appreciated my letting him see it. He also said that the press was going to want to know what we talked about.

He said, "I assume you are still for the Family Assistance Plan—welfare reform." I told him, "Yes, that was a plan that was too little, too late, but at least it was one step in the right direction"—that was the plan that had been devised largely by Pat Moynihan.

Nixon said, "Well, in the next session of Congress, I am going to fight for it tooth and nail, and if the Congress doesn't give it to me, there is going to be blood on the floor; you can tell the press that."

Well, I told the press that the president had said that, but there was no blood on the floor and he didn't fight for it, because it was not politically expedient for him to battle for it at the time.

Raymond Price We inherited the legacy of the 1960s, which I have called the second most disastrous decade in the nation's history after the 1860s. We wanted to get away from the screeching and shrillness of the 1960s and get back to civility and rationality. Nixon was trying to do domestically— broadly—the same thing he was trying to do internationally: to move power away from the center—following the rule that the best way to get people to behave responsibly was to give them responsibility; to try to reverse the period of the middle third of the century—the period of maximum governmental aggrandizement, driving all power to Washington—not only from the states, but from individuals. He was determined to reverse that. He also had a great respect for Middle America which, he felt, had been given rather short shrift by the intelligentsia and by the Washington establishment; he felt that there was a good deal of wisdom out there in the country. He wanted to get power away from the permanent Washington establishment; this, of course, was resented by the permanent Washington establishment, which includes much of the national media.

Howard Phillips I operated on the assumption that he meant what he said, which he obviously didn't. I thought he meant it when he talked about closing down the Great Society, and opposing quotas, and busing, and bureaucracy, and unbalanced budgets. The bottom line is that he did not have firm opinions—that most of his policies in the domestic area were brokerable. The very fact that he relied so heavily on Len Garment—who is every bit as liberal as Bill Clinton—as his domestic policy adviser shows his lack of seriousness of purpose in that area. Len had a lot to do with everything from the buildup of the National Endowment for the Arts to the creation of the Legal Services Corporation, the National Endowment for the Humanities, quotas, and the Environmental Protection Agency to a lesser degree; he had a whole cultural and social portfolio at the White House. He won almost every battle. On top of that, John Ehrlichman was a liberal, and Colson was not philosophically conservative—he's becoming more so now, but he still isn't. But Colson—for political reasons—reached conservative conclusions on many things. Haldeman was a conservative influence, as well, but the Nixon domestic staff was very liberal.

CIVIL RIGHTS

Maurice Stans Something came up almost immediately that was of considerable interest to him. That was what he called "minority capitalism." He made two speeches on the radio in the '68 campaign talking about the problem of blacks and their nonparticipation in the economy—the fact that something had to be done to give them a better break than they were getting. He had concluded that the answer was to give them a chance to be capitalists—not just jobs—figure out a way to have a growing percentage of them become capitalists. Then they become employers, and taxpayers, and we shift the whole burden in the economy for a lot of these people away from welfare and into being taxpayers. He had a pretty sound analysis of it at that point. We talked about it a bit in the first meeting I had with him. He said, "I don't think this is a good political move; it won't get us any votes. But we'll do it, because it's the right thing to do." He had a conviction that that was something that needed to be done.

In the next meeting I had with him, I said, "We have to enlarge the scope of this, because there are more than blacks involved; there are four ethnic groupings of people in the United States that are considered by the Congress to be minorities: blacks, Hispanics, Asians, and American Indians. I'd like to wrap them all together into one program and call it 'Minority Business.'" He said, "All right; let's do it that way." I said, "We have one big problem—that is, I can't start a program of this type without congressional approval, and without appropriations." From my experience in the Eisenhower administration, I knew this was a two-year process. I said, "There is a way to speed it up, if you're ready to do it." He said, "What's that?" I said, "An executive order of the president. There are a lot of appropriation accounts in existence that could be used to help minority business." He was tickled at the idea and said, "Send it over." By the first of April, we had an executive order from the president, giving us everything we could have gotten by appropriation or legislation. It was a very successful program. It was the first time the federal government had ever put into effect an organized program to help the minorities get a start—what Nixon called an equal place at the starting line.

H. R. Haldeman Coming out of his Quaker background, his view was that all people are equal—different, maybe, but equal. He clearly recognized the need for making progress in race relations, but he was adamant that it should be made not in a demagogic, show business way, but in a realistic way. The best evidence of this is in what he did, not on the integration of schools, but on the desegregation of schools, in a positive—not a grandstanding—way: not sending the troops in, but working with the responsible people at the state and local levels, to develop a climate that would accept desegregated schools; not doing it by forcible busing, that disrupted families and neighborhoods, but by encouraging the things that brought it about. George Shultz took a strong role in leading that effort, while—at the same time—John Mitchell, at Justice, was trying to avoid the grandstanding legislation, which required confrontation, rather than cooperation. The militants were impatient with that, because they wanted confrontation; they thought it would make things move faster. Nixon, I think rightly, felt strongly that it made things go slower.

Frederic C. LaRue The South had been crucial to Nixon in 1968; there was no way he could have gained the nomination without very solid support there. The Republican Party in the South was never racist; certainly, by 1968, it had become very moderate as far as civil rights was concerned. We had to implement the legislation—and to the extent that busing had to be part of it—this had to be: the legislation was in place, and the administration had to desegregate the school systems. This was accomplished in a relatively peaceful manner, and by 1972, the South had some of the most integrated systems in the country. And between 1968 and 1972, Nixon had become very popular in the South.

Raymond Price On the civil rights front, the biggest thing we confronted was the segregated southern school system. We did what people said couldn't be done; we integrated the schools peacefully. Nixon did that by deliberately reversing the conventional way of doing it, which had been to demonize the white South and beat these people over the head and demand that they rise to a higher moral plane; he made a point of treating them with respect—making them part of the process—and it worked. From his earliest days, Nixon has been a strong civil rights person.

Gerald R. Ford Dick Nixon believed fundamentally in responsible civil rights policy on the part of the federal government. I don't think that he favored mandatory busing; with that exception, he had a very balanced view. He didn't go as far as the liberals wanted, but he was more liberal than most conservatives wanted.

George McGovern The president came out against court-ordered busing. That may be understood in view of his constituency. The Democrats weren't all that excited about school busing, either; that subject didn't have a lot of friends around this town. I can understand the administration's reluctance to move on that formula; it is not the happiest way to deal with civil rights issues, so I never felt that that was one of their chief failings. Nixon was actually pretty good on civil rights questions.

James Farmer He was capable of doing very bad things or very good things with equal facility, because he believed in nothing. This is true in the civil rights area. He was, for instance, the strongest president on affirmative action—up to that point, both in government service, where government funds were used, and in the private sector, for instance, in the Philadelphia Plan, where the Nixon administration had fostered a plan dealing with the construction industry in Philadelphia [Pennsylvania] which mandated that any construction job done with government funds had to be integrated—the work force had to have a percentage of blacks involved at every level, which bore a favorable resemblance to the percentage of blacks in that part of Philadelphia.

Talk about quotas! That was pretty firmly quotas—even the AFL-CIO was screaming bloody murder on that one! The plan was dropped after the first term, when Nixon was asked in the campaign what his opinion was of quotas; he said he was opposed to quotas.

HEALTH-CARE ISSUES

Ronald Ziegler On health-care reform, if you read Richard Nixon's proposal—put out in February 1974—it has health care for everyone, employer mandates, pharmacy care, preventive care. It was far-reaching thought twenty years ago, stimulated by his ability—and his presidency—permitting people like Elliot Richardson and others to present that type of thought and allow his presidency to move forward.

Howard Phillips In the programs I oversaw—and tried to close down—the whole liberal agenda was being advanced. The abortion movement was a major beneficiary; they were able to use legal services projects throughout the country to develop litigative strategies. It's not that Nixon signed off on—or was aware of—every grant; it's that his subordinates did not want to do anything that would get him criticism in the press.

Donald E. Santarelli We were seriously thinking about health-care reform, welfare reform, court reform. We created the EPA [Environmental Protection Agency], and if Watergate hadn't happened, and Nixon hadn't been an unlikable person, he would have been a great president, because he managed issues and government very well. But he had a personality that didn't resonate with the public: he was stiff, cold, and uncomfortable. And he did not have the kinds of leadership skills that stimulate people's emotions—only their intellects.

LAW ENFORCEMENT

Donald E. Santarelli Nixon was very interested in the law enforcement issue, not because it made good politics—although it did; he was genuinely a lawyer at heart, and genuinely interested in the criminal justice system, and in the issue. He read voraciously all the memos we ever sent him. Bud [Egil] Krogh was my counterpart at the White House when I was at Justice under (Attorney General) John Mitchell; we worked very closely together, daily, and when we would come to a joint position, invariably, Mitchell and Ehrlichman would endorse it rather quickly, and it would go in to the president, who was anxious to talk about it. He would call Krogh and me on the phone, and call us in for conferences. In fact, I ended up doing all the congressional and leadership briefings at the White House on all the crime—and crime-related—issues, because Nixon just liked the issue; it was a favorite of his, and he was thoughtful about it. In one of our recommendations, we suggested that the president rid us of Mr. Hoover—in his last and less effective days. Nixon's annotations on the memo that came back were: "A good idea, but can't do until after the '72 election; the public wouldn't understand." It wasn't that he disliked Hoover. Hoover had just reached the point where he was widely understood to no longer be effective; he was just too old and rigid.

And the FBI was somewhat recalcitrant to assume any responsibility on the drug issue; Nixon was very concerned about how to deal with the issue.

It was building because there was very little response, on any front, to the growing problem of the public's perception of crime. The drug issue was just beginning to bloom. The culture in those days was very accustomed to safety, and the presumption of it; the country was accustomed to civility, respect for law and order, for property rights. And so the initial incursions into that—in part by a new drug culture—were very dramatically jarring to the public. Nixon believed that the judiciary had moved too far to the left; he promised to appoint strict, constructionist judges.

NUTRITION AND HUMAN NEEDS

George McGovern Nixon was actually quite flexible in terms of the issues I was interested in. I was chairman of the [Senate] Select Committee on Nutrition and Human Needs; every time we pushed them to go a little further than they were inclined to go, they did it. To whatever extent the food shipment program—the special program for women, children, and infants, and the senior citizens' program—Meals on Wheels—that whole range of nutritional and food assistance programs went, they had a pretty good record. I must say, we had great success with the Nixon people in moving things along on a related domestic issue: they pioneered a kind of negative income tax proposal that was not unlike the $1,000 I had proposed during the 1972 campaign. And partly under the influence of Pat Moynihan—who was then working at the White House—the Nixon administration was open to welfare reform and deserves some credit for that.

THE WAR ON POVERTY

Donald Rumsfeld I got in there and decided things needed to be sorted and sifted and that some things that weren't working should be discontinued, and the funds from those things put into areas that were working. So we tended to deemphasize a lot of the more radical things that were going on, where activities were being funded that were really antisocial, and to take the funds and move them into programs that were having greater success in actually helping people. I knew of no plan to ultimately discontinue it, although I continued to feel—as I think President Nixon and others in the administration felt—that my original judgment had been correct, that is to say, it is better—if it's possible—to have the departments and agencies reformed and changed in a way that they do what they are supposed to be doing in the first place, rather than duplicating it out of the executive office of the president. It did not make sense, ultimately, to have a major, multi-billion-dollar agency in the executive office of the president. The pieces should eventually be moved out to the departments and agencies that have the fundamental statutory responsibility for those activities.

At that stage, the so-called War on Poverty had had some success and, in addition, had had a number of negative effects. I can remember Mayor [Richard] Hatcher of Gary, Indiana, coming in to me once and worrying about the effect of OEO, where there was a lot of hype and press every time the OEO made a grant—Gary was a city which was half black, half white, and the constant hype about an OEO grant for some program for black people was creating a hardening of the crust between black and white, to a certain extent.

OEO had gotten to the point where a reasonable amount of the money had ended up going into radical organizations that were antisociety, and they were doing things that were, in some cases, illegal, and in other cases very irritating to the rest of society. A great many of the mayors and elected officials around the country were up in arms; people felt that the program had run amok. It wasn't just President Nixon who was sensitive to the problems in these programs; an awful lot of people were about ready to throw the baby out with the bath water because of anger over the way it had been administered.

One of the other problems was that there was an excess of rhetoric; President Johnson had talked about eradicating poverty *now*. In fact, the program had no prospects of doing that; in fact, there are always going to be some people at the lower end of the economic spectrum, and the society decided they wanted some sort of safety net for those people. And, in addition—properly in my judgment—they wanted to see if they could find some innovative programs that would conceivably help people move out of poverty. There was no assurance that innovative programs would necessarily do that.

5

Foreign Affairs

The Nixon administration dealt with a wide range of foreign policy issues, including the Vietnam War; relations with the then–Soviet Union—at that time the world's other superpower; the possibility of establishing relations with Communist China; tensions in the Middle East between Israel and several of her Arab neighbors; the continuing threat of Castro-type communist takeovers in Latin America; the status of Berlin; and relations with the U.S.' NATO allies.

GENERAL OBSERVATIONS

Thomas Moorer I met him during the 1968 campaign. He had a broad knowledge of domestic policies, but he was more interested in foreign policy. This is normally true except in the present administration: Mr. Clinton cares nothing about foreign policy; he doesn't spend as much time on foreign policy as he does on jogging. Nixon had a global view. He is the last president to have that kind of understanding of the world at large.

Vernon Walters Richard Nixon was the only president of the United States that I have been totally comfortable about leaving alone with foreign leaders. He knew what policy was, what U.S. interests were.

Joseph Sisco For Nixon, the number one priority was Vietnam; there isn't any doubt about that. Insofar as the Middle East was concerned, Nixon's view, geopolitically, was to look at the world in strategic terms; he looked at the Middle East as a test between the United States and the Soviet Union. Our policy there had two prongs: obviously, the special relationship with

Israel and the commitment of America to its security and survival but, at the same time, seeking to strengthen the fabric of relationships with those moderate Arab states that seemed to be committed to live and let live, and to coexistence. Mr. Nixon didn't follow all the details; that was not his style. He focused on the broad strategic decisions; the details were at the Kissinger-Rogers level. Kissinger had on his staff a Middle East man, Harold Saunders, who followed the issues in great detail and who kept Kissinger informed, so that we were, at the staff level, not only writing reports and cables, but were in daily contact with Kissinger's Middle East man at the NSC.

William Colby, deputy director of operations; director Central Intelligence Agency He is a brilliant strategist; he is just phenomenal. Kissinger would be the first to admit that he is not the originator of the big steps: the SALT [Strategic Arms Limitation Talks] agreement, the opening to China. The big steps were Nixon's. He was extremely good in the foreign field, and a good customer of intelligence—a very brutal infighter in the political sense. Some of that compulsion to be tough comes out in that bad language in the tapes. I never heard him use language like that.

Viktor Sukhodrev, interpreter to Leonid Brezhnev, General Secretary, Communist Party of the USSR The tremendous role played by Kissinger was seen to be major and very important. But Kissinger, for all his ego, would always say, when we got to an impasse in negotiations, "Of course, this is as far as we can go; the president will have to decide how much further we can go." So it was understood that while Kissinger was playing a major role, I would have to say that in all the negotiations with Nixon, he [Nixon] was very much in command. Nixon knew the business; he certainly was good in foreign policy—he had the expert knowledge; he didn't just read from prepared briefs; he could carry on a negotiation.

DR. KISSINGER

President Nixon chose as his national security adviser Dr. Henry A. Kissinger, a protégé of Nelson Rockefeller and a professor at Harvard University, who had served as a foreign policy consultant to both the Kennedy and Johnson administrations.

Although Dr. Kissinger's views were hawkish—in the context of the late 1960s—he was intensely involved in Nixon's opening to China, in fostering détente with the then–Soviet Union, in the negotiations with North Vietnam that led to the end of the long conflict there, and in dealing with the ongoing Middle East crisis.

Although technically outranked by Secretary of State William P. Rogers, a longtime Nixon friend and political associate, Dr. Kissinger functioned as the administration's point man on foreign affairs.

At the National Security Council, Dr. Kissinger put together a staff of young experts, many of whom went on to occupy prominent positions in later administrations. They include Lawrence Eagleburger, deputy secretary of state and secretary of state in the Bush administration; Brent Scowcroft, that administration's national security adviser; Anthony Lake, national security adviser to the Clinton administration; and Winston Lord, who went on to serve as ambassador to China and is currently assistant secretary of state for Far Eastern affairs in the Clinton administration.

Marshall Green Kissinger was brilliant in his own way, but he was self-seeking, self-aggrandizing. I don't think the president got the best kind of support this way: Kissinger played a role as an adviser and consolidator, but the president's principal adviser always has to be the secretary of state, or the system is not going to work. Kissinger was the first one to appreciate that when he became secretary of state. The reason he didn't use the system was fundamental: the president had almost a paranoia about leaks—he basically liked to conduct diplomacy secretly; he wanted to keep the cards in his own hands. When he found out that something leaked—which is inevitable in Washington—he then immediately suspected somebody in the State Department or in the Defense Department. The truth is that the leaks often occurred in his own White House.

Howard Phillips Kissinger was my international relations professor at Harvard; he gave me an A. I liked him; I thought he was the most conservative professor on campus. I enjoyed the course tremendously. At the time, what he said—compared with other things I was hearing at Harvard—seemed eminently sensible. He was clearly of the Rockefeller camp—and Nixon always felt he had to make his peace with Rockefeller.

George Romney, secretary of Housing and Urban Development (HUD) At the 1968 convention, I was staying at a house in Boca Raton. In the past, Kissinger had given me some advice in the foreign policy area. He called me and wanted to come and see me. He came out to see me, and he urged me to support anybody but Nixon. "Anybody," he said. So it was interesting the way things turned out.

We had some contacts during the first few weeks of the administration. I was interested in finding out more about Vietnam, because I had taken very significant positions on the subject. I was interested in knowing whether or not he knew if my discussion with Nixon about Vietnam had had any impact—I had gone to see Nixon after I accepted the Cabinet post, and we spent a good bit of time talking about Vietnam. I urged him to take the peace initiative. Kissinger indicated that after I left Nixon, in the Pierre Hotel, he called Kissinger and they talked about what Nixon and I had discussed.

Daniel Ellsberg In November 1968, right after the election, Kissinger spoke at Rand,* and said, "Nixon is a man who is not fit to be president." A month later, when he was offered a job [as national security adviser], he discovered that Nixon was a fine person. Kissinger also said in that talk at Rand, "I have learned more about Vietnam from Dan Ellsberg than from any other person"—I had briefed him on two occasions in Vietnam at great length, and he had followed my suggestions more than most people did. When I was being considered to write the first paper for Kissinger's National Security Council [NSC], he raised a question about my discretion: he said, "When I was in Vietnam as a consultant, Ellsberg had been very candid with me. I very much appreciated it at the time, but now that I am on the other side of the desk, I see things differently."

Hermann Eilts, ambassador to Saudi Arabia; deputy commandant, Army War College; ambassador to Egypt He would work you to death—he would work his own people to death; he was inconsiderate; he was not a leader in the sense that he looked after his own people—but as far as I am concerned, he was a first-rate secretary of state, although his style was never to go beyond telling the half-truth. I want to make it very clear that I am a great admirer of Kissinger; we would not be where we are today if not for his initial diplomacy: in one year's time, he succeeded in eliminating—for all practical purposes—the Soviet influence in Egypt, and in bringing Sadat, much against the wishes of his senior people, to our side. This led, eventually, to Camp David,† but none of that would have been possible without the skillful diplomacy of Henry Kissinger.

---

* A defense-oriented think tank located in both Washington, D.C., and in California.
† The Camp David Accords, establishing peace between Israel and Egypt, were signed in Washington, D.C., in March 1979, during the administration of Jimmy Carter.

Viktor Sukhodrev Over the Nixon years, Kissinger was very busy with his Vietnam policy, and he would usually make it a point during his frequent meetings with [Soviet Foreign Minister Andrei] Gromyko to outline— sometimes in great detail—the progress of his discussions.

He had a prodigious memory, and he would just reel off figures, dates, times, places. Of course, the Soviets were never really satisfied with the pace of movement toward a possible settlement. They would always urge him to be more vigorous, just as in the Middle East issue they would urge him to put more pressure on Israel—there was a feeling that the United States could bring the necessary pressure to bear and influence Israel, prob- ably more than the Soviets ever could—so there was always some tough talking on Vietnam and on the Middle East.

But Kissinger did give out a lot of information on what the United States was trying to do. Maybe Gromyko didn't always believe it, but the talks were very detailed and businesslike.

Vernon Walters I've never had difficulties with Dr. Kissinger; I'm told that this is an unusual circumstance, and that I should be grateful. Someone said, "I've never heard him criticize a telegram of yours, which is about as high praise as you can get." Kissinger did say, "Dick Walters is enjoying this so much, he would have paid us to let him do it." I often disagreed with Kissinger, but when I thought, Who could do it better?, no name came to mind, and no name still does.

George McGovern I continued to be very critical of administration policy, but he was always open to meeting me. When he was nominated to be sec- retary of state, I was on the [Senate] Foreign Relations Committee, and I telephoned him the night before the committee's vote and told him I was going to vote against his confirmation—not because of anything personal; I had a high regard for his intellect, and I wished him well, personally—but I said that this was a matter of principle; that I couldn't have completed a two-year campaign for the presidency that was directed against our policy in Vietnam and then vote to confirm him as secretary of state. He had been too identified with that policy, so I would vote no. He expressed regret about that, and said he hoped that I would change my mind, but, he said, "I understand what you are doing. I don't like it, personally." But even after that, I always had access when I wanted to see him.

Morris Amitay, legislative aide to Senator Abraham Ribicoff (D- Conn.) As a professor at Harvard, Kissinger would sometimes refer to his

German accent, but he would stay away from associating with anything Jewish. I knew Morton Halperin—he worked for Kissinger at Harvard, and I roomed with Mort's brother when I was at Harvard Law School. I recall once walking up to Mort, who was standing with Kissinger and using some Yiddish phrases. I saw Kissinger physically cringe.

Mohammed Fawzi, commander in chief, Egyptian Armed Forces; minister of war Egyptians hate Kissinger because they believe he is really a Jew.

H. R. Haldeman Henry did not have a wife at that time, and he didn't bring his starlets up to Camp David, although we urged him to consider doing so. But he wasn't interested in sharing.

Vernon Walters [During a secret Kissinger visit to Paris] I had a white cat—a very intelligent cat who did tricks and used to sleep at the foot of the bed. So the first night that Kissinger took my bed, I heard this wail, and Kissinger saying, "What is this cat doing in my bed?" I said, "Dr. Kissinger, it's his bed, and if you're nice, he may let you sleep in it." Then, I picked up the cat and took it into the living room with me.

Marshall Green Kissinger was a brilliant expositor: he could brief the press, bringing in all the points in a coherent fashion; he was superbly articulate. This was just what the president needed—somebody who had the same kind of vision of American supremacy in dealing with the other great powers. Kissinger wouldn't tolerate anyone else having the president's ear. When the president named me assistant secretary, before I was approved by the Congress, I went on a trip through East Asia—I was the first administration person to travel in that area, and I wanted to be sure that what I was saying to the leaders of those countries was, indeed, a correct reflection of what the president thought. So I took it upon myself—with the help of two friends—to put down on paper what I understood to be the president's views on all the major problems related to East Asia. Armed with this paper, I made an appointment with the president. He looked at the material, nodded, and said, "That's fine." Just at that point, the door opened and in came Henry Kissinger, obviously put out that somebody from the State Department got to the president, and met with him alone. That never happened again. The president showed the paper to Henry; he looked at it without much comment, and tossed it back on the president's desk, obviously quite mad.

THE RELATIONSHIP BETWEEN NIXON AND KISSINGER

John Ehrlichman They were jealous of one another; that caused a certain distrust on both sides. One of the reasons for the White House taping system was that Nixon wanted to be able to prove whose ideas were being carried out, and who was the originator; that it was him—and not Henry. At times, he despaired of Henry. I was the audience for some lengthy soliloquies about his problems with Henry: his personality, his complaints and threats, how difficult Henry was to work with. The relationship with Henry was of two people responsible for the same job, who were confederates, but rivals, each with an extraordinary personality—personalities which didn't jibe. They were always at odds with one another.

Raymond Price Nixon tended to be his own secretary of state; he was going to be a foreign policy president. He brought in Bill Rogers—a good and loyal friend and a good manager as attorney general under Eisenhower—to State; he was to run the State Department bureaucracy. Nixon saw in Kissinger a kindred spirit in terms of worldview—and this turned out to be a very good partnership. The care and feeding of Henry was one of the greatest burdens of the presidency, but he was worth it. Nixon was prepared to take the heat for unpopular things—which Henry didn't like to do; Henry liked to get the credit, a lot of which was due to him. But a lot of the credit Henry got was dependent on Nixon's courage and insights. Kissinger put together a first-rate policy staff at the NSC [National Security Council] and drove them mercilessly. There were times when I found it difficult to work with him, but he was a first-rate policy thinker, and a shrewd negotiator. He was very good at handling the press, even if he leaked a little more than I would have preferred. Nixon and Kissinger were a good partnership; neither one could have done it without the other.

Dwight Chapin Henry would spend hours in the Oval Office. He would come out and express agitation over the amount of time he had to sit with Nixon, but that is how Nixon got to decisions. Henry and Nixon were a great combination: you had a president who understood foreign policy; you had this incredibly bright piece of talent who helped to innovate. But I don't think Henry could ever have been what he was under another president.

Robert Hartmann They loved the glory of their positions. Henry was restricted by the Constitution,* so he didn't have anything more to be ambitious about. He was never really a threat, and he was well aware of that; being secretary of state was the best he could ever be in this adopted country of his, and Nixon must have felt secure about that.

Vernon Walters I have never seen anything to reflect that Kissinger had contempt for Nixon. I think that after Nixon became the monster and the beast, Kissinger would go to a party and make some snide comments about Nixon. Nixon said, quite frankly, "I know this. Kissinger likes to be liked. I understand that."

Herbert Brownell Kissinger's ways of operating were the same as Nixon's: they were great manipulators and schemers. On a personal basis, they were very simpatico. It may not be that Nixon took Kissinger in, but that Kissinger took Nixon in. In political terms, he was an operator who loved power more than anything else.

Marshall Green He had one overriding defect: self-aggrandizement at the other person's expense. He also talked out of two sides of his mouth: when he talked to his Harvard friends of liberal persuasion who came to the White House, he talked one way; then, he turned right around and talked differently to hard-liners. This was really silly because, after a while, people began to compare notes, so as time went on, he had more and more enemies. His book†—whatever its attributes—reveals a distortion of incidents to the extent that I was involved, which adds to his luster at the other person's expense. I think that Nixon saw through this, but he also saw in Henry the perfect person to carry out his policies—a man who had equally strong desires for fame and glory. Each of them saw the other as a friend poised with a potential dagger in his back; there is a little paranoia in both men.

Winston Lord Kissinger and Haig had a very complicated relationship; Kissinger respected his skills, but over a period of time, he began to suspect that Haig was improving his relationship with the president at his expense. Haig was more hawkish than Kissinger over Vietnam, so Haig—as chief of staff, with direct access to Nixon—would complicate Kissinger's bureaucratic position.

* The presidency was restricted to those born on U.S. soil.
† *White House Years* (Little, Brown).

Alexander Haig I have the utmost respect for both men in the foreign policy field. Kissinger is probably the most astute tactician I have ever worked with; that tactical skill is a product of vast historic knowledge and experience. Nixon, on the other hand, is a long-term thinker in the area of foreign policy; Henry is far more pragmatic than Nixon. So they made a very good combination, in that one reinforced the other. Nixon has a retentive memory; he remembers every individual he has ever met in the foreign policy field and has instant recall—even at this age. Of the two, he was the least credited with his talent. But history will take care of that.

Thomas Moorer Henry Kissinger is an extremely well-informed person, so far as history is concerned; he thinks that no matter what happens, it's happened before. He had a great sense of humor, as long as you were not laughing about him; he was very concerned and sensitive about his image. He and Nixon had what I would call a good business relationship; I don't think they were very close in the evening—going out with the boys. The relationship was such that Kissinger could always get the president's ear, and could call him at any time. The president was always giving Kissinger guidance, in broad terms.

Kenneth Rush Nixon was driving the engine in this area, no question about that. The relationship between him and Kissinger was one of father and child: when I'd be talking to Henry, and the president would telephone, his voice would shake; the whole tone of his voice would change. When I was with the two of them, together, Henry was very subservient; he was completely dominated by Nixon. Nixon was not a man you felt close to; Henry is a man you feel close to—or hate—but Henry has the capacity to make you feel that you are an intimate of his. But Nixon is a very thoughtful man. When I appeared on television, he would call me afterward with congratulations.

Hafez Ismail, national security adviser to President Anwar Sadat When Kissinger came to Aswan, he said to our minister of foreign affairs, "I am the president as far as foreign affairs are concerned."

Ronald Ziegler Nixon was very much driving the engine. Henry was a thought stimulator, and a thought contributor, and an individual who could carry out the president's general philosophy, but I know that Henry would support the idea that all of the initiatives were very much Richard Nixon's.

Winston Lord They were both driving the engine. Nixon genuinely understood foreign policy as well as any president ever has—and probably better than any recent president—so you had a conceptual, rather than ad hoc, strategy. They would have long talks and work things out. Nixon deserves the credit for making the big decisions—the tough ones. He gave wide latitude to Kissinger—who would take the general framework and implement it.

George P. Shultz Nixon was a very accomplished thinker and strategist. Kissinger is also formidable. I would prefer to think that they made a very good team, but I think that Nixon, clearly, was going to do the deciding in the end.

Alexander Butterfield Richard Nixon was behind so much of everything; he was truly the architect of his own foreign policy. I certainly give Henry a lot of credit. Nixon couldn't have done it without Henry's political science skills and sense of history, which made him a better political scientist. And even though the two fought all the time—not openly, but there was tremendous conflict—they still did things very well together.

Charles Colson It was a love-hate relationship. Nixon respected Kissinger. He knew he was sharp and devious, like Nixon himself was; therefore, Kissinger was a marvelous foreign policy negotiator. But Nixon also recognized that Henry could be a sycophant, at times, which he was, and never disguised very well. Nixon wasn't ready to throw Kissinger over the side until after the 1972 election. I was at Camp David with Nixon. We were standing in the living room, and he walked me into the hall—I couldn't figure out why. I now know, of course, that the hall wasn't bugged, but the living room was. Kissinger had just given an interview to the Italian journalist, Oriana Falacci. It was a horrendous interview. Nixon said to me, "He's going back to Harvard; that's where he belongs. I've put up with everything I am going to put up with. This is the end." But Nixon knew how to get the best out of Kissinger. Between the two minds, they weren't even in the same league: Nixon had a far superior intellect and capacity and ability than Kissinger. Kissinger was a shrewd operator; he knew how to maneuver a situation; he was a very good foreign policy operator—I would not call him a strategist. At least during the time that we worked together, Nixon did the strategy and Kissinger did the operating. They were a pretty good team when they weren't mad at each other.

William Rusher Kissinger was a hell of a lot smarter than [William] Rogers, who could not find the State Department in broad daylight with a flashlight. Essentially, Kissinger very much had Nixon's view of the world. They were, and are, both Machiavellians. You can divide the world into two types: moralists and Machiavellians. The moralists are not necessarily better, although they sound better, but it means that they believe in principles, and they operate—more or less—on the basis of principles. Jimmy Carter was a moralist, but a disastrous one. Nixon is a Machiavellian, which merely means that he was born without a perception of principles—an appreciation that one conducted one's life by them, that they were what politics is essentially about, and that they were to be abided by. Nixon knew that there are principles in this world, in the sense that he knew there was a law of gravity. But it was just a fact out there—like other facts. The same way with Kissinger: when you scratch him, one doesn't find beneath the arabesques, and twists and turns, anything that we could describe as a settled set of principles. As [Winston] Churchill said of John Morley, when he became Churchill's successor as chancellor of the Exchequer: "The Treasury mind and the Morley mind embraced each other like two long-separated, kindred lizards, and the reign of joy began." I think that Nixon and Kissinger embraced each other like two long-separated, kindred lizards.

CHILE

William Colby We had been concerned about [Salvador] Allende since 1964. As the 1970 [presidential] election in Chile neared,* we decided to devote a modest amount of money to some anticommunist propaganda. The election turned out to be a disaster because Allende had two opponents who split the vote against him; he won with about 36 percent of the vote, at which point President Nixon called in Dick [Richard] Helms [director of the CIA] and said, "As I understand the Constitution down there, since Allende got only a plurality—and not a majority—he must be confirmed by the Chamber of Deputies. You have about six weeks to work and make sure he doesn't get confirmed. And don't tell the State Department, or our ambassador. Just do it." That was a legal order at that time, under the statutes that set the CIA up. So Dick Helms started a project called Track

---

* The presidential election took place on September 4, 1970. Mr. Allende received 36.3 percent of the vote. Under Chilean law, the Chilean Congress would name the new president on October 24.

II. We sent a team down there that talked to the right wing and to the military, and they ran around for six weeks and accomplished nothing; it was too late, at that point, to affect the situation.

The one thing they did do was to be in touch with some people who had the idea that the military might be stimulated to move if the chief of the military, a General Schneider, could be taken out of the picture for a while, because he was a very strong constitutionalist. The idea was to kidnap him, so that the rest of the military could be stimulated to move against Mr. Allende. We talked to two different groups of officers and ex-officers. We stopped talking to the first group. We talked to the other group and supplied them with three weapons. They never made the attempt. The first group did, and in the kidnapping, Schneider was wounded and died a few days later. Now I'm not whitewashing the CIA, but it was clearly within the president's directive. Nobody meant him to be killed, but when you go into a situation like that, you have to count on a shooting taking place. That pretty well blew it when Schneider died; the chances of doing anything about Mr. Allende were over. Essentially, Track II was wrapped up and forgotten.

THE TWO CHINAS

Throughout his congressional career, as vice-president, during the 1960 presidential campaign, and well into the 1960s, Richard Nixon was strongly allied with the supporters of Nationalist China which, following the communist takeover of the Chinese mainland in 1949, was based on the island of Taiwan, formerly known as Formosa.

In the mid-1960s, however, Mr. Nixon began to reevaluate his China position—and to consider the previously unthinkable possibility of the establishment by the United States of relations with Communist China.

In rethinking his position, Mr. Nixon would both astound his political enemies and risk alienating a major segment of his conservative-leaning political constituency, as well as the right-wing leadership of the Republican Party.

John Ehrlichman The genesis of the trip is an article Nixon wrote in *Foreign Affairs,* before he became president.* I believe that he was convinced of the merits of rapprochement back in 1961. When he came into office, one of the first things he did was to call Kissinger in and say, "This is my for-

---

* Published in the October 1967 issue.

eign policy with relation to China. I want you to do what is necessary to accomplish it."

Alexander Haig The China initiative was Nixon's. Henry was very skeptical until he analyzed its potential consequences, and then he became the most effective tactical operator in getting it done.

Winston Lord You have to give both Nixon and Kissinger the credit—Nixon because he is the president. It was his clear feeling that we ought to move toward China. I think that he also understood that because of his anticommunist credentials, it would be easier for him than, say, for Hubert Humphrey. More importantly, he knew that China would become an important country; our approach to China would give the Soviet Union an incentive to have better relations with us, in that they might get a bit nervous about our dealings with the Chinese. Indeed, within months after the announcement of Kissinger's secret trip, we had an agreement on a summit meeting with the Soviets, as well as a breakthrough on SALT, and on the Berlin negotiations. Kissinger had, independently, come to the same conclusions, for the same reasons.

Within less than a month after the inauguration, there was a memorandum from Nixon to Kissinger which, in effect, said: I want to start getting in touch with the Chinese. Kissinger was brilliant in carrying out this approach, and in implementing the vision of the president. On the Chinese side, the incentive was about the Soviets; the two nations had just had a border clash,. and the Chinese were worried about their security. They also saw eventual trade and economic advantages in dealing with us as helping to modernize their economy. It also gave them a chance to break out of their diplomatic isolation.

H. R. Haldeman The opening to China came, from the beginning, from Nixon's initiative. He had made up his mind early on that he was going to work out some way of dealing with China. He saw this as one of his contributions to his overall objective of building a structure for peace—not just building peace, but building a structure that would maintain peace. You couldn't achieve that by ignoring a country that has one-quarter of the world's population, whether they were communists or not.

It started when we visited Pakistan, on the trip where we picked up the moon astronauts. Through [President] Ayub Khan [of Pakistan], steps were taken to start some exploration with the Chinese. The Romanian leader,

[Nikolai] Ceausescu, was also involved in the effort. Kissinger was a very valuable encourager, developer, and implementor of Nixon's concept.

Vernon Walters The Chinese were very concerned with secrecy. If you sent a letter to the State Department, they would make eighteen copies and, obviously, eighteen more people would read it. The Chinese knew we were meeting with the Vietnamese, but the Vietnamese did not know we were meeting with the Chinese. To my mind, the whole thing started with the idea of getting the Chinese to get the Vietnamese to accept some kind of a reasonable peace. That was the immediate reason for the opening to the Chinese. Vietnam was the wound that was bleeding.

Richard Helms, Director of Central Intelligence; U.S. ambassador to Iran The agency was not consulted, but it played a role, in a sense, because one of our station chiefs in Pakistan was involved in passing messages back and forth; he was asked to keep his activities secret, and he did so.

The agency certainly would not have been opposed to such an opening. I remember a talk I had personally with Lee Kuan Yew, who was then the top man in Singapore, who was then on a state visit to the United States. We had a long conversation, the point of which was that the United Stated had a great arsenal of goodwill among the people of China, because the United States had never taken any of its territory, as European countries had, and that he could not understand why the United States had not opened up relations with China.

He thought this would be accomplished; he felt it must be political considerations in the United States that made this issue such a difficult one to handle. I could understand what he was saying, because over the years there had been a great deal of domestic concern about who had lost China. As far as the agency itself [was concerned], there was no reason why we shouldn't have an opening to China.

William H. Sullivan The success of the Nixon overture to China, which could reciprocally be called the Chou En-lai overture to the United States, ultimately reversed the strategic balance in the world. Our strategy to that point was that we had to be prepared to fight two-and-a-half wars—one on the NATO front, against the Soviets; one on the Pacific front, against the Chinese, assuming the two of them were acting in concert; the half one was a brushfire war. The Soviets, on the other hand, had to be concerned with only one-and-a-half wars—one on the NATO front; and presuming that their alliance stayed with the Chinese, they didn't have to be concerned with a war from that quarter. When the situation was reversed and, for instance, the Chinese terminated the alliance they had with the Soviets—and more specifically, when they took some concrete actions like taking all those radar sites we had in Iran and putting them up in Western China—the Soviets knew that the roles had been reversed. So we, in effect, became a one-and-a-half-war strategic nation, and the Soviets became potentially a two-and-a-half one. So Nixon and Chou En-lai's moves were brilliant on the larger chessboard of geostrategy. This certainly was the most important geostrategic move in the second part of the twentieth century.

Viktor Sukhodrev The initial steps were done without the foreknowledge of the Soviet leadership. The Soviet leaders were always very wary of those steps that were being taken by the United States because of the state of relations at that time between the Soviet Union and China. It was a very sore issue; there was a feeling that it was an attempt by the United States to play the China card—to bring some kind of pressure to bear on the Soviet Union.

Nixon always used to say, in terms of the Soviet–U.S. relationship, that he—with his reputation as a red-basher—could get things through Congress, because no one would ever suspect him of being soft on communism, that was his line. So I always felt he was acting from that position vis-à-vis the Chinese, as well. But there was certainly some tough talking between the Soviets and the administration, especially concerning one phrase uttered by Nixon at a banquet in China, to the effect that, together, the United States and China can decide many of the world's problems. That cut to the quick. Where was the Soviet Union in this equation?

Marshall Green The immediate cause for the breakthrough was the fear in Peking of Moscow, and of scores of divisions on the borders of China. On Nixon's side of the Pacific, the right wingers of his party were dead set against mainland China; they were pro-Taiwan, so the president had to play his cards very close to the chest.

William Rusher This man had been the principal friend of the Republic of China in the United States for twenty years, and then he turned around, with cool precision—a politician without any principles at all. He proceeded to double-cross them—one of the greatest historical double-crosses of all time. He would justify having done it on the grounds that he was president and was fighting the Cold War. I have since asked what in the world we got from this; I don't see that he solved the problem of China at all. I suppose we got some listening posts in China against Russia. Now, I guess, we have listening posts in Russia against China.

H. R. Haldeman There was opposition in the White House. Pat Buchanan, who at that time was a major speechwriter, thought it was a sellout of the Taiwanese. Some of the president's backers in Congress, and in the country also, had that view. Nixon knew there would be flak, but that the ultimate results would override the opposition.

Charles Wiggins I didn't sense a political risk. I recognized the reality of the headlines—that only a Republican president could forge this break-through, and that, obviously, we had to develop better relationships to China; it was in the national interest. I didn't think that a Democratic president, given the pressure the Republicans would apply, could make that breakthrough, so I commended Nixon for having done this.

Ronald Ziegler I was one of the few people who knew about the opening to China before Kissinger went on his trip. I never heard the initiative discussed in terms of a political risk to the president: Is it going to turn off the conservatives? It was not a proposition that permeated the staff; President Nixon never talked to me in those terms. He really did feel that in the broader global sense it was the only thing to do.

Gerald R. Ford The China breakthrough was one of the master strokes of international diplomacy while I was in government. I had no advance warning of it. On reflection, I was surprised and very pleased; I had been as adamantly anti-Mao as Nixon, but in the changing world, I could see that there were good reasons for opening the door with China. It gave us more clout with the Russians. They didn't want us to get too close to the Chinese, so they became more flexible in their dealings with the United States. Also, from a pragmatic point of view, they were a billion people—with the largest landmass in the world. We couldn't ignore them in perpetuity.

Thomas Moorer He wanted to go to China, but thought that the joint chiefs might not like it. When I was asked about this, I said, "There are a billion people there; somebody has to get over and talk to them." The chiefs didn't have any objections. What we would want to see was any proposed agreement that had any military connotations.

Marshall Green I will give Kissinger and the president full credit for lining up the secret meetings that led to the breakthrough to China, but he could have brought me in. Why not? I wasn't going to divulge it to anybody; I am a disciplined careerist—far more so than some of these White House cohorts who had little background. I was in my office one morning—I had about three or four of my staff there, and one of them said that the ticker had just come across, saying that Kissinger, who was in Islamabad, had come down with a case of "Delhi belly" [dysentery], so he had decided to take several days off, and had driven up to a hill station in the mountains above Islamabad. I said to my staff: "That is ridiculous; the last thing anybody who is suffering from that ailment would want to do is to get into a bumping car and go way up in the mountains. You know, he's probably going to Peking." Then, I said to myself: By God. Supposing he has! Then I will be guilty of the worst damn leak that has ever occurred in history. So I said to everybody: "Hold it; don't leave this room. I want to talk to the secretary [of state]." I rushed upstairs and, fortunately, Rogers was there, and I told him what had happened. His face turned ashen. He said, "My God! You are going to have to go down there and swear those people to secrecy, because Kissinger has gone to Peking." So I went down and swore them all to secrecy. We could keep a secret.

Winston Lord The one thing we underestimated was the need for secrecy: the Chinese didn't want this leaking out; we didn't want to raise expectations, in case we failed—we hadn't talked to these people for twenty-two years. Having said this, we paid a price with Japan, in particular, and with other countries. They only heard about what had happened a couple of hours before the official announcement. It was a shock to Japan, which had been anxious to move ahead with China but, out of deference to the United States, had held back. Suddenly they saw us leapfrogging over them.

President Nixon's Historic Visit to the People's Republic of China

Marshall Green Pat Buchanan said to me on the plane* going out that the Chinese people had never been told about our men on the moon and wouldn't it be a fine idea if the president, in his speech in the Great Hall of

---

* President Nixon arrived in China on February 21, 1972.

the People, would pay a tribute to Chinese civilization by saying that last month our men on the moon had looked down at the Earth, and the only man-made object they could see was the Great Wall of China. The president said, "It's all very amusing, but no." He was right, because he did not want to run the risk of offending his Chinese hosts. This is one measure of the man's greatness—he could see these things in the right proportion.

The Meeting with Mao Tse-Tung

Winston Lord It was typical Middle Chinese [behavior]; they always like to keep you guessing whether you are going to see the emperor. They had not assured us in advance that Nixon would be meeting with Mao, although we had made it very clear that this was our assumption. We had arrived and had just gotten to the Guest House when Chou En-lai asked to see Kissinger. He told him that Mao would like to see the president within an hour, so it was then a matter of getting ready to leave in fifteen to twenty minutes. Now, that is not to say that we couldn't have located Secretary [William] Rogers and taken him along; it does mean that we had to move very quickly. Nixon wanted only Kissinger to accompany him; Kissinger has admitted that he didn't say to the president—as he should have—you should also have the secretary of state there. Kissinger asked me to go along; he did that for two reasons: first, I had been in charge of putting together the briefing books for the president and, in general, had the most information on China; and second, he needed a note-taker, as he would be too busy during the discussion to do this chore.

Kenneth Rush Bypassing the State Department was a deliberate pattern. When they went to Moscow and Beijing, Bill Rogers was treated very badly, and there were acrimonious clashes between Rogers and Kissinger in both places.

Winston Lord With a great historical figure, there is the danger that you will be impressed by personal charisma and presence because you feel you ought to be. Having said that, Mao—although physically fairly weak—did, nevertheless, strike you in terms of charisma and power; you had the feeling that if you were at a cocktail party and didn't know who he was, you would be drawn to him. And Chou En-lai, who was himself a very charismatic and impressive figure, suddenly became a different person when he was with

Mao—very deferential and reserved. Mao was more of a rural person—as opposed to Chou En-lai, who had a more mandarin, elegant, cosmopolitan style. Mao could be relatively crude and somewhat bawdy in some of his jokes and references. He liked to use somewhat weird images: in one of our meetings, in a discussion of emigration, he said, "We will send you 10 million Chinese women." We thought that this may have been his way of saying that he was having trouble with Madame Mao; that his wife was a pain in the neck.

The conversation with Nixon lasted for about an hour. I thought the meeting to be something of a disappointment. We were used to Chou En-lai's somewhat elaborate, mandarinlike presentations, conceptual and philosophic, as well as practical. Mao's style was completely different; he spoke in broad strokes, going from one subject to another, throwing out a couple of sentences—some of which we didn't fully understand. I thought it was a haphazard conversation, but the more we began to think about it, the more we examined the transcript of the meeting, we realized that Mao had hit the key issues—the Soviet Union, Taiwan, and Vietnam—in just a few sentences, sometimes directly, and sometimes in an allegorical way, stating the basic Chinese positions, which gave us a framework to enlarge and flesh out over the next few days.

The Shanghai Communiqué

Marshall Green The Shanghai Communiqué* could have been a disaster. It had been approved by Nixon and Chou En-lai and left the implication that we stood behind all of our treaties in East Asia, but it excluded reference to our treaty obligations to Taiwan. Kissinger was very mad at me for finding the mistake in the communiqué, because I put him in an embarrassing position vis-à-vis the president: he had bound Nixon to a document which was wide open to criticism from the right wing. There was a stormy session when the president found out about it. Kissinger wrote about the incident in his book, *The White House Years*. The president is storming up and down in his underwear, swearing he will get even with the State Department. My guess is that the president was storming up and down because he was mad at Kissinger for this serious oversight. I hope that the history will be written correctly.

---

* A joint communiqué issued on February 27, 1972, describing the results of the U.S.-China talks.

Winston Lord When the meeting came to a close, the Chinese said, "We will release the photographs taken at the discussion, and a communiqué saying that Nixon, Kissinger, and Lord met with Mao." But Nixon and Kissinger said, "You have to cut Lord out." They thought: it is so embarrassing that Rogers is not here; it will be even more embarrassing if both Kissinger and one of his assistants are here. So, with Rogers's sensibilities in mind, they told the Chinese—who must have been somewhat mystified about it—that no photographs should include Lord, and that his presence in the meeting should be a secret. Two years later, the Chinese gave me a photo, so I could finally prove I had been there.

Marshall Green Not having Rogers at the meeting with Mao was a terrible slap in Rogers's face. The Chinese were amazed that the secretary of state was not with the president; instead, he had Kissinger and some of his henchmen along.

GERMANY

Kenneth Rush I was in touch with Nixon throughout my time as ambassador in Bonn. Nixon, Kissinger, and I discussed the problems of Berlin, and the feeling was that the only way to make progress toward an agreement with the Soviets was for me to negotiate in secret. Rogers knew nothing about it; we couldn't use normal channels. In my embassy, I had no help, because no one knew what I was doing.

THE MIDDLE EAST

As President Nixon began to formulate his Middle East policy, he took into account the outcome of the June 1967 conflict—which came to be known as the Six Day War—namely Israel's conquest of the Golan Heights, the West Bank of the Jordan River, and the Sinai Peninsula.

President Nixon—as had several of his predecessors—articulated strong support for Israel's security needs while he hoped to develop a more even-handed Middle East policy, in which positive relationships could be established with the various Arab nations.

In an attempt to begin to implement this policy, Secretary of State William Rogers in 1969 made a proposal—which came to be known as the Rogers Plan—for Israel's phased withdrawal from territories taken during the Six Day War from Syria, Jordan, and Egypt, respectively.

The Rogers Plan was strenuously opposed by both the Israeli govern-

*ment and the organized American Jewish community, and the plan's failure
was a major factor in the decisions reached by Syria and Egypt in 1973 to
again go to war with Israel in attempts to regain their respective territories.*

General Middle East Policy

Hermann Eilts The details were driven by Kissinger, but Nixon had a very
deep interest in the Middle East; it was a region he knew something about.
He wanted involvement if it made political sense, and if it would help him
with his own image.

Morris Amitay Nixon and Kissinger viewed Israel in terms of their strategy
toward the Soviet Union. They realized Israel's importance, but were never
willing to go all the way because of the oil factor, and the State Department's conventional wisdom of not getting too close to Israel. It is very clear
to me—based on conversations with [Secretary of Defense] James
Schlesinger and with [Israeli Prime Minister] Golda Meir—that Golda's
bottom line on Kissinger was that as an American secretary of state he could
have done more for us; I also think that this is true. In a discussion on Israel
with Senator Ribicoff, Kissinger said, "I have to be very careful; Haldeman
and Ehrlichman are trying to cut off my balls." When he wanted the Israelis
to do something, he would say, "How can you doubt my intentions? So many
members of my family went up in the ovens."* That was Kissinger trying to
persuade, to cajole; it was part of his technique.

Joseph Sisco Golda had great confidence in Nixon as a man of strength.
There was also Nixon's characteristic of always being for the underdog, and
Israel—in that context—was the underdog. She believed that Nixon, the
strong anticommunist, was not going to allow Israel to go down the drain,
because she felt he saw the Middle East within the context of the
U.S.–USSR competition, so a defeat for Israel would be a victory for the
Soviets—and a defeat for the United States.

Mohammed Fawzi Our view was that America would support Israel
regardless of who was president.

---

* Numerous members of Dr. Kissinger's family were deported from Germany and killed in
the gas chambers of concentration camps during the Holocaust.

Kissinger on Israel

Morris Amitay In the White House, he had his non-Jewish boss and his non-Jewish associates. He could be as tough on the Israelis as anyone else.

Robert Mardian He came out here [Phoenix, Arizona] to make a speech eight or nine years ago. He suggested to the chairman that I introduce him, and I did. I told about the first time I met him, in what we called the Little Cabinet—Cabinet-level officials from each department. Henry was the representative from the White House. He said, "You expect me to talk about Vietnam. In Vietnam, we have a client and we can control our client; the Russians have a client, and they can control their client. In the Middle East, we have a client we cannot control; the Russians have a client they cannot control. Our problem today—and maybe for the rest of the century—is the Middle East." I thought I was saying how prescient he was. Well, three years later I saw him here at a function, and he said, "You're not going to introduce me again, are you?" I said, "No, why?" He said, "Well, I hemorrhaged for six weeks after the last one, as far as my Israeli friends were concerned."

Kissinger and Sadat

Hermann Eilts The relationship between Kissinger and [Egyptian President Anwar] Sadat was very close; Kissinger found Sadat a much more likable and much more flexible person than he had anticipated. Kissinger was very well aware that when Elliot Richardson had returned to Washington after Nasser's funeral at the end of 1970, he had spoken of Sadat as "Nasser's poodle," so Kissinger thought that Sadat must be something of a weakling, but he came away very impressed. At the same time, in Kissinger's typical fashion, he was a little condescending, because he felt that Sadat had been too easy. I mention this because later, in negotiations with Syria, he liked [Hafez Al] Assad, because he thought Assad was tough. Sadat wanted aid and continuing U.S. engagement in the peace process. At the same time, Sadat knew exactly what Kissinger was about; he was not fooled by Kissinger's effusiveness—his hugs—and by the secrets Kissinger would divulge—secrets concerning what some Israeli officials had said; Kissinger would tell these secrets with great relish, so as to show Sadat that he was being fair, but Sadat was never fooled by that.

U.S.-Egyptian Relations

Hafez Ismail Sadat received a message from Washington that the Americans wanted to raise the level of our contacts from the State Department to the White House. He was asked to send a personal representative to meet Nixon. I went, and on February 23 [1973], I was brought into the Oval Office. The president was very courteous and statesmanlike. I gave him a letter from Sadat, and he said that he hoped we could have a frank discussion. But, he added, he had no plan for the Middle East. He said he was not prepared to exert pressure on either party; he felt we had to work out a settlement that would satisfy both sovereignty and security—that is, sovereignty as far as Egypt was concerned, and security for Israel. Of course, at that time, there was not any trust between Egypt and Israel. He also said—referring to Watergate—"Despite my disadvantages, I will not promise anything I cannot implement." I told him I spoke for the other Arabs, as well as Egypt, and that what stood between us and the United States was America's financial and political support for Israel. I added that one day the United States would regret this: because of Israel's atomic capability, she would be more independent, and would be able to say no.

Hermann Eilts I got a call at the Army War College to come see Kissinger. He first spoke to me about Saudi Arabia; he wanted to know how to deal with King Feisal, whom I had known since 1948. Kissinger asked a lot of good questions. As I was leaving, he said, "By the way, I expect that when I leave Egypt in four or five days, we will be resuming diplomatic relations, and I would like you to go to Egypt as ambassador." On November 5, I received a telegram at Carlisle,* sent through the State Department, that Kissinger wanted me to meet him for breakfast in Karachi in two days' time. So I flew to Pakistan, and Kissinger was late for breakfast; we talked for fifteen minutes. He told me to go immediately to Cairo, so I am not sympathetic to foreign service officers who take months to get to their posts. I was briefed by Sisco, who told me to work closely with the Soviet ambassador to Cairo; my task was to organize the first Geneva conference.

---

* Site of the Army War College.

THE ROGERS PLAN

Joseph Sisco The Rogers Plan called for Israeli withdrawal from the Sinai to the international border, subject to several very important conditions: first, there had to be bilateral negotiations between the Israelis and the Egyptians; this was an absolute, categorical element of Israeli policy—direct negotiations between the parties—because this implies recognition. The conditions to be worked out were demilitarization of the Sinai; security arrangements for Sharm El Sheik; and the question of sovereignty and security with respect to Gaza, which before 1967 had been administered by Egypt. The Rogers Plan, when unveiled publicly, was a public expression of where the state of negotiations had gone between the United States and the Soviet Union. Mr. Nixon said to me, "I want a test of the Soviet Union as to whether they want peace in the Middle East, or whether they can live with controlled tension."

After that eight-month negotiation, the Soviets were misrepresenting the American position throughout the whole area, and were deriving a propaganda benefit from it. Therefore, we decided we would make public what the negotiations had brought about; neither the Egyptians nor the Israelis accepted it. Kissinger's suggestion, in his book, that the enunciation of the Rogers Plan came as a surprise, is inaccurate; Mr. Kissinger was fully au courant with not only the elements, but was kept fully informed, day by day. In the negotiations that occurred from March 1969, between myself and Mr. [Anatoly] Dobrynin,* which culminated in the Rogers Plan, the policy and negotiations were undertaken only after a detailed review—and in two NSC meetings at which Kissinger was a full participant; he was kept fully informed of every development in the negotiations and, at critical junctures when there were decisions to be made, he was part of that decision-making process. In fact, the record will show that those eight months of negotiations were probably the most fully recorded in the history of the Middle East— with blow-by-blow cable summaries. Therefore, I'm afraid that the record needs to show that Kissinger was fully part of the process though, clearly, he did not agree with the direction in which we were going; he says [in his book], very frankly, that he did not agree with the direction taken, and that he tried to undermine it. Kissinger basically did not want to be associated with the Rogers Plan.

* Ambassador of the Soviet Union to the United States.

First Dealings with the Palestinians

Vernon Walters When I was deputy director of the CIA, Kissinger sent me to see the Palestinians in Morocco, when they were hijacking American airplanes and shooting up Americans in airports. Kissinger said, "I can't send anyone else, because that would be negotiation, and the American Jewish community would go crazy. But you are an intelligence contact." I said, "Dr. Kissinger, I'm deputy director of the CIA. I'm probably number six or seven on their hit list." He replied, "I'm number one. That's why you're going." I went to Morocco, and before I went into the meeting—this was at a time when they [the PLO] were killing Americans all over the world—I said to the king, whom I had known since he was a little boy, "Your Majesty, I am going in there alone and unarmed. I hope this is true of the other side, also." He said, "Walters, I have this building completely surrounded by my troops." I replied, "Your Majesty, I'm not terribly interested in being revenged."

The War of Attrition

Mohammed Fawzi The War of Attrition° was a turning point: the Israeli custom was that wars would be of very short duration, but in the War of Attrition, they lost an average of three soldiers a day. That is why they asked the Americans to stop this war.

Seeds of the Yom Kippur War

Hafez Ismail The decision to go to war was taken by the Egyptian people back in 1967. The people understood that what had happened in the Six Day War was not a total reflection of the balance of power between Israel and Egypt at that time; they did not accept the results of the war. Nasser's view was: That which was taken by force cannot be taken back, but by force.

Mohammed Fawzi Nineteen sixty-seven was not the decisive battle. We lost Sinai, but we did not lose determination. So we started a new system with the Soviets for equipment and armaments, and we immediately began

° A prolonged period of artillery duels between Israel and Egypt along the Suez Canal in the period following the June 1967 Six Day War.

preparations for war with Israel. [Minister of Defense, State of Israel, Moshe] Dayan had said there had been a six-day war, and I said it is a three-years' war, because between June 1967 and 1970, we only stopped action for a ten-day period. I had an order from [President, United Arab Republic, Abdul Gamal] Nasser to be prepared for war with Israel no later than three-and-a-half years after the June 1967 war. Every week he surveyed my actions and had a step-by-step knowledge of the development of the Egyptian Armed Force.

Under Sadat, Egypt changed its policy 180 degrees, beginning in May 1971. He wanted a victory, but as easy a one as possible. When I described to him my plan for war with Israel in 1971, I mentioned that our anticipated casualties in crossing the [Suez] Canal at 30,000 men. He said, "Nasser can accept this figure, but I cannot." In 1971, we expected to win the entire Sinai by military action. Sadat was prepared to accept something less: a line running from El Arish to Ras Muhammed. In fact, Sadat wanted to cross the canal and then claim victory.

Arnaud de Borchgrave, foreign correspondent, *Newsweek* On March 26, 1973, six months before the outbreak of the Yom Kippur War, I saw Sadat. He understood that Egypt could not defeat Israel militarily; the purpose of the war would be to change the geopolitical equation, so he was mobilizing for war. He also realized that an oil embargo could result from a war with Israel. I immediately came back to the United States and called Henry Kissinger, who was then at San Clemente—busy with Vietnam. I said, "Henry, I have just come from Cairo, and I have important news for you; I must see you urgently." He said, "I can see you tomorrow for five minutes if you fly to California, or I will see you for lunch next week at the Metropolitan Club." So we met, and I told him what Sadat had said. He said, "I am not sure when and if a war will happen, but when it does, we shall restore some equilibrium between the Arabs and Israelis, which is essential for a peace process." He added that, "If that happens, we will, at last, be able to distance our Middle Eastern policy from internal domestic considerations," meaning, of course, the Jewish lobby. I, to this day, don't know if this information—with its advance warning as to what was going to happen—was relayed to Nixon.

Hafez Ismail If Nixon and Kissinger had taken a different attitude in early 1973, the war would have been averted: I met with Kissinger in March, in Washington. At that time, he said that Egypt had to make concessions. In May, I met with him again, in Paris, and I asked him if the United States would be prepared to make a statement respecting the sovereignty of Egypt over its territory. He said no, he couldn't do that, but perhaps he could make a statement along the lines of [U.N. Resolution] 242* and that, probably, the Israelis would accept this. I said, "No thank you. We have had a lot of experience with 242, and we want something more definite." But he refused; that made Sadat take the final step toward war.

The Yom Kippur War†

Thomas Moorer The Egyptians had new equipment with which to build bridges across the canal. They practiced over and over: they would go up to the canal, off-load, and begin to position the matériel and put it together, and then go back. They did that over and over, and all of a sudden, on Yom Kippur Day—when all of the Israelis were in the synagogues—they came across. When something like this happens, people like to say the intelligence failed. I tried to explain to people that if the United States had come out with a statement that the war was going to start and the war did start, then the media would say we started it, so in a situation like that, you have to keep your mouth shut. The Egyptians did a good job in deceiving the Israelis.

Joseph Sisco On October 5, in New York, we had seen both the Israeli and Egyptian foreign ministers. We had had reports of a possible use of force. At that time, we were sufficiently concerned to ask for a separate evaluation from our own intelligence apparatus. The Egyptian foreign minister said that there would not be an attack. He said this in good faith, so we now know he was not in the loop. The decision to go to war was held very tightly by Sadat, Mubarak, and the top military echelon. So when the foreign minister gave me his assurance, he was not lying to us. About three years later, he was a private citizen and he called me to say in effect: I really didn't lie to you guys; I just didn't know.

Mordechai Gazit, director general, Israeli Foreign Ministry; director general, prime minister's office On October 6, 1973, we had intelligence from an Arab source at 3:30 in the morning that the war would begin in the afternoon of that day, perhaps at sunset, or before six o'clock. At a

---

* A United Nations resolution passed following the Six Day War, calling for return of territories and the guarantee of secure borders.
† Which began on October 6, 1973.

meeting that morning, the chief of staff, General David Elazar, wanted to launch a preemptive bombing at noon. Prime Minister Meir decided not to preempt—particularly against Syria—because she felt U.S. diplomatic support for us would be reduced to nil if we fired the first shot. She thought Nixon was a friend, but we had experienced a carrot-and-stick approach from the White House over the issue of phantom jets from 1969 to 1972, and she felt Nixon wouldn't be behind her if we opened fire first.

Hafez Ismail The Americans, based on what the Israelis told them, thought that our troops would be drowned in the [Suez] Canal. It was quite a surprise. There were other surprises: the date—which was Ramadan; and the time—it was two o'clock [P.M.]. Nobody starts fighting at two o'clock. This was to give our troops sufficient daylight to cross the canal and then, during the night, to build the bridges and start sending over armored troops.

Vernon Walters We knew they had it in mind, but we didn't know when. This is human intelligence; you can tell a lot of things with satellites and intercepts, but as to what they intend to do, you can only be told by human intelligence, which is why so-called spies are important. Of course, the public has been fed all this pap by John Le Carré* and James Bond† We have never killed a member of the KGB,‡ and no member of the KGB has ever killed one of our people; that just shoots all these stories to hell.

Hafez Ismail We didn't even tell the Russians the war was imminent. They knew that we were going to war, but they did not know the date, nor the time of the attack. On the 6th of October [1973], our minister of foreign affairs was in New York attending a meeting of the U.N. General Assembly. Dr. Kissinger called him in the morning to tell him that the Israelis thought that Egypt was going to war. Kissinger went systematically from one stage to another. First, he tried to prevent war, but then he couldn't, so then he wanted our action to take place only in the area of the Israeli attack. When that did not happen, he spoke to Saudi Arabia and to Jordan, trying to limit the extension of the war.

The Israelis had a very excellent mobilization plan. They had to fight on two fronts: the Egyptian and Syrian. The Syrian front was the most serious, because of the proximity of the Jordan River, and to Israeli territory. The

---

* The pseudonym of British spy writer, and former British Secret Service operative, David Cornwall.
   † The fictional spy, "007," created by novelist Ian Fleming.
   ‡ The Soviet secret service.

distance from the canal to Israeli lands was 200 kilometers, so they first sent major numbers of troops to the northern front, and at the same time, tried to limit our advance. They had strong points on the canal, and a limited number of troops with small armored reserves, about 10 kilometers behind the front line.

Kissinger's Strategy

Morris Amitay Kissinger tried to fine-tune the outcome of the war so that both sides would be dependent on the United States, which is what ultimately happened. But it involved bloodshed from the Israelis and it robbed them of a decisive military victory; the record is clear that Kissinger advised the Israelis to absorb the first blow. Had the Israelis moved first, they could have seriously blunted the Egyptian attack. During this period—on two occasions—Israel's ambassador in Washington, Simcha Dinitz, told me he had Kissinger wrapped around his little finger. When I heard him say this, a chill went down my spine: I knew something about Kissinger—he was my former professor—and I knew that Dinitz was no match for Kissinger, experience-wise or intellectually. Kissinger played Dinitz just about right in terms of allaying Israel's fears.

Hafez Ismail The Israelis were surprised. They didn't expect us to cross the canal; they didn't expect us to reach the other side. Unfortunately, we did not develop the offensive. Perhaps previous experience did not encourage us to fight a moving war. Our initial advance of ten kilometers did not leave much room for deployment. We had to keep our main armored forces on the west side of the canal, and when we did move the armored troops east, it was too late; the Israelis had stopped the Syrian attack and were breaking out in the north. Damascus was very close to the front line, so at that point, the Syrians asked Sadat for help. This led Sadat to consider a second stage, with an armored division. When on the 14th we sent the armored division east of the canal, the Israelis—who had been able to build up troop strength in western Sinai—were ready. Our losses were very high, and the division was recalled.

On the 15th, at 3 A.M., the British ambassador in Cairo asked for an urgent meeting with Sadat. He had a message from Kissinger, who wanted a cease-fire, with troops going back to their original lines. Once that happened, he would send out a committee of investigation. We did not like that, because we had started the war. Then that evening, the Israelis started to push forward: they sent some troops across the Great Bitter Lake, while [General Ariel] Sharon prepared his attack, aimed at building a bridgehead across the canal. The next day, as Sadat was meeting with the legislature, he was told that Golda Meir had made a statement at 11:00 A.M. that Israeli troops were on the African side of the canal.

The bridgehead, which started with a very small operation, greatly expanded in the next two days. Our armor was with the Third Army, on the east side of the canal and—as a result—our defenses on the west side of the canal were weakened, particularly the anti-aircraft posts. We could not stop the buildup of the bridgehead. We made some grave mistakes: there was an argument between the chief of staff and Sadat. The military wanted to bring troops from the west side to fight on the east; Sadat wanted to attempt to close the Israeli advance from the east side. He reasoned: if you cross the canal eastward, you are victors; if you cross the canal westward, you have lost. So he refused to withdraw the troops from east to west.

Was the Resupply of Weapons to Israel Necessary?

In the first few days of the war, Israel experienced major losses of warplanes and armored vehicles as the Arab armies advanced along the Sinai and Golan fronts. The Israeli army also began to have critical shortages of ammunition and other supplies. This critical situation caused alarm in Washington, and resulted in a strenuous debate at the highest levels of the administration as to how and when the United States could furnish replacement equipment to the Israel Defense Forces. More than two decades later, the argument still rages as to what positions on the resupply were taken by the president and his key aides.

William Colby The key was that the Israelis came really close to disaster in the first two or three days. Their intelligence was no better than ours. Their defense plan depends upon mobilizing the reserves; it costs a lot of money to do this, so there is a disinclination to mobilize unless you get pretty clear warnings, and they—we—let the warnings go by. Once they started to win, our policy turned around almost 180 degrees; we were trying to hold them back from trying to go into Cairo. One of the ways of holding them back was to convince them that we were providing the supplies; that's where some of the tension between Kissinger and Schlesinger came up: Kissinger would say, "Why the hell aren't the planes there?"

Aharon Yariv Kissinger said, "The Russians will land helicopters amid the [Egyptian] Third Army if we don't supply them. Let's ask William Colby." He invited Colby to Simcha Dinitz's house, and Colby said, "It's not going to happen." For Dayan and Golda, the Russians were ten feet tall, so they wanted assurance, which Colby gave them.

Morris Amitay It is clear in my mind that Kissinger held up the airlift. Schlesinger's feet were set in concrete by national policy. That policy was drafted in the National Security Council by Kissinger; it called for supplies to go to Israel in graduation and moderation. When people in the Defense Department asked, "What do you mean by that?" he said, "One aircraft per day." During that time, I was told of a meeting at the White House when the decision was finally made to start the resupply to Israel: Nixon told Kissinger—who was still not on board for letting the supplies go—"I think we should send the stuff, Henry; the Israelis have bled enough."

James R. Schlesinger Kissinger was not in favor of the resupply in the initial stages of the war; that was quite clear. Toward the middle of the week, he began to change his mind. But on the Saturday on which the war broke out [October 6], we sat down and I worked out a number of options. It was the view of Kissinger and myself that the United States should not visibly be involved on the side of Israel if we could avoid it, in order to avoid creating in the minds of the Arab states that we were hostile to them. So the general position at the outset was to stay disengaged.

I sat down and wrote out six or seven options. The first option was the so-called zero option: no supplies, no equipment, just stay out of it. The next option was: all the supplies the Israelis could carry away in their own fleet— the El Al fleet—and commercial aircraft they could hire; they could take any supplies away and no major equipment items. A third option was that the United States would provide airlift. Well, Kissinger reported back to me that the president had chosen the option that the Israelis could carry all supplies away on El Al and commercial aircraft they had hired.

So, at the start of the week, my instructions were quite clear: it was what the Israelis could carry away without the United States seeming to be involved. The Israelis thought that, pretty quickly after the initial blows, once they had mobilized, they would quickly take care of the Arab states. That turned out to be wrong, but it was something they conveyed to us at the outset and, consequently, we were, in the early days, operating on that basis.

Mordechai Gazit The airlift was decided not because we asked for it. Our relations with the United States were not at a point where we could have asked for an airlift; this was beyond our imagination. I accept Nixon's version, which is that when he realized there was shilly-shallying going on in Washington, he felt the man who should have been doing something more rapidly was Secretary of Defense Schlesinger. He picked up the phone—as he writes in his memoirs—and said, "I am assuming responsibility; send everything you can fly." What worried the administration was what would happen after the war. They didn't want the Soviets to dictate the peace process. The airlift had tremendous psychological effect on us and on the Egyptians. But what turned the war was the great mistake the Egyptians made in coming across the canal with hundreds of tanks; they were pressured by Assad to do this so as to ease his situation on the Golan. But we had the advantage in mobile warfare. I remember the deputy chief of staff, General Yisrael Tal, saying—just two or three days before it happened—"If only they will cross, we shall put them to fire. Like torches they will burn."

Joseph Sisco The criticism of Henry Kissinger that he held back in the resupply in order to squeeze Israel is a very, very bad rap. For the first forty-eighty hours, even though the Egyptian and Syrian forces moved forward, we were assured fully by the Israelis that they could cope with it. Then, after two days, Israel's ambassador in Washington, Simcha Dinitz, came in as nervous as he could be. He reported that a near-disaster was about to take place. There had been a serious breakthrough with significant casualties and a major loss of matériel. When the resupply request came, Kissinger moved very promptly. The problem was in the Pentagon; we got all kinds of slowdowns. They were reluctant to undertake the resupply, talking, for instance, about a lack of transport. Henry, myself, and a number of us in the State Department got so exasperated that we finally concluded that the only way to get it done was for the president to direct the Pentagon to move. Nixon did this, and added that he didn't want a modest air resupply, but a very substantial one.

Helmut Sonnenfeldt It was a delay, as I understood it, that had to do with paying the insurance for the charter crews, since they couldn't use Air Force planes, and there was some holdup of getting these people properly insured—and other technical issues of that kind. Kissinger put it about to the press that he thought Schlesinger was stalling in order to put pressure on the Israelis, and then Schlesinger hit back. I do think it's true that at the very beginning Nixon and Kissinger didn't realize how badly things were going, so they didn't do very much, right at the start. But then, when they realized that things were not working out very well for the Israelis, they made their decisions—and then there were these delays, which frustrated them.

Vernon Walters Both Kissinger and Nixon wanted to do it, but Nixon gave it the greater sense of urgency. He said, "You get the stuff to Israel, now. Now. Now." There was the story of the American pilot who, after three refuelings en route, and a twelve-hour flight, landed in Israel, and—as he opened his canopy—he smelled fresh paint; the Israelis were painting out the U.S. star and painting in a blue one.*

William Colby We were all in the meetings on the resupply. Kissinger was sore as hell at Schlesinger; he thought he was dragging his feet. Schlesinger was not dragging his feet; he was trying to get the damn machinery to work. It took time. The physical thing was almost unbelievable—the way they supplied the aircraft to Israel.

James R. Schlesinger Around Wednesday or Thursday of that week, the Israelis began to feel desperate, and conveyed that desperation. The reason they felt desperate was that they had calculated their days of supply on the basis of three weeks of usage in the 1967 war. But they discovered that their usage of supplies was at a much more rapid rate than it had been in the 1967 war and, therefore, they were beginning to run down their supplies. They conveyed that to Dr. Kissinger. So around the middle of the week, I was urged—as was the secretary of transportation [Claude Brinigar]—to go out and find commercial airlift for the Israelis to reinforce, as it were, their own airlift, still keeping U.S. airlift out of the Middle East. The secretary of transportation reported back to me that he was unable to get anybody to come in.

We could, of course, have called up the commercial airlift if we had declared a national emergency, but it was very hard simultaneously to declare a national emergency in order to get the airlift and pretend that the United States was disengaged. The airlines, with the one exception of World Airways, took the view that if the U.S. government is not prepared to get involved in this, why should we? I recall Pan American saying: "Look, we have to fly into Cairo West every day, and we don't want to have our pilots shot. If, of course, you declare a national emergency, we're obliged to

---

* The colors of the Israeli flag are a white background and blue star.

respond, but we are not going to provide aircraft or pilots to Israel voluntarily." This went on through Thursday evening. By Friday night, I had a call from Kissinger, who was pretty frantic at that point, and I said to him, "If we're going to deliver these supplies to Israel, we are going to have to use U.S. airlift, or military craft; there is no alternative."

Well, as late as Friday night, Henry was hoping I could find some commercial airlift, but I said there was no way of doing that. A little while later, Haig called up and I explained the situation to him. So, late Friday night and early Saturday morning, we began to move supplies from the interior of the country toward the coast. They began to arrive at Dover Air Force Base—the principal point of departure. But we didn't have permission from the Portuguese to use the Azores. And only after considerable pressure did we get permission; that was sometime Saturday afternoon. All that time, supplies were piling up at Dover Air Force Base, so anyone who thinks it was our intent to use military airlift from day one, and that it was held back by the Pentagon, should look at the correspondence with regard to the use of the Azores base that was only sent out on Saturday, a week into the war.

On Friday night, in my conversation with Kissinger, when I told him we had to use U.S. military airlift all the way, he told me to get the Israeli attaché to agree that we will fly in under the cover of darkness, that the Israelis would unload the aircraft during the night, and that it would be on the way back before first light. So I had the attaché over to the Pentagon at about 1 A.M. Saturday morning, and he agreed to that requirement. But the agreement fell apart because, by sheerest chance, there were crosswinds in the Azores that day, and our planes were held up after they got permission, because they could not land; it was not until Sunday that the winds abated. So when our aircraft began to drop out of the sky on approach to Lod airport, in Israel, they did so in broad daylight. And there was a great big C-5A with a white star on each wing dropping out of the sky, and half the population of Tel Aviv turned out to see it; they stood around the airport cheering. It was very hard after that to keep the United States disengaged from the war in the Middle East.

Kenneth Rush Nixon wanted the resupply; Kissinger delayed, and blamed Mel [Melvin] Laird. He delayed for a very good reason: not because he didn't want to help the Israelis, but he wanted to make them feel that they owed the resupply to him; he could use this in his negotiations, as well as for his personal benefit. So he delayed, and the Israelis, at the time, thought that he was the hero who had stepped in and made Defense and Nixon come through. The fact is that Nixon was pressing like mad for the resupply,

Defense was ready to go forward, and Kissinger was holding it up by various means. But to be fair to him, Kissinger—by getting the Israelis to feel that way about him—was able to make them behave better than they otherwise would have.

Hermann Eilts My understanding is that, initially, Kissinger did not want to do anything. Kissinger explained that it was the secretary of defense who was objecting to resupplying the Israelis. The secretary of defense did, indeed, object; when Kissinger came around and persuaded Nixon to resupply, the Department of Defense continued to be opposed, partly because some of the weapons were going to be taken from U.S. units in Europe. Kissinger had initially opposed it, but then felt it was necessary, because they got a report that the Israelis on the fourth day of the war were feeling the pinch, and were very upset that we were not resupplying yet. And they were taking the lids off their nuclear weapons, so there was concern that if we did not do something, the Israelis—being in extremis—would possibly use their nuclear weapons.

Leonard Garment It was Nixon who did it. I was there. Different games were being played, but it was more Kissinger's game than Schlesinger's. Schlesinger couldn't really stand up to Kissinger if Kissinger took a strong position, so I think that Henry used Schlesinger for his own purposes in creating something of a mock battle. Henry was always trying to titrate the administration's support for Israel, so as not to get the Arabs angry: "We can do this, but we can't do that." There is a war going on, where people are not really making fine distinctions like that; they are shooting each other's heads off. It was like a real race track of history: in one corner, you had Henry Kissinger, who was now secretary of state and also national security adviser; over here is Al Haig; over here is the president. Mrs. Meir would call; the ambassador* would call. I knew these people because I had been doing a lot of the back-channeling to Israel—I was usually over in the old Executive Office Building, but during this period, I was in the White House, dividing my time between Watergate and the Middle East.

[Brent] Scowcroft is negotiating private charters to carry this stuff, but the insurance companies are very loath to insure these planes. Then they decided that they could fly a certain number of planes over a certain course, with a certain type of aircraft. It was very surreal. As this was going back and forth, Nixon said, "This is insane. I want every last goddamn airplane. We

---

* Israel's ambassador to the United States, Simcha Dinitz.

are going to be condemned by the Arabs one way or the other. It's going to be a mess, but we are supporting Israel on this." He just ordered Kissinger: "Get your ass out of here and tell those people to move." Boom! and then it went.

David Packard The Middle East situation is a very difficult issue, because we have to be on the side of Israel; we have too many Jewish people in the country to be otherwise. That biases it. The Egyptians had a pretty large force that crossed the canal and, as a result, we had to send Israel some of our best capability. If we hadn't done that, Israel might not have prevailed, so we had to do it.

Aharon Yariv During the war, we communicated with Nixon, Kissinger, and the top American echelon. Very quickly after the fifth day, we asked for equipment. The whole airlift business was Nixon. He determined it; he gave the green light. The airlift was very important and impressive, but it did not make a strong impact on the war—only on the last stages, when the tide had turned.

James R. Schlesinger With regard to major equipment items, my initial instructions were to provide no major equipment. Around Wednesday of that week, an issue developed about F-4s. The Israelis had purchased F-4s from McDonnell, and they were regularly delivered and, initially, I was told to hold them back. The president called up on Thursday, saying, "Go ahead and deliver the aircraft." After the start of the airlift, we began to deliver some major equipment items. But, basically, the equipment items the Israelis used to prosecute the war were the items they had at the outset of the war. We did, with some fanfare, load an M-60 tank on a C-5A and fly it to Israel. And I was told by some of our people who were in touch with the Egyptians that flying that single tank over there was one of the things they found most impressive about the whole airlift operation.

Mohammed Fawzi By the time the Americans resupplied Israel, the war was over. Sadat said, "I am not ready to make war with both America and Israel."

The Worldwide Alert

On October 24, 1973, the Soviets threatened to intervene, unilaterally, as the tide of war swung decisively to the Israeli side. A late-night meeting was

held in the White House Situation Room on how to respond to the Soviet
ultimatum. A small group of the president's foreign policy advisers—in
apparent consultation with the president—decided to issue an alert to U.S.
forces stationed throughout the world. This move led some of Mr. Nixon's
critics to suggest that the alert had been issued to divert attention from his
increasing Watergate problems, and to reassert his primacy in foreign
affairs issues.

Thomas Moorer [Leonid] Brezhnev had sent a nasty message to Mr.
Nixon. We knew that they were assembling their paratroopers in one place,
and were preparing to airlift the troops into Egypt. The message said: "Let
us go to Egypt together and put a stop to the Israelis' violation of the agreement." They had the capacity to airlift these troops; like us, they used their
cargo aircraft to transport troops. It was a very significant threat. The alert
had nothing to do with Watergate; it prevented the Russians from picking
up the war in Egypt.

Mordechai Gazit I received the message at 3:30 in the morning about the
Soviet airlift. My interpretation is that the assumption that Nixon or
Kissinger was making up the threat is terribly unfair. Now we know that the
Soviets were not all that strong, but at the time, this was not clear; it
appeared to be the real thing.

James R. Schlesinger Nixon had received a very sharp cable from Brezhnev. It was just after the so-called Saturday Night Massacre; it was just after
the first calls for impeachment came from the Congress, and we were quite
concerned that the Soviets believed that the American government might
not function. Therefore, we took very vigorous action with regard to the
placing of forces on the alert, virtually worldwide, in order to convey to the
Soviets that the American government was alive and well and was not distracted, and was quite capable of acting vigorously in support of its own
interests.

Alexander Haig Watergate complicated it; it didn't motivate it. The suggestion that Watergate did motivate it was the *Washington Post* party line. It
was such a bum rap, because we were all there, looking at the situation,
when we got the ultimatum from the Russians; all you had to do was read
the ultimatum to know that we had World War III in the making. They were
saying: Either you intervene with us in the Sinai to interpose neutral forces,
or else. The Russians and the Egyptians thought that the Israelis were going

to Cairo, which they could have done. Henry sent Harold Saunders* into the next room to draft a reply, and Hal sat down at the typewriter and came up with a draft. In effect, we said: No way. And in order to make it credible to the Russians, we knew that we had to take some dramatic steps to reinforce the message we sent, which would be unequivocally understood that we meant business; that is why we went into that alert. We also did some other things: Henry had been working twenty-four hours straight, so I did some things on my own to convey to the Russians that we meant business—diplomatic things.

Helmut Sonnenfeldt There was sufficient intelligence that suggested the Soviets might in some way, not fully understood, attempt to intervene. Therefore, since the American units in the Mediterranean were already on Defcon 3, the feeling was that we weren't certain. We saw funny things going on with Soviet naval forces—with their paratroop units—and there was the threatening language—or seemingly threatening language—in the oral note; we hadn't gotten it in writing, formally, but it had been phoned in by Dobrynin. The feeling was pretty unanimous around the table in the Situation Room that we needed—for practical reasons—to get troops back to base; the JCS were interested in getting the B-52s back from Guam to the United States. I think the unreasonable hope was that nobody would notice, except for the Soviets, and that this would reinforce our diplomatic response to their rather threatening note.

Hermann Eilts In the course of the three-week war, there was a time when we were almost at war with the Soviets; they had seven divisions they were prepared to deploy to prevent the Egyptians from losing entirely and they had invested billions of dollars in weapons the Egyptians had not paid for. So Nixon—actually, it was Kissinger—ordered all U.S. forces in the world to the highest alert. Everybody then backed off relatively quickly, but it was a reminder of the tensions between the two superpowers. My reading of the alert is that it was Kissinger who decided to do this. It did not have to do with helping the president on the domestic scene. Today, Kissinger will say that he made a mistake—that we should not have undertaken a global, nuclear alert.

Kenneth Rush The alert was Kissinger's idea, and was effective. We had information that the Soviets were putting nuclear weapons en route to

* Staff member, NSC.

Egypt. We wanted to scare them; Watergate didn't have a damn thing to do with it. Kissinger claimed he had checked with Nixon and had gotten approval, but we never did know whether Nixon approved; all we knew was that Kissinger said so.

Viktor Sukhodrev The Soviet leadership resented the alert. They saw it as an attempt to somehow break up what was beginning to be a cooperative relationship. But the important thing was that communications did not break down. Ambassador Dobrynin continued his ongoing, confidential talks—the so-called back-channel—with Kissinger. That was what kept things mostly on an even keel.

The Deliberations

William Colby The president was upstairs; Kissinger would go out, and then come back and say, "The president asked, Would you agree to this or that?" This reflected Nixon's personality: Kennedy would have had us all in a room—half of Washington would have been there; Johnson would have only half a dozen; but Nixon would have the argument go on among the various people, and then have the result brought to him, which is a little bit the way Eisenhower ran it—he being the general, he had the staff go through the options, come up with the recommended solution, and then a commander either accepts it or sends it back.

Thomas Moorer It's true that the president was not in the meeting. But those who say, "Kissinger went out to the bathroom and came back and said, 'The president says . . . ,'" that's a lot of nonsense. In a situation like that, you go in to the president, give him a quick briefing, and get a yes or no answer; you don't debate with him. I don't think that Kissinger would have dared to come back to our group and tell us he had seen the president if he hadn't.

Helmut Sonnenfeldt It was not unusual for Nixon not to have been in the meeting. It was a constituted group that was meeting at the White House. Nixon, in any case, did not particularly care to participate in meetings where he was under pressure to make a decision right then and there. He wanted to keep his distance, make up his own mind, not be maneuvered or put under pressure. Moreover, there were too many people in the room, and he didn't like large meetings.

Joseph Sisco Nixon was not a detail man; he had great confidence in Kissinger. It was not unusual for the president not to be in this type of meeting. The alert succeeded in that it brought the Russians back to the table at the U.N. Security Council and defused the potential confrontation.

James R. Schlesinger Quite clearly, it was unusual for the president not to be in the Situation Room. The meeting, initially called as a convening of the Washington Special Action Group, was later described as a rump meeting of the National Security Council [NSC]. At a meeting of the NSC, the president, who was head of the council, ought regularly to be present, but he was not there. General Haig would slip out of the meeting and go and confer with the president about what was going on, so that at each stage of the game he would return, having reported to the president what was being proposed, and saying that this was quite satisfactory from the president's standpoint. I certainly believe that Mr. Nixon approved the alerting of American forces, because that is the kind of action that he would take in a crisis. He was quite concerned about the thought that Soviet forces would be introduced unilaterally into the Middle East, as Mr. Brezhnev's note indicated. He certainly wanted to head that off. What, precisely, he agreed to in his conversations with Haig, and what, precisely, may have been left out, I do not know. But in general, he was in support of the meeting. Nonetheless, it was somewhat unusual, but those, indeed, were unusual times.

I think that Dr. Kissinger may have had general guidance from the president before the meeting; my recollection is that he stayed in the meeting throughout. General Haig went into the residence from the White House basement, the Sit Room, and would return, and it is my judgment—and this is only a judgment—that on these matters President Nixon indeed tended to put much more reliance on General Haig than he did on Dr. Kissinger. He relied on General Haig, as it were, to make sure that Dr. Kissinger was staying within the general guidance he had been given.

Alexander Haig The president wasn't in the session because it wasn't the place for him to be. We—the staff—would make a recommendation to him; I was on the phone with him. When we had gotten the ultimatum, Henry wanted to convene the NSC over at the State Department. I said, "You are [going to] like hell! You are going to convene the meeting in the president's house." So Henry pouted, but he was going to do what he was told; that is why we had the meeting in the Situation Room, where we always had these meetings. Can you imagine it not being there? It would look like the president was dead, or had already resigned; I wouldn't tolerate this, nor would the president. He asked me, "Should I come downstairs?" I said, "No. Stay where you are." If some think that Henry was arranging the decisions all by himself, that is baloney—B-A-L-O-N-E-Y. I got the president on the phone and told him what we proposed to do. He said, "Fine."

It is incredible to me how long it takes for the truth to come out. An honest press corps would have known later on, when I was secretary of state under Reagan, that I was the victim of Jim [James] Baker's leaks. In those years, George Bush thought that I was going to compete [by seeking the Republican nomination for president] in 1988; he got me so mad that I did go out and run—to keep the country from buying off on the likes of George Bush. He worked for me twice; he was a nothing.

William Colby Watergate never came up. They had read a message from Brezhnev that was very tough: either you stop the Israelis, we do it together, or we go in alone. The question was: Were they prepared to go in alone, with all the terrible prospects of direct Soviet involvement in the Middle East? My job was to find out the status of their troops. We knew that the airborne divisions were on alert—ready to move. But that night we lost the transports; we weren't quite sure where they were. Were they going back to pick up the airborne divisions? The issue was: What answer are we going to give to Mr. Brezhnev, and how do we phrase it? Our answer was that he wasn't going in alone. The alert idea came at the tail end of the conversation—that we ought to alert our forces in case something happens. We realized that all our forces were at Defcon 3, the whole Pacific region was always at Defcon 3, so we really weren't doing much by having our forces at Defcon 3. We were sending the Russians a signal, but we weren't thinking of scaring the world—but we did; it scared a lot of people.

Vernon Walters The Russians had three airborne divisions getting ready to load on aircraft, but they didn't load them; they understood that we were ready to go. Yet people say that Nixon was on the edge of insanity, doing crazy things.

Thomas Moorer It really wasn't a full-fledged alert. It changed the readiness conditions from ordinary peacetime conditions; we upped the whole thing a notch. The press made a great to-do of it—you would have thought we were about to go to war. When I went to a NATO meeting, I was criticized because they hadn't been notified; the point was, it was midnight here [in Washington] when we declared the alert, which made it six or seven [A.M.] in Europe, and none of those guys get up that early.

The Cease-Fire Negotiations

Aharon Yariv I was called up on Saturday, October 6. The chief of staff appointed me his special assistant. I served at his headquarters during the war, and was then appointed by Prime Minister Golda Meir as chief of the Israeli delegation to the cease-fire talks. There was one factor that had not to do with the Americans, but with Kissinger. He said, "What are you doing? You are selling out. And if you finish everything, I will not have anything to do in Geneva." That stopped the negotiations. He wanted to be in the picture. During the war, he wanted a cease-fire on the fifth day. Kissinger wasn't happy at all; he wanted a reversal of the situation.

Mohammed Fawzi Kissinger had told us he wanted to make peace between us and Israel. But, he told us, "I can't begin the conversation with Israel unless you make the theater 'hot.' To make it 'hot,' you should begin some limited actions, so I can interfere." Sadat listened to this directive from Kissinger and did as Kissinger said. But it didn't have to be limited; we had the forces to conquer all of Sinai without stopping.

Hermann Eilts Events on the ground in the Middle East required a certain openness. Nixon's sending of Kissinger to the region would not be hidden, the way the opening to China was; it was a publicly announced American effort to try to implement the cease-fire resolution, and to bring about peace in the area. There is no doubt that this was a total change in Kissinger's style: he was always more comfortable dealing secretly; even in Cairo, the talks were conducted between Kissinger and Sadat without most of Sadat's principal advisers being in the room.

Hafez Ismail On October 23, Sadat suggested that troops from both superpowers supervise the cease-fire, and send the Israeli troops back to the October 22nd lines of the bridgehead. The Russians were preparing to send an airborne division to Egypt, and would not have done so without agreement from Washington. Nixon told Sadat that he did not accept the idea of sending troops—that he did not want Egypt to become a fief of atomic war. He offered to intervene to stop the Israeli advance, and Sadat accepted his word. In his book, Kissinger says that he gave the Israelis the impression that while he flew from Tel Aviv to Washington, they could break the cease-fire and advance. At that time, we did not think that the Americans were not sincere. Looking back, I would say that everyone fights for their own interests. The United States was not fighting us; they were fighting the Russians. The Israelis were fighting us.

Aharon Yariv I met the Egyptians on October 24 [1973], at night, at kilometer 101. It was quite cold in the desert. An officer came up to me and said, "Look, the Egyptian general is shivering out of fright." I said, "No. He is shivering from the cold." I asked the [Egyptian] general if he would like to put something [warm] on. He said yes. And after about ten minutes, everyone was wearing an Israeli jacket. I had wondered, before I met the Egyptian general, should I extend my hand? But what if he doesn't take it? Then it occurred to me: he is a military man; I am a military man. What do military men do? They salute. On the second day, he said, "Finish Palestine; finish with Palestine." Then he said, "Sadat wants peace, but you have to give back everything." He was a proud man—a proud Egyptian, a proud Muslim, but he said, "You have to give back every inch." He never mentioned the Americans.

Israeli Prime Minister Golda Meir's Visit to the White House

Mordechai Gazit We met with Nixon in the White House in the beginning of November. The meeting lasted between a half hour and forty minutes, since Nixon had to fly to Key Biscayne afterward. His face was very reddish, as if he had five or six whiskeys. He told Golda, "I took three critical decisions on your behalf: the airlift, the $2.2 billion to finance the arms, and the confrontation with the Soviets in"—as he put it—"the precautionary alert." And then he whispered to her, "I can't do it again." By this we understood him to mean that he had his own problem—Watergate; that he was not very strong, and that he was saying the time had come for us to move along in the peace process. In the meeting, he said all the right things. He said, "You know, Mrs. Meir, when I heard you talk about your prisoners of war in Syria, I thought about you, because this is what I felt about our prisoners in Vietnam." There were two or three statements like this, which showed empathy—and you didn't expect a man like that to have empathy.

Aharon Yariv Golda wanted to come to Washington after the [Yom Kippur] war. Nixon was at the height of his Watergate problems, but you wouldn't know it. He was smartly dressed, well prepared. He made a first-class impression. He was very clear in what he said. He told Golda: "One, there will be no more airlifts; two, you have to give back territory." By this, he meant the Sinai; the West Bank and the Golan Heights did not come up. As Nixon spoke, Kissinger was sitting there, polishing his glasses. When we went out [of the room] Nixon asked my age. I said, "I am in my fifties." He replied, "You have young generals, not like ours."

Kenneth Rush She was a strong, tough, old woman. He liked sharp, tough people. She was a blunt, outspoken person—not without charm, however; ugly—well, Nixon was not too handsome. She was a fellow soul, you might say. They were two of a type, something like [President Ronald] Reagan and [British Prime Minister Margaret] Thatcher.

Aharon Yariv The relationship between Nixon and Golda was one of personal friendship. When we came to the White House they were sitting next to each other in armchairs, and he put his hand on hers and said, "You and Brezhnev would get along well together." Golda would refer to Nixon as "my president."

Golda felt very bad then. The morning we went in to see Nixon, she said, "Boys, if I die here, promise me you will take me back and bury me in Israel." [Mrs. Meir had lived in the United States prior to immigration to pre-Jewish State Palestine). She was a very strong leader. She was a grandma and the skies fell down on her. Her military advisers were split. After the war she asked me: "Should I blame myself for not mobilizing [the Israel Defense Force]?" I said to her, "How should you blame yourself? You had one general, [Moshe] Dayan, near you; a second general, [Haim] Bar Lev, near you; and a third general, [David] Elazar, near you. And you want to blame *yourself?*" But she couldn't get over the war. When I came back from Washington in August 1974, she said to me, "You know, Arileh, I am like a prisoner who knows the date of his release."

Nixon in Egypt

From June 12 to 18, 1974, President Nixon traveled to Egypt, Saudi Arabia, Syria, Israel, and Jordan. The highlight of the trip was the visit to Egypt, where huge crowds turned out to greet the president, who on June 14 signed an accord with President Sadat on the peaceful uses of nuclear technology.

Hermann Eilts The people in charge of advance for Nixon's trip to Egypt were the least sensitive group I have ever met: one was a used-car salesman from Delaware who was seconded for this business; the others were from the White House. They wanted to run the president's schedule. They expected the Egyptians to change all of their plans. For example, they said that Nixon would not ride in Sadat's car—he would only use his own automobile. When this got back to Nixon, he said, "No. I will use Sadat's car." He wanted the Egyptians to have their way on arrangements. Nixon made a great impression on Sadat because of his knowledge and balance; his comments on Arab-Israeli issues were persuasive to Sadat.

Mohammed Fawzi Sadat forced the people to come out and greet Nixon. The police brought the people by force to the train route between Cairo and Alexandria.

Hermann Eilts At the time, the Arab Socialist Union [ASU] was the only political party. It was used when Sadat—as Nasser before him—needed to mobilize the masses. Nobody held a gun to anyone to turn out, but the mobilization capacity of the ASU was used in a massive fashion in Cairo and Alexandria; it was intended to show that the Egyptian people were friendly to Nixon and to the United States. It was also Sadat's intention to show that he was a strong leader.

They traveled on a special presidential train; there was a nice car for the presidents. The train ride from Cairo to Alexandria normally takes about three-and-a-half hours; this trip was made relatively slowly, so that at each village along the way you would see the people mobilized. Some of them were very colorful—you would see horsemen galloping by, alongside the train. The conversation on the train was rather desultory—Nixon was obviously brooding about something and was more inclined to answer when someone spoke to him, rather than to initiate conversation. Mrs. Nixon tried very hard to keep the conversation going: she would say, "Oh Dick, look out there," pointing out something along the tracks. And sometimes she would say, "Dick, look around." Later, when we got to Alexandria, and there were huge crowds, Nixon's spirits were buoyed. When he left Egypt a day or two later, he was feeling chipper.

THE SOVIET UNION

Throughout his pre-presidential political career, Mr. Nixon had been considered to be a cold warrior who advocated a hard-line policy toward the then–Soviet Union—at that time the world's only other superpower.

From the time of his first congressional campaign in 1946 through his tenure as vice-president, Mr. Nixon had earned his stripes as an arch-foe of the Soviet system—witness his dramatic encounter with then–Soviet Chair-

man Nikita S. Khrushchev in 1959 at the site of a U.S. exhibition in Moscow, which came to be known as "the Kitchen Debate."

On becoming president in 1969, Mr. Nixon by necessity viewed the U.S.-Soviet relationship within the context of a complex set of problems: he had inherited the Vietnam War—in which the North Vietnamese were supplied and otherwise supported by the Soviet Union—from President Lyndon Johnson; he was also confronted with problems with which all of his predecessors since the end of World War II had grappled—the Soviet thermonuclear threat; tensions in Berlin and in other areas of Central and Eastern Europe, and in the Middle East.

While many Nixon-watchers expected the president to deal with these issues in the confrontational manner that had characterized previous U.S.-Soviet relations, he chose instead to seek a general policy of détente, and a specific policy of reduction in nuclear armament.

This policy shift was complicated both by the ongoing Vietnam conflict—which Mr. Nixon had claimed during the 1968 campaign he could end through implementation of a special plan—and by his hope of establishing dialogue with the People's Republic of China, then at odds with the Soviet Union.

Viktor Sukhodrev In all of Nixon's dealings with the Soviet Union, his main merit was that at the point when he became president, he realized that the arms race was beginning to get out of hand. It would seem now—looking at the archives—that the United States was probably aware, more than a lot of people in our country were, of how ruinous it was for the Soviet Union. But I think he felt it was getting out of hand for the United States, as well, and that the Soviet Union, with its great inner resources and the patience of its people—which, of course, was also based on coercion and the repressive system—could match the United States in arms. So he realized that the overriding concern was to reach some form of accommodation, and that is one of the things he will go down in history for.

Brezhnev was very sincere in his desire to cut down arms; he was sincere in his desire never to see a major war again. Whether Nixon and Brezhnev went far enough is another matter, altogether. But it was still a major breakthrough—two superpowers talking about the most horrendous of arms, and talking about ways to limit them.

But there was nothing Nixon did to bring down the Soviet system. This came much later; it was a generation change led by Gorbachev.

Vernon Walters It wasn't a question of anticommunism; it was a question of recognizing threats to the United States. The media made this some sort of a paranoia—to be strongly anticommunist. The Soviet Union was the first country since the independence of the United States to threaten our existence as a nation. It was not that we would lose a province, or an island; it was the first time since George III that anybody had the power to obliterate the United States as a nation. So being strongly opposed to that is not as bad as it was made out to be. Only a man of the right could have opened to the left. Nixon had a sense that he was the first leader that had a real dialogue with Russian counterparts. When Khrushchev said, "We will bury you," Nixon said, "Your children will live under freedom." Nobody quotes that now.

Gerald R. Ford On balance, most Republicans in the House and Senate understood it as I did. On the other hand, under no circumstances did they want any concessions or capitulation to the Soviets.

H. R. Haldeman He was a strong anticommunist; he did not soften in regard to it at all. What he did, programatically, was [to reason]: You may not like them, but they are there. Russia, at that time, was the other superpower; China was the population power—and potential superpower. Nixon realized that someone with his anticommunist belief and credentials was the right person to make the openings—not giving into communism, but communicating with those people, and trying to convey to them some understanding of what an anticommunist leader in this country would—and would not—tolerate, and what could be worked out. He was also able to do that in ways that a John Kennedy or a Lyndon Johnson couldn't.

Winston Lord The impact was immediate and positive. We had been, from the beginning of the Nixon administration, trying to improve relations with the Soviets, both through pressures and incentives. We had gone through some rough periods. Within weeks after the announcement of Kissinger's secret trip to China and the word that Nixon was going to hold meetings in China in February of 1972, the Soviets agreed to a summit, something they had held back on prior to the Kissinger visit to China. We got a Berlin agreement, an arms control agreement, and the whole Soviet relationship started to move forward.

Viktor Sukhodrev Brezhnev was present at the famous Kitchen Debate— you can see him in the photographs, standing to one side. When Brezhnev would meet Nixon, he would frequently recall that he was there. So Nixon was not an unknown quantity when he became president, but his reputation was not perceived to be a good one, or auguring anything too good in terms of Soviet-American relations.

It was a feeling of some concern, some wariness: here comes a newly elected president, with a history of red-bashing, a history of outspoken anti-Soviet attitudes. That was the general atmosphere in which the Soviet Union and its leadership confronted a new American president with a well-known history.

Yuri Barsukov The attitude of the Soviet leadership toward Nixon changed from one of very strong suspicion to one in which, by the end of Nixon's presidency, the United States and the Soviet Union had their best relationship of the whole Cold War period; Nixon and Brezhnev came to more agreements than had ever before been reached by the two nations. By the time of Nixon's resignation, the Soviet leadership learned that they could deal with this president.

Helmut Sonnenfeldt Kissinger met Brezhnev for the first time in April 1972, in the preparatory meeting for the summit—the secret meetings. I think Kissinger was intrigued with Brezhnev, and he was [in turn] intrigued with Kissinger. There was a lot of fencing around, a lot of testing—Brezhnev was trying to figure out how much authority Kissinger really had; Kissinger trying to figure out how much authority Brezhnev really had, in the Politburo setting; a lot of tactical bantering. Kissinger used some of his humor, and it turned out that Brezhnev had a certain coarse sort of humor as well. I got dragged into this because, for one reason or another, Brezhnev liked to play practical jokes, and I was considered to be the heavy, because of some stuff they had from their intelligence people concerning my previous jobs and attitudes.

Nixon knew these people a lot better than Kissinger did when Kissinger started, because he had been around in the Eisenhower administration, and had traveled quite a bit in his period out of office. I think Nixon thought he could do some business with Brezhnev. I don't think he had any illusions about Brezhnev's basic outlook and attitudes, but there developed fairly frequent contacts, both face-to-face and through letter writing. So there developed a recognition of how the other guy functioned and some of the weak spots that you could play on.

Nixon and Kissinger were both anticommunists, but there was this strain of realism which, by and large, held that the Soviets were a great power and we had to deal with them. We had no interest in getting into a war with them. Moreover, Nixon—whatever the detours were—wanted to extricate the United States from Vietnam and, consequently, he recognized from the beginning, as did Kissinger, that the Soviets would be playing some kind of a role in that process.

A lot of this evolved over a period of time. This was a little different from the attitude on China, where Nixon was on record in his *Foreign Affairs* article with a view that the United States at some point would have to recognize that China was a great country, with a large population, and we couldn't live in isolation from it. In the Soviet case, the process—and the possibilities of how to do business with them—evolved in their minds as time went on.

There was an assumption that the Soviets would be uneasy if they discovered that something was developing between the United States and China. A part of the opening to China had to do with putting pressure on the Soviets, so the assumption was that they would be uneasy, and it might induce them to be more malleable in certain areas of policy that we were concerned about, like Vietnam and the Middle East.

Viktor Sukhodrev Before Nixon actually came to Moscow in 1972, there had been a long history of contact—mostly with Kissinger, who would meet with [Soviet Foreign Minister Andrei] Gromyko, but also with Brezhnev, whenever Kissinger came to Moscow.

As progress advanced on the Strategic Arms Limitation Talks, there was agreement that Nixon should come to Moscow for a summit meeting. The SALT discussions were the centerpiece of the discussions, but the talks took place against the background of Vietnam. So it was a bold step to be talking about arms limitations against the background—and sometimes the intensification—of the war.

At that time, although Brezhnev was on the ascendancy, the official decision of the Politburo was to entrust the actual conduct of the negotiations to the Troika—Brezhnev, [Alexei] Kosygin, the prime minister, and [Nikolai] Podgorny, the president. Brezhnev was the general secretary of the Communist Party, which was the top job at that time. But the actual talks were entrusted to all three, so all three were always there, and all three spoke, Brezhnev kicking off on each subject and the others adding, in many ways for the record; they had to be seen.

Gerald Warren The Soviet officials were not very nice people. There was a respect between Nixon and Brezhnev, but no warmth. They might have given each other a bear hug from time to time, but it was not because they really liked each other. The police, the KGB, and everyone else in Moscow treated us rather shabbily. They roughed up the press corps when they could.

Winston Lord Brezhnev could be blustery and intimidating, but also friendly and warm; he had great changes of mood. Nixon did not get along with him as he did with Chou En-lai. Nixon worked very hard to get ready for his meetings with the Soviets. He was very good in these sessions. Brezhnev would speak at great length; Nixon would be briefer in his responses.

Nixon and Brezhnev got along quite well in the sense that they would, particularly over meals, get into a relaxed anecdotal mode. It could also be very tough; the mood could shift quite suddenly, depending on the agenda of both sides. But in each case, there was a respect for the other as a tough fighter who's fought his way to the top, despite odds. It was not great chemistry that could change history, but they could get along and discuss business. In the spring of 1972, just before we went to Moscow, Hanoi had invaded South Vietnam in considerable numbers, and Nixon had to decide whether to go. We bombed Hanoi and mined Haiphong in response, despite the dangers of their canceling the summit. They didn't cancel the summit, but Brezhnev felt an obligation to give Nixon very stern lectures so he could send a transcript to Hanoi to prove he was not selling out his North Vietnamese brothers.

Just four of us—Nixon, Kissinger, John Negraponte, a Kissinger aide, and myself—went out to his dacha to meet with Brezhnev, and we sat through four hours of very tough lectures from Brezhnev, and one or two other Soviet leaders, on Vietnam. Nixon listened patiently. When it was over, we went upstairs and they broke out the vodka and caviar, and the whole mood changed. It was clear they were going through the motions, although it had been a rough session.

Viktor Sukhodrev Brezhnev was a man who took his position of host in the typically Russian way: you can argue very sharply on certain subjects—like Vietnam—but when the session ends, you ply your guest with Russian hospitality; you smile at each other, because he is a guest in your home. Brezhnev took this very much to heart.

Kosygin was a more dour type, while Podgorny tried to play the tough guy. In his official utterances, Brezhnev could be very tough, indeed; he was reading from a brief that had been approved by the Soviet leadership. But the relationship did begin to evolve into an affinity between Brezhnev and Nixon.

In the period between the Moscow summit in 1972 and the summit in the United States in the summer of 1973, Brezhnev's star kept rising until he did, ultimately, become the one-man ruler, so in 1973, the return visit was by Brezhnev alone. At that summit, Nixon went out of his way to make his guest comfortable. We spent a good deal of our time in discussion—not in the White House, but in Camp David—in our shirt-sleeves, tieless. When we got to California—at Nixon's own private dacha—things were even more comfortable; the atmosphere was much warmer than at the White House, even though some serious negotiation was held there—notably on the Middle East. Brezhnev didn't get what he wanted on the Middle East; there was basically a stalemate.

No mention of Watergate was ever made during the Brezhnev–Nixon discussions. And Nixon was clutching at the straw in 1974, by trying to show that he alone, could really talk to the Soviets, trying as hard as he could to prove that he was the real expert in foreign affairs; that if the American people wanted real détente, rapprochement, agreements with the Soviet Union, he was the man. By the time of their meetings in the Crimea, they were good acquaintances, and they spent all of their time there together.

H. R. Haldeman He enjoyed his give-and-take with Brezhnev. It was chaotic: up and down; a lot of fun and good comradeship. But then Brezhnev would turn very hostile, banging his hand on the table, demanding this and that. Nixon would handle that very icily, and coldly, and say, "We are not going to get anywhere that way," and would not back down. He didn't respond in kind; he did not take the bait and get all charged up.

Helmut Sonnenfeldt There were some aspects of Soviet policy, especially in the White House, where some of us on the NSC staff—virtually all of us—were not fully informed, because these initial, so-called back-channel contacts between Kissinger and Anatoly Dobrynin were held very closely.

Maurice Stans In early October 1972, it was decided that I would go to the Soviet Union in my role as secretary of commerce. It was an interesting experience. I was there for eleven days and had access to anything I wanted to see. I visited a tractor plant; a steel mill; they showed me the financial statements of the GUM department store; I went to an oil field near Baku. It was as friendly a meeting as if I were representing California and negotiating with the state of Arizona. They were ready for this; [Alexei] Kosygin was the negotiator. He met me at the airport and we sat down and talked. He said, "There is no reason in the world why we can't open our harbors to your ships, and your harbors to ours," and we agreed on this in about five minutes. Finally, I got down to the last item on my list, settlement of the Lend Lease debt from World War II—this hadn't been discussed for twelve years. I said, "Mr. Chairman, the Lend Lease debt may impede our progress; I can't go back and ask the president to give you credits on agriculture without clearing that up." He said, "We will pick five people and you do the same. We will put them in a room together and give them a couple of weeks to work this out." The meetings took place, and this was settled on the same percentage basis we had settled this with other countries. Before I left I said to Kosygin, "We have had good discussions, but there is one thing I hope you will take care of: on the highway into Moscow there is a great big billboard with the United States pictured as a vicious killer, with a sword in one hand and a gun in the other, killing people all over the world. I don't think that will be a good entrance for President Nixon,* and the sign ought to come down." He said, "It will."

VIETNAM

During the 1968 campaign, Mr. Nixon claimed to have a plan for ending the Vietnam conflict. During his first year in office, he enunciated the Nixon Doctrine, in which it was stated that once the war was concluded, the United States would furnish its Asian allies with only the matériel, economic, and military assistance necessary for resisting aggression.

The president also subscribed to the recommendation made by Secretary of Defense Melvin Laird that the United States adopt a policy of Vietnamization—an effort to train the South Vietnamese to take greater responsibility for their own defense as the United States began major troop withdrawals.

At the same time, President Nixon, hoping to resume the Paris peace talks that had been deadlocked since the end of the Johnson presidency, suggested that the United States and North Vietnam establish a channel independent of formal discussions.

On August 4, 1969, National Security Adviser Henry Kissinger met with North Vietnamese officials Xuan Thuy and Mai Van Bo, commencing what would become three years of arduous, on-and-off, secret negotiations that would eventually result in the cease-fire of January 27, 1973.

---

* Who visited the Soviet Union the following spring, arriving in Moscow on May 22, 1972.

In pursuing his Vietnam policy—in which he claimed to favor "Peace with Honor"—the president confronted difficult realities: the increasing impatience of the U.S. Congress with the war; the safe return to the United States of the more than 325 prisoners of war;* the burgeoning antiwar movement—in which massive rallies were organized in a number of U.S. cities in October and November 1969;† the unwillingness of South Vietnam's president, Nguyen Van Thieu, to accept any settlement that would allow for North Vietnamese influence in the South; the seeming intransigence of the North Vietnamese negotiators—once described by Dr. Kissinger as "tawdry, filthy shits";‡ and President Nixon's fear of being the first U.S. chief executive to lose a war.

Bui Diem, South Vietnamese ambassador to the U.S.; ambassador-at-large I met with Nixon in 1968, at the Pierre Hotel, in New York; this was before the Republican convention. He had John Mitchell at the meeting, and I brought along Mrs. [Anna] Chennault.** It was a very cordial session. We had thought that Nixon, through his statements, was stronger than Humphrey; Nixon was known to be a very anticommunist politician during his whole career. This gave us the idea that he knew how to deal with the communists. I think that at the Pierre Hotel meeting he was already thinking of how the Russians could help the Americans to end the war.

Ronald Ziegler President Nixon really did want to end the Vietnam War from the outset; he did not want that war to continue. As he began to deal with it, I think he found that what he considered to be the U.S. totality of interests in foreign policy were that it would not have been good for the United States to unilaterally withdraw from the conflict.

William Westmoreland During the [1968] election campaign, he intended— and succeeded in—giving the impression that he had some new ideas that were going to solve the problem, but nobody knew precisely what he had in mind. What he ultimately had in mind was that he was going to withdraw at all costs, which he did. We pulled out our ground troops; we didn't pull out

---

* By the end of the U.S. involvement in Vietnam, 562 prisoners of war had returned to the United States.

† The antiwar movement intensified as a result of the late April 1970 U.S. incursion into Cambodia and the killing, the following month, of four students by National Guardsmen during a demonstration at Kent State University, in Ohio.

‡ *The Memoirs of Richard Nixon* (Grosset & Dunlap, 1973), p. 733.

** Widow of U.S. General Claire Chennault.

all of our air forces. Air power cannot stop a ground attack; it can render casualties, but is no substitute for people on the ground.

William H. Sullivan I think he developed the intellectual concept for this plan from an article that Kissinger had written in *Foreign Affairs* in the late 1960s. I think it was conceived in far broader terms in his 1969 statement at Guam, in what became known as the Nixon Doctrine—the general idea being that we would cease to bear the exclusive burden for these events, whether in Vietnam or somewhere else, and there would be more responsibility thrust on the people who started the whole thing.

George Romney He was a smart enough politician to indicate at the start of his campaign in New Hampshire that he had a plan for peace. That was another thing I wanted to check out with Kissinger after my conversation with Nixon at the Pierre. Kissinger said he didn't have any plan for peace at that point, and I don't think he had a plan for peace when he said that in New Hampshire.

George McGovern I don't think that Nixon had a plan to end the war; I think that it was more in the nature of a campaign hope than a concrete plan. It always seemed to me that the essential tragedy of the Vietnam policy was that he played it more in terms of the realities of American domestic politics than he did in the realities of Vietnam. To illustrate this, I didn't know Henry Kissinger well, but when Nixon was elected, I waited for a few months and then asked for an appointment with Kissinger. He asked me to come right over to the White House. I got over there at about ten o'clock one morning. He was in a small office at that time. I began by telling him that I thought he was in a very fortunate position, because there was a growing consensus that the war in Vietnam was a disaster; there was a general feeling that we should wind it up. So I suggested that they do just that— they weren't responsible for the war; they should just terminate it; just announce that we are going to get out. Henry answered, "I agree that the war is a mistake. I haven't been as forthcoming in my criticism of it as you have. I think that it is clear now that we never should have gone in there, and I don't see how any good can come of it. But we can't do what you recommend and just pull out, because the boss's whole constituency would fall apart; those are his people who support the war effort: the South; the blue-collar Democrats in the North. The Nixon constituency is behind the war effort. If we were to pull out of Vietnam, there would be a disaster, politically, for us here, at home."

So it became clear to me that they were planning that war policy not in terms of the realities that faced us in Asia, but in terms of politics here in the United States. It was very clear that the policy would be constructed along the line of: how you hold the Nixon constituency together and, hopefully, reach beyond that—to pull in the George Wallace people, because they were already starting to chart the so-called Southern Strategy of trying to develop an approach that would pull the South away from Wallace and into the Nixon column—which is exactly what happened in 1972, when Wallace was shot; that became the formula for the Nixon landslide: Nixon plus Wallace—which he didn't have in 1968, when he had Humphrey and Wallace to contend with. I never again could develop much respect for their Vietnam policy. I thought that they were willing to continue killing Asians and sacrificing the lives of young Americans because of their interpretation of what would play in the United States.

Morton Halperin It became clear to me, in retrospect, that Nixon's plan was to threaten the Russians with the destruction of North Vietnam unless they cooperated. But, at the time, it wasn't clear to me that he had any plan at all.

Daniel Ellsberg The plan counted on holding off an invasion by the North Vietnamese until the South Vietnamese Army could take over for the Americans. Thus, there had to be warnings—from the beginning of the Nixon administration—of escalation, mining, bombing, destruction of the dikes, and, possibly, an invasion of the North. I always felt that if an invasion did occur, it would lead, sooner or later, to the use of nuclear weapons. I had been in the Johnson administration, and had been in on the bombing plans. I had been critical of the bombing, and this criticism was very well borne out. When Nixon came into office, we had dropped 3.2 million tons of bombs on North Vietnam—compared to 2 million tons in all of World War II, including the two atomic bombs. I really didn't think we were facing a country that was about to surrender if we used another million or two tons of bombs. What was in the mind of the new administration was: We will do it better—and more savagely. The joint chiefs [of staff] wanted to give it a try, up to a point, but even they were not really hot on it anymore; they had been doing it for three years. Only Nixon and Kissinger—coming in fresh, and thinking: We know how to launch a threat campaign—could convince themselves that this was going to do the job. By the end of the first term, they had dropped 4.5 million tons of bombs—but to no effect. It was a dumb, reckless, and dangerous strategy.

Thomas Moorer When Nixon came into office, we had 49,500 men in Vietnam. Of course, in less than three or four weeks, the media was calling it "Nixon's war" when, in fact, it was Lyndon Johnson's war. I always felt that President Johnson didn't want to win the war; he was just trying to figure out how not to lose it. He was far more focused on the Great Society than he was on the war itself. He ordered me not to permit the wives of the men who were captured to say so, because he thought that would antagonize the public, and they would want to fight more than we were fighting. For the same reason, he never did call up the reserves; he didn't want people to be gone from their accustomed places.

William Saxbe When I came to the Senate in 1969, I got off on a real bad foot with Nixon: he had the new Republican senators to the White House on a one-to-one basis, and I said to him, "Look, this is Johnson's war, and you've got six months to wind it up and then it's going to be your war." And I was not invited back to the White House for two years, so I was amazed, later on, when he picked me to be attorney general.

The Domino Theory

Marshall Green In 1969, when Nixon came to power, what would the result be of our losing the war in Vietnam—in other words, just walking out? What price would we have to pay? At that time, everybody was referring to the old Eisenhower "domino theory," a series of falling dominos—Hawaii, eventually. In my opinion, that was a completely false conclusion: when I was ambassador in Indonesia in 1965, the communists were virtually in power, yet by the end of 1965, the communists were completely out. The result was that Indonesia, instead of being pro-communist was, all of a sudden, anticommunist; that was one domino that was not going to fall.

David Packard We were concerned with the domino theory, which turned out to be a misconception. But at that time, we believed that if Vietnam fell, it would result in the Chinese taking over the entire area.

Alexander Haig One of the great mistakes of the Nixon presidency was in not recognizing that the whole war had started wrong, that it could not be ended decently unless we carried it through in a more dramatic, forceful way. God knows—Moscow was not going to go to war over North Vietnam; through subsequent history, we know how weary they really were. In

Henry's compulsion to have détente and a dialogue, he got snookered. I wouldn't have done that; I would have said: Hey boys. We want to take this Hanoi out, and if you don't like it—and want to intervene—why, you may get it, too. That's what statecraft is; that is how Eisenhower settled Korea.* He told them he was going to nuke them. In Vietnam, we didn't have to use nuclear weapons; all we had to do was act like a nation.

The Secret Paris Negotiations

Vernon Walters Dr. Kissinger was "Henry A. Kirschman" on his secret trips to Paris. I had a housekeeper who was very interested in everything, and one day she came home and said, "I've just seen this man on television that you gave your bedroom to." I replied, "You think this man is Dr. Kissinger. Dr. Kissinger is the principal adviser to the president of the United States. If he came to Paris, he would be in the big embassy downtown, not in my apartment."

Arnaud de Borchgrave I was aware of what Kissinger was doing in Paris. I don't have any details, but I know from the girl he was taking out, Jan Cushing—she stayed with us at my in-laws' place in Gstaad, and she used to be in touch with Henry at the White House every day by phone—that there were some secret negotiations, but I didn't think they were going to lead to anything for a long time.

Vernon Walters I reported to Kissinger through an unbreakable form of code. It was a very tedious thing to encode and decode; it took hours and hours. Kissinger obviously didn't want this to go through the usual government channels. He would fire me a telegram at the end of his workday; it would be midnight in Paris. I would go down to the embassy and spend all night breaking a message that expected me to do something with the Vietnamese in the morning. And I would follow the instructions and meet with them, and then sit down for hours, encoding what I had done.

Bui Diem Ambassador Ellsworth Bunker briefed President Thieu about the fact [of the existence] of the secret negotiations—that conversation was going on. But the extent that Thieu was briefed about the content and nuances of these negotiations was a problem, so we were frustrated. The

---

* In 1953.

fate of South Vietnam was at stake, and we should have been informed. We were a small country, fighting for our life; the United States was a superpower, and to the extent that a superpower was going to decide the fate of a small country was a concern to us. This is a lesson to other people: in dealing with the United States, you have to take these factors into consideration. You cannot close your eyes. For the Americans, losing—or not losing—a war was just a chapter in American history. For us, it was the question of the fate of millions of people.

William Westmoreland This was a maneuver to try to withdraw with a minimum loss of face. The [joint] chiefs [of staff] were not really aware of the cast these discussions were taking; it was operated out of the White House, not out of the Pentagon, or the office of the joint chiefs. Basically, it was a political and not a military matter.

George McGovern I knew that such discussions were taking place; I got tipped off by a reporter. But I also met with the North Vietnamese in Paris, so I got filled in from their side on what was going on. They were hopeful that something could be done. They were unwilling to stop their military operations in the South in the absence of an agreement; they were unwilling to go very far in their negotiations as long as the bombing continued. I thought that they were ready to cut a deal if they could do it on terms they perceived as reasonable.

Vernon Walters Kissinger arranged my role, but the president directed me to do it. Otherwise, when Kissinger told me not to report to my superior in the embassy, or in the Defense Department, I would not have taken that from Kissinger. In fact, the president was specific when he said, "Do you recognize me as the commander in chief of the Armed Forces?" This arrangement was unique, in my experience: the [U.S.] ambassador in Paris did not know of my role, or of the meetings themselves. He knew nothing, other than that I was the military attaché to the French Armed Forces. Even the regular negotiating team that was meeting with the Vietnamese every day didn't know.

Marshall Green I was brought into the process near the end of the negotiations. In October 1972, President Nixon was interested in seeing if he couldn't strike a deal with the North Vietnamese based, essentially, on money that we would offer to bind up the wounds of war. The generous payments would run to around $3 billion or $4 billion for the Vietnamese if we could have a peace treaty, and the prisoners of war returned. The money would be given out over the next several years, in measure, as they abided by the terms of the treaty. I believe that Nixon really felt that this might do the trick; I don't think that Kissinger ever did—he was very cynical. By that time, he had been dealing with Le Duc Tho,* and had realized what a very difficult kind of person he was. The effort never came to anything; the offer was made and was water off the duck's back. If Hanoi had lived up to the terms of the Paris Treaty of January 27, 1973, we would have been held accountable before Congress; we would have had a terribly difficult time getting the money.

Alexander Haig At the time, everyone had suspicions that the North Vietnamese were lying; hell, they were duplicitous from day one—on every aspect of our negotiations. That wasn't the issue; the issue was: How do we at least get what prisoners had been accounted for out? And we did get the bulk of them out. We persisted in exploring every lead we ever had. I saw that not only in the Nixon-Kissinger era, but it continued throughout Ford and Carter.

William H. Sullivan I had a number of people assigned to the negotiations with the North Vietnamese in Paris, which was actually more camouflage than substance, and in due course, Philip Habib† and I became aware that something else must have been going on. That was in the early spring of 1972. I thought, if it was actually going on and substance was being done, the more the merrier. Back in 1968, when we first started the negotiations with North Vietnam, I was ambassador to Laos, and Averell Harriman‡ called me over to Paris because he knew that I had some associations in Vietnam that I had developed earlier, in the Geneva negotiations on Laos in 1962. His thought was that I could develop a back-channel. We never succeeded at that time. But I was delighted that somebody was doing this, and I assumed it was our friend, Henry.

Alexander Haig I was never opposed to a dialogue, exploratory discussions, negotiations. I am one who believes that you have to talk. I always believed that we should be talking to the Russians. What I was nervous about was that, as a nation—and this was not a Nixon-Kissinger problem, quite the opposite—we inherited a situation in which restraints were

* Chief North Vietnamese negotiator, Paris Peace talks.
† State Department official.
‡ Chief United States negotiator, Paris Peace talks, 1968.

imposed on our handling of the conflict, which were self-defeating and were never going to succeed [from] the Kennedy and Johnson administrations, and a whole, evolving distortion of the application of national power, which began with Korea, and blossomed to full, devastating consequences in Vietnam.

I did not think that we had imposed sufficient leverage on the Russians, who were the logisticians, the catechists, and the leaders of the conflict, with Hanoi being a proxy. We never understood that; only Nixon grasped the implication that the Chinese were not necessarily in the Russian camp on that—it was precisely the opposite; I remember a meeting with Chou En-lai, who in effect said: Don't lose. I was accused of taking leave of my senses with every journalist I talked to; I thought we should have taken the battle to Hanoi. We put constraints on the application of our bombing all through the conflict. We ultimately did settle the conflict because we did bomb Hanoi; that's when they came back to the table—and only for that reason. At that juncture, people had left the president; Congress was threatening impeachment. I can't be critical of Henry for accepting the deal—which I was skeptical would ever be carried out. It was driven by the people, the press, and the national mood.

Vernon Walters Kissinger thought the Vietnamese he dealt with were all intelligent. He thought Le Duc Tho was very intelligent, but he was exasperated by their dogmatic repetition of "You must show sincerity and goodwill"—all these communist slogans.

William H. Sullivan Kissinger was rather titillated by Le Duc Tho, because Tho was an authentic revolutionary, a guy who had lived a life of revolution and had spent a lot of time in jail. He was self-educated, but he could quote from Nietzsche, or could appreciate some of Kissinger's allusions to other Germanic philosophers, so Kissinger did have a certain grudging respect. But Tho could be more frustrating than almost anybody.

Winston Lord There was mutual respect between them though they may not have liked each other. Kissinger understood, above all, that Le Duc Tho was a rebel and a revolutionary; he didn't believe in compromise or negotiation; he thought that negotiation was to be used to wear down your opponent while you persevered on the battlefield. The North Vietnamese also played a double-leveled game, where they would say certain things in public—suggesting to editorial writers, congressmen, and peace advocates that they were flexible—but in private, they would be much tougher. Indeed, one of the prices we paid was for the secrecy of the negotiations, because we were much more reasonable than the editorial writers and congressmen gave us credit for. I remember reading in the *New York Times* and *Washington Post:* Why don't we offer this or that to the Vietnamese? We already had, secretly, and had gotten no response.

Vernon Walters Compared to the Chinese, I found the Vietnamese very dogmatic, very unpleasant, without much of a sense of humor, whereas the Chinese were different. The Vietnamese were very tough—true believers in communism. When I testified before Congress on the MIAs and was asked why we didn't get a list from the Vietnamese, I answered: "Le Duc Tho looked at Kissinger [during the Paris talks] and said, 'I don't know why I'm negotiating with you. I have just spent six hours with Senator McGovern [Nixon's opponent in the 1972 presidential race]. Your antiwar movement will force you to give me what I want.'" That was one of Kissinger's better days.

Winston Lord It was interesting, particularly toward the end, when there was sometimes progress and sometimes setbacks. Whenever we were tough with the North Vietnamese, they tended to be a little more flexible; if they thought we were getting soft on them, they would be tougher. Kissinger tried to establish some kind of personal relationship through humor. They had some laughs, but Kissinger was under no illusion that Le Duc Tho was suddenly going to be more flexible just to show friendship. The North Vietnamese were trying to have us not only withdraw our troops—which we, increasingly, indicated we were willing to do—but they wanted us to overthrow our friends as we left. So the sticking point was: Do you have a military settlement, alone, and leave the political settlement up to the two sides to battle out in the future? Or do you arrange the political future of Vietnam at the same time? We got to the point where we were willing to withdraw and even leave North Vietnamese troops in the country. That was what broke it with Thieu; but we thought that they would wither away because they weren't allowed to resupply, and it was the best deal we could get: to get our prisoners back, have the cease-fire, and then have the two sides struggle, politically, for the future.

Marshall Green My own feeling about Kissinger's secret encounters with Le Duc Tho in Paris was that had this been known to the world, there might have been a lot more sympathy for the president—and for Kissinger—in understanding how far they were going in trying to reach accommodation, and how obdurate, intransigent, and impossible these North Vietnamese

SOBs were. After all, Kissinger was making reasonable proposals, by our lights, but when you are dealing with the mentality of Ho Chi Minh and the others, you are dealing with a whole different kind of mentality.

William H. Sullivan We had achieved a fairly broad agreement by the end of October. Then we had that incident where Arnaud de Borchgrave went up to Hanoi and talked to Tran Van Dong, the prime minister, who put a whole different twist on the agreement—and it was exactly the twist that Thieu and his people were telling us was the way that they interpreted this. Then everything stalled, and Thieu submitted to us the changes we would have to make in the text as then agreed. Henry went back to Paris and put these on the table as a gesture, not believing that the Vietnamese would give us much of anything, whereupon the North Vietnamese reaction was to reopen everything that they had conceded to us before. This was when, I guess, Henry developed his reaction to them.

Nixon, at that point, gave us a charge: he said, "You have to convince me that progress is being made, or I will resume bombing." Henry met privately with Tho, I met privately with my counterpart, and we said, "Thieu really means this, and if you don't stop this backpedaling, you are going to get bombed—and heavily bombed. All you have to do is start making progress again." They turned up their noses. I remember Henry and I had a long walk in the drizzle in the back garden of the embassy residence, and he was going to have to go back to Washington. We concluded that he could not honestly tell the president we were making progress. Therefore, the inevitable consequence was that this was Nixon's way of, in effect, putting the decision to resume bombing on us—that we could not say there was progress. So he did begin bombing again. I think that the North Vietnamese felt that Nixon wouldn't have the political support to go back to that kind of bombing.

After Christmas, on January 1, I was sent back to Paris to meet with my counterpart to talk about resuming the negotiations. It was very clear to me in the meetings that they had been very badly shaken by the bombings. The principal reason, I believe, was that they had expended their supply of SAM-2 missiles and by then the blockade, and the Chinese collaboration with the blockade, would permit any of those missiles to be shipped either by sea or across China to Vietnam. In their view, they were naked before heavy bombing that they assumed would be even heavier. So they were bending over backward: I had a sore throat, and they brought in all sorts of Vietnamese prescriptions to make sure my throat worked; they backed off on every one of the points they had spent weeks dragging their heels on. In the course of two days of meetings, I got everything taken back, and we started making progress again. Without the bombing and the mining of Haiphong Harbor, they might have held out until the denouement of Watergate, which they saw coming; there was no doubt they were up to speed on Watergate.

The Cambodian Incursion

Arnaud de Borchgrave I was in Phnom Penh when Nixon sent troops into Cambodia.* There was never any doubt in my mind that he was trying to give us some breathing room for the withdrawal, by destroying the North Vietnamese and Vietcong base camps, which were just across from the Parrot's Beak.† Yet every reporter in Phnom Penh at the time said here is proof that he wants to expand the war. These were people with tunnel vision, who didn't understand strategy. I am sure that the Ellsbergs of this world thought the same thing.

Thomas Moorer There are three things Nixon should get credit for: The first is going into Cambodia—we were sitting there; the North Vietnamese were coming down and sitting right on the border, coming across into South Vietnam and killing Americans, and running back, and sitting down and smoking cigarettes. We had the right, under international law, of hot pursuit. The second is the Sontay Prison Raid—I felt that if we could get two or three of those boys back and let them tell the American people how they were being tortured it would completely reverse the attitude about the war. Nixon went ahead, even though we knew that they would not find anybody—the raid required that they come down the river in a helicopter, with the moon sitting right on the river; that happened only twice a year. We flew into the compound; the helicopter blew down all the walls. We had trained at Englund Air Force Base at night, and in the daytime, took down the model of the prison, so that the Russian satellites couldn't photograph what we were doing. Third was mining Haiphong Harbor—I had tried to get permission for that in 1964, when I was commander of the Pacific Fleet. The North Vietnamese had no defense industry; they were getting 95 percent of their supplies by ship. Kissinger said, "You can't do that; the Russians will sweep up the mines." But Nixon asked me to come in, and asked, "How

* On April 30, 1970, 70,000 U.S. and South Vietnamese troops invaded Cambodia.
† A military strong point inside the South Vietnamese border.

long will it take to make the plans?" I said, "I already have the plans." He said, "Will it leak?" I said, "No, it won't." After the mining, not one ship entered or left that harbor for two years, till we took up the mines ourselves. You can just imagine the result if we had done that in 1964, because every bullet that was killing American boys—and we lost over 50,000—was taken in there by ship, some by the British, some by the Japanese. But Nixon had the guts to approve the mining.

Nixon's War Management Style

H. R. Haldeman Nixon—unlike Johnson—never picked the targets on a map; he never micromanaged the war. He did make major decisions, though, such as the bombing of the Ho Chi Minh Trail, the mining of Haiphong Harbor, the bombing of Hanoi, and the Christmas bombing. There was a lot of agonizing, research, discussion, and pinning down of the joint chiefs, and going beyond the chiefs and talking about it to the commanders in the field. But that was not to manage the war; it was to understand the situation, so he could make what he believed—in his heart—to be the right decisions, because these were horrible decisions. Each of them involved an estimate of substantial U.S. and Vietnamese casualties. He tried to educate himself to make these hard decisions, but once they were made, he didn't go into: "We are hitting this village; let's hit that one." He would talk to the field commander, because there was some question in his mind as to the validity of the information he was receiving. He kept probing, but he did that in everything; he did that when we were planning a political campaign. He would never listen to one adviser; he would ask everybody. We would get into a car in a motorcade, and the local chairman [of the party] would be there, and Nixon would spend the whole motorcade [ride] pumping the guy on what the real situation was. He did this on Vietnam. He wanted to know, and he soaked up information like a sponge.

William Westmoreland My strategy was that in several years we would turn the battlefield over to the South Vietnamese. That involved training them and giving them better equipment so that we could continue to fight and weaken the enemy on the battlefield while we were building up the South Vietnamese forces. In retrospect, this may have been wishful thinking. On the other hand, theoretically, it worked. I couldn't see any other way out of the commitment; we were obliged to hold up our departure to give them a fighting chance.

Deception by the Administration

Daniel Ellsberg At a conference at MIT in early 1971, Kissinger was being criticized by both faculty and students. Kissinger said to them, "You are asking these questions as if we want to continue the war. I tell you, we are winding down the war, and it will continue to wind down." He then went back to Washington. I had said on a panel discussion that escalation was imminent. During the day, I was told by a journalist that a total news embargo on Vietnam was in effect for twenty-four hours; the next day, we learned that what was going on was the preinvasion bombing of Laos, and some twelve hours later, the invasion took place. This was what Kissinger had gone back to Washington to preside over, having told us several times during the MIT meeting that the war was winding down; he had come all the way from Washington to lie to this prestigious audience—or, as a state department official said later, "Kissinger was widening down the war."

Donald Segretti I was not a true believer in Nixon; I'm not a true believer now. I did not disagree with certain of Nixon's policies. I viewed him as somewhat moderate. When I was in Vietnam,* I could see that the war was starting to wind down—at least from my vantage point. I thought that was positive. I did not believe that we should fold our tents and pull out as rapidly as some thought. I wasn't a true believer in terms that I'm going to my death following him, but I agreed with his policies, in general, and thought that he should be reelected.

Thomas Moorer When we mined Haiphong Harbor, the State Department was afraid that the Chinese would come down and reinforce the North Vietnamese. The fact is that if you want to fight China, you have to go to China. They have essentially zero mobility; they are not going to all jump into a ship, or an airplane, and go fight somebody, somewhere else.

The Christmas Bombing

Arnaud de Borchgrave In the summer of 1972, I heard from the foreign ministry in Hanoi, telling me that my visa application had been approved. I went to see Kissinger at the Republican convention, in Miami, and asked

---

* During military service in 1968, at the time of Nixon's presidential campaign.

him why the North Vietnamese wanted me to come there—I had never even applied for a visa. He told me that they likely wanted me to visit the dikes they claimed had been demolished by U.S. bombs, so I sent a message to Hanoi saying that I wanted to interview the whole Politburo. When I arrived in Hanoi, they wanted me to take a week-long trip into the country-side to see the bomb damage. I said, "Either I see members of the Polit-buro, or I am out of here on the next plane." A little while later, I was told that I would see Prime Minister Tran Van Dong. It was a fascinating inter-view, which lasted three hours. I typed up 5,000 words and then submitted the piece to him. He put 2,500 words off the record.

I flew to Vientiane [Laos], where I knew our ambassador, and asked him to take me to the post office so I could file my story. He said, "It's closed; this is Saturday." I said, "What do I do now?" He replied that there was a State Department back-channel, but that he was not allowed to use it. I said, "I have 2,500 words off the record that are dynamite, and I'm sure that Kissinger—who was then in Saigon—would love to see them." In the car the ambassador picked up the phone and reached [William] Bill Sullivan, in Saigon. I explained what I had to him and Bill then told Henry. Kissinger said to me, "Okay, as long as I can see it all, and quickly." And at his press conference on October 26, 1973, he said, "Peace is at hand, but an interview in *Newsweek* has raised fresh doubts as to whether or not we and the North Vietnamese see the accords in the same way." Marvin Kalb said to Kissinger, "I don't see anything in the published interview that would raise fresh doubts." Henry had been referring to some of the off-the-record stuff; he had mixed this up with the material in *Newsweek*. He showed the off-the-record part to President Thieu, thinking that this would convince him, but it had the opposite effect: Thieu pointed to some of the things said by Tran Van Dong, and said, "This is why I can't sign." So the breakdown in talks was caused by this interview, and it led to the Christmas bombing.

H. R. Haldeman There was an absolute conviction on Nixon's part that, by the fall of 1969, he would have Vietnam settled, in the sense of a cease-fire and decommitment of the United States, and some means of protecting South Vietnam for free elections. He really thought he could accomplish that. He thought so because his intelligence information had led him to believe that there was an opening for negotiation. There *was* an opening, but while they played the role of being willing to negotiate, whenever a negotiation got to a point where something was being arrived at, they would back off, or shift. Henry, in his ill-advised public statement of November 1972, said that peace was at hand. He shouldn't have said this, because peace wasn't at hand—mostly because of the intransigence of President Thieu. This was a very frustrating time for Henry. He kept reporting: "We are on the edge of doing this." On the other hand, [Senator Edmund] Muskie [D-Maine.] and the Democrats in the Senate kept saying: "The North Vietnamese will agree to certain items," which Nixon had already agreed to. They were playing Nixon and Kissinger on a string, in a cat-and-mouse game.

Alexander Haig The "peace is at hand" statement was overplayed; it was like the day President Reagan was shot—Dear God! That was contrived by Jim Baker to keep me out of the White House;* they thought I was running for president. If they had had any brains, they would have known that nobody takes the job of secretary of state if they want to be in the White House.

Thomas Moorer I was the one who started the whole thing: I went up to see the president at Camp David. I couldn't wait to do the bombing; I wanted to get the POWs—that was my one focus. We had a policy under way to withdraw troops. I kept saying, "If you keep this up, and the only Americans left in Vietnam are the prisoners, you can't get them back without really laying it on them [the North Vietnamese]." Nixon said, "How can we do that?" I said, "These people only understand one thing: brute strength. They are professional revolutionaries. Until we demonstrate some brute strength, they will never turn the POWs loose." Many people said that that would just make them meaner than ever to the POWs. But, to Nixon's credit—and I think he never got enough credit—he went right ahead, despite opposition from several sources even within his own administration. He did it, and the other side couldn't wait to ask for a cease-fire.

William Westmoreland The Air Force had supported troops under my command, but when it came to the tactical bombing of North Vietnam, that program was not under my jurisdiction; it was under the jurisdiction of Admiral [Ulysses S. Grant, "Oley"] Sharp, in Honolulu, the commander of Pacific forces. As I remember it, when Johnson stopped the bombing of the North, Admiral Sharp resisted it.

Alexander Haig John Connally and I were the only two Nixon confidants in favor of the Christmas bombing. Then, when it got started, the admiral in

---

* On the day in March 1981 when then–President Ronald Reagan was wounded in an assassination attempt, General Haig, then the secretary of state, said, from the White House, that he was in charge.

charge of the Pacific got cold feet and wanted to terminate it immediately. There was a massive, in-house row. Thank God we had a strong chairman of the joint chiefs, and a good strong Air Force guy, who got that admiral over-ruled.

Thomas Moorer Mr. Nixon decreed that we couldn't bomb on a Sunday— that is, a Sunday in the United States, or in Vietnam. Well, because of the time difference, that stuck us with thirty-six hours for them to repair their anti-aircraft and missiles before we could start in on Monday. But we really let them have it on Monday and, according to the POWs, their guards ran away; it scared the living hell out of them.

Bui Diem A man came to South Vietnam from the North in 1975 and said, "Well, with the Christmas bombing, we thought you would finish the war and liberate us; now we are the liberators." In many ways, the American bombing was inefficient: a lot of bombs fell along the Ho Chi Minh Trail, but were not accurate. But the B-52 and carpet bombing and the Christmas bombing made an impression in the North; many people there came to the conclusion that if the bombing went on for a few weeks more, the outcome of the war could be different. But the United States lacked the will and didn't want to go to the end.

The U.S. Antiwar Movement

Bui Diem There was misunderstanding on the part of Americans about the war in Vietnam, and misunderstanding within the South Vietnamese govern-ment and public about the United States. As one living every day with the antiwar demonstrations, I understood the feelings of American public opin-ion, but it was difficult for me to convey these feelings to Saigon, because the Vietnamese government and people saw the United States as the superpower leading the anticommunist struggle around the world. They thought in terms of John Foster Dulles* with his moralistic statements; of General [Douglas] MacArthur† leading the war against North Korea; and all these impressions were left in the minds of the Vietnamese people. And so they did not under-stand the antiwar demonstrations in the United States. But having to deal with people who sent their children to Vietnam, I understood it.

---

* Secretary of state in the two Eisenhower administrations.
† General MacArthur was relieved of his command in 1951 by President Harry S. Truman, due to their difference of opinion over how the Korean conflict should be fought.

William Colby Given the turmoil in the United States, it was a very natural question as to whether any foreign influence was bringing it about. After looking into it, the CIA report was that it was an American phenomenon. We knew that some of the people [the antiwar protestors] had contacts with foreigners: I had the great pleasure of explaining to Bella Abzug* that her name showed up in our files. I told her, "If you go to a foreign country and walk into the headquarters of an organization whose soldiers are shooting American soldiers, there is no way I can keep your name out of the CIA files." In various countries around the world, we tried to cover the North Vietnamese and communist representatives; they had certain contacts with Americans—not necessarily nefarious—and we would pick these contacts up and put them in the file. The conclusion was that the phenomenon of the antiwar movement was certainly manipulated by Hanoi in its policies and technique used with the delegations—Jane Fonda† and that sort of thing—but that the movement here was an American phenomenon.

Thomas Moorer The country was in a state of near-anarchy; people were pouring blood on the Pentagon steps; lying down on Constitution Avenue, so that people couldn't get to work; parading every night. I don't know where they were coming from. They would have a line of buses a mile long; I think the communists were paying for it. Nixon was sensitive to the public reaction; he had a Congress that opposed every step—it was always trying to cut off the resources. All this had a deterrent effect, in terms of the speed with which he made decisions. He admits himself that the mining of Haiphong Harbor and the Christmas bombing should have been done sooner. But I can understand how he had to overcome all the pressures and the opposition; he was doing things that 99 percent of the government structure—not only in the Congress, but also in his administration—were opposed to.

John Dean I was not a Nixon man, if you will. I had not been involved in his campaign; I had not been one of his California clique; I didn't know anybody, other than a few people, in the White House when I went there. When the president of the United States walks into the room, you want to stand up and salute; I've seen people who I knew did not like presidents get

---

* The New York political figure who later became a member of the U.S. House of Representatives (D-N.Y.).
† The actress during her visit to North Vietnam in 1972 had gone on Radio Hanoi to appeal to American pilots to cease their bombing of North Vietnamese targets, as well as taking other stands that were perceived to be anti-American by the Nixon administration.

all pumped up as soon as they play "Hail to the Chief"—and in walks the chief; you can't help but get drawn into the excitement of where you are and what's going on. If you are a good advocate, you believe in effective advocacy; you get caught up in the advocacy you are trying to see happen. So I did get involved in many things and believed deeply in them. In others, I certainly was a little bit more detached and didn't believe in them. I thought there was a lot of overreaction to the antiwar demonstrators.

One of my jobs at the Justice Department was to negotiate with the antiwar demonstration leaders over permits for where they could march. During those days, that was a big deal. Could they go down Pennsylvania Avenue, or Constitution Avenue, when they shut the whole city down? I got to know a lot of these people. I was the same age as many of them. Just by a fluke I had not been sent to Vietnam; I had been in law school at the time that Johnson was escalating the war. It wasn't a war I particularly liked. I don't think anybody liked the war. So I empathized with these young people—and some of them were even older than myself—but in the process of dealing with them from the Department of Justice, I really took their position and would come back into the attorney general's big conference room and argue why they felt they should have this or that in a demonstration, or about the tenor in the way we dealt with them.

I thought the government at times far overreacted to them—I thought all this business with Hoover trying to paint them all as communists was crazy, just crazy. I dealt with these people. I didn't care if they were communists to start with; it didn't affect me as to whether they should have a right to march or not march. So I tried to temper that at times. But I was a middle-level guy, and all you can do when somebody overreacts at the top is to try to soften it a little bit when it comes down to you as to what finally is done. I think that some in the White House were ideological, but some of the young guys who I tended to talk to more openly saw it that way: Bud Krogh was able to distance himself. He could understand why they were marching and were angry.

Jerry Jones This Vietnam thing was clearly part of the reason Nixon got nailed and Johnson didn't. Those of us in there felt we needed to win that war, and that it really was a war against the Soviet Union and their imperial ambition—that we shouldn't kid ourselves that it was some little civil war down in South Vietnam. It was an imperial move by our major enemy; we had to stop it. But Nixon's problem was that he didn't stop the war, or finish it. The Nixon view was that the people who were against him on Vietnam were essentially wrong, and didn't have the interests of the United States at heart, and didn't see what, in fact, was happening, which was a sellout to the Soviet side. So everybody that went against you became an enemy of the country; there was a bunker mentality over the war issue. That then fed into the hardball plan that he used in the campaign and on the cover-up.

William H. Sullivan The antiwar movement was clearly something that agitated the president, because he saw in it the potential for political catastrophe. He fluctuated back and forth from demonstrating contempt. And then, of course, there was the famous incident when he went out to the Lincoln Memorial at 2 A.M.° and tried to communicate. I was not just encouraged, I was impelled from the White House to spend a lot of time on college campuses, talking to groups. I remember at the University of Wisconsin, I had to be taken out through the steam tunnels. Nixon was really concerned about the movement, in domestic political terms. This was underlaid in personal conversations I had with him, in a continuing contempt for these people.

Bui Diem Americans, by their nature, are very impatient people; once they decide to do something, they try to do it right away. In Vietnam, perhaps because of cultural differences, America saw the Vietnamese as not [being] up to the standards expected of them, so you jumped to the conclusion: Let's do it ourselves; we will do the job and give the land back to you. But it is difficult to do things this way, and the war dragged on. And after a while, America got tired, and said: Let's get rid of it.

William Westmoreland The American forces were confined geographically: we were not allowed to move into Laos; we were pretty much forced into a defensive posture strategically while, on the other hand, any time the enemy crossed into South Vietnamese territory there was no tactical limitation on them. It's not the policy of the military to fight a war of attrition, but that is what we were doing. But the staying power of the North Vietnamese was much greater than that of the great American public—particularly in view of the tremendous visibility given to that war—it being the first television war. Therefore, we were not in a very strong position to carry out the strategy that I outlined. All of these factors, which I was certainly aware of, led me to feel that we should pull out—in all fairness to the Vietnamese— we should arm them and try to prepare them to fight on their own.

° May 9, 1970.

Alexander Haig Who would ever have believed that in the wake of the agreement the U.S. Congress would begin to steadily reduce all support for Saigon? Why did that happen? It happened because Mel Laird sold the country down the river; he went up and made a deal on the Hill. He couldn't get out of that war fast enough, and he was not loyal to his president, in my view. And he drove [U.S. Army General] Creighton Abrams—one of the great soldiers of all time—into an early grave because he was pulling people out faster than the schedule called for. He wouldn't let the United States support Saigon when they went into Laos, when the cream of the South Vietnamese Army—the product of so-called Vietnamization—was destroyed.

Could the War Have Been Won?

H. R. Haldeman I remember Pat Moynihan pleading with him: "Mr. President, you have got to get out of Vietnam before it becomes your war; it's still Lyndon Johnson's war. Leave it as Lyndon Johnson's war and let it die." Of course, it did become Nixon's war. He wasn't successful in doing that because we never could get the agreement at the peace table. But what he did, instead, was to start the withdrawal of troops in the summer of 1969, and the Vietnamization of South Vietnam, by bringing their troops to replace ours.

Could Vietnamization Have Worked?

William Westmoreland Theoretically, Vietnamization could have worked, but we underestimated the toughness and persistency of the North Vietnamese: we had thought that there was a limit to the sacrifices the North Vietnamese government would want to take, but, as it turned out, they had more staying power than we had imagined—as a matter of fact—more staying power than was imaginable, at the time. They used the Ho Chi Minh Trail as a supply line, and it got to the point where it would have been very easy for us to cut it, but we were not allowed to. The person most responsible for the geographical confining of the war was Averell Harriman. It was irrational for us not to move into Laos.

William H. Sullivan Nixon thought if Mel Laird took the responsibility for Vietnamization and it worked, fine; we'd try it and give it a chance. He wanted to shove the whole thing onto the Vietnamese and get the United States out of there. So he bought into it, but he didn't have real illusions that the South Vietnamese, no matter what they were given in the way of the sinews of war, were going to prevail.

Marshall Green Nixon was absolutely right in trying to proceed with the policy of Vietnamization; it was the only solution. I do not think that Nixon would have gotten us into this fix had he been president in the preceding years. But he was saddled with it: he comes into office; he's got a war on his hands; he's got to liquidate the war; he has to do this on honorable terms. The only answer was to strengthen the South Vietnamese as we withdrew our forces so that, ultimately, it would be entirely a South Vietnamese responsibility. And if they couldn't meet their responsibility, it was not our fault. The president, I believe, began to feel more and more that the North Vietnamese could take advantage of the policy of a weakening of American involvement, and that they could simply wait it out and—at some point— come in, in strength, and it would be too late for us to do anything. It could have happened, so he tried to give evidence that we would not tolerate such an enemy reaction; we would show our teeth; we were going to be tough; we were going to take the heat—that was one of his favorite expressions.

My own feeling was: This is all very well, Mr. President, from that viewpoint. On the other hand, you have to consider Congress; the war is very unpopular; every time you go in for one of these things, it looks like broadening—like Cambodia, or Laos. Congress is going to come up with more and more restrictions; you are going to end up being bound by this same rope you gave Congress to bind you up with. And that was what was happening. So my rationale was to take the heat and get out, doing all you could to help the Vietnamese to protect themselves—which was very limited, I'm afraid, and just write it off as a bad deal. The South Vietnamese just didn't have the stuff—that's all. The North Vietnamese were far more determined.

Vernon Walters I learned much from talking to my contacts in Paris. It was obvious to us that the Vietnamese had observation on Da Nang Airfield; we couldn't figure out where from. I talked to a French friend of mine who had lived there and used to ride around on his bicycle. He said, "You go up to such-and-such a place, and you will find out where they are looking from." So they went up, and there they were.

Marshall Green It's been demonstrated that the South Vietnamese were incapable of carrying the war to the enemy; they were not the equal of the

North Vietnamese and the Vietcong—people who would come down the Ho Chi Minh Trail on a bicycle carrying a rifle that would probably kill the man the second time he fired it. With that kind of resolve, we couldn't win. This was a war of guts and resolve, and the degree to which these people had it was of absolutely maniacal proportions. We couldn't understand that any more than Henry Kissinger could understand, when he sat down with Le Duc Tho, how obdurate the man was.

Thomas Moorer That is nonsense. In the first place, they had the very latest AK-47 rifles; they had the MIG-21 airplanes; they had the SA-2 surface-to-air missile—and plenty of them; they had artillery that would outgun us. As I told Nixon, these people are professional revolutionaries. Look what they did to the French at Dien Bien Phu.* They only understand brute strength. I thought it was a mistake for us to put the army in the jungle and have high school graduates fight these coolies; that was a big waste of manpower. When Johnson made his famous speech, in which he said, "We seek no wider war; we will not invade North Vietnam; we will not overthrow Ho Chi Minh," I said to General [Earle] Wheeler, who was chairman of the joint chiefs, "We might as well come home."

Gerald Warren The president thought that the war was winnable on the terms he had developed: Vietnamizing the war; the steady reduction of U.S. troops; the bombing of the trail that fed the North Vietnamese and the Vietcong; the bombing of the related territories, which included Cambodia and Laos; and the bombing of North Vietnam—all of which, he believed, would end the war. Nixon did bring the war to a successful conclusion: he got the North Vietnamese back to Paris, where Henry Kissinger was able to come up with an agreement which may very well have held had Congress, under Mr. Ford, continued to fund the effort. But Congress chose not to do so.

Bui Diem My meetings with President Nixon were very businesslike: he constantly expressed the determination to see the war terminated under the American conditions—that is, continued support for the fight for freedom and self-determination in South Vietnam. He was very firm about this; he was of the opinion that somehow the war should be ended. Taking into account the internal situation in the United States, this was quite logical; but he kept insisting on peace with honor.

---

* French forces were overwhelmed at the fortress of Dien Bien Phu, in what became the Democratic Republic of North Vietnam, in 1954.

Gerald Warren His main conduct of the war was pretty honorable, and led to an honorable end. Now there are great differences of opinion over that proposition when it concerns Laos and Cambodia, and over whether the reporting at the Pentagon was as accurate as it should have been. All the peripheral things, which are not honorable, tainted the entire picture. They were the result of the desire to bring the war to a successful conclusion, and to do it with as much secrecy as possible, so there was a mania for secrecy— which is always a problem and which led to the excesses of Watergate. When the reelection effort came around, there was a desire to win a major, major mandate, so that with Vietnam behind him, the president could turn his attention to the Soviet Union, to China, and to doing something about reinventing the federal government.

Bui Diem Toward the end of the U.S. involvement, the language Nixon and Kissinger used was very blunt: we were presented with a kind of half-peace, with verbal assurances from the administration that they would do something later to help us. But with Watergate, these verbal assurances came to nil. We had not expected that support from Americans would collapse so completely.

Thieu Receives a U.S. Ultimatum

In January 1973, General Alexander Haig delivered an ultimatum to President Thieu from President Nixon stating that if President Thieu did not sign on to the agreement with the North Vietnamese, which had been worked out at the Paris Peace Talks, President Nixon would still initial it.

Alexander Haig We had a running dialogue with Thieu, and I had to be Lord High Executioner in that respect, because he wouldn't listen to Henry, but he would to me. I found Thieu to be a very honorable individual who had a good feel for the battlefield, and for what was happening in the United States. I'd say that by the time Nixon's letter came, he was very, very resigned that the string had run its course, and that if there was a reasonably graceful way for Washington to extract itself, then Washington was going to take it. Thieu believed, wrongly, that the United States would act if the accords were broken. When in U.S. history did we ever enter into an international treaty in which we didn't reserve the right to sanction violations?

William H. Sullivan I wrote almost all of Nixon's letters to Thieu. In fact, by that time, Nixon was so engaged in the Watergate business that I doubt he ever saw them; we usually cleared them with Haldeman. This was a long correspondence, in which we tried to bring Thieu aboard. It shows that a meeting of the minds was never achieved. I was hoping we could persuade Thieu, but in the back of my mind I assumed it probably wasn't going to happen. It would not have served Thieu's purposes to have agreed with our program.

Marshall Green Thieu was a politician seeking to continue his tenure. Some of his generals were very poor; they gained their positions simply because they were personally loyal to him. We should have rapped his knuckles harder than we did; I don't think we should have tolerated his sending of any irresponsible general to command divisions where our divisions were at stake, yet two or three of the worst generals were in charge of divisions that were between Saigon and the Parrot's Beak. But Thieu was a nice man. To be in power anywhere, you have to be a little bit of an SOB, a quality not lacking in some people in our government.

Alexander Haig Kissinger couldn't handle Thieu. I was a soldier; I had fought the war. They knew me; I was a quasi-hero in their minds. Thieu thought Henry was a little duplicitous—a little too quick to advocate Hanoi's line. And, in fairness to Thieu, he was right. He had one set of objectives; he wasn't living in an American milieu, in which public opinion and congressional dissent was going to destroy a president. It ultimately did, and had a major role in Watergate; I have no doubt about that. My God! What Nixon was accused of in Watergate is child's play compared to what Clinton is being accused of [in the Whitewater case].

William H. Sullivan Thieu had a little nephew, whose name was Na, who really didn't care for what Mr. Nixon was doing, because he saw exactly where it was going to be leading. So he fairly well led Thieu to be skeptical and reserved about direct personal relations with Nixon. I went to the only meeting they had—the one on Wake Island—which was a bit of a farce. Nixon was doing his "Hail Fellow, Well Met" thing which, in his instance, is always a little forced and artificial. Thieu was very reserved. I remember a goony bird collapsing in front of them as they were standing at attention for the rendition of honors, and I always thought that was the best symbol of the whole excercise.

George McGovern I went to see Thieu in 1971. He knew that I was an unabashed critic of the war policy, but he was civil. He didn't argue; it was more of a courtesy call. The night before I met him, a group of Vietnamese religious leaders had asked to meet with me, and I agreed to meet them in a church. There was an organized demonstration outside; lighted torches were thrown inside; stones came through the windows; it was a frightful situation. I was then an announced candidate for president and found myself hiding on the floor—under a table. Fortunately, there was a phone available, and I called Ambassador Ellsworth Bunker, who sent a force of heavily armed MPs over—and they broke up the demonstration. I never made any charge, but I wonder if that demonstration—and the violence—wasn't organized by either the Thieu government or pro-government forces, as a means of embarrassing me.

The Prisoners of War

William H. Sullivan The general feeling was that POWs and MIAs [missing in action] occur in all wars—that this one percentage of the casualties and those involved as POWs was not as high as in other wars. It didn't become politically active until the time that Ross Perot got involved, in 1969–70, when he started flying wives and other family members around; that attracted political attention. But in terms of the White House, I did not detect a great political reaction to the POW issue.

Marshall Green In the beginning, this issue should have been raised by the American peace groups to get an exchange of prisoners going. Instead, Mel Laird turned it into very much of a war aim; therefore, it made the prisoners all the more important as hostages. Of course, we couldn't end the war without getting our prisoners back; that was an enormous complication. The North Vietnamese were asking for a political solution in which there would be shared power in Saigon. This was something we obviously couldn't countenance. What you had to do was to sit back and grasp the nettle and say, What's at stake here? You had to look to some kind of defeatist solution, realizing that there was no alternative. That's all hindsight.

George McGovern I have always been troubled by the POW argument. It has always seemed to me to be a phony argument, because you never get prisoners released during the middle of a war; it is taken for granted that once a war is over arrangements will be worked out for the prisoners to be released, and I think that is precisely what happened. I don't think that the

North Vietnamese ever unduly held American POWs once the war had ended, so one of my personal complaints against the Nixon administration is that they elevated that POW-MIA issue to the point where you would think that that was the reason we were in Vietnam, ignoring the fact that it was the decision to go to war that created the prisoners in the first place. The Nixon people created an issue where none should have been.

Alexander Haig The key issue was: Were we naive enough to believe that a continued North Vietnamese presence in the South—under whatever ground rules—could result in anything but a disaster? That was the issue and Thieu was right and we were wrong; but we were wrong because we had no alternative.

Three Conflicting Views on the Vietnam War

Daniel Ellsberg In a personal sense, I do not have animus toward Nixon, as Nixon put it so well: "If you hate someone, it destroys you." That exemplified his relationship to me. If you ask me today what I think of Nixon and Kissinger, I have no personal animus toward them in terms of their relations with me. I do think of mass murderers when I think of them—of people who, without any justifiable excuse, killed hundreds of thousands of people with no good reason. I hope that Nixon will one day learn that, but it will never make right what they did—which was to prolong unnecessarily a wrongful war which led to the deaths of millions of Vietnamese and 20,000 Americans; that is blood on his hands, which is never to be washed off.

Vernon Walters If Nixon had remained president of the United States, 39 million South Vietnamese would not have gone into slavery. The day we stopped the heavy bombing because the Congress ordered it stopped, the North Vietnamese had one surface-to-air missile left. After that, it would have been a milk run. Ask our prisoners. The Vietnamese came to them and said, "When your people get here, you will tell them we have treated you nicely, won't you?" Nixon would have continued the heavy bombing, and they would have collapsed a week later. What defense did they have against B-52 carpet bombing? There is no defense. I have been asked so many times while abroad, "How come the United States, with all of its power, didn't win the war?" It's very simple: the United States was prevented from using its power by its own people. If you have ever seen a B-52 strike, you know that there are no human beings on earth that can withstand unlimited B-52 strikes. I've heard them [subjects of B-52 bombings] on the radio, gibbering like animals under it.

William H. Sullivan I consider that we are probably far better off now for having lost the war than we would have been had we won it. Had we won it—by our definition—we presumably would have had a divided Vietnam. We would have had to maintain U.S. forces in the South to protect the integrity of the South against the constant pressure of the North. By the same token, the Chinese probably would have had to maintain their lips and teeth policy with Hanoi, much against their own general instincts. And the opportunities for developing the relationship with the Chinese that led to the geostrategic imbalance that ultimately upset the Soviet Union and brought the Berlin Wall down would not have happened if we had won the war on the terms that Lyndon Johnson used to describe our war ends. It's a cynical thing to say—in view of the loss of life and the political turmoil in the United States. It was probably a better result than it would have been had we won. There are some pyrrhic victories that are not worth winning.

Part Three

The Pentagon Papers
and the Plumbers

In the spring of 1971, Dr. Daniel Ellsberg, a former Defense Department official who had been involved in the development of U.S. strategy for the conduct of the Vietnam War, decided to make public hitherto secret reports on the subject from the Kennedy and Johnson administrations.

This material, which came to be known as the Pentagon Papers, was given by Dr. Ellsberg to the New York Times, *which began publication of the papers on June 13, 1971 (the* Washington Post *published similar material on June 18–19, 1971).*

President Nixon and National Security Adviser Henry Kissinger were outraged at both the actions of Dr. Ellsberg and the New York Times. *The White House was concerned not only over the revelations contained in the Pentagon Papers and the possible detrimental impact their release might have upon secret negotiations then under way in Paris, but also over the possibility that Dr. Ellsberg might have possessed additional highly sensitive documents.*

Disclosure of the Pentagon Papers led to two crucial actions: the prosecution of Dr. Ellsberg in an attempt to inhibit further release of materials; and the establishment of a unit within the White House—known as the Plumbers—for the plugging of security leaks.

6

The Pentagon Papers

Daniel Ellsberg I had drafted a set of questions for Kissinger, called National Security Study Memorandum One [NSSM 1], during the transition. Then I went over the answers—about 500 pages of classified material—and helped Kissinger's aide, Winston Lord, draft a summary of the answers; that was in February 1969.

NSSM 1 showed that he had asked—of course, I had asked since I had drafted the question in his name—what effect mining Haiphong would have on the war in the South. I knew that an honest answer was: it will have no effect—it was true that most of the supplies were coming in through Haiphong—but all the intelligence agencies said: If you shut off Haiphong, they have more than enough channels from China—waterways, railroads— to get many times more supplies down than were coming in through Haiphong, so hitting Haiphong would have no military effect on the war; it would just shift supply routes.

I also knew that Nixon knew that—as would anyone who read this study. He decided to use the mining as a cover for renewing the bombing of North Vietnam—more heavily than Johnson had, using B-52s. This was not a way of stopping supplies, but of killing people and intimidating the leaders into feeling they had no choice but to meet his terms, which were to allow mutual withdrawal: the Northern troops would leave South Vietnam; the American troops would leave the country. So the mining and subsequent bombing would not be a response to an offensive; it was something he meant to carry out all the time.

When it turned out that Nixon and Kissinger were making the same mistakes their predecessors had, I felt a peculiar, strong obligation to try to head them off; my first steps on the Pentagon Papers were, in effect, to try to head them off. After all, the Pentagon Papers did not implicate Nixon; they implicated the Democrats. My first impulse was to get him to throw the blame on the Democrats. I thought: This is the only way a president can get out—if he can blame the situation on his predecessors. When I discovered what he was doing—and he wasn't getting out, but was reproducing what his predecessors had done, no more wisely than them—it was, to say the least, a tragedy to reproduce those mistakes and keep the war going. But I will go further: I don't think that the errors are worse than the crimes, when the crimes involve the killing of hundreds of thousands and millions of people; it is mass murder. It was mass murder under Johnson; it was mass murder by Nixon.

George McGovern Ellsberg came to me with those papers; he had first gone to Fulbright and wanted him to release them. He said, "No; that's against the law. I can't do it." Then Ellsberg came to me and I told him pretty much the same thing. I said, "Why don't you do it?" He said, "I could be prosecuted." So I said, "I am supposed to be prosecuted? I have been against the war. You were for the war; you were one of the architects of our policy. Why shouldn't you take the risk if you feel strongly about it? Why don't you take the risk of going to jail? Why do you ask a U.S. senator? I'm sworn to uphold the Constitution of the United States, and I've told young people who were against the war that if they can't fight, they should be prepared to go to jail. We are a society of laws, and I am not going to recommend amnesty until the war is over. As long as the war is on—and it is the law of the land—you either have to go or be willing to go to jail. I feel the same way about this: if these papers are as rich a lode as you say they are, then you probably have some obligation to think through whether it is worth breaking the law to release them. If it is, then you should be prepared to go to jail. But I am not going to tell young people all over this country that they should obey the law and then break it myself." He was very disappointed and—I think—somewhat indignant about it, but I turned him down the same day as Fulbright did.

A few days later, he released the Pentagon Papers to the *New York Times*. He had been such an advocate of the war that, and on intellectual grounds—he was a very bright guy—he seemed committed to the war effort. But it didn't surprise me when people reversed themselves; the same thing happened to Clark Clifford. With Ellsberg, I think he had an intellectual conversion based on his revulsion to the war itself. With Clark, he just decided that it was a no-win deal: no matter how many forces we put in there, we weren't going to prevail. I think that Ellsberg took the right course as a deeply concerned public official. He told me that he had gone through a very painful conversion. He said, "I just can't live with this; we are on the wrong track over there, and I have to get this material out." It didn't end the war, obviously. I was at a fund-raising party in New York when the editor of *Life* magazine came in with a big brown envelope—there were probably about eight people there—and he said, "I have some photographs here that are going to end the Vietnam War." They were color photos of the My Lai Massacre[*]—God! They were gruesome. But they didn't end the war.

Ben Bradlee I think it was an epiphany to Ellsberg. Ellsberg had been a hawk. I wonder what took *us* so long; I was very, very late to turn against our position in Vietnam. I had spent four years in the Navy. I thought of it as my country—right or wrong. I instinctively hated the dictatorial nature of communism, and equated the two. I didn't know anything about the Vietnamese people's own desire to be independent.

Daniel Ellsberg I saw Nixon's plan as a replay of what I had lived through in 1964, when I was at the Pentagon and taking part in secret planning for escalation during the election campaign against [Senator Barry] Goldwater [R-Ariz.]. I knew that the Johnson administration secretly planned to execute Goldwater's plan for bombing North Vietnam. But the public was not to know this, and it led to the dropping of 3.2 million tons of bombs, to no good effect. I didn't want to see that happen again, so I gave the Pentagon Papers to Senator [Robert] Mathias (R-Md.), not revealing anything about Nixon's plan, because the papers ended with Johnson, but revealing over twenty years of secret plans for escalation, lies to the public, plans to violate treaties, and plans to basically enlarge the war. I hoped that the public would draw from that that the current president might be doing the same, which I knew he was. Everyone had asked: "Why did Nixon get upset?" I had only revealed material about Johnson. But Nixon knew that I was revealing about Johnson what he was also doing, and that it would be just as serious if it became known that he [Nixon] was lying, as it would have been for Johnson. So he had to try to shut me up.

I had planned to introduce the Pentagon Papers into evidence at the

[*] On March 16, 1968, a unit of the U.S. Americal division, under the command of Lt. William L. Calley, killed more than three hundred civilians in My Lai, a hamlet in South Vietnam alleged to have been a Viet Cong stronghold.

draft resisters' trial of the Minnesota Eight; I was on the witness stand and had the papers in my briefcase. The defense lawyer asked me, by prearrangement, "What do you say about this statement by the president on our Vietnam policy?" I replied, "That is a lie." The plan was that the lawyer would then say, "That is a pretty strong statement. Do you have any evidence?" I would say, "As a matter of fact, I do have a lot of evidence for that statement, in the form of documents." Then I was going to say, "If you want the evidence, here it is," and then put the goddamn thing right into the record. At this moment, the judge, in a rage, asked the lawyers to approach the bench. He said, "If another one of your witnesses makes a statement like that in this courtroom, I will put you in jail for contempt. I will not hear criticism of the government in this courtroom."

In those days, to say that the president had lied was enough to get you into jail. Imagine—criticism of the government! We had eight people in jail, facing prison, and they all went to prison for protesting what they claimed was an illegitimate war—and they happened to be correct. They were supposed to conduct their defense without criticizing the government. The Pentagon Papers made a difference: I guarantee that it will be a long time—and it's been twenty years now, since any judge has said it to a defendant—before any judge will say, "You can't say the president has lied in my courtroom."

William Colby I think that he [Ellsberg] was affected by antiwar attitudes. He had worked for the government in the early days of Vietnam; he had been very forceful. My friend, John Vann,* thought he was really very warlike on the couple of occasions Ellsberg had come out to Vietnam; he wanted to go out on patrol, shoot, and so forth. He went to the Pentagon and was assigned to do part of that study. I guess that turned him; a number of our analysts were negative about the war—in the CIA and elsewhere. But he decided to work independently, and turn the documents over.

Arnaud de Borchgrave I remember Ellsberg in Vietnam, when he was very gung-ho, very hawkish: he used to go out on patrol in combat fatigues. I remember one famous incident when the officer in charge of a company told the troops, as they were taking a break, that Ellsberg wanted to keep going, chasing Charlie [the Vietcong]. I am not a psychiatrist; I can't tell you what happened to the guy; I can't tell you what happened to Mort Halperin. These guys became self-hating Americans. I never quite understood why. I

---

* A high-level U.S. official working on pacification programs in Vietnam.

had many tours in Vietnam; I was hit out there a couple of times, but it didn't turn me into a self-hating American. It opened my eyes as to how the media was setting the agenda and showing certain incidents way out of proportion. Ellsberg and Halperin somehow convinced themselves that the enemy was the United States.

Daniel Ellsberg Yes, I was in a fair amount of combat. Kissinger's story* is that I shot at civilians, which is absolutely false. The obsession of my life is to oppose terrorism and actions against civilians; that has been the basis of my aversion to strategic bombing. This is an amazing charge. I don't know whether he [Kissinger] believes it or not. There is a passage in my book, *Papers on the War,* where I describe myself as horrified to find myself in a little plane with a pilot who was shooting at people in black pajamas; people who John Vann later conjectured were possibly civilians. I did shoot, but only when I was being shot at, in combat, by Vietcong. I never saw the people I shot at; I was shooting at tree lines. I didn't carry a weapon at first because I was representing the ambassador, investigating pacification. Then I found out that if you didn't carry a weapon—and you weren't a reporter—the troops were constantly asking: "What are you doing here?" They had a reflex feeling that they had to protect you, so I started carrying a weapon in the field, and when everybody else was firing, I fired. But Kissinger's notion that I had anything to feel guilty for, or to apologize for, has not the remotest truth. As for those other charges—that I had sex in front of my children, for instance—that is bullshit; Kissinger was trying to say that I was a crazy person who had to be stopped.

A. M. Rosenthal We got hold of the papers, physically; they were brought up to New York. We had to set about processing these materials in our heads. Are they genuine? Of what value are they? How do we judge the secrecy of the information and the importance of publishing, or not publishing? I had a small group of people, headed by James Greenfield, the foreign editor. They sat down and examined the materials to determine if they were genuine. I had some horrible vision of a bunch of Harvard freshmen sitting up in an attic saying: We're going to get the *Times;* you be the CIA and I'll be the joint chiefs. We do take the issue of national security very seriously, although we don't always agree with its definition. So they spent some time going through the material, and determined by references and checks that they were genuine. And we also looked for information that we thought

* Related by Kissinger in his book, *White House Years* (Little, Brown, 1979).

might be really prejudicial to military security. We couldn't find any. We did find numbers on some documents which, as I recall, we cut out because there might be a way for a spy to trace this document with another from the same time period. Then we set up a team of reporters to see what the story was; they met in a suite of rooms in a Manhattan hotel. Among them were Neil Sheehan and Hedrick Smith. The process was kept quite confidential, which, for a newspaper, rather surprised me. All during this time, there was a concurrent discussion on whether we should publish the documents, or the analysis, or both.

Nothing like this had ever been published. When I first saw them spread out on my desk, there were banner headlines on many of them: Secret Report of the Joint Chiefs of Staff to the President; or CIA to Someone or Another. I had never seen that kind of thing before. It was like: God, what are we doing? The final approval had to be made by the publisher, Arthur Ochs Sulzberger. I thought he had to be involved, because I didn't know how publication would affect the future of the paper. The newsroom was all for publication, but there were people on other parts of the paper who thought we shouldn't be doing it—that it would be unpatriotic. I felt very strongly that we had to print the documents as well as the analysis—that without the documents there was no story. The documents would verify what we said, and if someone wanted to argue with our analysis, we could say: Go argue with the documents.

Another issue was that if we went ahead, should the material be printed in one paper, or should it be spread out over several days? I felt we had to spread it out, because the material could be undigestible in one bite. This argument went on for a couple of months. I gave the publisher the worst-case scenario. I said, "It is possible that the country will turn against us; the living ex-presidents will renounce us; that readers and advertisers would turn against us." Dealing with this issue was probably harder for Punch [Arthur Ochs Sulzberger] than for me. I knew, as an editor, that this was what we had to do once we had determined that there was no secret stuff. I also felt: How could we send reporters to Vietnam if we now had all this information and were hesitant ourselves about whether we printed it or not? He said, "You know, I have to see those damn things." I went down to my office and got someone to get me a grocery cart—I don't know where from—and I dumped them in there, took off for the fourteenth floor, and said, "Here they are. You want them?" And we decided to publish with the documents.

Bui Diem It was a shock; there were a lot of things in the Pentagon Papers we hadn't known about. With their publication, the South Vietnamese government became more careful about handling the problem. I had met Dr. Ellsberg in Vietnam; he was with General [Edward] Lansdale, who was a friend of mine. The fact that someone like Ellsberg—who had been deeply involved in the war—could change, made me aware that there had been a lot of evolution in American society about the war. I was very, very concerned about this; I didn't feel I could do much about it, because even more than the problem of Vietnam, I felt that American society was going through a profound change. So, kind of jokingly, I said to my friends, "Even if the war in Vietnam didn't exist, perhaps it should be invented."

A. M. Rosenthal We were printing on a Saturday, for Sunday's edition. We had an early deadline—about seven-thirty in the evening; it was very tense. We wanted to keep it confidential. The word was getting around a bit, and we didn't know what the impact would be. My secretary said, "There is a call for you from Daniel Ellsberg." I said to her, "I don't want to talk to anybody." I didn't know what he wanted to say, but I didn't want to hear it. We were ready, and the paper came out, and the most surprising thing of all happened: nothing. We thought we had the biggest damn story in the world—and it was; we knew its importance. It was a real history of the war, as seen from the inside—and what the presidents knew, or didn't know. It was like opening a huge box and seeing the different administrations walled off from each other, so they didn't know the impact they had on each other. But we did. But nothing—not a damn thing—happened. We thought it would be on the radio, on television, but nothing. The AP ran a little story, which was obviously a night rewrite.

The next morning, we turned on the television. There was nothing. It was very interesting, since the wire services didn't know what to do with it, and didn't move it. It was a Saturday night story; they probably had nobody around, so since they didn't move it; the television, which was dependent on them in those days, didn't do anything. And I thought: What, are we crazy? I must be insane. Nothing has happened.

It wasn't until David Brinkley, in the early Sunday evening news, said that something was going on. The story was hard to grasp. In those days we didn't make it easier for the reader; we didn't give them précis, or one, two, three, four. And then, on Monday morning, it all broke and there was hell to pay. Nixon and Kissinger were tearing their hair out. They knew what it was, all right.

Stephen Bull The mood was generally "us vs. them." If you recall the Vietnam period, you had the banshees screaming at the gates; 200,000 to

300,000 people around the White House and over at the Ellipse, and the like, and there were a lot of outside groups that appeared not to have the best interests of the United States at heart: you had people like Senator [Mike] Gravelle [D-Alaska] reading the Pentagon Papers into the *Congressional Record* so they could be made public; you had a guy like Ellsberg, who was taking secret documents out, and you would read about this in the *New York Times;* Henry Kissinger would go to the negotiations with the North Vietnamese, and the U.S. negotiating position would be printed in the newspaper. I guess we were paranoid; all of us were extremely defensive. As Henry said, even paranoids have enemies; just because you're paranoid, it doesn't mean they're not out to get you.

William Westmoreland [Publication of] the Pentagon Papers had a negative effect on the staying power of the American public.

David Packard I spent a whole day looking through those papers, and I couldn't find a damn thing in them on security. The issue was overblown; there was no imminent danger to the country at that time. I recommended that they let it go, but they did not agree with me. The president tended to overreact in situations like that; that was typical of his attitude. But that was a period when they were very sensitive.

George McGovern They were the official record and might have been embarrassing to some of our policymakers, but I can't see how they told the enemy anything they didn't know—or that would be destructive of our security. I went through them pretty carefully; they just showed how American policy was formed during the Vietnam period. I thought that they were very helpful from a historical standpoint, but I could never understand why President Nixon and Kissinger were so angry and alarmed: they didn't reflect unfavorably on them, because they weren't in office during the period.

Raymond Price Maybe, in retrospect, 95 percent of it was no longer secret, but even if there was 5 percent of a million pages that were, that is a hell of a lot of very sensitive stuff, which could do untold damage to the United States, its interests, and to the lives and safety of its people. And—at the time—one thing which Nixon knew and others didn't was that he was then in a very delicate stage of trying to engineer the opening to China. One of the critical things he had to persuade the Chinese of was that he could keep a secret. The Pentagon Papers almost undid that. And then, of course, the media got up on their high horses and said that it was outrageous of us to have any concern with keeping government secrets *secret;* all that mattered was the public's right to know—and fuck everything else. To me, it was one of the vilest episodes in the whole history of journalism.

Ben Bradlee I have yet to hear of the first secret, the first issue of national security. That's a terrible charge: to violate national security. You're really talking about treason. It makes my blood boil that somebody could sensibly charge me with treason. They were sort of reckless in talking about that, since the last event described in the Pentagon Papers happened in 1968— that was three years before the period we were talking about. People didn't understand that most of the journalists are patriotic. I had a top-secret security clearance when I was in the State Department for a year and a half; I know what a national security secret is. I also know what it isn't. We took many things out of the papers—like the names of the two CIA agents in Saigon—and Helms said, "That's really very nice of you, but those guys were taken out of there as soon as the study was ordered."

I only met Ellsberg six or seven years later. Ben Bagdikian* was in touch with him, but I have a feeling there may even have been a go-between between Bagdikian and Ellsberg. I know that Bagdikian got them from Ellsberg. It was very difficult to persuade our lawyers, and to persuade Katharine Graham,† because that was the first leap into public prominence that we had ever had; that was our first whack at it. William Rogers had been our lawyer, so his law firm was still representing us. The thing that made the *Post* lawyers hesitate was the television stations; we had three or four stations. It was perfectly clear that, had we lost the civil suit, they would pursue us on a criminal charge of revealing secrets. If they had done that and we had been convicted, we couldn't own television stations. They were putting $100 million onto the table. I thought that was a very bold decision from that point of view. Poor Katherine got hammered by us editors. We said, "If we are ever going to go first-class in terms of professional commitment on excellence in journalism, we have to do this." If we hadn't, we would have shot ourselves in the foot and taken ourselves out of the race.

Kenneth Rush Henry and Nixon both had obsessions about leaks destroying everything they wanted to do. They were both absolutely paranoid about leaks; each made the other much worse. Part of that was Nixon's feelings about the press; he wouldn't have the *New York Times* in the White House.

---

* A *Washington Post* reporter.
† Katharine Graham, owner-publisher of the *Washington Post*.

Henry pretended to be that way, but he wasn't; he was talking to the press all the time, giving them information. Nixon's fighting the press was a terrible mistake.

William Colby The mind-set in the White House is that everything you do is in the national interest; you are trying to carry out national policy. And somebody like this, who is obviously running at cross-purposes with you—and violating the rules by revealing this material to the press—is obviously the ultimate enemy, so they get emotional about it.

Raymond Price We didn't even know that the Pentagon Papers existed. Ellsberg stole them; the *New York Times* got them; and they set up a whole secret task force: they took hotel rooms so they wouldn't be caught; they had phony names—a team of about half a dozen people preparing their material, ready to spring it on us by surprise, which they did. All we knew was that there was a vast compendium of what, apparently, was very sensitive material; we didn't know what was in it. Nobody had given us a chance to vet the material—to recommend to the *Times* that it could be dangerous to print. They had the gall to do it—to spring it on their front page, and we went ballistic. They were arrogating to themselves the sole right and authority to decide for the United States of America what could and could not be safely and properly used—material from prior administrations on the most sensitive issues of the day—while we were in the middle of a war. It was absolutely outrageous.

A. M. Rosenthal We saw no necessity to consult with the government. I know that if we had consulted with them, they would have had the troops out—perhaps have gotten an injunction against us. Also, Mr. Nixon had not been president during any of this time. The question was: Should we consult with figures from previous administrations, going back to Eisenhower? I had first visited Vietnam in 1956, when I was the paper's correspondent in India, and I saw the military assistance people.

Richard Moore There was severe anger upon the part of the president that this kind of material could be leaked and published. We proceeded legally on the matter: we went to court against the *New York Times*, and people were not aware—because it was not properly reported—that while the vote was six to three in favor of the release of the papers, five of the nine Supreme Court justices agreed that serious damage had been done to the national interest—the notion that codes had been compromised in those papers, and that other governments would question whether they could do business with us if that was how we handled our secret material.

Robert Mardian Maybe 95 percent, or maybe 98 percent, of the Pentagon Papers could be declassified; I doubt it, but let's assume that. In the Pentagon Papers there was a disclosure of the involvement of the Canadians and several other nations. Canada, for one, denied having anything to do with Vietnam. This would be tremendously embarrassing. Also, if a Russian intelligence officer read the Pentagon Papers and tied what they read in there to the events that occurred, it would have disclosed the fact that the United States had a facility for obtaining information that, till that time, was unheard of. The National Security Agency had the ability to sit a block away and pick up conversations in a building. This is out now. It wasn't then.

I was in California making a speech and I read about the publication of the papers. I went directly to my office and didn't leave there from Monday to Wednesday. I went to New York to argue the injunction; we got a temporary restraining order. Then, bingo, the *Washington Post* started publishing, so I went back to Washington and I got a temporary restraining order. The *Boston Globe* started publishing; we got a TRO there. The *St. Louis Post Dispatch* started publishing. Here again you have Nixon's anathema with the media; he thought they were disloyal. He was very upset, not only with Ellsberg, but with the media. My inability to get to the bottom of it was probably the beginning of the Plumbers: Nixon wanted to know how well I was progressing with the Ellsberg case. I went out to San Clemente and I told him I was doing everything I could, within my legal powers, to nail him. I said, "I am doing everything I can, Mr. President." I wasn't satisfying him. My parting statement was that I was doing everything in my legal powers that I can, and as I was leaving, Haldeman said to me, "Mardian, you never come up with the right answers." That was the beginning, in my opinion, of the Plumbers.

John Dean My office was not a policymaking office; others made decisions they sent to me to implement. I was not consulted about any of the decisions relating to how to handle the Pentagon Papers, and I personally thought it was a tremendous overreaction. The likelihood of the Supreme Court invoking prior restraint just seemed so remote to me—and not a particularly good position to be in. I thought there were other ways to do it—to try to quietly but seriously go to the *New York Times* and the *Washington Post* and say: Okay, here are the parts of this revelation that could hurt our government, and here's why, rather than a blanket, you can't print any of it.

Because, clearly, some of it didn't affect anything, and—as we know, in retrospect—it is questionable how much harm was really done. So I thought it was kind of dangerous precedent—like Truman in the seizure of the steel mills; a little bit of overreaction. Now, our office was involved in dealing with the U.S. attorney's offices on that, and helping the solicitor general's office—Fred Fielding of my office went up to New York—so we were right in the thick of it. As far as the prosecution of Ellsberg [goes], we weren't involved in that decision at all; we read about that in the newspaper.

A. M. Rosenthal On Monday night I was having dinner, by pure coincidence, with Katherine Graham, in New York, and somebody handed me a note to call the office. The Nixon administration had moved against us, and the question was: Do we publish the third installment? We met that night, and our lawyers walked out on us—Lord, Day and Lord, which was headed by Herbert Brownell. They told us they would not represent us. I thought that it was a dastardly thing to do. We had a paper signed by Robert Mardian, one of Mitchell's deputies. My position was that we go ahead with publication. We had no court injunction; we had a statement from the attorney general, but I felt that without a court order, he was just one more lawyer. We had a big discussion about that.

We passed our first edition. We were supposed to go to press at nine o'clock; I was watching the clock. The news editor downstairs kept calling me and saying, "We're getting close"; so I called him up and said, "You'd better hold things up a while." I didn't say: Stop the press. I was not that dramatic. So we delayed the first edition. Then we decided to go ahead.

The next morning, the government got a restraining order. And we didn't have a lawyer. I said to Harding Bancroft, who was the executive vice-president on the business side—and an ex–State Department man—"Do you happen to know a constitutional lawyer? We need one in a hurry." He replied, "I do." It was the first time I had ever heard the name Alexander Bickel. But we didn't know where he was. He knew that he taught at Yale, so I went down to the night rewrite bank, because one of their talents is to find people. They called Yale and he wasn't there. They called California and he wasn't there. And they finally found him at his mother's house, in Washington Heights. So he came in and represented us.

H. R. Haldeman Kissinger was more incensed than the president was, at the outset. Kissinger was absolutely infuriated and, in his inimitable fashion, managed to beat the president into an equal froth of fury, not because it hurt Nixon in any way politically—because the Pentagon Papers didn't have any information about Nixon; they were all about Johnson and Kennedy—but because of the implication that a massive collection of top-secret, classified documents could be printed in the *New York Times,* with impunity. Kissinger's argument was not that the contents of the documents created any problem themselves, but that the printing of them did—in terms of our relationships with our allies, and with our enemies, because it convinced them that we couldn't control our own internal operations, and that we didn't know what we were doing.

When you are trying to play a game of world leader, this seriously castrates your ability to produce. This was the reason for Henry's concern, which I saw expressed to the president in a very vivid fashion. It wasn't hard to get the president churned up about this, because churning the president up on something against the *New York Times,* and people like Daniel Ellsberg, was a fairly easy project to undertake. Henry dramatized it tremendously, painting a despicable picture of Daniel Ellsberg, who was a protégé of his. So a legal effort was launched to get into criminal sanctions and have it stopped. There were also all kinds of other things, which got shot down in the legal process. Henry was understandably furious, because it [the Ellsberg situation] was jeopardizing his position at the Paris peace talks. Daniel Ellsberg knew exactly, at the time, what Henry was doing, and I think that Henry believed that he was sabotaged, or stabbed in the back, by his former protégé.

Morton Halperin Kissinger and Ellsberg had a professional relationship in the sense that they were both part of what was then a very small group of civilians who thought about national security issues. They had had a contact because Ellsberg had come back and worked with us on Vietnam at the beginning of the administration.

William H. Sullivan Kissinger and Ellsberg had worked fairly closely together at a time when Ellsberg was a flaming hawk. Kissinger's comments to me about Ellsberg certainly were pretty scatological, so I assume that reflected some animus.

Helmut Sonnenfeldt I don't think in Kissinger's case there was an animus that went back into the past. There may have developed an animus when this Pentagon Papers episode occurred. I guess he participated before that in some of the demonstrations: he shifted his ground.

Daniel Ellsberg My only formal relation to him was that I lectured at his Harvard seminar on two or three occasions. In that sense, I was not his student; he listened to me. In Vietnam, I briefed him on two occasions. The closest I was to him—and this probably proved to be of some embarrassment to him—was that I worked as a consultant for him in the preparation of National Security Study Memorandum One [NSSM 1]; I wrote his first presentation to the National Security Council. His bringing me into the government at the very beginning of Nixon's term suggests a relationship between us that didn't actually exist.

There is no question that Kissinger was a force pressing for me to be pursued; how much Nixon had to be persuaded, once it was explained to him, is a matter of conjecture. I think that there was something Kissinger was very worried about—a top-secret document [NSSM] on nuclear planning. I had checked that one out of the top-secret office but; ironically, I never got around to reading it in full. I scanned it and could see it had all of the old calculations: this many hundreds of thousands killed this way; this many that way. I was quite sure that Kissinger did not want the public to be reminded that he was one of the models for Dr. Strangelove. I think that he was nervous that I would put this study out, but I didn't.

Alexander Haig Kissinger, I admit, was very upset about Ellsberg, and he did drive the president's concern about it. We had no idea that there was this group of Plumbers that had been put there by Ehrlichman. His motive was to scare Henry; he was very jealous of him. Ehrlichman proved to be a man of far less character than he should have had. He is back now, and thank God, because he had some good fiber.

Daniel Ellsberg I was under the impression at the time that I must be breaking some law. I later learned that we do not have an official secrets act. We had no precedent for it; I was the first person prosecuted for giving information to newspapers. I knew that this was going to be a much larger disclosure than had ever happened before—a great challenge to the system, you might say. I presumed that I would be prosecuted and—if prosecuted—convicted. And that I would go to prison forever; I expected to spend the rest of my life in jail. I did feel, however, that they might decide not to prosecute, for political reasons.

Marshall Green What Ellsberg did was a stinging blow to Nixon. He wanted to handle it as harshly as he could. That is why he tried to bring Ellsberg to trial on conspiracy and espionage charges, whereas Rogers had recommended that he be brought to trial on a theft charge. Rogers knew that conspiracy and espionage would not stand up in court—and they didn't. I have no reason to believe that Ellsberg was passing secrets to the Soviets, but I can see how President Nixon was upset, given his passion for secrecy and his utter dislike of leakers.

A. M. Rosenthal About two years after we published the Pentagon Papers, I was in Philadelphia at a meeting of the Associated Press Managing Editors Association. They gave us a prize for printing the papers. Riding down in the elevator, I saw John Mitchell. I had this plaque, and he said, "You know, you ought to give it to me, because I got it for you."

And also at the convention, a man came up to me and said he was Daniel Ellsberg, and he would like to talk to me. It was the first time I'd met him. So we talked in my suite; it was a very interesting experience. He was mad at us; angry, because he said, in effect: You guys wrote the story, you fought it in the court, and now you've moved on to something else. He implied that we had kind of dropped him. As a matter of fact, we *had* dropped him in that sense. I think he resented this.

There was also something else that happens on major stories and in relations between the people involved and the newspaper: it was an enormous story—the biggest one we'd had, in some ways. But he was right: we went on to something else; the world went on to something else. For him, it was still the greatest event of his life; for us, it was not just another story, obviously, but we went on to something else. I am not saying he did not do other things, but I don't know if he did or not. But this was the pivotal experience of his life. He felt kind of lonely.

7

The Plumbers Unit

─────

The Plumbers Unit, whose members included presidential aides Egil Krogh, David Young, G. Gordon Liddy, and White House consultant E. Howard Hunt, was formed in July 1971 and operated from an office in the old Executive Office Building.

The unit would participate in the May and June 1972 break-ins at the headquarters of the Democratic National Committee (DNC), located in the Watergate office complex.

Bernard Barker, Participant, Fielding and Watergate break-ins I found a note at my home from Howard Hunt. This was the beginning of my involvement in Watergate. Ten years before, Hunt had been my supervisor during the Bay of Pigs; he was the area director, and I was working directly under him. When the Bay of Pigs ended in a fiasco, he left. When I found the note, I was a realtor.* The note said, "If you are the same Bernard Barker that I once knew, contact me at such-and-such hotel." It was signed "Eduardo"; that was the code name for Howard Hunt during the Bay of Pigs operation—a part of my life that was very significant because it involved try-

* In Miami, Florida.

ing to liberate Cuba. I had been born and raised in Cuba as an American. I was part of the American colony there; my mother was a Cuban. So when I got this note from Hunt, I became very emotional, because I had felt very deeply involved with him over Cuba. I answered immediately and went to see him. He was with his wife, Dorothy. The first part of our meeting was social, but I knew that he was not in town on a social visit, because he is on a much higher level socially than I am.

The next day, we went together to an event they have annually in Miami at the Bay of Pigs Monument. To a certain extent, he was incognito; very few Cubans knew him personally. It took another visit before Howard finally spoke to me about what he had in mind: he wanted to know if I would go ahead with him in the mission that ended up with Watergate, but at that time had nothing to do with Watergate. He described the mission as national security. He was out to stop leaks that had been hounding the administration—security leaks; things that were said in the administration got to the Soviet Embassy. They had information, from taps in the limousines, that all this information was getting to the Soviet Embassy. He said that he was going to activate a number of cells to create a group of people who would act on a national security case for the United States, so, of course, I said I would be very willing to do it.

Ronald Ziegler The Plumbers thing was not basically put in place to trod upon the Constitution. It was developed, maybe, with bad thinking, but certainly with thinking relevant to the context of the time.

H. R. Haldeman McCord, Hunt, Liddy—none of these names meant diddly to me. I had never met—and still have never met—McCord, Hunt, and Liddy, or any of these people. Hunt, they say, was working in the White House, but he was in the EOB [Executive Office Building]; I doubt if he ever was in the White House. Of course, it is basically the same thing; there were various presidential offices there. He was working on this Plumbers thing, I guess, and then becoming a project guy for Colson, as Ehrlichman had a guy, Tony [Anthony] Ulasewicz, doing things for him—surveillance things. I don't even know if they were illegal.

Lawrence Higby I couldn't have told you who Hunt or Liddy were; I'd never seen them. I did know about the Plumbers—that it was organized to try to get into serious leaks that the president felt were going on with relation to national security material. The reason the Plumbers came to my attention was because David Young* had the same job with Henry that I had with Bob, and then he was taken off it and put on this different assignment, which I thought was pretty unusual, because he was very close to Henry.

Alexander Haig Young couldn't hack it as Henry's assistant. He was a nice young man, but he couldn't hack it. The next thing we knew, he's over working for Ehrlichman, but we don't know why—I don't mean that in a denigrating way. He wasn't strong enough to handle the job of mothering Henry Kissinger; it ain't easy.

Daniel Ellsberg My strong sense is that Kissinger knew everything the Plumbers were doing, because they were effectively run by Egil Krogh and David Young, the latter being Kissinger's personal assistant and protégé. Young bought his freedom; he didn't go to prison because he had taken incriminating files on Ehrlichman, with which he bargained with the prosecutors. Then he went off to Oxford [University, in Oxford, England] where he is protected by several layers of tutors.

Seymour Glanzer, assistant U.S. attorney, District of Columbia; chief, Commercial Crime Section, U.S. Attorney's Office If one were to denominate the sources of information, it would be the middle-level employees at the Committee to Reelect [the President] and at the White House. One of the most important witnesses in the entire Watergate case was a person who is rarely mentioned: David R. Young. He was a critical witness in the cover-up case. I gave him immunity; I did it on a handshake. In those days, you could do that.

---

* From almost the beginning of our research, we realized that David R. Young, who had served on Dr. Kissinger's staff and was then assigned to the Plumbers, was an important potential source of information. We had a difficult time locating him but, finally, in the fall of 1993, we learned that he has an office in Oxford, England, at a company called Oxford Analytica, Ltd. We then placed at least six telephone calls to his office, and each time we were told that he was either in the office but not available or was out of the office. We were asked for our telephone number in New York, and we also provided our fax number, but we never received a reply. On both December 23, 1993, and January 10, 1994, we faxed letters to Dr. Young, providing him with specific information on the project and again requesting an interview. We followed up these faxes with telephone calls. But again, we were not put through to Dr. Young.

It is interesting to note that we have not received any response—even a negative one—from Dr. Young. It is obvious to us—as several of our interviewees have implied—that he is "in hiding" in Oxford.

One could also speculate that Dr. Young could be an important source of information on exactly what knowledge his former superior, Henry Kissinger, had concerning the activities of the Plumbers. It is possible that Dr. Kissinger knows much more about the Plumbers than he has acknowledged over the years. It would be hard for us to believe, based on our research, that Henry Kissinger would not have known why one of his key aides was taken from his staff and given another assignment in the White House.

Bernard Barker I asked Howard who he represented, and the answer he gave me really was something for the books: he said he was in a group at the White House level, under direct order of the president of the United States. This group was active in an operation of national security. I asked him, "Howard, why not the FBI or the CIA?" He said that this group was above the FBI and the CIA, and that those organizations reported to this group. The operations he described are what we refer to as "bag jobs." This is why I said to him, "If you are going to have bag jobs, why not use the FBI or CIA?" He answered that the FBI was hampered by recent Supreme Court decisions, and that the CIA could only act in cases outside the United States. I said, "Howard, we worked here, and created a brigade for the CIA." He replied, "We were representing a foreign power at that time, which was the underground in Cuba."

At that point, I stopped asking questions, because it was clear that Howard was what he represented himself to be: he had his office at the Executive Office Building [EOB]—later on, I met him there; he had been my boss at the CIA, and I was definitely convinced he was the real thing. What's more, I really believed for quite a while that we were back in the CIA, on some sort of operation I would not need to have explained to me. I don't believe that today, because everything he said to me turned out to be true: they did have a group at the White House level, which consisted of the "Plumbers," who were there to stop the leaks; the FBI and CIA did report to these people, and gave them assistance and materials to work with. I was surprised at the time that the operation was on such a high level. It was my understanding that Hunt had gained his position through Colson; he spoke a great deal about him.

William Colby I never knew much about the Plumbers; we tried to stay away from that. We did get entrapped into it in a couple of minor degrees— with the tape recorder and the red wig. Once Helms found out about the contacts, he cut them off; that wasn't our business. In terms of the profile on Ellsberg, Ehrlichman called [General Robert] Cushman, our deputy director, and asked if he could arrange for Hunt to get some help from the agency on minor items. Cushman said yes, and arranged for Hunt to get the red wig and the tape recorder. Hunt brought back some films and asked us to develop them, which I did. I remember looking at the material. I could not tell anything about it at all: there was some office building, and a license plate suggested that it was California. We sent the photographs to Ehrlichman; he knew exactly what they were—pictures of the doctor's office.

Richard Helms Not until he [E. Howard Hunt] began to make some requests from the agency for assistance did we realize that he was working for the White House—at the time he came to General Cushman and asked for a wig and one of those devices that causes one's voice to be altered.

Then, when another request from Hunt came in, he came to see me, and I began to realize what was going on. But the issue of Hunt's working for the White House certainly came to the agency's attention at the time of the wig request.

My reaction was to tell him [Cushman] to turn them off; not to provide any more assistance to Hunt on anything. I think that the reason, in retrospect, that Cushman went along with any of this [Hunt's requests] was that we didn't have any idea that the White House was up to these nefarious practices. It was not until the Fielding break-in that we came to realize this. In other words, we were not in the White House's confidence in any respect whatever about what they were going to do.

Any attempt to use previous history on this situation is bound to fail, for the simple reason that no White House that I know of had ever done anything like this before and, therefore, nobody was suspicious that they were doing it. It certainly didn't occur to me and it certainly wouldn't have occurred to the American public.

Bernard Barker I would call Hunt directly at the White House. At my trial, the secretary to the Plumbers* was asked: Who had access to their room? Who were the people who were allowed to call on the phone in the Plumbers' office? She said, "Hunt, Liddy, Young, and someone else, from Miami, by the name of Barker." I said to myself, Oh my God. I've had it.

* Kathleen Chenow.

8

The Break-in at
Dr. Lewis Fielding's Office

In an attempt to obtain derogatory information on the character of Dr. Ells-
berg, the Plumbers organized a break-in at the Beverly Hills, California,
office of Dr. Ellsberg's psychiatrist, Dr. Lewis Fielding.

Participating in the action, which took place on the evening of Septem-
ber 3–4—Labor Day weekend—were Bernard Barker and a team of anti-
Castro Cubans he had recruited at the behest of E. Howard Hunt.

Standing watch outside Dr. Fielding's office was G. Gordon Liddy,
while Mr. Hunt performed a similar function outside the psychiatrist's home,
lest he decide to leave during the burglary and head to his office.

Bernard Barker Two of the recruited men, [Felipe] De Diego and [Euge-
nio] Martinez, worked in my real estate brokerage. They were perfectly
qualified for the operation: De Diego had been a member of an operation
to capture Cuban documents; Martinez had made over 300 infiltrations into
Cuba as a sea captain. The job we were supposed to do involved trying to
locate certain documents pertaining to Daniel Ellsberg. Hunt said that they
had approached the FBI to do this operation, but the bureau said that
recent Supreme Court decisions prevented them from doing any more "bag
jobs."

Howard [Hunt] came down from Washington and told me it would be a surreptitious entry. We flew to Washington. I personally financed all the travel. Later on, Hunt gave me the money. I was also able to give the men I recruited money to make up for the time lost on their jobs. The exact philosophy behind the recruitment was defined by me to Mr. Hunt right from the beginning: we were not in this for money; the motive behind our assistance to him and his superiors would be their assistance to us—to liberate Cuba. This was one of the most difficult things for people to understand after Watergate.

Daniel Ellsberg I got Hunt's copy of the *Time* magazine cover story on me; it had been in his safe and was turned over to me at my trial after he had talked to the grand jury. In his copy of the article, he had circled the part that mentioned that Dan Ellsberg had a psychiatrist in Beverly Hills, so it could be that Hunt got the idea for the break-in from this.

G. Gordon Liddy Hunt is in the car, surveying Fielding's house—just in case he decides at two o'clock in the morning to get in his car and drive down to the office. I am right at the office, watching the guys break in, and staying in contact with them. Then Hunt says, "I've lost contact with Fielding. I don't know where he is."

Bernard Barker At first, we got delivery men's uniforms and tried to deliver some packages, and then leave the door open. That didn't work, so we ended up having to break the door down. We made a complete search of the files. I did find cards involving Daniel Ellsberg, but no file involving him. The office looked more like a financial center of stocks, bonds, and investments all over the world. It didn't even look like a psychiatrist's office, as far as the filing was concerned. Before we left, we threw drugs that Hunt had given us all over the floor, to make it look like a burglary. I told Hunt—who was in a hotel room in Los Angeles—that we didn't find a file on Ellsberg, just a card. He said, "We know this, but they don't," whatever that means. Later on, when we went to trial in Los Angeles, we found out that there was a guy in jail for that operation; he had been involved in drug burglaries and confessed to the Fielding break-in, so when we went on trial, they turned him loose.

Daniel Ellsberg [Dr.] Fielding later told me he didn't have any files on my personal conversations with him, but that he did have papers I had given him to illustrate the kind of work I was doing. One of them was the paper which had won the American Political Science Association prize for the best essay of 1970. The paper, with my name on it, was found on the top of a file. There is no question in Fielding's mind that the burglars had gone into my file and wanted him to know that; this was quite contradictory to what the burglars said. From that point on, Fielding had no doubt that it had been a White House operation against me. He didn't share this information with me at the time, because his lawyer had advised him: If this was a White House operation, don't get involved. He had also not told me at the time that the FBI had visited him before the break-in; he felt so guilty about it that he got a bleeding ulcer.

G. Gordon Liddy It was a national security operation—the same kind of thing I had done when I was in the FBI. It had no relation to Watergate, but where it got linked was when I briefed Dean on the Monday after the disaster at the DNC. We met at his request and went for a walk in the park. I said, "Since you are the action officer—the damage control officer—you need to know what these guys could reveal"; these are the guys we used in the Fielding break-in. Now Dean was counsel to the president, and I had every expectation that he would go immediately to his client, the president, and tell him. The fact is, he didn't tell him for nine months. So here is the president, sitting around in the White House, and wondering: Is it Colson? Is it Mitchell? What do you think? Bob Haldeman? And Dean was sitting right there—and he knows.

Donald E. Santarelli If I had sat in on a meeting with Liddy proposing campaign shenanigans, I would have said to Mitchell: This is crazy. You can't take the risk of this kind of crap. It's not valuable enough, whether it's legal or illegal. And similarly, if I had been asked to opine on whether it was constitutionally permissible to break into Dr. Fielding's office, I would have said: Yes, that is entirely permissible, once the president declares it to be a national security matter. Mitchell was not sensitive enough to the pitfalls of Washington. I didn't believe Mitchell to have had impure motives, or to be malicious, but to be not just careless, but unaware of how dangerous and fatal are the traps and pitfalls of high Washington office.

George McGovern I thought that it was one of the more shocking aspects of the whole Watergate episode. It always seemed to me, though, that when you add up all of the things of Watergate, the most serious part was the effort to cover it up, rather than anything you could technically describe as "the break-in." I don't want to minimize the break-in. It is just that that wasn't what bothered the Congress, or the country. It was the whole network of things they did to cover it up. That was the part I found shocking.

Bernard Barker When the Fielding break-in was over, it was quite obvious that this had been just one operation. We kept in touch with Hunt, who told me that he wanted to recruit a very large number of people, and that I was to start thinking in those terms. This turned out to be Operation Diamond, which I was in charge of. Diamond was to recruit personnel for all operations that were to come later. Included were street fighters and members of labor organizations who worked in Miami* hotels. We went to Washington on several operations, like the one when Hoover† died; there were hippies burning flags. I took ten Cubans and we took the hippies on and busted up their demonstration.

---

* Miami, Florida, site of the 1972 Democratic National Convention.
† J. Edgar Hoover, director of the FBI, died on May 2, 1972.

9

Who Ordered the Break-in?

G. Gordon Liddy We had sent a memorandum on the break-in plan, and Ehrlichman said, "Okay, on your assurance that it cannot be detected." To prove we had not spent the money on a party, we took photographs of the windows in Fielding's office; of the drugs we had strewn about to make it look like a junkie had done it; and of the broken files. Krogh was shocked when he saw the photographs.

Bernard Barker It was quite obvious that Liddy was Hunt's superior; Hunt told us that. The fact that Hunt needed to get approval was natural to me; even in the CIA he had to get approval. I never thought Hunt would order an operation like that on his own. It was my understanding that Hunt was the bottom man; on top of him was Liddy; on top of Liddy was Young; and on top of Young was Krogh. Hunt said that Krogh had been involved in an antidrug operation in Turkey; they were very seriously considering the creation of groups to fight drugs. They expected that to blossom here in America, and the group I would recruit would be very much involved in that effort.

Leonard Garment I remember very clearly Krogh's coming into my office and saying, in effect, that the instructions came out of the Oval Office. At the time, it wasn't a question for me of believing or disbelieving; it was a problem of comprehending. Ehrlichman had written a memorandum authorizing covert operations, as long as they were deniable.

Bernard Barker I don't know at exactly what point in the operation the names of Haldeman, Ehrlichman, and Mitchell came up, but it was quite obvious what we were dealing with; the names of those people came up. I told Hunt when I was recruited that what we wanted as compensation was assistance in the liberation of Cuba. He said that he would have to consult with Mitchell. Later on, he told me that they had looked very favorably on that. It was like a horse-trading thing.

H. R. Haldeman I don't know why the break-in happened. You must talk to John Ehrlichman about it, but he will profess that he didn't know anything about it, although he did sign off on it. Bud Krogh has the best answers. Henry [Kissinger] made a big point of Ellsberg's psychiatric imbalance and it [the break-in at the office of his psychiatrist, Dr. Fielding] was to try to document that, and use it to discredit Ellsberg in whatever fashion could be done.

Alexander Haig I wouldn't want to label Henry's paranoia about Ellsberg as the cause of the Fielding break-in. I don't believe that the president knew in advance about the break-in, but it would be hard to know what he did— or didn't—know. The real éminence grise of all this was Colson; he would get President Nixon in the bag—when I say "in the bag," all Nixon needed was one scotch; his toleration of alcohol is zero—and he could get pretty high. In an hour, he would get cold sober.

John Dean I learned about the Fielding break-in some time after Liddy went over to the Reelection Committee. Jack Caulfield [CRP employee, investigator, and undercover agent] told me that this guy is kind of a crazy man, and told me some of the things that Liddy had done. I didn't know who was the target at that point; I just knew they went to California and broke into some doctor's office. And they had done that right out of the White House. I was dumbfounded when Caulfield told me that. I knew it had been an Ehrlichman-Krogh operation. It was one of those things I wasn't supposed to know, and I just kept my mouth shut. Who would I go to? They all knew about it but me.

I am now very inclined to believe that Liddy and Caulfield were much closer than had been portrayed historically—that they were talking; that Caulfield told Liddy what he was doing; that Liddy apparently went up and met with Ulasewicz and tried, at one point, to recruit him. These were things no one knew back then, but I think, with hindsight, that was probably where Liddy was getting some of his ideas. He said: I'll do better what Caulfield couldn't do. Liddy says that, indeed, he was prepared to carry out the firebombing of the Brookings, even though Caulfield was not. He presented a plan to do it, even though I had turned that off at one point. It had not died, because Liddy was trying to sell it to Colson on the fact that he and Hunt could do it.

When I first learned of the proposed firebombing of the Brookings, it was from Jack Caulfield, who came into my office wide-eyed and said, "You're not going to believe what Colson has asked me to do, and it's crazy." And I agreed; it was crazy. I said, "Sit still. I'll deal with it," and I literally got on the next plane I could to fly on to California, where Ehrlichman was, and sat down and said, "John, this is craziness." And Ehrlichman kind of looked at me over his half-glasses and said, "Well, we'll see what we can do," and he called Colson and turned it off. But it hadn't turned off. I met with Ehrlichman in July; in September, Liddy and Hunt were still planning it.

John Ehrlichman It is highly probable that Nixon ordered the break-in at Dr. Fielding's office. It didn't originate with me, and according to Krogh, it didn't originate with him. For Colson to have been energized for such a thing means to me that Nixon was involved. There was money, which Colson—who had no independent source—got his hands on. The president would have had to turn that on and off, so circumstances—and a process of elimination—suggest it to me. Colson always uncritically carried out what Nixon wanted, without exercising any independent judgment. Nixon would not have realized the danger in the Fielding break-in; he loved that kind of stuff. I recall an evening at [J. Edgar] Hoover's house, where I listened to Hoover, Mitchell, and Nixon discussing "black bag" jobs that the bureau [FBI] had done, not just in foreign embassies, but against U.S. civilian citizens. That was dessert for them—great stuff—and they ate it up. They loved that stuff.

Robert Mardian Hoover used to refer to me as "that goddamn Lebanese Jew." I told the director: "He's not Lebanese, he's Armenian. He's not a Jew." He did things that were unbelievable to me. He would write me a letter—congratulations for this—but then his top people would send me the letter he had put out to them. One of Hoover's top aides told me about a bag job they were doing on the Russian Embassy. The ambassador and his wife were out, as were the security people; they had gone to some function. All of a sudden, they get the word that the ambassador and his wife and the security people are returning. I asked the aide, "What did you guys do?" He said, "Oh, the ambassador had an automobile accident going back." They used to brag about their bag jobs.

Raymond Price The president might have known about the Fielding break-in; it would have been appropriate—use just about any means—considering the magnitude of what we then thought we might be dealing with. From what we knew at that point—and what we were worried about—the Ellsberg situation could be absolutely calamitous. I would not have any moral scruples about it [the break-in] myself, even though it would obviously be dangerous legally. People tend to forget that this was wartime; you were dealing with the life and death of your servicemen—and with major betrayals of significant national trust.

John Dean It is impossible for me to believe that that was the first time he knew about it.° I have now seen tapes where it's very clear he's saying this is the first time he's learned something; he does this again with his memoirs. For example, I tell him about [Haldeman aide] Gordon Strachan; he says this is the first time he learned about that. But that is not true. Ehrlichman had told him a month earlier that Strachan was involved. I think Nixon was playing that for me and not for what it really was. Ehrlichman has indicated they were talking about it [the Fielding break-in] when they were walking down the beach.

I think that if Nixon had ordered the break-in at Fielding's office, Ehrlichman would have had it nailed down somewhere; that would have given him more of a potential for national security defense than he was able to mount in the case against him. I never believed that it was a national security break-in, and if it was, instead of using people on your own staff, why not use people who were supposed to do those sorts of things when they are necessary for national security? What often happened in the White House was that the general gave a broad policy decision and then the others had to figure out how to implement it. Much like the Brookings—when we ever hear the tape that he now said in his memoir he even authorized—the surreptitious entry into the Brookings—he might have said something similar, as far as: Well, let's get stuff on Ellsberg. That's the same thing they are looking for, in a sense. It's all in the same motif, so the overall policy was: Get it any way you have to; I don't care.

° In March 1973.

William Saxbe The order for the surveillance of Dr. Fielding was signed by Mitchell. He had requested it; it came over from the White House.

Samuel Dash, chief counsel, Senate Select Committee on Watergate Ehrlichman signed off on the Ellsberg break-in; I had the memorandum. Interestingly enough, we learned that all of [Jeb Stuart] Magruder's files for the Committee to Reelect the President [CRP] were sent over to the archives to record the history of the election. We thought we ought to look at these files, although our original view was that if you are a sophisticated obstructionist, you are not going to keep incriminating files; we thought that they would have screened the files. I sent some college students over to the archives with a subpoena; they found dozens and dozens of "eyes only," confidential memoranda—from Haldeman and Ehrlichman—admitting the dangers of the operations described, if they were caught. These memoranda were distributed to a small group, and Magruder was on the distribution list. I don't know if he ever read them. I think he got them, put them in his file, and then sent them over to the archives. When the White House needs approval for a specific action—by the president or a top staff person—a memorandum is written, with little boxes to be marked Approved, Approved with Qualification, or Disapproved. In the memorandum on the Fielding break-in, the approval box was checked with Ehrlichman's initials.

Seymour Glanzer [David R.] Young had the document that showed that Ehrlichman had ordered the break-in at Dr. Fielding's office. Without that document, it would have been difficult to deal with Ehrlichman.

G. Gordon Liddy Nixon probably was genuinely surprised when he heard about the Fielding break-in. Ehrlichman may not have shared it with him on the grounds of plausible denial. The most plausible denial is the truth—you just don't tell the guy—you don't go in to the president of the United States and say, "Boss, guess where our guys are going to break in tonight?" The same thing with Watergate; he didn't know the facts when Dean finally told him nine months later.

Richard Moore It is my theory that the president could have said: That son-of-a-gun! He has betrayed the country. Find out about him; we ought to hang him up by the nails. That guy ought to suffer and be punished—it's the theme of Henry II: "Will no one relieve me of this priest?" Somebody, probably Ehrlichman, reported this to Bud Krogh and said: The president really wants something done. They thought the psychiatrist might have information about communist ties, so my theory is that Nixon said: That fellow should not be allowed to get away with this. And it is translated into these two kooks—Liddy and Hunt—playing cops and robbers, and putting on red wigs and going out there.

WHY NOT THE FBI?

Daniel Ellsberg They didn't want to hand Hoover a blackmail capacity against the White House. An order to him to commit a crime [the break-in] would go into his safe as insurance against his being fired, so they couldn't give this domestic-type crime to Hoover; they needed a special unit for this. The background to all of this is the Huston Plan for domestic intelligence, which Hoover had first approved, then backed off from.

THE HUSTON PLAN

H. R. Haldeman It resulted from the president's having been informed by various sources that our intelligence system was not satisfactory. There was a lot of backbiting and infighting within the intelligence community that was part of the cause and the result of this inefficiency. He got tired of hearing this and not doing anything about it. He had a feeling that one of the great, glaring weaknesses was the infighting between foreign and domestic intelligence, and that, from his viewpoint, he needed the two to work together because we knew, for example, that some of the demonstrators and agitators that were very effective within this country in stirring up the rallies and anti-Vietnam [war] stuff were being trained in Algeria by foreign people. But we couldn't grasp what the relationship was between cause and effect, and that frustrated him.

So he called all these intelligence people into the Oval Office one day and said, "I am not going to tolerate this anymore. I want you people to get together. I am appointing all of you as an interagency intelligence task force, to come up with a plan to get good intelligence, properly evaluated and properly presented, in a timely fashion, to be presented to the president so that he can take action." He made Hoover chairman of the task force—which was a real slap at the CIA, and I think that was intentional. And he made a low-level staff person who was a buddy of Pat Buchanan's, Tom Huston, coordinator of the White House with Hoover and this task force.

The task force put a plan together; they all signed off on it. It became known as the Huston Plan, because he was the White House staff person who transmitted it to the president. The plan called for various means of domestic intelligence, interrelated to foreign intelligence. It was signed off on by J. Edgar Hoover, as chairman of the task force. No sooner was the plan signed off on and delivered than Hoover tiptoed quickly over to John Mitchell and said, "This is a terrible plan; it must not be carried forth." And Mitchell walked forthrightly in to the president and said, "I feel this is a terrible plan and must not be carried forth," and it was abolished.

There is a lot lying beneath the surface of this simple story, but most of it I don't know. It arose from the desire to beef up the quality, quantity, and usability of U.S. security information and intelligence, and it got sidetracked by internal fighting and, probably, an ill-conceived plan. But maybe it was designed to be ill-conceived, to make sure it was sunk. You can chalk that up to my paranoia, but I don't think it was paranoid. I believe it is a realistic appraisal of an inefficient group of organizations who, at that time, were not doing well within each of the agencies, and were not cooperating with each other in a way that would make them truly useful to the chief executive.

John Dean I liked Len Garment; I was open with him. I tried to convince them through him, at one point, that I wasn't going to be a scapegoat. What I was thinking of at that point was the Huston Plan, which I had taken, for my own protection, because I didn't know if they were going to blame that on me, too—the whole Huston Plan and the documents approving it. And it's nothing in a sense but a precursor to Watergate. Hoover, at the time the plan was developed, was having trouble working with anybody, on anything, and he didn't want his agents working with the CIA and other investigative agencies included in that plan. In fact, what we now know is that a number of things that were in the Huston Plan were actually going on; some of the mail covers and the wiretapping of newsmen were going on; one of the better-kept secrets around the White House was the fact they had been having electronic surveillance on newsmen. That's pretty amazing.

That alone—trying to put a national security cover on those things to make them palatable—that to me was in a whole different league than a bungled break-in at the Watergate.

John Ehrlichman Kissinger was preoccupied with Ellsberg. He very volubly explained to Nixon what a bad man Daniel Ellsberg was. He had been his student, his protégé. Kissinger had kept track of him for years, and he cited chapter and verse of what a threat to the nation he was, because he possessed a whole lot of secrets—well beyond anything in the Pentagon

Papers: the plans for missile counterattack, what was targeted, how the system worked. Kissinger convinced Nixon early on of the merits of Daniel Ellsberg. Without that, there would not have been the impetus when the word came that Hoover would not investigate Ellsberg. That probably would have been the end of it. Hoover didn't pursue the Ellsberg situation because Daniel Ellsberg's father-in-law, Louis Marx, was Hoover's very close friend. He was a toy manufacturer and he would bring toys to the FBI at Christmas; he would host Hoover at the race track; and Hoover forbade his people from pursuing Ellsberg. In fact, one agent got into serious trouble with the director. It was his case, and he had gone further than Hoover wanted. As a result, I think, he was demoted. The report came over to us from the assistant attorney general that he could not move the bureau against Ellsberg. Nixon saw the principle that secrecy had been violated as a serious problem.

Daniel Ellsberg According to the record, they were close friends, but they never met. Louis Marx had the nice habit of sending loads of toys out; he had a huge list of people to whom he would send them. Hoover was on that list. Marx was a conservative Republican who admired Hoover; he was one of his heroes, but he told my wife that he had actually never met Hoover. He was on a Friend of the FBI list, and the FBI would do him favors. He [Louis Marx] would have liked nothing more than to put me in prison; to him, I was a bad guy—a traitor.

10

And Why?

Bernard Barker Hunt asked the CIA to do a profile on Ellsberg. At first they refused, saying that the subject was a U.S. citizen; they could do one on Nikita Khrushchev, but not on Ellsberg. Then Hunt reminded them that they had produced a profile on the captain of the *Pueblo*,* and that if they could do one on him, they damn sure could do one on a man who might be a traitor. Well, they did the profile, but it was so stupid that they were asked to do it again. The second one was no better than the first. It was then, according to Hunt, that a decision was made to create a separate investigative apparatus. Hunt told his superiors that he knew Cubans in Miami who were loyal to him. That is how I was recruited—which he did on the basis of national security: they had decided to find out what was behind Ellsberg; what kind of person they were dealing with. They had traced some of the leaks directly to this sector. They were pretty sure his records were in the psychiatrist's office.

Richard Helms There wasn't any question that the request came from the White House. David Young requested it; the agency collaborated. We had done profiles like this on foreign leaders. It was probably, in retrospect, a mistake to have done this profile, but in was done, and it was done with my okay.

---

* Lloyd Bucher. The *Pueblo* had been captured by the North Koreans off the North Korean Coast and was said to be carrying surveillance materials.

I don't have any recollection anymore of what the criticisms [of the pro-file] were. I was amazed at the break-in. Since we had absolutely nothing to do with their analysis of what was going on—or with the break-in, or the problems connected therewith—I don't think I discussed it with the White House; it was none of our business.

G. Gordon Liddy We had asked the FBI to get his medical records, but they tried and failed. That was when we were given the task, in writing, to go in there and get the medical records. The FBI had said—undoubtedly from a wiretap—that although Ellsberg had terminated the services of the psychi-atrist, Fielding, some time back, he was nevertheless telephoning the psychi-atrist almost daily—at all hours of the day and night—revealing to him the most intimate details of his daily life. We figured if he was doing this, then—on something so central to his existence as giving out the Pentagon Papers—he might have told the doctor whether he was the one who had given the material to the Soviet Union; he might have told the doctor whether he was in the show with the KGB; he might have told the doctor what else he had—what plans he had. The doctor might have put this information in his files.

John Ehrlichman They expected to find evidence to corroborate what Hunt had been saying about Ellsberg's mental unbalance: that he was a drug user; he shot at peasants in Vietnam from a helicopter; he had a ménage à trois with two women. The catalog went on and on.

Robert Mardian The reason they went into Fielding's office was they wanted to show that Ellsberg was a sexual deviant, that he was crazy. The press was eulogizing Ellsberg, so the idea was: Let's show them what Ells-berg really is like. And, apparently, there was evidence that he was a sexual deviant, and whatever else he was going to the psychiatrist for.

Ben Bradlee When you think about it, it's like swatting a fly with an ICBM. What did you need to break into a psychiatrist's office for? My God. That's awful. Think of the trouble it caused them. The administration had the sense that people who were against the war were all hippies, commies, free lovers; they paraded topless, and they had committed the most egregious sins. Maybe, even, a lot of them were Jewish. Certainly Nixon—and some of those people around Nixon—felt that way.

Daniel Ellsberg Where Nixon got into trouble on Vietnam was that he chose ambitious goals that were hard to achieve: not a disguised defeat, but a practical victory. This strategy was likely to lead to an escalation of the war that had to be kept secret, and this had many consequences. If somebody threatened to blow the whistle, Nixon had to take action; he had to try to plug the leak, hence, the Plumbers. Specifically, he believed after I put out the Pentagon Papers that I knew his secret policy of escalation in detail; that I knew the nuclear target plan. I could have known this—I knew people who could have told me of it, but they hadn't. He thought I might have documents—he knew I had NSSM 1. So he knew that I had administration documents that I hadn't yet put out, so it was quite plausible—not paranoid—that I might know things, if revealed, which could be very serious for Nixon politically.

G. Gordon Liddy In the narrative part of the Pentagon Papers, there are constant excerpts and citations from top-secret code-word material—backchannel traffic. In the other part is the full reproduction of the entire texts of those documents. Ellsberg himself had said, "I gave the material to the *New York Times*." The FBI investigation determined that in the in-and-out logs, the accounting for the top-secret holdings of the Rand Corporation were a mess; people were going in and out, and not logging anything.

Daniel Ellsberg The fact is that Rand kept much closer control of top-secret material than anywhere [else] I had worked in Washington; top-secret material was handled very carefully at Rand and, in fact, there was not very much of it: about one to two percent of the total was top secret, and of that, perhaps one-tenth of one percent was not logged in. And I was the custodian of the Pentagon Papers. The material was in my safe; I didn't have to go to anyone else's safe. [Paul] Warneke, [Morton] Halperin, and [Leslie] Gelb had wanted me to keep the Pentagon Papers out of Rand's top-secret system. A year or so ago, Mort explained to me the reasons: they were convinced that someone like Walt [W.] Rostow,* in the name of Johnson, might find out the whereabouts of this material and insist that it all be destroyed.

G. Gordon Liddy They knew that Ellsberg had extracted more than the Pentagon Papers from there [the Rand Corporation], but they had no way of knowing what it was, because the logs were incomplete. They knew that Ellsberg had it stashed away somewhere. At about the time that Ellsberg said he gave this to the *New York Times*, the FBI's constant surveillance on the 16th Street embassy of the Soviet Union picked up the fact that some-

* National security adviser to President Johnson during his full term in office, 1965–69.

one had given the Soviets the whole shooting match, including the material not published by the *New York Times,* and God knows what else. Nobody knew whether Ellsberg was what a lot of people were characterizing as a romantic lover of the left—acting out of conscience—or whether this guy is in the show with the KGB, à la Kim Philby.* We didn't know, so we needed to find out as much about Ellsberg as we could.

Bernard Barker I believe that if a man is giving up secret information, that is treason. I believe that Daniel Ellsberg is a traitor to his country, and I believe that traitors should be dealt with much more strongly than they did [with Ellsberg].

Robert Mardian Ellsberg had stolen the top-secret documents from the Rand Corporation, and that is a crime, and it's under the jurisdiction of the Internal Security Division of the Department of Justice. But they were being published in all the newspapers, so it didn't add anything.

Jerry Jones The idea that somebody could dump what Nixon and Kissinger considered extremely sensitive material on the public record and have it printed was absolute treason. I think that they also felt a lot of their intelligence stuff was being compromised. Whether that is a rational view or not, that's what they thought; that's what I thought.

Yuri Barsukov I never heard about this idea that Ellsberg gave material to the Soviet Embassy, and the Soviet ambassador in Washington did not know about this. I only learned about Ellsberg from the publication of the Pentagon Papers in the *New York Times*.

Daniel Ellsberg The origin of the charge that I gave material to the Soviets is quite complicated: A double agent, code-named Fedora, who was an FBI source, said that a copy of the Pentagon Papers had been given to the Soviet Embassy. When I heard this, I thought: the Plumbers could have done that to set up an espionage slant against me; they had plenty of copies of the papers. After my trial, I began to get calls from reporters in Boston who told me, "There is a guy in prison here for murdering his homosexual lover, saying that he committed the killing in a dispute over the proceeds of selling the Pentagon Papers to the Soviet Embassy. He says that his lover got the papers from you, as blackmail on your homosexual affair with the

---

* A British spy for the Soviet Union, who fled to Moscow to escape arrest.

lover." My first impression on hearing this was: That's a funny one. Then, a couple of these reporters kept saying, "You had better take this more seriously; this guy sounds plausible." I said, "Does he have any evidence?" They said, "He is very detailed; he described this bar in Boston he saw you in on December 23, 1970." So I said, "Look, I don't go into bars, I never had a homosexual affair, and on December 23, 1970, I was on vacation in Morocco with my wife—and had been there for ten days."

It turned out that the man had told this story to my prosecutor, who realized the account was full of holes. But the man's lawyer gave us a transcript of what the men had said they gave to the Soviet Embassy. In fact, it was a typescript of exactly what had appeared in the *New York Times*. From Fedora, Hunt and Liddy got a report that the Soviet Embassy had a copy of the papers. Helms, on the other hand, discounted Fedora's story.

Raymond Price Nobody knew if Ellsberg had any additional material. We didn't know what we were dealing with. I don't believe the president even knew who Ellsberg was. Kissinger did—and probably had more animus, because he felt betrayed by Ellsberg, in whom he had trusted.

Leonard Garment The Fielding break-in, to paraphrase a nineteenth-century leader, was worse than a felony; it was a blunder. It was like a man-of-war, with all these poisonous, long, filamentlike threads hanging down, that can kill you; but right on top is the master intelligence for all of these spikes. The central decision made was: we are going to get information. How do we do this? We need an organization. The FBI isn't going to do this; J. Edgar Hoover is out dancing tonight. The CIA can't operate domestically, so we are going to have the Plumbers.

It's 1970—the counterrevolution; Cambodia; Kent State. The Huston Plan is no good, so we are going to have our own little intelligence organization. It does prove a point about American politics—that we have a system calculated to keep things reasonably in place by not having an intelligence operation, with bugging and black bag jobs and red wigs, in the White House. It's all so wonderful. How could anyone even dream up this story? So you have the Plumbers: Young is from Kissinger's office; Bud Krogh is Ehrlichman's guy; Liddy's for Dean; and Hunt's for Colson. Nobody could say: I didn't have anything to do with it. They were all in the act, both for its gain and its trouble. And the whole operation exists for Haldeman and the president. It's reasonably compartmentalized—they all have their responsibilities, except that Liddy is semipsychotic at the time; he's since recovered.

Their first operation is Ellsberg—the Fielding break-in. The Pentagon

Papers had been released, and they had gone through those crazy gyrations with Kissinger: everything is compromised unless we go after Ellsberg. Ellsberg is indicted. They are trying to discredit him; it's hard to find anything. There is talk of his throwing people out of airplanes; his relationships with men and with women. They can't find anything; they order a profile from the CIA. It comes back. It's like Psychology 101; the man has an anxiety neurosis. So they decide that they'll get the real stuff—this is Hunt, the writer of those forty-two novels written on the basis of real-life events that were fictionalized. Hunt's life consisted of the concoctions that were the raw material of his books; he couldn't find enough in his own imagination, so he did all these crazy things, and then he wrote about them in these completely mediocre books. So they go out there and do this insane thing, and take these photographs of themselves standing in front of the parking place with the name Fielding to prove that they were there.

11

Dr. Ellsberg's Trial

In connection with the release of the Pentagon Papers, Dr. Daniel Ellsberg was indicted on June 28, 1971, on two counts: theft of government property; and unauthorized possession of documents and writings related to the national defense. On December 29, 1971, a new, fifty-count indictment was handed down, in which Dr. Ellsberg was charged with misappropriation of government property; violation of statutes prohibiting the unauthorized use of classified information; and violation of statutes involving espionage and conspiracy. Included in the indictment was Anthony J. Russo.

The trial of Ellsberg and Russo began in Los Angeles on January 18, 1973, with Federal District Court Judge Matthew F. Byrne, Jr., presiding. Misconduct by the Nixon administration in two areas led Judge Byrne, on May 11, 1973, to dismiss the charges against Ellsberg and Russo.

On April 26, Judge Byrne had learned that a break-in had occurred at the office of Ellsberg's psychiatrist, Dr. Lewis Fielding, involving members of the Plumbers Unit. The following day, he read a Justice Department memorandum, in open court, describing the break-in, and ordered an investigation to determine if the defendants' rights had been violated.

Then, on May 9, Judge Byrne received a memorandum from Acting FBI Director William Ruckelshaus, disclosing the existence of a wiretap overhearing Ellsberg speaking on a telephone at Morton Halperin's home. When the judge requested the logs of the wiretaps, he was told by the Justice Department that the government did not have the logs, tapes, or other records pertaining to the overhearing. Byrne's dismissal of the charges precluded the government from retrying the defendants.

William H. Sullivan Bill Rogers and I discussed this at some length and we came to the conclusion that if they wanted to charge Ellsberg with anything, it should be larceny—stealing something valued at over $100. That would get him one or two years in jail, and that would be the best thing they could do. Instead, they pushed it to say that this was a great impediment to the American war effort; that we suffered serious damage. And they wanted me to be a witness in the trial, and I refused to testify because I said it wasn't, and I wasn't going to testify to the contrary. Instead, they got Phil Habib to go make these rather foolish statements. When he [Ellsberg] was acquitted, Rogers and I said that if they had gone for our $100 larceny case, they could have gotten this guy. Instead, they made a hero and a martyr out of him and lost their case.

Daniel Ellsberg During my trial in Los Angeles in 1973, I saw Dr. Fielding weekly, just to talk; he was someone who could see how I was reacting under the pressure of the trial. He told me, "I can't guarantee that my office is secure." I asked, "What do you mean?" He answered, "They could be tapping"—he knew that his office had been broken into, and that a bug could have been planted.

Richard Kleindienst The thing that blew the Ellsberg case apart was that it developed during the course of it that one of the assistant attorneys general found out that there were records in the Department of Justice that should have been turned over to Ellsberg's attorneys and had not been—not deliberately, but inadvertently. I had recused myself from the case. Henry Petersen [head of the Criminal Division, Department of Justice] was informed of this fact, and he went over to the president and told him we had to turn this material over to Ellsberg's attorneys. Henry related to me that the president forbade him to do it. On that day, I said to Henry, "I'm going over to talk to the president myself. And when I get back, I might not be attorney general." But I went over to see the president and told him we had to do it, and he said, "There's no problem about that." So it was the information that had not been disclosed to his attorneys that led to a dismissal of the Ellsberg case.

Robert Mardian There were things that killed that trial. One was that there was an overhearing of Ellsberg that was not disclosed. Those were the so-called Kissinger tapes. I had possession of the Kissinger tapes. They were not indexed. Everything else—all of the warrantless wiretaps—are indexed. And every time, before we go to court in a case, we would ask the FBI, "Do you have overhearings on any of these individuals?" In Ellsberg's case the tap had been on Morton Halperin's phone. Kissinger suspected him—that's why they call them the Kissinger taps; they were trying to find out where the leaks were coming from in Kissinger's office. All of those taps were out of channel; they were not indexed.

When Hoover was getting ready to fire William Sullivan—the FBI's associate director—Sullivan called me and told me, "There are some very sensitive documents that Hoover might use to blackmail Nixon." I was told five times that Hoover would be fired. The last time, for sure, they told me was on October 5, 1971. Five of his six top people were in my office, waiting for the call from the White House that they finally got it done; we never got it. In any event, Sullivan felt that Hoover might use this material to get his way with Nixon, so he gave the material to me.

I immediately called Haldeman. He talked to the president, who said, "Give them to Ehrlichman," and I delivered two suitcases. In there was the Halperin tap and there was an overhearing of Ellsberg talking to Halperin. After I left office I was back in Phoenix. I was interviewed by the FBI—Ruckelshaus was then the FBI director—about the whereabouts of the Halperin material; somebody had said they were destroyed. They wanted to know if it was true that I had destroyed the taps. I said, "No. On instructions from the president, I gave them to Ehrlichman." They were incredulous: "You're sure you didn't have them destroyed?" I said, "No. My instructions were to give them to Ehrlichman." With that, the FBI went to Ehrlichman's office and got them. They went through them and they saw the overhearing.

The FBI now did what they ordinarily would have done—they started indexing them, because it was going to foul up a lot of prosecutions. And in indexing them, they saw the overhearing of Ellsberg, and the Ellsberg trial was going on. I don't know whether there was any nexus between that information coming out and the meeting that Ehrlichman had with Judge Byrne. He had invited Judge Byrne to the Western White House. The crux of dismissing the case was that we had tried the case without informing Ellsberg of the overhearing. The Byrne-Ehrlichman deal was a side issue.

One aspect of the Nixon administration's style was demonstrated in the early spring of 1973, when a replacement was being sought for Acting FBI Director Patrick Gray. While the Ellsberg-Russo trial was in progress in Los Angeles, John Ehrlichman invited the presiding judge, Matthew Byrne, to San Clemente for—as the judge put it—discussion of a nonjudicial matter. At San Clemente, where Byrne met briefly with Nixon, Ehrlichman told the judge that the president wanted to know if he was available for the FBI job.

Judge Byrne has said that he informed Ehrlichman that he could not consider any position until the Ellsberg-Russo trial concluded.

Daniel Ellsberg At the beginning of my trial, the gossip columnist Dorothy Kilgallen said that Judge Matthew Byrne was the likely candidate to succeed J. Edgar Hoover, who was still alive. Some of my lawyers said that we should ask for Byrne to be removed as the judge presiding over my trial, but I was against the idea. In retrospect, I think that Byrne had reason to believe from his friend, Kleindienst, that the Nixon administration had its eye on him. At the trial, I noticed that the prosecutor—normally a very competent person—was not doing his homework, and he was very insubordinate to the judge; I could not understand this. But now, I believe that it was because he felt: the fix is in; this guy wants to be head of the FBI, so we are going to offer it to him, and so I don't have to work too hard at this trial.

Richard Moore The suggestion that the offer to Judge Byrne to be FBI director had any relation to that is absurd; the president was much taken with Byrne long before there was any Ellsberg case. Byrne was an Irish Catholic; he had been executive director of the Crime Commission's report. He was even a bachelor. He was perfect for the FBI job.

Part Four

The Second Administration

———

12

The 1972 Campaign

As President Nixon and his associates looked toward the 1972 election, they were mindful of the extreme closeness of the 1960 election—which Mr. Nixon lost to John F. Kennedy—and the 1968 election—where he narrowly defeated Vice-President Hubert Humphrey.

The mood in the White House was one of determination to squeeze out every last possible vote, and to develop the campaign organization and finances required to accomplish this task.

Mr. Nixon's first task was to convince his 1968 campaign manager, John Mitchell, to leave his post as attorney general and run his final election effort. Then there was the job of staffing both the Committee to Reelect the President and the Finance Committee to Reelect the President—the two organizations that would conduct the campaign effort.

The intense desire to win a mandate led the campaign into controversial and illegal areas, such as the "Black Advance"—or dirty tricks activities— and the development of intelligence operations, which would culminate in the break-in at the headquarters of the Democratic National Committee.

As the White House began its campaign planning in late 1971, President Nixon's potential rivals included Mr. Humphrey; Senators Edmund Muskie and George McGovern; and, possibly, Senator Edward Kennedy, who was seen as a rival even though his involvement in the summer of 1969 in the death of Mary Jo Kopechne at Chappaquiddick Island, Massachusetts, continued to be discussed whenever his name was mentioned as a presidential contender.

Another major factor in determining Nixon's strategy was the third-party candidacy of Alabama Governor George C. Wallace, whose American Independent Party had in 1968 won 13 percent of the popular vote. Wallace's 1972 presidential ambitions came to a tragic end on May 15, when a gunman* severely wounded him at a Maryland shopping center.

* Arthur Bremer.

THE RUN-UP TO THE 1972
PRESIDENTIAL CAMPAIGN

Charles Colson In 1970, as Nixon began to think of the off-year elections, he called on me and Harry Dent,* who were the only people in the White House with much grassroots political experience; Haldeman and Ehrlichman were not really politicians, nor was Mitchell. I had cut my teeth running political campaigns in Massachusetts in the 1950s, so we kind of talked the same language.

Hugh Sloan, White House aide, Scheduling and Appointments Office; treasurer, Committee to Reelect the President It was clear in 1971 that the president was under political attack, not only from the Democratic side, but also from Republicans—with announced candidates to the right and left—which forced a commitment to structuring the reelection effort, I would suspect, earlier than Nixon wanted. It was also clear that he intended to rely on Mitchell and Stans to run that campaign. Since both of them were Cabinet officers at that point, it was premature to have them step down, so that was the point at which they asked a number of us to step out of White House roles, or other government roles, to set up the initial campaign organization.

The campaign objective was to have a mandate—as opposed to the first election. In the first term, his interests were primarily international, and because of that—and the constitution of the Congress—there was a feeling that there was a limited ability to affect the domestic agenda, and that only with a much stronger mandate would he have that ability in the second term.

Maurice Stans I was having a good time at the Department of Commerce. I didn't want to leave; I had no desire whatever to get into that 1972 campaign. However, one way or another, they began prodding me about it—never directly from the president, never directly from Haldeman, but one way or another, I was asked: "Maury, are you going to get into the campaign and raise money again? Who else could do the job?" and that sort of thing. Questions began coming at me from different directions, and then I would get a question from, perhaps, Colson: If you got into the campaign, and the president won, what job would you like to have? Well, I didn't want a job; I was going to be sixty-five when the election was over. I thought I would like to retire.

---

* Southern political liaison, Nixon administration.

In December, [CRP official Herbert] Kalmbach came back at me and said, "Maury, the campaign is going to heat up pretty soon and they haven't found anybody that can take your place." At Christmas, I said, "Herb, this is all coming from the White House. Who is the guy I should talk to?" He said, "No. These are my ideas." I said, "Who do you report to?" He said, "I don't report to anybody." Well, he wasn't telling me the truth, of course—and I knew it and he knew it. I finally thought of it this way: if the head of the team wants you to take a certain position, and do a certain job, you ought to do it, or get out; I can't stay on and expect to stay on as secretary of commerce if I don't do what the boss wants me to do in the meantime.

I got a call from Nixon the day after I agreed to do it. He said he was delighted to hear it, and Haldeman and the others were highly pleased. I had for several months before that been meeting with Sloan and talking to him about what was going on and advising him, so I had given some sign of interest. The same thing happened to John Mitchell, I am sure; I am sure that the pressure built up on him, the idea that he was the only one who could run the campaign. John held out a lot longer than I did, until May.

Hugh Sloan You had had a change in the campaign law halfway through the election, where disclosure was required in the new law—not in the old one. This was money that had been raised in the prior period—and had been raised by Maury [Stans] with personal representations that there would be nondisclosure. I believe he felt a great personal obligation to protect the anonymity of people who had contributed in that earlier period. He asked me to prepare a final—in one copy only—report based on these cash books that could give him the contributors and the amounts related to that period. I gave it to him. Herb Kalmbach had been raising some money for Maury as well and presumably had done something similar. I guess I asked him, "Stans wanted one copy; what do we do with these things?" [the cash book], and Herb said, "I'm destroying these, and think you should do the same." I wasn't totally comfortable with this, but I knew there was, in effect, a copy with Maury, so I thought there was protection from that standpoint. That copy disappeared.

William Rusher In January of 1972, about twenty of us conservatives met with John Mitchell. During the entire meeting and afterward, as he greeted us, Mitchell was shaking like a leaf; he was as nervous and tense as could be. It was not us. Maybe it was Martha [Mitchell's wife, who was rumored to be mentally unstable]; she was enough to make anyone tense. But this was at about the time he was examining plans for the campaign.

Jeb Stuart Magruder, special assistant to the president; deputy director, Committee to Reelect the President (CRP) I'd say John was certainly preoccupied. After our first meeting, when we decided how we were going to work together with him still over at Justice as the attorney general, and me [being] the "director" of the campaign at that time, he said to me, "By the way, you are going to have to deal with my wife," so I became responsible for her, as well. That was a very different task.

Donald E. Santarelli He did not want to leave the job of attorney general to run the campaign, but there is a very deep-seated principle in America that when the president calls, you generally respond. Presidents are pretty good at using that line. I did not want to go to LEAA at all; I did not want to be an administrator. But the president was very insistent, and he did it very skillfully. He said, "I need you." It's very heady stuff. Then you had Haldeman saying, "If you don't do it, you'll probably regret it." Mitchell, like many people, did not see himself as adopting Washington as his new home. He disliked a lot of the trappings of Washington; he disliked the professional types who thought they knew it all; he certainly disliked the *Washington Post,* and it disliked him; so he wasn't comfortable in Washington.

Maurice Stans I don't think he disliked Washington. I think he had a problem with Washington, which was a very difficult one for him—and that was Martha. She was a strange woman; she misbehaved a great deal, did a lot of drinking and didn't conceal it publicly. She was a lot of fun when she was on the verge of it. I think John was embarrassed quite a number of times by Martha. He thought the place had too many temptations for Martha. I think he would have preferred to stay in Washington.

Jerry Jones Mitchell absolutely didn't want to run the campaign again—just like Stans didn't want to raise money again. President Nixon simply insisted: "We have to win this, and we are going to pull out all the stops and put the best team on the field, and you're going to do it." Lawyers don't run things the way managers do. So, at a policy level, Mitchell was "hands-on," but he was not really involved in what was going on. In fact, after the Watergate break-in, he was completely befuddled.

Richard Kleindienst I think the only reason he would want to get out of government was because of Martha Mitchell's problems. She was just handmade for the Washington press. She was a very volatile person. She had health problems—had been in some kind of care home before the election.

She was not completely mentally well; I don't say she was insane, but she had a lot of emotional problems. The press attention she was getting was very disturbing to John and to the president. Her total conduct was distracting to John; he knew he had to go home every night. My wife and I got to know Martha quite well. It was a very difficult domestic situation. Very, very volatile.

Robert Reisner, White House aide; assistant to the deputy director, CRP Up until March 1972, Mitchell was attorney general and supervised the campaign in only the most general sense. Magruder would go over to brief him, and sometimes Dean, who had the Justice Department account [as liaison], might join him. In this period, Mitchell overlooked some details that caught up with him later: in March, he was totally preoccupied with the ITT scandal, and with Martha, who was a problem at that time—she was really out of control. Mitchell was reduced by all of that; he was tired, and went to Key Biscayne. And, ultimately, some of his big errors in judgment occurred down there. In the spring [of 1972], he joined the Nixon Mudge law firm, in Washington—his office was directly across from the campaign [headquarters]—and he spent his time seeing political people from around the country, so he wasn't ever really involved in the operation of the campaign. Then, in June, everything fell apart.

Richard Kleindienst Mitchell pretty much delegated the day-to-day operations of the Justice Department to me. He was not only busy being attorney general, but he was also busy as a very close adviser to Nixon—one or two of Nixon's primary advisers; he was on the National Security Council. Because of his proximity to the president, he was able to erect a shield between the Department of Justice and the White House staff. I think John felt he, in effect, got Nixon elected as president; he was very proud of that fact. He was a very able man, a very good attorney general, a man of real breadth and capacity. The downfall came when he went over to the Reelection Committee.

RECRUITMENT OF CAMPAIGN PERSONNEL

Terrence O'Donnell I was a captain in the Air Force, and through Alex Butterfield—who had been a military assistant to my father, a general officer in the Air Force—I was introduced to Dwight Chapin in April 1971. I came on board at the White House in late May of 1972, and was initially assigned to the advance office, under Ron Walker, from June until the convention, when I worked in the control trailer as an assistant to Chapin, and I worked for him from the convention until the election, and immediately afterward I was assigned to work with Bob Haldeman. At the convention, I was working around the clock. It was a great experience to see all of it unfold. I was in charge of the president's box, making sure that various luminaries from the public and private sectors were present at all times, so that the television [cameras] could sweep and cover them.

Robert Reisner Magruder was a young man on the move—thirty-six at the time. He had all the marbles in his hand; it was a very fast-paced existence, in which the White House or the attorney general's office was calling. He put on the charm and said to me, "Come over here. You'll be in the middle of a national campaign. How many people get to see that? It will be great fun." I went back to the White House to see Fred Malek. I said, "I'm not sure I want to do this." He looked me in the eye and said, "You'd be out of your mind not to do this," so in November of 1971, I joined the campaign.

G. Gordon Liddy When Ehrlichman became head of the Domestic Council, they needed a replacement for the job of counsel to the president. This was no longer a high-powered job, so they looked around for a nerd and came up with John Dean. He inherited two men: one was John Caulfield, a former New York City police intelligence agent, and through Caulfield, Anthony Ulasewicz. They did off-the-books investigations. They didn't need the FBI to do political stuff: they had their own guys. Dean realized that the way to increase his influence was through political intelligence, so when Caulfield—to Dean's dismay—decided to resign to set up his own detective agency, Dean—to his horror—realized he was going to lose his operative, so I was recruited. I worked under Ehrlichman and Krogh. When I had something for the president, I would give it to them. Mr. Ehrlichman would take it in to the president, and he would report to me what my grades were.

THE COMMITTEE TO REELECT THE PRESIDENT (CRP)

Frederic V. Malek We helped to staff CRP, but Mitchell essentially had Magruder there as his front-line guy. When I went over to CRP as deputy director, after Watergate [the break-in], I didn't think it was well organized or well directed. I thought it was a loosely formed confederation of people. I think I brought a lot of organizational discipline to CRP. We put a lot of emphasis on our field operation; we had a lot of money to spend.

Robert Odle, Jr. I was asked to be one of the first five people to organize the Reelection Committee. Many people were critical of President Nixon for having an independent reelection committee, separate from the Republican National Committee. What they overlooked in that criticism is that, at the time—before China and other successes had had a chance to settle in— he had two challengers for the nomination: [members of the U.S. House of Representatives] John Ashbrook [R-Ohio] from the right and Paul McCloskey [R-Calif.] from the left. Although there was never any doubt that Nixon was going to be the nominee, he could not technically use the Republican National Committee. I remember being assigned to get a name for the committee, and I went to Bill [William] Safire—who didn't spend as much time on it as he might have, and came up with Citizens for the Reelection of the President. We later changed Citizens to Committee, but we never realized the acronym CRP [CREEP] would arise. I always kidded Bill about that.

Alexander Butterfield Haldeman formed the committee. He had one of his junior aides, Gordon Strachan, as the liaison between him and the committee, and the president met with John Mitchell, the head of the thing, almost every night, over in the EOB [Executive Office Building].

Jeb Stuart Magruder Nothing was done in the campaign that I did not basically initiate. I formed the advertising agency, the November Group; I set up the polling situation; we set up the group that developed the campaign strategy; we set up every group, and everything, that related to a political campaign.

John Mitchell asked me to run the campaign, in a sense. He was still at Justice. Obviously, all decisions that I recommended went first to Mitchell and then to Haldeman. I can't think of any decision that I asked for that John ever turned down—or was then turned down by Haldeman—except for the one decision that I asked them to make, which was to fire Liddy.

G. Gordon Liddy The 1972 campaign was coming up. Bud Krogh called me and said, "John Dean wants to pitch you on something." He added that he wanted to be at the meeting. I said, "You have a right to, because I am working for you. Besides, any time you have anything to do with Dean, you ought to have a witness." There had been a political intelligence plan called Sandwedge, developed by John Caulfield, who was working for Dean.

Dean thought it was inadequate; he wanted an all-out intelligence plan. I said to him, "You are talking about a lot of money." He replied, "How about a half million [dollars] for openers?" That had been the whole budget of Sandwedge, so he recruited me right there, in Krogh's office. I went over to CRP as general counsel; that was to be my cover. Dean had promised me a whole platoon of Republican lawyers to do the work, while I spent all my time on political intelligence. It didn't work out that way; I was working all day as general counsel and all night as the intelligence guy.

John Dean Jeb Magruder called and asked for somebody who could come over to CRP and be general counsel, which was important because our office was doing a lot of the work and it was taking up a lot of time, and it was growing increasingly difficult for our small staff to do our work and do the Reelection Committee's work also. My first reaction was that a good candidate for that job was David Young. He and I had just been flying all over the country, interviewing Supreme Court nominees. I liked David; he had a nice manner. I mentioned this to John Mitchell, and we talked generally about the job; it was either in that conversation—or sometime around there—or in a conversation with Haldeman, that the idea [of intelligence] was raised.

One of the things we were very concerned about was demonstrations and demonstration intelligence, and that the committee not be totally relying on government information—which may or may not be something we should be sending to them. We didn't know. So they needed to be aware of that and, of course, the White House itself is always interested in political intelligence, so it was agreed that whoever was general counsel should handle these types of problems as well. And at about this time, Jack Caulfield had been trying to sell his Operation Sandwedge, so that is why this whole idea of political intelligence, and campaign intelligence, and demonstration intelligence, all came up, and Mitchell said, "This is something I want the general counsel to really handle out of his back pocket; it's a small part of the job." That was my understanding.

I talked to David Young, and he was interested but said, "I don't know if anyone else will let me go." So I went to talk to Bud Krogh about it, and he immediately said, "No. There is no way that we can let David Young go to that job." But, he said, "I've got somebody that I'd like to suggest for that job," and that was Gordon Liddy; that's where Gordon Liddy came from. I didn't become a champion of Liddy. I didn't know Gordon Liddy; at that time, I didn't know Liddy had been a part of the Plumbers and involved in the Ellsberg break-in. I learned all that much later. After Liddy went over to the Reelection Committee, he and Magruder were apparently oil and water; that became apparent very quickly. My office had dealings with Liddy, and I opened my election law files for Liddy to use, and he came over and used them. I've discovered there are a number of memos back and forth between my office and Liddy on election problems.

Jeb Stuart Magruder The first time I met Liddy was when John Dean called me and said, "Mitchell and Haldeman would like you to consider this guy for general counsel."

My response was, "Well, I've already got one who's doing fine." Dean's response was, "This man can do more than that."

Every other person I had hired had the approval of Mitchell, but they were people I knew. This guy comes over and starts talking this kind of "Gordon Liddy talk." I said to myself, I don't want this guy over here. And he tells me about his special capabilities. I did not know what he was talking about. So he leaves, and I call Dean and say, "I don't want this guy."

Dean replied, "There is a problem. You had better talk to Haldeman and Mitchell." So I talked to John and he said, "Haldeman really wants him hired over there. Maybe he can do some other things for us." I was still not sure what this other stuff was, so I called Haldeman, and he said, "Jeb, we want you to hire him." So I said, "All right," and we hired him.

Donald E. Santarelli Liddy ratcheted himself up. When he was at Justice, I could tell he was not suited for the usual roles: he was too restless and more operationally oriented than lawyerly oriented, so we sent him to the Treasury Department, where he would be a coordinator between Justice and Treasury on law enforcement activities. Liddy would report to me, but the Treasury people had a problem with us on turf matters, so we moved him out of that job and Krogh said, "I want him to work for me." I said, "Fine." And then I wrote a memorandum to Krogh: "Don't let Liddy operate unsupervised." The next thing I knew, Krogh told me that Liddy had been assigned the job of counsel to the Finance Committee of the Committee to Reelect.

Hugh Sloan We had a specific need for a legal counsel as we went through the campaign. Stans told me he had been asked to consider Liddy, from the political side of the campaign. He interviewed him and hired him. In a day-to-day sense, he was professional. I've often wondered when he had the time to do what has subsequently been ascribed to him. He put in a lot of hours on issues related to the campaign. He seemed perfectly normal at meetings—not the raving lunatic he has subsequently been described as.

In hindsight, you began to see the potential—the time he came back from Magruder with a budget ostensibly for campaign security, and it was in cash; it's sort of odd to have your legal counsel involved in those types of activities. This started the whole discussion about cash disbursements and the lack of control. Rather than approving and paying bills, you were giving money to the political campaign without any controls at all on how it was spent. The first issue was when Gordon came to me with regard to $83,600, which was a significant sum—particularly in cash. He told me Magruder had signed off, and if I had any questions about it, to talk to Jeb. I did talk to him to verify, and then went to Stans and wanted him to be aware of this, because I had a certain discomfort. He said he would talk to Mitchell about it. I was concerned that as treasurer I was being asked to disburse funds in a way that was off pattern to anything else we had done in the campaign to that point.

Stans came back to me and said, "Go ahead." One of the issues I had raised was the purpose of the funds. That was one of the early flags in my mind—where he said, "Go ahead. That's the political side's business; you don't want to know and I don't want to know." That troubled me. But not having a basis for knowing there was anything particularly wrong with it, it was just a discomfort level. Later, it became very significant.

Robert Odle, Jr. I reported to Jeb Magruder, and through him, to John Mitchell. While Mitchell was still attorney general, he was looking at broad campaign issues; when he came to CRP, he was quite involved. He did not like leaving a Cabinet post to go to work in a campaign, nor did Maurice Stans like leaving that lovely office the secretary of commerce has to come to CRP to raise money. But Mitchell knew that it was his manifest destiny to run Nixon's last campaign.

Donald E. Santarelli Maurice Stans is one of the finest people I have ever known, but I also knew him not to be the kind of guy who could supervise a person like Liddy. Maury Stans was not prepared for Liddy, because Gordon was an activist and he would do things covertly, as well as overtly, and get into trouble. Liddy needed a guidance system; left on his own, he would make mischief. I told that to Krogh; I said, "Don't let him go to that job, because Stans won't supervise him, and he'll just get into trouble." I had no idea of what was going on—that the job was a cover for Liddy to run his Plumbing operation.

Maurice Stans Gordon Liddy was handed to me almost by coincidence at a time that I was looking for a counsel to the committee. We had legal questions of various types: Can we take money from a foreigner? I'd call the White House and talk to Dean or one of his subordinates. Apparently, that registered when they wanted to get Liddy out of the Committee to Reelect and put him somewhere else. They called me and said, "We understand you're looking for a counsel; we have one surplus over here. He is a good lawyer, very smart." So the next day, he was on my payroll at the Finance Committee. He did a good job; he was a good lawyer. I immediately made him a member of my management committee. I had a daily meeting of the top six people in the office. Liddy sat in on those from the beginning; he participated; we kept minutes of everything that happened at those meetings. There was never a suggestion by him, or anybody else, that something should be done that was illegal. The part he played was very valuable to me. And he never, ever discussed the idea that he was doing something that was contrary to our idea of what he was doing, within my knowledge.

So I was sure as hell surprised when I learned of his involvement in these other activities. I called up John Mitchell and asked, "Do you know what Gordon Liddy has been doing?" He said, "I'm just hearing about it." I said, "Well, he's on my payroll. What should I do about him?" He said, "That is your decision, but if it were mine, you've got to get rid of him pretty fast." So I called Gordon in and I said, "Gordon, I have a problem with you. I don't know what to do with you." He said, "I understand your situation. This thing is getting entirely too hot. I know too much. We don't need to discuss it. I know that I have to go." I said, "I have no idea what you were doing." He said, "That is right; I was told not to tell you." Later on, I was annoyed that they had played that kind of game with me. I had a feeling that this must be the way elections were handled: keep the guy under cover. He covered it very well, too. He'd say, "I have to go up to New York for the weekend to visit a relative, and I probably won't be in until noon on Monday. Is that all right?" I said, "If you get all your work done, it's all right with me." I have a lot of respect for Gordon since then—the way he stood up and refused to be pushed around by Judge Sirica.

Robert Reisner There was a highly honed sense of concern that our office at CRP should be made secure. There was a great deal of security, in that sense, that I think was excessive. But you have to remember that a national campaign is the focus of considerable attention; all sorts of people call in, and people are always sneaking around. One day, a Russian called and asked to meet me. I asked Magruder about it, and he told me to call David Young, on Kissinger's staff, who advised me not to return the call. In October, one of my friends at the campaign told me, "I had the greatest time last night at the Russian Embassy." I'm a very close friend of this guy, and he named the person who had called me months before. I thought to myself: what an idiot I am.

"BLACK ADVANCE"

Jeb Stuart Magruder There was no "director of Dirty Tricks" that I know of; these things were happening all over the place. Chapin had Segretti; we didn't even know about that. We had some people in Muskie's campaign; we had Muskie's driver, early on. There were some things that were initiated by us because Haldeman kept pushing for information, and Mitchell wanted some information. I had been in campaigns before. This was not new—hiring a secretary and having her go over to the opponent's headquarters and volunteer.

There was always some of this stuff going on, and Colson was involved; he had all sorts of things going on, himself—somebody sent a thousand pizzas to a Muskie fund-raiser; it wasn't us—all sorts of people sticking their fingers in the pie.

We couldn't stop these activities. There were all peers. Chapin was a friend of mine; I had no idea he had anything going. With Colson, it wouldn't have done any good to complain, because we were mortal enemies at that time. Mitchell and I griped about it, but it didn't seen to have any effect.

The tone for this was clearly set at the top. There were many times we would get orders from the president when I was at the White House to do things to get back at people who had written columns, or made negative newscasts, and a lot of times, we played a game; we would send back memos claiming this or that happened, when nothing had happened. We had satisfied this voracious appetite for getting the enemy.

Donald Segretti I was a captain in the U.S. Army—in the judge advocate's office—and was contacted by Mr. Chapin and Mr. Strachan regarding working for the reelection of the president. I went back to Washington, D.C., and met with both of them. At that time, it was not explained in detail what it [my work] would be. It has come to be known—as I learned later—that it is called "black advance." I went to work for them in that category in the early part of 1972. There was no written plan; it was something that evolved over time. They were primarily interested, in the early stages, in difficult issue questions, press conferences, things of that nature—perhaps pickets relating to those items, at appearances [by the Democratic candidate or campaigners].

At that time, Mr. Strachan was working for Mr. Haldeman, and Mr. Chapin was Mr. Nixon's appointments secretary, so I assume they were working for those people—the president. It was never mentioned that they were working for the Committee to Reelect the President [CRP] or some other entity; that was never discussed. There was never anything written— or told to me—that: We have discussed this with the president, who wants you to do A, B, C; it never worked like that. I suppose it doesn't in real life, either. I was still in the army at the time. I really didn't know what I was going to do after I got out. I was going to get a job with a law firm and prac- tice law. But this seemed like a unique opportunity to work, essentially, for the White House, and for people I had known for a couple of years and respected, and was comfortable with. I asked, "Why would you like me to get involved in this? I have been in the army. I was trying cases, not cam- paigning. Why would I be a good choice?" The answer was, "Because nobody knows you." That was a good reason, but the other side was that it had downsides: I really didn't have the experience to do things in a proper context. I'm not going to blame anybody. I can tell you that now, as a man- ager of something, I try to keep a pretty clear, hands-on overview of things. But these were busy people; maybe they didn't have the time, or maybe they didn't want to take the time. I don't know.

Dwight Chapin I was told to get a person like that. Don came to mind. He was very bright and nondescript; he was the perfect guy. I always had this in the Dick Tuck vernacular; these things had always been a part of all cam- paigns I had been in. Did it belong in American politics? Probably not. Is it there? Yes. Did it belong, coming out of the White House? Obviously, I would say no. Did it [emanate from the White House]? Yes, it did. I did it, and I paid a hell of a price for it, and Don has paid a hell of a price for it— disproportionate, in my judgment, to the prices that should have been paid. But Segretti's escapades and my involvement in those escapades were multi- plied dramatically by this thing called Watergate—which was entirely sepa- rate. Watergate happened and—as Woodward and Bernstein went at it—

one of the first things that bubbled up was Segretti. This led to me, and was one of the first openings into the White House. To my mind, it exploded disproportionate to its magnitude. I am not condoning what I did. I am saying that it got way out of proportion. The point is that its actual significance was its use as a battering ram to get into the White House.

H. R. Haldeman This started out like a Dick Tuck operation: let's get out and hassle them like they hassle us. There was probably inadequate supervision of a guy with an overly stimulated imagination. What I realized afterward—which I realized to a degree, but not sufficiently, while I was there—was the tendency for overkill when some suggestion, or even hint of a suggestion, comes—presumably from the White House, or Oval Office—that something ought to be done: people tend to overreact as it works its way down the line. I think you had a lot of that in the Segretti thing—that so-called "dirty tricks" department: in the Plumbers, in the leak business that sprang out of Ellsberg, and what led to Watergate. You went from reasonable people who knew what the president wanted—and why—to people who didn't have any contact or knowledge of the president at all, and who were getting draconian orders that they then took draconian measures to carry out.

There is no question that the president put the heat on me to get better knowledge of what Muskie was saying, and in the primary period, what the other Democratic candidates were saying about each other, and the policy statements they were making. I was perfectly used to that: I had managed his [President Nixon's] 1960 [presidential] campaign. I had worked with Murray Chotiner [longtime political associate and adviser], and I knew how Chotiner ran campaigns. One of the specific orders I gave to Chapin—and it probably got to Magruder at CRP—was that they were to tape every statement Senator George McGovern made at any session where there was public access. This was not bugging him; this was pretending to be a reporter—using a tape recorder to tape him, or paying a reporter to do so. We did both of these things, which I consider to be perfectly honorable dishonorable things to be doing in a political campaign, in order to get on record, so that we can say that, "On December 13, at 3 A.M., in Arlington, Texas, Edmund Muskie or George McGovern said, 'I will never do this.'"

So we say we want to know that kind of stuff, and what happens? Somebody at the White House—Gordon Strachan, or somebody—calls Magruder and says, "The president is up in arms again, because we are not getting any information: he has asked what McGovern had said at this meeting, and no one can give an answer. So get someone out there and get these things covered." Magruder doesn't know what do to about these things; he's a little PR man from Los Angeles who is struggling in the Reelection Committee. But he's got this guy, Gordon Liddy, who has a CIA background, and so he calls Liddy and says, "Find out what's going on." So Liddy runs out and starts tape-recording the Democratic National Committee; this is Dick Tuck gone awry.

He [Liddy] was a sophisticated guy, politically. He pushed right up to the edge, but he knew where the edge was, and he did a pretty good job of not quite going over it. Segretti was a young kid who Dwight and Ron Ziegler had known from college. They said he was a great guy to do this stuff: he had a great imagination. Well, he had a greater imagination than good judgment called for. I don't know the specifics of all the stuff, but I know the results of some of them; they were not proper results. If some of them had come off, they would have been regarded as being just as funny as the stuff Tuck did. If they come off wrong, they backfire.

Some [of Segretti's operations] were beyond the pale, and some were okay, but were done wrong and, therefore, backfired. The president didn't know about Segretti. We pushed for what we called "a chaplain's friend," which was a code word Murray [Chotiner] used, and he always had a legitimate, credentialed newsman in a campaign who we paid off, who would report to him of what was going on in the enemy camp. He would call in every night and say, "Such-and-such is happening; somebody is fooling around with someone's girlfriend," and you would know what the opposition was worrying about. So we were pushing to get a chaplain's friend, and we got one—and we got reports. The unfortunate thing is that, by excess, some of the normal "dirty tricks" became abnormal ones. Then they all got tarnished by the same brush. Some of them were absolutely inexcusable. Unforgivable. And the Watergate break-in is still inexplicable to me, because there is no reason to have done it that I can figure out.

John Dean If you put him in the context of Whitewater, which they are trying to make into a scandal, and you put in Segretti, who was a minor scandal during the Watergate scandal, Whitewater is to Segretti as Segretti is to Watergate. He could have been a major scandal; he wasn't because there were so many much more major things that were going on. He was a college prankster who was still doing college pranks. It was more than a Dick Tuck operation.

George McGovern We had suspicions, from time to time, that there were people inside our organization, because certain things would happen, indicating that somebody in the opposition camp must know where we were going and what our strategy was. I was surprised at what a small-potatoes operation it was—kind of frivolous. Segretti always seemed to me like a lightweight, frivolous character. It seemed almost embarrassing for an incumbent administration to come up with such a Mickey Mouse operation. I never took that stuff very seriously. I don't think it hurt us any.

Donald Segretti People got painted with very broad brushes, and I don't think that's fair. Some of the people who became involved—people I know—are genuinely good people. You have to remember that there are people who get into circumstances that don't really go to their heart and soul, but they end up doing things that they regret later. Egil Krogh comes to mind as a very upstanding, responsible individual who got involved in things that—with hindsight, if he thought about them—were probably not appropriate. Mr. Strachan is a very upstanding, responsible individual; I think Mr. Chapin is, also. The real decisions—where a lot of these things developed—were at the next higher level; that's how it evolved—with Haldeman and Nixon. I think that their decisions started these things going, and that the tones of campaigns are set by those who are really right at the top. Unless the tone is set properly, and the rules are laid down properly, you are going to have problems. I don't think that the tone was set properly.

Dwight Chapin The Segretti situation probably owes its origin to a sense that the other side was always pulling things, so let's make sure we do the same; let's make sure they get what they are giving us. I don't remember Segretti's having met Hunt and Liddy in Miami; I wasn't continually in touch with him; I was heavily involved in the planning of the China trip. I'd get calls from Don. He'd come to town a couple of times. I met him once at the Hay Adams.* I don't think I was aware of a lot of the things he did. In his world, that was all that he was doing; in my world, he was out there. When Don testified, he told the prosecutors: "When Dwight hired me, he said, 'One of the reasons we are hiring you is that you are a lawyer; you will know what is right and what is wrong.'" That caused horrible problems for the prosecutors who were trying to indict me. They couldn't indict me for what Don did.

---

* A luxury hotel in Washington, D.C.

SEGRETTI'S MANDATE

Donald Segretti My experience in politics was extremely limited—I would underline extremely. I was not an operative, nor a political professional. No plan was ever presented to me in writing, or otherwise, so I had no plan—even a general plan. I expected that I would be subjected to something they would state they wanted me to do. I was told that I could live in Los Angeles or New York, or wherever I wanted, because I would be doing a great deal of traveling, so I moved back to Los Angeles, where I had grown up. My mother was quite ill, so it seemed natural that I would be on the West Coast.

At some point, it was set up that I would receive a bimonthly payment through a lawyer in the area, Mr. [Herbert] Kalmbach, whom I had not met. I met him and, for a period of time, did receive bimonthly checks, not in large sums—relatively modest money. The first thing I did was to travel to New Hampshire because the primary was coming up, and I was requested to make contact with some local individuals who were involved in the campaign, to see if there could be some "black advance" set up. I met up there with someone working in the campaign and told him what I wanted to do, and I was told that I really shouldn't use my name. I went back up there and told the man what my name was, and I guess he called Washington—or somebody—and it got back up to the people that I was involved: there is somebody up here wanting to do "black advance." What's it all about? I received an urgent phone call—it was either Chapin or Strachan who made the call—that I should not be so open with what I was contemplating doing. So I did not go back to New Hampshire after that.

I traveled primarily to the primary states. I was not given a schedule that said these were the places to go, but it was worked out that we would have primaries in New York, Florida, Texas, etc., and those were the areas that I should go to and make contact, to start making arrangements for activities. In some weeks, I met individuals who were interested in doing such things; in others, I didn't make any real contacts. It is a great exaggeration to say that I hired fifty people; I may have talked to fifty people, but I did not hire them.

There were probably three or four people that I worked with regularly. It was not all that structured, nor was it an all-encompassing, cohesive apparatus. Even the name *apparatus* is misleading, and connotes something different from reality. I was not getting calls from anybody at CRP; it was the individuals at the White House. I never had any contact with anybody at CRP—

with one exception: at one time, I did have contact with Mr. Liddy and Mr. Hunt, in Florida. At various times, I was told of issues to focus on; it was coming from Strachan and Chapin. I can remember one issue that they really wanted to hit on: the issue of having a black running mate; they tried to make it an issue in the campaign—that was with Senator Muskie. He made some comments that he did not feel it made political sense to have a black vice-presidential running mate. That seemed like normal politics to me.

G. Gordon Liddy We started getting word that there was some guy going around, being active. I was supposed to be running the whole thing; at least, I thought I was. Actually, Dean was running everything. We thought that this person running around was a Democratic plant. People were calling in, saying someone is representing himself as a Republican; he's probably a Democrat. We looked into it and found that the person was Segretti; then we found out that he was working for Haldeman, of all people, so he wasn't a Democrat at all. I was annoyed, because I had been told I was in charge, but everybody was running operations all over the place. I complained and was told, "Okay, you run him."

Segretti wasn't doing the kinds of things we were interested in; he was doing "dirty tricks," as it is correctly known—sending in all these pizzas, and things like that. So Hunt and I said, "We have to get control over this guy." We met with him in Miami, and played "good cop, bad cop." There he is, wearing his three-piece, New York suit, standing out like a sore thumb in a rundown hotel in a sleazy neighborhood. I said to him, "From now on, you are going to do what Hunt tells you to do, because Hunt is unstable; so don't kill without receiving orders." You could only pull this on a poor, little, naive guy like Segretti. He started to tremble. I talked about getting his knee caps broken—I'm the good guy; I will try to protect you, but watch out for Howard. Afterward, we gave him some minor chores. He was a very minor figure, and I was surprised that it was thought that he did anything worthy of going to jail.

Donald Segretti I was told that they could assist me with making contact with some individuals down there. I met them on one occasion in Florida— an unusual pair. It was a strange, bizarre meeting: I was staying at a motel outside Miami, or perhaps in Miami. They came up to the motel room, and one of them went and turned on the television, or radio, relatively loudly; I guess they were concerned with being recorded. We talked for fifteen minutes to half an hour, and they left. I didn't really have their true names; I don't remember the names they gave me. I found out their true identities when I was in Los Angeles and picked up the newspaper one day and read about the Watergate break-ins. My first reaction was: "These people must be crazy"—it was a normal reaction—and wondering: "What is this? What's really going on here?"

At some point—in my meeting with them, or later—they gave me the name of a printer, because it was decided to get some stationery printed by the other candidates—the contenders for the Democratic nomination. I was told by my contacts in Washington to meet them [Hunt and Liddy]: "They are good people, and you can have confidence in them." I think that all the activities that were looked upon as improper—and were, in many instances—were shielded from Mr. Nixon. Looking back, I wish that the lines in the directions to me had been much clearer, because I didn't have any of that. I don't think that what Dick Tuck did was proper, so for Nixon to say it was only Dick Tuck items—and I don't think we have a full accounting of what he did—even that type of activity is improper. There didn't seem to be any fences around what we should or shouldn't do. The only thing that was said was that this should be done very discreetly and secretively. That aspect of it gave it a different varnish. I suspect that was how they had conducted campaigns in the past. We are in office; we are popular; we have all the power of the presidency; and we are going to have a degree of vindictiveness and vengeance—getting back at them for what they have done to us. That office has a great deal of power, and sometimes comments and statements by those at that [power] level result in people taking actions that maybe they didn't contemplate.

George Romney I had an experience with Martha Mitchell after I was out of the Cabinet, and about several months before she died. She was our house guest. She was the first one to indicate that John Mitchell had to resign as chairman of the Committee to Reelect Nixon; she was the first one, as far as I knew, to sense that something was very much amiss. I said to her, "Martha, did you say that because you were aware of the break-in?" "Oh, no," she said. "What I learned was that they were pouring huge sums of money into the McGovern campaign. And that's what incensed me." If you take a look at what happened during that period, the dirty tricks were designed, in my opinion, to undercut the strongest Democratic opponents and to ensure that Nixon would run against McGovern, as the weakest of the Democratic candidates.

THE POSSIBLE OPPONENTS

Stephen Bull As I recall, we acted as if there was no serious challenge. McGovern's name did not come up.

George McGovern I thought my chances were at least fair. I knew it was uphill, but I thought I had a shot at the nomination for several reasons: first, during the 1968 convention, once Humphrey was nominated, I immediately went up to the platform and held up his hand, receiving a very favorable reaction from the party; and having long opposed the war, I had the [Eugene] McCarthy-[Edward] Kennedy wing solidly in my corner—by then, Robert Kennedy was dead, and Teddy had run into the Chappaquiddick thing and more or less disqualified himself; Gene McCarthy just kind of dropped out after 1968; and Hubert was still pursuing the war pretty much in line with where Johnson had been; Ed Muskie said that he didn't think the war was a major issue—this really hurt him, in not taking a straight-out position of opposition to the war. So under those conditions, I thought that if we started early, and organized at the grass roots, and got the women, the young people, the antiwar crowd, some from labor, and the environmentalists, there was enough to win the nomination.

We targeted Wisconsin as the first place we might win, but we very quietly put a lot of time and effort into New Hampshire, and that is where we stopped the Muskie bandwagon. I didn't win there, but the press thought I did, and played it that way. Of course, there was some feeling among Democrats—and the Nixon people may have thought this also—that if Teddy really wanted the nomination in 1972, he had a really good shot at it, but I decided a week after Chappaquiddick that I had a more or less clear shot at the nomination.

Jerry Jones I joined the White House in 1971. At the time, Muskie was ahead of us, so the mind-set as we began thinking about the campaign was: we are going to be challenged; let's get ready for a tough one. Then, of course, Muskie faltered and McGovern came on board and ran a simply miserable campaign, and we ran quite a good campaign, and it wasn't close at the end.

Terrence O'Donnell The White House staff felt very solidly that McGovern could be handily defeated. This huge operation developed, however—and the massive fund-raising—and no stone was going to be left unturned, which I blame for the ultimate problems. The Watergate break-in was absurd; what possible good could come out of bugging Spencer Oliver's phone? It's overkill of the worst kind, and reckless beyond belief. There was that enormous amount of money—$60 million spent—and the desire to leave no stone unturned: Nixon had been through enormous political disappointments, and he wasn't going to let this one slip away. This permeated from the president through to Haldeman, and then on through all the layers of staff, into the campaign. But there was no certainty that Nixon was going to win; and the White House was in battle stations all the way through the summer and fall.

G. Gordon Liddy Remember that Watergate happened before the Democrats had selected their candidate. Yes, McGovern was in the lead, but we were of the opinion that any time Teddy, the last remaining [Kennedy] brother, had wanted to claim his legacy, or wrap himself in his brother's bloody coat and say, I want the nomination—he damn well might have gotten it, and we thought he'd be a lot tougher than McGovern. If the June Watergate operation had succeeded, we were going to go that weekend to McGovern's headquarters and do the same thing. And then, the rest of the much modified—and truncated—Gemstone Plan would have been followed. We had a flow chart for the implementation of the plan, and we would have followed it right through the operations in Miami, after the Democrats had selected their candidate. The alternative to Nixon was President McGovern. I would have done a hell of a lot to stop that. It's almost as bad as President Clinton, for God's sake.

Alexander Butterfield I was privy to something that has never come out: that there was a guy on the White House staff—a sort of catch-all guy; a former Secret Service agent who had been on Nixon's detail when Nixon was vice-president. They used him when Teddy Kennedy started getting some popularity, and Nixon was worried. They put him back on duty, on Teddy's detail.* Of course, they thought Teddy was fooling around; they were going to get some information on him; he must have a lady someplace. So he made weekly reports to Haldeman. I was aware of that. It's abuse of power, technically, and I imagine that LBJ did worse things.

Charles Colson In early 1972, the polls showed Nixon and Muskie in a dead heat. It was not until Nixon's speech in which he revealed he was

---

* Candidates who received a certain percentage in polls merited Secret Service protection.

engaged in secret negotiations with the Vietnamese that Muskie's position was undercut. Even after Muskie faltered in New Hampshire, we still thought Humphrey could be difficult. None of us ever dreamed that McGovern would get the nomination. If we had, we would have laughed our way through the campaign. I was Nixon's chief political adviser during this period, and it looked like a very close race until the Democratic convention and the McGovern nomination.

On July 12, George McGovern was nominated at the Democratic convention in Miami. But before he could begin the campaign, McGovern was hurt by two organizational failures: the inability of his staff to have the candidate give his acceptance speech during prime-time television; and the selection of Missouri Senator Thomas Eagleton as his running mate—a choice that would prove to be short-lived when information was made public concerning Eagleton's history of mental problems.

George McGovern It was a nightmare for me; it was one of the most costly mistakes of the campaign that we frittered away that prime time when the country, for the first time, could have seen me on my turf, in control. It was a disaster. It was a very foolish thing in retrospect, in that my people who were running the convention—Gary Hart and Frank Mankewiecz, and to a certain extent Larry O'Brien—felt that we'd run a rather unstructured convention all along, and we had talked about the politics of openness and everybody is invited to the table and that you shouldn't put restrictions on people who wanted to talk. Since my nomination had been decided, the focus then shifted to the vice-presidency, and there were all those groups that wanted recognition: the antiwar crowd, the young people, the women, the blacks, the Chicanos, the environmentalists; everybody wanted a piece of that national television time. In retrospect, I should have called over there and said to Larry O'Brien: Goddamn it; let's wind this thing up. I want to get on the air by no later than ten o'clock. Instead, we just let them drone on and kill that time with superficial things that really added nothing to the convention.

The selection of Eagleton more or less followed the traditional pattern of letting it go until the last minute and then, suddenly, you begin to think you have to have a running mate. We put that together in a hurry; that was a mistake. He was everybody's second choice. I tried to get Kennedy to run—frankly because I thought he would attract attention to the ticket, and votes, and money and organizational power and manpower; he'd have been very helpful. Then I tried to get the governor of Florida, Reuben Askew, and I tried to get [Senator] Abe Ribicoff [D-Conn.], and then Mondale, and right down the list. I had a lot of good people; they all said no. People like Mondale, Kennedy, Ribicoff, or Gaylord Nelson said to me, "You know, Eagleton wants that job. Why don't you give it to him? He's a bright, able guy." Mike Mansfield thought he would be great. I couldn't find any hesitation about him, so finally, by a process of elimination, I called him about fifteen minutes before the deadline and told him we were thinking about him.

He said, "Well, I'm going to say yes before you change your mind." And that was it. I had no suspicion about his background—and nobody I talked to had any suspicion; a couple of people had told me they had seen him loaded after a party or two. I later discovered that the reason for that was that he was on sedatives, or things to deal with his mental problem, and that—combined with liquor—made it impossible for him to drink. But we had no warning about it. I spoke to political reporters in St. Louis, and talked to Senator Stuart Symington [D-Mo.], and to the governor, and nobody knew anything about the mental illness; he was a manic depressive, and had been for about twenty years. He had gone through rather extensive electric shock therapy. The Eagleton nomination and blowing the acceptance address timing were the most costly things [of the 1972 campaign] that, obviously, I would do differently, if I had them to do over again.

THE EAGLETON PROBLEM

George McGovern I had to virtually force Eagleton to leave the ticket. I had no power to remove him. Once you are nominated by the convention, the candidate cannot say I don't want you anymore. I told him that I just didn't think we could go forward in light of the controversy that was swirling around his past, and in view of the fact that he had not seen fit to tell me about that. I felt—on a man-to-man basis—he should have the decency to step down. He finally said that he would if he could be in on the drafting of the statement as to why he was stepping down. He wanted to make clear that there was nothing wrong with him emotionally, or mentally, but that he was doing it to avoid controversy. It put me in a bad position politically as the iron hand persecuting a man who was perfectly all right, perfectly stable, sound emotionally and mentally in every way, who was stepping down purely because I thought it would create a controversy. In retrospect, I think that politically, laying aside any of the risks involved in putting somebody like that that close to the White House, it might have been better to stay with him, because I got hit on two grounds: first of all, carelessness in picking somebody with a history of mental illness, and secondly, indecisiveness in picking him and then dumping him.

One of the Nixon ads was of a coin with my face on each side. The coin kept flipping; you would see one face, then it flipped and you would see the other. I guess for the first time in my public career, I gave the opposition the chance to say that I was indecisive, confused about what I thought on a particular issue: one day, I'm a thousand percent for Eagleton, the next day, I'm asking him to leave the ticket. Believing we had been hurt by the Eagleton matter, I tried to get somebody I thought would be a reconciling person to pull the whole party together. So I went to Mansfield, and to Humphrey, and to Muskie, and all three turned me down. So then I went to [R. Sargent] Shriver.

Alexander Butterfield Bob [Haldeman] once intimated to me that they had stuff on Eagleton—that electroshock therapy. They were just waiting to spring it—waiting for the right time; they knew that it would be explosive. They had something else on McGovern—something about cowardice.

Morris Amitay Shortly after the Democratic convention in 1972, Ambassador Itzhak Rabin asked me to arrange a meeting for him with George McGovern. We met in Senator Ribicoff's apartment in the Watergate. Rabin had asked me to put to George some of the tough questions he might be asked during the campaign. In answer to one question, it was apparent that McGovern did not understand that you can't keep all U.S. [aircraft] carriers on station at one time; it also became clear that he was unfamiliar with the geographic borders of Israel. Rabin was usually very taciturn, but I could just sense that he was sitting there, saying to himself: Oy vey! This man could be president of the United States!

President Nixon was renominated at the Republican convention in Miami Beach on the night of August 2, by a vote of 1,377 to 1. The delegates also renominated Vice-President Agnew, thus putting a formal end to Mr. Nixon's wish that Agnew be replaced on the ticket by John Connally, who Nixon appeared to prefer as his White House successor in 1976.

In the months before the convention, the president had realized that Agnew had a large, growing, and vocal constituency among the silent majority—so crucial to Nixon's own political ambitions—and had proved himself to be quite an effective campaigner in the 1970 congressional election.

Howard Phillips The Nixon-Agnew relationship was virtually nonexistent. By 1972, it was clear that if Nixon had not been so cautious a politician, he would have much preferred to have someone else as his running mate. It was clear that he wanted Connally to succeed him. One of the great ironies of history is that Mel Laird was able to talk Nixon out of picking Connally as his choice for vice-president when Agnew stepped down. Laird had been actively pushing Ford. A couple of days before the decision was made, I had lunch in the White House Mess with a White House aide who was pushing Ford. They frightened Nixon into dumping Connally, not realizing that Agnew was 100 percent impeachment insurance, Connally was at least 80 percent, and Ford was about zero. So Nixon made the most stupid move of all in his vice-presidential selection.

David Keene John Connally was a guy whose only real ability in life was that he could con presidents; they all thought he was pretty impressive. Nixon was taken with Connally. It was general knowledge very early that he was toying with the idea of replacing Agnew with Connally. There were a lot of people urging him to do this. They saw some advantages to this: One, they liked Connally's toughness and the fact that he was a former Democrat. He was just the kind of character that Nixon was attracted to. We took steps to make sure that didn't happen. We arranged for a lot of people around the country to express support for Agnew, particularly among Republican activists and conservatives.

Raymond Price The relationship between the two men started out well. Agnew was included on domestic issues; he took on some of the hard battles and established a certain reputation as one who weighed in where others dared not tread. He built his own constituency, which was one of the factors that kept Nixon from picking John Connally as his running mate in 1972; he certainly wanted Connally as his successor—there is no doubt about that. But by then, Agnew had built such a large constituency—and Connally being a new recruit from the Democratic Party, it couldn't have been done without leaving a lot of blood on the floor.

THE THIRD-PARTY FACTOR

George McGovern Had the bad breaks not taken place, the election would have been a lot closer. But what turned the election into a landslide was something I had no control over, and that was the shooting of Governor

Wallace. Wallace was stronger in 1972 than he was in 1968; in primary after primary, he was my toughest competitor. He won a number of primaries; he won both primaries the day he was shot, in Michigan and in Maryland. He was tough, and in my opinion, had he not been shot, he would have taken 12 to 14 million votes away from Nixon; then you would have had a real horse race. That was what he did to Humphrey in 1968, except that he wasn't as strong then. I suppose that one other thing was George Meany's endorsement of Nixon: he told his Executive Council [AFL-CIO] that he couldn't see any difference between McGovern and Nixon; that hurt us with organized labor. I had about an 85 percent approval rating on their scale; Nixon about 8 percent. It was over Vietnam. I'd say that George Wallace, George Meany, and the mistakes of George McGovern—the three Georges—all hurt us quite a bit.

Gerald Warren There was concern because of the third-party aspect; that made it uncertain. The president wanted everybody, particularly the campaign staff, to work doubly hard to make sure that money was collected to put on a credible, winning campaign—and one which would produce a mandate. I think that that extra push gave some of the people the feeling that they could go out and raise money in nontraditional ways.

CAMPAIGN ORGANIZATION

Jerry Jones I was John Mitchell's assistant at the campaign, trying to help him audit the field organization. Then, after Mitchell left, I put together the fifty-state campaign organization with a team of superb young guys. We spent a ton of money from July to November—about $20 to $25 million—on the field organization, more money, in fact, than President Ford had in 1976 to run his entire campaign.

Frederic V. Malek I thought that Nixon would be reelected, but I didn't think it was a slam dunk; we had to work very hard, and I had no intimation that we would win by such a large majority. The president was not involved in the day-to-day operations of the campaign. The product, however, was developed in the White House—his positions on issues and plans for the second term.

Stephen Bull I am not sure how much he enjoyed meeting people. He is a very businesslike guy; he was uncomfortable with small talk. He is a very good politician. I'll bet that if you sat down with him this afternoon, he could tell you who the county chairman is in some obscure county in one of the smaller states. He relished the game of politics. In the 1972 campaign, he made very, very few appearances; as the polls started widening in the fall of 1972, states that had originally been scheduled were crossed out.

Herbert Klein Part of my role in the 1972 campaign was to do a lot of traveling. I went about 100,000 miles on my own to speak to press groups. I felt that having been in touch with people across the country, I had more of a sense of what they were worried about than did people in the White House, who were sort of hunkered down and didn't get out that much.

Terrence O'Donnell Dwight Chapin was active in planning the "surrogate" operation, a very aggressive operation to get the administration out and speaking on behalf of the president. Due to the availability of funds prior to the Federal Election Commission rules, and fund-raising success, they used the "sandwich" technique, in which they could put a surrogate in a given city before and after George McGovern appeared there: if he visited city X, the day before he arrived someone would be there, criticizing his policies and asking questions, which he would be confronted with when he came in; and then, the day after he left, someone else would be in that same city—in that same media market. It was an aggressive and awesome campaign operation. There is no question that there was too much money floating around then, which I think was part of the problem. Dwight was also responsible for coming up with the so-called "line of the day" that was put out through the surrogates—the issues to be addressed on a given day. He had Bob Haldeman's trust and confidence.

Hugh Sloan The question is not if there was too much money, but was the money spent appropriately? I know that Stans felt there was lack of control, and lack of discipline, in his mind, in terms of the spending; it was a runaway budget. He felt there should be precise goals in terms of effective budgeting on the political side. The actual spending for political objectives would primarily have been signed off on by Magruder and Mitchell.

13

The New Administration

Soon after he assumed the presidency, Mr. Nixon began to develop plans for the reorganization of the executive branch of government. He assigned industrialist Roy Ash to head a commission to examine the issue and to make recommendations. In the period after his victory in 1972 and before the beginning of the second term, Nixon and his associates gave considerable thought to restaffing the administration. Some officials would be asked to leave, while others would be reassigned. One of the interesting aspects of the Nixon presidency is the fact that key personnel, such as George Shultz, James Schlesinger, Elliot Richardson, Kenneth Rush, and others, each served in several capacities during those years.

Terrence O'Donnell After the election, I was up at Camp David for several weeks, working with Haldeman. There was a small staff there working with the president: Haldeman, Larry Higby, Ehrlichman, and his assistant—Todd Holland, Ron Ziegler, and Diane Sawyer. Everyone in the administration had been asked to submit their resignation, so it was a time of some significant tension in Washington, as the president went up to the mountain—and stayed up there. There was great uncertainty; rumors would filter down that he was interviewing people—which he was—for jobs that were filled by incumbents who were unaware that their days in those jobs were numbered. I helped the military aide to operate the little "airline"—the helicopter that would fly people who were being interviewed back and forth.

Frederic V. Malek What the president was trying to do was to make the statement: We are going to keep most of the people, but we are going to ask some of them to leave; this is the time to face up to our mistakes in personnel and to get some new, committed, hard-charging, capable people in key jobs. Let's get the best people possible for the second term. So, to start with a clean slate, the policy was to ask everybody to submit their resignations, but to let them know that we didn't expect to accept many of them. This way, we could reinforce the loyalty of those individuals who were reappointed. It just didn't work out that way. We had been led to believe that we would be able to act very quickly—that the vast majority of people would be told immediately that they were not going to be affected. That didn't happen, because Colson convinced the president that we needed to dig deeper and have more ethnics: Irish Catholics, Italians, Poles—a group representative of America. So a lot of matters were put on hold, and these resignations sat there for a long time, and people were getting angry.

Jerry Jones About six of us did the "spent volcano" analysis on who should leave the administration. Then Malek went to OMB, and I became head of the White House Personnel Office in January 1973. Of the 550 presidentially appointed positions, 208 were open, and I had to restaff them. In the middle of that, the Watergate thing was flapping around and causing unbelievable problems in trying to staff those jobs. In the first term, we had done a lot of work, looking at who was out there, and how they were performing. When you think about the 550 presidentially appointed jobs, there are a lot of ways to measure performance. Our tendency was to try to measure it on a technical basis: Were these fellows doing a good job?—and, by the way, have they been loyal? But there really wasn't the loyalty test that you might think.

Haldeman really wanted us to find the very best people. I believed the political view should be taken into account. I don't think that people can serve a president well unless they really buy into his program. I saw what happened when you had people out there who wouldn't buy in—and who were, in some way or another, trying to subvert him and the program politically. So when we sifted through the people, we were trying to do two things: to replace those who had not performed technically, and to replace those who had not been willing to support the president politically. It was a technical and political screening, but most of the decisions were based on the technical evaluation. There were exceptions—almost the entire Department of Defense was wiped out. On a substantive basis, that was probably the wrong thing to do. I think the DOD had performed brilliantly in Vietnam; the problem was that the president and Secretary Laird simply didn't get along very well—there was not much trust—and the president wiped the entire DOD out.

George P. Shultz One of my daughters was twelve at the time, and she asked my wife, "Can't Dad hold a job?" In my case Nixon regarded these changes in positions as promotions and, in a sense, they were. Nixon believed that second terms were worse than first terms, because the same people do the same work, and they are tired and lose their creativity, so we should shake things up; he wanted the second term to have creativity and energy. That was the theory of it, but it was done in an appallingly brutal way; it just left people stunned the day after the election. These people, who had worked hard, are called into the Cabinet Room and told to resign. It was cruel, particularly as it was done by Haldeman, in his very straightforward way. But some of the realignments made sense. He thought of [Caspar] Weinberger as someone who tried to be careful with money, so he put him at HEW [Health, Education and Welfare]; he thought of [Eliott] Richardson as someone who was always trying to spend money, so he put him over at [the Department of] Defense, because he wanted Defense to spend more. He had a rationale for these moves.

Kenneth Rush After the 1972 election, I was asked by President Nixon to become secretary of state. He asked all his Cabinet secretaries to submit their resignations, but Bill Rogers refused. Nixon, who didn't like to give bad news to people, asked Haldeman to call Rogers and inform him that I was to succeed him. Rogers insisted on seeing Nixon. As a result, Rogers was told he could stay on until May. At the same time, Kissinger wanted the job; Henry said he would leave if he were not given the position. I was to be his deputy.

Dwight Chapin I don't think that Nixon pushed Bill Rogers aside. From the outset, Nixon was going to be his own secretary of state. Rogers was a lot of things Nixon wasn't: he could get into all of the right places at all of the right times; he was every inch a gentleman. He was the kind of lawyer who would follow his client's instructions, and Nixon was his client, so he was put into State. Meanwhile, here is Kissinger, this youngish guy—forty-one or -two. He comes bouncing in: bright, funny, clever. But he is also an agent of the president; this scenario was run by Richard Nixon. If Nixon hadn't been around, Henry would have self-destructed. He has his own hang-ups and idiosyncrasies.

Jerry Jones In April 1974, General Haig asked me to become staff secretary, with the additional duty of being the custodian of the tapes. The staff secretary is an unbelievable job; essentially, it is the president's In and Out boxes. The guy who controls the In box dictates to the people who are trying to get memorandums and, particularly, decision questions in to the president. We had quite a structured system to do that; people didn't simply run into the Oval Office and say, Mr. President, I need you to decide. There was a very formal process, and the staff secretary controlled it. Then, when the decisions came out from the president, the staff secretary communicated them, so I essentially got to read everything that came in and out of the Oval Office.

INSIDERS EVALUATE THEIR COLLEAGUES

Charles Colson

Herbert Klein Colson, who I think was one of the meanest people I ever knew, was recruited by Bryce Harlow, one of the gentlest people I ever knew. He was recruited to fulfill a job of relating to outside organizations. Colson first came to my attention when there was a potential postal strike; he had a reputation in knowing how to deal with unions. He was assigned to these outside organizations, like the supporters of Vietnam, and that is how I used to see [H. Ross] Perot in his office all the time, which made me worry about Perot. If Nixon made a speech on Vietnam, I looked at my job as finding out afterward what people thought; Colson felt it was his job to get everybody to say, "The president did wonderfully"—he would get the labor unions to say this, or the American Legion to have telegrams sent in. He became a part of the inner circle because he could provide a bright light on a dark day. Nixon, on occasion, would be angry; he'd say, "I think we ought to punch that guy on the nose," and if your name was Herb Klein, or Bob Haldeman, or Bob Finch, we'd ignore it, and in a couple of days, he'd say, "You never really did punch him, did you?" Colson's nature was to punch him twice.

H. R. Haldeman Colson was a [Capitol] Hill guy; he had worked for Senator [Leverett] Saltonstall [R-Mass.]. Bryce Harlow knew him as very bright, very eager, very energetic, an upcoming young politico. At some point, the president came up with the thought that we needed to have somebody at the White House who went beyond the Harlow congressional relations thing, and into general relations with interest groups around the world. That was the first place that I had heard of Chuck, who came in with recommendations from Bryce. He thinks he had known Nixon before that. I don't think that Nixon thinks so, and I don't think so. Nixon, from his viewpoint, probably made him feel like he had known him before; that's one of a good politician's knacks. He became both an advocate for outside interests—labor, ethnic groups—to the White House, and was lobbying, in effect, from within, for the interests of these people, to the extent that their interests coincided with White House interests, and could, therefore, satisfy both parties.

As it turned out, Chuck was—and is—what I would classify as a true zealot. When he was a marine, he was a zealot marine—which the marines strongly encourage; and now he's a zealot Christian—which the evangelical Christian movement strongly encourages, and he's doing a wonderful job with the prison movement. And, in a lot of cases, he did a very good job in what he was doing at the White House: he fought for these causes; he was building a new coalition that Nixon was trying to leave as a legacy for the Republican Party, making it a majority party. Chuck really worked at that, but in his zealotry, Chuck also was given to listening to the president's worst ideas, taking them as marching orders, and carrying them out.

I should have realized this with Chuck; this was another of my mistakes. I really welcomed Chuck, because he absorbed a lot of time with Nixon that I used to have to sit through—listening to him rant about somebody who's got to be done in, or thrown out of an airplane—and did nothing about. Chuck sat and listened, and wrote it down, and went out and did it. I caught him short on a number of things, from time to time, and really tore him apart for carrying out that which he should have at least had enough sense to talk to me or someone else about, before he went out and did it. But he said, "The president said, 'Don't talk to Haldeman about it; go out and do it.'" Well, that was the president's way of saying, "Get it done, regardless of what the cautious people say." I don't know that any of these things were what you would call White House horrors. I think that they were evidences of bad judgment; things we could have done more smoothly and effectively.

Jerry Jones The reason Colson was so important—and the reason that Nixon's first term worked out the way it did, and one of the reasons I was fairly close to Colson—was that Colson had the idea and the thrust of carrying out the whole idea of the silent majority—the essentially blue-collar, typically ethnic, formerly democratically oriented, here in the Northeast and around the major cities. We pushed that very hard in many of our appointments—certainly in the organization of the personnel work in 1973; we tried to reflect the appointments to that group. That's why Colson was so important to Nixon; the silent majority was the way Nixon thought he could be reelected against a liberal Democratic challenger. Obviously, it was very successful.

Donald E. Santarelli Colson had an enormous influence on Richard Nixon, and he used it to a fare-thee-well, and he's publicly apologized for it for the rest of his life. Richard Nixon's Achilles' heel was his sense of personal insecurity. He never, never could understand why he wasn't the darling of the Republican liberals and/or the establishment Republicans—the Rockefeller crowd; the rich Republicans. This bothered him greatly, and Colson played on that sense of insecurity and brought him tidbits, in the same way that [J. Edgar] Hoover brought previous presidents tidbits, to both ingratiate himself and aggrandize his appearance of power. Colson was always full of ideas that would appeal to Nixon's weaker side; the line was always: Let us confound your enemies—and Nixon did have a weakness on the subject of enemies, and when he lost John Mitchell as his guide—his lodestar guidance system—when Mitchell left to run the [1972] campaign, Colson became more ascendant—he was more proximate, anyway, with an office just across the way, so that he could barge into the Oval Office pretty easily. Those were interesting times. Colson was very seductive; he tried that on me, too. I saw Colson using the new majority as his theme, but he always had what I would call rifle shot ideas—specific projects. I saw what he was up to. Even though I was pretty young, I didn't want to be part of that.

Leonard Garment Along came Colson. There is always that tiny little slit in a subordinate vein or artery that causes death; you don't know that you are bleeding to death until it is too late. Colson may have been an evil genius. Haldeman let him in. I don't think that he appreciated the extreme to which Colson carried his craziness in order to establish a very special role with Nixon, and how complex this relationship was—what attracted Nixon—that sadistic Colson quality: get a man by the balls, and his heart and mind will follow. I know that there is redemption for everyone, but for a lot of people redemption is a kind of high-level act of deceit. It just outrages me now that Colson would receive awards like he was a Mother Teresa, when he did the most outrageous things and was part of planning which put all kinds of lives in danger; in some instances, there were plans that came out of the Colson shop which involved homicide. Haldeman couldn't kick Colson out because he was, generally, too effective in what he did.

Ronald Ziegler The only way that Colson got into the loop was that Richard Nixon let him in. Nixon could have stopped Colson, but I also think that Haldeman, Ehrlichman—and Colson—never faced up to what they could have stopped. I said this before Bob passed away—God rest Bob's soul. If you read their books, none of the men really confronted the shortcomings that led to the tragedy of Watergate, so I don't think that the fact that Colson went out and did what President Nixon said, and others stopped and waited, means much of anything except that if Colson had stopped and waited, something else would have taken place.

Frederic V. Malek Colson developed a personal relationship with Nixon. He was very outspoken, very aggressive, and conservative—with a forceful political philosophy. Nixon liked this and identified with Colson. When that began to happen, Colson had the ability to influence Nixon's thinking. He was also able to execute Nixon's directives without a filtering process. That was not a good thing because, at that time, Colson was a little too extreme, perhaps, in some of his thinking and actions. He had some good ideas—having a new majority representation in the administration, for example. But he wasn't the person who was attuned to the fine points; he was, philosophically, a black-and-white-type person.

Jerry Jones He organized himself very well; he had a yellow legal pad for each issue. The president would call him, and he would grab about seven or eight of those legal pads and run to the president's OEOB office next to his. Colson was always a gentleman to me—extremely cordial, a very nice man. I was not involved in the political operation he was dealing with. My sense is that he and Nixon sort of fit; they sort of fed off each other. I don't know that Colson had the brakes to say, no, let's think about that. They were too much alike; they were both hardball players, and they knew how to do it, and enjoyed it. There are not a lot of checks in the White House; people can go a long way down an incorrect path before they ever get pulled in. That was not occurring when I was staff secretary. I came in after the horse was out of the barn.

Dwight Chapin Haldeman and Ehrlichman would come out of Nixon's office and take a break; Colson would come out and get into action. Nixon loved this, but there was a danger there. A number of times, Bob tried to tell Chuck: "When you come out of there, tell me; do not start things before you talk to me." But Chuck—by God! The commander in chief has just told him to go do whatever, and he's going to do it. I was horrified one day: I was in the Oval Office and the president called Colson in, and Chuck turned on a machine and taped him. I said, "Chuck, does the president know you are taping him?" Chuck answered, "I just do this so I will have notes to follow up." This was back in the days when they had those IBM belt things; I've always wondered where those belts are.

John Ehrlichman I was surprised by the Nixon-Colson relationship. We had a very good staff system, and the Nixon-Colson relationship cut across that system; it short-circuited it. Nixon bridled against the staff. The staff system, in a sense, required him to arrive rationally at decisions, where Colson did not, so he was able to vent his spleen, and had someone who would do things for him that, on judgment, the rest of the staff wouldn't have done.

Herbert Klein I had a number of broadcasters in from small stations to meet with Nixon in the Cabinet Room to discuss the FCC* and other issues. Colson had planted someone in the meeting, a man from South Carolina, who stood up and said, "We want to endorse you." I interrupted, "That is not the purpose of the meeting, but we thank you for your thoughts," and I cut it off. Colson and Nixon went into the Oval Office, with Colson saying that I had screwed up. Nixon said that I had egg on my face, or I didn't have my head screwed on properly—a couple of things of that nature. Later, Nixon apologized to me.

Robert Reisner Chuck Colson probably had one of the most brilliant, innovative political minds [of the Nixon administration]. It's another one of the tragedies of Watergate that someone as creative and innovative as Colson was would let himself go as far astray as he did. If Colson had stayed on the path, he might have created a Republican Congress in the 1970s. He and Nixon used to get together and strategize. Nixon, who was a clever political thinker, had picked one of the most interesting political minds to talk about these things with, and because of that, Colson picked up all sorts of secret missions and, as a result, built up an enormous empire in the White House. He had all sorts of groups: Catholics for Nixon, Labor for Nixon. He was the one who came up with a lot of the thinking about the peripheral urban ethnics, and that drugs and crime were issues for the Republican Party. He was in a state of perpetual conflict with the people at CRP, and he was part of the group that ultimately tried to make CRP a front for what was going on—that the real campaign was going to be run from the White House. In many ways, it was.

* The Federal Communications Commission, a regulatory agency.

Howard Phillips Colson did a great job for Nixon; he was one of the saving graces of that administration. He basically told the truth to Nixon; he talked reality to him. Colson was not motivated by ideology. He was very liberal. In the 1970s, I gave a speech at a conference that was very critical of the Great Society. Colson got up and said, "This is an outrage. I am going to rip up my prepared remarks, because this is terrible." I was amazed. I buy into the fact that Colson encouraged Nixon to act on his best impulses, which is what the liberals call his worst.

One of the worst things that can happen is to have disloyal employees who thwart the clearly expressed, carefully considered decisions of the person to whom they are accountable. Nixon had a bunch of self-serving prostitutes who thwarted his legitimate directives. Most of the people on his staff didn't believe the things Nixon said in his promises to the American people; they opposed what I regard as the "good" Nixon—his good instincts. Colson knew how to talk to men senior to him as peers. He had a level of brass analogous to John Connally's. He had a degree of confidence and certitude which Nixon himself lacked and wanted to have. There weren't many people in politics who were not a threat to Nixon—who could speak as a peer or protégé to Nixon; he looked on Colson as a peer-protégé.

Richard Moore He appealed to the president's naive side—some people thought the darker side. Colson was a gung-ho guy; he was ready to do anything—walk over his grandmother's grave—to get it done. In one of his first meetings with the president, Nixon wanted to get out support for racial fairness in the construction industry. He said, "If you have to break all the china in this building, get people to do this." The president enjoyed talking about fighting back against our opponents, and Colson liked that kind of thing. When I went over from the Justice Department to the White House [in 1970], John Mitchell said, "Look out for Charlie Colson. If the president ever gets into real trouble, it will be his fault."

Daniel Ellsberg Colson has said several times on the air that in the course of his born-again experience, people reminded him: You are supposed to apologize—to make amends to every person you have wronged. Since he had gone to prison for pleading that he had wronged me, the natural question interviewers asked him was: "Have you apologized to Daniel Ellsberg?" And on each occasion, he said yes. I got the impression that his born-again experience had not been complete since, in fact, I had never heard from him; there was no apology.

Maurice Stans He would call me to ask if I had gotten any money from specific people. I never knew him very well, except in a few instances when I would ask him for information. He would send me a memo back—many times profane—saying, "We've got to do something about this bastard; he's going to ruin us if we let him go ahead." He is a very smart guy. He has demonstrated that by the organizations he has built up, and the work he has done, in recent years.

Richard Kleindienst He was a very bright, able political operator, in a very tough way; I had dealings with Colson before Watergate occurred, and he was just a tough son-of-a-bitch. That is why, as a Christian, I am gratified that he did have a conversion, because if there was ever a man that needed it, it was Chuck Colson.

Bernard Barker I did meet Colson after Watergate. He came up to me one day; I had never spoken to the man before. He said, "Mr. Barker, have you found God lately?" I looked at him and said, "No. I never lost Him."

John Dean I've often thought, reading over my tapes—and feeling my relationship as it was evolving between myself and Nixon—that he knew that Colson was on his way out and he was grooming me as his next Colson. But I didn't have the same mentality that Colson had; I couldn't have done the things that Colson did. So it never would have worked. I'm sure glad that didn't happen. As to how Colson got in there, well, the president has to deal through his aides and there are only so many hours in a day that Haldeman and Ehrlichman could sit there and listen to this stuff. Nixon discovered me; he enjoyed talking to me; found me relatively intelligent, so this stuff started pouring out.

Raymond Price Bob Haldeman told me in a conversation at his home—when he was on a weekend furlough from jail—that he blamed himself for the Colson phenomenon. He explained that he was spending too much time listening to Nixon talk politics; he couldn't get his work done. Colson was steeped in politics; he had worked for Senator Saltonstall and he could talk to Nixon for hours on political matters, releasing Bob for other things. This was his fatal error; he'd created the Colson monster. I think of Colson kind of clawing his way to the top by pandering to the president's worst instincts. Colson is a strange bird; I don't have much respect for him. Nixon always had around him what I call "sentinels," whom he could trust not to do the things he said to do. Haldeman was one, Rose Woods was one, I was one, and Mitchell was one, also. I once asked John, "Who is Colson's constituency, anyway?" and he replied, "The president's worst instincts."

John Dean

Herbert Klein Ehrlichman had been head of the General Counsel's Office, then head of the Domestic Council. He wanted to keep control of the General Counsel's Office and he needed someone weak there. Mitchell wanted someone in the White House so he could keep track of Ehrlichman. Dean came from Mitchell's shop, so that's how he got there. Nixon wasn't looking for the greatest legal mind to solve his problem; he thought it [Watergate] was a political problem. Dean was someone he could listen to, or dominate, or take or not take, so I don't think that he looked for the strongest person around; Buzhardt and Garment were much stronger.

Fred Fielding, assistant counsel to the president; deputy counsel to the president I was aware that John Dean would go meet with Mitchell or Dick Kleindienst; that was something he did all the time. He would talk about it. Every time he'd come back and regale me. He'd say, "I was up at Mitchell's apartment. We did such-and-such." But he would not say anything substantive about what he was doing. He later explained that he wanted to keep me out of it. I have to take him at his word, if that's what he personally says to me. At one point, I almost resigned, and said to one of his friends that I couldn't help John because half the time I didn't know what he was doing. John Dean was a very ambitious man. He wanted to do things later in life. He wanted to be ambassador to France; he used to take French [language] tapes and sit in his office and listen to them while I worried about business.

Richard Kleindienst If he had put down a prior employment in Washington, D.C., when they gave him a full field check, he never would have gotten into the Justice Department; he lied about that. He came into my office one day and said, "Boss, I've got a chance to be counsel to the president." I said, "You are out of your mind. You can't be counsel to the president; you have to be a peer for that." A week later, he came back and said, "It's too good an honor. I'm going to take it." I said, "Junior"—I used to call him that—"this is a big mistake on your part. You are not going to be counsel to the president; you're going to be a robot up there, run by Haldeman and Ehrlichman." I think that is the way they treated him and, as I understand it, that is one of the reasons he tripped over at the end and had these fantastic recollections. He is an amazing character; I don't think there is an ounce of morality in him. To have pulled off what he did—and in the manner in which he did it—is one of the most amazing stories. I think John Dean thought he could pull off almost anything—and he almost did.

Donald E. Santarelli He was extremely ambitious without portfolio. I met him when he was one of the minority counsels to the House Judiciary Committee; he had preceded me in that job by about six months. I found him to be interesting, lively, witty, and intelligent, but highly opportunistic. His tendency was to piggy-back on the work of others and synthesize it into his own work, and, like the three little pigs, to get up early in the morning and go use it as if it were his—a tendency I did not admire. But John was very effective in ingratiating himself, and so he ingratiated himself with the Congress, the attorney general, then with John Ehrlichman. I was so exercised about that that I made a lot of noise and was told by the then–deputy attorney general that if I didn't stop fighting with Dean, I would be fired. He didn't have the power to do that since I was a presidential employee and in those days enjoyed a warm relationship with Mr. Nixon.

But when Ehrlichman selected Dean to fill his old title as counsel to the president, I really went ballistic; I thought that John was in over his head in that job, so I went to Ehrlichman and said, "I've known John Dean for a long time and I've worked with him. I believe that you have given him a charter that exceeds his abilities. But, primarily, I believe him to be too much of an accommodating opportunist for you to get what you want in a counsel. That is a sense of independent judgment." Ehrlichman's response was that he knew what he was getting; I assumed that to mean that Ehrlichman was interested in filling the slot with someone who would not be independent of him—not a threat to him, but subservient to him, and controlled by him. I went to others in the White House—to the point where I received instructions to shut up. My view was that the counsel to the president was supposed to be his conscience, not his lackey; there were plenty of those on the White House staff, but the counsel had to be able to say: This won't work; this is wrong; this is not authorized by law; or this is high risk. John was not of that view until, of course, he got an assignment he could not handle—the cover-up.

Donald Segretti I met with Dean once in Washington. He is a very personable man, but he is also a different study: he has a very appealing voice—it gave people a great deal of comfort. But there is more to that—under the surface. When I met him, I needed some legal assistance; I was in an arena totally different from anything I had ever been involved in. It's hard to sum up somebody's motive in a couple of sentences. If I had to do it, I would say: the survival of Mr. Dean, and his own interests. I have run into him out here [in California]. I have no tremendous animosity; those times are closed. I occasionally talk to Chapin and Strachan; I think they are good people—they got involved with something they didn't really think about at the time, as did I.

Jerry Jones John Dean was a very strange fellow: he was clearly brilliant, but he was not touchable in terms of having a relationship; I never, ever, was able to be close to John in the sense of having any sort of a personal relationship. I would typify him as an extremely ambitious guy who—a lot like Magruder— put ambition and career progress ahead of morals, judgment, and ethics, and got over the line. That office handled all of the FBI field investigations for the Personnel Office and had to give me an opinion: Yes, this person is okay to handle this job. I did not deal with the FBI; Fielding and Dean did—and particularly Fielding—so I had a lot of interaction with that office.

Stephen Bull In the Watergate days, I couldn't figure out where this guy was coming from, and for a number of years I was almost giving him the benefit of the doubt, thinking that the guy did pay the penalty—even though he brought down the president. But I have come to realize—and I don't think you need to go through the first year of law school to realize it— that the principal job of a legal counsel is to keep a guy out of trouble. For whatever reason, he [Dean] did not keep his boss out of trouble. If he knew of all these things going on over at the Reelection Committee, he had an absolute moral obligation to blow the whistle and say, "You can't do this"; but he never did. He can write his books about blind ambition* and all the rest, but because of his own ambition, and his own selfishness, he brought down this president. He can justify that every minute of the day, and say what a rotten bunch of scoundrels the rest of us were, but I think that he was the scoundrel there who just didn't know right from wrong, and to this day he won't admit it; it was his failing as a human being.

Raymond Price There was a time when I considered Dean an ally in shooting down some of Colson's crazier schemes. Later, I discovered how he operated—what his agenda was—and I realized I had misjudged him; he really was a snake.

* *Blind Ambition: The Watergate Years* (Simon and Schuster, 1976).

Alexander Haig Dean was an absolute snake. I wouldn't let him into my office—this was *before* Watergate. When he was assistant counsel, he came slithering in one day on behalf of Ehrlichman; he wanted me to send a military plane to Latin America to pick up a guy named Robert Vesco.* I said, "Who is this guy, Vesco? Is he a military man? Is he in government?" Dean replied, "No. We want him up in Washington; we have to talk to him about some business." I said, "You are not going to use taxpayers' money for that, so get out of here." That's the kind of weasel he was—and, of course, he double-crossed Nixon. There was no excuse for what he did to Nixon, even if he was totally right—which he wasn't.

Robert Odle, Jr. Dean was a competent lawyer, and was very nice to me, but I don't think that there was a moral compass there—or a great, overriding dedication to principle. The people who watched him at Justice don't have a great view of him. You would have a meeting and kick around ideas; the next thing you knew, your ideas would be on a piece of paper he would send someone with his name on it. He's not the kind of guy I'd trust my wallet—or my wife—with.

Bernard Barker This guy, Dean, is a piece of excrement as far as I'm concerned; people like that make me puke. Here was a guy who was a nothing, who becomes an assistant to the president of the United States. He takes advantage of this position; he marries this beautiful doll,† who wouldn't normally even look at a jerk like him. When the time comes for him to give the man loyalty, he says: No. I have to take care of myself. To me, he's nothing but a coward. I don't believe anything he says. If I were ever to criticize President Nixon, it would be for choosing people like Dean; he should have known better.

John Ehrlichman

Richard Bergholz When Nixon was president, he dispatched Ehrlichman to come out and tell the Editorial Board of the *Times* what a great program the Family Assistance Program was. It was an amazing, liberal program by

---

* A financier and fugitive from U.S. justice who had made a $200,000 contribution to the Nixon campaign. In April 1974, Nixon aides John Mitchell and Maurice Stans were acquitted by a New York Federal District Court jury of a charge of having accepted the Vesco funds in exchange for taking his side in a dispute with the Securities and Exchange Commission (SEC).
† Maureen Dean.

Republican standards. There were ten or fifteen people sitting at an oblong table, and Ehrlichman was running down all the wonderful things that are going to happen under FAP. I said, "John, how are you going to pay for this?" And he just snapped at me and said, "I know you; we have a file on you; we know all about you." Now, this can only be a carryover from 1962 and 1968, when I had been covering Nixon. Was he reflecting Nixon, or was this his own personal feeling? I thought it was Nixon. My sense is that before he came out here, he had been briefed on everyone who was going to be at that meeting.

John Dean He [Nixon] picked Mitchell for the events prior to the Watergate break-in, and I became the candidate for the post-break-in period. I think a lot of that was John Ehrlichman maneuvering and positioning, saying, we will have Dean fall on the sword. I think he was involved in Nixon's August 29 [1972] statement—and to this day he is trying to perpetuate that. He is sitting in Atlanta, feeding Roger Morris° all this stuff for his work. This is John's life; he is trying to rewrite history. He is, I gather, a very bitter person. I told the BBC people something that they later came back and said stuck with them. I said, "You're going to meet with Ehrlichman and Haldeman. You're going to find Bob is kind of straight and a little terse; John Ehrlichman is going to be absolutely charming and delightful. But by the end of your relationship, you are going to respect Haldeman and have no respect for Ehrlichman. They came back and said, "You are absolutely right."

Alexander Haig

Alexander Butterfield In October 1973, Nixon took a United Airlines flight out of Dulles† at five o'clock to come to San Clemente during the oil crisis [embargo]; it was to get good press. I was furious, because the FAA [Federal Aviation Authority] has a responsibility when the president travels; we have to keep all airplanes 25 miles from his airplane. I blew up; I wasn't careful about it, and it got out. One other administration official was quoted as saying how stupid it was, and I raised hell. What a dumb, goddamn idea. Haig said to me, "Alex, you have this man climbing the walls here." So I wrote a letter of apology to the president.

° A Nixon biographer.
† A major airport serving the Washington, D.C., area.

Robert Hartmann Haig, in his dealings with Vice-President Ford, thought himself the president; he thought he was serving Nixon's interests. At some point—like St. Paul on the road to Damascus*—he saw a blinding light and decided that Nixon's interests were best served by his resignation. He was ambitious, unlike Haldeman, who threw himself on his sword for Nixon.

Raymond Price Obviously, Haig was hiding things from the president, including his Woodward connection. Later, when Woodward was causing so much grief and Haig was not leveling with us about the connection, we wondered why not.

Jerry Jones Buzhardt and Haig were, perhaps, roommates at West Point; Butterfield and Haig were at the Pentagon together; and Woodward was probably tied in to them, so there were some interesting ties that no one, at the time, understood or appreciated.

Bob [Robert] Woodward, reporter, *Washington Post* I never knew Haig when I was in the navy. I never briefed him; it's all bogus. If you check on that you will see it's just not true. I deny it; Haig denies it; there is no one who will come forward and say it. And if I had briefed him, what would be the big deal? This certainly would be a matter of record; people would know and I would have acknowledged it a long time ago. It just didn't happen.

William Saxbe I have great admiration for Haig; he held that office together; he was the president toward the end. Nixon seemed so engrossed with what was happening to him and in self-pity that somebody had to watch the store, and it was Haig.

Howard Phillips He was a personable, attractive, fanny-kisser.

H. R. Haldeman

Jerry Jones I have worked for four chiefs of staff: Haldeman, Haig, Rumsfeld, and [Richard] Cheney. Haldeman was absolutely the best of the group in terms of administrative skills and ability. He made that system work.

---

* A New Testament reference.

Alexander Butterfield Haldeman was the president's alter ego; he was like the assistant president. He was every bit the authority that Sherman Adams* was, I am sure, in the Eisenhower days. He was not called chief of staff; there was no such term then. Haldeman was invaluable, but he was very abrupt with everyone; he was all business; he did exactly what Richard Nixon wanted him to do. People thought Haldeman was arrogant when he testified,† but people forget that we—the White House staff—hated the committee; they were trying to harm our man.

Frederic V. Malek Sometimes Nixon would go off on a tack that was too aggressive and went too far, and Haldeman would be a very sensible moderator. He was probably one of the most underrated public servants; he was a hell of a good executive. A strong chief of staff. Totally loyal to the president.

Rocco Siciliano As I was leaving the administration, Haldeman asked me to come over for a talk. I had a litany of complaints: my number-one criticism concerned control from the White House. He just listened and didn't say much; it was a catharsis that he was letting me get it out of my system. Of course, nothing happened as a result of the meeting, but—to his great credit—he listened.

Raymond Price I happen to be a fan of Bob Haldeman. I think he did a very good job, both in the campaign and in the White House. To me, he was a model chief of staff; he kept himself strictly out of the policy process; he was the honest broker and made sure that all sides were represented.

Donald E. Santarelli He was very efficient, very effective, in his management of what was then a much simpler process, and he served Nixon as he wanted to be served. Nixon liked Haldeman's coordination. Haldeman's initial approach—to stay out of the policy aspects—was very healthy. As time went on and the burdens of the government became greater, he began to be more politically oriented. Aside from his personality, and his personal style, and his desire to have young people around him who were very subservient—you could argue as to whether that is in the president's best interests—it seemed to work for Mr. Nixon in the beginning. But as time went on, and with Mitchell's departure and the tendency to get more involved in policy went on, I don't think that it was in Mr. Nixon's best interests. But Mr.

---

* Mr. Adams was forced to resign after it was disclosed that he had accepted a vicuña coat from industrialist Bernard Goldfine.
† The Senate Watergate Committee.

Nixon liked to be managed, and in the beginning, the Haldeman-Ehrlichman team served his interests.

E. Howard Hunt

William Colby If you are running spy operations, you have to be very solid. Hunt was always a romantic; he wrote those spy novels.* We have had our romantics and they have gotten us into trouble, but the agency doesn't have control over former employees. If Helms had known about Ehrlichman's request for help, he would have said no. But that is what happens in a bureaucracy. The reason Ehrlichman went to [Lieutenant General Robert] Cushman [deputy director, CIA] was that Cushman was an old friend, who used to work in the White House. When Helms found out what was happening, he cut it off.

Bernard Barker I am both disappointed in Hunt and understanding of him: I am disappointed because it is hard to see your superior in the accuser's bench, accusing you of doing the thing he ordered you to do. But then, I can't forget that Hunt was a great man—that he had fought behind the Japanese lines in [in World War II]; that he had lost his wife† and had gone to pieces. In a way, I think that Hunt thought he was doing the right thing by cooperating. But if he had asked me, I would have said: "Howard, don't do it, because what would you say to the Cuban colony involved in the liberation of Cuba: 'I did this for the liberation of Cuba, and then I turned state's evidence.'" I would rather be dead.

G. Gordon Liddy Hunt had been involved very heavily for the agency in the Bay of Pigs, at a pretty high level. He had a great emotional, as well as career, involvement in it: he was very close to the Cubans; he felt they were betrayed. The Cubans really believed that the Nixon administration was their best bet for going in and getting rid of Castro and liberating Cuba. They would say, "Use us; use us; use us." After Hunt's turning, I never really spoke to him again. Some while ago—at an anniversary of the "Firing Line"‡ television program—I found myself at the next urinal in the New

---

    * Mr. Hunt is the author of many spy novels.
    † Dorothy Hunt, killed in the crash of a United Airlines plane en route to Chicago, in December 1972. Mrs. Hunt was carrying $10,000 in cash, thought to be money toward the Watergate burglars' defense.

York Yacht Club's rest room, and I think we nodded. He ratted because of his age, the fact that he was sick, and because he was destroyed by Dorothy's death. In that marriage, she was psychologically stronger.

G. Gordon Liddy

Frederic V. Malek The first time I knew about Liddy was when I was appointed White House liaison with the 1972 campaign. I met Liddy, who was then counsel for the Committee to Reelect, and thought he was a little weird, but Jeb Magruder and others over there spoke well of him.

Fred Fielding I met Gordon Liddy on an airplane flying back to San Diego [California]. Somewhere in the bowels of the White House is a memo that I wrote to John Dean, saying, "This fellow, Liddy, is indeed a strange person." I was concerned. It wasn't anything criminal; it was his manner—there was something about him. Subsequently, I had some dealings with him when he was general counsel at CRP. I recall one time when we went over to the Justice Department to meet with Henry Petersen, head of the Criminal Division.[*] I was there representing the White House, Liddy representing the CRP. It was a straight legal issue, but I remember thinking afterward—and I checked the dates out—here was Liddy, sitting there, kidding Henry about smoking cigarettes, and it's either two days before or after—he had broken into the DNC for the first time, and here he was, talking to the head of the Criminal Division, just as cool as a cucumber.

Robert Odle, Jr. Liddy came over to CRP because I don't think anybody at the White House wanted to put up with him, he was such a nut. We needed a lawyer, because the campaign laws were changing. As we later learned, Liddy was going to have some other responsibilities as well. Dean and Krogh didn't want him around the EOB [Executive Office Building], so we got him. The day after the break-in, when I saw him running around the office—looking for a shredder and trying to figure out what to do—I realized that he had these other responsibilities. He didn't get along with Jeb [Stuart Magruder] because he didn't like to take orders from a younger man, so he went off to the Finance Committee, where he worked for Mr. Stans, who was much older than he.

---

[*] Henry E. Petersen, assistant attorney general, who was in charge of the Justice Department's Watergate investigation.

Alexander Butterfield Liddy was a guy no one ever knew. After the break-in, I was called and asked if I knew Hunt. I said, "There is no Howard Hunt [in the White House]." I didn't even have to look in the [White House] directory; he wasn't in the directory. How about Liddy? I said, "There is no guy named Liddy." Now, I was wrong there; just wrong. He was so many rungs down that he was a guy you never heard of.

Robert Reisner Liddy remains a fascinating figure. He was introduced at his first [campaign] staff meeting as a "super sleuth." When Magruder said that, Liddy pulled him aside and was extremely angry: "You are going to blow my cover." It was clear that Liddy had other duties beyond being a general counsel; he didn't tell people what he was doing, but he wore it as a badge of honor. What Liddy was up to was sneaking around—and letting people know he was sneaking around. He was also acting as a lawyer for the campaign, filing for primaries. At first, he was located near Magruder; then his office got moved. He and Magruder had a lot of disagreements and, ulti-mately, Liddy resided in the Finance Office. I think that all this stuff about Maurice Stans supporting Liddy was a bum rap; Stans knew Liddy had other duties, but I bet he didn't ask—or wish to know—what Liddy, who was a very free operator, was doing. Liddy was a very colorful guy, but he also came on as being quite bizarre as an individual.

Robert Odle, Jr. I was blown away when I heard that McCord was in jail; I was his boss. I wasn't surprised when I came to hear about Liddy, because he was such an odd duck. One time, I was in a meeting and my wife was waiting for me. When the meeting ended, she said, "I've just met Gordon Liddy. I was sitting there, and he said, 'Would you like to learn how to kill somebody with a pencil? You make sure it has a big eraser; you put that in your hand; you make sure the point is sharp; and then you put it through the soft palette. Generally, it will take them out.'"

Jeb Stuart Magruder As I said to Gordon Strachan one day, walking across the street, "This guy is Adolf Hitler." And he said, "Well, at least he's our Adolf Hitler." I had no use for Gordon Liddy back then, any more than I do now.

Jeb Stuart Magruder

Robert Reisner I was in charge of the paper that flowed in and out of Magruder's office. He was a secretive guy—that was part of his charm and power. He was always doing political deals. He had these long action lists of things he wanted done; sometimes they were very cryptic: he would call someone and say, "Have him do the following . . . " Sometimes it was hard to see the mosaic.

Jerry Jones Magruder was a lovely fellow trying far too hard to be pleasing. My sense is that he would do what he had to do to please whoever his boss was. He had been Herb Klein's deputy in the White House Communications Office; he was sort of a Haldeman protégé put under Klein, trying to bolster his administrative abilities. He was then put over in the campaign as the organizer, with the thought being that a lot of the political input would be coming from the White House team: Haldeman, Chapin, and Colson. Magruder was simply going to be an organizer, and later, as people peeled off of other positions—like Mardian, Kleindienst, Mitchell, and others— Magruder would recede. But as it worked out, that didn't happen. I am sure that the president and Haldeman discussed how all of that was going to be phased in and proceeded on what they thought was the phase-in of the A team.

Robert Odle, Jr. Magruder was very efficient, very well organized. If he had been a partner in a law firm, he would have done well at leveraging—at finding associates to work on projects. I wouldn't argue with his later statement that he lost his moral compass.

G. Gordon Liddy Magruder is the kind of guy who would piss in your pocket and tell you it's raining. There is just no substance there. He was a glorified gofer. He was happy because he had the appearance of power.

James McCord

Robert Odle, Jr. McCord worked for me. We were terribly worried about security, because Nixon campaigns were looked at pretty closely—and sometimes ruthlessly: Jack Anderson* had a habit of hiring people to go through the trash.

David Wilson We had a significant amount of coordination with the Secret Service in the Counsel's Office; we developed a role when the antiwar

---

* A nationally syndicated columnist specializing in exposé-style reporting.

demonstrations were going on. In that context, the only connection I had with McCord—and the reason I knew who he was—related to that. At one point, the Secret Service called and said, "We wanted to let you know that there is going to be a demonstration in front of the Headquarters to Reelect the President; we don't know if they [the committee] have been advised of this, but they may want to take precautions to avoid an incident." I didn't know what to do with that information, so I ended up calling Rob Odle at CRP and telling him about this information, and saying, "If you have someone who handles these things, he ought to be dealing with it." He said, "Yes, we do; we've got Jim McCord. He should know about this. I don't know what he is doing, because nobody has told us of this information."

Half an hour later, I had a call from McCord. He said, "I just want to report to you that there is going to be a demonstration here, in front of the office." I said, "Thank you very much; that's just what I told you." That was my one contact with McCord. When I saw his name as one of those arrested in connection with the break-in, I knew who he was—and clearly, he should not be involved in such a circumstance. I didn't know Hunt at all; I had never heard of him, nor did I know of the existence of the Plumbers. I knew both Bud Krogh and David Young, personally, well, but I didn't know what they'd been doing.

Bernard Barker Jimmy came to me during the Watergate trials and asked me to turn state's evidence; he said he was not going to be a scapegoat. I told him that not only would I not do this, but that he shouldn't either. I said, "Look, Jimmy, you are going to have to shave every morning and look in the mirror. This is too big for someone like me. When something is this big, leave it alone; it will take care of itself." He was also involved in some investigation regarding the Jewish people; it was one of two or three things he was involved in that he was going to expose if they didn't give him immunity. I said, "No, Jimmy. There is nothing behind this, except that we are caught, and we have got to take our punishment." Mentally, Jimmy was not prepared for things to go wrong; the appearance of power caused these people to think that they had connections and would not have problems, so they broke down.

Robert Reisner He came to the committee [CRP] from the CIA and, over time, he didn't seem very different from security people who were former FBI agents, or other agents I've known; he took delight in talking about security matters. In retrospect, I think that he was wildly out of date in his understanding of technology: he would answer my questions about devices, but the true security professional would not have taken so much time to tell a twenty-five-year-old assistant about bugging devices and how they worked. He was a terribly nice man, who got caught up in a terrible, life-changing set of circumstances because he wanted to be helpful—and because he was fascinated by the "tradecraft" that he had never himself participated in. It's tragic that they got him involved, because he was vulnerable.

John Mitchell and His Wife Martha

Robert Reisner Mitchell was clear-sighted enough to know what had happened in the White House—to see how Nixon's worst instincts had been controlled and fed by the rise of Haldeman and Ehrlichman. While Nixon could go to his study—with his yellow pads and Richard Nixon pens—and think about Russian-Chinese relations, he probably also got together with Colson in his office in late afternoon, or would come storming into his office in the morning, telling Haldeman things like: It's those guys in the Labor Department doing it to us again. Find out who they are; we need to fire them! So there was this White House apparatus which geared up around carrying out his instructions. This was something Mitchell didn't want to spend his time on. I think that Mitchell took on the campaign for much the same reason he later allowed himself to be ruined as a political figure: he did it for Nixon, so that he would somehow be a balance-wheel, to moderate what he later referred to in his testimony° as these "White House horrors."

Donald E. Santarelli Mitchell got a bum rap, but he was also careless. Washington is a mean place, where the rules of civility have ever been eroding. In the 1960s, there was great reverence for the private lives of people who served in government. But when Mitchell came to Washington in 1969, he did not understand that it was a place with increasing disrespect for privacy and missteps of a minor nature—when you're in a Cabinet job, you tend to see the big picture; you don't pay close attention to the small stuff going on around you. Mitchell did not pay attention to the dangers and risks of the small stuff—like Liddy's activities; the campaign chicken-shit stuff. He should have recognized that the small items are the ones that bring big men down. He didn't appreciate the degree of long knives, and how fatally they can cut.

He was not a man trained to be attorney general, and not a man trained for the job of prime minister that Nixon thrust on him; he did not have a his-

---

° Before the Senate Select Committee on Watergate.

tory of government experience. He was very willing to listen and learn—a man who recognized his limitations and tried to rise up to what was expected of him and, perhaps, more was expected of Mitchell than he was prepared for. Certainly, he didn't expect the extraordinary visibility and searchlight examination of his conduct; he wasn't trained for it. If you are going to run in the Kentucky Derby, you'd better be a thoroughbred. Well, he wasn't quite prepared for the track. He was a very open, honest, and honorable kind of guy. I was proud to work for him.

William Ruckelshaus Mitchell took a bad rap. He was not a public man; he was about as unconcerned about his own reputation as any public man I've ever seen. He really thought that much of what was being written and said about him was so far from reality that it was laughable. I can remember a conversation with him in which I said I believed that it was important for him to be portrayed as concerned about issues involving justice in order to be an effective attorney general on behalf of the president, even if he didn't care about himself. A lot of the publicity he got, particularly during the early stages of the administration, was unfair and unwarranted. He did very little to try to offset it.

Then, he ended up hiring [Richard] Dick Moore after a year or so of the pummeling, to help him with his public image. It got better for a time; then, of course, it declined again when he went over to manage the Committee to Reelect the President. But he was a man who really didn't care very much about what the public thought of him. If you take that approach, you are potentially going to get into a lot of trouble, because your popularity—or unpopularity—was going to reflect on the president, and it wasn't irrelevant to his own success, or that of the president, because he was correctly perceived as being very close to the president.

Donald E. Santarelli Nixon was extremely reliant on John Mitchell. I often saw Nixon in Mitchell's presence because I would go with him in my position as associate deputy attorney general, because crime was the interesting issue to Mr. Nixon. Then, I began to go on my own, because Nixon would simply call for it, and Mitchell said fine, that he didn't need to be there. The president was reliant on John Mitchell for more than just the Justice Department function: it was widely said in those days that John Mitchell was the prime minister of the administration and, in the three years he was attorney general, he did, in fact, function that way. Mr. Nixon would expect support from him, or opinion, or reaction, or responsibility, for issues far broader than the normal Justice Department functions.

In Cabinet meetings, the president would keep a close eye on Mr. Mitchell, who had an informal signal system with the president—that is, the president would occasionally wax on, perhaps longer than needed, or would get off-track on the substance of the subject, not often, because Nixon was an extraordinarily bright guy, but when you are the boss—particularly the big boss—of an organization, people do not tell you much that isn't wanted to be heard, so you can easily get off the track. Mitchell was really very much the station master of those Cabinet meetings; Nixon would keep an eye on him, and if Mitchell became agitated, he would jiggle or puff on his pipe with some vigor. Nixon would get the signal and switch subjects, or terminate that line of conversation; if Mitchell looked serene—and that was really the only word for it—Nixon would go on.

Raymond Price John loved Martha very much. He did not want to be attorney general; he knew that Martha had a problem and he was afraid that the pressures of Washington would send her over the edge. And, of course, it turned out that he was right. Nixon persuaded him by his sense of duty to the country; he knew that John would respond to this. So John came to Washington, and it ended up destroying Martha—and destroying him.

Donald E. Santarelli He was very distracted by Mrs. Mitchell. He was genuinely attentive to and—at the time—in love with Martha; he did everything he knew to accommodate her increasingly bizarre personality. There was a time when she was extraordinarily popular; she was a real Washington phenomenon. One of my responsibilities at Justice was to be in charge of relations with the professional legal world. Inevitably, requests for Mitchell's attendance at conventions or events included a request that he make sure to bring Martha along. It got to the point where you felt they were more interested in having Martha there than having John. She was a celebrity, but she was an errant juggernaut, and so Nixon and Mitchell were very attentive to managing Martha, because John was not comfortable otherwise, and she had every potential for being what she finally became—an embarrassment.

When we would have high-level meetings at the Justice Department and Martha would call, John would take the call right in the middle of the meeting. When Mitchell and the president were meeting and Martha would call, John would take the call, and often the president would get on the line and greet her warmly. Nixon—who treated women in an old-fashioned, respectful way, and was gracious to all women—was especially warm to Martha, in part because he was entertained initially by her liveliness, and in part because he was terribly reliant on—and affectionate of—John

Mitchell. Great efforts were made to accommodate Martha; she had an FBI detail—and for a while a Justice Department car—until it became an issue in the press; then we raised the money for it privately. Martha was not included in state secrets or political strategy; she just enjoyed being a celebrity, and whatever it took to be one—like a moth drawn to a flame, she was drawn to it.

Dwight Chapin At one point, I was made the Martha Mitchell contact at the White House; you haven't lived until you've been the Martha Mitchell contact. I would get her calls—at all hours, and in all kinds of conditions. At the Waldorf* the morning Nixon found out he'd been elected, he's standing there with John Mitchell, Haldeman, Ehrlichman, and myself. Nixon puts his arm around Mitchell's shoulder and says, "John, in a little while we are going to pack up and go down and visit Ike,† and then we are going to Key Biscayne to get this show under way. I want you to be on that plane." And this tear comes down John Mitchell's face, and he replies, "Mr. President-elect, I think I'd better go up to Connecticut and take care of some things with Martha." She was in an institution there. John loved that woman. How many men, at that moment in time, would have done that? He could have gone up there two days later. He was really in love with that woman, madly in love.

Leonard Garment Martha was a problem for Mitchell. During the campaign, I would be working late, and Martha would call my wife in the middle of the night and say, "Are you wondering where your sonny boy, Lennie, is? He's out having a frolic with sonny boy John." Those phone calls were probably duplicated hundreds of times over. But as the song goes, "Yet he loved her." He was proud of her; she had that manic zest. He didn't know what she would do next—go over the edge, or the parapet. At the end, he was very much distracted and not thinking clearly—which is an explanation, not an excuse.

Kenneth Rush She was drinking too much, and calling the press, and having delusions. I knew her quite well; she was a sad case of an alcoholic. She distracted John Mitchell so much that he didn't push this Watergate idea away from the crazy people. John was a compromiser, a very nice, fine man, in many ways. Nixon thinks he let it get out of hand.

---

* The Waldorf-Astoria Hotel, in New York City, Nixon's election-night headquarters.
† Former President Dwight D. Eisenhower, then a patient at the Walter Reed Army Hospital, in Washington, D.C. Nixon's postelection visit occurred on November 6, 1968.

Robert Odle, Jr. At CRP, we called Mrs. Mitchell "the account": she always thought that people were trying to kill her. Some of us wished they had. It was more difficult for John Mitchell than we ever knew, but he never complained about it; he was never disloyal to her. He was such a fine man. His whole life was full of kindnesses.

G. Gordon Liddy We knew that she had a severe alcoholic problem—episodes lasting about seventy-two hours. When she was sober, she was a very charming woman. She was colorful: she would make calls to the press; she would throw his clothes out of the apartment [window] and someone would have to go down to Fifth Avenue* and pick his pants up—not the kind of thing you usually associate with attorneys general.

William Ruckelshaus Martha was extremely vulnerable because she had no sense of what the role of the wife of the attorney general ought to be—what she should, or should not, say; she was far too outspoken. Many of the reporters who discovered her after a couple of months abused their access to her. She would often speak off the top of her head, and was very quotable. I don't think this ever hurt the attorney general's relationship with the president, but it did hurt him publicly, because a lot of people who were opposed to the administration saw what she was saying as reflective of his own views. That was not altogether wrong; she was sometimes repeating what he had said to her in private. My impression of him around his wife was that Mitchell was more amused than distracted by her; I don't think he took her views on public issues very seriously. And while their relationship obviously became very strained over the course of this, it didn't seem to have much effect on his ability to concentrate on the issue at hand.

---

* The Mitchells maintained an apartment on upper Fifth Avenue, in New York City.

Part Five

"This Thing Called Watergate"

14

The Atmosphere That Engendered Watergate

In mid-1971, Richard Nixon began to look ahead to the following year's presidential election—his last political race. As he and his associates developed the outlines of their campaign strategy, they set as a primary goal the creation of an overwhelming victory—a surge of votes that would produce a mandate, allowing Mr. Nixon to intensify his efforts at détente with the Soviet Union; widen the breakthrough he had achieved with the People's Republic of China; conclude the Vietnam War with "peace with honor" and the return of the American POWs; propel his legislative program through a Congress that would, inevitably, be controlled by the Democrats; and gain a measure of revenge against those in the political sphere and in the media who he perceived to be his opponents.

The electoral mandate would also bring Mr. Nixon personal, political validation and would forever banish the memory of his loss to John F. Kennedy in 1960, as well as his razor-thin victory over Hubert Humphrey in 1968. If all went as planned, the long journey, which had begun in Orange County, California, in 1946, would culminate in a massive demonstration of political clout, and a signal from the electorate that his vision was in harmony with that of mainstream America.

In the view of Mr. Nixon and his colleagues, the creation of a mandate would require not only skilled political professionals and unprecedented levels of funding, but would also call for intensive intelligence-gathering activities focused on his potential presidential rivals.

Almost from the start, the campaign was marked by the development of schemes for questionable, if not illegal, intelligence-gathering operations that would—with or without the personal sign-off of the president—result in criminal harassment of his opponents; break-ins at the headquarters of the Democratic National Committee; and illegal financial campaign transactions. These activities would, in turn, lead to a cover-up, setting in motion the chain of events that would lead inexorably to Mr. Nixon's resignation.

Stephen Bull You have to look at Watergate within the context of the times. The times were tumultuous: there was great unrest throughout the country—civil unrest; antiwar activity; people getting shot on campuses; political violence abounded; there was uncertainty about motivations. Because communism is dying away now, it's easy to say, "Isn't it kind of frivolous to be so concerned?" But back then, it wasn't. Secret documents* were being published with impunity in the major newspapers; you had to wonder what things were coming to. While some things are not justified, maybe they're a little more understandable. The thing that isn't is why they went into the Democratic headquarters in the first place; I don't think any of us will ever really know the answer. My guess is that, to this day, Nixon hasn't a clue as to why those guys [the Watergate burglars] went over there. He didn't know who those guys were—Martinez and Barker, and the rest of those guys.

Maurice Stans There was a compelling feeling: Nixon had a hard time with Congress his first term; a lot of things he proposed didn't go through. His basic concept was that he had to win big to increase the size of his mandate from the people. That idea permeated his campaign organization; it permeated the White House; and I think everybody was working on the idea that the bigger the vote, the better the next four years were going to be. I think that is what swept Gordon Liddy into the play—that swept so many others into the play. Gordon Liddy says, "Let's get a bunch of girls on a ship down there at the Democratic convention." The whole idea of getting a look at the records in the Democratic National Committee was a wide-swinging approach to: How can we get something on one guy or another that will help us in the campaign? And it ran wild, and got out of control.

---

* The Pentagon Papers, for example, published by the *New York Times*.

G. Gordon Liddy There certainly was the feeling of "us against them"; it was no secret that the establishment media were not members of the Nixon fan club. But there was no extrapolation from that, therefore: We can do anything. We were just playing by the rules. They are not the rules you are going to read about in civics books, but they are the rules.

Robert Finch There was a mentality among some of those who were running the 1972 campaign, because many of those same people had been involved in the gubernatorial election in 1962 [in California, in which Richard Nixon had lost to Edmund "Pat" Brown, Sr.], and they thought they had been "jobbed," so they weren't going to be "jobbed" again.

Richard Moore Undoubtedly, the president had said more than once to Haldeman: I hope you are sure that we are finding out everything. They are always doing it to us; I hope we are getting intelligence. Then, I think Haldeman said—and that would be Magruder's chance—Jeb, the president is determined that we find out as much about them as they are finding out about us, and he wants to know what we are doing about intelligence, so be sure that we are on the track. This was Jeb's license to decide to get Dean to hire Liddy, so that we would have an apparatus to find these things out. Magruder was eager to please Haldeman; that was his ticket to the future.

G. Gordon Liddy On four occasions, someone tried to penetrate our defense at CRP, but failed. I can't say it was the Democrats, because nobody was apprehended, but I don't suspect the British Labour Party. In 1964, the Goldwater office was burglarized. Files were taken; a wiretap was in place. But the difference was that nobody could be identified with the Democratic Party, or anybody else. But it wasn't the Irish Republican Army.

Charles Colson We used to look at politics as warfare: Democrats and Republicans; liberals and conservatives. Nixon had been badly treated when he was out of office. We had believed at the time—and later had good evidence—that our campaign plane in 1968 was bugged. We knew that the IRS had come after a lot of our friends in the Kennedy-Johnson years. It was the IRS issue that made Watergate explode: we felt we were in a war, and now that we were in power, we were going to use that leverage. When Nixon was elected, the *Washington Post* had an article saying that Nixon's coming to Washington will be like Hitler's coming to Paris; we didn't feel very welcome. It was a "we vs. them" attitude which, probably, to a degree, was exacerbated by Nixon's personality.

I remember going to a luncheon in honor of Max Raab* when he left the Eisenhower administration. Nixon and [John F.] Kennedy were there. Kennedy gave a witty, two-minute speech. Then Nixon got up and said, "I won't do as well as Senator Kennedy did." It was almost a chip-on-the-shoulder attitude. Kennedy had been to Harvard; Nixon had worked his way through Duke [University] Law School. It was the other-side-of-the-tracks mentality; they really didn't like each other. I ran into Kenny [Kenneth] O'Donnell† at the airport, after Watergate. He said to me, "How did you ever stand working for Nixon? JFK never trusted his mental stability." There was that kind of feeling.

---

* Maxwell B. Raab, staff assistant, Eisenhower administration.
† Kenneth P. O'Donnell, special assistant to President John F. Kennedy.

15

The Break-ins

THE BREAK-INS PRIOR TO JUNE 16–17, 1972

On the night of May 26, 1972, a team of Cuban refugees led by Bernard Barker, a Miami realtor and Bay of Pigs veteran, attempted to break into the headquarters of the Democratic National Committee (DNC), located in the Watergate complex in the area of Washington known as "Foggy Bottom."

That attempt failed when the men were unable to open a door to a staircase that led to the DNC offices.

During that same night, another attempted break-in, at the presidential campaign headquarters of Senator George McGovern*—then one of several possible opponents of President Nixon in the coming election—was thwarted by someone's presence at the entrance to the building.

The following night, May 27, the Cuban refugees' second attempt to enter the DNC's headquarters ended in failure when, having entered the Watergate complex, they were unable to pick the lock on the DNC office door.

Attempting yet another entry there during the night of May 28, Barker and his associates—Virgilio Gonzalez, Eugenio Martinez, and Frank Sturgis, along with CRP security chief and ex-CIA employee James McCord—were finally successful in entering the DNC offices, where they photographed documents and planted wiretaps on the telephones of both DNC Chairman Lawrence (Larry) O'Brien and staff member R. Spencer Oliver.†

---

* Senator McGovern would not become the Democratic Party's candidate until nominated at the Democratic National Convention on July 12.

† Executive director of the DNC's Association of State Democratic Chairmen.

Bernard Barker In the first entry, in May, Gonzalez told me he had forgotten to bring the tools he needed. When I told Liddy and Hunt, they said, "Oh God." I told them I would take care of the situation, so I went to the airport and put Gonzalez on a plane to Miami. Then I called my wife and said, "Pick up Gonzalez, go with him to his house to pick up the tools, then go back to the airport and send him back to Washington. Then, report to me, or I will have to scrub the mission." She followed through, and Gonzalez came back to me. Later that evening, Hunt asked me: "What did you do about Gonzalez?" I said, "I have solved the problem." He was very happy.

JUNE 16–17, 1972

Less than one month later—during the early hours of Saturday, June 17, following an evening of preparation—Barker, his team, and McCord made their second successful entry into the DNC offices, only to be discovered and apprehended, setting in motion the series of events that led to the resignation of President Nixon.

Soon after their entry into the DNC offices, a security guard noticed that strips of tape had been attached to the front door of the CRP office— they had been placed there by one of the burglars. The guard removed the tape, but in an act that seems strange—as they were on a secret mission— one of the burglars reattached the tape to the door, and in another inspection, the security guard noticed that the tape had been reaffixed to the door, and he then notified a supervisor who, in turn, notified the police.

On arresting the burglars, the police confiscated their cameras and electronic surveillance equipment, as well as a large amount of hundred-dollar bills—money that would later be traced to the Finance Committee to Reelect the President.

As the men were being taken to the Washington, D.C., jail, where they were charged with second-degree burglary, Plumbers E. Howard Hunt and G. Gordon Liddy—both of whom had been present for a time in another part of the Watergate complex as the burglars proceeded with their work in the DNC offices—began to remove potential evidence from the Executive Office Building (EOB), shredding some money and delivering other funds to attorneys who Hunt had retained to represent the arrested men.

Bernard Barker Hunt told me that in this operation I was going to have a "hitchhiker"; he would do some telephone tapping and would be under me. My job would be to search for and photograph documents. He said that they had evidence that McGovern was receiving money from Castro, and receiving donations through groups like the Black Panthers,* so that when I looked at documents, I should check for nonnormal contributors; they especially wanted to see contributions that have some indication of [emanating from] a foreign country. I went over hundreds and hundreds of documents. When I found any that had these characteristics, I would give them to Martinez, who would then photograph them. I personally checked [Lawrence] O'Brien's† desk. All I could find were all kinds of bottles of liquor. I thought to myself: this man must be drunk twenty-four hours a day for the amount of whiskey he had. I didn't even know who O'Brien was, nor did I care; I had complete, maximum trust in Hunt, who had been my superior at the Agency [the CIA]. I later found out, at one of my trials, that I had been conditioned by the CIA to accept any order emanating from Howard Hunt as a legal order, and I did. I realize now that I was conditioned.

George McGovern There were a couple of reporters who said something to the effect that we were receiving funds from foreign governments, but this was totally without foundation; we were accused of taking money from Castro, but we never got a dime from any foreign government, or from any foreigner.

USING JAMES McCORD

G. Gordon Liddy McCord had originally been a special agent of the FBI. Early on, he went over to the Central Intelligence Agency [CIA] and was a "tech"—a very high-level "tech"; he would go to your embassy abroad and check to see if it was bugged; he was a big expert—a genuine "wire man." The only reason I used him was that all the people I had lined up had drifted away while I was waiting for an answer. So in desperation, I go to the only guy I know—and that's McCord. It was an error—I knew that it was an error at the time; I gambled and lost on that. The problem was that McCord could be connected to us; there was no alias. He was employed by CRP.

Bernard Barker It was the first time I had met McCord. At the time, I thought he was a technician. He was also CIA, but not like me. He was office CIA—Washington CIA; he had never before been "behind the cur-

---

* A militant black organization headquartered in Oakland, California.
† Chairman of the Democratic National Committee.

tain," like Hunt and me. Jimmy was very likable, a very nice guy. It was made out that McCord was working with Liddy and I was working for Hunt. At the time, I wasn't completely convinced about Liddy. He was Hunt's boss, but he was kind of a strange person. Besides, I understood he had been Treasury and FBI, not CIA. I didn't trust the FBI; as a matter of fact, I never liked FBI people, so the fact that McCord was with Liddy made me very guarded. I made it quite clear that he was to follow my instructions. I went in and started my work, and the photography. I asked McCord how he was doing. He said that he had finished about 80 percent of his work. We started watching him—he looked a little nervous. He was having problems, so I said, "My key man knows telephones. Would you mind if he helped you out?" He said, "That's fine." So Gonzalez helped him. Hunt came up to us after the mission and was very proud; he said that McCord had told Liddy he would work with Barker any time; any place.

G. Gordon Liddy Hunt and I were over in the hotel;[*] we were on transceiver contact with the people on the inside. We first got a query from the guard, [Alfred] Baldwin,[†] across the street, who had seen some people on a higher floor. He asked if any of our guys were wearing hats, or cowboy clothes, or looking like hippies. We answered, "No. Our guys are wearing business suits." He said, "There are some guys dressed like hippies coming down from another floor." Then, all of a sudden, he said, "They've got guns; they've got guns." We then tried to contact our guys, but because the transceiver squawked, they had turned down the volume, so they couldn't hear us. Finally, they reported, "They got us." At that moment, I knew that we had to do two things: first, we had to clean the place as best we could— and the best way to do that was to take all the equipment and boldly walk right through the police—like we own the place; second, we had to get to the lawyer. The plan was to quickly make bail—the guys had alias documentation—then have them vanish. The lawyer who was to do this, Douglas Caddy,[‡] said, all of a sudden: "I don't know how to do this; I'm not a criminal lawyer. I'm going to bring in another attorney." So we couldn't get them out of there.

Jeb Stuart Magruder One of the great mistakes of all of this is that Liddy passed himself off as this great burglar. I've often said, "How do you reference-check a burglar?" Bud Krogh recommended him as having been suc-

---

[*] The Howard Johnson Hotel, across the street from the Watergate complex.
[†] Alfred C. Baldwin, III, former FBI agent hired by James McCord.
[‡] C. Douglas Caddy, original attorney for the Watergate burglars.

cessful with the Plumbers—whatever that meant. I didn't even know what that meant; I had no idea what Liddy had done. I knew that he had worked for Bud, but I didn't know what the Plumbers meant. I didn't know anything about the Fielding break-in. All Krogh told me was that Liddy was good at gathering information. They pushed him off on me because Bud wanted to get rid of him.

Bernard Barker We were into so many operations by that time that it never occurred to me that we would go back to the DNC. I had already been given a briefing on working with the Howard Hughes* organization, and working with Interpol on planning the drug operation—by that time I had increased the number of recruits to about 120, all of whom had been involved in the Bay of Pigs—to gather intelligence on the drug people. Special squads would be trained to go in and waste these people at their bases and centers of operation. During that first operation at the DNC [in May], I had discovered a room full of files, so they said, "Let's look at that room; use a whole night." Hunt told me that, "We have verified what you reported; we didn't know about this before." There was also the need to change the tap; that was McCord's job. We got caught before the operation ever took place. We were told by Hunt, by radio, that the building was being searched, and that we should keep low. That was the wrong order; they should have said, Get the hell out of there!

AFTER THE ARRESTS

In the hours after the burglars' arrests, a trail of evidence began to grow, linking the White House—through Hunt—and the CRP—through McCord—to the break-in. And complicating the situation further, both Hunt and McCord had CIA backgrounds.

As the FBI pursued its investigation, high-level White House and CRP officials were increasingly concerned as to where the investigation might lead, bearing in mind that the 1972 presidential election was less than five months away.

During a series of meetings and telephone conversations with one another, these officials discussed options for damage control, including destruction of files and other potentially incriminating materials.

In addition, some of the officials were aware of meetings that had taken

---

* A billionaire industrialist.

place with Attorney General Mitchell at his office on January 27 and February 4, 1972, as well as at Key Biscayne on March 30, during which White House and CRP staff had discussed detailed plans for intelligence-gathering operations against the Democrats—including the break-ins at the DNC's Watergate complex headquarters.

Bernard Barker We had been told that if something went wrong, we would receive all kinds of assistance. I really expected the attorney general to give an order to turn us loose, until they started fingerprinting us and the FBI said, "Mr. Barker, what are you doing here?" Then I knew we were in trouble. So, you keep your mouth shut and your eyes open. The only thing I could think of saying was what I had said when I was a prisoner of war in World War II: my name, rank, and serial number—like I was in the army.

Robert Mardian The ridiculous part of my being indicted in the Watergate scandal resulted from Jeb Magruder testifying that Mitchell told him to tell me to get a hold of Liddy, to get a hold of Kleindienst, to get the burglars out of jail before their identities were disclosed, which is the stupidest thing you can imagine. These guys all had fake CIA identification, but they were all fingerprinted; any lawyer would know that their identities were already known. The other thing here was that Liddy was going all over town trying to locate Kleindienst; he found him at Burning Tree.* First of all, if Mitchell wanted to send a message like that—which is utterly impossible for me to believe—he'd call Kleindienst, his former deputy, and say: See what you can do to get them out.

Dean called me from Manila and said, "You'd better get your ass back here right away; we've got trouble." He called from Manila; I thought he was in Washington. I didn't get back to Washington until Monday night; he was back on Saturday. He'd already interviewed Liddy. He'd gotten the straight poop. So when I interviewed Liddy and told Mitchell, in Dean's presence, what Liddy told me, John Dean is sitting there, acting surprised: "Did he say that? Oh, my gosh." He'd already heard all this.

Richard Kleindienst Right after the break-in, on Monday morning, I was in my office with Henry Petersen, and John Dean came in. Henry and I had agreed that I would go out to San Clemente and tell the president he had to make an immediate announcement to the public: whoever is responsible for

---

* A country club near Washington, D.C.

this will be prosecuted. John Dean—who at that point was counsel to the president—said, "I'm going out to San Clemente this afternoon. I'll tell him." I said, "Okay, John. You tell him."

That was a big mistake. Henry, before he died, and I always agreed that that was a mistake. I don't think Dean ever told the president. I should have pursued it. I guess I'm somewhat responsible, because I relied on John Dean to do something I should have done myself.

Seymour Glanzer At the preliminary hearing, the U.S. Attorney's Office was opposed to bail, saying that there was a danger of flight, and Jack Anderson got up in court and said he would take it upon himself to be Frank Sturgis's custodian; it was clear from what Anderson said that he and Sturgis had a longstanding relationship. Had the judge followed the prosecution's advice and refused bail, the case probably would have been broken immediately. As we now know, McCord could not have taken twenty-four hours in jail; it was only when faced with imprisonment that he started to break. Under today's laws, the burglars would have been held, but in those days, there was a more lax attitude, and they were released on bail. That helped the cover-up because, being free, they were able to seek support and monetary assistance through their lawyers and others.

Robert Mardian When we landed in Washington Monday night, I was handed a summons and complaint; the Democrats had already filed a lawsuit. Mitchell said, "You're going to have to handle it." I was the attorney of record for the Republican National Committee and the Committee to Reelect the President. I had to find out what the hell had happened if I was going to represent the committee; it was my job to find out. I interviewed practically everybody who could give us any information. Liddy tried to explain to me that there was no way he, or anybody, could be identified. The Cubans wouldn't talk; they were soldiers. I said, "You were in this hotel room; you had dinner there; you used the toilet; there must be fingerprints all over the goddamn place." He says, "Look, we pulled a lot of jobs right under your nose and you never caught on," and that is how he started telling me about Dita Beard*—I had had eighty FBI agents looking for her—and Liddy said, "We pulled her out of town and you never found her."

Then he told me about the break-in at Ellsberg's psychiatrist's office. He

* A lobbyist for the International Telephone and Telegraph Corporation (ITT) who was escorted from Washington by G. Gordon Liddy at the time of the Senate confirmation hearings for Richard Kleindienst's appointment as attorney general. Ms. Beard was subsequently located by the FBI in a Denver hospital.

said, "My group had to do it because you couldn't handle it"—I was the assistant attorney general in charge of that case—"You couldn't get the job done, so we had to try and do it for you." That is what Mitchell called the White House horrors. I had never practiced criminal law, and Liddy is dumping all this stuff on me. He said that he had the go-ahead from Mitchell. I asked, "Personally?" He said, "No. Magruder was the go-between." He was relying on what Magruder said, that Mitchell said it was okay.

Jeb Stuart Magruder Gordon Liddy called me in Los Angeles and asked me to get to a secure phone; he wanted me to go to some Air Force base, or someplace. I went back to the table and said to LaRue, "I've got to call Liddy on some reasonably secure line," and he replied, "Well, use the pay phone," which was as good a secure line as you could get.

I called Liddy from the pay phone in the Beverly Hills Hotel, and he told me about the break-in, and about McCord. That was the part that sent me through the roof; I was devastated by McCord's involvement. My first thought was that we were in deep trouble. I didn't think at all at that time anything other than, Wow, we've got a problem. I talked to LaRue and to Mardian; we talked to Mitchell; Kleindienst was contacted by someone, not by me. At some point that day, or maybe the next day, I talked to John Dean. I didn't even know where he was. I called the White House and they patched me in to him. Haldeman selected me to go back and work with Dean to try to see what was going on and to try to contain the situation as best we could—find out what was really happening.

Robert Reisner On June 17, Magruder was at the Beverly Hills Hotel. I reached him as he was leaving for a breakfast meeting and told him about the arrests. He broke off the call quickly and then called back—for Liddy. Late Saturday afternoon, I was at home and received a call from Magruder. He told me to go back to the office, find a file—or package—that was in the left-hand drawer of his desk, and give it to Rob Odle; I think that Magruder did not want Odle going through his desk. It was perfectly classic Jeb Magruder that (a) it was not an inconvenience to direct me to leave home and drive back down to the office; and that (b) it was necessary to compartmentalize his life so that taking the file folder out of his desk and handing it to Odle was something he needed a third person to do; it was typical behavior. I do not know what was in the folder; it could have been Liddy's plans, or material they got when they were in the Watergate the first time.

Robert Odle, Jr. Magruder was in California, and he wanted certain files not to stay in the office over the weekend. Bob Reisner put the files in my briefcase. I took them home and put them in my closet. I guess that Magruder was afraid of an FBI subpoena. I thought: the DNC was burglarized; it might happen to us, also. I was scared to death. I took all my budget files home.

Jeb Stuart Magruder I was concerned that the materials in the file that Rob Odle took home would put us all in jail. In retrospect, I should have saved it all, but I didn't. I got rid of all the memos and, later, the Gemstone file.

Hugh Sloan The issue, in my mind, was that I had thoroughly convinced myself that the campaign had done it—or that people in the campaign had done it. At the time, I believed it was purely an issue of the campaign—for whatever reason—and I wasn't getting any personal satisfaction from the people I was talking to, in terms of my understanding it, or getting direction on how the issue was going to be resolved. So I went to Ehrlichman and Chapin and talked to them about: "After all, it is the White House's campaign, and you have to get into this and resolve it, because it is not being resolved at CRP and, clearly, there is an involvement."

Ehrlichman interpreted my remarks—by virtue of his response—as being a personal liability concern, because he said, "If you need help with a lawyer, I'll be glad to help you, but the main thing is to get through this election." Dwight's attitude was more of a, "Gee, you're a little overwrought. Why don't you take a vacation?" kind of thing. So there wasn't the kind of response, in my mind, that you would expect, such as: we know about it; we're dealing with it. It was taken more on the basis that *I* had a problem in terms of being overly concerned, or overwrought, even to the extent of having a legal problem.

FIRST LEARNING OF THE BREAK-IN

Richard Helms I heard about it on Saturday evening, from Howard Osborne, who was then director of security at the agency. He called me at my apartment and told me that this break-in had taken place and that material had been found indicating that, possibly, Howard Hunt was involved. So that was the first I heard of it, and my reaction was one of amazement, obviously, and concern as to what Hunt was up to. But he was not working for us, and so I really didn't get that concerned about it.

I knew him, because he worked for the agency for a long time. I was surprised that he went to work for the White House, but that was none of my doing. The White House never checked into the Agency when they hired Hunt. I assume he did it out of what he believed then was a show of patriotism; he was working for the president. But I was surprised, nevertheless.

I was not in touch with the White House; the only thing I did do that same evening was to try to locate Patrick Gray, which I finally succeeded in doing in some hotel in Los Angeles, and telling him that these people who had been involved in the break-in had been hired by John Ehrlichman, and that this was something he ought to keep in mind, because he was obviously going to get involved in this burglary.

William Colby I went to the daily nine o'clock meeting Helms held with senior staff. We were all sitting around, saying, "Here is this story about the break-in; apparently they have arrested several former CIAs. Do any of you guys know anything about this?" No. Nobody knows anything. Helms's position was: we are going to catch a lot of hell, because these [men] are formers. We knew they were working in the White House, but as to what they were trying to do there, we didn't know. Helms's direction at the end of the meeting was to stay away from this thing; it is not our business.

Robert Mardian At the minute the Watergate break-in occurred, my wife and I were with John and Martha [Mitchell] in California. I was there by accident; I was supposed to be playing golf with Kleindienst at Burning Tree. And on Thursday, Mitchell said, "Reagan"—I had been Reagan's state chairman in California—"wants you there; you are the only one that knows the players." There was going to be a meeting between the California regular party chairmen and the Committee to Reelect. Our committee had a chairman in each of the counties in California. This was a meeting between the regular county chairmen and the Committee to Reelect chairman. I was to go along to make the introductions.

We were just leaving the Beverly Hills Hotel and there was a limousine for Mitchell, Reagan, and myself. I started to get in with John—Reagan was already in; he had come to pick us up—and Magruder tapped me on the shoulder. He said, "Bob, John said for you to come with us; we've got a problem." I said, "What kind of problem?" He said, "A slight problem." I said, "Well, if it's a PR problem, you're the guy to handle it," and I started to get back into the limousine. He said, "No. John wants you to come with us. I've got to explain it to you."

Well, Tom Reed, who had been the California state chairman, was with me and, as he testified—and they asked him if he was with me at all times—supposedly I went and made a telephone call—and he testified under oath, along with my wife—that "I never left Mardian's side; he was my meal ticket." He had had a falling-out with Reagan and wanted to get back to talk to him. We got in the back-up car. Fred LaRue was there, Magruder, Tom Reed, and myself. So I'm trying to get Magruder to tell me what it is he has to tell me. He points to Reed—in other words, he can't talk in front of him. So we get to the hotel, and in a room opposite the room where the big meeting was taking place, Magruder—I think LaRue was there too—told me about the break-in. Then I got a call from Rob Odle—he was practically in tears. He didn't know what to do; he was telling me about Liddy. I never did get to go to the meeting. There was a luncheon after the meeting, where there were only about eight of us, and Mitchell was scheduled for a press conference afterward. I thought: this is going to be it, but not one question came up on the break-in.

John and I ended up going back to the hotel together after the meeting, in the limousine. He asked me what I thought the political consequences would be. I said, "If they don't find any electronic devices, it will be a boys-will-be-boys operation, and that will be it."

Bob Woodward I learned about the DNC break-in on Saturday morning, when the *Post* city editor called me in. Actually, the phone call woke me. My feeling at first was: this is a local burglary—kind of a typical story. My visual picture was of a little storefront office some place in downtown D.C., where four people had offices—the local Democratic Party in the District of Columbia—and that a Xerox machine had been stolen, or something like that.

It's like getting in a bath and turning the water hotter and hotter; you don't feel the incremental increase in temperature, because it's going up so slowly and you're already so hot. I mean hot, in the sense that the story immediately had CIA people, rubber gloves, hundred-dollar bills. So at eleven or twelve o'clock that morning in the office, I had a very different impression of the story than I did when I was awakened. If you were to graph it, it just kept going up and up and up.

Robert Odle, Jr. We were having a meeting the day we found out about the Watergate break-in. Just before lunch, someone came up to me and said, "Did you hear, Mr. Odle? There has been a break-in at the Democratic National Committee." I looked at some of the folks in the room and said, "That could never happen here, because I have this great guy working for me, named James McCord," not knowing as I spoke these words that McCord was in the slammer.

Maurice Stans I picked up the paper that Sunday morning at home and I said to myself: that could happen to us; maybe somebody will hit our place next, to see what they can learn from us. I didn't know if it was a money search, or a document search, but the first thought I had was that it could happen to us.

John Dean I did not hear about it in Manila, contrary to some people who tried to pitch that—not that it would make any difference. I first learned about the break-in when I landed in San Francisco, on Sunday, June 18, 1972. I was planning to stay in San Francisco because I was tired—I had been on an airplane a long time, flying from Manila—and it seemed like a good way to break up the trip before I went back to Washington. So I called my deputy to check in, because I had not talked to the office in five or six days at that point. Fred Fielding told me that there had been a break-in at the Watergate and that he thought I ought to come back. I argued with him; I said I didn't see why I should come back. It really wasn't until I got back that Sunday night that Fred told me the burglars were apparently found with a check from Howard Hunt that would tie the White House in, and that is what he was concerned about. My initial reaction was, "It's Chuck Colson"—because of Howard Hunt—that Colson had been responsible for ordering the break-in at the DNC, using Howard Hunt somehow. I went to bed that night. There was nothing I could do about it.

I always figured that with all the craziness that was going on, something like this could happen. Let me piece together something that preceded this. It could have been the Brookings affair instead of the Watergate affair—the fire. All one has to do is read Richard Nixon's memoirs and realize that Nixon was right at the middle of that whole thing—that he was the one that wanted the entry into Brookings, and he even writes in his memoirs, "surreptitiously, if necessary."* I think this is a nice soft spin on what he probably told Colson; it was probably to get in there, and get that stuff—however you have to do it. So when Watergate happened, it just seemed that the inevitable had caught up, because of all this kind of craziness. I had also

* *Richard Nixon*, p. 512.

learned by that point the fact that there had been the break-in at Ellsberg's psychiatrist's office. I had learned about the fact there had been the wiretapping of newsmen. I looked around and saw a whole bunch of serious trouble at that point.

David Wilson I read about it in the *Washington Post*. It made an impact: the article mentioned a lawyer, Douglas Caddy, who appeared that evening when they [the burglars] were brought up for arraignment. When I saw that name it jumped out at me, because Douglas Caddy was one of the people John Dean had brought in on the election law research project. I had met him and knew who he was, and I immediately said, "What in the world is he doing representing those people at two [o'clock] in the morning?" I called Fred Fielding, and his first comment was, "You must have an early edition of the newspaper." I said, "Why is that?" He said, "Have you seen the real names of the people who broke in? Among them is James McCord," at which time I essentially knew that there was a major problem, because I knew who McCord was—that he was head of security at the Reelection Committee; and that if Caddy was somehow involved in it, and McCord was involved in it, somehow Liddy was involved, because knowing how law offices work—and how general counsels' responsibilities work—I assumed that Gordon probably had some tie into the security operation, or some responsibility for it. I had very much a sinking feeling that there was much more involved here than a mere break-in. I remember meeting with Gordon about a week after the break-in, and having a very strange feeling that he was looking to me for some sort of message. Of course, I had no message for him, but he seemed very uncomfortable.

Hugh Sloan I learned about the break-in by reading about it in the newspaper the next morning. That's when Gordon had passed me in the hall in a bit of a panic and said, "I made a mistake; I used somebody from here, which I told them I wouldn't do." Once they started, in subsequent days talking in the newspapers about the hundred-dollar bills and the fact they were in sequence, my own mind quickly made the association of the fact it could very easily be the money I paid Gordon Liddy, in cash, out of the committee's funds, so that in my own mind it was obvious pretty quickly that the campaign organization was involved in it. Then, of course, when McCord's name came out, it was even more clear what had happened.

Robert Reisner I was in my office that Saturday morning when someone— it may have been Liddy, because I remember seeing him that morning;

Powell Moore[*] and I met with him concerning his talking to the attorney general—told me that McCord had been arrested. The moment I heard about the break-in, I thought: something is wrong here; Liddy was in the office—walking around like a guy would look if he had been up all night and something was terribly wrong. So from the first day after the break-in, Liddy was connected in my mind with the fact that something was going on.

Jeb Stuart Magruder On the Tuesday following the break-in, I suggested to Mitchell that he go to the White House and tell them to drop them. He came back and said, "We can't do it." He never gave me a reason.

Well, there is obviously a reason: the Ellsberg [Dr. Fielding] break-in; drop Liddy and Hunt and you know what they are going to say. And the five Cubans, as well. And then the president is really in trouble. That, in a sense, is more serious.

Their hope was that, somehow, the damage control could stop with Liddy and Hunt, if they were "taken care of," but [U.S. District Court Judge John J.] Sirica outfoxed them all by giving them these unbelievably long sentences.

Robert Finch I remember my wife's having been concerned about it; I don't think I paid much attention to it. Those of us who were in the inner circle—Shultz, Don Rumsfeld—would ask, in the early morning sessions with Haldeman, Kissinger, or Nixon, what was going on, and we didn't get any indication from any of them of any White House involvement.

H. R. Haldeman When I heard that McCord was involved, I thought: somebody over at CRP has screwed up and they have a problem. You have to put that in the context of Nixon's orders to me—and from me to all of the White House staff—that the White House staff was not to become involved in the political campaign operations; we were setting up the Reelection Committee under Mitchell—and over there [at CRP]—so as not to get the White House involved in; bogged down in; diverted by the campaign, so when a campaign problem came up, it was the Reelection Committee's problem, not mine. I viewed it that way, and it was a stupid mistake on my part. I'm readily willing to admit that. We maintained liaison with the committee. All the scheduling of surrogates—all of that sort of thing—was to be done outside the White House. If it had been the White House's problem, I would have handled it in the standard staffing fashion: it would have been

[*] Spokesman for CRP.

staffed out, dealt with, and disposed of. It wasn't that kind of problem until a lot later. By that time, it was beyond control.

Stephen Bull Most of the campaign activity went on at the Committee to Reelect the President [CRP]; we had never even heard of half the people who were working over there, so when we saw in the paper that some people from CRP had been arrested for breaking in [at the DNC], we didn't know who they were. We were puzzled by the whole thing. At the time, there was no particular concern; there was no intimation that anyone at the White House was concerned [involved]. Howard Hunt had been characterized as a White House staff member—he had an office there at one time—but he wasn't a White House staff member as any of us would have defined it, and none of us had ever met him—had not even heard his name—so we didn't think that the White House was involved.

Herbert Klein I was in Washington that Sunday. I read two paragraphs way deep in the *Washington Post,* so I knew it had occurred and I thought that it was peculiar, but I had no sense that it had anything to do with us, or who these Cubans were, so until more things started to come out, I had no sense that it was tied into the Committee to Reelect the President [CRP]. Once the story came out, I would find that I was picking up the *Washington Post* in the morning and learning about things I had had no idea were occurring. As it went along, it was apparent that it was still a mysterious factor.

16

Who Ordered the Break-ins?

Many scenarios have been developed in the years since the break-ins at the DNC's Watergate headquarters as to who ordered them: Was it the president himself? Or aides acting on what they believed were the president's orders or wishes? Was it the distracted John Mitchell? Or aides acting on their own, either to curry favor with their immediate supervisors, or for other personal reasons? Or was it the CIA? Or another, as yet unmentioned individual or group?

While some of these scenarios contain plausible elements, absent any compelling evidence, one cannot draw any conclusions. And so, the question of who ordered the break-ins remains the whodunit of the late twentieth century.

THE COLSON SCENARIO

Seymour Glanzer Colson had no direct role in Watergate. He was not an enviable person; he had been acting in the most egregious fashion in the White House; he had bad press and a bad image, so he was targeted to be a central person in Watergate, but he wasn't. We had written a ninety-page report before the special prosecutor came in, putting the whole case together. In it, we pointed out that Colson had no direct involvement. We also pointed out that while Robert Mardian had slight involvement at the outside, the case against him should not be proceeded on; that was counter-manded, and he was indicted. Colson was indicted on a charge of violating civil rights; he claimed he was not guilty of this and would go to trial, so he pleaded guilty to obstruction of justice. He had become a born-again Chris-tian and he said, "I did do something I'm ashamed of; I had arranged that if material taken from Dr. Fielding's office was detrimental to Ellsberg, I would leak it on the Hill [Capitol Hill]. That would likely have had an adverse effect on Ellsberg, who was then on trial, so—in a sense—I was denying Ellsberg a fair trial." They said to Colson, "Will you plead guilty on this?" And he said, "Yes. I'm guilty." But without that plea, how in the world could you prove the case?

Leonard Garment I am sure that there are things that were not recorded, where there was a lot of pressure put to bear to get something done; these people had an assignment: what the president wants is information about Larry O'Brien; O'Brien had him spooked for decades. He thought: Why can't you guys get the stuff for me that I know is there? When Colson called Magruder and said, "Get off the stick," and Hunt and Liddy are in Colson's office, if anybody can believe that before and after that conversation—and in other conversations with Magruder—it wasn't made clear what this was all about, then they really do believe in Santa Claus. Colson was so clever; he thought ten moves ahead: I'd better get something from Hunt, and I'd better have a tape-recorded conversation. They had a very hard time figur-ing out how to indict Colson; they finally got him on that defaming Ellsberg craziness.

Howard Phillips I've always had great affection for Colson. I knew him from Massachusetts politics in the 1960s. He consulted me before he pleaded guilty. We spent a long morning together at the Ramada Inn in Tyson's Corner [Virginia], and I said, "Chuck, it's a crime for you to plead guilty; you haven't done anything criminal." He said, "You're right. I haven't. But the legal bills are such that even if I win, I'll lose my house, and I do feel badly about some things, and basically, I can't take it anymore." I said, "Chuck, you are basically serving your head up on a platter to your enemies, and they are not entitled to it. All you did was fight the good fight." But God makes all things work together for the good, I guess.

Frederic V. Malek I think that Magruder ordered the break-ins. Mitchell may or may not have known about it; I don't believe that the president or Haldeman knew about it, but I do believe that Colson knew. Colson was continually pounding on Magruder, who was basically running the campaign at this early stage—because Mitchell was only there part of the time; he was distracted by the problems he was having with his wife at that time, so he was drinking a lot—and for most of the time, he was still at the [Department of] Justice. So Magruder was running the show. And Colson was really a tough customer. He's mellowed and changed, obviously, but he was a tough guy, and Magruder was scared of him.

One of the things Colson pounded on was the need for better information—better intelligence—on what was going on on the other side: You guys should have more information; why don't you? So, based on what I know, Magruder was looking for ways to get better information, partly because he felt it was needed, and partly to satisfy Colson; Magruder didn't want Colson to criticize him to the president, because he wanted a nice job in the next administration; he wanted to be head of ACTION;* he had told me about that. So he didn't want to get on Colson's bad side, because Colson could be influential—and vindictive. My guess is that he authorized the break-in. I don't think he concocted it—that he had that kind of mind that would conclude: Yes. We have to break into Larry O'Brien's office. He had these Liddy types around, and they would come up with lots of different schemes that fit into the kind of netherland none of us had experience in.

Jeb Stuart Magruder I was guilty; the fact that other people above me were also guilty doesn't mean that I'm any less guilty. I wish they had told the truth earlier—Haldeman, Ehrlichman, the president, Mitchell.

All this stuff to try to revise history to indicate that none of them are involved is unfortunate. But now, obviously, Haldeman and Ehrlichman have decided to tell the truth. I'm glad they finally indicated that neither Dean nor I, alone, were the culprits.

Charles Colson The break-in remains a mystery to me. I never could figure it out. If someone had come to me in May 1972 and said, "Look, we can find out what is going on in McGovern's headquarters; we can put a spy in there," I probably would have said, "Go ahead and do it." If someone had come to me and said, "We can plant a bug in Larry O'Brien's office at the Democratic National Committee," I would have laughed them out of the office. That's a waste of time; you'll never get any information out of the DNC.

* A government agency.

THE DEAN SCENARIO

H. R. Haldeman I believe the bugging was done at Dean's* insistence. He conned Magruder into ordering the bugging; then he conned all the rest of us into doing everything we did, step by step, along the way, thinking he was a key one of us. There is ample evidence to support the thesis that he was not. I think we were had. At first, he was simply trying to protect himself. As things got worse, he realized he had to start throwing bigger fish into the pan in order to protect himself. I think he thought that by throwing me and Ehrlichman in, he could satisfy the prosecution, and he may well have rationalized that—in that way—he could save the president. But he was perfectly willing to throw the president in when he had to do that; it was a case of self-preservation. He got away with only a couple of months in prison, and he's living a good life in Beverly Hills [California] now.

Donald E. Santarelli I don't believe for a minute that John Dean's motive in Watergate was personal. I do believe that the idea of the break-in appealed to the sort of skullduggery approach to politics. The tapes reflected something that was often discussed in the Oval Office and in Nixon circles: Why could the Democrats get away with what the Republicans can't? That was very much a corrosive element in Mr. Nixon's world—the double standard that Hoover and the FBI had ; Lyndon Johnson and his henchmen; and the Democrats, in general, could get away with what Republicans could not get away with. That meant using the IRS to investigate—or audit selectively—all the little pressure points of government abuse that had been engaged in: character assassination; the selective leaking of confidential information; all the little tricks available to government. Nixon was bothered by that, not so much that he wanted to do these things, but that he couldn't do them if he wanted to; that was his Achilles' heel.

So somebody like Colson would appeal to him on that front: Let's do it; the Democrats got away with this; why can't we? Why are we held to a dif- . ferent standard? And John Dean played into that scenario; it was one of his stocks in trade. In part, you had someone like Liddy proposing these things all the time, and Liddy, whom I knew very, very well—in fact, I'd hired him for his first job in government—was a guy looking for pyrotechnics, the grand play, a role for himself; he loved the idea of being a feudal knight in

* Mr. Dean, who is currently in litigation over an account of his behavior during the Watergate period contained in a recently published book, was thus unable to discuss certain areas of our inquiry.

search of a liege lord; he saw himself as a black knight; he was always proposing hare-brained schemes because it was in his personality to do this for president and for country with what he thought were his talents—a James Bondian grand play. The DNC break-in was concocted in part by Liddy and his little gang of operatives. And John Dean's approval, or disapproval, would have been part of the tendency to look for things that earn you stars or spurs.

Robert Reisner I can't imagine that Dean was the mastermind; I just don't believe that he could have conceived of, and directed, the burglars into the Watergate. But he was a very powerful guy—an independent actor—who was much more influential in the process than he later appeared to be when he testified before the Senate Committee; he testified as if he was asked to do these things. He didn't get to be counsel by accident; he got there because Ehrlichman and others perceived him to be the best successor as White House counsel, because he could get the job done. He was the keeper of many secrets and a very effective inside player. It's intriguing to imagine that in the highly compartmentalized structure that was created—where Colson and Dean and Haldeman and the campaign all ran independent operations—they didn't tell one another what was going on, and where there were very few senior officials with the experience to review actions, that this kind of environment led people to do things that were wrong. A good example of this is the wiretapping of the White House staff and reporters. It is not astonishing to imagine that this might happen if they had a national security crisis; what is astonishing is that it could go on for eighteen months. There was no review process in the White House.

Leonard Garment John Dean is smart and feverishly ambitious. He was recommended by Krogh and Magruder; they had highly sensitized smell organs when it came to who was prepared to do dirty things. But Dean was not the architect of Watergate; he was not the architect of the whole intelligence plan which gave rise to it; he was not the one who said: I want information on what every one of my adversaries is doing; he was not the one who thought they might lose the election to Muskie; it wasn't Dean who calculated that everything had to fall into place like pinballs on the great geostrategic machine, for Nixon to be strong in the summer of 1972. It was Richard Nixon who said: I want information; I'm not going to risk this campaign; it was too close last time; there are people who have information I want. From that point on, everything else was implementation.

G. Gordon Liddy Dean was the highest-level person to sign off on Watergate. Colson may have suspected we were up to something of dubious legality, and he was smart enough to say, "I don't want to know anything about this; I don't have to know to get you a decision." It's very weird. I was in the courtroom when he pleaded guilty; this guy had gotten this religious epiphany and was feeling guilt and that he should be punished. So he and the prosecutors invent a noncrime to which he is perfectly willing to plead guilty. And this judge, with an IQ of half a glass of water, says, "Fine." So off Colson happily goes to jail. And he's been with Jesus ever since.

Seymour Glanzer It is unclear to this day who ordered the break-in at Watergate. The only people who really knew what they were doing—and were acting in a very direct criminal fashion—were people like Liddy or, more importantly, people like Dean. He was very knowledgeable about what was taking place; he understood the ramifications of all of this; he was the linchpin. Dean was heavily involved in all of these matters. In his two meetings at the Department of Justice, on Gemstone, he was the only participant who knew that what they were doing there was a conspiracy to obstruct justice—to violate the law. He knew that these meetings were terribly incriminating. Mitchell didn't know the implications; he had no knowledge of criminal law. In fact, when they told him about Gemstone and what they planned to do, he told them this wasn't what he had in mind. Even Dean admits that that is what Mitchell said. It was over these two meetings at the Justice Department that Magruder committed perjury, and the person who promoted that was no one else but Dean. So there was one person who knew and understood everything.

David Wilson In August [1972], when the president said in a press conference that he had appointed John [Dean] to do the Watergate investigation, I watched the conference on the television in Dean's office. Apparently, it was the first time John had heard he was to conduct the investigation. We looked at him in the sense of: Gee, we didn't know you were doing that, and John didn't immediately blurt out, I didn't either; he gave us the look of: yes, there are things going on here that not everybody is aware of. But clearly, he may have at that time been concerned that he was being set up; there was clearly an attempt to make Dean the fall-person on it. I assume the president was involved; that Haldeman and Ehrlichman were involved; that he was one of the ones who was going to be found responsible—he had connections with Liddy; apparently, he was responsible for bringing Liddy in. I think that part of John's strategy in going public the way he did was that he essentially knew he was being set up to take full responsibility and it would be his word against the president's.

Fred Fielding The August 29 Nixon press conference was the first time that I knew that Dean was supposed to be conducting an investigation, and he told me, when I kidded him about it, that it was the first time he, too, had heard about it. He told me that there was no Dean investigation, and there certainly was none that I knew of.

Ronald Ziegler I don't know whether Dean was or wasn't pursuing an investigation; all I know is that it was easy for me and my staff to accept the proposition that he was, because he gave us all of our guidance: from the outset, the guidance to the press office on Watergate was from Dean's office. He was playing a very legitimate role for the president as his general counsel and was more or less a liaison with the other appropriate investigative bodies on the break-in and the surrounding areas. What I said—and my staff said—relevant to Watergate was based on written memoranda and guidance provided to my office by Fred Fielding and Gerry Warren, so when the president of the United States says that his general counsel is conducting an investigation into this matter, you say two things: I'm sure he is; and you don't want to make any comment from the White House that will in any way be prejudicial to the ongoing, legitimate investigative procedures. I've never seen a Dean report, but God knows how many bizarre things have taken place. I don't know if he ever did it or not. He denies it.

John Dean The press conference* occurred in San Clemente. It so happened I was in California at the time and had really planned to go down and watch it that morning. For some reason I didn't, and I turned on the press conference in my hotel room in Newport Beach, and when the president got to this question about appointing a special prosecutor and said, "Well, I don't think that's necessary because we have the FBI"—and he names a whole list of investigations—"plus I have my counsel; Mr. Dean has conducted an investigation and nobody presently employed in this administration is in any way involved"—I was literally dumbfounded. My first reaction was: that's pretty neat—the president saying that I'm his counsel; my second reaction was: I'm being set up, because I haven't conducted an investigation. They'd put me out there, giving every one at the White House and in the administration a clean bill of health. I don't know that is a fact. If that

---

* On July 29, 1972.

turns out wrong, the guy who is going to take the fall is yours truly. So then I began worrying about it.

There was no investigation; all I was doing was to try to keep abreast of what was going on. We were involved in a cover-up. It wasn't an investigation; it was how to deal with making it go away—and with damage control. Something that must be understood—and it is very important and is often missed—is that I think that the White House firmly believed it could withstand a full investigation of Watergate—that nobody in the White House was really involved in the ordering of the break-in of the Watergate. Did people have the knowledge about the fact that there was somebody there with that kind of mentality? Yes. Were they actually involved in the conspiracy to break in? No. I know I wasn't.

I didn't know the criminal law at the time, but I instinctively had renounced it and departed from the conspiracy, and no one else, to my knowledge, had really entered into the conspiracy to break into Watergate. Now, maybe Haldeman—through Strachan—had been directing Liddy to stop Muskie and start looking at McGovern; we don't know. Maybe on tapes that may be released we will find out. But I think, based on what's known, the White House was pretty comfortable that if they just go off and investigate the Watergate and stay away from everything else that Hunt and Liddy had done, we can survive this. The problem was that these guys made the demands for money, and to say that this was humanitarian funds is not terribly credible. This was a cover-up. Ehrlichman has always tried to say that Angela Davis* is entitled to a defense fund; why aren't these Cuban Americans entitled to a defense fund? A jury didn't buy that either.

Lawrence Higby It is one of the more fascinating mysteries of modern politics; it ranks in some ways—and I don't mean to sound perverse—with the Kennedy conspiracy. It's clearly somebody who had his own personal motive, which would make some sense for Dean if you believe one theory; or somebody trying to shine and show how good they are—which to me would lead you inevitably to Magruder. But that's speculation.

I am sure that Haldeman didn't have prior knowledge; I would have known that. We laughed about some of the stuff that did happen: there was something where the driver for Muskie hated Muskie and was giving somebody over at CRP some of his mail.

---

* An Oakland, California, political activist associated with the Black Panther Party.

Dwight Chapin Magruder would do anything for Dean—anything. That has got to be understood: Dean was golden; he was a chosen person. Dean established an aura among his peers—and those below—of being exceptionally bright—at least perceived to be so; very wired in with the president and with Haldeman. He drove a Porsche, he had this beautiful woman on his arm, and he was very stylish. He had this beautiful townhouse; he was counsel to the president. Now, that could all be very superficial, but in the composite of power, he appeared to have it. Jeb is a pawn to that kind of person, so if Dean calls him with an instruction, Jeb isn't going to say, "Well, thanks, but Bob [Haldeman] has to confirm this to me." So, bang! Jeb is off!

Herbert Klein Some say it was personal on the part of John Dean, who was a lightweight, but I can't think of a good reason for it—and I'm sure Nixon couldn't either. It was a plan that came from subordinates that, I suspect, was approved by Mitchell without really knowing what he was approving.

THE MITCHELL SCENARIO

John Dean Liddy had his first meeting with Mitchell on January 27th—I had no idea there was going to be a meeting; I had no idea of the subject matter of the meeting when Jeb Magruder called and said, "There is a meeting in Mitchell's office; we would like you to attend, and Liddy is going to present his plans." I had not talked to Liddy about them and I hadn't talked to Magruder about them. When Liddy presented his plan, I was dumbfounded. I mean, I thought it was unreal; I thought it was absurd; I thought it was crazy. And I was really surprised that Mitchell didn't throw him out of the office at that time—really surprised.

I went back and reported to my superior, Bob Haldeman, what I had heard—a meeting that amnesia has, unfortunately, affected Bob's memory of, although it's on a number of tapes, and he told a number of people back twenty years ago what had happened. He now says, "Well, Dean just reminded me of that meeting so many times that I believed him." That isn't true. I can vividly recall my meeting with Bob Haldeman and his saying, "Yes, I agree that the White House and you shouldn't have anything to do with these plans of mugging, bugging, wiretapping." I thought it was over at that point.

A day or so before February 4th, I get another call from Magruder that Liddy is going to present his revised plans. Again, I have had no conversations between the first meeting and the second meeting other than my alerting Haldeman to the problem. I went to the second meeting. I really was reluctant to go; I almost didn't go to that meeting. I arrived late, and as soon as I got the gist of the meeting—now, instead of having three charts, they were down to small letter-sized paper and the chairs were up closer to the attorney general's desk—I realized that they were discussing the same things. I picked up the tenor of the conversation and I was incensed. I really threw a wet blanket on the meeting. I said, "These aren't things that should be discussed in the office of the attorney general." And that ended the meeting; it was like spraying a hose on everybody. I felt that was the only thing that could and should have been done. Yes, that is what happened, and after that I really thought that the Liddy plans would just go away. I thought no one would ever approve this; I thought no one, in fact, would ever bring it up again. I thought that no one was giving Liddy any guidance at all as to what was expected of him—and wanted of him. In hindsight, I realize that Gordon Liddy is the kind of person that if you give him just a millimeter, he will take a mile; he runs to his own drummer. And all he needed was the millimeter—and he kept pushing and pushing, and selling his own plan, because this was his future.

Jeb Stuart Magruder Dean tried to separate Mitchell at the second meeting. He told Gordon to just deal with him, or with me. And then we had a third proposal from Liddy; it was one of twenty-eight or thirty decision papers I brought down to Key Biscayne with Fred LaRue, who was my closest adviser, as he was Mitchell's adviser. This was the last item on the agenda. We had a good meeting. John was very good at this; he was bright, incisive, with a very good political mind. He wasn't distracted. To say it was an unwitting sign-off would be to rewrite history.

From then on, I met with him every day at eight or eight thirty. He would go over all that was going on in the campaign and, of course, this would come up periodically; it was not an issue that went away. He would ask, "What's Liddy doing?" And then, when we got the first Gemstone file, I brought it in to Mitchell and said, "It looks worthless to me," and sent it over to Haldeman through [Gordon] Strachan, and one or the other of them said it was worthless, too, and we called Gordon Liddy in and indicated that he ought to go back in and get something worthwhile. The first had conversations of no consequence which—by the way—did not include Larry O'Brien.

Robert Reisner In January [1972], a meeting was set up in Mitchell's office with Liddy, Dean, and Magruder. At the time, I didn't know that its purpose was to discuss Liddy's plan. As they were getting ready for the meeting,

Liddy needed an easel. He asked me to call the attorney general's office to see if they had one. I asked Mitchell's secretary, who didn't have time to look, so we found an easel at CRP. Later—in the spring of 1973—Magruder wanted to claim that Liddy wasn't at the meeting, or that a plan had not been presented. So when they came to me and said, "McCord remembers an easel," the question was: Did I recall getting the easel? It was a matter of determining who was lying. Magruder said to me, "What do you mean, remembering the easel? Nobody remembers it." I was standing in Fred Fielding's outer office at the time; Magruder was screaming at me: "Don't you realize this could lead to impeachment?" And I said, "I don't know what it could lead to, but I have to tell what I remember."

Jeb Stuart Magruder He [Liddy] comes into my office and tells me he is supposed to prepare some plans. I said, "Okay, if that's what they want you to do. Put them together and I'll set up a meeting with Mitchell," and that's what I did. I had never seen the charts before the meeting. That is very unusual; I never would have done it this way with anybody else, but Dean indicated that this was okay—this was what Liddy was supposed to do. Then I saw the charts and realized what he was talking about.

At the first meeting, John said, "Well, Gordon, why don't you go back and get this down to some reasonable level?" He sort of used the money [issue] as being out of line with reality. At he second meeting, Mitchell said, "Well, let's forget about all this stuff; maybe you want to think about the Watergate thing," or something like that.

G. Gordon Liddy At the second meeting in Mitchell's office, he didn't know what was going on. He told me to burn the charts I had prepared. I was furious, and chewed out both Dean and Magruder. I said, "Why are you putting me in a position of selling something to a guy who doesn't want it?" They said, "You don't understand Mitchell. He is trying to tell you that the budget is too high." That was when Dean said, "I don't think you should get the answer through this office." I was discouraged; the people I had lined up were waiting and waiting. So Hunt and I went to Colson; he didn't want to know what it was about. He cut me off as I tried to explain. He said, "What you want is a decision on something, is that correct?" I said yes. He replied, "Okay. I'll get you a decision." Subsequently, an aide to Magruder told me that Magruder, who was in Florida, had just spoken to Mitchell. He actually said, "You have a 'go' on your plan," which I understood to mean that Mitchell had authorized it. It is clear that that never happened; it is Dean being in business for himself. Dean's later claim that he had objected to the plan as given in the two meetings in Mitchell's office is bullshit; it was a Dean operation.

Jeb Stuart Magruder He [Mitchell] was a full participant; the presentation was to him. Dean was there, representing Haldeman and the president, in a sense, and I, representing the campaign.

Liddy worked for me. He had seven charts—the seven activities Liddy wanted: capture the antiwar leaders and put them on a plane and drop them off in the middle of a desert in Mexico. Some of that stuff was almost hilarious if it wasn't serious, because he meant it.

Six of those ideas were discarded, but this Watergate thing kept coming back—clearly because of the Howard Hughes issue: O'Brien. O'Brien was a consultant to Hughes; they wanted to find out if O'Brien knew anything that would prove negative. Neither Mitchell nor Haldeman ever told me exactly what the connection was. I knew it had to do with Hughes, because it had come from Hank Greenspun of the *Las Vegas Sun*. They were interested in it.

Dwight Chapin He [John Mitchell] is at Key Biscayne. He's been up all night with this woman [Martha Mitchell] on one of her binges. Here come Magruder and Liddy, and they make this presentation, and John [Mitchell] does a "Well, okay, but we'll deal with that back in Washington." It's in his testimony. I believe it; I don't believe he approved what was supposed to happen. Knowing Jeb, this thing took off. If you go to the psychological makeup of some of these people, Jeb was a pleaser; he had to prove himself—be in this action. Once, he pulled up in this limousine. I thought, oh God, Haldeman would die if he saw this. At the White House—believe it or not—they helped us keep our reality in check; we served there at the pleasure of the president; life was short; we were going to be there for a limited period of time. Maybe we were conned. Here's Jeb, whose ambition has run amok—I think he wanted to be a Cabinet officer; God knows what he thought he could end up being. This sense of power was just out of line, when you take Haldeman's taskmaster style and put Jeb on the receiving end. Had Jeb been reacting to a Finch, or to a Harlow, it might have been much different; the system was so managerial and demanding in terms of response. You get a guy like Jeb Magruder out there, and he's like one of those little model planes: he comes whipping back from Florida and this thing is off and running, and I don't think that Mitchell knew.

Frederick LaRue We had a lot on the table at that meeting. I had asked Magruder about this item the night before and he had told me that this was something that John needed to make a decision on. I said, "We have a lot of decisions to make. If we get to that item all right." So I put the Gemstone plan at the end of the agenda. Mitchell never signed off on that scheme or plan whatever the hell you want to call it. I don't think he ever signed off on it. I know damn well he didn't at that meeting. I remember it vividly. There were questions about it; it was a ludicrous plan. If you want to bug some-body, why the DNC? It was not a well thought-out scheme. The essence of a good political campaign should be to avoid major mistakes. This was a major mistake. It was not signed off on at that meeting. I say that unequivocally. And in my opinion, Mitchell never signed off on it.

John Dean I don't mean this unkindly about John Mitchell—and I said it while he was alive. I don't think that John Mitchell was as sharp and as bright as a lot of people give him credit for. I think that he got overwhelmed by a lot of these things. I saw it happen when I was at the Department of Justice. When I was having to brief him on things he was asked to testify about, he was not somebody who could quickly assimilate a lot of informa-tion. I think on Liddy, he would puff on his pipe and give it a little time, and think: this is crazy, no one is going to go anyplace with this. Yes, he may have been preoccupied with Martha, but he was also making day-to-day deci-sions. I don't think this was Mitchell's cup of tea; I don't think he liked this kind of stuff but he thought somebody at the White House did, and so he wasn't about to say out the window you go, Mr. Liddy. These things had come over from the White House before. They had very definitely come over in the form of the Huston Plan and other things; I am uncovering little things now that suggest that this couldn't have been any surprise to Mitchell—that this was the way they were thinking at the White House.

So many things like that go to natural deaths in government; no one ever approves them, so they never go anywhere. I thought that this was what had happened to Liddy's plans; I thought he was over there working with the Finance Committee; the election law problems were complex, and massive, and difficult, and time-consuming. I had no idea the guys over there were planning burglaries. I mean, I had no idea.

Robert Odle, Jr. Gordon Liddy is the most persistent man you will ever meet; he just will not give up. In those kinds of meetings, John Mitchell would find it hard to get tough, or nasty, as opposed—for instance—to Haldeman or Ehrlichman. I can see this meeting: Mitchell would have puffed on his pipe and said, "Well, Gordon, that's not what we had in mind; can you come back?" And Liddy did come back. At the meeting in

Florida—I gather that Mrs. Mitchell was in one of her moods, coming into the room, screaming—this happened when they were at the end of the agenda, and Mitchell said, "Okay. Just go handle it." I can't imagine someone with John's intelligence and long-range view of things wanting all of that. There is another theory—that Haldeman wanted it and that they did it to please him. But Mitchell had no need to please Haldeman; he was his equal, or greater, in the eyes of the president. I can see Jeb Magruder wanting to please Haldeman in that sense, but not Mitchell.

Raymond Price I don't think that Mitchell knowingly signed off on Gemstone. He was at Key Biscayne and drinking heavily at the time—probably on his eleventh martini—and what probably happened was that Magruder came to him with a list of many items—and this was the last item. And if Mitchell was paying attention at all, it was modest attention, and Magruder chose to take this as authorization.

Jeb Stuart Magruder Mitchell signed off on the Watergate break-in in Key Biscayne; I think we all reluctantly signed off. None of us were interested in it at the committee; we were pushed, first by Colson, then by Haldeman. We were continually told that the president wanted it done.

All of us had worked in the White House, and all of us understood what the president wanted. Usually, if Haldeman said the president wanted it, it *meant* the president wanted it. Haldeman was not the one who used the president's name carelessly. I had many notations on my memos that would go over to the president which would indicate that these types of activities were certainly acceptable to him, and not only acceptable, but desired.

There is the question of what he was aware of. I wasn't even aware of when Liddy was going in the first time—the exact date.

Robert Reisner What Magruder later said was that he sought approval for Liddy's plan. He called me and said, "Find Liddy and tell him that it's approved." But I am still not clear, to this day, what it was that was approved. Magruder's message to me was typical; I would probably pass twenty of those messages a day. Later, people made a lot of the conversation because Magruder did. It was Magruder saying: "You see, I didn't do this on my own; I was given permission by John Mitchell." It's not clear to me what he got permission for—what the plan was that was approved. I have a memory of Liddy saying, "What do they mean? How fast do they want me to get going? What are they talking about? What kind of a deal is this?" It may be that my memory of this is colored by history—in which I now know that

Liddy thought it was such a joke that they would start and stop. It also may be mixed in with later encounters with Liddy.

Samuel Dash I think that the break-in had been approved by Mitchell. There was the so-called Gemstone Plan; they were operating like undercover agents; these "spies" had letterhead with "Gemstone" written on it. In the show and tell Liddy gave Mitchell in his office, he was putting the whole plan out, and the only reason Mitchell disapproved it the first time was that the budget was too high; Liddy had to come back with a smaller budget, which limited itself to the break-in—and that was signed off [on] by Mitchell at Key Biscayne.

Richard Moore Mitchell got a bad rap; he never authorized the buggings. When he resigned as attorney general, he went to Florida before moving into the campaign, and that is when Mr. Magruder went down to see him. And he came back and said the deal was on—the bugging of the [Democratic National Committee] headquarters. That was totally false: he was a man who had a rather strong compulsion not to tell the truth. He called me the Sunday after the break-in and left word that Mr. Mitchell was calling me. I went into the office that morning for other reasons. I called Mitchell back—they were in a hotel in Los Angeles—and got Magruder on the phone. He told me about the break-in, and that McCord had been arrested, and that he was a contract employee of the Committee to Reelect, and that Mitchell wanted to know my views, and whether we should publicly identify him first, or wait till it came out. Magruder was excited to be in on something dramatic, important, and romantic, and he was enjoying his role. He wanted to be able to tell Bob Haldeman that we are covering all the bases.

H. R. Haldeman I know that there is a lot to be said about Watergate, because we still don't know who ordered the break-in and why. When you look at some of what he said, and the way he reacted, I have to wonder what Nixon's thoughts really are in all of this, in the sense of why he raised the Bay of Pigs issue and why he agreed to call in the CIA. Both John Ehrlichman and I had the feeling that—as Watergate became a matter of concern in 1973—he was afraid that he may have either ordered Mitchell or Colson to do something, or perhaps he didn't order anything, but realizing that people sometimes overstep, that somebody in there—either Colson or Mitchell— had ordered the Watergate break-in, or had been involved in the break-in, and he was concerned with the effect that would have on him, and on the 1972 election. I think that John and I, deep down, thought that Nixon's concern was that Mitchell was involved. Then I got to thinking, maybe it was Colson, but he wasn't as likely to protect Colson as he was Mitchell if, in fact, he thought that was what he was doing. But he also wasn't likely to protect anybody at the expense of the presidency.

Robert Reisner I am not sure, in retrospect, what Mitchell did. I am not sure that the story that he said, "Get those guys out of there—this is crazy," is true. Mitchell was a gruff guy. People inferred what they thought Mitchell meant; he had a kind of dampening effect. To the extent that he had to leave the campaign immediately, I wouldn't be surprised if he was taking a fall for Haldeman, Ehrlichman, and a lot of other people.

H. R. Haldeman It was at that time a second-rate burglary. We should have treated it properly—as a second-rate burglary committed by one of our people. I think now—and have always thought—that the president was afraid that one of our people was John Mitchell, or Chuck Colson, and therefore was not willing or anxious to take the kinds of steps that he knew I would take. But he never stopped me: he never told me not to do anything, as you can see in the tapes.

Richard Kleindienst I am confident that Mitchell didn't know anything about the Watergate break-in. I'm now confident that Nixon didn't know either. You'd have to know John. Three people could be in a room with him and he'd say something, and in the manner in which he said it, one person could interpret it one way, another person another way, and the third person yet another way. That was his personality and rather understated manner of speech. While that takes care of the break-in, he all but admitted in his testimony in the Ervin hearing that he probably knew about the cover-up and did nothing to stop it, because he didn't want to have McGovern elected president. If John had gone over to CRP in the beginning of January, the kind of personnel that worked there never would have been there.

Robert Mardian Mitchell is accused of being one of the prime people; he didn't know anything about it, believe me. I knew John Mitchell intimately well; we were very close; my wife was probably the last friend poor Martha ever had—I'd come home and Martha would be at my house, and John would phone and ask, "Is she there? Send her home." I am convinced Mitchell had no prior knowledge that they were going to break into the Democratic National headquarters. That is the stupidest thing: They had five candidates at the time. They each had their own committees. The most sterile place in the world to get information would be the Democratic National Committee. If you want to get the dirt on one of the candidates—if McGovern was the lead one, go into his headquarters if you want to find dirt. None of the five candidates would give any information to the National Committee.

Mitchell thought that here, again, Nixon—he had an anathema for Howard Hughes because Hughes had gotten his brother, Don, mixed up in that $205,000 loan; Mitchell knew as attorney general that Larry O'Brien was in the pay of Howard Hughes while he was the chairman of the Democratic National Committee. It was Mitchell's opinion that the White House crowd was trying to get the goods on Larry O'Brien to embarrass not only him but Howard Hughes. That is what Mitchell believed. And Nixon thought it was the crazies over at the Committee to Reelect the President who didn't know anything about politics, who were going to break into Democratic headquarters.

Gerald R. Ford It was the most stupid political action I've known in my long career in politics; I have not the slightest idea why anybody would undertake such a stupid action. On the following Monday, I had a meeting with John Mitchell and Hugh Scott [member, U.S. Senate, R-Pa.] to talk about our campaign for 1972; Hugh was the Senate [majority] leader, and I was the House leader. I got to the breakfast meeting early and sat there talking to John Mitchell. I said, "John, did you know anything about this stupid thing of breaking into the Democratic National Committee headquarters?" He looked me right in the eye and said he had had nothing to do with it— had no knowledge of it. That was pretty strong language from somebody who had been attorney general. Quite honestly, that assurance from him was a factor in my strongly supporting President Nixon up till the last. Now, I think that Mitchell lied to me.

Fred Dalton Thompson, chief minority counsel, Senate Watergate Committee I thought John Mitchell was a very sad case. Here is a guy with a great reputation as a lawyer—attorney general of the United States; I had his certificate of appointment on my wall in Nashville when I was assistant U.S. attorney. I never thought I would meet him. When I did, I was interrogating him; he was a broken man. I don't think he did it for money. He was a good soldier and took the rap for some others in some respect. He probably signed off on the break-in in an offhand sort of way.

THE CIA SCENARIO

Robert Mardian Mitchell thought it was Nixon going after Larry O'Brien. I know for a fact that Mitchell was convinced that maybe not Nixon himself but people trying to aggrandize themselves with him [would] get the goods on Larry O'Brien and expose Howard Hughes. When he told me that, I said, "John, the outfit that they used was Intel"—they called it the Mullin Agency then but it had been Intel, which was a CIA front, but it was a Howard Hughes organization, and Hunt worked for Howard Hughes. I told John, "That's the craziest thing I've ever heard of. You're not going to get Howard Hunt to go after his true employer"—who was Howard Hughes. The Mullin Agency was still a CIA front operated by Howard Hughes people.

William Saxbe The president thought that the CIA was involved in the Watergate break-in.

Jerry Jones I know that Senator [Howard] Baker [R-Tenn.] thought all along that there was some very strange thing with the CIA that he never really understood: it appears to me that McCord and some of the others were probably still in the CIA. I think that the CIA knew that the break-in was occurring; I think that the Democrats knew that their phones were being bugged.

Raymond Price I suspect that the break-in can be traced to Howard Hunt, who—in his various roles—tried to ingratiate himself with the director of the CIA, the president, and Howard Hughes, from whom he expected to make a lot of money; all the targets at the DNC headquarters were of much more interest to Hughes than to us. This was especially so in the case of Larry O'Brien—when you take into account that he was then the Hughes's $100,000-a-month fixer in Washington. Also, so many things from the Kennedy assassination traced back to the same people, and my guess is that some of the connections might have been so politically damaging that they might have destroyed the agency's usefulness. Hughes was at the center of the attempts to assassinate Castro, as was Hunt. To me, the most likely origin of the break-in was Hunt trying to go after Larry O'Brien—not in his DNC capacity, but in his Hughes capacity.

John Ehrlichman Walters had not been aboveboard. The memoranda of conversations that he prepared after the fact—several months after the fact—didn't square with the facts, as I recall them. I think that there was a lot of contrivance on Walters's part to protect himself and the CIA.

Richard Helms The CIA was never behind the break-in; the CIA had nothing whatsoever to do with the break-in. I said that before the Ervin Committee; I say it again, now, even more fervently.

THE NIXON SCENARIO

George McGovern I always assumed that it led up to the president— maybe not the details, but the general parameters were known to him—and he might not have said, Go down there and see what they are doing at the National Committee, but I think that there was a mood and an atmosphere created there that made those folks feel they were doing what the boss wanted.

H. R. Haldeman Nixon never would have ordered—and I wouldn't have— any surveillance of the Democratic National Committee. We might have ordered trying to get a plant into McGovern headquarters—something like that—but never the National Committee, because we had, as professional politicians, total disregard for the Party Committee as an effective political entity, in terms of anything of a highly sensitive nature. You just wouldn't do it from a practical viewpoint, let alone the moral, or legal, or any other viewpoint.

We knew there was smoke: Larry O'Brien was getting a $150,000 annual fee from Howard Hughes while he was chairman of the [Democratic] National Committee. And the Democrats, over the years, had made very effective political hay over Nixon's ties to Howard Hughes, which were pretty remote: He [Nixon] was never getting any stipend from him [Hughes], although his brother [Donald Nixon] did get a loan from Hughes. Of course, the place they went into [during the burglary] was on the exact opposite side of the building from Larry O'Brien's office; the guy they bugged was Spencer Oliver.

John Ehrlichman I have no evidence that Nixon ordered the break-in. The Fielding break-in and Watergate are insulated from each other by time and events, so I have a whole lot of trouble in extrapolating from Ellsberg to Watergate. The Fielding break-in did establish a weakness—in a structural sense—a vulnerability that continued to dog the administration, and particularly Richard Nixon and me, throughout that period of time. The pattern had been established. Entries were nothing new; they were nothing new in the Kennedy and Johnson administrations. That kind of activity has been going on in this country for decades. The Fielding break-in was the first one I knew about in the Nixon administration, but I have no doubt that the Bureau [FBI] was doing that kind of thing the whole time; as long as Hoover was there, they were in that business. At the dinner I attended at Hoover's house, along with Mitchell and Nixon, there was talk about operations at the new Russian Embassy, against the Cuban mission, against other embassies, and against some civilians. I have forgotten who the civilians were, but I can vividly remember the discussion.

Jerry Jones I would be absolutely amazed if the DNC had been broken into without Nixon's having asked that it be done. First of all, that's a pretty high-risk kind of thing to be doing; perhaps then it was thought that one could do that and be impervious to being caught, but the fact is that it was a fairly major political risk. After all, this guy is running for reelection. Why in the world would some underling, like Magruder, take it on himself to break into the DNC? It just wouldn't happen. It had to come from higher up. And why would a Mitchell, or a Haldeman, or a Colson even, take that kind of risk without the president wanting it done? It would be amazing to me, knowing how the place works. I certainly wouldn't have taken the risk: Hey, I've got this great idea; let's go break into the DNC. We won't tell Haldeman or Mitchell, or anybody; let's just go do it. No one that I ever worked with would have thought of doing that—ever. There was—and still is—a cute way of trying to structure deniability to a president; you could see it in Irangate, with Reagan and [Oliver] North. Perhaps they attempted to construct a deniability thing where Nixon said: It would really be wonderful if we knew what was going on over there—and winked, and that was the authorization to try to find out.

Richard Helms I can't imagine his ordering the break-in, but on the other hand, there has been so much material that has come out about Watergate in the intervening years that I had never seen. In fact, it was only comparatively recently that I finally saw some documents indicating the extent to which President Nixon was trying to ensnare the CIA in the business of the break-in and the whole Watergate affair.

Obviously, at that time I was totally innocent of the White House's effort to put the whole blame for this affair onto the agency: it's now clear that this was what they were doing. But I certainly had no sense of that at the time; it never occurred to me that the president of the United States would want to perform an operation of this type against an agency of government.

The whole handling of the Watergate business—from the day of the break-in on through—was very difficult for the agency. If we had known that it was the White House that was trying to do this, we probably would have defended ourselves in quite a different way. There would have been a public relations battle. But my whole objective was to keep the agency from getting ensnared, caused by all the leaks to the newspapers coming from what I thought was the FBI. Maybe it *was* the FBI, with the White House pressure behind it.

In any event, questions have been asked by lawyers as to why we didn't come right out and say: we did this; we didn't do that. The whole point was, there was no privacy at that particular time on anything that was going on in the investigation. The FBI had never been known as a leaky organization before, particularly in matters of criminality, so it was a very difficult situation to handle.

I may have made mistakes, but nevertheless defended the agency as best I could, because I realized that the end result would have been the end of the agency. No only would I have gone to jail if I had gone along with what the White House wanted us to do, but the agency's credibility would have been ruined forever.

George Romney My personal thoughts were, as I heard that some of the staff people were involved, that Nixon had to be involved. I never was aware of anything that Haldeman and Ehrlichman and Mitchell did that Nixon didn't approve of; they were 100 percent loyal and supportive, so I knew the minute their involvement became apparent that he had to be involved.

My impression of Nixon is that he is the brightest and ablest man we've had in the White House since World War II, in terms of his overall, total grasp of things; I think he is a tremendously competent, informed individual. He had the desire to do domestically things as important as what he'd done in the foreign field in his first term. He knew he would have a Democratic Congress, and he wanted to get an overwhelming mandate in the election of 1972, so that Congress would approve his domestic program. So what happened was tragic not only for him but for the country. He's always been very willing to do politically whatever he had to do to accomplish his objectives. That's been his undoing.

John Dean I don't know if the president was involved in ordering the break-in; I have never seen any evidence myself that the president was aware there was going to be a break-in at the Watergate. If you ask me if the president knew there was somebody over there collecting intelligence, or that might have that mentality to break in, I would take even money, right now, that some day a tape is going to come up that shows that it is pretty clear; I think there are tapes that hint at that right now. On one of the tapes that had been released publicly, it says Haldeman said to the president: You know, we knew there was something going on over there. There are also documents that certainly indicate that Haldeman knew, through Strachan, what was going on over there, and it's hard for me to believe some of that didn't seep to the top. But I don't have any evidence that he [Richard Nixon] knew there was going to be a break-in at the Watergate. I've always believed that what he said in August 1972 is essentially correct.

Bob Woodward There is no conclusive evidence, whereas there is conclusive evidence on other parts of the criminal activity—specifically the cover-up. I just don't know. You can lay out a possibility that he would have. He seems to take great pride in the claim that he didn't know. It makes no difference; these were his people, doing his bidding in the most unskillful way; they were doing what he wanted. There is nothing on the tapes where he expresses shock: My God. What happened? Who were these people? Who did it? There is none of that. There is a kind of: We collectively have this problem and have to deal with it. Nixon has always been a political gut fighter. He never gives ground. Why admit mistakes? Why clean house? You hunker down. It was the bunker mentality which was all part of Nixon—part of his presidency, of going into the Oval Office, or that EOB office, and sitting for hours and reading, or talking to Rebozo, or Haig, or Haldeman, endlessly, and not dealing much with the outer world. Compare his schedule with the schedule of somebody like Bill Clinton. Clinton is all over the place: talking to everyone. Nixon was almost born in a bunker.

Alexander Butterfield When I heard about the break-in, the clear, obvious first assumption was, of course, that the White House knew. These things don't "happen." Anything of the magnitude of the break-in at the headquarters of the Democratic Party—who is going to do it? We're going to do it, of course. It was one of the many little things we did. Now, I wasn't in on all those little things, because it wasn't part of my job. There is still no question in my mind that it emanated from the Oval Office; that is why I am not a fan of Richard Nixon, to this day. He says that he was wrong, but what he means is: I was wrong not to keep a more watchful eye over my zealous young aides. But that's all baloney. He directed everything.

Maurice Stans Nixon had nothing to do with the Watergate play; he was on the sidelines; they didn't tell him. But when they did tell him, he was as surprised as anybody could be, and he took the natural step of: How do we protect our folks that got into this thing? Lyndon Johnson had done the same thing in other circumstances, as had other presidents, and it seemed to him to be pretty natural to try to defend his organization, particularly with an election six months away. The normal reaction in a case like that is: How do we control the damage? That doesn't mean you have to do anything illegal, because there are ways you can control that damage by squelching a bit of knowledge without anybody having to perjure himself. But the people who were involved in it had an entirely different view of it. When they got to that point, John Dean, McCord, and a few others couldn't take the pressure, so they decided to tell the story from their side. And, of course, that drew others in, and the circle began to increase—all the way up to John Mitchell.

Samuel Dash I believe that Richard Nixon and Haldeman knew of the plan prior to June 17th. According to his testimony, Dean was surprised when he attended the meeting in Mitchell's office. He went to Haldeman and said that Liddy has a cuckoo plan and the White House shouldn't have any part of it; Haldeman would brief the president every morning on things of that nature. I think he told the president about the plan, but may well have said, But Dean says it's cuckoo and we shouldn't have a part in it. When the burglars were caught, Liddy met with Dean on the 19th, and according to Dean's testimony, said, "I should be punished and executed; I'm a Catholic and I can't kill myself. I'll stand on any street corner in Washington and you can shoot me with a machine gun."

Dwight Chapin There is a person who goes all the way back through this whole thing, and that is Murray Chotiner. He was in the White House—he had an office in the EOB. He leaves; the break-in happens. Murray was the operator for Nixon on God only knows what—somewhere outside the channels; he was a marvelous political manipulator and handler. I always had terrific respect for his abilities, but God knows what he was up to. When I was a young man working in the 1962 campaign, I was asked to deliver something to Bob Finch's office in downtown Los Angeles. The door opens and the room is filled with cigar smoke, and there are Vic Lasky* and Murray

---

* A journalist of the conservative persuasion.

Chotiner—like a classic picture of the Tammany Hall* back room. When I think of Murray, I always start there.

Terrence O'Donnell I was always convinced that it was due to the overzealousness of staff at a level way below the president, or Haldeman. Bob was an extremely bright, capable guy, and I didn't believe—and still don't believe—that he would be party to giving an order to do something like this. I viewed it as campaign-based excess, overzealousness, bad judgment. I do not believe the break-in was White House–initiated at all. The post break-in activities are better documented. There, I think, it first became a media campaign and management problem, and then it crossed over—absent good legal advice and sound reasoning—into misconduct, which—because I'm a lawyer—I blame to a large extent on the lawyer, John Dean, because when you have trouble in an institution, you need a good house lawyer who will say: We can do this, but we cannot do that, because in the long run it will make things worse, and it could bring down the presidency, and I will not permit that to happen. John Dean was a young person at that time, who had enjoyed tremendous advancement. He had lousy judgment; he was not an experienced lawyer and he was coming up with ideas to manage the problem—which pleased his bosses, but were wrong, in hindsight. An experienced lawyer would have known that if you started down that road, sooner or later it would all collapse.

Alexander Butterfield These aides weren't going to go out and do anything on their own; they would never jeopardize the president's position. For this to happen, it would have to have the okay from Haldeman—or at least tacit okay. He would never do that without telling the president—not in a million years.

Fred Dalton Thompson If I had to guess, a bunch of very ambitious and bright young men with more money than judgment decided that this would be a neat thing to do. They sold it to higher-ups, and they did it. It's hard, in retrospect, to believe they were concerned about George McGovern, but politicians are paranoid by nature.

Vernon Walters Nixon never knew anything about Watergate until they got into trouble and they came to him and said, "You have to help us." Richard

---

* A New York City institution of Democratic machine politics, known for its "smoke-filled rooms."

Nixon was too intelligent to have bugged the Democratic National Committee. These junior people did it—got in trouble and screamed for help. He had very incompetent subordinates. None of those men were of real capacity. He needed bureaucrats, and that's exactly what they were.

Robert Hartmann Nixon may be as puzzled as we are as to who did this damn fool thing. Jerry [Gerald] Ford did not believe that Nixon had crossed the line of aiding and abetting a felony, and up to that point, despite all the shady things that were leveled at him, Nixon had never crossed the line of knowing illegality. The idea that Nixon—as intelligent as he was, as good a lawyer as he was, as smart a politician as he was—was dumb enough to do some of the things he was alleged to have done was hard to believe.

Alexander Butterfield I was called before the House Judiciary Committee to contradict something the president had been saying right along: that, essentially, "While all of this was going on, these young guys got carried away. I was busy with affairs of state." The guy is a detail man; he knew everything that was going on at CRP—Haldeman ran CRP. All the CRP people were from the White House: Malek, Magruder, Liddy.

David Wilson I don't think there is any question, in retrospect, that the president was—certainly after the fact—knowledgeable about what went on. He went into a very understandable defensive posture politically: he thought he could stare this down, stonewall it, make it go away. He tried to do that and—in the very unusual circumstances—failed. Within that situation, there were people who were going to have to take responsibility, and whether it was going to go up to Haldeman, Ehrlichman, or Dean, or whoever, someone would have to pay the price—which was not just being fired, or humiliation, but going to prison. The problem with Watergate was that it was not limited to the burglary, but ballooned into all sorts of evils of the Nixon administration, some of which were truly reprehensible things, and others things that had been done in other administrations. But they all got jumbled together, and when this was going on, politically it was difficult to separate any of it out.

Alexander Haig I don't think that Nixon knew about the Watergate break-in before it occurred. I do think that John Mitchell knew and that Nixon tried to protect him—and this became fatal for him.

Philip Lacovara, deputy solicitor general of the United States; counsel to the Watergate prosecutor I would doubt that he personally ordered the break-in, just because there is no evidence from all that's come out to indicate that he was involved in that stage. And with all the people who have talked so far, I think it's likely if that had been his role, somebody would have 'fessed up by now. I relate Nixon to Henry II and the assassination of Thomas à Becket: Will no one give me the head of this meddlesome priest? I believe that that is the way Nixon and his aides related.

17

And Why?

Many theories have been advanced as to why the break-ins at the DNC were ordered. On the face of it, these activities appear to be inexplicable, and perhaps they were, and are. Or perhaps there were reasons why someone would undertake these actions: Were the president and his senior aides concerned about his possible opponents in the 1972 presidential election? Or were they seeking derogatory information with which to embarrass DNC officials? Or was someone seeking to discredit the president?

George McGovern I never knew the purpose of it. In retrospect, you wonder why they bothered about it; they had such a lead in the polls—and the power of incumbency—but I've always felt that the president worried about us having some information about him that could be damaging, and he wanted to foreclose the possibility of a last-minute revelation of some kind. I always had the feeling it was more of a defensive move than an effort to find something that might embarrass us.

Hugh Sloan The confusing thing is that by the time the Watergate break-in actually happened, the political landscape had cleared up a lot. The president was ahead at that point, and there certainly weren't the kinds of pressures that would lead you to think people would get desperate and do these kinds of things.

Bob Woodward The question of the reason for the break-in has become a red herring. If you really look at the testimony of the burglars, and Hunt and Liddy, and their writings and books about it, it was a broad fishing expedition into the opposition headquarters. It was a reflection of the Nixon paranoia about the other side: we need to know what they are doing; get dirt on the other people. This idea that there was one Rosetta Stone that people were looking for just does not hold water at all. The answer is in the chronology. If you look at when the idea was set in motion, in the meetings in Mitchell's office in January and early February, and you look at the newspapers of those days, you see the condition of the Nixon reelection effort in February 1972. It was thought that Nixon was very vulnerable politically—that the Democrats were going to put up a formidable candidate; that the issues of the war and the economy were not good for Nixon. There was a momentum to the plans. It had been wound up and it's not that you couldn't stop it; it's that the mentality was not there to stop it.

G. Gordon Liddy At CRP, I was under Jeb Stuart Magruder. Three minutes into my first meeting with him, I knew I had a problem because he started poisoning the well of Gordon Strachan—saying that Strachan would want copies of my reports, but that I should not give them to him. I said, "Wait a minute. If the White House wants certain things, they are entitled, and I will give them to them." Magruder then announced to the staff: "Gordon is going to be in charge of 'dirty tricks.'" I got my instructions through Magruder, but it was quite clear to me that they weren't from him; he wasn't a self-starter type. So when I was asked by Magruder, "Do you think you can get into Watergate?" I said, "Yes. But to what end? We are going to hit them later in Miami* after they have chosen their candidate."

John Dean When you take the break-in as an isolated incident, you have that question: Why? If you put the Watergate break-in in the context of everything else, it was just another in a pattern. People say, we've got all these concerns and questions about why the break-in. Well, hell! They would have been breaking into McGovern's headquarters the same night they got caught at the Watergate. It might have been the Brookings. It might have been Ellsberg's psychiatrist's office. This is a pattern of activities. There are probably places I don't even know about. This was their second break-in at Watergate. It was because of this mentality that was coming out of the Oval Office, that's why.

* Site of the 1972 Democratic National Convention.

George McGovern I think that the Nixon people thought that I was an honest, decent person—maybe naive—but that I wouldn't be involved in anything scandalous involving finances, or anything like that. If they had assumed by the middle of June that I was going to be the nominee, they had very little reason to be snooping about anything relative to me; there was nothing in the DNC headquarters or in my campaign headquarters that could have helped them, or that could have hurt us; there weren't any scandalous letters or crooked records, so I think they must have known that I didn't operate that way. If they were trying to trap me with some blonde, there would have been an easier way to do it than breaking into our campaign headquarters—I don't want to imply any totally virtuous record on that score, but I never really thought they were after me, or after the committee.

I think they thought that maybe we had something on them; we didn't—not really. We knew about the ITT matter; I talked about that publicly. There had been some talk about money laundering in Mexico. We knew how the Vietnam War had been manipulated for political purposes. But I said all these things publicly; I didn't have any bombshell, and we didn't have any investigative team looking into Nixon. Why we didn't, I don't know.

Ben Bradlee If you put me up against the wall and gave me my life, I couldn't explain it. I think they were looking for dirt. What could they use on Larry O'Brien? I think it was all bullshit. They had these sorts of engines in Hunt and Liddy that were driving them to do something. They had all the money in the world. They couldn't spend it fast enough.

Charles Wiggins Those who were planning the campaign in 1972 were planning about a $60-million effort. It was a highly structured organizational plan. One of the major issues of a campaign is security. There was a slot for security, and there was a name suggested; it was Liddy. The next thing they had to do was to allocate a budget for each one of the responsibilities, and that involved the process of these nominal people given the responsibility for various functions of the campaign marching down to the attorney general's office, and the attorney general was acting improperly in a dual role at that time, and he listened to them present their budgets. It was in that context that Liddy presented the proposal to John Mitchell of this bizarre effort to conduct counterintelligence of the Democratic Party, including breaking into the Watergate headquarters and seizing their materials.

I think it was an idea conceived in the mind of Gordon Liddy. He presented it to Mitchell and Dean in the years before 1972 as just an idea—as a justification for his budget. Mitchell turned it down; he smoked his pipe, and grumbled, and said this was not the kind of thing that he had in mind, and sent Liddy away for the purpose of conducting another effort to come back with a modified plan. So Liddy probably sold a plan that was excessive at the outset for security for the campaign. And Mitchell bought off on it, and then here was the problem of execution. There was no good reason for this at all; there was no necessity of breaking in.

John Ehrlichman I am not sure that there was any purpose in planting the bug; it has never made sense to me. I like the theory that they went in to find the call [girl] ring* trick book. There wasn't anything happening in that office of a helpful political nature.

G. Gordon Liddy The FBI never found a listening device near the office of Larry O'Brien. The burglars didn't go near there, although those were the orders I gave. When they went in, they put a device on the telephone in the office right outside the office of R. Spencer Oliver.

Arnaud de Borchgrave The French intelligence service had a team which, after Nixon was brought down, looked into the origins of Watergate; they were convinced that there was some kind of conspiracy. In 1980, the chief of French intelligence gave me the synopsis of a report his service had put together on what had happened at Watergate: the operation was an attempt to embarrass Nixon to the point where he would be brought down. As best as they were able to reconstruct what had happened, it had been organized by the Cuban secret service—the DGI—perhaps at the behest of the KGB. Today, this sounds ridiculous, but at the time Nixon was considered to be a danger to certain people in the KGB, or the Politburo, because of his opening to China and other issues.

I gave Nixon the synopsis. He read it in front of me, kept a copy, and—to his credit—never once mentioned it. The report said that two of the Watergate burglars—Eugenio Martinez and Virgilio Gonzalez—were double agents since the Bay of Pigs, working for the CIA and the DGI, so this was a third-rate burglary designed to be discovered. Of course, to Liddy and Hunt—who considered themselves supermen—this notion is preposterous.

---

* It was rumored that a call girl ring was being operated out of the DNC to service party VIPs, using the telephone of Spencer Oliver, who had no connection to the enterprise.

WILL WE EVER KNOW THE TRUTH
ABOUT THE BREAK-IN?

Perhaps one day, as more of the Nixon administration tapes are released— according to the National Archives, as of March 1994, only 63 hours of approximately 3,000 hours of tapes have been released—one scenario will emerge and all of the speculation will be laid to rest.

But this day will not arrive as long as Mr. Nixon's injunction against the tapes' release remains in force.

Ronald Ziegler This is the startling thing about Watergate: it's twenty years later, and I still don't know who ordered the break-in; certainly no one had admitted that they ordered it. Did the president? Did Dean? Did Magruder? It is an extraordinary set of circumstances; why doesn't somebody just come out and say, "I ordered it," so we can clear all of this up. It seems so simple. Bob has now died, but if you just got Ehrlichman, Colson, Dean, and Fielding to sit down in a room and tell the truth, it wouldn't be a mystery.

David Wilson After I left the White House in early 1973, it was somewhat terrifying just to read the newspapers every day and to think: Is there something that I have been involved in that will turn out to be highly improper? Did I get sucked into something that I was not aware of? The more it came out, the more I discovered that John [Dean] was right in the middle of it— which I had never really believed before I left the White House. I had no idea he was playing as active a role as he was—that he had ended up taking over responsibility for the cover-up and actually had been involved in the payoffs; I had always assumed that John was much too savvy politically to allow himself to get into that position. I don't know why he did—whether it was out of ambition, or that he needed to be more personally involved in matters that he wanted to make certain would not come forth; there were a lot of games being played on a lot of different levels. But the final word has not come forth and, perhaps, never will.

Ben Bradlee Eventually, we'll get close to the full story. They're still writing books about the Lincoln assassination, and certainly, the Kennedy assassination.

Jerry Jones It is really interesting to me that there are four or five people who have never talked about what they know: Dean is one; I am not sure that Magruder ever completely discussed how all of these things worked; Mitchell never did; and Nixon never has. I think that Haldeman was truly amazed at a lot of this stuff. I don't know that he was completely aware of what was going on; he has said that he wasn't. I believe him. How all of that fit together, and who did what, we still don't know the story. It will be a mystery until the guys talk. Until then, we are all the victim of conspiracy theories; one can erect wonderful structures—as some do—on what appear to be little pieces of facts, but until these fellows talk, we won't know.

John Ehrlichman It would not be characteristic of Nixon to make an admission, even a deathbed one.* If he has a safe deposit box, it probably contains—if anything—a defense.

THE COVER-UP

The president had special concerns: as he writes in his memoir, Richard Nixon, *he had first learned of the break-in on June 18, while at Key Biscayne, upon reading of it in the* Miami Herald; *and on the following evening, while returning by air to Washington, he was informed of the involvement of a CRP employee.*

The president's concern was highlighted on June 20, when the Washington Post, *citing "federal sources close to the investigation," reported that Hunt's name had been found in the address books of two of the Watergate burglars, and that he had been identified as a former CIA employee who had worked at the White House as a consultant to Charles Colson.*

The Washington Post *article and the news that the DNC had launched a $1 million civil suit against CRP were indications to President Nixon that the Watergate issue would surface during the 1972 presidential campaign. Soon after reading the* Post *article, the president conferred with H. R. Haldeman to discuss the Watergate situation, among other issues—a discussion, it was discovered the following year, after Alexander Butterfield's revelation to the Senate Watergate Committee of the existence of a taping system in the Oval Office and elsewhere, that had been taped and then obliterated, in what became known as "the 18½-minute gap."*

---

* Mr. Ehrlichman and most of the other individuals quoted in this book were interviewed prior to Mr. Nixon's death.

During the next few days, the president conferred with Colson, Mitchell, and other key aides. At the same time, the FBI was conducting its own thorough investigation, and had traced money in Bernard Barker's Florida bank account to CRP.

Then, on the morning of June 23, and again in the early afternoon, the president met with Haldeman, who told him that, "The FBI is not under control," prompting the decision to ask CIA officials to tell Acting FBI Director Patrick Gray to back off from the Watergate investigation, as it could lead, according to the president, to conclusions that would be "very unfortunate for both the CIA and the country . . . and for American foreign policy."

Following the afternoon meeting, Haldeman and Ehrlichman met with CIA Director Richard Helms and the agency's deputy director, Lt. General Vernon Walters, to convey the president's request that Gray be told not to pursue the FBI's Watergate investigation.

Haldeman then met with the president, for the third time that day, to inform him that the CIA would cooperate. The taped contents of these discussions between the president and his chief of staff, released on August 5, 1974, would become known as the "smoking gun" that would inextricably link the president to the burgeoning cover-up of the involvement of both the White House and CRP in the Watergate affair.

H. R. Haldeman John Dean called me on the morning of the 23rd [of June 1972] to give me a report on the Watergate investigation. This was not surprising, because he was the White House counsel and was riding herd on the agencies who were doing the investigating. My notes show a number of things that I wrote down while he was talking to me on the phone. From that phone call, I went into the Oval Office for my normal meeting with the president. At that meeting, it is clear that—because you can compare my comments on the tape with my notes—I was reading from my notes. What I said was that John Mitchell suggests—and Dean agrees—that you should have the CIA talk to the FBI and tell them not to get into it. The way to handle it is to have Walters, the deputy head of the CIA, call Pat Gray and say: "Just stay the hell out of it; this is business we don't want you to go any further in." In other words, it is not the president's idea.

Nixon's response to the suggestion, which astounded me, was very much picking it up and telling me to meet with the CIA. What they were concerned with here was tracing the money trail. The reason for the concern was not, as far as I knew, as far as Nixon knew, and as far as, I think, what

Dean knew, that it would simply reveal a major donation from a Democrat that we had committed ourselves to not revealing, because in those days, you could take donations that you didn't have to report. We got big donations from big Democrats, including some from Hubert Humphrey's state [Minnesota]. This was one of them. As it turns out, when they traced the money trail, the money that was washed [laundered] in Mexico was the actual cash that this Democratic donor had given to the Reelection Committee.

It sounds so stupid now: Why would we care? But we did care, because we were told, "You can't let this out." The president said, "Call Helms and Walters over, and you and Ehrlichman meet with them and tell them that they are to tell the FBI not to pursue the investigation of the money sources." And, he said, "It may get into the Bay of Pigs thing." The president said that to me, so I said it to them [the CIA]. When I did, Helms just became unglued—he started screaming irrationally: "We had nothing to do with the Bay of Pigs; it had nothing to do with us," disclaiming everything, which, to this day, surprises me. I still don't understand. I've asked Nixon. I've never gotten an answer from him. I don't know what I was saying to Helms that caused this reaction. But I think Nixon knew, when he told me to speak to Helms, what the reaction would be. He wasn't too surprised when I told him.

Richard Helms To this day, I have no idea why the president thought that threatening me with the Bay of Pigs would have the slightest impact on me. After all, everything about the Bay of Pigs by that time was a fully public matter. What harm was there left in that old saw?

I don't know anything about it. I had never discussed with anybody in the Nixon administration getting rid of Castro. They didn't have anything else to bring up, I guess. They seemed assertive to me; they were carrying out a mission, and they just laid it on the table—bang, bang, bang. I believe that Haldeman later wrote a book—I never read it—and that he said I had all kinds of strange expressions on my face. That is all nonsense. I was just surprised at the thrust of the meeting; I didn't know what they were referring to half the time, but when you get an order from the chief of staff of the president of the United States—which is obviously a presidential order, because they made it clear that it was—you obviously think twice before you throw it overboard and pay no attention to it.

It took a little bit of time for us to sort out what was behind this, and we never did come up with a sensible conclusion, except that I checked carefully to be sure there wasn't something going on in Mexico that I hadn't been told about. When I found out that wasn't the case, I just said, "We are not going to have anything to do with telling the FBI what they can do, or what they can't do."

I told Walters, while he was getting into his car to go over to talk to Patrick Gray, "the agency has a delimitation agreement with the FBI about what they do in foreign countries and what we do; all I want Gray to do is to abide by that limitation agreement. We will abide by our part and leave it at that."

Seymour Glanzer You have to understand that *cover-up* is an elastic term: when you put it together, it looks like there is a pattern, but there is no pattern to the possible motivations. I don't believe that the evidence will support the notion that Nixon initiated the cover-up—a cover-up in the criminal sense. Nixon and his group were concerned about the political ramifications and the decisions they made were fueled by these considerations. Later on, there may have been a recasting of the motivations.

Ben Bradlee He went to a cover-up because he didn't trust those people; he thought he couldn't control them. What other explanation could there be? I suppose you slip into a cover-up. I don't suppose you say to yourself: Here's a fork in the road and that's cover-up and that's non-cover-up. You make little bits of decisions and you say: Well, we have to pay the legal fees for those Cubans, and you may have someone who's a little more sophisticated than a fanatic—and a fanatic like Hunt, and before you know it, you're in up to your throat.

I suspect that Nixon had some sort of understanding that generically there was a lot of dirty work going on. But whether he knew that on such-and-such a night they'd break into the psychiatrist's office or into the Watergate, I kind of doubt. But nowhere is there anything in the record that I can find where he said: You did what? You broke into a psychiatrist's office? Jesus, it's illegal. That's quite amazing. You think of the politicians you've known, or your relatives—your father. They would have said: You can't do that. You have to get rid of those guys. But, of course, he couldn't; he was in on it and all his buddies were.

Richard Helms The political didn't even enter into it at that point. As far as I was concerned, I was being asked about an operational matter; that was what was concerning me: What did they have in mind? What were they up to? Because, I want to point out, that for a fellow working in the executive branch—and I had, for many, many years—it did not occur to me that a president of the United States would be asking me to perform an illegal act right in the White House itself.

You can imagine that we were a bit surprised. In retrospect, all of this looks terribly simple, but at the time it was very confused: I had never heard of the expression "money laundering" at the time; I didn't even know what it was. We were dealing with a whole bunch of things that had nothing to do with the agency at all and with which we were not familiar.

It was the president speaking, and you never know what information the president has that you don't have—they have all kinds of sources; they have all kinds of people they talk to, and anybody who thinks you can say the president's wrong about that lives a very dangerous life in the executive branch. I wanted to be careful and check things out before I decided exactly what had to be done.

Ronald Ziegler At one point, Haig and I had a meeting with a group of leading lawyers, but assuming that there was a cover-up—which he knew about—President Nixon's will would not be extraordinary. Also, Nixon looked at the issue as more of a political than a legal problem. When you look back at it, the bottom line is that his legal situation was pretty ineptly handled; no strong legal defense was put forth. It was not because competent lawyers were not around him; it was just ineptly handled. But on the other hand, maybe the complexity of it all left no alternative. When this is all sorted out in the future, those who engage the problem will generally find that there was nothing that deeply, inherently bad about it—that there was extreme, excessive behavior and clearly an intrusion on people's constitutional rights that should not have taken place, yes. But it was all pretty marginal. However, it looked to be quite serious for our democracy, so I don't mean to denigrate the scope of the tragedy. It's probably best that it was uncovered, but ultimately there is not going to be some major, hidden, smoking gun behind it all. How easily it could have been turned off.

Alexander Haig Nixon genuinely believed that he had never directed anything that was blatantly illegal; he did, however, as we now know. Not being a politician, I think I can say this: The life of a politician in America is sleaze. He lives by it; he eats it every day. I didn't realize this until I started to run for office. But there is hardly a straight guy in the business: as Nixon always said to me—and he took great pride in it—"Al, I never took a dollar; I had somebody else do it." And he never did. I know that. A lot of things he was accused of in taking money he was never involved in, and after Watergate was over, they were never again alleged. I would get orders from him to do certain things that I knew were blatantly illegal, and I'd say, "Aye-aye, Mr. President." But I wouldn't do a damn thing. The next morning I would go in and say, "Mr. President, you didn't mean what you said yesterday?" He would answer, "Of course I didn't. Thank God you didn't do that." That is part of his nature.

Frederic V. Malek The president did not have all the facts; Magruder would have been covering his ass big-time on this, so Nixon wouldn't know what Magruder knew. I am sure that Nixon believed Mitchell when he told him that he didn't know. Nixon probably thought that the stonewall approach had an extremely high probability of success, so why have an embarrassment in the middle of a campaign, just before our convention?

Hugh Sloan Magruder asked me to limit the amount of money I would say I had given to Liddy; this was followed up by Fred LaRue. Magruder put it in the context of perception—that a number like that wouldn't be understood—and "Don't you think you could reduce the number?" The initial $83,000 had grown to about $199,000 at that point; there had been additional disbursements. When I told Magruder I couldn't, he said, "You may have to," which may have implied pressure from somewhere, but it never came other than from LaRue's conversation with me. He asked, Had Jeb talked to me about this money issue? And I said yes. He asked me to change the numbers. I told him I wasn't prepared to do that.

John Dean If you talk to a number of people on the White House staff, you know there was a very limited access to the president. Even after Watergate, his lawyers couldn't get in to see him. That's just the way Nixon wanted it; he didn't want a lot of people coming in to see him. I think the reason he started dealing with me is that Haldeman and Ehrlichman got tired of it. They had other things and this was becoming increasingly time-consuming. By then, I had somehow proven myself to them as someone who could carry this load. A typical example of the problem is what I told Haldeman on June 23rd—the "smoking gun" morning—and you look at his notes. He didn't convey to the president everything I told him; he spun that, for his own reasons, his own way. And the president was denied some vital information.

John Ehrlichman Nixon knew things that I didn't know—about how he had been involved in the cover-up early on, in manipulating the FBI and CIA. I was unaware of that. It wasn't until I listened to the June 23rd tape that it dawned on me that the president had not told all to the American people in the spring of 1973. I had suggested that he tell all, but he had knowledge, early on, that he would have had to explain away.

Jeb Stuart Magruder I was certainly aware that we were trying to use the CIA and the FBI to cover up the break-in. The president's claim that, in his July conversation with Pat Gray, he ordered Gray to go ahead with the investigation is unbelievable to me. The cover-up went on; [Herbert] Kalmbach continued to raise money; John Dean helped me prepare for my testimony at the grand jury. Haldeman was absolutely aware of all this, and if he was aware of it, the president was aware also.

I still had my White House pass; I was still running the campaign—even to the point that Haldeman wanted me to get someone into McGovern's headquarters in July so that we could get his schedule further in advance than the press release was telling. By July, it was clear that we were going to win in a walk. Even with the problems of the break-in, they were still talking in those terms.

Ronald Ziegler We thought that the May 1973 statement went well, but there were so many proven and unproven charges that came forth after that. You have to keep in mind that a good part of the Watergate story—and the demise of Richard Nixon—rests on an unproven allegation that undermined his authority to lead. That doesn't mean that he was brought down by unproven charges, but it is historic fact: there were unproven charges about his children, land deals, his taxes—a lot of things that were headlines, that tended to undermine public confidence in the president. The break-in was irrelevant in what became Watergate; the relevancy is the cover-up. The fact that the president lied about his early involvement to politically contain it led to the loss of confidence and the failure to lead.

Richard Ben Veniste, deputy special prosecutor, Watergate Special Prosecution Force There was certainly sufficient evidence of the president's involvement. Removing all other considerations, if you looked at the case simply as another case of criminal conspiracy to obstruct justice, the president's role was substantial, and it was a role employed by the president with knowledge of the facts, and was not a result of a mistake by him—a mistake based on an incorrect perception of the facts rather than as a mistake in intent, which it certainly was.

Charles Colson The investigation into the Bay of Pigs was a comedy of errors; Nixon never had anything to do with that. You would have to know the chemistry of Howard Hunt—what a romantic idealist Hunt is. He came to the administration to be part of the Plumbers operation, which started very innocently as an effort to stop leaks. He was a guy who had been in middle-level CIA operations all his life. He was a bureaucrat. He had retired, but he never got over the spy novels and the romantic notion of James Bond. So he gets into the White House and has access to all these cables. He comes in one day and says to me, "There is a reporter fishing around about the Diem assassination and the Kennedys' role in it." I told him to go ahead and find out what he could. I should have picked up on this, but I didn't. I later discovered that Hunt went to my secretary's desk, got some equipment and a typewriter, and forged a cable—which he then gave to a reporter—before telling me what he had done. That is the genesis of the forged cable.

Fred Fielding They found that Hunt had a safe in the basement of the old Executive Office Building. Dean called me at about seven in the evening and said, "I am busy. Can you go down with Bruce Kehrli, of Haldeman's staff, to open the safe?" So I was involved in drilling open the safe, inventorying the contents, and turning them over to Dean. The interesting thing was that there was a gun in there, and the next day, when we were turning the stuff over to the Secret Service, they didn't want to take the gun. So I told them that if they didn't take the gun, they wouldn't get anything. Dean told me that Ehrlichman had told him to "deep six" the material. I said to Dean, "Tell him that too many people know about it. You can't destroy it; you're destroying evidence." The Kennedy stuff meant nothing to me, except that it looked like someone was fabricating something—just because there were so many copies.

John Ehrlichman Dean gave Gray the contents of Hunt's safe; it came in two sealed envelopes. But I have no idea what they were. When Dean described them to Gray as "political dynamite," I assume he referred to the Nixon administration, but I don't know. There is no question that Hunt was doing things besides the Fielding break-in: he was planting articles about the Kennedys; he was seeing Dita Beard on the ITT case; he was all over the place. Colson was undoubtedly telling Nixon what Hunt was doing.

John Dean I have put together a lot of pieces here that I didn't know were sitting around—as to when Colson actually learned about all this and went to Ehrlichman, and Ehrlichman called a meeting over in his office, and all this business. The problem was that there were very politically sensitive files in Howard Hunt's office. No one knew at that point that he had dumped a bunch of stuff from his Watergate break-in in the safe; apparently, he'd put in bugs and a briefcase that belonged to James McCord. So he had come over from the break-in to his White House office, thinking that was a secure place. What this did was to bring the Watergate break-in right into the White House. It was an incredible move actually.

I was not present when the safe was opened. I'd gone off to another meeting in Mitchell's place. The contents of the safe came to my office—Fielding was up there when they opened the safe. We went through this stuff, and it was very clear that Howard Hunt was counterfeiting cables that would put the Kennedy administration right in the middle of the Diem assassination; they were trying to feed this stuff to a *Life* magazine correspondent. There were documents, stacks of cables that had been gone through—razor blade stuff that had been Xeroxed, and cover memorandums saying: will send this to the *Life* reporter. There were also files relating to the Dita Beard stuff. There were also personal letters that belonged to Hunt—apparently, he was having some marital problems at the time. There were address books and other things. It was not until much later that the question of the Hermès notebooks came up.

The question was, What do we do with all of this stuff from Hunt's safe? I went over and told Ehrlichman what we'd found, and that's when he said to me, "Well, you drive across the river at night"—he suggested I "deep six" the suitcase in the [Potomac] river and shred the documents. I went back to my office and told Fred Fielding, "This is dangerous. How many people have looked at these documents?" "For openers, you've looked at them; I've looked at them. The secretary saw us in here with all this stuff, and it's all going to vanish?" I said, "Give me a break." That was one of the signals I should have recognized. Had I been a criminal lawyer and thinking about obstruction of justice, that would have sent bells going. I wasn't a criminal lawyer. I realize now that the counsel to the president in that particular White House should have been an experienced criminal lawyer; maybe that would have prevented some of the things that happened from happening.

G. Gordon Liddy The significant material that came out of Hunt's safe was the operational notebooks that he had on everything. Dean has admitted that he took them; he has admitted that he destroyed them.

Richard Kleindienst I don't believe that what Gray did with the materials from Hunt's safe had any effect on the integrity of the FBI's investigation, or the work of the Department of Justice.

Hugh Sloan The committee hired some lawyers at the beginning of the investigations. I tried to get people's attention by saying, "You know, they are obviously going to be following the money and the audit trail, and I am going to be subpoenaed shortly. It would be really nice if somebody would talk about it and give some guidance as to what the committee might do about it." At my initiative, I went to see the two lawyers, Kenneth Parkinson* and Paul O'Brien,† and said, "I am going to be subpoenaed and this is the issue: let me tell you what I know, since you are not coming to me to ask me what I know." So I spent a fair amount of time with them, and what they told me was, "If that's the case, we are clearly being lied to by other people in the committee. We need some time to deal with this. Is there any chance you can travel or be out of town?" In hindsight, this was an obvious attempt to avoid being subpoenaed. They said, "We can't tell you to go, but you'll get a call from somebody."

So Fred LaRue called me at home and said, "Can you join Maury Stans, who is fund-raising out in California?" I said yes. They said, "Well, it would be really good if you spent the night in a motel at the airport," which just heightened my level of discomfiture, because the reason for doing this obviously was so I wouldn't have a process server pounding on my door before I got to the airport. So when I flew out West, my discomfort level got to the point where I decided I'd rather deal with this alone—and personally— rather than where an organization was involved, and where there would be a conflict of interest because the lawyers would be representing people on the committee, who were clearly involved.

When I resigned‡ and got back to my house, the FBI was already staking it out. I invited them in and we chatted. They said, "The prosecutors will want to talk to you. Presumably there are only two reasons why you resigned. Either you are personally liable and are trying to separate from the committee, or the reverse—where you are resigning because of discomfiture and, therefore, you have information that is valuable." They said I should get a lawyer before I talked to the prosecutors—this was a Friday. They added that I should have one by Monday. I spent a weekend with a lawyer, only to have the lawyer call me on Monday and say that his firm decided they couldn't take any more controversial cases. I believe it came out that they'd had a telephone call from John Dean, suggesting that they not take on the case. So I had to start all over again, and my new lawyers set a date with the prosecutors to review what I knew at that point. It was pretty

---

* Kenneth W. Parkinson, an attorney for CRP.
† Paul L. O'Brien, an attorney for CRP.
‡ July 14, 1972.

clear to me what my obligation was: just answer the questions that were asked of you, as honestly as you could.

WALTERS GOES TO THE FBI

William Colby Ehrlichman called Walters and said, "Would you go over to see Pat Gray and tell him that this is a matter of some CIA interest, and to be very careful about the investigation." Walters did this and then came back to the office and asked me, "What's this about a CIA interest?" I answered, "I don't know anything about a CIA interest; let me go down and ask at the working level." I came back in the afternoon and said, "There is none at all," at which point Walters called Gray and told him that. He had, innocently, thought we did, went to Gray, checked it, and when it was clear we didn't have an interest, went back and told Gray. Dick Walters would never do anything wrong—not in a million years; he would salute and do what he was told, and then check it. Gray passed along the request, but he didn't pass along Walters's correction, so the investigation was called off, period.

Robert Reisner I assume that Kissinger and Nixon knew that Walters was being taken upstairs to the second floor of the West Wing to talk to Haldeman and Ehrlichman. It is hard to imagine that they did not know that a high CIA official was being led past their offices.

Alexander Haig Before I went over to the Pentagon, I was sitting in my office one day and saw Dick Walters walk out of Haldeman's office, white as a ghost. I've known Dick for thirty years, so I went over to him and said, "What is wrong?" He kept on walking. I think that was the day they tried to get him to cover up—which he refused to do.

Vernon Walters I thought they might have something going against Castro in Mexico. That's why I spoke to Pat Gray. That was on a Saturday. When I got back to the agency [CIA], I had a search done and found out there was nothing going on in Mexico City. So on Monday, I told John Dean, who, I had been told, was in charge of the whole thing, that there was no operation of the CIA that might be endangered by the pursuit [of the Mexican Watergate connection]. I thought he would tell Pat Gray, which was how naive I was at the time. He didn't tell Pat Gray. When Pat called me a couple of days later and said, "I can't hold this up anymore," I said, "But Pat, I told

Dean to go ahead, and I thought he told you." He replied, "No, he didn't tell me." Pat was one of the innocent victims of this. I feel very sorry for him.

Donald E. Santarelli Pat Gray was Kleindienst's closest confidant; he was also a close confidant to Mitchell—he was part of the inner sanctum of the Justice Department. Kleindienst, particularly, had a high regard for Gray as a tough guy, and Gray tried very hard to create that image: the close-cropped hair; the ex-submarine commander. Gray was involved in the hot issue of the day—the antiwar movement. We were very, very concerned about the protests undermining government, and Nixon's efforts to get the United States out of Vietnam. There was a great deal of discussion about this at Justice, and Pat Gray was a daily visitor to Kleindienst's office to plot strategy.

I remember Kleindienst asking me, "What do you think of Pat Gray as FBI chief?" When Hoover died, we had all rushed into Kleindienst's office and had a conclave and asked, "What do we do now?" The first thing we decided was to secure the famous Hoover files. We all marched down the hall on the fifth floor, to Hoover's office, only to find that there weren't any files. It's not that somebody had cleared them out. He didn't maintain a special set of files of any significance; it was just selective leaking. Pat Gray's problem was that his training and background created an inherent conflict between serving his president and serving his country, so what he did as acting head of the FBI was very much motivated by the high notion of protecting the commander in chief and containing a scandal, rather than illuminating it and bringing it to a public conclusion.

H. R. Haldeman They did go to Gray, but it resulted in nothing, because the FBI didn't call off the investigation. Pat Gray called Nixon and said, "Your people are doing you some harm." So Nixon told Gray not to back off. There's a game in there, somewhere, that I still don't quite understand. John Dean was lying when he said, "Mitchell suggests, and John Dean agrees"; he had not even talked to Mitchell. So he used Mitchell to authenticate that line; he used me to authenticate the line going back the other way; and gets me into the meeting with Helms and Walters to transmit the thing. And I end up in the smoking pistol. There is a Dean motivation here. There is no question that in there, somewhere, we—Nixon and I—did something that triggered something that caused some reaction—a series of reactions—because there are some strange things that Walters did after that, that don't make any sense; things I could never figure out at my trial.

John Dean If you look in Mr. Nixon's memoirs, you see something that is very interesting. First of all, his account of those first few days after he returns from Florida are apparently all based on his reviewing the tapes of those days. Buried in the acknowledgment of his memoirs° is the revelation that he sent one of his secretaries into the archives to type all the tapes between June 20th and July 20th, and again of May 1973. It appears that what Mr. Nixon has done is to take not a smoking gun, but smoking cannons, and put the best buffing on them he can to make them look presentable, because if you read those memoirs closely, in those first few days after the break-in, you will see that, first of all, Mitchell had suggested somebody cut off the FBI several days before this conversation on the 23rd—I think it is on the 21st or 22nd; it's not quite clear from the memoirs which day it is. So Mitchell had already been trying to tell Haldeman that the FBI is running wild and somebody's got to cut them off.

I talked to Mitchell on the evening of the 22nd. When I got back from Pat Gray's office, the first person I called was John Mitchell. We discussed Pat Gray's theories—one of which was that the break-in was a CIA operation and this is something that is landed on not only because of what Mitchell wants, but because of what Gray wants, in how to handle the situation. Incidentally, I didn't know on June 23rd that Haldeman and Nixon had met on this. The reason that this is a hot issue is that the FBI was about to uncover Campaign Act violations; Stans was very upset that he was going to get bagged into Watergate—so he is livid. This is all going on—and understandably. So there is the pressure coming from Stans and from Mitchell, and they are all coming down. And, my God, the FBI is about to start plowing right into the Finance Committee and contributors who have been promised anonymity, and all the problems that this opens up. This is what is really going on.

Richard Nixon adds one little spin on this and that is his concern—he had not felt all the pressure of the campaign finance issue—he is concerned about what Howard Hunt has been doing at the White House, generally, and sees this as a nice vehicle to deal with national security matters; he can put it under the national security umbrella. So there are two agendas, it appears: one is how to deal with the campaign finance problem, and the other is whatever Nixon thought were the national security activities of Howard Hunt.

Seymour Glanzer The U.S. Attorney's Office viewed the Watergate break-in as a serious offense because it involved wiretapping. This was what

° *Richard Nixon*, page x.

brought in the FBI; a simple break-in would have stayed with the [Washington, D.C.] Metropolitan Police. When the burglars were arrested, the police found evidence almost immediately that there was an illegal surveillance; there were bugs there. So we investigated all avenues to put the case together for an indictment. At that point, there was a great deal of political pressure—both publicly and privately—saying that we should indict the burglars immediately. Senator [Sam] Ervin [D-N.C.; chairman of the Senate Watergate Committee], for example, wanted only the burglary case brought; he wanted a half-formed case brought. So did the media, but that was not the professional thing to do; you couldn't leave the far more serious violations uninvestigated. That, in turn, really opened up all the other aspects of the so-called Watergate scandal, because then all these other things—the trail of money to and from Mexico—could be explored. These were matters that arose out of the need to determine why anyone was conducting an electronic surveillance at the DNC, and why these particular individuals were involved, which was another problem, because when they were arrested, they all seemed to have CIA ties—and at least one of them had connections to the media.

18

The Senate Select Committee on Watergate and the Appointment of a Special Prosecutor

---

In an atmosphere of continuing revelations in the media on the break-in and other Nixon administration campaign acts—and following guilty pleas by the Watergate burglars in Federal District Judge John J. Sirica's Washington courtroom—the U.S. Senate on February 7, 1973, voted—by a margin of 70 to 0—to establish a Select Committee to conduct a full-scale investigation of the Watergate break-in and related efforts against the 1972 Democratic presidential campaign. The committee, consisting of four Democrats and three Republicans, would be chaired by Senator Sam Ervin.

Samuel Dash I am a registered Democrat, but I have not been a partisan Democrat, nor have I been involved in politics. I had been district attorney of Philadelphia and a trial lawyer. I'd known Senator Ervin slightly; I had testified before one of his committees. In early 1973, he called and asked me to come in and consult with him on the issue of the kind of resolution that would be necessary to give the Senate Watergate Committee the kinds of powers it needed. He also asked me to recommend names for chief counsel. I gave him some names, but it never occurred to me that I would be one of them. A couple of weeks later, I was at home with a cold when Sam Ervin telephoned. He said that he had hundreds of lawyers—even some judges—

who wanted the job of chief counsel; he also said that he didn't know these people's motives, so he decided that he was not going to appoint anyone who asked for the job. Then he said, "I've looked around the country, and you are the man I am looking for. The committee has approved you. Will you accept the job?" I was flattered, but I had teaching responsibilities at the [Georgetown University] Law School. I spoke to the dean, Adrian Fisher, who said to me, "I hope that you told Senator Ervin yes." I said, "How could I? I have classes." Fisher said, "Call him back before he changes his mind."

THE COMMITTEE HEARINGS

Samuel Dash The Senate had voted unanimously to set up the committee on the condition that it would have a minority counsel. I thought that was quite appropriate, since the Senate majority was Democratic, and we were investigating a Republican administration. They picked a fine person, Fred [Dalton] Thompson.° He made it very clear in an early meeting that his basic loyalty was to Senator [Howard] Baker [R-Tenn.], the vice-chairman, but that we would work together. Although Baker was up front and publicly presented himself as favoring a bipartisan investigation—"What did the president know, and when did he know it?" was his favorite quotation—he was, in fact, partisan; he did everything he could to help Richard Nixon, and I, not being a politician, got aggravated at times. I learned about it primarily from John Dean, who had witnessed some of the meetings between Baker and President Nixon, and I brought this to the attention of Senator Ervin, whose only response was, "Well, poor Howard. I guess they are bringing pressure on him." It was probably natural for Senator Baker to be very much concerned for what it might do to the Republican presidency, and I was, maybe, naive in how I assessed it.

I wanted to develop hearings that would be educational in nature—that would actually tell a story to the public in a way that they would understand it, so I decided to divide the investigation into three parts: the break-in at the Democratic National Committee headquarters and the cover-up; the dirty tricks part of it, which had to do with political espionage, which was at a height that had never occurred before; and the illegal campaign financing. I gave each of my three deputy counsels an area, and in order to encourage them to really go at it hammer and tongs, I decided that each, in his turn, could question witnesses during the televised hearings. This was a good

---

° Later to become an actor, portraying administration officials in films.

chance for them to gain public attention, so they became three competing teams, and it got to the point where they almost became enemies. To this day, a couple of them still don't talk to each other.

I told Senator Ervin that I would have to pick my own staff—not a political staff, or a Senate staff, but some of the most experienced prosecutors and trial lawyers in the country. I also wanted sufficient budget, and time to take the trail wherever it might lead. In his typical way, Ervin responded: "You wouldn't be any good unless you asked for those conditions." We worked together very closely, and I found him to be a man of great integrity and a fundamentalist on the Bill of Rights.

Vernon Walters When I came down to that Watergate Committee, Sam Ervin said to me, "Explain your relationship to Mr. Nixon." I said, "Mr. Chairman, if I do not tell this committee of my admiration for Mr. Nixon's personal courage, I would be hiding part of the truth from you. I sat in a life-threatening situation with him [in Caracas], and he was cool as a cucumber." Curiously, Sam Ervin said, "I happen to share your regard for his courage."

Samuel Dash Very early, Senator [Lowell] Weicker [R-Conn.] asked me to come to his office. He said that he respected what Ervin and I were doing and thought we were working with integrity; therefore, he wanted me to tell Ervin that he would support us and we would have his vote. That was very important, because all we had at that point was the majority vote of four Democrats to three Republicans; to give a witness immunity under the statute, you need a two-thirds vote, and Senator Weicker's committed vote gave me the two-thirds pretty much in my pocket. That took a lot of tension off me. Senator Weicker really became a member of the majority almost throughout the hearing.

Fred Dalton Thompson There is no specific charter for a minority counsel; it is by nature an awkward position. The goal of the committee, as a whole, was to find out and disclose facts. On the other hand, it is, by its very nature, a partisan endeavor. Technically, my role was to serve the three minority members of the committee and to supervise the minority staff. I had two jobs, as compared to the majority counsel. Part of my job overlapped what he was doing, but I also felt an additional responsibility to make sure that partisan advantage was not taken. From time to time, we had problems. During the public testimony, things got out of hand on a few occasions. I remember Ehrlichman's testimony: the audience became rather boisterous; there was uncalled-for clapping and hissing.

From time to time, the staff overreached; it tipped off the press. But I always like to think—in comparison with what could have happened—with all the pressure, the stakes involved, that things got along pretty well, both from the committee and the staff standpoint.

Appointing a Special Prosecutor

In the early spring of 1973, the Nixon administration came under increasing pressure to appoint a special prosecutor to deal with the Watergate incident and related events and abuses of power. This pressure intensified when, on April 30, the White House announced the resignation of Attorney General Richard Kleindienst—the second Nixon attorney general to resign in the wake of Watergate.

In an effort to control the damage caused by Mr. Kleindienst's resignation—which occurred at the time of the resignations of Haldeman, Ehrlichman, and Dean—the president nominated Elliot Richardson, a moderate Republican and member of the Eastern establishment, as his new attorney general. Richardson, who had been secretary of defense, quickly announced his intention of appointing a special prosecutor, and in his confirmation hearings, suggested that he would give this official, whom he soon revealed to be Harvard professor Archibald Cox, complete independence. The White House was enraged at Mr. Cox's selection, as he had been an associate of John F. Kennedy and had served as solicitor general in the Kennedy and Johnson administrations.

Concern of Mr. Nixon and his associates over Mr. Cox's appointment was heightened when members of the Kennedy family attended his swearing-in ceremony as special prosecutor on May 25. President Nixon had been warned about Mr. Cox by Haig and other aides, and by Henry Kissinger, who told him that Mr. Cox had been "fanatically anti-Nixon all the time I've known him." While there appears to be some dispute as to how well the two former Harvard colleagues did know one another, it is a fact that Mr. Cox's daughter had worked as a secretary to Dr. Kissinger at Harvard.

One of the ongoing controversies regarding the Cox appointment is what, specifically, the Special Prosecutor was mandated to investigate. Cox claimed that his charter was far-reaching and included not only the break-in, but all potentially criminal activities arising out of the 1972 presidential election, while the White House believed there should be a more limited scope to his responsibilities. What is known for certain is that Cox could select his own staff, could grant immunity to witnesses, and could only be removed for extraordinary improprieties.

Of the Special Prosecution Force's eighty professional staff members,

*seven of the eight most senior members had served in the Kennedy and/or
Johnson administrations.*

Archibald Cox, Watergate special prosecutor I was first asked whether
I would be available, which is short of an offer of the position. I was giving a
series of lectures out at the University of California at Berkeley. Elliot
Richardson, who had been a student of mine and had followed a path not
dissimilar to mine—we had both been clerks to Judge Learned Hand; we
had both gone to work at Ropes, and in Boston—telephoned and asked if I
would be available.

I told him I would certainly think about it: Was it fair to the Harvard Law
School? I had been away a good deal. The morning before, I had awakened
totally deaf in my right ear. Before I could do anything else, I must get an
explanation of that. So that was the first call. Later, we talked by telephone
and he offered me the position, which I had been urged by [Harvard] President [Derek] Bok to accept.

We did negotiate the terms, but most of the terms under which he was
prepared to apply to a special prosecutor had been worked out by Richardson and the Democratic members of the Senate Judiciary Committee.
There were two that I insisted upon, which were added: I should not have
the subordinate's usual duty to tell his superior anything of great importance
that I learned that was relevant to the subject; and that I should have the
right to go public whenever I thought it advisable.

Robert Bork Nixon made a mistake in pushing Kleindienst out at a time
when he was wildly unpopular with Congress; that meant he had to get a
new attorney general confirmed, and they could attach any conditions they
wanted to the confirmation. When Richardson was at his confirmation hearings, they insisted that he appoint a special prosecutor and give him a charter. Cox was one of his professors at the Harvard Law School, so he
appointed Cox, who was a close ally of [Senator Edward M.] Teddy
Kennedy [D-Mass.]—when Cox was sworn in, Teddy and his family were in
the press photos. That, of course, gave the White House semi-hysteria,
because they thought that the special prosecutor was a tool of Kennedy's—
and the Democratic chieftains—to get Nixon. Politically, Nixon made an
unwise choice, but that was not the fault of Cox.

Richard Kleindienst I had tried to get a special prosecutor from the very
beginning. It wasn't until Richardson's hearing before the Senate Judiciary

Committee that the concept of the special prosecutor came up and he agreed, from the very outset, that there should be a special prosecutor. If I had been in his position, I would have agreed to that myself. The only problem was that in order to get Senator Kennedy and other liberal Senators to go along with the whole concept, they told Richardson, in advance, that if he would take Archie Cox as the special prosecutor, his confirmation would sail right on through. Elliot Richardson agreed to that without prior consultation with the president. That was an agreement that was bound to fail from the very outset.

Archibald Cox is one of the brightest and most gifted lawyers in the country, but he was also one of the most articulate spokesmen for the liberal wing of the Democratic Party. He had been very much involved in Jack Kennedy's campaign in 1960—that is not the characteristic of an impartial special prosecutor. It was doomed to failure from the very outset because Archie Cox expanded his perceived function and role, far beyond the Watergate situation, so that it turned out to be a special prosecution of the Nixon administration, generally speaking. Nobody ever contemplated that. You can't have that kind of a person in that kind of office under those circumstances.

Archibald Cox My recollection was that it was not confined to the 1972 campaign—that it involved allegations of wrongdoing by the president, or any other senior officials in the administration, and any wrongdoing in the 1972 campaign.

There were some things in which he [the president] thought I had exceeded my authority. In one case, at least, it was a matter of expenditures at San Clemente.

When these questions arose, someone in the White House—perhaps President Nixon—would tell Attorney General Richardson to tell me to stay within my charter. Richardson would talk to me, and I was always able to satisfy him that I was within my charter.

Raymond Price The president was appalled when he found out that Richardson wanted Cox as special prosecutor. Cox had been a Kennedy political operative all his professional life. I think that Elliot—who is a very honorable guy—genuinely felt that by choosing Cox, he was selecting someone who would be beyond public suspicion, but he made the fatal error of choosing someone who could not—under any circumstances—have the trust of the president. Politics were in Cox's bones; he put together a staff drawn, overwhelmingly, from the Kennedy and McGovern political campaign staffs.

Richard Ben Veniste Was Cox's staff political? That can be answered simply with a "no." As far as my credentials are concerned, probably the most significant case I had ever been involved with was the prosecution of a chief assistant to the Democratic speaker of the House of Representatives. That investigation was launched under a Democrat—Robert Morgenthau.* I also prosecuted the law chairman of the New York City Republican Party, under a Republican-appointed U.S. attorney, Whitney North Seymour, Jr. Both Morgenthau and Seymour have reputations for being apolitical, as does the office of the U.S. attorney for the southern district.

Personally, I was never in politics. I was a registered Democrat; I would say that, probably, most of the young lawyers were Democrats—there were some notable exceptions, such as Philip Lacovara, who was a registered Republican. I never saw any overt hostility, or overt political bent, by anyone on the staff. Certainly, Archie Cox had no such bent. If we were to analyze his performance as special prosecutor, I think one would have to say he gave Mr. Nixon every benefit of the doubt, and indeed, in some cases, to the exasperation of more seasoned day-to-day prosecutors—or, perhaps better put: prosecutors who had day-to-day experience prosecuting cases in recent years. Mr. Cox had the tendency to reinvent the wheel; even though something was an accepted procedure—as prosecutors would use it on a regular basis—he would step back, reflect, and say, "Is that really fair? Is that the way we should go here?"

Seymour Glanzer Cox is an esteemed and venerable professor, but he never prosecuted a case in his life; he wouldn't know how to prosecute a case if he tried; he doesn't know how to put a case together. He did have a very able staff, and although there were Democrats on it, that would not have made a difference. In my experience, prosecutors bend over backward to avoid the suggestion of being influenced by their own political affiliations.

Archibald Cox The prime requirement was to fill the almost total gap in my experience. As I told Elliot Richardson when he asked if I'd be available, "Why me? I've never prosecuted anybody for anything." His answer was,

* Federal Prosecutor, southern district of New York.

"You could hire yourself a prosecutor; you have a reputation with the American Bar Association, with members of the Senate and others on the Hill."

I needed people with investigative, prosecuting experience. We did go looking for people of that caliber. In terms of younger people, it was a matter of choosing from the applicants, rather that going out to recruit.

There came a time when we made some conscious effort to think about: Shouldn't there be some Republicans on the staff? But, predominantly, the staff remained non-Republican, although one of the very senior people had been in the office of the solicitor general—a highly prized position to be in—under a Republican attorney general, and I think that the staff person was himself a Republican.

Philip Lacovara When Archie Cox was appointed, he set out trying to create what he considered a model prosecutor's office. He did not have much criminal background, having been a labor law professor. There were two things that called my background to his attention: first of all, as a former solicitor general in the Kennedy administration, he instinctively looked to the solicitor general's office as a place where he might find some talented lawyers; secondly, a Harvard Law professor whom he brought down as a consultant, Jim Vorenberg, had been head of the appointments committee at Harvard Law School when I was offered a faculty appointment, so he introduced me to Cox and they asked me to come over as the principal lawyer in the Watergate prosecution office. So my title was counsel to the Watergate prosecutor.

Officially I was responsible for all the legal and policy issues—that is, the handling of the legal analysis of the constitutional questions that were anticipated even then, particularly executive privilege. There was, even at that point, the question: If the evidence might indicate that President Nixon was a culpable part of any conspiracy to cover up the responsibility for the Watergate break-in, would he—as a sitting president—be subject to criminal prosecution? So my staff was responsible for advising Archie, and the individual subject matter task forces, on the legal and policy issues that we were going to be confronting. Those were the official factors in my charter; the unofficial factor that I think was viewed as somewhat helpful was that I was identified as a Republican in an office that tended to have a number of very politically active people of a more liberal stripe—from Archie Cox on down to the new people fresh out of law school. The notion that there was a somewhat seasoned Republican in the office in a position of some responsibility was thought to be reassuring that this was going to be a serious exercise, not a political witch-hunt.

I would divide the senior-most people in the office from some of the younger staff people. In the four months or so of his tenure, I never recall Archie making a comment about President Nixon that I would regard as partisan or politically animated. There were some real concerns about the propriety of what President Nixon was doing, but I never got a sense that Archie Cox's motivation in any of the decisions that were being taken had a political dimension. I think that the same thing was true of the deputy special prosecutor, Henry Ruth. The younger people—some of the young ex-prosecutors, people just coming out of law school or clerkships—the median age was quite young. I would say that many of those people—either as a result of the Vietnam War, or other aspects of their own political consciousness—started out assuming the worst about Richard Nixon and virtually everybody else around him. But I don't think that was true of Cox. I don't know whether Archie ever assumed the worst, but he never manifested that that was why he was doing what he was doing.

Richard Ben Veniste When Professor Cox was appointed to be independent counsel, he decided he would select a staff of legal scholars of unblemished reputation—people who were leaders of the profession; above reproach—and then he decided, as an afterthought, that he might need somebody who would know which way to face in court, if the case ever got to court. I was in that second category. I was an assistant U.S. attorney in the southern district of New York, and they were looking for people in government with prosecutorial experience; I had prosecuted some official corruption cases, as well as some organized crime and racketeering cases, and was fairly experienced for a federal prosecutor in these kinds of matters. When I started, I was one of a number of people who were assigned to the Watergate Task Force—which meant the Watergate cover-up conspiracy. Jim Neale was the head of the task force, and I was his deputy in seniority. We had a number of brilliant lawyers with us; we had a very strong bench. In that regard, it was a remarkable opportunity to work with so many talented lawyers. After Jim Neale left—which coincided with John Dean's guilty plea and Archie Cox's firing—I inherited the mantle of chief of the task force.

Samuel Dash Initially, I greeted the Cox appointment with great expectation and delight; Archie Cox had been my former Labor Law professor at Harvard, and I respected and liked him; we were friends. When he came to Washington, the very first thing I did was to go over to the Justice Department to meet with him and to offer all the help I could give him. By that point, most of our investigation was fairly complete, in terms of the documents we had subpoenaed. We were the first congressional committee ever to use a computer for investigations; our entire database was on computer; the Library of Congress trained my assistants on it. I told Cox, "I'll give you everything."

The first thing Archie Cox said to me was that while there was plenty of need for the Senate Watergate Committee before he had gotten to town, now that he was here, there was really no need for us to continue. He added, "Why don't you close the investigation?" I was a little shocked. I said, "There is a separation of powers; our role is different from your role. You are going to investigate a criminal case, using the grand jury and, ultimately, prosecute; you will have tunnel vision of what you are looking at. We have the job, under the Constitution, for legislative purposes, and public inform- ing purposes, to expose the entire scandal. We have to act fairly and quickly, because it seems to me that the public ought to know, as quickly as possible, what happened." I asked, "When do you expect to even be ready to go to trial?" He replied, "Maybe two or three years." I said, "That is going to be quite a long time for the public to wait. I can't believe that Senator Ervin or the committee would agree that just because you are here and, obviously, will do a very professional job, that we ought to stop what we are doing." He then said, "I'm going to fight you as best I can."

Richard Ben Veniste Mr. Cox was very clear that he didn't like the fact that the Ervin Committee was conducting a parallel investigation; he thought that this complicated his job. Naturally, he gave the committee appropriate deference, as a lawyer and also as a professional, but there were not, to my knowledge, meetings or cooperative efforts.

Fred Dalton Thompson This is a structural question: Archibald Cox took the same position that Robert Fiske is now taking in the Whitewater investi- gation; Sam Ervin took the same position that Senators [Alphonse] D'Amato [R-N.Y.] and [William] Cohen [R-Maine] are taking. It's two groups of peo- ple trying to do their job, but they have different purposes. The key is to carry out the job without interfering with each other. It's not easy.

Seymour Glanzer The Ervin Committee had a hundred staff people, but what difference did that make? The most important threat was from the special prosecution staff. All that the Ervin Committee got was a lot of headlines; they didn't prosecute anybody. The problem is that if you mix up political motivation with law enforcement motivation, you will usually have an aberrational result. While they had good headlines, and provided good television fare, the fact is that the work was done in the grand jury and in the trials, and that is what forced Nixon out. He wouldn't have been forced out simply by Congress; he was forced out by the fact that the investigation was proving every day that he was either criminally culpable or the most incompetent U.S. president. Either way, he would have been impeached.

Fred Fielding Were they outnumbered? You bet they were; they were fighting on three or four fronts at the same time. Just looking at it from a large-case management situation, they were outnumbered; if you go head to head, they were outgunned. They were fighting on too many fronts. But the main issue at the time was that there were the documents.

William Ruckelshaus I don't think that I have ever been involved in a legal matter in which the sides were equal. That is the fallacy of the advocacy system; it postulates equal advocacy on both sides—from which a disinterested judge will arrive at a conclusion. They are never equal if you think of the prosecution as an array of people dedicated to proving the accused guilty, as opposed to trying to dig up the facts in a disinterested way. Then it is an unequal battle.

On the other hand, if the defendant—in this case, the president—has truth on his side, that's a tremendous advantage; he is the one who is in possession of the facts more than anyone else. Therefore, I don't think that out of this apparently unequal distribution of forces there will necessarily come an unjust result as long as the accusers—in this case, the Justice Department, which is part of his administration—are doing the best they can to ensure that the process is fair, and that we are trying not to indict the accused unjustly, but to get at the facts, and see that justice is done. I know that that was my goal; I know that it was Elliot Richardson's goal; and I think that, by and large, it was Archibald Cox's goal. While he could be perceived as having a differing political background, he was extraordinarily sensitive and, therefore, pulled back in many cases from pursuing leads about issues the White House complained about that were off the mark as far as the Watergate crimes were concerned.

Every time I would get a complaint from Haig about Cox's people—or about Cox himself—moving against some aspect of the charges against the White House that was unrelated to Watergate, and I would inform Cox, he would pull back largely I think because he knew that he was perceived as being politically friendly to the Kennedys and, therefore, his investigation would be suspect if he wasn't scrupulous about what he did.

Fred Dalton Thompson When you turn a whole town of young investigators—whether they be staffers or members of the press—loose on a person or a group of people, you are almost, by definition, going to run into problems. The minority counsel is one of the few things thrown into the mix to try to balance that situation.

On May 17, the Senate Select Committee began televised hearings climaxed by the appearances of John Dean, who on June 25 read a 245-page statement into the record acknowledging his own participation in the cover-up, and describing the president as having had some knowledge of the cover-up since the time of the break-in; and by White House aide Alexander Butterfield, who on Monday, July 16, startled the nation with his revelation of the White House taping system, following a closed-door session with committee staff on the previous Friday.

Samuel Dash When Dean was fired by the president, he was saying such things as he thought he was going to be a scapegoat. I thought it would be very valuable to get his cooperation. I called his lawyer, who put me off for a while because Dean was talking to the prosecutors. Dean wouldn't come into the Senate Office Building because he was frightened; he thought that if a Republican senator or a staff member knew he was coming in, this would be leaked back to the White House, and he felt he'd be killed. So I had to arrange to see him without anyone's knowing—except that I did get Ervin's permission. I would go out to Dean's home, or to his lawyer's office in Rockville [Maryland]. I set up what I would call nonmeetings: I said to Dean, "I will talk to you, but I am not really here; if I think that what you have to tell me is worthy of immunity, I will so recommend; if not, I'll walk away—we never met, and you are not in jeopardy."

Initially, Dean was not credible; he only wanted to tell what others did, and he was lily white. That didn't make sense; he knew too much not to have been very much involved in the conspiracy. Several times I started to walk away. I told him it would not be helpful if his testimony was not credible.

Dean's lawyer supported me, so bit by bit, I got Dean to put himself in the middle of it. He had taken from the White House a number of documents that corroborated quite a bit of what he said. I really began to believe him when I called him in Florida and said, "John, we are following up the possibility of [the existence of] tapes; would you be concerned if we actually found tapes?" My assumption was that if he had been lying to us, his response would be negative. In contrast, his response was instantaneous: he said, "Great; if you can get tapes, it will back up everything I said." He was not afraid that a taping system would prove him a liar. I had tried to shake him every way, but his consistency, his responses, satisfied me that he was telling the truth. As it turns out, the tapes do basically support his testimony.

Fred Fielding At the time, Dean's testimony seemed credible—and incredible. He'd obviously had a lot of time to prepare; he's obviously a smart fellow—a quick study. There were so many things he was talking about that I knew nothing about. Dean obviously got into a bad situation and let it get worse. It does no good for me to ascribe motives to any of these people—that they collectively intended to bring down the president. I don't think that they thought they would do the harm that they ultimately did to the institution. But in fact, they did.

One of the highlights of Dean's testimony was his recounting of a meeting between him and the president in the Oval Office on March 21, 1973, when he told Mr. Nixon of "a cancer growing on the presidency."

In this discussion, Dean told the president of the involvement of Mr. Nixon's chief associates—including Mitchell, Haldeman, Ehrlichman, Magruder, Colson, and himself—in the Watergate and Fielding break-ins, and in the cover-up. He also informed the president that Hunt had told a CRP lawyer that unless he received an additional $120,000 before his March 23 sentencing, he would tell "seamy things" concerning his activities in the White House. (In the days immediately following the DNC break-in, White House officials learned that the burglars had been promised funds for legal assistance and maintenance, should they be arrested. Throughout the remainder of 1972—and into early 1973—payments were made to the Watergate defendants. Although the White House would claim these funds were disbursed on humanitarian grounds, it was not difficult to believe that in fact the payments could rightly be characterized as "hush money.")

Dean also told the president that on March 19, James McCord had written to Judge Sirica, alleging that he and other Watergate defendants were under pressure to remain silent, and that the break-in involved a higher echelon of Nixon aides.

At some point in the conversation, Haldeman joined in, and the three men discussed the demands of Hunt and the other burglars for funds—which Dean estimated at $1 million. The president indicated that this sum could be obtained, and he endorsed the payment to Hunt. But in the next several weeks, the president realized that the payments would not make a real difference as the investigations intensified, and after Judge Sirica read McCord's letter in open court, and following indications that Dean had retained a criminal lawyer and was meeting with the prosecutors.

John Dean I had already told him some of the things I would mention on the 21st. But the way I thought I needed to approach it was to give him the benefit of the doubt: Here is an empty slate for you, Mr. President; here is the problem. What I was desperately trying to do—and what I hoped would happen—was that he would say, "This is a terrible mess; it's got to stop this minute." That was the exact reason I went in there; I didn't try to point the finger at anybody; I didn't try to absolve myself. People have said, "Well, you didn't say this or that." What is amazing is how much I got in. I had not prepared a note; it was totally extemporaneous. I was trying to recollect things I hadn't thought about. He had a very good overview. I am sure there were some small parts he had learned. When you look back in the early tapes and his memoirs, you know he knew a lot of the stuff. Paying money? Well, he was the first one to suggest it.

At the end of the meeting, I was disappointed. I knew we had big trouble. If you listen to my voice on that tape, I'm pretty down by the end of the meeting. I hadn't tried to distort, but I tried to put the most serious consequence picture on everything. I tried to paint it as black as I could without painting it blacker than it should be, and I'd failed. I had not sold him and, frankly, I just didn't know where to turn. I failed because Richard Nixon wanted the cover-up to go on. He'd been in it from day one.

I think he wanted it to go on for multiple reasons. First of all, there was no easy answer: the Watergate break-in involved so much more than the break-in at the DNC. That was the problem from day one; it involved the Ellsberg matter and all the things that this unraveled. It involved campaign finance problems; it involved personal friends of the president; it involved his staff. I don't know that Bob Haldeman ever 'fessed up to Richard Nixon—even years later, after the memoirs—as to what exactly he knew and when he knew it; I just don't think he did. When something like that goes wrong, everyone is embarrassed; they are concerned about their own liability. I'm sure Haldeman had to think: My God, I knew about those meetings! I approved Liddy going over there. So there was no easy answer from day one, because of everything that had gone on before.

If the Watergate break-in had been an isolated incident, the president could have dealt with it. I often thought, had he come forward right at the outset and said: Here's what happened; these guys also did some national security things. I can't condone any of it, he might have survived. It would still have been a form of cover-up, because he never would have 'fessed up everything. But he might have survived. Instead, it was one lie built on top of another lie, built on top of another lie, until they all started crumbling down.

Samuel Dash By the time we learned about the tapes, John Dean had become available to us. I had prepared Dean for his week-long testimony. Up until Dean, there was no evidence that the president was involved in any way. John Dean, as a young counsel to the president, was the only one who gave eyewitness testimony of being in the Oval Office with the president, conspiring to obstruct justice, and conspiring to get money to pay off the burglars. It was John Dean's word against [that of] the president of the United States. I said to Ervin that we wouldn't be able to draw any real conclusions about the president, nor would an impeachment committee or any prosecuting officer, because the issue was: Do you believe in John Dean or the president of the United States? The answer should be, and has to be, the president of the United States, so the only way Dean's testimony could have impact is if it's corroborated.

Richard Ben Veniste Before I was selected to join the Prosecutor's Office, I recall having watched portions of the Senate Committee hearings—particularly Dean's testimony. I was extremely skeptical of it; this was a young man who was telling a story that to me seemed remarkable. For one to believe that the president of the United States could have this man working for him—and revealing the kinds of things Dean was testifying about—it seemed extraordinary. And by that time, I had a relatively high threshold for surprise. Of course, that threshold was raised considerably by subsequent events.

William Ruckelshaus On a credibility scale of one to ten, Dean was an eight. He was pretty credible; he had a remarkable memory. I knew John Dean at the Justice Department before he went to the White House—we were involved with a lot of the negotiations with the demonstrators against the war, who were very active at the time—and my impression, from watching him on television, based on my own knowledge of him, was that he was telling the truth. It was his version of the truth—one is bound to have some gaps, or lapses in memory, and to shade it in one's own direction, even if only subconsciously—but I give him high marks in terms of what he was saying.

Frederic V. Malek At the time, I liked John Dean. He was a sharp young guy. We related a lot; I saw him every day at the White House staff meeting—we even traveled together a number of times. His testimony shocked me; I couldn't believe that he was turning on the president. I wasn't sure he was telling the truth; I thought he sought to do this either for personal gain or to save his own skin at the expense of the president. I don't think that John was a man totally driven by conscience; I am not sure what his motives were. But I have no animosity toward him. I guess that, in retrospect, he probably did what he thought was right. And maybe it was. I don't know.

John Dean I stand on every word of my testimony; I wouldn't retract a word. Do I have some mistaken dates? A few. Given the fact that I had no access to any documents other than newspaper clippings, it's amazing that I didn't miss more. But I wouldn't retract a word of my testimony; I believe it as much today. In fact, I can prove more of it today than I even said twenty years ago.

Richard Moore There is a will to believe in issues of this kind; certainly, anyone who was anti-Nixon was quick to believe whatever Dean said. But while much of Dean's stuff was correct, it was totally blown out of proportion. The so-called Enemies List was a Colson-Dean game that never went any further; the president never saw the Enemies List. Dean, it turns out, hadn't told the president earlier the things he testified to—in other words, What did the president know? When did he know it? Dean antedated that, yet the mass of testimony he gave added to his credibility.

Samuel Dash Cox said, "I am going to talk to the chairman of the committee." We had such a meeting and Senator Ervin said that, "It is more important that our committee get at the truth and tell other people about it than that some people go to jail," so he turned Cox down. We ultimately went to court—primarily over the issue of our granting immunity to John Dean and Jeb Magruder. This was because Cox took the position that if we put Dean and Magruder's testimony under immunity on television, it would prejudice the trials.

There is plenty of Supreme Court precedent that has addressed the issue: one of the best cases was where Cox, as solicitor general, representing the interests of the Congress, took the position that Congress shouldn't be interfered with, even though it could prejudice criminal trials—and he won that case—so I cited Cox on the case in my argument before Judge Sirica, and he had to agree. Ultimately, we had a very cooperative relationship with the Special Prosecution Force; they couldn't give us information because of the secrecy of the grand jury, but every new piece of information we got—every new witness, every new document—we continued to convey to them.

Richard Ben Veniste With respect to Dean, we found that their immunization of him—and the related fallout—made it extremely difficult to prosecute Dean; one of the principal objectives was that this man should be held accountable. It took some considerable thought and ingenuity to find a path by which Dean could be convinced that we were serious about prosecuting him, even if it meant delaying other prosecutions based on his testimony. We were going to do that if he hadn't pleaded guilty.

Samuel Dash We began an investigation strategy to see if there was any record of Oval Office conversations by designing what we called "satellite charts": we took each of the principal targets—Nixon, Haldeman, Ehrlichman—and put them in the center of each chart. Then we charted out all of the people who on a daily basis would come in contact with each of the targets, whether they were gofers who got coffee, secretaries, assistants, or aides; these people would bear witness every day to transactions—how many may have bought a tape; how many may have transcribed a tape. In the real world, we make tracks; the powerful people are not usually aware of the little people around them, but the little people are very much aware of the powerful people, so they observe an awful lot.

Alexander Butterfield Everybody who went through that committee had a prior session with the staff to weed out unimportant things. I wasn't on the original list. That was a credit to Haldeman—the fact that we kept things pretty quiet at the White House about who did what to whom. We didn't see reporters. If you did see one, you had to get Haldeman's permission, and it had to be to promote the president: Haldeman had said on the day we were sworn in by Chief Justice Earl Warren, "Everything that we do as a staff should be to promote the president and his image, and to enhance our chances for a second term, because in this modern world you cannot do in one term what needs to be done."

Samuel Dash We had hundreds of witnesses come into different rooms in the Senate Office Building to meet with my staff. We would ask a lot of questions—and buried among them was the question: Did you ever see tape transcripts; did you ever know that somebody was buying tapes? Butterfield was called because, according to our charts, he sat outside the president's office. We had no idea that he knew anything; only three people knew about the taping system: Haldeman; his assistant, Lawrence Higby; and Butterfield.

Haldeman and Higby had not admitted anything about the tapes when we talked to them; when we called Butterfield, he knew that we had talked to the others, and he did not want to commit perjury. A question was asked by a member of the minority staff—based on a memorandum we had received from the White House, which was their recollected reconstruction of a conversation between the president and Dean. The staff person—in an exploratory question—asked if this reconstruction could possibly have been a tape recording. Butterfield said something like, You probably know this, because you've already talked to Haldeman, but I might as well tell you that it's not just one recording; I supervised the putting in of a taping system that went twenty-four hours a day for two years. That was the explosion.

WHY THE TAPING SYSTEM WAS INSTALLED

Robert Finch After the 1968 election, Johnson asked us to come by the White House. I think it was Joe Califano* who grabbed me and pointed out the [taping] mechanism Johnson had in there. Nixon was in, talking to Johnson, and Califano said to me, "You should see this, because you have to decide whether you want to take it out or leave it in." It was a fixed set with a few locations, and it also had to be turned on by the president, or someone he designated. I asked Nixon when we were down in Florida: "They have this set in there; do you want me to leave it in?" and he said, "Oh no. I want to take it out; I don't want the damn thing in there." It turns out that it was a much better arrangement than the one Haldeman—or whoever—installed. The one Haldeman put in was voice-activated, so you had thousands of hours of tapes.

Alexander Butterfield I didn't get any guidance, but I didn't think they wanted any tin-horn, fly-by-night thing, so I said, "Yes, let's make it a sophisticated system." I didn't know that it was going to be voice-activated. They said it was voice-activated, but it wasn't in the Cabinet Room or in other places, just in the Oval Office.

Ronald Ziegler I never said to Nixon, "Why did you install the tapes? Don't you realize what a foolish thing that was, and how it may have brought down your presidency?" But I did talk in general terms with him, and I am quite convinced that he was repulsed by the Johnson system and had it

---

* Joseph Califano, Jr., a White House aide to President Lyndon Johnson.

taken out. He did not like the process of taping people; he felt awkward about it. The only way he could bring himself not to feel awkward about it was to have the system he was encouraged to put in—I am sure by Haldeman. He only agreed to it when Bob convinced him that a system was appropriate for history, but I am convinced that he did not have it installed for the purpose of catching people in traps—using it for clandestine reasons. It was simply to record history and to use it as a record of his presidency—as he felt others had done. He could have survived if the system had been destroyed.

H. R. Haldeman He [Nixon] had said all along that I was to tell nobody about the existence of the tapes. Rose Woods didn't know we were making those tapes. At one point, I said to the president, "The tapes are piling up and you may want to get someone to transcribe them." And he said, "Absolutely not"—this is before Watergate—"They are not to be transcribed, and no one is to listen to them, except you or me."

Terrence O'Donnell The day I went in to interview with Dwight Chapin for a job, Alex Butterfield said to come and see him when the interview was over, so I went down the hall to his office. The president was gone, and Alex took me into the Oval Office. He showed me the panic button under the desk, and I was walking around the office, and he said, "You have to be careful in here; there is a lot of really trick stuff." I thought that Alex was referring only to the security apparatus to call the Secret Service. But, of course, the taping system was well ensconced by that time.

Alexander Butterfield The taping system was so elaborate; the microphones were embedded in the surface of the desk. I never dreamed that the Secret Service would go to that length to do this thing. Most of the conversations at the president's desk were hard to hear when coffee was being served.

Stephen Bull The taping system didn't record all conversations, and some conversations were almost unintelligible, just by the nature of the system. It was not a sophisticated system.

Kenneth Rush The reason for the taping system was twofold: first, they were a chronicle of history that only Nixon would have; second, the tapes would protect Nixon against Henry Kissinger and others; he knew that everyone was an egotist, and that Henry was a supreme one. At times, he forgot the system was on. The recording was so poor that many errors have been made in their transcription.

Lawrence Higby I know exactly why the taping system was installed: the president wanted to make sure that there was a clear record available on the major decisions he was making, particularly with regard to foreign policy, and wanted to be sure that in the history those decisions would be written about correctly—and not in Henry Kissinger's eyes. He felt that Henry and others kind of courted the press, whereas he had made a lot of the tough decisions and he wanted the record to show, ultimately, what he had done.

The reason the system was so comprehensive was because the president was an absolute klutz when it came to things mechanical. Therefore, what Haldeman asked me to do was to make it voice-activated. Bob told me to get it done, and I went to Butterfield to get it done.

Obviously, by the tonality, the language, the frankness, and brashness, the self-doubt that you hear as you go through the tapes, the collection was never contemplated for public release; it was to be the president's own personal and private record. I don't think he ever intended even Bob Haldeman, or Henry Kissinger, or anyone else to hear it.

Alexander Butterfield There is absolutely no doubt that the system was [installed] to help Nixon write his memoirs; he did have a strong sense of history. We already had a fairly elaborate system in place called Memos for the President's File, of which I was the custodian; I was the person who beat people around the head and ears to get their memos in. Everyone who was in with the president was in with someone else. That someone else at first had a pad and pencil in hand and took notes, but then we quickly realized that that was inhibiting to the visitor. Then we said, "All right. You don't have to remember everything; just give us the sense of the meeting—the president's mood, any little things of interest that happened during the meeting, or any comments made."

As soon as the meeting was over, I would be responsible for taking the person back to the West Wing Lobby and saying good-bye. Then I was supposed to go by my own rules straight back to my dictaphone—everyone had one—and spit that out; forget the punctuation; we just want the substance: "The president was in a good mood; he saw so-and-so today." It was half a page to a page. These memos were on every single, solitary meeting the president had, many of them with his own staff members—staff members that weren't in the inner sanctum even though they were senior, like Pat Moynihan. He was very senior, but he was a Democrat, so he was always suspect, so he was never in alone with the president. The same with Arthur Burns. We never left Arthur Burns in by himself, even though he had great stature; he was a guy that Haldeman didn't trust.

There were a lot of people we didn't trust. Any visitor from the outside, even the president's old Duke Law School professor, had someone go in with him. Usually for this type I went in, because my office adjoined the Oval Office; I was the handy person when those little things came up. It would be a short meeting—ten minutes; he would get some cuff links, and he would be easy to write up. The Memos to the President's File was in place for a year and a half before the taping system came along. I thought: maybe we can forget this file, because it took a lot of my time. It was really a waste of time to get people—especially like Henry Kissinger, who tended to be delinquent, anyway; he had a big load. He was in there with heads of state and the meetings were very substantive, so the Memos File had to be more lengthy. It was hard to get Henry; he didn't want to waste his time with this sort of administrative business, so he was tremendously in arrears.

William Saxbe When I would talk with Nixon when I was attorney general, he would spend most of his time telling me how [President Franklin Delano] Roosevelt did this and [President John F.] Kennedy did that—and about all those other presidents who were taping in the White House.

Vernon Walters Johnson recorded Nixon's campaign plane. Kennedy recorded his brother and his wife. Roosevelt had recorded [presidential adviser] Bernard Baruch's love life, although more out of curiosity of how an eighty-two-year-old handled it. When Nixon did this, he was a threat to American democracy; the Constitution was in peril. The fact is, there have been recording systems in the Oval Office before Nixon and after Nixon. Everyone acts as if this was a one-time situation, done by this strange, complex, inhibited weirdo. It wasn't.

John Ehrlichman I suppose a psychologist would say I was aware of the taping system. I had an inkling of it; nobody ever told me. But in the contretemps of March to April 1973, Nixon told me he had John Dean on tape. I thought: That is curious; I wonder how he rigged that up so Dean didn't know. I never inquired.

Alexander Butterfield No one ever mentioned the tapes once they were in, which was sort of interesting. The president was never in any way intimidated by them. I think he was totally oblivious, or acted oblivious, to the fact that they were in. He didn't curb his language.

Raymond Price Most people imagine that the language in the tapes was quite different from what it actually was. I remember, when we were up at Camp David and we were working on the speech with which he would release the White House transcripts, Ron Ziegler coming in to see me and saying, "My God, 'expletive deleted,' that's all anybody is going to see." He was right, of course. Nixon's basic concern wasn't the language; it was the Bible Belt and things like "goddamn"—that was the level of profanity—and maybe an occasional "shit," or something like that. But as soon as the transcripts came out, everybody put in his own imagination—it's a very interesting psychological thing—whatever longshoreman-kind of thing he imagined might have been there, and then began to believe that that was what it was. Nixon is not a foul-mouthed guy; he is not as straitlaced as his public persona sometimes is.

Maurice Stans In my years with Eisenhower, I found out that profanity is a tool of the presidency; he could get mad as hell and cuss about some person or other, particularly about somebody he wanted to get rid of. I heard that Truman was very profane at times. It was a way for a president to let off steam. I wasn't surprised that Nixon did it, though I didn't have much occasion to observe it myself.

John Ehrlichman He had not shown that side very much to me; but the minute I left the room and [John] Mitchell was left behind, then they got very coarse. He presented different sides to different people; that was part of his political essence: he could be what you wanted him to be. The briefing papers prepared for him on people he was going to meet were directed that way. He is the Queen of Hearts in *Alice in Wonderland*. I think that he forgot about the taping system a lot of the time. There were things he said to me that he never would have said for the record, for example, that blacks are ethnically inferior; he wouldn't have wanted that in the historical record. I have no doubt that in that instance he was responding to the stimulation of the discussion. Presumably, he had sort of an a priori intention of cleaning all of that up.

Alexander Butterfield The thing was only used for a year and a half. The Secret Service came to me—I was the liaison with them and the FBI, supposedly; I learned later that a lot of things went around me that I didn't know about—and said, "We are having storage problems for this stuff; we have so many tapes." They changed a couple of spools daily. I said, "You will have to solve it yourself; find another closet someplace." They kept the tapes across the street, in the Executive Office Building, in all kinds of cubby holes that only they had access to. I said once to Haldeman, "We ought to get some secretaries—get a room on the top floor of the EOB, off limits to everyone else—and get them typing, because this stuff is every word of every day; it's going to be voluminous, to say the least." But we never did that.

THE CLOSED-DOOR SESSION

Alexander Butterfield I said to myself, if they ask me about the tapes—if they ask a fuzzy question—I'll give a fuzzy answer. I never in a million years dreamed they would ask about the tapes. But I was so aware of the tapes that I had a little game plan if it happened and—lo and behold—it happened; I couldn't have been more surprised. They opened by throwing this memo at me. It wasn't a memo; it was a true transcript. It said "P" and it had some verbatim stuff there, and then it said "D"—I guess for Dean. They said, "Where might this have come from?" I said, "Gee." I'm thinking: I know where it came from—the president had great retentive powers, but not this good. This looks like something verbatim. And to my great relief, they got off that subject. About four hours later, it was Saunders'* turn. He picks up this paper, which had been lying there for four hours, and says, "Mr. Butterfield, John Dean, in his public testimony,† had said that, 'One day, I was in the president's office and, uncharacteristically, the president got up from his desk as I was about to leave, came over and put his arm around me, and walked with me to the door and said something in lower tones, which made me, John Dean, think: I wonder if he was taping me at the desk.'" That got the staff guys thinking about the tapes.

Finally the question came directly. I had said, "Well, there was a little recording device the president had; it was called a dictabelt. Those were for things to family members, maybe to an ambassador. And Rose [Woods] would take those dictabelts and type them." And then a little while later, this guy Saunders said, "Mr. Butterfield, was there ever any other kind of tape-recording system in the Oval Office?" I said to myself, that's the direct ques-

---

* A Senate Watergate Committee staff member.
† Approximately two weeks earlier.

tion that I had hoped wouldn't be. And my first reply was, "I hoped you fellows wouldn't ask that question." I said, "Yes, there was." They said, "What was it like?" So I just told them.

Lawrence Higby I was shocked, because I had been questioned a number of times on areas that scraped dangerously close to my having to reveal them. I had been told by Haldeman early on that the tapes were something covered by executive privilege that should be taken up by the White House lawyers if that question was ever asked of me. I went to Haig after spending a particularly grueling session up on the Hill, in which I was apparently going to be brought up before the Watergate Committee the next day, and they were kind of briefing me and asking a bunch of questions. I was asked: Was I aware of any other tapes? The president dictated dictabelt tapes. They asked: Was there anything else? And my lawyer coughed—it interrupted the line of questioning—and when we came back to the line of questioning, they never asked the question; they went on to another question. Then, two questions later, they asked if I was aware of any cash payments to anybody. I said yes, that I was aware of the $175,000 cash payment that we had given to Senator Lowell Weicker to help his campaign, and one of the gentlemen who was questioning me was Weicker's appointee to this group, and he like fell off his seat, and they immediately concluded the briefing session, and then called me that evening, and said, "We don't think there will be any need for you to testify."

I'll never forget—I left that meeting and went back to Haig and said to him, "Are you aware of the tapes?" He said, "There is no big deal about the tapes; everyone is aware that the president would sometimes dictate for his diaries." I said, "No, no. Not *those* tapes. Don't you know the Oval Office is bugged and, I think, the EOB office?" And it was like he went white. My impression was that up until that conversation, he had no idea that that stuff was in existence. He dismissed me immediately and marched into the president's office.

Helmut Sonnenfeldt When I heard about the taping system, I was particularly irritated because those of us who were in the Oval Office when, for example, foreign visitors came in, were under the strictest orders to take verbatim notes—as though we were court reporters, which we weren't. The State Department style of writing memoranda was indirect speech—third person, and not direct quotations. But in the Nixon administration, you had to write memos as though they were verbatim, and we frequently had to make up words that rang true, but we couldn't swear to. So when I and others heard that this damn stuff was really on tapes, it was quite infuriating, because we spent hours and hours dictating these damn things.

Ben Bradlee If you add up rubber gloves, hundred-dollar bills, notebooks with the White House telephone number, Spanish-speaking people, you say, "Oh, this has got to be interesting." It built so gradually; it got to be more and more interesting. Certainly, when McCord went to Sirica, then you said, "My God, I can't believe this." Then the story of Patrick Gray destroying documents; and Mitchell—the attorney general of the United States—committing crimes; and then, finally, when the tapes came out; I knew about the tapes through Woodward, who had heard about them the day before [Butterfield's testimony]. But I didn't believe it. He said, "There are tapes of every conversation." And I said, "Sure." I couldn't believe it. I still can't believe it.

Leonard Garment When I heard about the taping system from Higby, it didn't seem like a terribly big deal to me. He came to see me because he knew he was going to be examined by the Senate [Watergate Committee] staffers, and he told me about it. There were so many things going on at that point that nothing surprised me; if they had said, the building is fifty feet up in the air, I wouldn't have been surprised. Higby said, "Butterfield knows about it, Haldeman knows about it, some Secret Service men know, and I do." Of course, Ehrlichman knew about it, because in one of the tape-recorded conversations before he resigned, he says: "Either you, Mr. President, or Bob [Haldeman] has to listen to the March 21st tape." Higby asked me, "What should I do? I need some guidance."

Later on, there was some criticism that I should have told him—and somehow contrived to tell everybody—that they were to claim presidential privilege, on the ground that anything having to do with White House facilities was covered by executive privilege. A rather extraordinary theory of executive privilege, it was later imposed on the Secret Service. I didn't think of it at the time; I wasn't that smart. Nobody else thought of it. I told Higby, "If they ask you, 'Is there a taping system?' you answer truthfully. You don't have to volunteer, but be careful that you don't dance around it. Don't get too fancy; you'll end up with a perjury problem." I am not sure whether Butterfield called and asked the same question, but I would have told him the same thing: You don't have to volunteer, but don't get too close to the line; don't try to fool them. Higby got quite close; he had a hard time for some period after that, but he got away with it; he somehow slid away.

Alexander Butterfield I went in at two o'clock on Friday, the 13th of July 1973, and I imagine that it was just like staff sessions that others had gone through. I knew—far better than the staff—that when they got this information about the tapes, it was the first time they were hearing it. As I was talking, I admired how composed they remained; I knew it was big, big, big. As soon as the meeting was over, they couldn't get to their bosses fast enough. I will say that they closed the meeting in a very smooth fashion. I said to them, "Before we part, I know what I've told you is dynamite. I'm worried about how it is going to be handled. I hope you will handle it maturely." One of them said, "Mr. Butterfield, we want to tell you that your testimony was so straightforward." I said, "For all I know, you got this from Haldeman or Higby, or someone, and were just checking me to corroborate." I knew goddamn well that they didn't get it from anyone else. I knew that Haldeman would never tell about the tapes. It doesn't mean that I was that less loyal; maybe it does.

Samuel Dash On Friday afternoon, July 13th, I was in my office. I had been working almost around the clock; the next day was my wedding anniversary and I had promised that I would come home for dinner, so I was packing my bag when Scott Armstrong, one of my assistants who had been in the staff session with Butterfield, called me on the phone and said, "I've got to see you." I replied that I would see him in the morning. He said, "This is important." I answered, "Scott, everything is important to you; I'll see you in the morning." He says again, "I've got to see you." So I said, "Come on up; you've got a minute." He comes into my office—his eyes are bulging; he is sweating, and he says, "The president bugged himself; there is a tape recording." I then call my wife, and I next call Senator Ervin, and out of his memory comes some quotation from the King James version of the Bible—something like: "Didn't they know that no matter they tried to hide, they would be uncovered. " We now had that evidence that would corroborate John Dean.

Archibald Cox We had fairly good relations with Sam Dash and his staff—not 100 percent, but good enough—that they might have told us, but they might not. To my recollection, we learned from Butterfield's disclosure that there were tapes.

If we could get the tapes, there was a way—so far as the cover-up was concerned, or the responsibility for the original break-in at the Watergate was concerned—that might lead to what otherwise was coming down to: Who do you believe?

Fred Dalton Thompson When a staff member told me on Friday night of Butterfield's meeting with the staff, I was surprised and intrigued. I also wondered if the material was incomplete—that surely they wouldn't have kept anything that was damaging and perhaps the material could even be exonerating—that Butterfield had been sent to the staff on purpose to disclose the existence of the tapes. As circumstances moved along, I was proven to be wrong about those thoughts.

Somewhere over the weekend, I talked to Fred Buzhardt. I told him, "You guys had better plan on gathering up your tapes and getting them down here; we know you have them." I don't know to this day whether he had been aware of the taping system or not; he was very vague in his response to me.

Archibald Cox Our very quick response was: we will have to get the tapes. We realized from the beginning that we would have to subpoena them; Fred Buzhardt and the lawyers in the White House had been refusing, generally, to supply what they would have called White House documents, so we knew that a request wouldn't do us any good.

As we thought about the legal issues that lay ahead, I became convinced that it was important to subpoena all the tapes—there was too much danger that a court would regard this as a fishing expedition—and that we must identify as best we could the tapes that were most important.

We had some material to help us do that: early on, the White House had provided us with all the secretaries' logs of telephone calls and visits, so when we saw there was a conversation between President Nixon and Attorney General Mitchell on the morning after the break-in, it was a pretty good guess that if they had had anything to do with it, there would be some discussion about it. Or, indeed, if they hadn't had anything to do with it, there would be some discussion about it. There were eight other tapes we chose that one could identify as likely to be key ones. The Ervin Committee subpoenaed them all, and its suit was thrown out.

Before we moved, we discussed the problems we thought we would face. There were very difficult legal questions: Is the president subject to legal process? You go to the older books on constitutional law and they tell you that the president is not subject to legal process; he is the head of an independent branch of government, not answerable himself to the court.

Then, there was a claim of executive privilege, which wasn't easy either: suppose we get an order that is confirmed by the higher courts, and the president simply says, I won't. What do you do then?

John Dean I had left town after my testimony to the Senate Committee. Sam Dash asked me to come back; he said there was something very important. So he and I, and my lawyer and, I think, Jim Hamilton° met, and Dash said, "What would your reaction be if all this stuff was on tape?" and I said, "I've always told you that I thought some of my conversations were taped." He said, "No, I'm talking about everything." I answered, "I think that's terrific." I was one of his key witnesses, and he was testing me—as he later admitted. I said, "If anything, I've undertestified; I've tried to remember things the best I can." I later learned that I'd mixed up conversations a bit. But if there were tapes, I couldn't have been more pleased. I knew it was all over. They had learned of the tapes on a Friday. We met on a Saturday, and Butterfield testified on a Monday.

I racked my brain after Haldeman testified about the fact that didn't Nixon say to me, after I said we need to raise a million dollars, that that would be wrong. I said to myself, that isn't my sense of what he said. He kept bringing the money back up; that we have to pay. So I couldn't believe he ever said it was wrong. There is only one way to establish that, indeed, he hadn't said that. That is through the tape. On the tape he is reacting to what I have said about executive clemency, and I am saying, you can't do it. How would I ever prove that without the tapes? So it was my word against the president of the United States—against almost anybody at that point.

I felt very comfortable that the tapes had been discovered. But I had been suspicious there might be taping. As I testified, I was suspicious because of Nixon's behavior when I met with him on April 15, 1973; he had been asking me lots of setup questions. When he didn't exactly like to hear what I said, he would try to rephrase the questions. I said to myself: Hey. There is somebody making a record of this. I'm not dumb. Then when he literally got up and walked around and was kind of whispering around flower pots and said, "I was foolish to talk to Colson about clemency for Hunt," he was obviously hiding from a microphone. I thought: This is crazy; I'm being taped. Also, during my testimony there was some very specific language from my conversations with the president. I said: "Boy, I can't remember. Can Richard Nixon remember those kinds of details?" So I was very suspicious.

Samuel Dash Immediately [after] my staff told me, I informed Ervin, and we got Butterfield in for questioning. He was then chairman of the Federal Aviation Administration [FAA] and was very reluctant to be a public witness;

° A Senate Watergate Committee staff member.

he said he had to go to Russia to negotiate a treaty. But Ervin said, "No. You are not going to Russia," and we made Butterfield our next witness when the hearings resumed on Monday morning. That weekend was one of the few times that the Senate Watergate Committee didn't leak its information, so Butterfield was our surprise witness, who provided information that appalled—if not shocked—the world.

Alexander Butterfield I had talked to Howard Baker, the co-chairman of the committee, over the weekend. I told him about my testimony to the staff, not knowing he knew about it from the staff. He let me tell the whole story. I said, "I hope I don't have to testify," since I was off to the Soviet Union at 6 A.M.; I didn't want to be held up. Baker said, "No, I don't think you will have to," and he led me to believe that he would support my not testifying. So, Monday morning, I was in the barbershop at the White House, watching the hearings, and I got a call from Jim Hamilton, and he said, "They want you to come up and be the first one on this afternoon." I got mad. I said, "I won't be there; I am just not going to jump through a hoop for you guys." He said, "Well, I will have to tell the chairman what you have just said." On TV, I saw him walk behind the chairman and whisper in his ear. Then the phone rang again. It was Jim, saying, "The chairman says if you're not in his office at twelve o'clock, he'll have federal marshals pick you up on the street." Of course, I knew he wasn't going to send federal marshals, but what he was saying was: You'd better get your ass up here, Mr. Butterfield, because we need you.

I wasn't nervous or upset, or mad. At least I had a haircut, and had a nice suit on. So I went up there. I said, "First of all, I want to apologize for what I said to Mr. Hamilton, because I still don't think I should do this; I'm very peripheral to all this. Why don't you ask one of the central people? Ask Haldeman, when his turn comes." They said, "No, you're the one who told the staff; you should be the one who tells the country." I went into the bathroom, washed my face and combed my hair, and thought about what I should say.

Leonard Garment I had been away for the weekend. When I got back to Washington, I was asked to come to the White House. Doug Parker, who worked with me, and Fred Buzhardt were in my office. [Senator] Howard Baker had alerted the White House on Saturday that this was coming up, so I called Butterfield and he asked, "What is going to happen? Can you represent me?" I said, "No; you'll have to get your own counsel, but you won't have any problems if you tell the truth." Monday morning, I was in Haig's office, and Butterfield called me from a barber shop and said he had been served to testify forthwith. At least he was getting a haircut; he may have had the idea that he was going to be on national television.

Alexander Butterfield At the end of the thirty-minute session, I said, "I was called up on short notice; I didn't have time to seek counsel, and I just hope I haven't said anything today that, by revealing the existence of these tapes, preempted the president, or said anything today that he may have wanted to say in his own time—for his own purposes." People who don't like me say, "Why didn't you just not say anything, Alex?" When I came back from my trip to the Soviet Union, nobody would sit next to me at a sub-Cabinet meeting.

Mr. Dean's testimony before the Senate Watergate Committee and information given by him to the federal prosecutors was damaging to the president, but not enough so as to bring about impeachment. As the committee and the special prosecutor sought ways in which to obtain White House documents, Mr. Nixon became ill, and on the evening of Thursday, July 12—the day before Alexander Butterfield's revelation to the Senate Watergate Committee staff of the existence of a White House recording system—was taken to Bethesda Naval Hospital suffering from pneumonia.

As Mr. Nixon recovered, he and his top aides, along with attorneys Leonard Garment and Fred Buzhardt, debated the question of what to do about the tapes, which would now obviously become the subject of subpoenas by the various investigative bodies.

Samuel Dash The president was taken to the hospital with what was described as viral pneumonia. I think that he was under stress; whether he was having a breakdown or not, I don't know. That weekend he was in the hospital [Senator Howard] Baker told Fred Buzhardt that we knew about the tapes, but he got a noncommittal response; it was never believed in the White House that the tapes would be found and, if they were, that they would have to be turned over. Richard Nixon had a perception of the presidency—and his power—that was absolute. He didn't invent the imperial presidency, but he believed in it.

Alexander Haig I got the president into Bethesda Naval Hospital. He was very, very sick. My assistant, George Joulwan—now the NATO commander—came in and said, "General, you are not going to believe this." He flipped on a TV in Haldeman's old office, and there was Alex Butterfield—who I had known in the Pentagon when he was an Air Force officer. As I heard his testimony, I thought: Oh my God. And I ordered that the whole taping system be ripped out immediately. I didn't ask the president or anybody. I just said, "Tear it out." When Nixon says, in his memoirs, that I called him that Monday morning to tell him that Butterfield was going to testify, he is wrong. I didn't know about it until I saw him on television.

Leonard Garment We had a question: the president was in the hospital; nobody had thought to go and harass him over the weekend about what the hell we were going to do. I immediately asked Doug Parker to look into the cases on subpoena and destruction of tapes. This was an immediate issue: Do we keep them or get rid of them? We talked about it and then went over to the hospital to see the president.

Doug had located the leading case and its decision—which had been followed over and over again—said, rather clearly, that it is not necessary to have a subpoena actually served for there to be an obstruction of justice accomplished in the destruction of the subpoenaed material; if you know that the material is going to be subpoenaed, and if you destroy it, that's an obstruction of justice—a Grade A felony. And it had been announced by Senator Ervin, in the clearest possible terms, that they wanted those tapes, so the law was clear that destruction of the tapes would be an obstruction of justice and would qualify, arguably, as an opening count in an impeachment petition.

When we went out to the hospital, we didn't assign each other roles, but the general feeling was—most of the books have this totally screwed up—that Fred Buzhardt was a very sound lawyer, very careful and prudent, a canny Southern Pentagon lawyer, a West Point graduate, a really very honorable man, and he was not about to do anything crazy, so he would not dispute the fact that there was a problem in destroying the tapes. What I basically said was that destroying the tapes would be a felony, and could be count number one in an impeachment petition.

My recollection was that Al Haig took a rather neutral position. He was sort of doing the right thing: he was the chief of staff; he was not making the decisions for Nixon; he was trying to have the different points raised, which was appropriate. Buzhardt was making the political argument that yes, it's a felony, but it's going to be a very big headache having these tapes around, and if it's done, it could be done in a way that the president could survive it. I don't think that anyone there really pressed hard for destruction of the tapes, because then you became parties to crime. But Buzhardt did make the point: Are they really going to make a big deal out of this? The president can't be indicted for an obstruction of justice; he would have to be impeached—and who was going to impeach Nixon over this?

I didn't dispute that. I said at some point, "We don't know what's on the tapes—whether they are good or bad—and without knowing what is on them, it's very hard to make a recommendation that we should take this or that risk by destroying or keeping them. Are they incriminating, or exculpatory? You have said, sir, that you don't want anyone in the world to hear these tapes." Then, Nixon said that Haldeman had heard the March 21st tape and considered it helpful; it would support his position against Dean, and there were things elsewhere that were helpful, so why commit a felony if what you have is helpful?

We had a discussion about logistics: How do you destroy the tapes? How many tapes are there? There must be a lot of tapes. Who is going to destroy them? And where? And how? Who is going to burn them?—John Connally's idea of a bonfire on the lawn. The Environmental Protection Agency [EPA] will come and arrest you—you have to file an environmental impact statement before you do that. It was easy for these people to say, "Pile the tapes up on the lawn; get on national television." Of course, the police are liable to drive up suddenly to intercept the commission of a felony, and the whole thing will be like a Mack Sennett* comedy.

Herbert Klein Haig told me that Garment and Buzhardt went to see Nixon in the hospital. Garment said that you couldn't destroy the tapes, as they were evidence; Buzhardt said they were not. Nixon told them he would let them know in the morning. In the morning, he said that he felt sure that if you burned the tapes, it would be evidence that there was something you had to destroy, and you couldn't do that secretly by this time. Secondly, they were the property of the president and couldn't be subpoenaed.

Leonard Garment What Nixon says in his book *[Memoirs]* about insisting he not destroy the tapes is not true. I wish I could claim such a historic role.

Alexander Haig At about 8:30 P.M. on the evening that Butterfield revealed the existence of the tapes, we met at the hospital. Every angle of the issue was discussed. Buzhardt was a very wily, cornpone lawyer and a Southern politician. He was very careful, but the basic thrust of his advice

---

* The silent filmmaker noted for bathing beauties and slapstick scenes.

was: Get rid of the tapes while they are still yours; the minute they are sub-poenaed, they are public property. The president got so mad at the advice from Len Garment [not to destroy the tapes] that he threw both of them out of the room and asked me to stay behind—I remember this as if it was yes-terday. He said, "Al, can you imagine getting advice like that from your lawyer?" He was a lot more vitriolic than I would want to see in print, because Len is a friend of mine. I told the president, "You have to get rid of the tapes." He said, "Al, I have to sleep on it."

I went back the next morning; he was feeling a lot better—they had been giving him antibiotics the night before and he had been feeling very badly and had a high fever—and he said, "Al, I've been thinking about it. I don't know what I'll be accused of by Haldeman, by Ehrlichman, by Dean and people around him. Those tapes are my protection." Whether he believed it or not, I can't say. But I didn't and it disturbed me greatly, so I discussed it with Buzhardt and he said, "I can tell you somebody who's in your camp very strongly, and that's Spiro Agnew." So I called the president and said, "You should see the vice-president"—Agnew was in deep trouble already but the public as yet did not know the scope or depth of it.

I met Agnew at the door and took him inside. Agnew looked down at the president—who was wearing a dressing gown—and said, "Boss, you've got to have a bonfire." So, to imply—as Nixon does in his memoirs—that I was against burning the tapes, or getting rid of them, is absolutely wrong. What was not wrong was that I was not going to do it. Back in the White House, I met with Fred Buzhardt, who said, "The president's decision is a mistake and it could have profound consequences." He then added, "From this day on, don't you ever be alone in a room with a tape; don't ever listen to one, or even touch one." That was the best advice I've ever had.

Ronald Ziegler I sat in on a meeting. I don't know if Buzhardt was there, but certainly Len and Al were, and we exchanged points of view on the issue. Generally, what was concluded—as best I can recall—was that any destruction of the tapes would certainly place the destroyer in legal jeop-ardy. I remember someone's saying, "Who's going to do it? King Timahoe?" [the president's dog]. In other words, the process itself had moved so far along that there would have been grounds for a clear charge of obstruction of justice. At that point, the Senate hearings were taking place, and we were well into the process. The point is that everyone who looks at the period knows that human beings are not going to make that type of judgment based on the technicality of whether or not the tapes had been subpoenaed: if you look at the news coverage and the focus of attention on anyone involved in it, if you had been involved in the possession and destruction of the tapes, you certainly would have without difficulty projected that there was about a 100 percent likelihood of your being charged with a crime.

Alexander Haig I called the [White House] lawyers and asked, "What can we do?" Fred Buzhardt said to me—in front of Len Garment and then privately—"He's got to get rid of those tapes. They are his property, and you know how he talks in the Oval Office; you would think he was Beezelbub* reincarnated"—that was his style. Len Garment said no; and he not only said no—he denies this today, but I know it is so, and Nixon does also—Len said, "If you do this, I am going to have to resign and attack the president for destroying evidence." What I didn't know was that when all this broke, Len—who is a very clever guy—had been up to his law firm in New York, getting a ruling from his colleagues as to what he should do, and they told him, "Don't let him burn the tapes; they are evidence." Well, the fact was that the tapes were not evidence until they had been subpoenaed; they were Nixon's private property. You could argue that he used public funds—the stenographers and all of what ultimately evolved out of all those arguments—but up to that time, nobody in our history had ever challenged the right of the president to have diaries—or anything else.

Leonard Garment It was up in the air at the end of the discussion. We said, "All right. We will keep thinking about it." Who was going to light the fire? Nixon wasn't going to do it, the Secret Service wouldn't, Al Haig wouldn't, and neither would I. There were also questions as to how many tapes there were, how long it would take to burn them. Then, Nixon said, "Look, I want those tapes in my personal possession, under my personal control." I don't recall the issue coming up again.

Alexander Haig I told Buzhardt and Garment, "I am not going to be the interpreter for you and the president. You are his lawyers, and this is the most important judgment he'll ever make." At that point, I wanted to see the tapes destroyed, but I wasn't going to do it because I would have gone to jail. And Fred said, "If the president asks you to do this because of your feeling that it should be done, for God's sake, don't do it; let him use a low-level Secret Service man."

---

* A Philistine god and a character in John Milton's *Paradise Lost*, ranking next to Satan in deviltry.

REACTIONS TO BUTTERFIELD'S REVELATION

Raymond Price It is a mystery to me as to why Butterfield divulged the existence of the tapes; there are a lot of things about his role that are mysterious to me. The feeling among the White House staff was that he didn't really have to tell the committee—that he could have avoided it. And I don't think he told anybody in the White House until Sunday that he had told the committee staff on Friday; he gave us no time to prepare.

Philip Lacovara I don't remember hearing about it until that public session. Whether anyone from the task force might have heard from somebody on the Ervin Committee staff I would doubt, because at that point there was more rivalry than cooperation. Not rivalry in the sense of political vainglory—we had very different views of our respective responsibilities. So it is not likely that anybody on the Ervin Committee staff went out of his way to call someone from the special prosecutor's office to say: Hey, guess what. There's terrific evidence that we just learned about, and we're sure you'd want to know it even before we go public with it.

My own reaction to hearing about the tapes was: this is too good to be true. And there was a real concern that we were being set up—that there would be a great flurry of activity that we would be sucked into and we would find either that these tapes were not audible, or were incomplete, or were duped. This is the prosecutor's general cynicism: don't believe anything you see or hear; treat everything as a trap. So my reaction was: this just doesn't sound right; it can't be. It would be too easy for them to have made contemporaneous recordings of a conspiracy. It just doesn't happen.

Fred Fielding When I heard about the tapes, my reaction was: I guess that will settle the question of who is telling the truth. Nobody had a sense of what had happened. Here you suddenly had two of the very closest people to the president and the counsel to the president—very powerful people in charge of big things—ousted and accused of doing all sorts of criminal things. You have to close your eyes and try to imagine what it would be like to have grown up in this society and all of a sudden you were told, from the outside, that they were evil and had done these things; it was very tough to try to figure out what had happened. I suspect that part of President Nixon's problem was that he didn't know. I don't know that Haldeman knew about the break-in. Ehrlichman worried because he had a break-in on his hands.

Everybody is making decisions and recommendations based on what they know—and upon what they are concerned about coming out.

Rocco Siciliano I couldn't believe the tapes; I just didn't believe that a president would have tapes in his office. I don't know about the cursing; I can't say that I was ever witness to a lot of cursing. I was not surprised by the ethnic remarks; in my generation, there was still a tendency to equate people by their ancestry, religion, and color. Nixon belonged to that generation.

Jerry Jones I was absolutely amazed when I learned of the tapes and I was amazed all the way through. One became more and more amazed not so much that a president would want to record conversations—I think that makes sense—but that there would be such a systematic way of trying to do it: the Lincoln Bedroom, Cabinet Room, OEOB Office, Oval Office. It was managerial overkill—an idea run wild. Then, of course, not only to do that, but to record very compromising conversations was just insane. I couldn't believe it.

Philip Lacovara To say that the tapes are raw and unpresidential is an understatement. I had thought of myself as a pretty worldly person, but when I first heard the tapes—and putting aside the fact that I was a Republican and had supported the president on the Vietnam War—I really felt as if I had been kicked in the stomach when I first heard the actual conduct of business in the Oval Office; worse than a locker room. It's conceivable that President Nixon does not want any more of that exposed than is absolutely necessary. There is no reason to think he and his associates were more tawdry in discussing Watergate than in discussing congressmen, or foreign leaders, or any of the other people who would be tracked in those conversations.

While it is difficult to speculate what President Nixon thinks, or knows, is on the other tapes, it would not be surprising that he would be concerned that those other tapes would reveal involvement in deplorable activities—maybe even unrelated to the ones that were related to the overall Watergate investigations; he was in office for five and a half years.

Raymond Price I first learned about the taping system from Len Garment, the morning that Butterfield was going to testify before the Senate Committee. I remember Len—in a bit of a frenzy—grabbing me and taking me into the Xerox room and asking me—kind of nervously—how I would react if I knew that the president had been taping conversations with me. I said that it wouldn't bother me—after all, nothing I had said was secret to him. And if the tapes were for his use only, so what? Apparently others reacted differently. Johnson had urged Nixon to keep his taping system, but at first Nixon didn't want one. He finally decided it would be useful to have it, basically as a historical record, since it was an absolutely 110 percent established constitutional principle that he would have total control over his tapes. They would also be a protection to his being misrepresented by others.

Ronald Ziegler I was not aware of the taping system until Butterfield's announcement; he made it known to the [Senate Select] Committee staff first, and then the word came filtering back to us that he had informed people. I was startled not from the standpoint of the fact that there was such a system, because there had been enough folklore about Lyndon Johnson— even the press corps joked about how he taped people—and I assumed that there was some national security system; even when you are that close, you assume that there are things occurring that are really none of your business to know about, but the scope of it was surprising, even though I did not understand its scope when I was first told. Later on, when you looked at the tremendous volume of tape, and how absolutely incompetent the system itself was, then it really became startling: incompetent in its installation, effectiveness—totally incompetent in all of its aspects.

Richard Kleindienst I was surprised when I found out about the existence of the tapes, and my surprise went beyond that when I found out at the end of my service in the administration, when I was having telephone conversations with Ehrlichman, that he was taping these conversations. He would call me and say, "The president thinks you ought to do this or that," and I would say, "John, I can't do that, and you shouldn't, either." If I had answered yes on any one of these, I probably would have gone to jail.

Samuel Dash Some have called finding the tapes an accident, but that was not really true, because Dean gave me a clue in the course of my examination of him which led me to believe there may have been a tape: he said that at one point in a discussion with Richard Nixon in the Oval Office, Nixon stood up and went to a bookcase and sort of whispered, "I guess I was foolish to promise Colson that I would give clemency to Hunt." Dean says he asked himself, Why is the president whispering? Maybe he's taping the conversation and didn't want that to get on the tape.

Leonard Garment I don't think that any human being has—or can—read all of the published tapes, unless they were forced to do so at gunpoint in order to induce a psychosis. One weekend, I had the Blue Book* and I also had the official transcripts from the archives. I was all set for a weekend of reading; I was going to read the Blue Book from cover to cover. I just couldn't do it. I got ill—nauseous. Then I realized that these people proba-bly got ill, nauseous and dizzy, themselves in this kind of vertiginous exercise they were involved in; they knew they were in a death spin—like being in an airplane where the wing is torn off. Knowing that, they were still trying to figure out how they were going to land—to make an elephant fly. It's amaz-ing how they kept trying. And if anybody reads the tapes, they can't figure them out, because they're all code.

Essentially, what Nixon was trying to do was to bring Haldeman and Ehrlichman peacefully to the execution chamber without having to give them sedatives or tie their hands. He knew just what he was doing; he had that capacity for that brain of his to work on two, three, or four levels. One level would be an absolutely literal exercise to deal in very concrete terms with what was before him, and believing that; at the same time, at another level, trying to create a certain effect—weakening their resolve to hang back, but not to anger them. He was always trying to create self-interested volitional activities, knowing that unless he could get them to go quietly, peacefully, and loyally, they would kill him.

Alexander Butterfield I am sure that I am on his [Nixon's] "worst" list now, because the revelation of [the existence of] the tapes was never sup-posed to happen. I just answered the questions that came; I gave what I knew. I've read that, "Butterfield must not have known of the impact this would have." I wasn't that dumb about it. I knew the impact it would have. I knew that it would change the complexion of the investigation from: Is John Dean right? Is the president right? to Let's get the tapes and find out. I was very concerned about the overseas image. That's a naive concern, looking back, but I was worried that people like Golda Meir and Prime Minister [Harold] Wilson† would know that they were taped in my presence, and

---

* On April 29, 1974, in response to a request by the House Judiciary Committee for addi-tional tapes, the White House released a 1,308-page document entitled *Submission of the Presiden-tial Conversations to the Committee on the Judiciary of the House of Representatives* by Richard Nixon. The Blue Book—so described due to the color of its soft cover—contained transcripts of forty-six taped conversations related to Watergate. The Blue Book caused a national uproar and revealed a president who used profane language, was contemptuous of others, and was cynical and vindictive.

† Of the United Kingdom.

that would be embarrassing. I knew that Richard Nixon wouldn't want me to do what I did. People say, "Why didn't you just say 'I am not going to answer that question'?" Well, I don't know. Maybe deep down inside, I wanted to. But I just answered the questions and let the chips fall where they may; and I knew where they were going to fall.

Richard Ben Veniste We had no inkling that there would be such things as presidential tape recordings. Initially, we reacted to the news that there were such recordings with considerable skepticism—that this might be some sort of trap, and there might be recordings created for the purpose of discrediting Dean. So when I actually sat down and listened with my own ears to the initial tapes that we received, I had no idea they would be so devastating to President Nixon.

Seymour Glanzer The only thing of importance that happened at the Ervin Committee was [the disclosure of] the tapes. The person who divulged their existence to the committee had been questioned several times by the U.S. Attorney's Office; he was asked if he had any other information. He did have, but he withheld it from us. Actually, way before Butterfield revealed the existence of the tapes, we had subpoenaed the White House for tapes; we didn't know if they had any tapes, so we said, "If they exist, we want them." Buzhardt reported to us that there were no tapes. Later, when they looked for the subpoena, nobody could find it but we knew we had issued a subpoena. Butterfield was a high governmental official* and he should have been fired for not telling us what we wanted to know.

George McGovern I wasn't horrified; I was just startled. We learned later that he didn't invent that technique. I remember vividly what happened when that [Butterfield's testimony] came over the Senate cloakroom television: I was standing next to Senator [John] Pastore [D-R.I.], and he laughed and said, "They may have everything taped, but you can be damn sure that before the sun goes down tonight there won't be any tapes." Everybody thought that—there were eight or nine senators in the cloakroom at the time, and everybody, including me, figured they would be in the oven before sundown. And that would have been very easy to do, because all he would have had to say was: I don't want to embarrass President de Gaulle,

---

* At the time of the Watergate investigation, Butterfield was serving as Federal Aviation Agency administrator.

or Helmut Schmidt, and all these heads of state or senators who have been in here talking to me about judicial appointments. And, as far as I can see, that is the only harm these tapes can do, and just to make sure we are not embarrassing anybody, I have asked my secretary to dispose of all of them. I don't know why he didn't do this. I can tell you that in the Senate it was just taken for granted that this would happen; every senator was embarrassed: Jesus, I told him what a lousy judge this guy would be. Is he·going to let that out? Everybody had something they wouldn't want out that was said in that Oval Office; I wouldn't want everything I've said to presidents leaking out.

The senators also would have said: that will keep them from nailing him. But if he had sold it on the grounds that these were confidential matters—that he never would have taped heads of state and senators and congressmen and governors and reporters, he never would have put those things on tape if he had thought there was any chance it would embarrass any of them—some politicians would have breathed a sigh of relief if he had destroyed the tapes. I think some of them wished [Robert] Packwood [member, U.S. Senate, R-Oreg.] would have burned his diaries, too.

On July 18, 1973, two days after Mr. Butterfield's revelation concerning the White House taping system, Special Prosecutor Archibald Cox wrote to Mr. Nixon, asking for eight tapes of presidential conversations. On July 23, the president rejected the Cox request and informed Judge Sirica, on the 25th, that his release of the tapes would jeopardize the independence of the three branches of government. Cox then obtained a show cause order directing the president to explain why he should not be compelled to release the tapes. On August 29, Judge Sirica ordered the president to turn over to the court eight tapes requested by Cox, so that he could decide if they should be presented to the grand jury. On August 30, the president announced his decision to appeal Judge Sirica's ruling.

THE 18½-MINUTE GAP

In late September 1973, Mr. Nixon's secretary, Rose Mary Woods, began—at his request—the transcription of tapes subpoenaed by the special prosecutor. One of the tapes Ms. Woods had worked on was the record of a one-hour-and-nineteen-minute, June 20, 1972, conversation between Nixon and Haldeman, whose notes of the meeting indicated that the Watergate break-in had been a part of the discussion.

While it remains unclear how it happened—and whether by deliberate act or accident—an 18½-minute gap exists in the tape, covering that part of the conversation that Haldeman's notes indicated related to Watergate.

The confusion over the June 20 tape was heightened by the fact that the president, at first, did not believe this specific tape had been included in the subpoena. Then, on November 15, he learned not only that this assumption was incorrect, but that what Ms. Woods had originally reported as a 5-minute gap was actually an 18½-minute gap.

The 18½-minute gap in the Watergate discussion of the June 20 conversation greatly troubled Mr. Nixon's attorneys and cast renewed doubt as to the president's credibility. In his memoir, he writes that, "Most people think my inability to explain the 18½-minute gap is the most unbelievable and insulting part of the whole of Watergate." *

Richard Ben Veniste We were concerned for the security of the tapes. That concern was heightened when we learned that one of them had this 18½-minute gap. When we made application for the court to take physical possession of the original tapes, I had made a suggestion to Professor Cox— and he rejected it—saying, "We can't make such an argument based on the possibility that someone might alter or destroy the tapes; we have to give the president the benefit of the doubt." That underscores the way Professor Cox operated.

Alexander Butterfield That is the first meeting when the president came back from Key Biscayne; he is talking to his top aide, Haldeman. I am sure it was purposeful; that's when he had to say, "Bob, what the hell happened to those bastards? I thought you told me this thing was going to be . . . "

Samuel Dash My guess has always been—based on the sequence of events—that the gap was Haldeman briefing Nixon of what Liddy had told Dean on the 19th; it would take about that amount of time to tell that story. It was very important later on that this conversation not be on the tape, because Richard Nixon had been telling the American people for almost a whole year that he had known nothing about this until Dean came in in March of '73 and told him everything. Although that wouldn't show approval by the president, it would show some knowledge—at least as far as Haldeman was concerned—that there was a plan.

H. R. Haldeman I have no idea how it happened; it was long after I was gone.°

Philip Lacovara When I heard that that testimony—shucks your honor; we just discovered that in one of these recordings we have to turn over there is a gap of approximately 18½ minutes—my reaction was: They really are stupid. Nobody is going to believe that that is an accident. There is a principle in the law of evidence called spoliation, which is the inference that one may draw from the destruction of evidence, that if it was destroyed, it really must have been damaging. And that inference is often more damaging than the evidence, because you can let your imagination wander, and perhaps think the worst about it. So my reaction upon hearing about the gap was: They're really clumsy. They're willing to go to this length to try to hide something. They're just digging the pit deeper.

There were elaborate acoustical tests done with experts; the government spent a fortune on this. We had hearings: Rose Mary Woods testified about how it was all her fault. I think the general assumption was that the president himself did that. The people on the task force who were following these tests and were intimately familiar with all the stops and starts and how long each of them went, they were confirmed in that opinion, because of their view, which may have been motivated by an attitudinal point concerning Nixon, that the president was a notoriously clumsy and physically maladroit person, and that is exactly the way he would have had to do it in order to try to make sure he had gotten it erased: he would have to go back and forth, and back and forth, because he was not a master of technology.

Archibald Cox People have written to me advancing every conceivable explanation. I have no reason to prefer one over another. In the first place, I am illiterate about such machines. It is not implausible to think that the wrong button was pressed, without meaning to erase it. If I were listening to some tape played back on a dictaphone machine, I think the chances are pretty good that I would push the wrong button.

Richard Nixon and I are about the same age; I don't think that he was a mechanical genius, either. So there are only two people who can tell us: Rose Mary Woods and Richard Nixon.

Stephen Bull The erasure occurred precisely the way Rose Woods described it. Here is the reason: She had a tape recorder that I obtained for

° Haldeman was forced to resign on April 29, 1973, effective on the following day.

her. The reason I did was that, originally, there were nine or ten conversations that were subpoenaed, and Rose set about to do the transcripts of them. She was having the darnedest time on this little tape recorder—pushing the button down and typing as fast as she could and then stopping it. So I called the White House Communications Agency and said, "Can you come up with some sort of device that has a foot pedal, like a stenographer's machine?" They came up with an Uher machine.

After the resignation, I was out in San Clemente with him [Nixon]. An enterprising young reporter for the *Santa Ana Register* newspaper ran across a woman who ran a medical transcription service. She had the same Uher machine and she was experiencing erasures. Somehow this reporter learned about it and went over and interviewed her. While he was sitting there, he actually witnessed an erasure taking place. Apparently, what was happening was that there was an inherent malfunction of the machine, so that when it was reversed, it inadvertently activated one of the record heads, which had the effect of erasing. I was one of three suspects in the erasure; the president, Rose Woods, and I had access to the tape. The guy who was after me was Richard Ben Veniste. I remember talking to him in September and October, saying, "Hey, look. Here is a good explanation of what happened." And the special prosecutor's office just rejected any outside explanation. I think that the reason it was rejected was twofold: One, they had already gone public—the erasure itself had become a kind of cause célèbre; secondly, Nixon had resigned the presidency and it almost didn't matter anymore.

Leonard Garment You can't speculate about guilt or innocence when no determination was made; no charges were filed; nobody was indicted; and the experts disagreed. Subsequently, experts said that these fellows missed the point—the machine could have had other problems. I had an experience that may bear on this: My son, who is a concert clarinetist living in Spain, sent me a tape he had made of a collection of solos by an artist who played with Count Basie's band—he stripped out the band music and just had the solos. I was listening to the tape and suddenly—right there—is exactly the same noise I had heard on the 18½-minute tape—a very special noise; it sounds like a rasp, the harshest sound your ear can imagine, a very distinctive sound. It lasted for about a minute and a half and then went back to normal. And I thought, My God! It's the same sound! So I called my son, and he told me there were loose screws in the transcription machine. Now that is exactly the position taken by the Uher people—the manufacturers of the White House machine.

Stephen Bull Common sense tells you that you don't erase 18½ minutes of tape and leave damaging portions at the beginning and the end. If I had done it, that whole tape would never have seen the light of day. It just didn't make sense; either you do it or you don't.

James St. Clair, special counsel to the president We hired an expert from Stanford [University, California], who looked at the equipment and found a defect: the power supply would cut on and off. We were able to make it quite clear to the judge [John Sirica], and whoever else was involved, that this was a very interesting problem—that indeed, if the machine isn't working, and the power supply goes off and on, then you get this blank. It was obvious to me that if someone wants to wipe out the tape, they push a button and it wipes out the whole tape; you don't have this off and on stuff. I don't think the judge wanted to have that opinion. With all due respect, I think he would have preferred that we did, in fact, wipe out portions of the tape. So he let it run over to the grand jury, and the grand jury never did anything about it. We won that one.

Richard Ben Veniste There wasn't sufficient information available to support a prosecution on the tape gap. What was established was that Ms. Rose Woods's explanation of what had occurred was discredited by the scientific panel that came in and essentially invented a new technology. That was an extraordinary process. The inescapable conclusion made by this jointly appointed panel—appointed by the White House and the special prosecutor's office—was that the tape was deliberately erased, that the erasure involved a number of steps, and that those steps were inconsistent with accidental erasure. We sort of narrowed it down to who was responsible, but it would not be fair at this point to speculate on that. But there is a record established showing who had access to the tapes; there were a few contenders.

Jerry Jones In retrospect, it is fairly clear what happened: there was some incriminating conversation on that tape that somebody—either President Nixon or Bob Haldeman, or Rose Mary Woods at their direction—erased. Perhaps they were even thinking about re-recording over it and they weren't able to do it, and then simply ran the eraser over it four or five or ten times, and completely destroyed it; somebody had the tape and listened to it, and there was a problem there, and they erased it. The other thing is, going back to the mind-set, no one really ever thought that those tapes would be taken away from him; no one ever thought that executive privilege would be breached.

19

Why Didn't Nixon Destroy the Tapes?

Stephen Bull I knew about the taping system before it became public. It seems to me that had he destroyed the tapes, it would have appeared that he was destroying any claim to exculpatory evidence, and therefore, would have something to hide. I always believed that the tapes were going to vindicate the president of any involvement in Watergate; I figured he was waiting for John Dean and the others to get way out on a limb, and would plunk a tape down someplace that would prove he [Dean] was lying. If you have evidence that will vindicate you, you don't destroy it. Maybe that was the reason.

John Dean A lot of people have said he could have. I don't think he could have destroyed the tapes at that point. Here's what happened—I haven't looked at this for a long time, but this is generally correct. If you run this to ground, you'll see that it was a sequence of events that followed that prevented him from destroying the tapes. After Butterfield revealed their existence, the Senate sent a subpoena on the tapes and the courts were immediately involved. For Nixon to destroy the tapes he had to order somebody to do it. That person was suddenly going to be obstructing justice, and was going to have to be prepared to go to jail for the president. I'm sure the Secret Service agents who were custodians of the tapes knew that immediately. So what would Nixon do? Go over himself and stack the tapes up on the South Lawn? Not likely. He probably didn't even know physically where they were kept. So if he had even had the passing thought, he would have had to have given orders that would result in other people going to jail—people who might have said, I won't do it.

And as Leonard Garment has said publicly, they always thought they could beat this on executive privilege. I think there was this belief for a long time that this magic of executive privilege would somehow prevent all this from coming out. What they didn't anticipate there was that there was also evidence of criminal behavior and that the court would pierce executive privilege for purposes of a subpoena on a criminal matter. It got out of hand. The real problem was that the Nixon White House wasn't full of a lot of good criminals; they were pretty bungling.

Jerry Jones I felt that once they had been revealed, the president should have destroyed them. I never understood why he didn't. I have always been mystified about what happened there. Here was a brilliant man, who had been through political wars since the mid-forties, who allowed himself to be destroyed by something that he had it in his power to deal with. There are two theories: one is that he feared that the Secret Service had another copy, so if he burned his, bootleg copies would begin to turn up that he couldn't control. I don't believe that there were other copies. The other theory is that he never thought the tapes would be subpoenaed and there was a lot of good stuff there in terms of the historical record that he wanted to preserve and use in writing his memoirs, and maybe it wasn't so bad—he had Dean in there, and he was trying to use the tape system to excuse himself and essentially to put the blame on Dean, or on others. So perhaps he thought there was enough of a trail that he could at least cloud the issue enough so that it wouldn't be a problem.

Fred Fielding From hindsight, there clearly was a window of opportunity. I don't know what the president knew—and when he knew it—about the break-in, but boy—talk about the perfect window of opportunity! Nixon obviously had a longer window of opportunity than we know to destroy the tapes; he knew that they were there. Perhaps he thought that the tapes could never be discoverable by compulsion of law. He may have often forgotten about the system, because if he had really been thinking about it, he never would have said some of the things he said; he is a smart man—a terribly intelligent man.

Archibald Cox Could he have destroyed the tapes secretly? That is most improbable. The volume must have been considerable. They were kept by the Secret Service. In a situation of destruction, the Secret Service and others in the White House would have been aware of it.

If that story got out, it would likely have the effect of the 18½-minute-gap tape [the suspicion as to why he destroyed the tapes]. If he could have cold-bloodedly considered this, he might have said that the suspicions that would have been aroused were worse than revealing the material.

In addition, one must have in mind that destroying evidence is itself a crime. Then, one has to consider what advice he was getting from his lawyers; there is at least some reason to think he may have received pretty categorical assurance that he would win the tapes case.

Charles Wiggins He didn't want to destroy the tapes in a hasty manner when all the precedents would lead him to believe the Congress could not reach this material. If his lawyers advised on the basis of the laws that existed at that time, then they would say: Mr. President, you may retain this material collected in your own office in the White House, free from any interference by the Congress; it's privileged. I think he felt there was no way the Congress would be able to produce it, so there was no need to destroy it. Now, the Congress turned out to be stronger than the president thought. On the other hand, I can understand him believing it was unnecessary to destroy the tapes, because the risk that the Congress would ever receive and listen to them was very remote.

Gerald Warren The man had a great sense of history. Every speech he gave had references to historical figures—people he knew personally or through study. He felt strongly that he had an obligation to history—that the tapes would buttress his views and how he dealt with world leaders. The tapes would make the record clear to future historians as to what really happened during his presidency. I do not think he recognized the danger in the tapes, from those even few conversations that have become so notorious and were so poisonous to his presidency. His overall respect for history is why he kept the tapes.

Bobby Baker When Watergate occurred, I had been a good friend of Bebe Rebozo for many years, and when the question of the tapes came up, Edward Bennett Williams—who had been my lawyer and who liked Nixon—said to me, "As a lawyer, I would be disbarred if I advised President Nixon to burn the tapes. If you want to help the president, go see Bebe and advise him to tell President Nixon that those damn tapes are his, that they are his personal property, and that he ought to go out to the back of the Rose Garden and burn them." I went to Bebe and told this to him, so I was sure that Nixon got this information; anything you told Bebe, Nixon was sure to hear about. I told [Lyndon] Johnson about this, and he said, "That is about the best advice Ed Williams had ever given to anybody." I'll never understand why Nixon was so damn dumb as not to burn the tapes.

H. R. Haldeman John Connally called me one day, here in California, long after I had left [the White House] when he found out about the tapes. He said, "Bob, you have to get hold of the president and you have to tell him to take those tapes and, in the dark of night, have them piled up in the Rose Garden under heavy guard, and in the morning, bring the press corps out to the Rose Garden and have the president come out and say, 'These are the tapes that I had made of all conversations in my offices. They are presidential property; they are invasions of privacy if they are heard by anybody other than me and, therefore, I am now setting them afire." Connally always had a flair for the dramatic.

I told the president what Connally had said. He asked what I thought, and I replied, "I think you ought to hang onto them. They are your tapes— your key to writing the history [of the presidency], and if we ever get into a real bind on this Watergate stuff, they are going to prove what we said— and didn't say." They proved what we did say; they didn't prove what we didn't say. I had not listened to many of the tapes. There were certain, specific ones I did listen to, like the "smoking gun" tape. I realize it's unbelievable today, but I did not think they were a problem; I thought they were a help. At that point, I was on the firing line. I was wrong consistently through this Watergate thing. You make one mistake and it tends to compound itself.

David Wilson I assumed that the tapes would vindicate him—that they were protection against people making false statements of what happened in meetings with him. They would also help him if he wanted to write memoirs. He thought that the tapes would put him in a better light than they, in fact, did; I am sure that he had no inkling how bad it would look when you saw the actual language, and the petty things, and the prejudices. I suspect that he thought he would always be able to control the material.

Leonard Garment Haig, Fred [Buzhardt], and I all agreed that destroying the tapes would create a very strong impression of guilt. On the other hand, there were various people—Agnew, Connally, Nelson Rockefeller—who were calling Nixon in a frenzy, urging that he destroy the tapes. Well, of course, these were the people who were on the tapes, and were terribly compromised by them, so you could understand why they were saying: Destroy the tapes.

H. R. Haldeman Why did I recommend that he not destroy the tapes, which I did? I felt—and I guess I convinced him, and I think he felt anyway—that the tapes would exonerate us; they were our last line of defense as far as the legal case was concerned. But also, he had total control of the tapes, and nobody could come near them. In American history, from George Washington on, the president's papers were the president's papers—and these tapes were his own. We both continued to think that nobody could touch them: they were executive privilege, which Congress couldn't touch; neither of the other branches could. Of course, the Supreme Court saw otherwise, and out they came.

William Ruckelshaus He did not destroy the tapes for two reasons: First, he wanted to write the definitive work on the presidency, and this source of information was a gold mine to him because, at that point, he had sole access to them. He thought he would have the ability to select whatever he wanted out of those conversations, and either make them available or destroy them, or push off access, in time, to the rest. That is not unique among presidents. Second, I think he felt that the tapes were worth a lot of money. All his life, he had been concerned about his financial condition; prior to the time he moved to New York, he never made any money. While he was in New York—and he was not there for very long—he began to accumulate some income. If he wanted to sell the tapes, they were worth a lot of money. If I had known that he was taping our conversations, I would have been a lot more profound.

I also think that one of the reasons he didn't destroy the tapes is that it never really occurred to him that he would have to give them up. He really believed that they were his tapes; they didn't belong to the American people, or they weren't discoverable by Congress, or by the Supreme Court—that in this whole penumbra of separation of powers, that executive privilege would ultimately prevail, and he would be able to keep those tapes.

Samuel Dash There may also be a financial consideration here: there is evidence that a tax attorney told Nixon that the tapes, unlike his papers, did not fall under the IRS restriction for deductions, and that if he kept a complete tape history of his presidency and then donated the material, he would have a remarkably large deduction. But I think that the more important factor was the arrogance of power.

Donald Segretti There was a feeling in the small group around the president—and with the president—that they had a great deal of power; that nobody would ever get to the tapes. I think that maybe they didn't believe that there would be many items on the tapes that would be adverse to them. And, after a period of time, they were reacting to events, and the events overcame them. Also, they did not think downstream: I can remember a discussion at some point—a statement that, "We have certainly played this thing wrong; the handling of it has been terrible." There was a great deal of ego—arrogance. I believe, to some degree, in the "bubble" theory: When you enter that office, you enter an enclosed bubble. You can look out and see what's going on, but you have no real feeling about what is going on in the world; a lot of it doesn't come through that bubble.

Seymour Glanzer He was keeping the tapes as a record and never thought this information was subpoenable, so he didn't, on his own, share the tapes when they were discovered, and he didn't enlighten his lawyers. A lot of people have criticized St. Clair for not listening to the tapes—for accepting Nixon's word that there was nothing important on them. A more resolute lawyer would have said: I don't care what you say; I want to listen to those tapes.

Alexander Butterfield Those tapes were terribly important to Richard Nixon. Also, you feel very powerful at the White House. The whole Watergate question was a thorn in his side. It looked for a time as though it was getting out of hand, but I don't think that they ever thought they wouldn't eventually win. Cover this up; cover that up: this is the White House. You can do anything. He didn't know how big that snowball was—how quickly it was accumulating discontent in America, and how fast it was coming down the hill—until it was too late.

Arnaud de Borchgrave [Adnan] Khashoggi,* Rebozo, and others were telling him to burn the tapes. Nixon told me that he had never thought it would reach that stage where the tapes would be subpoenaed; he had an imperial view of the presidency. He told me in 1980, "Look, I goofed. I made a mistake. I screwed up."

---

* A Saudi Arabian industrialist.

George McGovern I was surprised at how extensive the cover-up was and the degree to which they were willing to go. I have never understood why Nixon didn't try to cut his losses, unless he attached enormous importance to keeping that record for publication purposes, or in postpresidential days. That doesn't seem like enough of a reason, but he may have attached great significance to it and wanted to make sure he never had to surrender the material. In retrospect, it seems so clear now that I am wondering why they didn't consider at the time saying: We made some mistakes; my guys got out of hand, and I was negligent, and did some things I am embarrassed on. I've never understood why they didn't do that and throw themselves on the mercy of the public. I think that would have been the end of it, but Nixon has shown he is a more perceptive politician than I am.

Richard Moore I saw the president a number of times after he left office, and almost each time, he'd say, "By the way, Dick, did you recommend that I destroy the tapes, or were you on the other side?" The fact is that I didn't make any recommendation, but my view was that withdrawing the tapes would be an admission of some kind of guilt—that he had something to hide. I felt that it was proper to put them out in the way we did, but I underestimated the effect of all those obscenities deleted—the language which turned a lot of people off, but which would have been just a nuisance, except for the "smoking gun" tape. In that conversation, the president was not thinking of criminality; he was trying to avoid giving the Democrats a political gift by having the connection to the committee established. He told Pat Gray, on July 6th, to go ahead and find out everything we had to know. The FBI had the damnedest investigation ever, in terms of agents' hours trying to figure out what connections there were. The intention was not to obstruct justice; the intention was to avoid the political embarrassment, but that's not the way the courts saw it.

Jerry Jones When you look at Nixon from the outside, you say: brilliant politician, extremely able political operative, a guy who had seen every possible political situation you can imagine, and a brilliant analyst. And then, he makes every mistake in the book. You then have to ask: Could it be psychological—a death wish in his subconscious that led him to make a series of terrible decisions because he didn't feel he deserved to be president? Or else, were people helping him along in a conspiracy that he didn't really ever see? If he had been sitting there the first day after the break-in and said: Somebody broke into the DNC—why that's incredibly stupid—why did we do that? We are going to win this election; why would we risk that? Fire

Magruder; fire anyone who had anything to do with this; apologize to the DNC; I'll go on television tonight and I'll say: Some of my people did this; I'm horrified; I've canned them and I have asked the attorney general to begin to pursue all legal remedies; this shouldn't happen in American politics; we are going to deal with this—that would have been all of it.

There must have been something that kept him from doing this, so you have to go back to the question: there must have been something before. There was: if he canned those fellows, it would have shown the Ellsberg burglars—the Plumbers group. Would it have shown some of the other things their little secret service had going there? And would there have been a political problem? Yes. Were the people involved—like Magruder, Dean, and Mitchell—operating from something Nixon asked them do so? Perhaps. So when he made a judgment—or didn't make a judgment—you have to assume that he was looking at a picture none of the rest of us had, and that he was making rational decisions, as he saw them, trying to make the best decisions, given what he knew.

Then, you have to construct what he could have known that led him to make those decisions, and the obvious answer is that either he ordered the break-in, or else, if he had turned Magruder, Dean, and Mitchell, and others out—and turned them over—what would they have said that would have injured him more? Therefore, he needed to protect them, and so he took a course that protected them, which—in protecting them—killed himself in the end. My experience tells me that he knew something—that he was making decisions that were rational to him, based on what made sense to him. I don't think that he made stupid or unanalyzed decisions; so one has to assume there were things blocking him from doing what, in retrospect, would have called for a course of action. Why didn't he burn the tapes? There is a rational reason he has yet to tell us.

Kenneth Rush He could have destroyed the tapes. I urged him to do it. When I was to go over to the White House as his counselor in December 1973, I was going to have the tapes destroyed the minute I got there.

20

Why Didn't Nixon Deal with the Problem Sooner?

William Ruckelshaus He may have underestimated its importance; he may have known how deep the knowledge and involvement in the break-in went in his administration, even though he may not have known of the break-in, and found it unacceptable that he would have to let people like Haldeman, Ehrlichman, and Mitchell go. Clearly, when something like that happens, the best thing to do is to immediately excise the people who were involved—no matter how close they are to you—assuming, obviously, that you are not yourself involved, and do it quickly, no matter how much it hurts to do it.

Richard Helms At that short compass, any thoughtful person would say, Well, hell. This is some kind of political caper; it's going to be totally dis-owned and thrown overboard, and it's not going to amount to a hill of beans.

It was only President Nixon's decision, obviously, not to make some kind of statement and end the thing in twenty-four hours that caused it to go for-ward with what turned out to be a big cover-up. This was one of the oddest things: that President Nixon, who was so critical of the competence and intelligence of other parts of the executive branch of government, would make a mistake as really stupid as this one. Because if he had said, This is a political caper that these people at CRP have perpetrated and I disown the whole thing; it won't happen again, this thing would have been over in twenty-four hours, except for the trial of the burglars, who actually were performing a criminal act and had been caught. Politically, I couldn't have imagined it would have anywhere near the effect that it finally had.

Alexander Butterfield He could have said, early on, "Look, this is what I did." When guys started going to jail, that's when I sort of turned on him. The public can be very forgiving. He could have said, "Yes. We did these things; we have been concerned with secrecy," and he wouldn't even have had to say he directed it. There would be this tremendous uproar, but it would only last two or three weeks. He could really have gone down as a great president, because he did so many good things domestically as well as in foreign affairs. So I changed during that year [1973], when I went before the [Senate Select] Committee [on Watergate].

Not only was I helping them sort things out, and telling them how the staff worked—the relationships aide-to-aide and president-to-aide—I made it clear that he was a detail person; he insisted on which pictures hung in the West Wing Lobby, which we redid during his presidency; he is the guy who took the swimming pool out and gave it [the space] to the press. The press used to sit in the lobby; that's why they built the press room—to get those crummy-looking press guys, oftentimes with their wrinkled suits, out as dignitaries were coming in to see the president; it wasn't a fitting environment. He did pay attention to affairs of state, because he was a twenty-four-hour president, but he would decide what day King Timahoe got a bath; whether it would be this Thursday or that Thursday. I am trying to point out that the man ran everything.

Herbert Klein I suggested that some of the staff be fired, but it wasn't done, I think, because there was a great deal of confidence on the part of the president and others that—there had been similar problems with Lyndon Johnson and Jack Kennedy, and previous presidents—if you just weathered it out, it would go by and there was no need to wipe it all clean in that kind of dramatic form. I think it was a case of underestimating a Democratic Congress, and also the press, and the press was accentuated because Woodward and Bernstein were pretty much unknown, and yet had come forth with all of this, so others were being asked by their editors, "How come you didn't know anything about that?" The whole press situation fell completely apart; it was a pretty disgraceful chapter in the relationship between the White House press and the press secretary.

Donald Segretti It could have been managed very early on, so that his presidency would have survived. He would have had to stand up and say, What I know about the break-in, how it happened, who was involved. I suspect he would have mentioned his good friend John Mitchell, maybe Mr. Haldeman, maybe others around him. He may not have been prepared to do that—for all sorts of reasons, like loyalty, friendship. Also, they were so close to him that he would be tainted, too. Maybe it would not have swallowed him as it did. But it would have taken a very courageous individual to do that.

Dwight Chapin There is some tenet here—some axiom: if he's dealing with things *out here,* he is one kind of master; if it is an attack on one of his people, or a leak, he shifts, and is less skillful. It becomes personalized; you have a different skill level—a different intellectual basis. It may go back to Hiss, to Helen Gahagan Douglas—a setting up of patterns. Why doesn't he cut his losses [on Watergate]? What would Eisenhower have done? Bang! Get him out of here! Save the presidency!

William Rusher If, early on, he had said, "I don't know what the hell all this is about, but I don't like it; I won't permit it; and I have appointed some special prosecutor who hates my guts to clean it out; let the chips fall where they may; if it turns out that Pat [Mrs. Nixon] was involved, she can go to prison, too," I think that the American people might have taken it very well. In retrospect, I bet he would do this if he had his life to live over. Of course, if he had been a moral man, he would have done it instinctively.

Bobby Baker Had Nixon said: The buck stops here. These guys work for me; they were stupid, and I'm stupid, please forgive me—had he had Herb Klein and Bob Finch at the top of his inner circle at the time of Watergate, they would have been smart enough for him to have survived. But Haldeman did not have what I call "the Washington smarts." And I could never understand Haig being there—you have Colson and Haig; those were the kinds of personalities Nixon didn't need.

H. R. Haldeman I should have put a duty officer on it and said, Find out who ordered this. We have to fire him and find out why he did it. We have to disclaim any involvement in it, and nail whoever was involved. That is what we should have done, and would have done, but we didn't do that. I didn't think it was a problem; I didn't worry about it . . . and it went down a hill in a hand basket fast, from there. But it could have stopped, and should have been stopped.

Vernon Walters He [Nixon] asked me afterward, "What should I have done?" and I said, "If you had said, Ehrlichman, Haldeman, and other people who are loyal to me have exceeded the bounds of what is permissible and I have been required to request their resignations. . . . " The truth will out. People have found out that he was not threatening American democracy or freedom; he was not planning to violate the Constitution, or start a war, to save his own position. He was in a tough spot, with some stupid subordinates who had made serious mistakes, and he, out of loyalty, had supported them. That is what happened at Watergate.

Arnaud de Borchgrave I went to see Ron Ziegler in January 1974 and said, "It's all over for the president"—I had attended a meeting of *Newsweek's* senior editors and they said, "It's all over. They have him cold; they have all the goods necessary to bring him down, but it is going to be strung out." Ziegler replied, "Arnaud, I don't know what you are talking about; what you are saying is absolute nonsense." Much later, when I talked to Nixon in 1980, I told him about my conversation with Ziegler. He said that Ron had never mentioned it to him. He said if Ron had told him what I had said, he would have taken it very seriously. Who knows? Things might have turned out very differently.

21

Damage Control: Finally Letting White House Staff Go

In mid-April, the president learned from high Justice Department officials that Dean and CRP Deputy Director Jeb Magruder had implicated Haldeman and Ehrlichman in several Watergate-related acts. Haldeman was said to have received transcripts resulting from the May break-in, and that he controlled a secret $350,000 fund, while Ehrlichman was implicated in the Fielding break-in and in the destruction of material from Hunt's White House safe.

After hearing this, Mr. Nixon pondered whether he should now ask Haldeman and Ehrlichman to leave the administration. The latter were reluctant to do so, and suggested that Dean be fired. Nixon wanted to retain his two closest aides, but was fearful that if fired, Dean would tell everything he knew and implicate the president in the cover-up. Thus, on April 29, Nixon met separately at Camp David with Haldeman and Ehrlichman and extracted their resignations, which were announced to the nation in an Oval Office broadcast at nine the next evening.

Dwight Chapin I had been in Ireland. My plane landed on a Sunday and I took a White House car to the office to check my mail. At about four-thirty in the afternoon, the phone rings; it is John Dean saying he wants to see me the next morning. He comes in and says, "Have you given any thought to what you are going to do?" I said, "John, what are you trying to tell me?" He says, "I've gone out to California and talked to Segretti." I call Haldeman and he says, "Come up and see me at Camp David tomorrow." I was blown away. The next day, I fly up to Camp David, and I am informed that this guy, Sam Ervin, is going to hold hearings, and that Colson and I are potential public relations embarrassments and that it would probably make sense for us to move out of the White House. I am thirty-one—still a young person. This is tragic news. I'm crying; Haldeman is crying. I go into the bathroom. Kleindienst is crying. It is a mess, and I don't know about any of the Watergate stuff.

Terrence O'Donnell Bob was a tough taskmaster, but he had a good sense of humor; I got to like him a lot. I was shocked and disappointed when I learned he was going to resign. It's not that it came without some warning, because the drumbeat—and the press coverage in the weeks preceding the resignation—was ever-increasing. But I was still very inexperienced, and I didn't think that someone who was really the number-two person in government—aside from the vice-president—would ever have to resign.

Richard Kleindienst I had made up my mind, as a result of conversations with George Shultz, Barry Goldwater, and a couple of other people in government, about the fact that I had to resign. I was going to see the president on Monday. On Sunday,° when I got home from church, I had a call to come to the White House and take the helicopter to Camp David. I walked into the room and said, Mr. President, I'm glad to see you, because I have something to tell you." I told him what I wanted to say, and he replied, "That is what I wanted to talk to you about. I am announcing the resignations of Haldeman, Ehrlichman, and Dean, and I want to announce your resignation at the same time." I said, "You can't possibly have me do that." And he was very, very distraught, and said, "You've got to do this thing as a personal favor. This is my last chance to start over again."

Unbeknownst to me, Elliot Richardson was nearby and had overheard this conversation. He and I left that meeting to go down to Washington in the helicopter. I had to write my resignation statement, which they never published. And Richardson said something to me I'll never forget as long as I live: "Kleindienst, I wouldn't have done what you did for that man, or for anybody else on the face of this earth."

Nixon wanted a fresh start. I had to recuse myself from any participation

° April 29, 1973.

in Watergate so I was, in one respect, half an attorney general. I think that in his own mind, looking at it from his interest and not without regard to mine, he could have let me resign or done that one or two days before. But I think he had an overwhelming desire, in terms of his own self-interest, to start all over again; it was not fair to me. But I was a Cabinet officer, and a longtime political friend of the man who was president of the United States. He's distraught; his government is in peril; and I guess, in a situation like that, while the impulse would be to say: The hell with you, Mr. President, that is not fair to me, and I'm not going to agree to it—you are part of a government that's beleaguered.

John Dean When I was on my way out of office, the person I recommended was someone I relied on tremendously during the whole time—and I had tried to do this in a way that wouldn't compromise him. This person was Henry Petersen, assistant attorney general who headed the Justice Department's Watergate inquiry. Everyone thinks that I got FBI reports. The FBI reports were meaningless to me. They were months after the fact. You couldn't anticipate anything from them. It was Henry Petersen who kept me fully informed, and he knew exactly what he was doing; he was not investigating everything he could investigate. The whole Segretti thing—that sat around and around and really didn't get to the criminal stage out of Washington; it came out of Florida, with a U.S. attorney down there who was the one who prosecuted Segretti. So Henry Petersen was someone who was willing to look the other way.

I had told Henry right after the fact, "This is serious, Henry; the White House can't take an open investigation. It will wander into things that are disastrous," and he didn't need to be told more. I had met with Henry over the years and one of the things we talked about was the mentality at the White House—that somehow a case could be fixed. You couldn't fix a case once it was in process. They don't go away; you can't turn them off like that. At one point, Chuck Colson came to me to do something with some labor person, and Henry and I had these conversations that you can't turn off an investigation once it's started. I understood that perfectly. Henry had been in the criminal division for years. Everyone says Johnson was the master at turning off these cases and he could control the Department of Justice. Henry said, "This is not possible, John," and he gave me examples.

So, throughout Watergate, the person I principally looked to was Henry Petersen: What do we do now? I've got a person who is going to be asked a question in front of the grand jury; that question is going to open up something that is not really relevant to the Watergate break-in. What do we do?

*Among the measures that President Nixon undertook was the recruitment of
personnel to deal with his mounting problems.*

Alexander Haig I was living at Fort McNair—back at the trade I loved—
and happy as a pig in the sunshine. I started getting calls from Ron Ziegler,
commiserating on the problems in the White House—the president's
plight—and what he should do. At first, I looked on it as an old friend calling an old friend. Then, when I was on my way to Fort Benning for a conference, the night before I left, I got a call that did worry me a little bit: Ziegler
was saying, "The president wants to know what you think." I wasn't that
close to the president then. Henry made sure of that; nobody who worked
for him was close to the president—I don't mean that to be as nasty as it
sounds.

When I got to Fort Benning, there was a call during the first course of
the luncheon; it was Haldeman. That was it. And believe me, I said, "No." I
said it would be wrong for the president, and wrong for the country, for a
military man to be in there in the current environment. And besides, I had
just spent a year trying to get out of the White House. I said, "Bob, you have
to go back to the president"—I knew the president was listening on the
line—"and tell him that if he wants this done, I will do it, because I am a
soldier. But I prefer not to, and if I do it, it should be temporary." He called
me back during dessert, so they made it appear that they were really discussing the question, but I think the president had made up his mind. There
has been a lot of rumor and innuendo that, "Haig was ambitious; he wanted
the job all along. " That is just crap. But be that as it may, my other mandate
was that I wouldn't touch Watergate; I didn't know anything about it. But
within twenty-four hours, I was up to my neck in Watergate. You couldn't
run the country; you couldn't do the president's business without dealing
with Watergate.

James St. Clair I had taken my family to Florida. When I got to the hotel
room, the phone was ringing. It was Haig, asking me to come up to Washington right away; I didn't even empty my suitcase. Haig wanted to talk to
me about representing the president. He wanted me to have some sense as
to what would be involved, and what some of the documents looked like,
because some of them, standing alone, were rather tough, particularly some
of those with John Dean.

Herbert Klein A few months after I left the White House, I was asked to
come and talk with Haig and Ziegler about Watergate. I went to Key Bis-

cayne and had dinner with them. The idea was, would I take a leave from my new job and come back to the White House and handle only Watergate matters; I would be given full control over everything communicated on Watergate. I said that I was in a new job and would probably turn it down, but I would be willing to talk to the president. So we got on *Air Force One*, flying to Washington, and the time came to talk to him. Sitting down with the president and saying "no" to him is not very easy. To my surprise, he did not pressure me at all; he said, "I know that you have a new job. It would help if you could come back and handle this, but if you don't, I sure understand." He gave me every opportunity to decline if I chose to. I've always remembered that as his being someone who was pretty thoughtful; it was a different side than you sometimes hear of about him.

Kenneth Rush In December 1973, Al Haig called and said that the president wanted me to come to the White House to be his counselor in charge of everything having to do with Watergate. I spoke to the president and told him that I hadn't practiced law in years and had never practiced criminal law. He replied that the lawyers could handle these matters and would report to me; this would allow him and Haig to concentrate on running the country. I asked Nixon, "Have you told Henry?"—Kissinger was then engaged in shuttle diplomacy in the Middle East. The president said, "Who is more important, me or Henry?" I answered, "You, of course." I told Henry about this conversation and informed him that I did not want the job. Henry prevailed on the president by saying that he could not conduct his shuttle activity without me at the department, so the president decided that the country came first, and I stayed at State. If I had gone to the White House, it would have been the worst thing that ever happened to me.

Robert Bork I came down to Washington on June 16, 1973. Within a month—maybe less—Al Haig called and asked me to drop by his office. I did not know Haig at the time. I went over there, and he asked me to resign and become Nixon's chief defense attorney. He was very persuasive; he made it sound like the republic was going to burn unless I took over. Their legal operation was in vast confusion. He knew that I had organized large cases when I was an antitrust lawyer in private practice. I had just enough sense to say, "Give me twenty-four hours." I went home and talked to my wife, and to my Yale colleague, Alex Bickel. The upshot was that it was a job I did not want.

In the morning, I saw Richardson and discussed it with him. I then went over to see Haig, and gave him five reasons: one was that I would have to hear the tapes—I can't take the job if I don't know what the facts are. The answer to that was, "No. Nobody can hear the tapes." I remember saying, "How will people know that I'm in charge of the legal operation? Will you give me a title?" Haig responded, "No. You'll be the only one with access to the president." I said, "That's wonderful. If I give him an answer he doesn't like then I won't have access; I'll be sitting there with a phone that doesn't ring." Haig said, "That's very perceptive of you."

James St. Clair I met with the president in California for an hour on New Year's Eve. It was getting close to midnight, and he and Haig and I had a drink, and then I went back to Boston the next day. Nixon was in full command of his faculties; there were no tears in his eyes. I recall his making it clear to me that if I were to represent him, it would only be in his capacity as president; he wanted to make sure that I realized I was representing the presidency, not him personally.

Samuel Dash I think that St. Clair was so delighted to represent the president that he did not treat him as an ordinary client. If I had the president as a client, I would have gone to him and tried to find out everything I needed [to know] to make sound decisions, and then give him very hard advice. St. Clair didn't try to do that. The information I received was that he wasn't talking to the president; he was getting his information through Haig. I would never represent a client if I could not talk to him alone.

William Rusher At one point, when Watergate was getting pretty thick, I was on the TV program "The Advocates," on PBS. I was getting well known as a kind of conservative bully boy of a legal disposition, and a fellow in the White House, who had come from the FBI, called me on some pretext and said—as if it had just occurred to him—"I don't suppose you would be interested in becoming special counsel to Mr. Nixon?" I felt the wings of history rustling by. I replied that I had been out of the practice of law for about twenty years, so he let it pass. Shortly afterward, James St. Clair was picked as Nixon's lawyer. Who knows what might have happened if only I had said yes.

22

The Atmosphere of Watergate

Gerald Warren I was in the center of that storm: things happened during Watergate that hadn't happened before. Rumors would be floated on the Hill [Capitol Hill] and be reported on the radio wire. These rumors were read on local radio stations without being checked out.

Lawrence Higby It's hard for us today to remember the almost super-charged environment that we all lived in and acted in on a day-to-day basis—the way we talked; the way we conducted business; our views of what was happening to our country. Way up at the top in Washington was this white-hot debate. The president would go to bed every night and there were people out there marching with candles. Every time he tried to speak, people were shouting and saying terrible things about him; spitting on his kids. There was no sense of civility in the country.

Alexander Haig At that time, the president was still very popular out on the hustings, but not so in Washington, where the press hated him. The press has always hated Nixon; that goes way back. He'd be the first to say that he contributed to it. I don't think anyone would have laid a glove on Richard Nixon had he not had those tapes. At the time, I had no idea that there were tapes.

Robert Reisner You didn't have the sense that Nixon was ordering things. He was removed; he was more concerned with policy. It was the few people who were around him. Haldeman was the voice of the White House; he was a very severe person and presence.

Stephen Bull Surprisingly, the Watergate period was a fascinating time—almost an enjoyable time, in its own perverse way. You hated to see what was happening to the president, and the presidency, and to the people—you never knew what the next day's headlines would bring. But there was humor—a lot of macabre humor—and there were good people around there. John Ehrlichman was one of the favorites, and although he came across on television during the Watergate hearings as this hard-nosed, grim, stern visage that peered out at the American people, he was really a good guy; he had a good sense of humor: if there was a practical joke someplace, even though he would not precipitate it, he'd probably go along if it was worthwhile. There didn't seem to be a great deal of internal jockeying for position; there seemed to be a pretty good sense of loyalty to the president. Most people thought they were going to spend a short time there and then go someplace else, so they weren't looking to walk over someone else—or for self-aggrandizement.

Susan Porter Rose Watergate was like trying to grasp a cloud; there was nothing to get hold of. There was a great element of disbelief as Mr. Nixon's presidency was winding down. I felt resentment toward some of his staff; I felt he was really ill advised. I am highly critical of any staff person who would not counsel the president to take the straight and narrow.

Frederic V. Malek We couldn't imagine that the president wouldn't survive; none of us had the foresight to think of that. I believed in the power of the presidency; I was awed by the presidency. I had grown up in a lower-middle-class, ethnic environment near Chicago; I'd gone to West Point; I believed in following the directions of the leader—the chain of command—and I certainly didn't think that the president could do anything wrong.

William Saxbe As the months went on, Nixon became more difficult to talk to. I had a lot of questions—like the ITT case—that I wanted to talk to him about. But all he wanted to do was talk about his problems and how he was being put upon. These conversations were a waste of time, so I would go to see Al Haig. I don't think that the president was too rational in those days; he was filled with self-pity; he rambled. I had other problems: I was having problems with Kissinger on wiretaps. I felt that it was important to discuss this with the president, but I just couldn't get through to him. I could get to see him, but I couldn't get any sense out of him.

Gerald Warren In his dealings with me, the president always acted in an honorable and professional way; he did not seem preoccupied by Watergate. I thought his work with Kissinger in the Middle East was extraordinary. There was a lot going on that was beneficial, not just to the country [the United States], but to the world.

William Ruckelshaus Haig would call me during this Watergate period and fly into a rage over something that he alleged Cox to be doing, and I'd say, "Al, for God's sake, I don't know anything about this. Calm down." He would just carry on. Then he would call me back about five minutes later and say, "I apologize for that outburst, but you can guess who was standing in the room." It's conceivable that he wasn't telling the truth—that he was by himself, and he realized that he hadn't acted very well, and saw that as an excuse—but he did it more than once.

Alexander Haig There was hardly a day when we didn't have to put out a major bonfire. *Time* and *Newsweek* had the habit of calling me on Friday night and saying, "General Haig, we have this report that Richard Nixon and Bebe Rebozo own a bridge on Paradise Island, in the Bahamas, and have been collecting a dollar for every car going over it." I said, "You can't mean that." They said, "Absolutely." I would then tell them I needed to check the story out; I'd get the president out of bed—or whatever was necessary—and shoot the thing down. Then I would call up the magazine and they would say, "It's too late. We've already finished the story." I'd say, "Are you going to print a retraction?" "Oh no! we can't do that."

On another occasion, *Time* called me that they had just had word that the Teamsters [Union] had just bought the president's house in San Clemente; they claimed to have the story on unimpeachable sources and would run it on Monday morning. I then worked with the lawyers all of Friday night to put together the evidence that this wasn't true, and when I called *Time*, I was told, "It's too late. It's gone to press." I don't think our society has ever been so enfeebled by hatred and bias against a president. I am not trying to say he was innocent; he wasn't. But the blood lust was incredible.

Bob Woodward There was so much there, so much buried, so much secret. If the story had gone along for months and months with no new revelations, it would have died. But the mine was deep and rich, because there was so much going on that was secret, illegal, improper, ugly, embarrassing. If there hadn't been that, there wouldn't have been the story.

Robert Reisner On October 11, 1972, I was in Indianapolis [Indiana] with Clark MacGregor, the campaign chairman. He was having a press conference with Mayor [Richard] Hudnut, and this advance man came up to me and said, "The White House is on the phone; they want to tell you to get MacGregor on the telephone with them." I said, "We can't do that; he is talking to thirty reporters." I picked up the phone, and it was Ron Ziegler. He was an aggressive guy, and he said, "You have to get MacGregor on the phone—now." I said, "I can't. Why don't you tell me what you want?" Ziegler said, "I want to know how he is handling this Watergate thing." I said to myself: this is October 11—the break-in had been in June. We had questions asked of us every day. Woodward and Bernstein were national figures by this time. What on earth are these guys in the White House doing?

Gerald R. Ford In the last three or four months, he was very critical of some of his critics—that they didn't appreciate that he was so preoccupied with foreign policy and big decisions on China and his negotiations with [Soviet General Secretary Leonid] Brezhnev, and he didn't have time to focus on domestic politics and Watergate. He really believed that he was misunderstood.

Thomas Moorer Once the president was very involved in Watergate, he would sit at the NSC meetings apparently in heavy thought until someone mentioned foreign policy, and it was just like giving him a needle; he would spark right up and get right in the middle of the conversation.

Robert Odle, Jr. When Haldeman or another staff person went to Nixon with an issue he was not in charge of, or interested in, he did not think the issue through. He never was in charge on Watergate, and didn't want to deal with it. If you could listen on a tape of Kissinger talking to him about China and a tape of someone talking to him about Watergate, you would hear two different Nixons: in the former case, a Nixon very much in charge; and in the latter, a Nixon nervously reacting to something he didn't have to do with, didn't understand, or want to have anything to do with. When he did not want to deal with an issue, he was not the most pleasant guy in the world.

Terrence O'Donnell After Bob Haldeman resigned and I was working in the scheduling office, I was personally concerned about leaving at the time Bob left, because Watergate was in high gear. As a lawyer and a young person without a job knocking on a door, and they say, "What did you do?" and you say, "Well, I worked for Bob Haldeman," you might have a problem in getting a job. So I told General Haig that I wanted to stay on board and he said he had heard good things about me and he knew my father, so he would be very happy to keep me on. But if I didn't mind, he wouldn't keep me in his immediate office, because he thought that my last two bosses were, unfortunately, "going to the slam," as he put it—and he was right. My time in the scheduling office was frustrating because we kept coming up with ideas to get the president out, and he—as time went on—was preoccupied with Watergate, and it was harder and harder to get him out, around the country. Finally, it got so bad that there were not too many places that he could go and receive a warm reception, or could go without great risk.

William Saxbe It was a regular Cabinet meeting. The president was going on and on about a rather involved program for an injection of money to pick up the economy—there had been a substantial decline in 1974. It was proper to be concerned, but things were collapsing on an almost daily basis, and it looked like a conviction on the impeachment. So, as Nixon was going on, I said, "It is great to talk about what is going to happen next year, but I think we should talk about what is going to happen next week." I'll never forget this: he looked at his papers, put them under his arm, and walked out of the room; he never said a word. Maybe I shouldn't have said it, but there was a real crisis in government.

23

Corruption Charges Against the Vice-President, His Resignation, and Choosing His Successor

Amid the Watergate turmoil, charges of corruption came to light concerning Vice-President Agnew.

Alexander Haig I had a call from Attorney General Richardson that he had to see me right away. He came to my office and said that in all his days as a state prosecutor he had never run across as open-and-shut a case of multiple crimes as what he had on Agnew; he said that there were forty indictable crimes. I said to myself: God! We've got the worst of both worlds: a president who is on an impeachment trail, and a vice-president who is guilty of felonies. We have a double converging impeachment, where the results of a popular election won overwhelmingly by Richard Nixon would fall into the hands of the Democratic Party. The Speaker of the House* was at that time under a doctor's care for alcoholism; I realized that the Democrats knew this, as did the _Washington Post_. Agnew was no Boy Scout; he was one tough guy; he didn't want to give up that office—and everything he had built up in his life—without a struggle. But the evidence was overwhelming: he took money in his vice-presidential office, in envelopes, repeatedly. The case drained Elliot Richardson, psychologically

* Carl Albert (D-Okla.).

and physically, to the point where he was almost a vegetable. In my view, that probably affected his handling of the Cox situation.

Stephen Bull His access to the president was somewhat limited. I remember seeing a one-page summary in the president's out-box sometime during the summer of 1973 of all the charges pending against the vice-president. I knew of all this for almost a month before it became public. It ate me up inside; I could hardly sleep; there was no one I could talk to, and I knew that this thing was going to happen at some point. I remember feeling relieved the day the *Washington Post* carried a banner headline revealing the details of the allegations.

Raymond Price When Agnew's troubles—which we had not known about—began to surface, Nixon was reluctant to believe it; he told me that Agnew had looked him in the eye and said that the charges weren't true. With what Nixon had been through himself over the years, he was reluctant to disbelieve his vice-president, and he knew that many people in Maryland—including the prosecutors—were out for Agnew's scalp. He also didn't have that much trust in Richardson, who saw Agnew as an adversary. But finally, the evidence was conclusive and Agnew had to go.

William Ruckelshaus The case was overwhelming, and got worse and worse for him the longer it went on. We took the point of view of devil's advocate in the Justice Department; we tried to make sure that the witnesses were absolutely impenetrable—that their stories held up. We used lie detector tests and all kinds of ways of trying to break them down, just to be sure that we weren't unjustly accusing the vice-president, and their stories just continued to strengthen.

AGNEW'S INDICTMENT

Robert Bork Richardson took me over to the White House and I did most of the arguing about why we had to indict Agnew. He had to resign; otherwise, he was going to jail. The Department of Justice was wavering about whether there was a constitutional problem in indicting him; the White House was against the indictment because Agnew's core constituency was the same as Nixon's, and they figured that they would alienate whatever support Nixon had left. But once it came out that he was on the take, I thought he had to be indicted.

David Keene Agnew's defense plan was to be impeached. He sent a letter to Carl Albert, but it was given to Rodino,° and Rodino read the letter and said, "Tell him to fuck himself." That was the reaction, so we knew that wasn't going to happen; they knew they were going to get him anyway. Agnew felt he was a victim of a conspiracy, in the sense that the charges against him were the result of his having acted no differently than any other politician in the Maryland system had, and that he was caught on the cusp of a whole different set of values coming in. That you were judging people by rules that didn't apply at the time the actions took place. He was very bitter about all that.

But he is not bitter anymore. He saw me last year and said, "You know, you can never escape your past. I was in Copenhagen on business and I was walking down the street, and this guy comes walking toward me—this middle-aged guy who looks like he was the last guy to escape from Haight-Ashbury before it collapsed—and all of a sudden he froze and looked at me, and he pointed at me, and he said, 'You're Spiro Agnew!'" And Agnew said, "Yes, I am." And the guy put out his hand and said, "Lay some rhetoric on me, man."

Howard Phillips Agnew was a man of extraordinary pride; if anything, that was his great weakness. There was a lack of humility, which brought him down. That lack of humility and his pride made him view the idea that he might spend time in prison as the worst possible outcome. He felt that the least dishonorable way out was to resign; he was torn by that decision. Frankly, I believe that he was betrayed by his lawyers; it was partly because he had not played in the big league before and was not getting a level of advice that would have led him in the right direction. The reason he was indicted was that people wanted to get at Nixon, and in order to get at Nixon, they had to get Agnew first. Nixon was a fool to let that go forward. He encouraged the harassment of Agnew; he thought he was getting the heat off himself if he put heat on Agnew. It was the old story of the crocodile eating you last—but the crocodile has a big appetite.

AGNEW'S RESIGNATION

William Ruckelshaus Agnew either had to plead nolo [contendere] or go through the trial, which would have greatly embarrassed him and the

---

° Peter Rodino, member, U.S. House of Representatives (D-N.J.), and chairman of the House Judiciary Committee.

administration and—I am convinced—would have ended in his conviction. There was great consternation in the White House; it was the last thing in the world they needed, given the progress of the Watergate investigation, and all the furor it created: to have a greatly weakened vice-president, and one—as the evidence began to build—who was clearly involved in activities outside the law, thereby jeopardizing his continued presence in the administration. I supposed that there is another side to this, because, as he became weakened and left the administration, it strengthened the president in one sense, because there was nobody behind him, at least until Ford was selected. Of course, it wasn't in the interest of the president to have the vice-president be the first in history to be driven from office.

Howard Phillips My relationship with Vice-President Agnew had become closer. I was the one with whom he chose to spend his resignation day. He invited me to join him, and we went down to Trader Vic's.* I saw a man in extraordinary pain, who realized that he had held the whole world seemingly in his hands and—as a result of personal, moral imperfections—had let it slip away. There was tremendous pain there. I sat with him for about three hours as he reviewed the events and eased his pain with gin.

David Keene The day after Agnew resigned, he called me into his office at about nine in the morning. He said, "We were riding in this morning, and one of the Secret Service guys told me that you are thinking about going back to Wisconsin." I said, "Yes, I am thinking about this." He said, "You can't leave this town under these circumstances. You tell me what you want to do, and I'll spend as much time as I have to, and do whatever I can, but don't leave town; stay here." That was pretty good advice—for a guy who had just resigned to be asking his security detail: "What do you hear about people? and What do I need to do?"

Can you imagine Nixon doing that? In fact, one of the conditions of Agnew's resignation was that everybody who worked for him had to be taken care of. Nixon didn't understand that.

A day or two after Agnew resigned, I had lunch with the *Wall Street Journal* reporter who had broken the story on Agnew. He said, "You know, I covered Maryland for a long time. For all I know, it's probably true that Agnew was the most honest governor that served in that state in the entire time I covered it. But he was the only one that went to Washington." On the other

---

* A Washington restaurant featuring Oriental-style cuisine.

hand, I am certain that they had enough evidence to get him on some things—which is different than saying he was necessarily a criminal. But also, a lot of what was publicly talked about was overblown, and Agnew was, throughout his career, used by people in Maryland. One of his weaknesses was that his highest value was loyalty; once somebody had been loyal to him they could abuse the trust and the loyalty, and did. I think he was guilty of some crimes, and that it was the result of the system, and that the overall case was way overblown.

Richardson didn't like Agnew; they were ideological enemies—Agnew used to do great imitations of Richardson. I am one who really believes in the politics of class, and Elliot Richardson probably thought that anyone like Spiro Agnew was probably slimy, and certainly tacky, and didn't deserve to be in any high office.

I remember when Elliot ran a few years ago for the Senate in Massachusetts and lost the primary, and lost sixty points during the campaign. A friend of mine had run the campaign, and he told me that by the time the people went to the polls, they realized it really was Elliot Richardson that was running, and unless they sang in the Episcopal Church choir, he didn't have the faintest intention of representing them anywhere, or anytime—and that is Elliot when he is sober. The fact of the matter was that if you put yourself in the position of a Brahmin from Massachusetts, as he was and is, and think about his political career and then you have him look at Spiro Agnew, he would be disgusted by Agnew—before he knew what Agnew did or didn't do. This is a group of people who wouldn't hire the Irish, let alone a bunch of Greeks.

CHOOSING A NEW VICE-PRESIDENT

Stephen Bull My guess is that if it had been left to Richard Nixon, John Connally would have been his nominee. For political reasons, Ford could be more helpful; impeachment proceedings were starting to develop back then.

Yuri Barsukov Ford was not known to the Soviet leaders, and they were surprised when President Nixon nominated him as his vice-president. After the resignation, they were surprised that they had to deal with Gerald Ford as president.

William Ruckelshaus It was clear that the president—as weakened as he was—had to get someone who could be confirmed quickly by the Congress. That was why he chose Jerry [Gerald R.] Ford. Based on conversations I had with the president, his first choice would have been John Connally. He sang Connally's praises; he liked his strength, his independence, his self-confidence, his ease with people, as opposed to the president's unease. The president admired captains of industry.

Robert Hartmann Nixon had [member, U.S. Senate] Hugh Scott [R-Pa.] and Ford come to the White House for the stated reason of discussing the mechanics of the Twenty-fifth Amendment in submitting his vice-presidential nominee to the Congress. Nixon saw each man separately. When Scott left, he invited Ford in, and started the conversation by praising [Henry] Kissinger. He said that the United States must continue to seek rapprochement with the Soviet Union, and that in picking a vice-president, he must be sure that the man was in agreement with his foreign policy; he wanted to be reasonably sure that if the vice-president succeeded to the presidency, he would keep Henry on—at least through the transition period.

Gerald R. Ford It's my understanding that President Nixon preferred John Connally; he had very strong feelings toward him. But Connally had the milk scandal, and lots of Democrats didn't like the fact that he had switched parties. There was no question that Connally would have great difficulty in getting confirmed. I was very sympathetic toward him; I told him before I became vice-president that if he ran in 1976, I would support him.

The other potential [vice-presidential candidate], Nelson Rockefeller, would have had difficulty in being confirmed because of conservative Republicans. The third alternative, [Ronald] Reagan, would have had trouble because the liberal Republicans would have opposed him. So the three people at the top of the ladder all had problems in being confirmed. On the other hand, the House Republicans all signed a petition—which I had nothing to do with—which they sent to Nixon, urging that he nominate me. Probably the most persuasive reason why I was nominated was Speaker [of the House] Carl Albert's [D-Okla.] saying to Nixon: "If you want somebody who can get confirmed most quickly, it's Jerry Ford."

Alexander Haig Nixon had already committed to John Connally to have him on the ticket for the second term. After Agnew left, Nixon said to John that he would have to come to Washington. John was a thoroughbred—one of the most remarkable people I have known in politics. He wanted the job, but when we had to call and tell him no, he said, "We have to do what is right for the president." He was a high roller; a big-stakes guy in the school of Lyndon Johnson. I admired him immensely, but the fact was that Ford could be confirmed.

24

The Saturday Night Massacre

On October 12, the U.S. Court of Appeals for the District of Columbia upheld Judge Sirica and ordered the president to turn over the tapes subpoenaed by Cox to the judge, who would then be free to give them to the grand jury after his review for personal or national security material. The Appeals Court decision reinforced a decision made earlier by Nixon that he had to get rid of Cox, who was not just investigating Watergate, but was also looking into possible abuses unrelated to Watergate. The president and his associates came up with a compromise in which they would supply the judge with typed summaries of the conversations instead of the tapes themselves. To answer questions of verification of the summaries' accuracy, Buzhardt suggested that Senator John Stennis, a Mississippi Democrat, listen to the tapes and verify the transcripts.

From October 15 to 19, the administration, the attorney general, and the special prosecutor engaged in a round of discussions concerning the efficacy of the so-called "Stennis compromise." By the end of the week, it was clear that Cox could not accept the proposal, and that Nixon was moving closer to removing him from office. In examining the president's actions during that week—and his overall strategy of attempting to retain total control over the tapes—it is clear that the Stennis compromise was a ploy aimed at putting Cox into a position where the special prosecutor had to reject the compromise out of hand. This action—taken by Cox at a press conference on October 20—and his refusal to resign set the stage for his firing—an event known as the Saturday Night Massacre, which, in turn, resulted in the so-called "firestorm" of national reaction.

Archibald Cox On a Saturday, the court of appeals ruled against President Nixon on the issues he had appealed from Judge Sirica, ruling in our favor on the issues we had appealed, the question being whether the Special Prosecution Force could be present when the tapes were shown to Judge Sirica.

The court had granted a stay for seven days to allow a petition for *certiorari*. So the ball was in the president's court. We had considered what we would do if we won the case, but the president says, I won't. He has the power, the muscle.

We began discussing this sometime in September. It presented an agonizing dilemma. At a staff meeting, we discussed what sanctions there were. One suggestion was that we have him cited for contempt of court. Someone—not thinking very hard—said, "We will move to strike his name from the list authorized to practice [law] in the district court in the District of Columbia."

Another suggestion was a coercive fine—so much a day for each day he does not comply. That seemed to me to cheapen the whole question, turning it into a matter of money, when the real question was a struggle for the rule of law—by this I mean the ancient rule, going back before the Magna Carta, that the highest officials—including the King of Britain—are subject to the law.

Then someone suggested that U.S. marshals are subject to court order— Let's send a squad of marshals down to get the tapes. A voice said: "It won't be the White House guards; it will be the marines." Another voice said: "Yes, and they will be dressed in those fancy Nixon dress uniforms."

I began to have visions of a Gilbert and Sullivan opera. Furthermore— and very much part of the dilemma—if you force a confrontation and lose, aren't you going to hurt the rule of law by revealing its weakness? Under these circumstances, what do you do if your background is—as much of mine was—in the labor management relations field? As a neutral, you find a compromise, so I was very willing to find some kind of compromise that would not back off from the essential job I had undertaken to do and, at the same time, respect enough of the powers of the president to satisfy Richard Nixon.

Consequently, when Elliot Richardson broached this to me on Monday afternoon—two days after the court of appeals decision—I was very ready to listen. We talked very late that afternoon. During the next two days, we talked back and forth.

Richard Ben Veniste We received two sets of tapes: the first set of tapes were in response to our grand jury subpoena. The president resisted turning them over, and this caused the wheels to come into motion that culminated in the Saturday Night Massacre. Thereafter, the president turned over the tapes that had been subpoenaed, with the exception of one which, it was explained, had never been recorded, and another, which had, as it turned out, been erased. Among the first tapes was the March 21, 1972, "Cancer on the Presidency" conversation—and that is the one that knocked my socks off; it was as though I'd been hit with a lightning bolt when I listened to it. I could not believe that the president of the United States had engaged in that conversation.

Charles Wiggins As a matter of objective fact, without the tapes the evidence against Nixon was slender. The tapes were the crowning glory; they were the event that produced the impeachment and, probably, it may not have occurred but for those tapes. On the other hand, those who started the investigation believed that Richard Nixon was a venal person and that he had made sufficient political errors to justify his impeachment, and they undertook to impeach him.

I know that I sound very political and very Republican in my approach to this matter, but I honestly didn't believe that the evidence was sufficient to justify the impeachment of Nixon; the evidence just wasn't there. There was lots of evidence with respect to the misconduct of others, but those people were not subject to impeachment. It was necessary to attribute the misdeeds of others to the president, even though he had no knowledge of them or participation in the acts. I thought the president was unfairly condemned by reason of the misconduct of others.

William Ruckelshaus It started on the Monday after Agnew's resignation. I was on the way out to Grand Rapids [Michigan] to oversee the horde of FBI investigators who had gone into the city to check into Jerry Ford's background. I stopped by the attorney general's office before I left for Michigan, and he turned to me and said, "We have an even worse problem than Agnew." I said, "That's not possible." He said, "Yes, it is"; they seemed determined to try to stop Cox and have him discharged. My reaction was, "Don't worry about that; once they face the reality of it, they'll never do it." That shows how little I knew. Then it got worse and worse as the week went on.

I came back early on Wednesday evening from Grand Rapids to help Richardson manage the problem. But it became increasingly clear that they were determined to confront Cox and to get rid of him. The attorney general was trying the Stennis compromise, and a lot of other things, to see if he couldn't work out some solution short of the final confrontation; he was working very hard to find a compromise, so we didn't discuss the question until Friday night as to what would happen if the president actually asked him to discharge Cox. I knew that night that he [Richardson] wasn't going to do it. I didn't think it was a hard decision; I thought it was very clear that Cox had not been doing anything other than what he was supposed to do. And while, in one sense, I was only the instrument of the exercise of presidential power, if I fundamentally disagreed with what he was going to do—it had to be fundamental; it couldn't be just that my opinion differed from his—then I had no choice but to say no, and resign, or get fired; it didn't matter. I sent my resignation over at the same time that Elliot sent his. That evening, Ron Ziegler announced that Elliot's resignation had been accepted, and that I was fired. On Monday, Al Haig announced that both our resignations had been accepted.

William Saxbe One day, after I didn't go along with some things that the president and Haig asked me to do, Haig said, "We can get another attorney general." I said, "Fine, but I'm not going to resign; you are going to have to fire me. You would have been a lot better off if Richardson had taken that attitude." I always felt that Richardson, in flouncing out and not sticking it out, had done the president a disservice.

Ronald Ziegler Archibald Cox and the people who served with him were operating in an extreme way in the use of power. My feeling is that we took certain right actions and had correct conduct in dealing with the whole investigation—which anybody who looks at it with an unbiased mind would agree were the right things to do. Cox deserved to be fired. That doesn't mean that the cover-up should have succeeded; it simply means that Archibald Cox should have been fired because he was a partisan extremist in the pursuit of Richard Nixon. He was not conducting a balanced inquiry into the process; he was conducting a politically biased inquiry into the presidency of the United States.

Richard Ben Veniste It was dramatic. We really had no idea what would happen, or how the president would react to the Cox press conference. We knew that it wouldn't be good. We had taken certain precautions: there was a great deal of concern about the president's emotional stability, and that was heightened by the fact that the FBI was sent to our offices to seal our files. We took precautions in the sense of ensuring that certain documents wouldn't be subject to a preemptive strike, if it came to that; they were secreted in various unlikely locations in Washington.

Raymond Price I was off on the eastern end of Long Island, without a telephone and with a transistor radio. I had taken the weekend off to help a friend build a little house. My own conclusion was that it was not necessary to force the president to do this politically suicidal thing in firing Cox. We had expected a reaction to the firing, but not that much of one; it was actually a hysterical reaction—it was as if the world were coming to an end because the president had fired a member of his administration for insubordination.

Robert Bork Richardson did not take me over to the White House on the order to Cox and the Stennis compromise. I wish he had, because nobody thought to ask: What happens if Cox refuses the order? The White House assumed that Richardson would fire him; there was a big battle on whether that was a valid assumption or not. Haig has the view that Richardson was on board; Richardson denies it.

Alexander Haig The president wanted to fire Cox, but Elliot said, "No. You can't do that. Let me offer him this compromise, if it's approved by those involved, particularly Senators Ervin, Baker, and Stennis." And they all bought in; it was a done deal; we were celebrating because we thought we had finally gotten the tapes off our backs. At that point—on Friday night—Mel Laird called me and said, "Have you talked to Elliot Richardson?" I said, "What do you mean? He was here today; he knows everything that has happened." Mel said, "You'd better talk to him."

I tried to reach Elliot, but he wasn't home. After waiting a while, I tried again, but without success. I finally went home and then reached him at his home. I said, "Elliot, are you with us? This is your plan." He said, "No, Al. I'm sorry; I'm not." His voice was very slurred. I said, "Where have you been?" He replied, "I've been with Cox." I said, "Don't tell me this; you are going to tell the president."

The next morning, Elliot came in—at that point, we were on the verge of war in the Middle East—and the president said, "Elliot, wait until this international crisis is over." Richardson had guys around him who wanted him to run in 1976; they put out the story that after Richardson resigned, I said to Ruckelshaus, "Your commander in chief has ordered you . . . " That is totally untrue. I had sat with Elliot and the president; when Elliot said he was not going to withdraw his resignation, he said, "Here is what is going to happen: Haig will call my deputy and ask him to take the job, and he will turn it down; he should then call Solicitor General Bork, who will accept it." And that is exactly what happened. Ruckelshaus and Richardson were feeding this crap to the press at the most incredible level I've ever seen.

Archibald Cox His proposal was absolutely unacceptable to me; what became the Stennis proposal would have meant that I got nothing usable as evidence. Furthermore, while I had complete faith in the personal integrity of John Stennis, I was very much aware of several factors: one, he was in a weakened condition, just recovering from gunshot wounds suffered in a recent robbery°; two, he had a very broad view of national security and secrecy; third, the plan was that Fred Buzhardt would prepare a paraphrase, or transcript—it wasn't clear—and have that typed up, omitting the things that he thought were either not relevant, or of national security, and that John Stennis would be given the transcript to hold in front of him while the tapes were played once—no provision for enhancing anything that was hard to hear—and we also had to take into account the fact that Fred Buzhardt had once worked for John Stennis; they had a very close relationship.

Except for the fact that John Stennis was—and still is—a man of great personal integrity, everything else was so geared that for me to accept the proposal would be, in effect, to give up my undertaking to the Senate and, indirectly, to the American people, to pursue evidence in the courts to challenge claims of executive privilege.

I made a counterproposal, which included having three people, including Stennis, listen to the tapes without restriction on the number of times, and to have them appointed officers of the court. But that was not acceptable to the White House. The final break-off on those negotiations came when Charles Wright† called and had a try at persuading me to accept the Stennis proposal, to which he added conditions which made the unacceptable even more clearly unacceptable: that I must never go back to court again to get any evidence; the summaries of these eight tapes would be all that I could ever get. It was clear that I couldn't sign on to that.

By then it was Friday and the question was: What is the White House going to do? Are they going to the Supreme Court? The morning was very busy, because Dean had just pleaded guilty. Once that was over, it was a matter of spending the afternoon biting your nails, waiting to find out what the White House was going to do.

Eventually—very late in the day—just before the deadline for the eleven o'clock news and the morning newspapers, they did release the Stennis compromise, saying that Senators Thurmond and Baker approved, which they now deny.

There were just a few minutes for me to give the press some kind of

---

° Senator Stennis was shot outside his Washington, D.C., home during a robbery attempt.
† University of Texas law professor and Special White House legal consultant on Watergate.

response. I said, "I intend to carry out my duties on the terms on which I accepted them," meaning to imply that I would continue to seek evidence, which had been a very explicit part of my testimony to the Senate before Elliot Richardson had been confirmed as attorney general.

Richard Ben Veniste I don't think that any reasonable person could have thought that the so-called Stennis compromise was a viable alternative to obtaining testimony. I think that Professor Cox was very clear in explaining the reasons why it wasn't during his press conference, which immediately preceded his being fired. In hindsight, I think that it even looks shabbier— even Stennis, I think, repudiated the spin that the president had put on his proposed involvement. And there were other things, which were not discussed by Mr. Cox in the press conference: Mr. Stennis's later recitation of what the president had ascribed as his agreement; and the facts that Mr. Buzhardt had a very close relationship to Senator Stennis; that Senator Stennis thought he was going to be receiving summaries and not tapes; and—in terms of physical acuity—Senator Stennis had been the victim of an attack—he was shot in the head—and he was already of somewhat advanced years, and we noticed that, in listening to some of the tapes, you really had to have very good auditory capacity to be able to make them out. So, these were the practical reasons—that went beyond the legal reasons—which Professor Cox gave.

One should also be aware of the fact that the summaries could not be used in a trial. Agreeing not to request evidence was certainly inconsistent with the charter under which Professor Cox accepted his position, and I think that he quite rightly pointed out that the public would not have expected him to do otherwise than pursue available evidence to find the truth.

Philip Lacovara If we had fallen for the Stennis compromise, the other side would be laughing today; it was never a serious option from our standpoint, for a couple of reasons. The premise of having a political figure serve as the mediator just didn't seem right. It was not an orthodox way to proceed. It came up only after we had sued and gotten favorable decisions on the constitutional issues. But the other part was, it really wasn't the selection of a truly neutral person or one, frankly, who was capable. Stennis, even when he was in much better health, was not regarded as a real heavyweight. He had just been shot, so his health was marginal at best. It's a little bit like saying: Let's have an arbitrator. How would you like my wife to be our arbitrator? Hardly a sensible or realistic suggestion.

There was no basis for the Nixon people to assume they had a deal. What may have been giving them a greater degree of optimism that they could avoid the confrontation was that we kept the door open to some sort of compromise or settlement. But they were willing to go no further than irrevocable delegation of responsibility to John Stennis, and that just seemed to us not a viable alternative.

William Ruckelshaus I don't think that it was a nonstarter in Elliot's mind; I think that it might have been in the White House's mind. There is no question that it was a bad decision; the president would have gotten a better deal, and it is clear that his men would have. The decision [not to go with the compromise] was based on Cox's being too close to getting the facts and not being in control of the president. He was doing what he was supposed to do, which was to investigate these allegations, and the last thing they had in mind when they fired Cox was [his successor, Leon] Jaworski. They assumed they could fold it back into the Department of Justice and control it through the department.

COX'S FIRING WITHIN THE CONTEXT OF SEVERAL EVENTS

Robert Reisner During a two-week period in October 1973, Agnew pleaded nolo contendere and resigned; John Dean acknowledged that he was a conspirator and agreed to plead guilty to a felony count; Archibald Cox asked for the tapes; and as they negotiated back and forth, the October War breaks out—for reasons independent of all this. At one point, the ARAMCO partners brought the Saudi foreign minister to the White House to talk about the possibility of an oil embargo. When you look at the documents that had to do with the energy crisis, and you juxtapose them with the events leading up to the Saturday Night Massacre, you can see that Nixon was totally distracted. It may be that the system overloaded in October 1973, and it was beyond the capacity of this tightly controlled White House to handle all of these new events at the same time. By that time, Haig was chief of staff, and whether he was completely balanced in his handling of things is an interesting question.

Leonard Garment Four or five events took place more or less in the same time slot: the resignation of Spiro Agnew; the nomination of a new vice-president, Jerry Ford; the outbreak of the Yom Kippur War; the tumult with Cox; and on that day, the crisis with the Soviet Union was brewing. The president asked me to call Richardson and ask him to hold his resignation until the following Wednesday or Thursday because of the problem with the Soviets. He said, "How can I get planes to Israel?" He knew that I was a strong supporter, and so was he, by God!—the previous week he had done wonders for Israel on the resupply with the C-5As—breaking the Kissinger-Schlesinger logjam—saying, "Get every goddamn plane that can fly. We are going to be condemned by the Arabs anyway, so we may as well do it right." I saw his finest moment, and that was terrific; and Ford was terrific; and I think he got carried away, so he thought he could do [fire] Cox, and do it on his terms; it was like a wave of optimism and strength.

Richard Ben Veniste We were stunned, along with the rest of the nation, that this naked use of force would be employed. After all, we were all lawyers; the president himself was a lawyer; we had all been dealing with these matters in lawyerlike ways; and we expected that this would be resolved in the court, not by the president firing Professor Cox without cause—and without obeying court orders, but rather by using executive powers to force us to terminate our investigation. This was scary; this was not America with a *c*; this was Amerika with a *k*.

COX'S PRESS CONFERENCE

Robert Bork I was in my office on Saturday morning, and when the time came for Cox's televised press conference, I watched in the office of the department's press person. The moment it was over, Richardson's assistant stuck his head in the door and said, "The attorney general would like to see you." I went in, and there were Richardson, Ruckelshaus, and a couple of the younger people. We discussed the situation, and Richardson finally said, "I can't fire Cox. Can you fire him, Bill?" That was the first time it had really occurred to me that I was the third in line—and last in line—under the department's regulations. Ruckelshaus said, "I can't fire him." Then he asked me, "Can you fire him, Bob?" I said, "Let me think." I walked around the room while they talked about something else, and I finally said, "Yeah. I'll fire him, but then I'll resign immediately afterward." I knew that Cox was going to be fired; the question was, How much blood was going to be shed? Richardson then asked me, "If you fire him, would you then resign?"

I answered that I didn't want to be viewed as an apparatchik.* He said, "If you fire him, don't resign; the department needs continuity." Then the phone call from the White House came through. Richardson went over there and, after much argument, he had to resign. He came back to the department and said to Ruckelshaus, "You can expect a phone call, Bill."

Archibald Cox I suppose if anyone had said to me, Won't the result of this be that you will be fired? I would have responded, I guess so. I truly think this was not important in my mind at the time.

The most important thing was that the rule of law should prevail; the president must comply with the law. This depends whether the people in a moral and political sense, will rise up and force him to comply with the law. Will they understand what is at stake? Because, ultimately, all their liberties were at stake. That was in my consciousness, and also deepest in my makeup.

My wife and I, and our eldest daughter, went back home to nearby Virginia. The phone rang. It was Elliot Richardson. He said, "Let me tell you what is going to happen." He said he had been instructed to dismiss me and had refused. He added that Bill Ruckelshaus had done the same. Then he said that "Bob Bork is acting attorney general, and he is going to dismiss you."

So then it was a matter of settling down and waiting for the word to come, and it seemed like forever before anything happened. We were only twenty minutes from the White House. After about an hour, a messenger showed up at the front door with a letter from the acting attorney general, dismissing me.

DEALING WITH HAIG

William Ruckelshaus Haig put it every way he knew how: as a military officer, he put it in terms of a crisis in the Middle East—how it would weaken the presidency if I didn't carry out his order—and I said, "Well, why do you have to do it tonight? Why not wait a week or two?" I told him that I had been thinking about this for well over a week—since they had been forcing the issue—and I didn't think that I could fire Cox. I mentioned that Bob Bork was up in Elliot's office, and I knew I would go get him, if he wanted me to, and that maybe he'd do it. I knew that Bob would; we had talked about it that morning. It was the first time that Bork had been confronted with what was going on.

---

* Classic bureaucrat.

Both Elliot and I told him what he might be confronted with as a result of what the White House planned to do. He was very angry about it; he knew that he was going to have to make a decision pretty quickly. He mentioned more than once that this was not what he had thought he was signing on for when he became the solicitor general of the United States. But he said he would do it because he felt that it wasn't his controversy; it was between the president and an employee of the Justice Department, and that it was his obligation to carry out—as the instrument of the exercise of presidential power—what the president wanted done. I said, "If that is the way you feel about it, I would encourage you to go ahead and do it; if you don't, there is really nobody left after you, and while the president can appoint somebody from the department as attorney general to do it, that would, indeed, throw the thing into further disarray." It seemed that it would be better to have somebody in the chain of command willing to carry out the president's wish than for him to have to appoint somebody to do it.

"YOUR COMMANDER IN CHIEF ORDERS YOU . . . "

Robert Bork A call came through from Haig, and Bill [William Ruckelshaus] went down to his office to take it—that was the famous "Your Commander in Chief Orders You . . . " Bill came back up and said, "Bob, you are going to be called to the phone in a minute," and I was. Haig did not ask me to fire Cox; he was afraid to get another no. He asked me to come over to the White House, and added that he was sending a car to pick me up. I went down to my office and called my wife, who had no inkling [of what was about to happen]. I said, "I think I am going to have to fire Archibald Cox; if you have anything to say, say it now." There was a long ahhh, and then she said, "Why don't you call Alex Bickel?" I tried to reach him but he was out playing tennis.

So I went downstairs and there was the limousine, and there was Leonard Garment in the right passenger seat, and Fred Buzhardt in the rear, looking very much as though they were afraid I would escape. They took me over to the White House, and Haig began to talk to me about how the president couldn't be faced down in public like this; there was a foreign policy crisis on—the October Middle East War [Yom Kippur War]. I said, "I'll fire him, but I haven't decided if I will resign immediately afterward." Haig looked as if he didn't care much—just as long as I fired Cox.

Charles Alan Wright offered to draft the letter. I said, "Make it terse," and he did, and that was that. After I signed the letter, I went in to see the president. I'm not sure whether it was my psychological mood, or whether it was physical fact, but it seemed to me that the room was quite gloomy, and the president was very gloomy; he knew it was a disaster for him—and he hadn't planned it. When he said, "Do you want to be attorney general?" he wasn't offering me the job; he wanted to find out what my motive was. I said that it wouldn't be appropriate—and it certainly wouldn't have been; I couldn't profit in any way from the firing of Cox. So, we chatted for a little while, and then I went back to the department, and up to Elliot's office. We had a poignant talk, because he was going and I was staying—in circumstances that were less than ideal. And then we went to the garage together and drove off.

Leonard Garment I was in right at the end. I realize now that while I did some things that were useful for the administration, I was, for the most part, a Potemkin lawyer—pretending, and thinking I was a lawyer, but not having much solidarity, because Nixon didn't want me getting involved in what was a very complicated and highly controlled operation he was running, to try to wait out this grinding, Edgar Allan Poe process, where he knew that the ceiling was coming down. The last person he needed running all over the place was me. Therefore, I was not there when the idea of what to do with Cox was generated, but I was brought in later. The momentum was such that I didn't even think of stopping it. John Osborne, the journalist—and my best friend in those years—remembered years afterward that I had come over to his house to have a drink with him and his wife, Trudy, in the late afternoon on the day after the Saturday Night Massacre, and that I was in a state of absolutely unlimited euphoria, and John said, "After you left, Trudy and I said, 'Len's lost his mind.'"

William Ruckelshaus One of the great ironies of Watergate, it always seemed to me, was that if the president hadn't been so determined to ensure that Cox hewed the line—and finally, that Cox had to leave—many of the people who ended up being prosecuted under the rubric of Watergate Crimes never would have been; Cox would not have pursued them. [Leon] Jaworski [Cox's successor as special prosecutor] had no choice; he was perceived as the White House's choice—therefore, he had to pursue every line of inquiry his staff or anyone else recommended, in order to prove that he was not biased in the other direction. Cox would have been much more inclined to let people like Mitchell and Kleindienst go, so as not to be accused historically of being partisan.

Robert Bork Nixon did not want the Saturday Night Massacre; he was sick that night. He assumed that Richardson was going to fire Cox—he thought that since Richardson was in the meeting when this whole policy was framed, he was on board; Richardson said he was never on board. The whole thing is murky. On Friday evening, I called Richardson and congratulated him, because I had heard that he had worked it out with Cox. He was very gloomy, and said that Cox was not going to go along, so I knew that there might be trouble, but it never occurred to me that I might become involved. That is an example of not thinking ahead.

Alexander Butterfield I became increasingly disenchanted with Richard Nixon as the summer wore on, and the fall came, and there was the Saturday Night Massacre, and I saw people, who I thought were wonderful, become pawns—victims—of the system. That's when I wished he would say, Wait a minute; none of my guys are going to prison. We made some mistakes here, but they were all made here—with me. He would never do it, so I am not a Richard Nixon fan at all. On the other hand, I certainly recognize his attributes, and I will say a lot of good things about him, because they should be said.

THE FIRESTORM

Archibald Cox The public reaction against President Nixon—what Alexander Haig described as "the firestorm"—was so great that the president was forced to change his position and send his lawyer to court to say he would comply with the order.

The only answer to the question of: What is there to set against the power of the president who challenges the rule of law? is the people's realization of the importance of the rule of law. By the people, I include all the vehicles through which the public expresses itself—politicians, the press, and so forth. So I knew the reaction was going to be critical. I had been a teacher of constitutional law and solicitor general, so I had thought about Supreme Court decisions.

William Ruckelshaus I had no idea that the firestorm was going to happen. Being in the middle of it, there was no way you could predict it. A lot of it had to do with the way it was portrayed on television—the fact that virtually all the reporters in Washington were at a party Art Buchwald[*] had at an indoor tennis facility, so they all heard about it at once and dispersed.

---

[*] The syndicated political humorist.

Ben Bradlee Cox had received an iron-clad guarantee from the president and from the attorney general that he would be absolutely free to follow this investigation wherever it led. And then they turned on him as soon as it led anywhere. We were playing tennis at Buchwald's tournament. One by one: Ben Bradlee, call your office; David Brinkley,* call your office. If I had known something like this was going to happen, I wouldn't have been at Buchwald's.

Robert Bork I knew that there would be a lot of trouble about the firing, but I didn't anticipate the intensity of it. Everything I did then, I'd do again—with one exception: I would hold a press conference and say: "Don't get excited; Cox is going, but nobody else is." In fact, Nixon and I discussed that—that the office would continue; his only words on it were: "I want a prosecution, not a persecution." He viewed what was happening to him as a prosecution, I think, because of the Kennedy connection. I wasn't asked to fire anybody else, and I wouldn't have fired anybody else. Later on, the special prosecutor's office filed their report and said that they hadn't missed a day's work because of the Cox firing; they asked me if they could see the tapes, and I said yes. But I was new—I had never held a press conference in my life—but if I had held a press conference that night, and explained that Cox was going, that it was inevitable, but that nothing was going to stop the investigation, maybe there would not have been such a "firestorm."

Richard Ben Veniste In all of the confusion that surrounded the attorney general's—and his deputy's—refusal to follow the order that Alexander Haig had transmitted to them from the president, by the time Mr. Bork got around to firing Archie Cox, they said nothing about firing the staff. So we met thereafter—it took on the aspects of Hansel and Gretel; we were huddled somewhere, off-premises. Our offices had been occupied, sealed. We discussed what we ought to do—and what we could do. It was clear that there was much work left to be done. There were some people who advocated that the staff should resign. I took a very strong contrary position. I said, "Probably everyone thinks we've been fired, so no one will notice if we resign. Who cares? But if we don't resign, it's possible that somehow either the court, through its supervision over the grand jury, which we have been working with, or the Congress, can breathe life back into our organization. We are the ones who have the most information, and are the best organized

* Co-anchor of NBC's evening network news program.

at this point about the matters which are under investigation. So we ought to stay put, watch how things unfold, and then make an application to the court to determine what will happen next."

That's what we did, and when Mr. Jaworski was appointed, he had a full staff, which was operational and which he was able to rely upon. This was, I think, an extraordinary oversight on the part of the president if he wanted to derail the investigation because he knew that it might ultimately lead to his impeachment.

Philip Lacovara As that week was drawing to a close, the firing of Cox became a possibility. We had some contingency plans. After the deadline had passed and the president had refused to yield, Archie knew the fat was in the fire. He had to decide whether to yield, knowing that if he didn't, the consequences could be quite severe for the country as well as for him. While the possibility of his being dismissed was entertained, I don't think anyone saw it playing out quite the way it did.

That Saturday night, virtually the entire office mustered. I was at a dinner party when I heard the news coming over the radio. I—and virtually all the other lawyers and the secretaries, messengers, and others—appeared at the offices of the Special Prosecution Force between eight-thirty and nine o'clock. Henry Ruth and I—as the two senior people—began sorting out what to do. We convened the staff in the library and told them what we knew. I had reached Bob Bork at home; I had known him in the solicitor general's office. I wanted to know what he understood the firing of Cox to mean for the future of the special prosecution office. Not, do we still get paychecks?, but what has happened to our investigation? And in what—in my judgment—was the Nixon-Haig miscalculation of greatest consequence, all they had done was to direct Bork to fire Cox, not to do anything about dissolving the Watergate Special Prosecution Force. So the charter—the regulations Richardson had issued when he came in as attorney general— remained intact. And Bork told me, "I've got no instructions from the president to do anything other than fire Mr. Cox, which I believe the president has the constitutional power to do. But as far as I know, your office is still intact." So I reported that to the staff and said that, as far as I knew, we were still in business.

We arranged to meet with Archie, who was in hiding that Sunday. Monday morning, we went into court because of disputes we had been having with the FBI; they had been ordered to impound our office. We got Judge Sirica to issue orders instructing the whole government not to interfere with the work of the Special Prosecution Force, so over the weekend, we had orchestrated a campaign to make sure that the investigation could continue, even though we were temporarily leaderless. I am sure that Nixon must have been absolutely astonished when he woke up on Monday morning and realized we were still in business.

25

The Struggle for the Tapes

—————

The demand for tapes, documents, and other White House and personal records did not end with the firing of Archibald Cox. If anything, the investigative bodies, the Special Prosecution Force and the House Judiciary Committee, stepped up their activities in the late winter and early spring of 1974.

In late April, Mr. Nixon, in an attempt to placate the House Judiciary Committee—then deep into hearings concerning possible impeachment proceedings—released edited transcripts of White House conversations. This material, included in the so-called Blue Book, contained many instances of profanity and other coarse conversation, as well as expurgations of important discussions. The issuance of the Blue Book led to further demands for the tapes, which resulted in greater resistance by the White House to provide them.

Mr. Nixon and his attorneys believed that the tapes were protected under the principle of executive privilege; that they were his possessions and his alone and, therefore, not subject to outside scrutiny or control. The struggle over access to the tapes led to a major constitutional confrontation.

On July 8, 1974, Special Prosecutor Leon Jaworski and presidential attorney James St. Clair argued their respective cases before eight justices* of the U.S. Supreme Court as to whether the president had to give up the records of sixty-four subpoenaed conversations.

On July 24, the court ruled 8–0 that Mr. Nixon had to turn over the material. This was a calamitous development for him, as one of the tapes included in the subpoena contained the record of the June 23, 1972 conver-

———

* Justice William Rehnquist recused himself, as he had served as an assistant attorney general in the Nixon Justice Department.

sation in which the president—in an Oval Office meeting with Haldeman—
approved the suggestion of a cover-up involving the Watergate break-in.

Exacerbating the situation confronting Mr. Nixon was the fact that the
president had not shared the contents of the June 23 tape with his family
members, attorneys, key aides, and congressional defenders—all of whom
had been claiming that there was no direct evidence of the president's
involvement in a cover-up.

ST. CLAIR'S APPEARANCE BEFORE THE U.S. SUPREME COURT

James St. Clair I had worked quite hard to get ready. I don't recall that I thought that the court had already decided the issue; I guess now that they had decided it before the argument. I felt that it had gone well. When I got back to the White House, the president felt that way also. He thanked me for doing a very good job.

Raymond Price Jim St. Clair was a very good and very bright guy, but was the wrong guy for the job. He was a very good criminal attorney, but this was a political thing; while his legal case might have played very well in a courtroom, it was not the one we needed at that point. The president was very well served by Charles Alan Wright; I thought he did the constitutional arguments brilliantly, and I thought they were 100 percent right. The problem was not with Wright, but with the courts; they determined to go along with the flow rather than with the legal precedent.

There is also another element: our lawyers were so vastly outnumbered and overburdened; we had ten lawyers who not only had to handle all of this, but all the routine legal work of the White House—which is quite extensive. Up against us were over one hundred from the impeachment committees and the special prosecutor. They were intensely political; they were out for blood; they kept throwing our people off-balance with lots of demands for this and that, which kept them from doing the work of the case, so they didn't have a chance to do their job.

William Ruckelshaus The attorney from Texas [Charles Alan Wright] who was advising Nixon on his right to withhold the tapes gave him bad advice; it was bad advice, at least, according to the Supreme Court. But I also think that he was under enormous pressure from the president to take that decision, so I don't know whether he advised him poorly or not.

Robert Bork I think that there was a lot of anti-Nixon feeling on the Court; the pressure in this town was so great. I thought that they had no jurisdiction on the tapes question. Someone asked me, right before the decision was announced, "What do you think is going to happen?" I said, "This is not Nixon's day"—I knew that he was going to lose, and if he lost, it was going to be unanimous. The situation would have been a mess if the Court had said: we have no jurisdiction, so you can't go for the tapes. The whole government would have been in suspension, with nobody able to do anything. That is what, I think, drove the Court.

William Ruckelshaus On a lot of decisions that involve issues of national moment, the Court strives mightily to come out with a unanimous decision. They used to do it in civil rights cases and, particularly where they are making new law which has an impact on the country, they try very hard to come up with unanimous decisions; they recognize that any dissent on the Court would divide the country and provide ammunition for those who oppose the decision and, thereby, keep the country in sort of an ambiguous position relating to those kinds of policy. I thought they would decide [the tapes issue] unanimously.

I thought they were right; once it became clear that there were recorded instances of evidence involving these nationally prominent activities—I can't think of any more prominent activities, criminal or otherwise, in the history of the country—even though in the possession of the president of the United States, that would lead to information clarifying what had happened, it seemed to me that it was going to come out—that the Supreme Court would simply override the president's interest in holding onto those tapes by insisting that they be released to the prosecution. As the president became weaker, and as his actions—particularly where he became involved in the discharge of myself, Elliot Richardson, and Archibald Cox—gave the impression, at least, that he was trying to hide something, it became more likely that they [the tapes] would be released. The Supreme Court is not immune to the strength of public support, or nonsupport, for the president or the congressional branch.

Philip Lacovara From the very first inkling about the existence of the tapes, Cox and I began counting noses on the Court, because we were trying to figure out where a constitutional confrontation would take us. One of our concerns was: suppose we get a decision that is nominally in our favor and the president disregards it and the courts can't do anything with it. Archie didn't want to be the person who precipitated a confrontation that might involve a Pyrrhic victory that would be destructive of the courts.

The flip side was: suppose we lose and there is some sweeping announcement about presidential prerogative; the president really is above the law. Will we have done the country much benefit, going after these tapes in this piddling criminal investigation, if the consequence is that the Court expands presidential immunity?

We thought we probably had six votes. But—as Nixon had made clear—he would not necessarily be intimidated by a six-to-three decision; that would not have been a definitive ruling to him. We never assumed a unanimous decision was likely.

REACTION TO THE SUPREME COURT DECISION ON EXECUTIVE PRIVILEGE

James St. Clair *Surprise* is not the right word; *disappointed* is. I would have been surprised if the decision had not been unanimous. Here you have the head of the judicial branch [of government] dealing with the head of the executive branch, so if it had been a five-to-four decision, you would never have stopped reading about the pros and cons; the Court would not look impressive with that close a decision. I was in California [after the decision came down] and was asked to meet the press and tell them that the president was someone who recognized that the law has to be complied with: whether you are president or not, you must follow the law. He had always argued that the rule of law was the rule that governed this country, so he confirmed that, through me, at this press conference.

26

Did the President Have to Resign?

On July 27, Mr. Nixon received another serious blow when the House Judiciary Committee—by a 27–11 vote—passed its first article of impeachment. There would eventually be three* charging the president with engaging in a course of conduct to obstruct justice in the Watergate affair.

As July came to a close, pressure mounted for Mr. Nixon to resign. His resignation became a virtual certainty on the afternoon of August 2, when Representative Charles Wiggins, the California Republican who had been Mr. Nixon's most ardent advocate on the House Judiciary Committee, came to the White House and read the transcript of the June 23 tape. Wiggins insisted that the tape be made available to the committee, lest he, Wiggins, be liable to a charge of obstruction of justice. White House Chief of Staff Alexander Haig and Mr. St. Clair promised the congressman that the material would be released on August 5.

Over the weekend of August 3–4, as he pondered his rapidly declining options, Mr. Nixon received conflicting advice from family, staff, members of Congress, and close friends. When the June 23 tape was released on Monday, August 5, the overwhelmingly negative reaction it engendered convinced the president that he would not only be impeached by the House, but would also be convicted by the Senate and forced to leave office. This realization caused the man who had survived so many crises to begin making final preparations for informing the nation that his presidency was at an end.

---

* The second impeachment article dealt with abuse of power; the third charged the president with unconstitutionally defying its subpoenas.

Philip Lacovara There was a strong case against Nixon, largely based on the live testimony of Dean, who turned out to be a reasonably good witness whose version of events was largely corroborated by the tapes. When Dean was giving his first days of testimony before the Ervin Committee, he was testifying largely from memories, or from notes, about conversations that had taken place. And although he may have gotten one or two days mixed up, his recollection even of terms used was surprisingly accurate. With the testimony of Dean, plus the tapes, plus the normal inference to be drawn from information about how the Nixon White House was organized, and about how Nixon was working closely with Haldeman and Ehrlichman on virtually all of these issues, and was getting regular briefings from them and was aware almost from the day of the break-in that there had been White House involvement, I think it would not have been a difficult case to make.

It would have been much harder without the tapes—maybe impossible. Any one-on-one case is difficult to make. In this situation, you had not only the president denying Dean's public accusations; you had Ehrlichman, Haldeman, Mitchell, and others going up before the Ervin Committee, and before the grand jury, denying what had taken place. So you would have had a three- or four-on-one case, which would have been extremely difficult to make if there weren't contemporaneous tapes showing what actually happened.

Stephen Bull I think, had it been John F. Kennedy, it would have been a different outcome. Just talk about the tapes. You would believe that Richard Nixon was the only person who tape-recorded conversations. To this day, there is a whole load of tapes sitting up there in Massachusetts from the Kennedy days. I thought he was going to fight it out. That's his nature—not to surrender. I think it was the preponderance of opinion of confidants that he'd have to do it—that it was a battle he would not win, in spite of the fight he would put up. He could have won the battle and lost the war. He might have avoided impeachment. He might have won the trial in the Senate. I think he would have put up a furious fight. I think his own inclination was to fight it out.

Charles Wiggins The scope of the investigation of Nixon was immense. There were a number of organizations around the country who were openly hostile to the president. They were publicly invited by the staff of the Judiciary Committee to submit any information they had against Nixon. This covered a whole range of matters; there were fifty-four or -five distinct issues that were under investigation by the committee. They were fed information by organizations from all over the country, and then the committee would undertake to investigate them. There was the break-in and entry of the Watergate complex, that was the Watergate episode; then there was the matter of the Plumbers; there was a matter of income tax invasion that was attributed to Nixon; there was the bombing of Cambodia; and many others that would boggle the mind concerning the scope of the investigation that were unrelated to Watergate but were just against Nixon's administration.

Every time the investigation proceeded one step further, it was covered massively in the press, so I didn't have much hope that the president would survive this assault against him. I was hoping that even if we lost in the House that perhaps the Senate, which would act in a judicial role, could almost be shamed into doing the right thing. But I was losing faith in that, too. Of course, it turned out that we didn't have the opportunity of a vote in the House, let alone the Senate. So my heart was sinking in the spring of 1974.

H. R. Haldeman In the climate of the time, he could not have prevailed. There was too much piled up—too many interests in seeing him not prevail, and all working together, in a sense, to see that he didn't. I don't think he could have survived the impeachment proceedings.

Gerald Warren By the time Watergate came along, Richard Nixon had expended a lot of political capital. He had some support out in the country-side, but conservatives were questioning him over some issues, particularly the opening to China; his arms control agreements were not totally embraced by everyone; his early work on family support was not understood by every-one; his wage and price controls were terrible mistakes. All of that diluted his support on Capitol Hill, so there was no one willing to stand up for Nixon for very long. The tapes killed him. Had it been another president, the reaction would have been different. But I don't know if the outcome would have been different.

H. R. Haldeman Containment was exactly what I thought we were work-ing on in the early days of my involvement in the Watergate tapes: to con-tain the congressional investigation to Watergate, per se, and not let it go into a great witch-hunt, which was exactly what it did do, sinking the presi-dent. I thought we were doing perfectly legitimate things to contain the case, whereas what we were actually doing, I see now, was trying to obstruct justice: we were trying not to contain, but to conceal—to go beyond legiti-mate containment into illegitimate cover-up. I didn't think we had anything to cover up; I wasn't worried. I figured that somebody did it, but it wasn't us. If Hunt goes to jail, if Mitchell goes to jail, that's too bad, but there they are. I knew I hadn't done anything, and I assumed—or thought—that the president hadn't done anything, and I still don't think he had.

Samuel Dash If he had destroyed the tapes and made a public statement that they recorded heads of state and many matters of national security, and he had made the decision to destroy them as president, I think that the country would have agreed with him. If he had done that, I think he would have served out his presidency. The disclosure concerning the tapes came at a very difficult time for Richard Nixon: just before the disclosure, we had asked the White House for documents, and it seemed that they were stalling, so Senator Baker said to Sam Ervin, "If you call the president and ask for a meeting—or ask that he give us the documents—I think he will let you have them." We were all in a room together just before we found the tapes. Ervin is told that the president is on the line; he gets on the phone— we could only hear Ervin's part of the conversation—and he starts off by saying, "Mr. President, this is Sam Ervin." Then we hear him say, "We are not out to get you, Mr. President." His face is getting flushed. He then hangs up and says to us, "The president is screaming at the top of his lungs, 'You are out to get me; you are out to get me!'"

Charles Wiggins The cards were stacked against Nixon—deliberately stacked. How did it come to pass that the House of Representatives elected to try to impeach Richard Nixon? To ask that question calls upon a person to understand what it is that moves the House to do things. In the case of a major political step, a resolution—as in this case—it must be introduced by a member, but that doesn't even begin the process. This is a situation in which the speaker has to play a direct role; the majority leader has to play a direct role; those people who are close to the two leaders, without question, met in the speaker's office to discuss this problem of Richard Nixon, and they elected to go with the resolution; they decided to put the power of the Democratic Party behind that, and to pursue it. I know that with respect to major issues, this is how it occurs. These people decide among themselves that this is a project that they wish to pursue. They didn't undertake that project to lose; they undertook it to impeach Richard Nixon.

Gerald R. Ford If Nixon had destroyed the tapes, there would have been no solid, concrete evidence of a cover-up. The tapes were the key evidence that he had participated in obstructing justice. If the tapes had not existed, the situation certainly would have been quite different.

Richard Ben Veniste There was a case without the tapes. In my view, it would have been a very difficult case—and, perhaps, one that would not have been brought. I don't know that I would have recommended a prosecution; I don't know that I would have recommended that the grand jury issue an indictment along the lines of the one which was issued, if we had not had the information in the tapes. It would have been very difficult; there would have been a number of people testifying contrary to Dean—as they had in the hearing—and without the tapes, which absolutely corroborated Dean—I'd never in twenty-five years of experience as a trial lawyer seen a witness so absolutely corroborated—and looking at the circumstances, where Dean did not know that his conversations were being recorded, and comparing his version to the actual tapes, showed that he had an extraordinary memory, and if anything, he was somewhat conservative in the way he portrayed the president—and the president's statements.

Archibald Cox A lot of evidence was developed after my dismissal. In the few weeks—even the days—before Butterfield's disclosure, you had John Dean's testimony and some circumstantial evidence that we had to confirm it. We had a constant string of denials from all the people at the White House. At that point, unless something new came out, it would have been pretty much a matter of credibility.

There was more circumstantial evidence developed concerning Dean's testimony, much of it developed by the Special Prosecutor's Office. Maybe by mid-1974, if the tapes had not been available, the situation would have been different from that of June 1973.

Charles Wiggins I think that the special prosecutor would have chosen to indict the president on some count of obstructing justice. They may have been able to convict the president on the basis of the June 23rd tape, but I don't think that all the other allegations of misconduct that are subsumed in the idea of Watergate would have had any relevancy in any criminal prosecution of the president. He was on the outside of all of these things.

Robert Bork He was as well served as he could have been; once the existence of the tapes became known, he was doomed. His attorneys didn't know he had the tapes; it came as a bombshell to everyone, including Haig.

But I think he was also doomed before that: if there had never been a special prosecutor, the U.S. Attorney's Office was making the case. They turned over to Cox a ninety-page file with the evidence they thought they had; they had the goods on many people, including Nixon. In the file, there was a handwritten note in the margin of a document, beside Nixon's name, "Constitutional problem?" I'm not sure if it was put there by Silbert's* or Cox's crowd.

Richard Ben Veniste Certainly, we considered indicting the president. There were different views: that the matter be presented to the grand jury, and that the indictment be superseded—that is a legal term—to include the president, who was clearly—on the basis of the evidence involved—furthering the conspiracy to obstruct justice. There were others who thought that the initial indictment that was scheduled to be tried in January 1975 should go forward, and that consideration of whether or not to prosecute the president be deferred until that prosecution had concluded. I was of the latter view; I did not think that it was in the national interest to proceed at that point against the president; we had been through a tremendous trauma. The matter was reflected by President Ford, that he had no intention of considering pardon for Nixon at that time. That seemed to provide assurance that this could be dealt with later—and that it might have been possible to achieve some kind of disposition of the matter subsequently. Then, of course, President Ford issued the pardon.

Seymour Glanzer What Nixon said on the tapes indicated a very high involvement in efforts to suppress the case—to block it, to mislead it. He could have been convicted in a criminal case, there is no question about it, based on the tapes, and where the trial would have taken place: the federal government is not popular with the residents of Washington, D.C. You couldn't go to trial with Dean's uncorroborated statements; you could tell this by what happened in the Mitchell-Stans trial, in New York, where he testified without the tapes and there was an acquittal, despite a strong government case. When the jurors were interviewed following the verdict, they said that they would not believe Dean more than they would a cockroach; he got destroyed on the witness stand.

Samuel Dash The Senate Committee hearings were not a trial; we didn't follow all the rules of evidence. We made it very clear in our final report that

---

* Earl Silbert, original Watergate prosecutor, U.S. Attorney's Office.

we weren't attempting to determine guilt or innocence; it was fact-finding for legislation, period. Therefore, the Watergate period ends with the pardon—with no acceptance by Richard Nixon of guilt. There is that remaining question: Was he railroaded? Was he treated unfairly? Was it because he was not a popular president? Whatever the reason, there is a question mark. It seems to me that what the country needed was judicial judgment. I never would have wanted Richard Nixon to go to jail, but we needed a judgment for the people's sake—and for history's sake: yes, you're guilty; or you're innocent.

Richard Nixon was my president, and when I started the investigation, my greatest hope was that it would not go to him. When I found out from John Dean about the conversations, I was very saddened. I don't have any personal vendetta against Richard Nixon. I do believe that Watergate represented a tremendous crisis in democracy—that Nixon's abuse of power was such that we came close to a serious constitutional crisis, a crisis that was stopped only by the early revelations of the Senate Committee. It was also a healing experience, because it allowed the country to understand the powers of Congress and the president. But what the president did was not a peccadillo and not a third-rate burglary; it was a very serious abuse of his office. I personally believe that he should have been indicted, and should have been convicted; there is no doubt in my mind that if he hadn't resigned and it had gone to the Senate, he would have been convicted and thrown out of office.

Seymour Glanzer If Nixon had had a good criminal lawyer, the lawyer would have taken the tapes and destroyed them; Edward Bennett Williams would have done this. Also, a good criminal lawyer would never have accepted a subpoena. But Nixon chose academics—people like Professor [Charles Alan] Wright. Once the subpoena—and the jurisdiction of the Court—was accepted, Nixon was doomed. The lawyer could have said that Nixon was not subpoenable. I told this to [Earl] Silbert at the time—that if I was Nixon's lawyer, I would not allow myself to be served. What would happen? The subpoena would be given to the U.S. Marshal Service to serve. But the marshals work for the president; he could tell them they were not to come to the White House. That would have been the end of it: the president is not subpoenable.

The actual destruction of the tapes could have been done on the grounds of executive privilege; Nixon could have claimed that there was material that was completely sensitive. He couldn't be impeached on that basis; it wouldn't get through Congress in a million years. Not Cox, not Jaworski, not anybody would ever, ever suggest that an indictment be returned on that basis. They wouldn't have done a damn thing. He would have completed his presidency. Nixon's people made bad moves. They were not good chess players; Bobby Fischer* would have won.

Leonard Garment I gave Nixon a legal view which was correct. Looking back on it now, and considering the way it all went, I think that he would have survived the destruction of the tapes—put them in a couple of garbage cans and pour acid on them. There would have been a big hullabaloo for a time—a lot of yelling and screaming—but he would have survived. There are plenty of ways you can destroy tapes. After all, if you can mash up Jimmy Hoffa,† you can get rid of tapes.

Alexander Haig In December 1973, totally unknown to me, Pat Buchanan and some others had somehow gotten in to see the president and said that he had to let it all hang out. In that sense, they were right, so he authorized them to transcribe some tapes, which they did. I didn't know that this was going on. In mid-December, we had a meeting Pat had asked be convened, and he said, "We have all of these tapes put together and we are going to release them." I said, "Why didn't I know about this? I'm the chief of staff"—I had these problems with Nixon; so did everybody else who worked for him; he'd be playing six or seven alleys—"Pat, I'll tell you; this is not going to happen on my watch until I've read everything that's in them"—this had to do with the eight or nine tapes that had been subpoenaed. I gave a copy to Bryce Harlow and said, "Don't do anything until we have both read the material."

When I finished reading it, I knew that Nixon would never survive—no way. It had nothing to do with guilt or innocence. It was a moral question. I called Bryce, and we concluded that Nixon could not survive these tapes, even though they had been doctored. So I went to the president and said, "I urge you not to release this material; you won't survive." And the whole idea was scuttled, and the president went down to Key Biscayne, mad as hell at me.

---

* The chess champion.
† Mr. Hoffa disappeared from public view in 1975 and has not been heard from since. Rumor has it that his body was placed in a trash compactor and then buried in the New Jersey Meadowlands.

27

The Resignation

Charles Wiggins During the period after the Judiciary Committee voted in favor of impeachment, I undertook to meet with groups of House members to state my view as to why the president shouldn't be impeached. On August 2, during the course of one of those meetings, my office received a call from General Haig, and when I returned to the office, I saw the call slip from him. This was the first time Haig had ever called me. I returned the call; he wanted to know if I could come down to the White House, because there was something he wanted to discuss with me. I had no notion of what he wanted. At around two o'clock I drove my car down from the Capitol to the White House, parked in the area between the Executive Office Building and the White House—where I'd never parked before. I went in the side entrance of the West Wing. There was a Secret Service man who recognized me and took me upstairs, and after speaking to a secretary, in just a moment or two, Haig came out and led me back into his office. It was the first time I'd ever been in the West Wing of the White House, the first time I'd ever seen the office of the chief of staff.

When we entered the office, James St. Clair was there. I noticed a little stack of white papers in the middle of the desk. We sat down around a conference table, and Haig said that he was supervising the reproduction of certain tapes that had been subpoenaed. He had come across a tape from June 23, 1972,* and he felt it bore upon the problem before us, and that I had a special interest in it. I had been aware of the conversation on the tape,

---

* Known as the "smoking gun" tape.

based on our questioning of Haldeman in the committee about that conversation; this was before we knew about the existence of the tapes. I recall that Haldeman had said that this Watergate issue had come up, and that he had briefly discussed it with the president.

The contents of the tape had been typed out and was on the desk in front of me. Haig asked me to read it. It was clear to me that it was part of a verbatim transcript, but not the whole thing. As I read the material, it implicated the president personally. The idea was that the president was personally involving himself in conduct that could be described as obstruction of justice; I picked this up immediately upon reading it. I was stunned. I didn't have any idea that the president had engaged in that conversation; the oral statements of Haldeman before the committee did not reveal that the president had done that. This was the first evidence that I had seen at all that the president personally was playing a role in what I think could be fairly described as an obstruction of justice. It was very minor; I don't think it justified the impeachment of the president, but on the other hand, it was criminal misconduct committed by the president of the United States.

I asked Haig how long they had had this information. He said, "Just very briefly." I then told him that having disclosed it to me, they had disclosed it to the committee—that I was going to tell the chairman about the presence of the tape. He replied that he understood, but he asked me if I would hold off for the weekend—this was a Friday—and do it on Monday, because the president, that day, would make a statement about the tape. I agreed, and it turned out that the president did disclose it himself in a statement on Monday.

I was really heartsick. I didn't give up. I had recommended in the meeting that the president ought to consider resigning. They indicated to me that there had been some discussion with him about this. My feeling was that, coupled with the multitude of things that had occurred before my reading this tape, this probably was the straw that broke the camel's back, and that he ought to consider resigning rather than face impeachment. I thought it was all over—at least in the House of Representatives—that the House would impeach the president and do so decisively after that disclosure was made. I saw no chance of recovery in the House.

The atmosphere in Haig's office was charged. Perhaps I'm being unkind to Al Haig and to St. Clair, but nevertheless, I'm telling the truth. I had a sense that they were protecting their own rear ends; that they were being excessively wordy in saying what they had not done, what they didn't know. They were trying to impress me that they were blameless of any misconduct that had occurred on the part of Haldeman and the president. I wasn't trying to assess the blame. I asked them when they had learned about this information, but that was the only question that I posed to them about their involvement. But I thought they were excessive in trying to describe their own innocence.

THE "SMOKING GUN" TAPE

James St. Clair I am satisfied that I was furnished all the information that I wanted to know—and then some. There was only one tape that I was not furnished with until nearly the end of the proceedings, which led, ultimately, to his resignation.

Lawrence Higby The way the "smoking gun" tape reads—versus the way Haldeman gave it to the Senate Committee—there clearly is a discrepancy. I confronted him on that. I said, "You lied; you didn't tell the truth." His only reaction was, "All I had was my notes," and I did see his notes. If you had believed the notes, you could have given the testimony again. He said, "I didn't have the tape"—which I don't think he ever did have. He said, "I clearly made a mistake."

Jerry Jones On the June 23rd tape, the reason I knew that the game was over was that I was called by Al Haig from California and told to take the tape to Fred Buzhardt, on the president's orders, and I did. And Buzhardt took it, listened to it, and handed it back to me in about two hours and said, "It's all over." I went back and looked at my entries. The tape had only been listened to twice before, both times by Nixon, the last time in May. That was the first time it was clear that Nixon was implicated, even though he must have had a hand in thinking about what to do to at least prevent political fallout.

Leonard Garment To call the June 23rd tape a "smoking gun" is silly. Do you call something a "smoking gun" when somebody has been dead for three days? What is "smoking" about it? He was dead once he gave over the tapes to Judge Sirica; after that, everything else was anticlimactic.

James St. Clair I felt then, and still do now, that this was a situation that was rectified within two weeks. So in terms of a negative impact upon the government, it should not have had the importance that was ultimately attached to it. This is a permissible argument, but more so in the courtroom than in the public domain. My view is that the conversation cannot be important if it never came to fruition. As soon as the attorney general called up and said, "The FBI can't seem to do the work they were told to do," Nixon said, "Go ahead and do whatever you want to do." If you were in a courtroom talking to a judge, this would be a good argument, but we weren't talking to a judge.

Up until the June 23rd tape, I am satisfied that impeachment would not have been voted in the House [of Representatives]. A member of the House Judiciary Committee had asked: "Where is the smoking gun?" So they found this two-week variation, and there was the "smoking gun." And even if they had voted impeachment, there was a group in the Senate that would have prevented a successful trial. So, had it not been for the "smoking gun," I think we would have prevailed. The June 23rd tape seems so crucial because it was made so crucial.

Gerald R. Ford The "smoking gun" tape came to my knowledge on the Friday before he resigned. That was the first time that I was absolutely convinced that President Nixon was going to be impeached by the House and most likely would be convicted by the Senate. Prior to that time, I said—and I still believe it today—that there was not sufficient evidence to result in a conviction—maybe impeachment, but not a conviction.

THE LAST DAYS

Mr. Nixon's last days in the White House remain a source of fascination and controversy. Some of his close associates claim he was irrational, while others say the president was in full control of his mind, emotions, and office until the very end. On the evening of August 8, Mr. Nixon told the American people of his intention to resign, effective at noon the following day. Then, on the morning of August 9, as a helicopter waited on the White House lawn to transport the president and Mrs. Nixon to Andrews Air Force Base for the flight home to California, Mr. Nixon bade farewell in the East Room to a somber and—in some instances—tearful audience of staff and associates.

Stephen Bull We were exhausted, and not so much from lack of sleep as being emotionally drained. It was very, very grim in the last month. We had had two trips in June, to the Middle East and to the Soviet Union. We came back and went to California in July, and were back in Washington just about a week or ten days before the resignation. Everything was just unraveling:

the "smoking gun" tape; the Supreme Court decision; the increasing number of prominent Republicans calling on President Nixon to resign; and then—finally—the total collapse. I learned that he would resign when, on August 7, Jack Brennan* said that a family member had asked that preparations be made to go West.

Howard Phillips On July 18, 1974, Nixon made a deal with Senators [Jacob] Javits [R-N.Y.], [Mike] Mansfield [D-Mont.], [Walter] Mondale [D-Minn.], and [Robert] Taft [R-Ohio] that, in return for his being able to continue to receive subsidies for his Watergate lawyers, he would sign into law the Legal Services Corporation, which Garment was pushing. He had promised me and some Republican senators that under no circumstances would that happen. Then, on July 25, 1974, the very same Republicans, led by [Senator] Howard Baker and Bill [William] Brock [R-Tenn.], who had opposed its creation, voted for it. And on July 31st, I came out for Nixon's resignation. I made clear in my statement that it had nothing to do with Watergate. I think that Watergate was absolutely petty and was simply a means that was used by the left to derail significant policy changes which Nixon did intend to implement following the 1972 election. Watergate was a very flimsy pretext for ousting a president.

Donald E. Santarelli Nixon needed someone to advise him as to what to do—whether or not to resign. It was purely in his power to step up to the plate and take the medicine rather than to hang on. That's how I got fired: on June 4, 1974, I said, "The president is disabled; he cannot recover. He should resign for the good of the country, and let Jerry Ford carry on as the president." Well, you can't say that when you are a presidential appointee and expect to survive. I didn't.

William Rusher In the very last days of his presidency, a delegation of Republicans went to the White House to tell him that the numbers were against him in the Congress. They found him in the Oval Office, with his feet up on the desk, apparently without a worry in the world. He reminisced about Yorba Linda and his youth, and they realized that they did not have to tell him what they had come to say; he already knew. My interpretation of that is that there is in Nixon—as in many high achievers—a will to self-destruction that only becomes manifest at the point of total success.

---

* Lt. Colonel, U.S. Marine Corps, an aide to the president.

Raymond Price I only came to the conclusion that it was going to end when I saw the transcript of the key part of the "smoking gun" tape, which Haig showed to me on Thursday, August 1st. He called me over and said that the president wanted me to start working on a resignation speech, so he showed me the transcript. I had been gearing up to fight the impeachment battle, but as soon as I read the transcript, I felt he should resign—not for any ethical reason—it was something we could have handled if we had known about it a year earlier—but at that point, we were so politically weakened, and we had built so much of our case on the claim that he was trying to get all the facts out, that this was clearly going to be fatal—and if it was going to be fatal, it was better to get it over with quickly.

George McGovern I didn't think the resignation would come that fast. I'd thought he'd hold on for a while, so I was surprised. A good percentage of Democrats in the Senate were hoping it would not come to a trial; they didn't relish that at all. I don't remember being bloodthirsty myself. I had every reason to be, but I don't recall saying much about it one way or the other. I thought the House did a very good job in the way they handled it, and I think if it had come to a vote in the Senate, the Senate would have voted with the House, probably enough so that it would have been a clear decision. My guess is that the Senate would have gone along with it somewhat reluctantly. I am sure in Nixon's mind he saw resignation as the least painful and degrading way to handle a rather unhappy situation.

Raymond Price The family really wanted him to fight on; they did not want him to resign. Pat Buchanan proposed to me a two-step approach: we were going to have to deliver the transcripts to the court on Monday, the fifth; we should put out the transcripts and put out a statement explaining, from Nixon's perspective, what he meant and what he was trying to do, and then see what the reaction was. If the reaction was as bad as we expected, then go ahead with the resignation, so at least the president, his family, and everybody will know it wasn't just a few people panicking. I asked Pat to come along to Camp David on the weekend. It was very difficult for us to pin down all the facts. The reaction was as bad as we had expected when we put the transcript out on Monday. On Tuesday, the president decided to go ahead with the resignation. I started the resignation speech while he went ahead with the pretense that he was going to fight on. He met with the Cabinet, with the congressional leadership—going through what he felt were all the appropriate motions to cover all the bases before making the announcement, which he did on Thursday night. I talked to him extensively through that period. Of course, he was not happy, but he was determined to try to do it in the right way.

The President's State of Mind

Alexander Haig Until he left office, that man was in control. He was distraught. He was in a personal crisis of unprecedented magnitude—all he ever wanted to be was president. But of all the presidents I have known, he was the most thoughtful, the most generous, with those with whom he worked. No matter how difficult it was in those last days, I'd go in, and he'd ask how my family was.

Philip Lacovara There were concerns that the president might do something dangerous in the last days. There had been the suggestion that the alert during the October 1973 Middle East War had been precipitated for domestic political purposes. As the president's position in the late spring and into the summer of 1974 became more grave, there were concerns that a military action was not out of the question. We were assured by back-channels in the White House that if—as somebody put it—the president picks up a red phone, nobody will answer it. So it was somewhat reassuring to know that there were cool heads saying: we are not going to gamble the country for the protection of Richard Nixon's political interests.

Jerry Jones I saw the president in various Cabinet situations; I saw him the night he made the television address, when he had the Hill guys down, and at his farewell in the East Room. He was obviously under considerable stress. The government—in terms of his being a part of its functioning and the decision process—simply went on auto pilot, and the junior staffers—about twelve of us—basically did the work for several months, Haig and the president being completely occupied. In terms of Nixon's having been out of his mind, unable to perform, I don't think so; we would have known. He was under great stress—a huge emotional burden—unhappy, extremely sad, maybe panicked. But not able to function? Out of his gourd? No, I don't think so. Haig wove through the endgame there with unbelievable skill. He and Nixon did that together; it was brilliantly done for our country. If Nixon had been out of his gourd and unable to function, I don't think it could have been done so well.

Raymond Price On Wednesday night, while Woodward and Bernstein had Nixon talking to the pictures and chewing the rug,* I had finished up at the office at around 1 A.M. and had gone home. At about three-thirty, I got a call from him; he had been thinking more about the ending, and he spun out his thoughts to me. I went back to sleep, and he called again, with more thoughts. He called a third time, at about four-thirty or five; we worked out what became the final part of the speech. So, he had been thinking this through while they had him eating the rug; he had been on the phone with me. He was absolutely rational—really thinking through the substance of the speech and what had to be done.

Ronald Ziegler I can say absolutely without question that any report that Richard Nixon at any stage of the process—particularly the last weeks and the final days—was less than stable was absolutely a total violation of historic fact. I was there; I was with him as much as any other man. Obviously, there was emotion involved, but not extreme emotion; there was total understanding and a totally balanced view of the fact that he had lost his ability to lead. He did not lose control of his emotions; he was not erratic. He was balanced and knew exactly the course he had to take.

I guess I'm one of the few people—together with Haig and some others—whose firsthand observation of the man during that period will have to prevail someday, because Woodward and Bernstein's speculation on that period is not correct. Were there tears? Yes. But not at that point from President Nixon; the natural sense of tragedy—and the natural reactions to tragedy—occurred. Did Richard Nixon talk nostalgically to me? I was the last one to see him the night before he resigned. Yes. He talked nostalgically. Does that say he was off the wall? He was walking calmly through the White House that he had worked so hard to achieve, reflecting on paintings or whatever else is on the White House walls; that's not off the wall.

A fact that supports the reality of what I am saying is that he accepted my proposition—and I had the support of Diane Sawyer, Frank Gannon,† and others—that the departure should be televised. I said, "Mr. President, your departure has to be communicated, so that the American people—within their own minds—can bring closure to this tragic period. You simply cannot get into an automobile and drive to Andrews [Air Force Base] and get into an airplane and fly away, because the people, in their observation of the

---

* The *Washington Post* reporters' account of the preresignation period in *The Final Days* (Scribner's).
† Members of the White House Press Office staff.

transfer of power, will not be able to bring closure to it. No matter how diffi-cult it is, you have to shake hands with President Ford—in full national view—because if you don't, the people will not witness the peaceful transi-tion of power, which is so important." He bought into that totally.

He also agreed—at my suggestion—to address the staff on live television. If you look back at the speech he gave in the East Room—referring to his mother—it was a catharsis for him and also for the nation to see the tragedy of a fallen leader. His willingness—and knowledge of the importance of doing it nationally, and to have the transition of power shown—shows the stability of the man, not the instability. And his survival in California and the many books he has written since August 1974 tend to support my proposi-tion. If you accept the proposition that he was emotionally unstable and couldn't deal with reality, he would have walked into the Pacific with a bot-tle of Chivas Regal under his arm.

THE FIRST MENTION OF A PRESIDENTIAL PARDON

Robert Hartmann Haig told Ford on August 1st, when he met with him alone for forty-five minutes. After Haig left the office, Ford called me in and said, "Bob, what I am going to tell you must not go any farther than this room." He was staring at the ceiling, his face grim; he looked like a 200-pound blocker had just hit him. He told me that Haig had read a transcript of the June 23rd meeting, and that it was even worse than he had thought; it was devastating. It proved that Nixon knew about the cover-up from the start. Then Ford said that Haig reported that Nixon wasn't sure what he was going to do. He then reviewed for Ford the dwindling options: the president could declare himself incapacitated and turn things over to the vice-president until he was acquitted or removed by the Senate. This upset me, and I told Ford that nothing in the Twenty-fifth Amendment would prevent the president from taking back his office any day of the week. Then, he said, Haig had talked about the possibility of Nixon pardoning himself before resigning, which his lawyers thought he had the power to do, or of resigning and then being pardoned.

I asked Ford what he had said in reply. He said, "I told Haig I would think about it." This was almost the worst answer Haig could take back to the White House, because Ford had told Haig he was, at least, willing to entertain the idea. I said to Ford, "You should have taken him by the scruff of the neck and thrown him the hell out of here, and then immediately called a press conference to explain why."

I could see that Ford had not grasped the momentous impropriety of Haig mentioning the word *pardon* in his presence.

Alexander Haig It is totally untrue that I raised the question of pardon with Ford. He swore in the House Judiciary Committee that this was totally untrue. A series of options was given to him, including pardons: the president can pardon himself; you [Ford] can pardon him. There were five options written by Fred Buzhardt, and when he discussed the last one with me—on pardons—he said, "Al, this is a very, very controversial one and you have to be very careful about what you say when you go over it." What I didn't know was that there were men around Ford who wanted him to be president, and wanted to get Nixon out as quickly as they could—and Mr. Hartmann was one of them. As I met with Ford, Hartmann was hiding behind the curtain. After Ford became president, I went to him and said, "You ought to fire this guy; he is going to do you in, Mr. President." Ford said, "Al, I will handle it." I replied, "You have given me my answer; I am going to leave." And that is why I left.

Jerry Jones My strong recommendation to Haig was that he be pardoned. As staff secretary to Ford, I was sitting right in the middle of the government, and the Nixon problem was such that none of the other issues coming before the government could be dealt with; this was going to be our agenda forever; it had to be ended. The issue was being used for political purposes: he would have been indicted and the trial would have occurred in September of 1976, and it would have been used to defeat Ford; it was a giant whirlpool that was sucking us all into this sordid problem. There would have been a huge show trial; Ford would have been on the back burner and would have looked befuddled. As this circus went on, Ford's chances of doing well would have been far less than they were in having made the pardon.

Raymond Price If Haig did raise the question of a pardon with Ford, it was not on a quid pro quo basis. When the pardon became an issue, I thought it was essential—quite apart from the personal interests of the people involved—for the national interest. Len Garment and I put together a memo for Ford, making the point that it was clear that he was not going to be able to govern as long as that little piece of red meat was hanging out there; the press would not focus on anything else—would not let him do anything else—as long as they had a chance to put Nixon on the gibbet. The only way to stop it was with the pardon.

Gerald R. Ford Haig had met me in the morning on August 1st, but he came back in the afternoon. In the second meeting, he presented to me five or six different options that he said could take place. As I recall, one was that Nixon could pardon himself; another was that I would agree to pardon him after I became president. None of them were what I considered proposals; they were just what the White House was talking about. To make certain he would know how I felt, I called him back the next morning and told him, "Al, under no circumstances should you and the president consider anything we discussed as something I would do." I had Bryce Harlow, Bob Hartmann, and Jack [John O.] Marsh [Jr.]* listening as I read a statement to Haig, clearly indicating that I had nothing to do with any of the five or six options Haig had discussed.

Robert Hartmann Nixon knew that Jerry Ford would never let him go to jail. What was bothering Nixon at the time was not just the impeachment process, but the possibility of his indictment on additional charges—which would still be hanging there without the protection of executive privilege. In fact, before Ford issued the pardon, he had Philip Buchen† inquire of [Special Prosecutor] Leon Jaworski about how many high crimes and misdemeanors there were to which the president might be vulnerable if he were not still president. Jaworski came back with a long list of possible violations of criminal law, so from their long association, Nixon knew that Ford would not let him rot in jail.

Alexander Butterfield I thought he should go to jail. Most people don't see it that way; they think the poor guy suffered enough. Most people believe him. I feel positive that he was involved and had to give the nod. And, incidentally, he may have given the nod when they broke in thirty days earlier. Technically, he could say: I didn't know they were going in. It may be true that he didn't know they were going in that night, but I know that Haldeman had to know.

DISCUSSION OF PARDONS FOR KEY AIDES

John Ehrlichman Haldeman was discussing pardons. His lawyers worked up a brief on the subject; it was quite persuasive. Haldeman tried to get the

---

* An aide to Mr. Ford.
† Ford's lawyer.

president to read the brief, but he called me and said that Haig was blocking his calls to Nixon. My own view at the time was that I didn't want a pardon. This shows how unenlightened I was. I also knew that Nixon was getting strong advice against the pardon idea.

Alexander Haig I talked to Bob Haldeman several times about his request for a pardon. I don't know why Nixon didn't do it, but I think he felt that it would be more gasoline on the fire. Haldeman was a selfless, loyal White House chief of staff, and a highly effective one. You never saw him at the Cabinet table; it would have been inconceivable for him to have sat there. On the other hand, in the Reagan years, [White House aides] Jim Baker, Ed Meese, and Mike Deaver *were* the president; you couldn't serve in his administration without knowing that Reagan was a cipher and that these men were running the government. You also knew that Reagan had some principles, and that he was stubborn. Thank God for that. But you also knew that there would be trouble, because these weasels—who had never done anything in their lives to justify that kind of power—had it all, using Mama.

H. R. Haldeman The president called me the day before he resigned and told me he was going to resign. I said I thought that was the wrong move for him to make, but, as always, I would support whatever decision he took. As I got to thinking about it, it occurred to me—I realize it's self-serving—that it was of value to the president and to the country that a final act for him that would be a very wise move would be to issue a blanket pardon for everybody connected with Watergate, and a blanket pardon to everybody who was illegally involved in the Vietnam War draft resistance; there was still legal action pending against those people. My argument was that this would eliminate Vietnam and Watergate—the two major traumas of the Nixon presidency—as upfront issues, so that Jerry Ford could take over the presidency and move forward without carrying the load of Vietnam or Watergate. It seemed to me to be a good idea.

I was obviously naive; my wife told me it was a stupid idea. I guess the president decided that, too. I communicated the idea to the president through Haig. I'm not sure it got to the president. John Ehrlichman thought he had communicated it through Julie [Nixon Eisenhower, the president's daughter], but I don't know if it ever got to the president. In any event, he decided not to do it.

Should he have pardoned us? Probably not. I think I'm better off now, having not been pardoned. There were about six years when I didn't think that; they were pretty miserable years. Now that it's all over, and looking back—this is my wife's view—somebody has to be convicted. A pardon says that everybody is guilty, and nobody will ever know who, and that is an unsatisfying solution. I paid the price, and that's over with. There are people who have argued that I should have tried to get [President Ronald] Reagan or [President George] Bush to pardon me, but I have never tried to do that. Today, I would not want a pardon. I was convicted and served my time; I know what I did and didn't do, and I am perfectly happy living with my knowledge. I believe that the system failed in the sense that it convicted innocent people, or convicted people of the wrong crimes, at least. I have a very solid personal relationship with the [former] president and intend to keep it.

LEARNING THAT THE PRESIDENT WOULD RESIGN

Ben Bradlee The first person to tell me that Nixon was going to resign was Barry Goldwater. It was the day before he resigned. He said, "Goddamn it, you can't use this. If he picks up the *Post* tomorrow morning and it says he is going to resign that day, he won't do it." Goldwater was absolutely convinced that the resignation was essential. He was a hidden friend of mine; nobody knew it. Goldwater wanted him out. We wrote a story that talked about the increasing pressure on Nixon to resign. I made some great rationalization that he hadn't really made up his mind. When Goldwater told me of the resignation, I wondered if the old bastard was right. Nothing could surprise me anymore.

We didn't need his head on a platter. We were right; we didn't need vindication. When that jerk, Ziegler, got up there and apologized publicly to the *Washington Post,* that was enough for me.

Gerald R. Ford President Nixon asked me to come into the [Oval] Office after [Senator] Hugh Scott [R-Pa.] left.* He urged me to retain Henry Kissinger. I told him that I had worked with Kissinger for a long time, I was a strong advocate of his policies, and therefore, it was my intention—if and when I became president—to retain him, which I did.

There were just the two of us. He sat behind his desk in the Oval Office; I sat on a chair on his left side. He was very calm—very straightforward. He told me that he planned to resign the next day at eleven o'clock. After he

---

* Senators Scott and Barry Goldwater (R-Ariz.) and Representative John Rhodes (R-Ariz.) went to the White House on August 7 to inform President Nixon that he would not survive an impeachment vote and urged him to resign.

made these comments, we chatted for ten or fifteen minutes about our longstanding friendship; how we had worked together since 1949; about how he had campaigned in my congressional district; how I had come to California; how we had spent a lot of time together, socially and otherwise. Once the business was over, it was a chat among old friends.

I was saddened that a friend of mine, who had twice been elected president of the United States, was in a position where he had to resign from that office. I was sad because of what was happening to him, and it didn't give me any personal satisfaction, because I had never sought the presidency. On the other hand, once I knew that I was going to have that responsibility the next day, I felt very confident about my ability to do the job: I had dealt with major issues in the Congress; I had been the Republican leader for nine years; I had dealt firsthand with presidents from Eisenhower to Kennedy, to Johnson, to Nixon; I had, fortunately, been on committees which were of major consequence in foreign policy and military strategy. So I was torn between being sad about a friend having to go through this tragedy and, on the other hand, my conviction that I was ready for the job.

Hermann Eilts I received instructions to inform Sadat; they came about twelve to fourteen hours before the resignation was announced in Washington. I was to tell Sadat of the resignation and to assure him that President Ford would continue Nixon's policy with respect to Egypt, and that he would keep Kissinger in office. I got Sadat out of bed early in the morning. It was a shock to him. He made a comment about Watergate's being insignificant; he was convinced that the resignation must be due to Nixon's health—his phlebitis.

Viktor Sukhodrev The Soviet leaders were surprised that Nixon had to resign. They couldn't really understand, although they were reading the *Tass* reports, and reports from Ambassador [Anatoly] Dobrynin, in Washington, on what was happening and of something they regarded as a minor occurrence; they couldn't believe that the president had given the instructions.

So until the very last, they couldn't accept the notion that a president could really be impeached. That word doesn't exist in Russian. The word used was *impeachment*; that's how the Soviet leaders learned that word. It exists now in modern Russian politics, and a couple of years ago, that word was used in the Russian Parliament in connection with [Russian President Boris] Yeltsin. Brezhnev couldn't bring himself to believe that Nixon was in all that danger.

When Nixon left office, he became a nonperson to the Soviet leadership, just as Khrushchev had when he was kicked out. They no longer shot people, but became a nonperson.

Yuri Barsukov The leaders in Moscow really believed that Nixon's attitude toward the Soviet Union was a reason for the Watergate scandal, and I think they were right. They were surprised that he had to resign, because this had never happened before to an American president. The resignation stopped the progress that had been achieved in the relationship between the Soviet Union and the United States. I don't understand, even now, how a president who was elected in 1972 with an absolute majority could—in a year and a half—be out of office.

Raymond Price At the time I was drafting the Thursday night speech, I did not know that he was going to do the Friday morning East Room appearance; he prepared it all himself that Thursday night. The family didn't know that the cameras were going to be there. I was surprised to see them. I had thought that doing the Thursday night speech we were doing his final public event as president.

Bob Woodward We've never written about it. I remember Carl and I didn't have a story to write. We were in the newsroom watching the speech and they brought up bologna sandwiches. There was a sense, somewhat, of bewilderment [over] what had happened; what did it mean—a genuine sense of having worked on this for over two years and not knowing a lot; not understanding the consequences. There was no feeling that we had been vindicated, or of fulfillment.

He suffered a great, great loss. That farewell speech is one of the great spontaneous moments in history. And to give him credit, he sensibly—as he said—impeached himself, and saved himself and the country a great ordeal. He deserves great credit for doing that—for seeing that he'd lost.

THE PRESIDENT BIDS FAREWELL TO HIS ASSOCIATES*

Terrence O'Donnell It was a wrenching experience: there was sadness, anger, uncertainty—all kinds of emotions—in the East Room, and then in following the president out to the lawn. And shock—because I never

---

* August 9, 1974.

believed that no matter how bad it was, it would end up driving the president out of office. Many of us on the staff had thought: this will pass; it can't be as bad as the newspapers say; it will come around. But the staff was not privy to the legal deliberations, to the tapes, to the innermost councils.

Frederic V. Malek We felt deep disappointment in President Nixon—at what he resigned for: deceiving us and the public. He had done wonderful things in terms of world peace and developing a meaningful and coherent foreign policy. We thought he was, in many respects, a great president. But his actions were disappointing—deeply so. He lied; he continuously lied. He continuously deceived us—as well as others.

Robert Odle, Jr. There was in the Nixon rubric a little too much of a desire to get back—to get even; there was the dark side, which would occasionally get out, and to which others would play. I think that Richard Nixon understood that himself; he dealt with it beautifully in his farewell speech in the East Room. At the time, people said he was losing his mind: he talked about his mother; he almost fell apart. But if you go back and read that speech, it all hangs together. He said, "Don't hate. Never hate. Hate destroys you."

Jerry Jones In the East Room, I was quite angry with him. I felt he had let us down horribly; that he had done things he hadn't needed to do—things that were not right—and subverted the whole reason I was in the government. I didn't see a Republican being elected again for the rest of my lifetime. So I was quite upset with him in the end. I am, in part, still angry; I think I see things in a somewhat more rounded view than I did then, but essentially, I was quite angry with the guy for letting us down and selling out what we had all worked so hard to achieve on the country's behalf, on his behalf, on our own behalf.

Roy Ash If you looked around that room, you saw grown men and women crying. It was very, very emotional and moving when he left. But that wasn't the end of the story. We went to lunch. Afterward, we were back with President Ford; the government was in business again. It was amazing how the transition of government took place from hitting the bottom to in a couple of hours—with lunch in between—being right back in business. The important part is not the emotional part at the bottom, but how quickly we were in full-scale business again with the new president.

AT THE HELICOPTER PAD

William Saxbe When he made his dramatic, family-surrounded, tearful speech, and then walked to the chopper, I thought it was high drama—like somebody had choreographed it. I felt that, under the circumstances, he was a little overly dramatic.

Robert Hartmann After the Nixons got on the helicopter, I went to Bill Timmons's° office. He had a bottle of scotch on his desk and a drink in his hand. He poured me a little tumbler full and said, "To the president," meaning Ford. I said, "To the president," meaning Nixon.

Gerald R. Ford It was about the way we had felt the night before, when we went to bed and held one another's hand and offered a little prayer, which I often used—Proverbs 3:5–6: "Trust in the Lord with all thine heart; lean not on thine own understanding. In all thy ways, acknowledge Him and He shall direct thy path." That is the way both of us felt.

Leaving the White House and Heading West

Stephen Bull Nobody asked me to go; I just did. I'm not sure how we decided who was going and who wasn't. Those of us who should have gone did. I was on the helicopter, and then on the plane, with the president. It was grim, very, very, very quiet lifting off and leaving for the last time; every other time we had gone to San Clemente it was with all the accoutrements of the president and the presidency: people, and staff, and lots of activity. We had been there a week or ten days before, and there had been all that activity. Now it was just like a ghost town, and that is the way it remained.

At San Clemente

Ron Ziegler I was with him on the helicopter and I was with him in San Clemente for almost a year after the resignation. I saw him daily—on many days, hourly—and there was not one sentence uttered by the man—not one thought in the year I was with him—about coming back politically. On the

° Congressional liaison.

contrary, there was a disciplined approach in his persona and in his spirit not to allow this to destroy him as a human being. His actions then were to keep his intellect and selfhood going so that this tragedy would not destroy him as a person. That is what he focused on and what has proven to be his success after the tragedy.

Were there memories? Yes. Was there bitterness? Surprisingly, no. Was there blaming the press? No. Were there long-winded discussions—tirades—over the ill treatment he received from the *Washington Post?* No. Was there confusion at the actions of his men? Yes. I sat there with him in enough private moments of discussion—of reflection—to say that I don't believe it is naive to say, absolutely, that Richard Nixon was—and still is—confused about the complexity of Watergate. Certainly, he knew his mistakes—although he has not fully addressed them, although he did, to a great extent, in his memoirs. He does not give up any responsibility; he accepts the wrongdoings of the period. But he is still confused about the motivations of his men; I think that he will go to his grave confused about this.

Stephen Bull Regardless of the circumstances, he was still a former president. He was going to receive mail; he had to answer it. I had to get him set up with stationery and postage, and to figure out how he could—and should—operate.

NIXON'S POSTRESIGNATION ILLNESS

Robert Hartmann Nixon was really dying. I was in the Long Beach [California] Memorial Hospital, and talked to Pat and the girls. Ford was supposed to go in and see Nixon, but the door lock in Nixon's private room jammed; Ford started to open the door and couldn't. Nixon, who was filled with tubes—one going down his throat; one in his nose—was left alone in the room for twenty minutes. They had to send someone outside to climb the wall to his floor and break the window. Nixon was capable of faking, but there was nothing faked about that illness. If Ford had waited for the illness to pardon Nixon, he would have been cheered.

Gerald R. Ford I've never seen anybody who was so sick come back and live: he was attached to tubes; he could barely recognize me. I am glad I went. I got a lot of criticism for it, but it was the right thing to do. If he had died and I hadn't gone, I would have felt even worse.

28

The Pardon

In the days immediately following the resignation, the Special Prosecution Force debated the question of whether to ask the grand jury to change Mr. Nixon's status in the Watergate cover-up from that of an unindicted to an indicted co-conspirator. As this discussion continued, President Ford and his aides were beginning to experience problems and complications arising from Mr. Nixon's resignation. These difficulties—which were, to some degree, inhibiting the Ford administration from getting on with the process of governance—would be compounded if the ex-president were to face trial—and, possibly, incarceration.

On the morning of Sunday, September 8, 1974, President Ford announced to a stunned nation that he had granted Mr. Nixon a "full, free and absolute pardon" for all offenses he had committed—or may have committed, or had taken part in—during the period from January 20, 1969 through August 9, 1974.

Gerald R. Ford I was urged by some of my advisers: Why don't you wait until he is indicted or impeached? Why don't you wait until the trial? Why don't you wait until he is convicted and appeals to the Supreme Court? We had, in my opinion, had enough of the headlines and public diversion from more serious matters, and the only way to clean the desk was to do what I did, when I did it. With the passing of time, I am even more convinced that I was right.

Philip Lacovara My advice was that Jaworski ought to be talking to the White House about getting President Ford to make the pardon decision; I never urged that President Ford should issue a pardon. The point that I made—which may have gotten garbled in translation—was that the worst position for the prosecution of the Watergate cover-up defendants was to have lurking over the proceedings the possibility of a pardon, which would complicate everything—make the jurors uneasy about whether they should be convicting these people, while the primary culprit, President Nixon, was absent from the dock.

And also, a lot of psychological resources were going into the question of the what-to-do-about-the-president issue. The constitutional issue—to the extent that there was one—about whether a sitting president could be indicted had evaporated with his resignation, but there was the question: Should he now be indicted and added to the group of defendants who were about to go on trial in October of 1974?

President Ford had taken some soundings, with public musings that he might be willing to pardon President Nixon. So my advice was that if he was going to do it, he ought to do it sooner rather than later; get it clarified, not have us indict and have a pardon issued, or have us go through the process of adding President Nixon as an additional defendant and then having a pardon complicate the proceedings.

John Dean To me, the difficulty with the pardon is how Nixon could be the only person to qualify for it; I think it was unfair to pardon Nixon and not everyone else. Bush, for example, when he slipped in that pardon for the Iran-Contra people at the end, got everybody who had any problem and cleaned it all up. It just happened, and no one ever really said anything. Ford could have done the same thing; it might have softened his pardoning of Nixon by pardoning everybody. It's hard for me to believe that Nixon didn't do it himself; he was the one who should have done it. He didn't because this would have been a total admission of guilt. He is always ready for another day and another fight.

John Ehrlichman Ford was correct in pardoning Nixon; the White House would have been dead in the water for a year or more if Nixon had been impeached, tried, or both. Ford's hands would have been tied behind his back. If Nixon had been charged, I think he would have been convicted of anything the government wanted. The climate was absolutely poisoned; it had been so conditioned by television. It is hard enough to get a fair trial in

Washington, D.C., under the best of circumstances. Nixon certainly had been engaged in a cover-up; the government could have proved that.

Donald E. Santarelli Jerry Ford's pardon of Nixon was an extraordinarily heroic act. He did it for the highest public policy reasons. I was involved in it and can recall the discussions that the country should not be subject to the president in the dock—no matter who he is. The destructive nature of the effort to impeach President [Andrew] Johnson after the assassination of Lincoln was not lost on any of us: it allowed the radical Republicans in the Congress to engage in Reconstruction abuses [following the Civil War] for the next twenty years because of the disability of the executive as a result of the impeachment proceedings. All of Ford's advisers—and Ford himself—took that view, that whatever Nixon did or didn't do was not relevant; what was relevant was how destructive to the nation the process against Nixon could be, at a time when presidential leadership was vital. The disability of a president allows all the rats in the bilge of the ship to take it over.

The suggestion that the pardon was some kind of a quid pro quo with Ford is pure bullshit. I've always been irritated by that suggestion. Jerry Ford is not that kind of guy; he wouldn't have done anything like that; he's just too decent. In granting the pardon, he acted knowing he was committing close to political suicide. But he felt it was for the good of the country. He is a simple, noble guy.

George McGovern I didn't resist as strongly against the pardon as the public did. I was in a Methodist church in Watertown, South Dakota, and right in the middle of the sermon, the usher handed me a note. It said that President Ford had just pardoned Mr. Nixon and there were a number of reporters who wanted to know what I thought. Well, I didn't think that it was all that bad; it seemed to me that it would save the country a lot of grief and partisan wrangling. I was speaking at a Democratic picnic out at a park that day, and when I got out there the crowd was in an uproar; they just thought it was awful. I was up for election then, and the next day I was campaigning in the southern part of the state, in a very Republican area, and they were outraged.

And I began to realize this was going to cause serious trouble for Ford, who at that time was riding the crest of good feeling. I figured: if South Dakota thinks this is a bad idea, it's not going to go down very well everywhere. I did think it was better to complete the judicial process and then consider a pardon, but I have to confess that I talked to Goldwater just about the time Ford did this and suggested to him that maybe it would be a good thing if there was a pardon. He didn't think so.

Gerald R. Ford I gave no thought at the time to the possible impact upon the 1976 election—I would have been elected president if I had carried Ohio and Hawaii, or Ohio and Delaware, or if I had carried New York. The pardon was a factor, not the most important factor, but there were a good many diehard liberals who hated Nixon; who wanted him strung up; and never forgave me for removing that possibility. But I believed then—and believe today—that it was the right thing to do. I had come to the conclusion that I had an obligation—which was my own decision—to spend 100 percent of my time on the problems of 230 million people. And I had found out in the first month of being in the Oval Office that I was spending 25 percent of my time listening to the lawyers from Justice; the lawyers from the White House, advising me on what I should do about Mr. Nixon's tapes and his papers. Well, that was a poor distribution of my time.

I had the problems of a growing economic crisis; our allies were uncertain as to what this change [in administrations] would bring about in our relations; we were apprehensive about what the Soviet Union might do. I felt I had an obligation to spend 100 percent of my time on the problems of 230 million people, rather than 25 percent of my time on the problems of one man.

Jeb Stuart Magruder You don't accept a pardon if you're not guilty; you accept the pardon because you are guilty. Therefore, in this case, it was a pardon before serving any time, or sentencing, or conviction. In Agnew's case, he had to list out a bill of particulars. I think that would have been appropriate [in Nixon's case]; it would have made a lot of difference to Ford's situation, and helped him tremendously.

Stephen Bull Politically, it was probably the best move that Jerry Ford could have made. People say that it was his undoing, but I disagree. Think of the timing: this was September 1974; if he was going to run for president, he would be right in the middle of the trial of Richard Nixon. I am not saying that he did it for political purposes, but the result was that it got Watergate out of the way—and got it off the back of Nixon's vice-president, Gerald Ford. President Nixon called me into his office and told me about the pardon and said it would occur the next day; he was matter-of-fact. I can't characterize his attitude toward it; to me, the acceptance of a pardon suggests acknowledgment of wrongdoing, and I didn't feel at the time that he was guilty of the crimes that were being attributed to him, and I still don't. It would have been a terrible period. The pardon put a punctuation mark on it; it was the beginning of the end.

William Ruckelshaus If you look at all the evidence in the cover-up—that was the specific crime he was charged with—there probably were violations of the criminal law in what he did. Whether he would ultimately have been tried and convicted, I don't know. My own view is that President Ford was absolutely right in pardoning him; we had to get that behind us. There is no question that he could have handled it better; he could have better conditioned people for what he was about to do. But the action itself was absolutely right, both in terms of the interest of the country—which has to be paramount over all other interests—and in the interest of justice. The former president wasn't going to suffer any more than he already had; it almost killed him. I don't see what would have been gained by going through a trial. I continue to read about all of the unanswered questions about Watergate. Maybe there are some, but it is the most investigated crime in the history of man. I don't think that there are any important unanswered questions.

Philip Lacovara When the grand jury indicted the cover-up defendants, they specifically named the president as an unindicted co-conspirator, so they had already decided that there was enough evidence to charge him with criminal responsibility, although they elected not to indict him. After the resignation, there was very strong pressure from the younger members of the Watergate Task Force to move quickly to indict President Nixon. I think it was partly motivated by their desire not to have this whole effort become a side show—going after the lieutenants, when the field marshal would be skirting free. The other part of it was more of a tactical judgment. It would be—in their view—a more difficult case to prosecute successfully if the main culprit—using an organized crime scenario—if the head of the crime syndicate isn't there, but everybody knows he was pulling the strings and the only defendants are the button men, or the soldiers. It's not the kind of thing that plays as well with a jury, so there was a rationale for moving quickly to indict the former president.

That was the period of the to-ing and fro-ing with the White House over whether it was fair, decent, honorable—the American way—to indict this man who had been hounded out of office and publicly humiliated and was nevertheless on his way to his grave. I think that when push came to shove, Leon Jaworski would not have authorized an indictment. I should say that the grand jurors themselves were quite eager to issue a new indictment against the former president, and that Leon appeared before the grand jury and urged them not to act in haste, but to await further advice and recommendation. Within a few weeks, the pardon intervened and made that whole issue largely academic.

Seymour Glanzer As far as the pardon was concerned, you are talking about a nation that could have convulsed into some unforeseen thing. You would be dealing with a very dangerous situation: one-third of the country did not believe for a minute that Nixon had done anything wrong and, probably, another third didn't care. The fact that Nixon stepped down was a godsend; otherwise, we would have had a civil war.

Bobby Baker Nixon could be absolutely certain that Jerry Ford would do what he asked—and he did. And Ford destroyed himself; he would have easily beaten Jimmy Carter in the 1976 presidential race had it not been for the pardon. I have no question that Nixon asked him for the pardon.

Gerald R. Ford I had no personal contact with Nixon before I made the decision—or after I made the decision. Four or five days later, he called to thank me.

Bob Woodward The pardon made sense; it was a way of ending the issue. Extracting the pound of flesh? That would have been silly. It was all about the exercise of power, and Nixon was out of power, so there was no sensible reason not to. At the same time, I was distressed by the pardon. The best deals are without an explicit agreement. I think that through the good offices of Haig, and Price, and Garment, what amounted to a deal was made, and it made sense.

Archibald Cox I said at the time—and continue to think—the pardon violated the principle that all individuals, powerful and powerless, rich and poor, must stand equally at the bar of justice after they are charged with criminal wrongdoing. He was excused from that.

I tend to think of it in terms of an incident in the wee hours of the morning at O'Hare Airport.* I had just flown in from an ABA [American Bar Association] meeting in Honolulu and was waiting for my luggage. Nearby were maybe three baggage handlers and three taxi drivers, and I heard a voice saying, "Archie, Archie." I didn't see anyone I recognized; it turned

* The airport serving Chicago, Illinois.

out to be one of the baggage handlers. When you have an experience like this, you learn how friendly the American people are. The next thing I know, a little knot—six or seven people—have gathered around me. "Think he'll be indicted? Think he'll be indicted?"

I said, "Look fellows, I've been fired. I don't know if he'll be indicted." Then the word went around: "If it had been me, they would have put me in the pen."

Charles Wiggins I thought it was one of Jerry Ford's most important acts. It was clear that there was a great sense of frustration on the part of the majority that they didn't have the right to impeach the president. They thought they had the votes to impeach him, and that somehow that was mooted by the president's resignation. And they wanted to proceed with criminal prosecution of the president.

I don't think they thought that through at all. I don't think they understood the involvement of the public mind in a criminal prosecution of the president; it would have been all-consuming for, perhaps, a period of eighteen months. We didn't need that at all in the country at that time; we really needed to put that behind us. When he assumed the presidency, Jerry Ford's principal obligation was to put Watergate behind us, so I thought he acted wisely in ending all possibility of criminal prosecution by pardoning Nixon. There is no doubt it hurt Ford politically, but I thought he had acted in the public interest, and I was proud of him for doing it.

WOULD NIXON HAVE BEEN ABLE TO GET A FAIR TRIAL?

Samuel Dash I believe that Nixon could have had a fair trial on the evidence. Do you try a former president of the United States in a criminal courtroom? One has to look at the trauma that might occur in the country. I felt that the American people would not only be able to stand such an event, but that it would be good for the people to see that even the highest authority can be tried under equal justice under the law. The opposite was demonstrated, particularly by the pardon: here was a situation where the highest subordinates went to prison, but the president—who had played a significant role—got off scot-free. This left a tremendous scar on our concept of justice: I would get letters from judges who said, "I've got a young black man in for burglary; how can I sentence him when the president is free? Where is our justice system?"

Philip Lacovara He would have had a fair trial and, perversely, it's because of the amazing ignorance—and I use ignorance in the technical sense—of many of the jurors. One of the things we found in connection with some of the prior prosecutions, even before Watergate, the Ellsberg break-in case, and some of the other cases—and what certainly played out during the *voir dire* of the prospective jurors—was the very high percentage of citizens of the District of Columbia who hadn't the foggiest idea what Watergate was all about. Many of them hadn't even heard the names of the key defendants: the Haldemans, Ehrlichmans, Mitchells. Of course, they knew who Richard Nixon was, but I believe it would have been possible to have gotten a jury in the district composed of people who could honestly have said that they would decide the case on the basis of the evidence in the courtroom.

And that reflects two assumptions: one, that they probably didn't know very much about what had happened outside the courtroom—certainly they didn't know very much about the details, other than that Nixon had resigned because of something to do with Watergate, whatever that was. Second, Richard Nixon never did anything to me; I'm not going to send him to jail unless he did something bad. So I believe that had there been a prosecution, it would have been possible to have gotten a fair-minded jury—not necessarily the kind of jury you would say ought to be disposing of high matters of state—people who don't read newspapers, or when the television news comes on, are only interested in the ball scores.

Fred Dalton Thompson From a legal point of view, he would have received a fair trial. But within what is considered a fair trial legally there is a great array of things that can play out. Any time you have an individual being tried in the midst of his opponents, it's very difficult to get what most of us on a common-sense basis would call fairness. Washington, D.C., was one of the two places in the nation that voted for George McGovern.* It was also the hotbed of publicity.

Ben Bradlee I had absolutely zero stomach for seeing the president of the United States on trial for anything. But, it seemed to me that, as President Ford was holding all fifty-two cards and Nixon had none, I would have gotten out the document that they drafted for Agnew and just read it in court, just made him admit it—a specific series of crimes. Today, people are teaching about Watergate who were six years old when it happened. You don't get any sense that these [Nixon] people mocked the system of justice. They

* In the 1972 presidential elections.

mocked it. It seems to me that they should have exacted something in return for the pardon. I would have given the pardon, but I would have been in no hurry to give it, and I would have said to Nixon: You have to acknowledge your own culpability. Then Ford could say: I have hereby pardoned him, but Richard Nixon has signed the following statement.

Most people think of Watergate now as [Robert] Redford, and Jason Robards, and Dustin Hoffman. That's what these kids see; they think it's quite a good movie.*

Gerald R. Ford Nixon's statement from San Clemente was not as forthright as I would have preferred. However, there is a U.S. Supreme Court decision in another case involving a presidential pardon:† there is a simple sentence in that decision which says—in effect—that the granting of a pardon is an indication of guilt, and the acceptance is an admission of guilt. So, from my point of view, I have the backing of a Supreme Court decision that his acceptance of a pardon is an acknowledgment of guilt.

Richard Kleindienst I only fault Jerry Ford for one thing about the pardon: that he waited as long as he did; he should have done it immediately, because you just can't have Richard Nixon on a witness stand, with three steel balls in his hand,‡ with sweat pouring down his forehead, being prosecuted.

---

* *All the President's Men,* in which Robert Redford, Jason Robards, and Dustin Hoffman starred.

† In the case of Andrew Johnson, who succeeded to the presidency following the assassination of Abraham Lincoln in 1965. Mr. Johnson was not, however, impeached.

‡ A reference to Captain Queeg, a character in Herman Wouk's novel, *The Caine Mutiny.*

29

The Media's Role in Nixon's Downfall

Kenneth Rush Nixon knew nothing about the break-in, but when it was brought up to him, he did what every president has done: he covered it up—like Johnson and Kennedy. He had drifted into it. What turned Watergate from something small into something massive was the situation involving the Vietnam War—the hatred of Nixon by a major part of the press that was tied to Vietnam. Before that had been the Jerry Voorhis and Helen Gahagan Douglas campaigns [in California]. Melvin Douglas,* her husband, was Jewish, and the Nixon people brought the Jewish thing into the campaign, which was a very bad thing to do. Nixon was guilty of some very bad things in his campaigns, and he antagonized the Eastern press very badly. The hatred of the *New York Times* and the *Washington Post* toward Nixon was unbelievable; they would do anything to get him. I don't think that any president has had to bear this kind of hatred since Lincoln.

A. M. Rosenthal Press and government are often in adversarial positions. I would be surprised if most reporters and editors did like Nixon. They tended to be liberal; he was not. He also did things that were against the prevailing liberal climate in this country. But that does not mean that the animus became part of the coverage of Nixon, so I don't think his downfall was the result of animus by the press. I think this was the result of the [Watergate] cover-up.

* The film and stage star.

Ben Bradlee Nixon did not like reporters. Neither did Lyndon Johnson or Jimmy Carter. But Nixon was constantly blaming the press for a multitude of sins, and reporters didn't like that. It's not a question of disliking him personally; we never got close enough—I certainly never did. If you said to anyone in the Nixon administration that you represented the *Post,* there was kind of a McCarthyesque response: you gotta be a commie; you gotta be a silly, lily-livered liberal, and you can't be a human being. And after a while, that wears you down.

I remember thinking that Nixon was really an awfully difficult man in 1962—I covered that campaign in California—whereas Pat Brown was friendly; he was just like a little puppy dog. Nixon was so remote, and uncomfortable, and so unnatural—not easy to like, from my point of view.

In the middle of Watergate, we started worrying about the question of the perception of some that we had an animus against Nixon; we bent over backward the other way—the times we had stories ready to write and I held back and said, "No. We have to go another mile; we have to get another source." I felt we might be accused of being motivated by animus rather than fact.

Vernon Walters Nixon felt himself besieged by the media and, quite frankly, he was: the idea of this man winning the largest number of electoral votes since George Washington—this man about whom they had said, "Would you buy a used car from this jowly-cheeked pig?"—this drove the media absolutely insane; they had to get rid of him. It was not a professional thing with the media; it was an emotional thing, and it became emotional, also, with Nixon. He fell into the trap. He did not understand that things he was doing had now become "mortal" sins, whereas under Johnson, or Jack Kennedy, they were "venial" sins—such as recording.

Raymond Price It was the scent of blood—the thrill of the hunt with a quarry they had been after for years. It was a stampede; no one was going to be left behind. The hate was so thick in that town that you couldn't have cut it with a knife.

Gerald Warren Ousting Nixon was the goal of the *Washington Post.* I really believe that Bob [Woodward] and Carl [Bernstein] were on a personal crusade to bring down a president. Others at the *Post,* and at *Newsweek,* the *New York Times,* and CBS were a lot more professional and seasoned than Bob and Carl were. I think that, having been beaten on the story for quite some time by two young reporters, they felt: Let's do it professionally; let's follow this through. If it means the president falls, so be it. But let it be based on facts, not on suppositions.

Bob Woodward Does anyone make that charge—if it is a charge—from a position of knowledge? I don't think so. If you look at *All the President's Men,* it's not a pretty story. We made mistakes. We tried to go to grand jurors; we didn't follow up things; we didn't publish the existence of the tape story [on Saturday, July 14] because Bradlee thinks it's a B+, or whatever. We tried to learn the lesson of Watergate early: lay things out as they happened. I never detected any political motivation. We got very involved in the story, and it became a form of combat; there is no question about that. We tried to do our job and, in fact, if you look at it, our coverage was pretty conservative.

WOODWARD AND BERNSTEIN

Gerald Warren Some of their tactics were reprehensible. I think that journalism lost its purity during that time. The ends were worth it: you could do anything, because you were working on the holy cause of bringing down Richard Nixon. That offended me greatly, as a journalist and as an American. But I will pay them [Woodward and Bernstein] tribute for staying with the story until the end. I just wish they had been more professional about it.

Raymond Price There is nothing to Woodward and Bernstein's account that the president was inebriated [during a December 21, 1973, dinner at the White House]. [Senator Barry] Goldwater was threatening to go off the reservation in the Senate; he was critical to the president's position there. He was at the dinner on crutches; he had just been in the hospital. Goldwater—who, I think, was Woodward and Bernstein's source—was verging on senility at the time. I told Woodward and Bernstein that they had it all screwed up; I think that a couple of other people told them the same thing. They chose to ignore this. They are totally dishonest reporters; nothing they say should be taken as fact. There are things in *The Final Days* that are true, but there is also a lot of fiction—the versions of the people who cooperated with them, with a lot of their own embroidery. They put thoughts in my mind which were not remotely there—which they obviously had no source for. This is just the way they operate.

Bob Woodward Barry Goldwater said he was inebriated. There is a book that said we got this totally wrong. It was an interesting exercise; it was literally going to Nixon's daughter: Was your Dad drunk? What is she going to say? Goldwater and other people who were there said what we reported. I think Goldwater, when the book* came out, said he looked in the index under Goldwater and everything that was reported was accurate. He's the kind of person who will deal with reality.

Haig, in his latest book, *Inner Circles,* says we got things right. Yes, he was worried that Nixon might commit suicide. If you take that, and Kissinger's memoirs, and ninety others, and tapes that have come out, our book is not only correct in the specifics, but in the overall theme of the ordeal, emotionally, that Nixon was going through. That book will get better and better with time, when people 'fess up, or something comes out. There are his loyalists, who somehow feel that putting it *[The Final Days]* down will rehabilitate Nixon. He hates it, of course. The book got it right; it's stunning in its reportorial precision.

Ronald Ziegler If a person in my position gets into that subject, it can easily be translated into the assumption—or point of view—that somehow the press is being blamed for Watergate, or bringing down the president. I've never said that; I don't feel that; and Richard Nixon, in his most private moments in discussing the matter, does not feel that. I am not the perfect one to judge the Woodward/Bernstein reporting approach of that period. I will say that—not in relation to Woodward and Bernstein's book, but in terms of the contemporary history of that period—a lot of what was attributed to me as firsthand quotes was never said; a lot of thoughts I was supposed to have had were not had, and there were a lot of things which I did and said that were not accurately reported, an example being the role I had in the Haldeman and Ehrlichman firings.

And you constantly read that I had no access to the president. Even President Nixon in his memoir—using my notes—says that after the firings, I was alone with the president, looking out the window at Aspen Lodge, and he said, "Well, Ron, it's all over." And they wrote—and perhaps President Nixon recalled it this way—that I assume he was saying that the specific circumstance was over, and he meant the entire presidency was over. I knew what he was talking about; I knew he was referring to the fact that he felt it was all over—that he could not survive.

---

* Woodward and Carl Bernstein's account of Nixon's last days as president, *The Final Days* (Simon and Schuster).

William Rusher The interesting thing about Woodward and Bernstein is that they never got anywhere; why they won all those prizes is a good question. They suspected something was wrong, and jumped up and down, and yelled, but the guy who broke Watergate was John J. Sirica.* He was known as "Maximum John," because he liked to give long sentences. He first sentenced the Watergate defendants to long terms, and said he would confirm the sentences in six months. This gave them [the defendants] time to think, and they all yelled, except for Liddy. I said so much in a column, and months after it appeared, I got a letter—under the Gothic print: From the Chambers of Judge John J. Sirica—saying: "Dear Mr. Rusher, Someone has given me a copy of your article. I am glad that somebody is ready to tell the truth. Sincerely yours, John J. Sirica." So, he agreed with me that he was the guy who busted Watergate—not Woodward and Bernstein.

WAS THERE REALLY A DEEP THROAT, AND, IF SO, WHO WAS IT?

Ronald Ziegler I think that "Deep Throat" was a compendium of different sources; I'd be happy to be proven wrong relative to that assumption. If there was a "Deep Throat," we should know by this time who it was. After all, time has passed; "Deep Throat" wouldn't have anything to lose. Woodward and Bernstein would only be contributing to contemporary history if they said who it was.

Bob Woodward Exactly what happened is laid out in *All the President's Men*. I can't, without naming the person or providing more details, go any further. There was a person; it's a he. It would be absurd for it to be a composite. Suppose there were two people and one of them emerged and said: I was half. This would undermine everything.

I would disclose the identity of "Deep Throat" at his death, or with his permission. There is no formal agreement, but it is stated and understood.

Why does this take on such a mystery for people? Reporters have sources who are confidential. I've got lots of sources who are confidential, for life. I'm asked a lot about "Deep Throat." I understand some of it; I don't understand all of it, because reporters who try to get to the bottom of things inevitably have confidential sources. A lot was clandestine about it. The

---

* The U.S. District Court judge who presided over Watergate-related trials.

stakes in the story were very high, so it's larger than it was at the time. He was one of many sources we dealt with; he's not been identified publicly, so there is a mystery about it.

"Deep Throat" was crucial, but not determining; it was important to have somebody who was in that position to provide—and if you look at it very closely—sometimes specifics, but sometimes this drive to get to the overall, to the thematic lines in the story and the nature of the behavior in the White House. In the history of it, in the way we wrote it, it's all exactly the way it happened. But it's more important, perhaps, because of the air of mystery about it now than it was to us as we were writing the story. But it was that underpinning—that sense that there was somebody there who says: this is all true, and awful; and says: look for the theme in this.

Raymond Price When I was researching my own book,* I tried to run down a lot of theories—and candidates—for "Deep Throat." I finally concluded that he was a fictional invention for dramatic purposes; he didn't fit anybody who would have had access to the kind of information they claimed he would have access to.

Vernon Walters "Deep Throat" was an invention to justify some pretty good guessing. Why has Bob Woodward never given us a day when he saw Bill [William] Casey [a former director of the CIA, now deceased, who was the subject of another Woodward and Bernstein book, *Veil: The Secret Wars of the CIA 1981–1987*]? Everybody in that position has a daily diary of who he saw, and who was there. In the Casey situation, there were bodyguards, and there was his wife; either his wife or his daughter was at his bedside every day until he died. So my own view is that "Deep Throat" is as nonexistent as Woodward's visit to Bill Casey.

Alexander Butterfield For a while, people were saying that I might be "Deep Throat," because I'm the guy who told about the tapes.

John Ehrlichman A reporter told me that it was between the first and second manuscripts [drafts] of *All the President's Men* that "Deep Throat" appeared: Alice Mayhew, the editor [at Simon and Schuster, the publishing house], turned the first manuscript back to the boys and said it was not juicy enough. And then "Deep Throat" appeared as a plot device.

---

* *With Nixon* (Viking, 1977).

Robert Hartmann If I had to make an even money bet, I would say Haig; if I had to make a long shot, I would say [David] Gergen.* I think that it was not a single person. Remember that neither Haig nor Gergen has—in their various incarnations—ever been seriously blackballed, or criticized, by the *Washington Post*. You would be hard put to find anyone connected with the Nixon White House who, if they misstepped even a little, hadn't gotten something from the *Post;* even when Haig was making an ass of himself as secretary of state,† he never got his fingers rapped. Whoever "Deep Throat" was—if there ever was such a person—had exceptional access, and had to have a motive for doing this, and I can't think of any motive that would amount to much, except buying one's immunity for the future.

Bob Woodward For me to get into the motivation of "Deep Throat" is to lead into identity problems, so I'm not going to go down that road. The question of motivation is interesting, and when it is answered, it will make a little more sense.

Robert Reisner Hunt and Liddy's activities as Plumbers would have been very well known to Kissinger and Haig, because David Young was part of Kissinger's staff. I have always thought that Haig, if he wasn't "Deep Throat," was part of the composite.

Alexander Haig What a lot of people don't know about Watergate is that the FBI knew more about the subject than anybody, and was feeding the press; that was Woodward and Bernstein's "Deep Throat." I only realized this when I was researching my own book. I always thought that "Deep Throat" was someone around the White House—Len Garment or Dave Gergen. It had to be somebody who was very coherent and also had a collective picture, and only the FBI had that, because they were working intensely on it.

Arnaud de Borchgrave I am willing to bet my life that Haig was not "Deep Throat."

Robert Mardian It turned out that they were right for all the wrong reasons. If you read the reports that they were printing in the *Washington Post* prior to the Senate hearings and the trial, and compare it to what they wrote

---

* Appointed communications director by President Clinton, replacing George Stephanopolous.
    † Haig served as secretary of state in the first administration of President Ronald Reagan, 1981–82.

in their book, it's far different. In other words, what they were writing at the time couldn't have been coming from anybody who really knew what was going on. It had to be somebody who was picking up bits and pieces without an overall view of the situation. I kept saying: "Who could that be?" Well, based on what Al Haig's position was and what he knew, and what Len Garment knew, Garment was, in my opinion, not a great lover of the president, although he came from that Nixon law firm; I knew from day one that he didn't respect Nixon. Reading what I was reading, and trying to put together who could fit this, based upon the interviews that I'd had with everybody, I said, "Len Garment." I could be dead wrong.

Leonard Garment I wish I could prove that I was "Deep Throat"—I'd be monumentally wealthy. I think it was David Gergen if it was anybody; it was in character to sneak. Put him under oath and ask him if he was "Deep Throat," or not. Anyway, I think that "Deep Throat" is the silliest damn hype in publishing history. My understanding—and I have it on reasonably good authority—is that the first draft [of *All the President's Men*] didn't hold together, and Alice Mayhew was smart enough to say: It needs a hero—somebody to bring the pieces together; it also needs a Greek chorus. And that was "Deep Throat."

Howard Phillips I think it was Len Garment; if you check it out, it's hard to find any basis on which that can be disproven. But there's another aspect to it; it may have been George Shultz. The best evidence I can give for this is a speech that Kay Graham gave at a party at her house during the Reagan administration, when Shultz was under a great deal of criticism from conservatives. A number of people present at this party—in Shultz's honor—were diplomats. One of those present told me, in confidence, that Kay Graham praised Shultz; she said that on many nights during the key days of Watergate, George Shultz would come to her home through the back door and fill her in on what happened at Cabinet meetings during that day—and at other meetings involving Nixon administration officials. My source for this statement by Katharine Graham is unimpeachable. Shultz is the Benedict Arnold of the Nixon administration. Whether he was "Deep Throat," I don't know.

Ben Bradlee No way. She never told me about that—or anything remotely like it. The people in the Nixon administration who were allowed to talk to Katharine Graham you could put in your ear; Pete Petersen and Kissinger were the two people that we ever saw. Elliot Richardson also, but he didn't count. He was not really one of them. I've known him since I was a child. In retrospect, Richardson was so pure. If you know anything about Boston—I come from Boston—they can be a lot of things. They can be slow; they can drink too much; they can do a lot of things, but they're incorruptible. Archie Cox, the same way. Elliot had held many jobs in the government, and he had a "Mr. Clean" reputation.

Seymour Glanzer All Woodward and Bernstein did was to follow in the wake of the investigation; they didn't do any pioneering work. The real question on "Deep Throat" is: What difference did it make? "Deep Throat" didn't give them anything. It's like a red herring; all he does, according to their book, is to keep saying, "Follow the money." That's ridiculous. Everything they got was the result of following in the wake of the investigation. For example, their article about the Mexican connection was the result of an investigation started by the Miami district attorney who, after learning we had subpoenaed the banks, issued his own subpoena, asking them to deliver to him what had been given to us. He got the information from the banks, gave it to Woodward and Bernstein, and they published an article as though they had discovered it.

Ben Bradlee I don't answer questions about that, but there was a "Deep Throat." I maintain that somebody could enter every reference to "Deep Throat" into a computer in some binary way—in Washington, out of Washington—and enter all the candidates in, and you could figure it out. Don't try your candidates on me.

30

Watergate with Hindsight

Dwight Chapin I was the first person indicted; the first person convicted. When I went into the grand jury room, I had no intention of lying. That has always bothered me, because I don't lie. I've rationalized that I'd had a magnificent experience [in service to the Nixon administration] and that therefore it was all worth it. But it has been a problem—and continues to be something I will have to live with for the rest of my life. I still happen to believe that the overall experience overrides all of that.

Jerry Jones I had a great deal of respect for Nixon's mind. I was there because I believed in the conservative view of how America should work, which is individuals doing their best with a small government that enables a level playing field. My loyalty was there, far more than to Nixon, that somehow this conservative view could begin to prevail. I thought that Nixon did the best he could in attempting to steer us in that direction. I had a very high regard for his ability; I still do. I had so much confidence in his ability that I truly felt he was surely smarter than to do what appeared to have happened. I believed that for quite a long time, in spite of the fact that I was staff secretary and was literally the only person with access to the tapes; I had them locked in a vault in a secure room with a guard posted outside; I was the only one who could get into the room—the only one with the combinations to the locks—and if anyone, including the president, wanted to hear a tape, they had to get it through me and sign a receipt. They had to give the tape back to me, and I had an entire notebook on where those tapes had been, who had listened to them, and how long they'd had them.

As I began to do that job, particularly as the issue of could the president be forced to turn them over was being heard—I was the one who was giving the tapes to Fred Buzhardt, who had the job of listening to the tapes that the president would allow him to listen to, and I also had the job of preparing the big Blue Book that we gave to the Senate on various conversations we had transcribed—I didn't believe that the president was the culprit—and a lot of us who stayed there didn't think so. It's amazing, in retrospect, but at the time, it appeared: Magruder's stupid; Colson's a shark; yes, they overstepped; probably Nixon even tried to prevent the political damage from hurting him. So what? But did he really do it? Did he really order it done? None of us really believed that he did—at least I didn't.

Maurice Stans The whole thing became a nightmare for me: my wife was ill; I was investigated for three years before it was over. Nothing on Watergate was ever attached to me. They finally started to see if they could find some campaign violations on me or my organization; it was a hell of an experience. At one point, they said they wanted a concentrated period of interviews with me, extending over a period of a couple of weeks. My wife was in Florida recuperating, so they allowed me to go there every Friday evening if I would come back every Tuesday morning. They examined me on over 300 separate topics.

They told my attorney they had a hundred charges on me. We knocked them down—every one was wrong, based on misinformation, or misdates. Finally, they got down to where they had five charges left. My lawyers said, "You should drop these remaining charges." The prosecutors said, "How can we? We have spent so much time on this; the press has given him such play; we have to find something." So they said, "We will let him off on five misdemeanors; that will be a $5,000 fine."

The public never understood how brutal the investigations were, and the tactics were. It was a politically motivated affair once it became an open matter. It was great meat for the media—for the investigative journalists. There was no end to it. There was an excitement there, a momentum, a witch-hunt under way.

One day, the Italian banker, Michele Sindona, came into my room with a briefcase and offered me a million dollars in cash to help the campaign. He said, "I don't want anything in return. I just want to be assured of one thing—that there be no publicity." I said, "Gee, Mr. Sindona, that's a tough one, because the law specifically says I've got to report every contribution over a hundred dollars." He said, "Well, I have it here in the briefcase. Can't you take it without a name on it? Or some other way? So that it isn't reported? Spend it any way you want to in the campaign." I said, "I'm afraid that would be putting you in jeopardy, and putting myself in jeopardy, and I don't think I want to do that." I had the presence of mind the next morning to write him a letter and say exactly that. That letter was later introduced in his trial, when he was charged with fraud in the bank, and it was given to the prosecutors who were after me. It didn't make any difference to them at all. A million bucks; I could have taken that million bucks and put it in my own pocket and nobody would have known. So yes, it was a witch-hunt all the way. No sense of equity in it at all.

John Dean One of the disappointing situations that my current litigation has visited on me is that I thought that some of the people who got caught up in Watergate didn't deserve to be caught up—and to go to jail. After learning the way these people still talk after twenty years, I think the best thing I ever did in my life was to go down there and blow the whistle on them, and I just wish I had done it sooner. These were not nice men. To stop them from being in government, and having a future in government, was the best thing I ever did. Given the mentality I had at that time, as well, it was a good thing to do.

If Watergate had succeeded, what would have been put into the system for years to come? People thinking the way Richard Nixon thought, and thinking that is the way it should be. It would have been a travesty; it would have been frightening. Nixon absolutely set the tone. None of these things would have happened in Nixon's White House had he not wanted them to happen. Because the things he did not want to have happen, trust me, did not happen.

I'll tell you what he is going to have to deal with for eternity: his tapes. He had been very effective in covering up, or perpetuating the cover-up, if you will, for twenty years. Very effective. Only minuscule information has come out and this is amazing. It's been a legal fight, but at some point it will be difficult to institutionalize that fight, to prevent those from coming out. When the tapes come out, we will have a fairly complete picture. We will have one of the most complete pictures of any presidency, because, in a sense, it is electronically recorded. I think this material will show why Watergate—and why Watergate because it was the mentality of Richard Nixon to have those sorts of things.

Robert Mardian I went through an awful lot. I think—as the appellate court said—my case could have been tried in a day and a half; I sat there for four months. The trial cost $675,000, which I thought on my acquittal was going to be reimbursed to me. But by that time, the committee that had the trust funds had dissipated practically everything. My friend, Judge John J. Sirica, sentenced me to one to three years in prison; I had a large family. I don't look back on those years as happy years.

I feel a lot of anger toward people like John Dean—who, I think, was the prime mover. Jeb Magruder—who sat there and perjured himself, I can't forgive him; there is no way I could. I am a Christian; I believe in God, but those two men I can never forgive for what they did to my life. Not just mine, but my wife's, my kids', my brothers', sisters', nieces', nephews'. It blows my mind that Magruder could under oath insist on telling the story he told. That is the only thing that got me indicted.

Dwight Chapin Colson's a friend, as are Haldeman and Ehrlichman. The only ones I don't see are John Dean and Jeb Magruder; I just choose not to. I have real problems with Dean—in the sense that he says he couldn't get to the president. That is just B.S. in my mind, because if he saw this cancer, he could have gone in there—and gone right to the heart of it. I think that his manipulation was immense. Nixon's style, his patterns, allowed for a Dean to maneuver this thing.

Donald Segretti I was in total shock for weeks, months. It took a number of years for me to close the book on this. In a sense, I'm a little surprised that I'm even talking about it today. I was picked out of normal life, and all of a sudden, I had a different life. At some point, I was pretty much on my own. As things started unfolding, I had a variety of problems—in terms of worrying about how I was going to eat—what I was going to do for a living; what my future was going to be. Everything was turned totally upside-down, so I was in total shock.

I'd gone to a lawyer and was told he could help me. I found out that everything I was telling him went back to Washington, and from Washington it went to the Senate Committee, and from there it went to the newspapers, so I really didn't know where to turn. At some point, I was told that everything was going to be coordinated through John Dean. I was told that there was a lawyer out here [in California] that I could see. I went to see him. He was a very nice man—an older gentleman in a very large law firm. He said, "I want you to write down everything you did, everybody you saw, and so on." So I did. I learned later that everything I told him went back to Mr. Dean, and Mr. Dean gave it to the people he decided to give it to—people who were not friendly to me, in a legal sense. I really felt I was out in the cold then. It was at about that time that I broke off totally with everybody concerned. I went to a lawyer I had gone to law school with, and the two of us were on our own.

Bob Woodward Watergate was probably a good thing for the country; it was a good, sobering lesson. Accountability to the law applies to everyone. The problem with kings, and prime minsters, and presidents, is that they think they are above it, and there is no accountability, and that they have some special rights, and privileges, and status. And a process that says: No. We have our laws and believe them, and they apply to everyone, is a very good thing. No one died; the country got through its foreign policy and economic times quite well, and it was a great moral lesson for people. I happen to believe in the essentially conservative idea that concentrations of power are unsafe and that those concentrations of power need to be monitored and held to account regularly. Watergate did that like nothing else that ever happened in this country.

Richard Moore One footnote to Watergate has always annoyed me—the canonization of Judge Sirica. In his book, Sirica writes that when Mr. Stans and Mr. Mitchell were on trial in New York in connection with a political contribution, I noted that Dean was an important witness against them, and the defense attorney questioned him severely about whether he was testifying in order to get a lighter sentence. [Dean had pleaded guilty, but hadn't yet been sentenced.] So I decided, when it came to the trial of the seven, that I would see to it that the issue couldn't be used, so I sentenced Dean in advance of the trial to a stiff sentence. Now, if ever there was an obstruction of justice—to use sentencing power to support the credibility of a key witness against the defendants! If anybody should have been impeached and gone to jail—by his own admission—it was Sirica. Dean complained bitterly to the prosecutor, saying, "I thought that by cooperating I was going to get a break, and Sirica hands me this sentence." The prosecutor said, "John, don't worry. Just wait until the trial is over. You'll see." And just days after, Sirica commuted Dean's sentence to time served. But in the adulation for Sirica, anyone who mentioned this was brushed aside.

James St. Clair I think that Judge Sirica was prejudiced against the president, but not to the extent that he would call night day. He had an attitude of concern about the president. My view is that he never should have sent the issue of the tapes to the grand jury. The worst thing about it was that Sirica had employed experts from Boston to advise him on this problem. They found the defect, and repaired it, so no one could ever examine the machine in the exact condition it had been in when used by Rose Mary Woods.

John Ehrlichman There are eight or ten crystal-clear examples of misidentification of people in the tapes, some of which we called attention to in the trial. Sirica just waved this off; he was in a rush to justice. He was a totally incompetent judge—one of the worst I've ever seen. He was not a smart or attentive man; he kept falling asleep.

Frederic V. Malek We had some revolutionary plans for improving the management of government; that is why I stayed and put together my team at OMB. We wanted to manage the government with more pinpointed priorities of coordination—to be more businesslike. A well-run major corporation starts with a vision; you have a strategy of where you are going, long-term. You are not thinking of the four years of a presidential term; you need to be thinking about the problems of this country in the year 2000.

Lawrence Higby The big loser in the whole thing was the country. It was clear to me, because I spent so much time after the election at Camp David with the president, Haldeman, and Ehrlichman—when they were laying out the second administration—that the president was going to take on a lot of the sacred cows in tough domestic issues that he couldn't get to until Vietnam was resolved. If he had been able to get past Watergate and get on with those issues, in terms of government spending, reordering, and modernizing the government, we would have been a very different country than we are today, because you would not have gone through the whole Jimmy Carter fiasco, and the overreaction to Carter, in Reagan. Nixon had the Ash Commission; he had already moved to getting four or five super-Cabinet officers instead of the traditional twelve.

Robert Hartmann Alexander Butterfield is still the mystery man for me. Why did he spill his guts about the taping system, and who was he working for? I've often wondered if he was a plant for the CIA or some other agency. There are all kinds of untold tales around this thing, which will never be known.

Stephen Bull As we look back on Watergate now, it seems as though it's in a nice, neat little box; you just open it up and it's all there. It wasn't: there was a series of events—and allegations—it's important to emphasize allegations; this was a series of events, activities, accusations, and revelations from June of 1972 until the resignation. A lot of things that fell under the umbrella of Watergate weren't related to the break-in; they were things that people didn't like about the Nixon administration—whether it was the GSA [General Services Administration] shouldn't have spent $10,000 to put up a bulletproof windshield out at San Clemente; to a question of impropriety, or actual misdeeds, of a federal employee; or lying to a grand jury. There was a steady downward trend: every time we thought it was over, something else would happen.

The seminal date was when Haldeman and Ehrlichman resigned; Kleindienst resigned, and Dean was fired.* Then, the ball game changed; it was just a new place: different people, a different focus. You started to assume a defensive posture: almost everything you did would be put in the context of Watergate, in one way or another.

I remember one of the great events in the White House during the time I was there was the dinner for returned POWs [from Vietnam].† It was a neat event. We had finally gotten these guys home. There was a huge tent on the South Lawn. And even there, the press were accusing the Nixon people of staging this event to deflect attention away from Watergate.

Ronald Ziegler When you talk about the significant side of President Nixon's administration, you have to talk realistically about its shortcomings. I am no apologist for the tragedy of Watergate; it was really—in all sense of the word—a tragedy. Unnecessary, expensive. And hopefully, future leaders and administrations will have learned something from it. But you get discouraged when you see the actions of many of the administrations that succeeded Richard Nixon's.

Howard Phillips Nixon used to say, "We must be part of a cause larger than ourselves." He neglected his own advice; he permitted Watergate to become the dominant issue of his second term. Nixon didn't exploit the fact that no one has a more powerful microphone in the entire world than the president of the United States. Instead of going on the offensive for a conservative agenda—which I think would have saved him and rallied support for him against the Washington establishment—he permitted the establishment to define the question facing the nation. To me, that was his ultimate political blunder and failure of strategic thinking—his most decisive failure.

* April 30, 1973.
† May 24, 1973.

He was a great tactician: the "Checkers" speech was a great tactical effort; the Latin American visit in, which he was stoned was a great tactical thing; he was tactically effective in the Kitchen Debate with Khrushchev; he was tactically effective in the way in which he handled Goldwater in 1964. But he certainly did not show strategic vision in the way in which he ran his gubernatorial campaign in 1962, so I think he always showed himself to be a better tactician than strategist.

Bernard Barker I think that Richard Nixon was a very good friend of the Cubans; he had been involved in the Bay of Pigs.* Eventually, he would have been better than any other person in the process of the liberation of Cuba. In 1972, I thought: Nixon will never have to run again, so he can do what is in his heart concerning Cuba. His best friend† was a Cuban. Nixon was an anticommunist; he was the ideal person for the liberation of Cuba, as opposed to what we might have had in McGovern—a pro-Castro guy: I have photos of him with Che Guevara;‡ his daughter was at the University of Havana; he is an extreme liberal. Perhaps all of this motivated me to like Nixon more and more—to the point where I thought that giving your entire loyalty to this man was the logical thing [to do].

George McGovern As far as my daughter was concerned, she did attend the University of Havana, but I made no effort to hide that. My daughter could not have been there by 1972; she was born in 1955, and she was a college senior when she went to Havana—she went to school there for about one semester—but she would only have been twenty in 1975, so in the 1972 election, she would have been about seventeen—even I wouldn't have had the nerve to have my daughter going to school in Havana on the eve of a presidential campaign; this would have had to have been after 1972.

Raymond Price It was very sad and tragic—and not just a personal tragedy, a tragedy of monumental proportion. I felt very bad for the country; I thought we had thrown away an awful lot. In the midst of what he was doing, he was so cavalierly cast aside on such petty stuff—in an orgy of political opportunism. I thought then—and I still think—it was a political lynching. The biggest reason we screwed up so badly in handling Watergate was that we were all stumbling around in the dark—the president included—not

---

* As vice-president in the Eisenhower administration, he was a chief proponent of the operation.
† Bebe Rebozo.
‡ A close associate of Fidel Castro, who was killed in Bolivia while involved in attempting to bring communism to that nation.

knowing what we were dealing with, or how, or who might be involved; he was getting different stories from the different players, each with his own ax to grind—or ass to cover, so if he had tried to say what had happened, he couldn't have.

Basically, the fatal error was confronted after the fact: he addressed it as a political problem rather than as a law enforcement problem—and in addressing it as a political problem, he was given a way to make it go away pretty much the same way that FDR [Franklin Delano Roosevelt] or JFK or LBJ would have. They would have gotten away with it; he didn't. They didn't have opposition Congresses; he did. If he had just gotten on his high horse at the outset and said: This is a horrible abuse of law and propriety and we will get to the bottom of it, and cut off every head of anybody who has touched it—and if anybody would have been able to find out what heads to cut off, and enough blood had flowed in the streets, the demons might have been appeased.

James Wrightson Nixon corrupted a lot of good guys; they were not bad people when he met them. They may have been arrogant, but they were not bad people. And he got a lot of guys in jail. I mean, talking about corrupting the youth, he did it. I would like to ask him, "How do you feel about that?"

Ben Bradlee Compared to the people who served Kennedy and Johnson, these people seemed second-rate. I am delighted that Colson got religion and he's helping people. He was a mean son-of-a-bitch. I don't feel very sorry for these people. They paid their price; let them go on now; I don't want to interfere with them; I don't think they have to pay it again. Nixon, maybe, has to still pay, but he does—he absolutely does.

Herbert Brownell I can't forgive him for the handling of Watergate. He was Jekyll and Hyde.* It was a 75 percent Jekyll and 75 percent Hyde!

---

* A reference to Robert Louis Stevenson's literary character who, as Dr. Jekyll, was mild-mannered, and, as Mr. Hyde, was a monster.

Part Six

Nixon's Post-Watergate Rehabilitation

31

Has Nixon Been Rehabilitated?

All of the individuals in this section were interviewed prior to Mr. Nixon's death on April 22, 1994.

Gerald Warren He is a man of great substance—great gravitas. His successors [as president] have not been either, so people look up to someone of substance and gravitas for help in analyzing events happening in the world today. He is respected for his mind, and for his ability to analyze foreign and domestic issues.

Stephen Bull I underestimated him. The guy is just smarter than the rest of us. I shouldn't be at all surprised that he is back. The guy is just so darn smart, and dedicated, and patient. He almost died out in California [after the resignation]. People are not aware of it. After an operation, he went into shock. The buzzers went off. The heartbeat was already stopped. I guess clinically he was dead. They all rushed in and resuscitated him. It was that close a call.

George McGovern He has handled himself very well; he has concentrated on foreign policy, which the country has always thought he had special skills in handling, and stayed away from constitutional issues and domestic politics. He speaks about broad things on which there is rather general agreement, like the necessity of supporting Yeltsin. These are marvelous issues for a former president to be identified with because they are so presidential.

Plus the fact that he keeps churning out these books. Not that they are masterpieces, but they are not bad, and they show he is a serious, thoughtful man. He really has worked at rehabilitation. I don't know that that has been his purpose, but he has had a legitimate life since he left the presidency, and I think he has probably earned some measure of rehabilitation.

Bob Woodward A rehabilitation to what? To political power? No. Nixon knows a lot about foreign policy. His views are always interesting. Quite frequently right; quite frequently wrong.

To standing as a commentator and observer? Yes. But Rush Limbaugh and a whole range of people—left, center, and right—have that status in a country that practices free speech, so it doesn't surprise me. And in my view, candidly, he's a freak—an oddity. He resigned the presidency; he broke the law; he was disgraced. The people who really forced him to resign were the Republicans. He keeps portraying Watergate as some sort of media, liberal, Democratic, trumped-up operation. It was the Barry Goldwaters and the Charles Wigginses, on the House Judiciary Committee; those are the people who did Nixon in.

The period between 1974 and 1994 is when Nixon is conducting a strategic war against history. That's fine; that's his job. It was George Will[*] who said: There won't be any Richard Nixon grammar schools or parks. Well, maybe there is one now, somewhere in the country, but there's not going to be a Richard Nixon Center for Justice, or a Richard Nixon Audio Center.

His problem is that he will lose the struggle. There is such a mountain of evidence. The historians are going to read what I've written, and what others have, and look at it rather dispassionately. But then they will say, My God. We've got the tapes of the conversations; we have all of this sworn testimony from hundreds of people. They will look at that and will see the fundamental, namely, that everyone adheres to the law; that is what Nixon thumbed his nose at.

Philip Lacovara I have certainly mellowed over the years. I have said during several presidential campaigns—looking at the candidates on both sides—that in my view, the person best qualified to be the president of the United States is Richard Nixon. He is obviously a very, very flawed person; there is little question that he helped organize serious violations of federal criminal law, for which he avoided punishment. Nevertheless, he had a lot to offer the country and still does. While I have thought that we were gulled

[*] Syndicated columnist and author.

by the assurances of his lawyers in 1974 that he was at death's door and would be answering a much higher judgment than a jury could return in a very short time, it really hasn't bothered me that he has been able to make a contribution to the public debate on issues.

Fred Dalton Thompson If he can be of assistance in terms of world peace, or to our president, I have no problem with that at all. Whether you agree with the pardon or not, he was dealt with under the law and the Constitution, and I have no inclination to feel in any way hateful toward an eighty-year-old man.

I am constantly surprised at the resilience of certain politicians. I think most people would want to go into the woodwork. Nixon has come back from utter worldwide humiliation. He still wants to be a player. Certain people have remarkable stamina and desire to come back.

Bobby Baker Nixon has a world constituency; the Europeans look at Watergate like we are silly damn fools. They are right: you notice that no world leader ever refuses to see him; he has a line of communication that anyone would be a fool not to talk to him; he's become an elder statesman. He's probably done better in retirement than if there had been no Watergate.

Kenneth Rush Nixon was looked upon in some quarters abroad as our premier statesman. His standing in China and Europe was very high. After I retired in 1986, I visited China. When I arrived, they gave me the suite Nixon had used in the [Government] Guesthouse. As we traveled around the country, the officials knew I was close to Nixon. All I heard was Nixon, Nixon, Nixon. They served me the same food they had served to Nixon. The greatest tribute you could get was that you were close to Nixon.

Hermann Eilts The Egyptians would never accept Watergate as being very serious; for them, it was a minor affair. They never really believed that Watergate—the kind of thing that happened all the time in the Middle East—would eventually lead to Nixon's resignation. When Nixon came to Egypt in June 1974, he gave every impression to Sadat that he was going to stay on. This kind of talk fitted into the Egyptian perception that surely this Watergate business is nonsense.

Robert Odle, Jr. We don't know the half of what Nixon has done in recent years, because we are not privy to the phone calls and correspondence presidents like Reagan, Bush, and Clinton don't want to publicize for their purposes, and he doesn't want to, for his. It's the "iron butt," and his incredibly long view of history.

Dwight Chapin While a lot of men would have sat and thought: This is the end, he is a self-renewer. He would sit and think: In the darkest hours, Churchill thought such-and-such; or Konrad Adenauer* once told me . . . ; or Chairman Mao made this point . . . He is interested in who he is, where he is, and what he has to deliver, and it is in that formula how history will remember him, and that is very important to him. There is in the man a sense of destiny, of history.

Raymond Price In 1974 and early 1975, I spent a lot of time with Nixon, talking about his future. I always assumed he would come back; he is a remarkably resilient person. It took about thirty years for [Herbert] Hoover to be reevaluated; twenty years for Harry Truman. I thought it was going to take a lot less [time] for Nixon, first because the pace of everything has quickened—the pendulum swings a lot faster; second, the passions of 1974 were a product of absolute mass hysteria—and hysteria doesn't last. As the hysteria faded, people began to look with a different perspective and began to ask a lot of questions, just as the Europeans never stopped asking. The reason Nixon has advised presidents here and abroad is that they want to hear from him, because they respect what he has to say; they know that he has an extraordinary grasp of how the world works, and he never stops working at it.

Gerald R. Ford I have always felt that he was the best president, during my time, in the area of foreign policy. Today, he is still the most knowledgeable person who can best explain the world, geopolitically. Anybody with that talent, if he handles himself properly—and I think that Nixon has—is going to be listened to; therefore, it isn't surprising to me that he's been pretty much accepted. There isn't much talk about Watergate; when Nixon is mentioned, people talk about his knowledge of foreign policy.

Winston Lord It is appropriate for him to be consulted. He is a man of great experience and geopolitical perspective, and I think it is entirely appropriate to get his views. I often agree with him; I sometimes disagree with him. He made some mistakes and history will judge those, but if you

* First chancellor of the Federal Republic of Germany.

are trying to formulate foreign policy, it serves the national interest to get his views.

Frederic V. Malek It is a very healthy thing for the country, as well as, of course, for him. After all, he is one of the best minds in the country in the area of international affairs. Did he lie and do something bad? Of course he did. Was he a little paranoid? Sure he was, but nobody's perfect. It doesn't mean that he shouldn't have the opportunity to express himself and to lend his brilliance for all of us to absorb, and use, and build upon in the area of foreign affairs—and that is what he is doing. It seems to me that it behooves us as a country to take advantage of a unique talent like that and not to tarnish the value of that advice by the fact that he did something twenty years ago that many would regard as immoral.

Jerry Jones I was investigated; I had to have a lawyer; I was in front of the grand jury; I was accused, with Maurice Stans, of selling ambassadorships. The idea up on the Hill as this became very partisan was: Let's kill every one of these young Republicans, so that we never see them again; there was a real witch-hunt attitude that went way beyond the event and became a pretty nasty process. From that perspective, one begins to view it as more a political war game than a huge ethical blunder, and I think that the American people have begun to see it in that context, or Nixon never would have been able to come back. And they have also begun to see that he did some things awfully well.

John Ehrlichman He has come back several times; he has an inner ambition that wouldn't let him sit still. He has a very long-headed view of history. He has been working at this [his comeback] ever since the helicopter ride from the White House. He's wined and dined press that we couldn't have anything to do with when he was president; he has really worked to clean up his image.

Daniel Ellsberg I wish we had a culture in which a Nixon, or a Johnson, or a Kissinger's advice could basically be dispensed with when they have spent ten years killing as many people as they did. I don't think we need them or should have to rely on them. I would say that I dislike Kissinger more than I dislike Nixon, but that is just a personal feeling.

Samuel Dash Despite the fact that he has a good record in foreign affairs and other things, I think that the true measure of an American president is his adherence to—and belief in—our Constitution. I don't believe that he should be hounded, but I don't believe that he deserves any kind of senior statesmanship [status]. His books, his columns, fine; whatever opinions he has, he should write about; he can be listened to. But it should always be remembered that this was a president who betrayed the trust of the people and failed in his most important responsibility—to see to it that the laws are faithfully executed.

Bob Woodward The mistake he has made is in not going the whole distance and saying: I really screwed up; I obviously broke the law; and saying he's sorry and has learned a lesson. But there is a resistance to it—that it was some public relations screwup; that he mishandled it; and mistakes were made, but not going the distance to say he broke the law. Nixon was a criminal president. Maybe we've had other criminal presidents, but the evidence is overwhelming. The thing that stares him down as much as anything is that, after the final tape came out, all the Republicans switched their votes, saying they would vote to recommend impeachment. Instead of learning the wisdom of confession, maybe he should go into the therapy that Chuck Colson gives. But it's his nature, and what is interesting about him is that he loves the arena and he's always in there—and he's always struggling.

Fred Fielding It surprises me that Nixon could dig down into that reservoir and be so determined as to avoid listening to what people were saying and, instead, to play to his strong suit; his power to do that is very significant. Nixon is a national asset which we can't use fully. His understanding of international relations is phenomenal; his evaluation of domestic politics is encyclopedic. There are a lot of people like that, but the foreign policy aspect is unique. His rehabilitation would be important if we could use him, but that won't happen; that is one of the costs of Watergate. I am not saying that in sympathy to him because he made his bed; he lies in it.

Howard Phillips To this day, I have a personal regard for Nixon; I have great regard for his intellect, and for his resilience and his courage. He certainly had a wonderful wife in Pat and two wonderful daughters; that says something about a man. He's not all black in my eyes, but he is not a philosophical soulmate, by any means. It seems to me that he made a Faustian deal; he chose reputation and paid for it with his soul, and he's getting reputation, but he's lost his soul. I regret that. I still feel an affection for him, but I'm very disappointed.

Bob Woodward I disagree very strongly that he has been rehabilitated. It's like the three-headed monkey in the circus: he's a bit of a freak. People are interested in him in the same way they are interested in Madonna, or other celebrities, because he does have stamina and endurance, and he has fought a rear-guard action against history to try to blot out what happened and encourage people to forget.

It's sad, but it's also endearing, that somebody so old would keep trying to "out, damned spot!"* The record is so voluminous on Watergate; there is nothing like it, let alone the records; the testimony; the special prosecutor's work; the Watergate Committee in the Senate; the House impeachment inquiry. It's the most investigated event of all time, perhaps even more so than the Kennedy assassination, because there are so many witnesses to it.

Ben Bradlee I don't think he's been rehabilitated. You can talk about that, but he hasn't. What's the obituary lead going to be on Richard Nixon? The first American president to be disgraced and to have to leave office. That's his legacy, and he will never rehabilitate himself out of that. It will be down at the bottom of the obit that he wrote books, and it will be said that the books were written to try to rehabilitate himself.

A. M. Rosenthal The lead in his obit will say he was the first president to have to leave office. If this is not the first sentence, it will have to be close to the first sentence. Anything else would be ludicrous. But that won't be the end of it. The obituary will talk about other parts of his life, good and bad. Any obituary that would not include his intellectual powers would be derelict—powers and failings.

Leonard Garment The secular equivalent of religion is the miracle of the human spirit enduring under unendurable circumstances. Some have suggested that Nixon could have made a real statement of apology after the pardon—that he had done wrong; had let the country down. But he just wouldn't do it that way. It took him fifteen years to do it his way—the slow way. The whole story should be told with Frank Sinatra singing, "I'll Do It My Way."

---

* Lady Macbeth, in William Shakespeare's *Macbeth*, V:1.

32

Have You Heard from Mr. Nixon Lately?

George P. Shultz He is a remarkable person; he has tremendous fight in him. He feels he has a lot to say, and wants to be part of the action. Every once in a while, I will say or write something, and he will call with a comment. He is very much into public issues.

Herbert Klein I had dinner last night with [Governor] Pete Wilson [of California]. He had called Nixon on his birthday,* and the conversation was about the Super Bowl. Pete was impressed with what he called Nixon's "catholic" knowledge of issues: he wanted to know about the economy in California; he said the three areas he wants to concentrate his interest on are Japan, China, and Russia.

Frederic V. Malek The last time I saw him was in March 1993; he came out to Palm Springs and spoke to a group of major Republican contributors. He stood at a microphone, without a note, and gave a sixty-minute talk on world affairs, and then answered questions for another forty-five minutes. It was a virtuoso performance; none of us had seen anything quite so impressive. He is smarter today—more reflective, more profound, and more articulate than he was as president.

---

* Nixon's eightieth birthday, on January 13, 1993.

John Ehrlichman The last time I heard from him was a perfunctory phone call the Christmas after I was fired. I tried to subpoena him as a witness during my trial, and he fought that tooth and nail. I haven't heard a peep from him. I don't understand why people want to hear from him.

Dwight Chapin I am in touch with Nixon periodically; I send him letters and get notes from him. I feel good about it. The people who need to hear from him have some inner need for validation: Nixon asked them to be involved in a cause bigger than themselves, and they would like their families and friends to know that they were involved in such a cause. When I got out of prison, I took my daughters to see him. He told them that I made a contribution—that I had been very important to his presidency. That did it for me; it was a very proud moment and meant a great deal to me.

William Rusher As he has "grown" in recent years, I have come to think less of him. Eventually, he has noticed that, and I think that, officially, we are now on poor terms.

Howard Phillips I was invited to dinner at Saddle River more than four years ago. Pat Buchanan set up a get-together; there were supposed to be five of us there. I drove up to New Jersey. About an hour before the scheduled time of arrival, I reached the Saddle River exit on the [Garden State] Parkway and called my office to get final directions. They said, "President Nixon just canceled the dinner." No reason was given, but I'm sure it was because he didn't want to see me and had just discovered that I was on the guest list.

G. Gordon Liddy I have had correspondence with him. He has been particularly warm to me. I was not going in and out of the Oval Office and yet he has signed letters to me, "Richard." I felt that was remarkable. He is just a nice guy.

Philip Lacovara About two years ago, I went to a private briefing that he gave to major contributors. I went mostly out of curiosity. He gave an absolutely stupendous briefing on his view of important domestic, economic, and foreign policy issues. He spoke for forty-five minutes without notes. I know how he does this: he rehearses before a mirror. But here is a man who is eighty years old, having been at death's door when I had last seen him twenty years ago, standing up in front of the party faithful, wowing them, and then answering questions with a degree of humor and historical insight and common sense. He was on stage for almost two hours—completely in control of himself and his audience. And I said to myself: I'm glad he didn't die in 1974. Should he have been prosecuted? Probably yes. But in the grand scheme of things, maybe the country is better off that he is doing what he is doing now.

I had my picture taken with him. As I went through the receiving line, I introduced myself. There was the glint [from Mr. Nixon]: I know this man— and by that time I was off-stage. We hadn't seen each other in twenty years. If I had had the chance to engage in conversation on that occasion, I would have told him I was glad to see that he was still active in public affairs because, despite Watergate, I think he represents an important point of view, with a much more rigorous approach to policy issues than many of his successors have had.

A. M. Rosenthal I have a correspondence with him. If he likes something I write, he will write me a letter, and I answer him. He writes books; people consult with him; he's invited to the White House; he's treated as an elder statesman. If that's not rehabilitation! It's not that people are saying: let's forget all about Watergate. But that is not his objective. His objective is to say: I'm still here, I'm still alive, and I'm not going to crawl into a hole. I admire him for that. He has shown more courage and determination than anybody I know.

Ben Bradlee I was in St. Martin just recently with my family. Nixon left the day before we arrived. I'd have died for an interview with him; I'd have died for it.

Eleven years ago, we were in St. Martin and he was there with Rebozo, and Mrs. Nixon, and about twenty or so Secret Service people. I knew the owner of the hotel, who told me Nixon was there. I brought a tape recorder because I thought that I might accidentally catch him with his guard down, and we could sit down on the beach and talk—just like two human beings. He and Rebozo would walk down the beach at four-thirty every day. We were already down the beach in a little cabana. Jann Wenner,* a friend of mine, called me when Nixon and Rebozo started down, about a hundred yards to the left of us. My wife and I went out on the beach and turned away from Nixon, and started walking down the beach, and about fifty feet later, we turned around, hoping he would at least have to say: How do you do?

* Publisher of *Rolling Stone* magazine.

When we turned around, the beach was empty. He'd spotted us; people saw him turn just as soon as he saw us.

Donald Segretti I don't know whether I would desire a confrontation with him. It would be fascinating, now, after so many years, to just chat with the man. He is a great historical figure. Perhaps if I did, I would have greater insight and feeling towards him as an individual.

33

Mr. Nixon's Legacy

Herbert Klein There is no way that you can erase Watergate; he was the first president to have resigned and then to have been pardoned. It will be there, but my sense of history is that he accomplished so much that his international reputation will be key. No one remembers all the domestic scandals Truman had. The shame is that Nixon will not be recognized for many things he did do domestically. For example, he did more for school integration than anyone else—more than Lyndon Johnson; he did a tremendous amount for civil rights.

James St. Clair No one is going to forget Watergate. It will not disappear. Most people, nowadays, say he is tough; he hangs on; he is coming back. That's the kind of person he is. He's pretty resilient. He hasn't gone into an insane asylum. It was a terrible experience, but he has buckled down.

Leonard Garment Watergate is overstated by a factor of fifty. The hatred of Nixon was ideology triumphant. He had become the symbol of everything that went wrong for the opposition; he was very good at rubbing that in. He had had two very progressive terms as vice-president; he helped get rid of [Senator Joseph R.] McCarthy [R-Wis.]; he got many things together in the form of antidiscrimination enforcement in employment.

Susan Porter Rose In April 1983, Mrs. Nixon invited some staff people up to New Jersey* for lunch. The president came in and was center stage; he

---

* At that time, the Nixons made their home in Saddle River, in Bergen County.

took over. He is a presence; there is no question about that. Here is a brilliant man—maybe the smartest person ever to be president—with ideas in his head that are almost irrepressible. When you peel away Watergate, it will be remembered as a brilliant presidency.

William Rusher He cannot shake the fact that he is the only president of the United States who resigned under fire. Fundamentally, he does not—and, I think, cannot—perceive what we are all doing here. He's not the only one like that, by a long shot, but he became president, so it mattered. He is just another light that failed.

Herbert Brownell In the long run, his successes in the foreign affairs field will predominate. That won't happen for some considerable time; it will take another generation. It will never change until the last reporter who reported on Watergate dies. But look at people like Napoleon, who did so much good—and so much harm. The tendency of history is to select the significant. Watergate has no significance in history; it's a chapter in criminal law; it's nothing, compared to the opening with China. Historians will be much more interested in the positive developments which Nixon is responsible for.

Howard Phillips If the liberals write the history, Watergate will not be a major part of it. Nixon has already been rewritten from the liberal standpoint as a significant foreign policy president who got us out of Vietnam; who opened the door to China; who did nothing to undo anything he inherited from Lyndon Johnson; who gave us Harry Blackmun and others on the Supreme Court who paved the way for abortion on demand. Conservative historians will probably say he was a man who flew his flag under false pretenses; who betrayed his cause; and who was a major disappointment.

George McGovern Watergate will be seen as one of the spin-offs of the Vietnam War; Vietnam will loom as the major tragedy, and Watergate—and the paranoia behind it—was one of the spin-offs from that. I have always thought the two were part and parcel of the same scenario. In my opinion, Vietnam bagged two presidents: Johnson and Nixon. The Watergate break-in itself will be seen as a rather trivial incident; the cover-up certainly won't be excused, but I don't think it is in the same category as the Vietnam War.

Winston Lord Watergate will still be a significant factor. Obviously, as the years go on, it takes on a somewhat more modest profile, and I think that

that process will continue. I think that future historians will look at it as totally unnecessary, that if the original crime—if you want to call it that—had been admitted to by the Nixon administration instead of being covered up, that issue would have been squashed in its infancy. I think the historians' main conclusion will be that it was a lost opportunity, because when this Watergate started, Nixon was well poised, at least in foreign affairs, for a lot of constructive initiatives. He had just won reelection by an overwhelming majority; there was wide support for the agreement with Vietnam; he had opened up to China with great success; he had achieved tremendous progress with the Russians and was beginning to make some progress on the Middle East. So all this offered attractive terrain for further accomplishments by his administration.

Instead, because of increasing preoccupation with Watergate and then the impact on his relations with Congress, the impact on his public support—and therefore his impact as a world leader on foreign policy—began to slow down when it was poised for major success. The relationship with China began to slow down. You could argue that the agreement with Vietnam began to unravel, partly because of Watergate. So Watergate will be looked at as an obviously important event in driving him out of office and slowing down what was a very promising momentum in foreign policy.

Frederic V. Malek I think that he will be judged as an extraordinary strategist and intelligent chief executive who advanced the position of America in the world dramatically but, at the same time, had a fault running through his character that bred a certain amount of paranoia that caused him to resign from office. You have to conclude both of these; you cannot take one without the other.

Richard Kleindienst The judgment of Nixon is always going to be mixed. He has a resiliency; he also has some very strongly held views and attitudes about the country. Personally, he has been able to surmount the bitter days that preceded his resignation and go back to his better self—to the broader Nixon. He is a valuable asset to our country. It takes a man of great fortitude and strength to shuck off the disaster in which he found himself, and still be able to write meaningful books and be available as a counselor to a president. This is the other side of Nixon.

Ronald Ziegler Watergate will be very much a part of the Nixon presidency; so will the fact that he survived, individually and spiritually, with the ability to create, to write, to think, to be involved. But I also think that future historians will see Richard Nixon as being probably the last president who gave the men he surrounded himself with the ability to lead with ideas and be creative in their thoughts as to what would be a better society.

H. R. Haldeman I don't think it's surprising that he'd come back. Watergate dropped a huge black curtain over all that Nixon had accomplished. As time goes on, that curtain very slowly dissolves. Watergate never goes away; it is a permanent factor, but it isn't the only factor in the Nixon presidency. There are a lot of major positives, which have, historically, to become more and more clearly perceived as time puts them into perspective, and you get past the emotional context of Watergate, and the emotional hatreds of the anti-Vietnam [movement]. I had arranged to co-author my book with an eminent, well-known historian, a Pulitzer prize–winning, wonderful writer. The day before he was to come to Los Angeles, where I was then living, he called and sounded like he was in tears; he is a very sensitive guy. He said, "I'm calling to tell you I can't do the book. I realize that I am a historian, not a reporter, and this whole matter is still too emotional to be dealt with by a historian." But that fades, as all emotional things do, and reason comes along into a recognition of the enormous contributions that Nixon did make. He is a brilliant man.

Raymond Price When you get to another generation—to a point where you don't have people with a personal, emotional, or professional interest in the demon theory—he will be ranked among the best of presidents. I think that he will be viewed as one who took a nation in crisis—both domestic and in war—and dealt with that crisis with the most difficult of political circumstances: with the opposition Congress, the violently unpopular war, and the violent discord at home, and made remarkable progress, shaping a new world internationally by redesigning the relationship between the superpowers by bringing China back in the right way and for the better; he made a major contribution to the future peace of the world. He was a great innovator, and the great tragedy is that what he was trying to do was cut off in midstream.

John Ehrlichman He told me one time that he intended to go through his presidential papers by a fireplace; he would go through them one by one, and cull out the things he didn't want history to notice. I suspect he probably intended the same treatment for the [Oval Office] tapes. He was going to destroy things, so that what was left to history would be his selective version.

William Saxbe He is not going to go down as a very great president because of the things he did in Watergate. A lot of his problems were because he surrounded himself with a bunch of Nazis, rather than people who had faced the electorate over the years. He is not a victim—when you are a president, a congressman, in public life, you can't get by by blaming other people. One of the things I don't admire about him is that he did try to blame it on other people. When you have clowns like Haldeman and Ehrlichman and some of the other ding-a-lings in the White House, you can't blame anybody but yourself.

Gerald R. Ford I am not sure that historians in the next century who were not there will understand the turmoil the country was in during the Watergate period; I don't think, thirty years from now, that anybody who goes back and reads things will understand the intensity—and the controversy—that exists. If you weren't there, you don't understand it.

John Dean Someone once said to me, "What is Richard Nixon's presidency without Watergate?" This same person—if someone had asked him the question—would have answered it by saying, "Nixon's presidency without Watergate is Hitler's Reich without the Holocaust. How do you separate them?"

Kenneth Rush The world is worse off because of Watergate. Nixon had achieved so much; he was the only man who could have accomplished rapprochement with China and détente with the Soviet Union. In the Middle East, the October [Yom Kippur] War followed because we had Watergate, so Watergate was one of the catastrophes of our age.

Ben Bradlee It's a truism in American history that the right always has to open new ground, especially against a leftist enemy. I can't think of a Democratic president who could have gone to China. My God, if you ran for alderman in Boston and you said you were for recognizing Red China, they'd beat you. I think his achievements in China were great. I don't rate the Kitchen Debate in Moscow as a great achievement of anything, except that a master of public relations, [William] Safire, managed to commercialize it pretty well.

I think that Nixon was naturally more comfortable in foreign affairs. But I think that Watergate stains his whole presidency. You can't avoid it; you can't write an obit about Willie Sutton* and not talk about robbing a bank.

---

* An often-convicted bank robber of the mid-twentieth century, now deceased.

Alexander Haig I wish that Watergate would be a footnote, but Nixon will always be remembered for it because the event had such major historic consequences for the country: a fundamental discrediting of respect for the presidency—the integrity of the office; a new skepticism about politics, in general, which every American feels to this day. Respect for the institution of the presidency has historically been a vital aspect of the success of this country. We've had scoundrels in that office; we have had saints and mediocre people. But respect for the institution has guaranteed effective government, and when you destroy that, and maul it, it's not a cost-free ride.

Fred Fielding In the next one hundred years, his role in international affairs will be viewed as very significant and [it will be thought] that he was a flawed man who had good domestic ideas, as well, but that his flaws and the collective failure known as Watergate prevented them from coming into being. If there is a legacy, you should consult the Nixon White House Telephone Directory; I found a copy from the period of just before or after the break-in, and if you go down that list of names, you will be amazed at the people who were in the White House at that time—people who have been instrumental over the past twenty years [in American life]; they were staff people that Nixon brought into the government.

I would think that young people would want political service *because* of Watergate. It makes it a lot easier to impress upon people in government that they should cross the t's and dot the i's because you have seen a Watergate; you know what it does to people—and their lives—and how easy it is for people to get into trouble with no venality in their intent.

Samuel Dash My students, who were five years old at the time, know nothing about Watergate. They tell me that their mothers have told them that I had something to do with Watergate, and I have to remind them that I didn't go to jail; that I was asking the questions, not answering them. In time, there is a lot of forgetting and revisionism and maybe when it's looked back on—and particularly as people will look at Richard Nixon—the ultimate record will be different. That is unfortunate, because I really believe that we should have in our history a recollection of a near-miss. I think that it was tragic for Richard Nixon, personally. He was a very able and talented political person. Unfortunately, because of his personality and how he perceived the world around him, he allowed himself to get into a situation, and to have aides who betrayed him. His is a tragic case, but I don't believe that it deserves forgiveness.

Charles Wiggins I don't think the problems of Richard Nixon will go away in just a generation. In short, he will not be remembered for his good deeds with a simple footnote discussing Watergate; he will be remembered, rather, as the president who resigned in the face of Watergate. I think that he has recovered somewhat in public esteem in the years since Watergate, but he has not recovered absolutely. If he were to announce tomorrow to be a candidate for some office—dogcatcher, or governor of New Jersey—the press would jump on him for the Watergate episode, saying that he is unfit. They haven't forgotten yet, and maybe they will never forget; and maybe it's not fair that they forget. This is an event that should be remembered. But I remember Nixon otherwise. I think he is one of the outstanding presidents of the twentieth century.

John Dean I have no animosity toward Richard Nixon. I have tremendous animosity toward those who are trying to pervert history now, either for profit or their own reasons, to exculpate themselves from Watergate. When I see a Bill Clinton calling on Richard Nixon, I think he is a resource. There are not many people who have sat in that office. There are things that Nixon could share with other presidents that could be invaluable to them. The man is not unable. If Clinton were to call on him to ask how to handle Whitewater, I think he might find a better source of advice; if he were to call on him to ask how to handle the dissembling Soviet bloc, Nixon probably has got some pretty good thoughts.

Vernon Walters I think that Watergate will be remembered as a trivial incident. People will say, "How could they have forced the resignation of the president of the United States over an issue like this?" Or, some may say that the president lied to us. Well, if the president told the truth all the time, the stock market would bottom out. You cannot judge the president of the United States by the same rules you judge everybody else by.

James R. Schlesinger The substantive actions of the Nixon administration will be viewed with great regard, particularly in foreign policy. That was Nixon's area of principal concern; he performed exceedingly well in that area. With regard to domestic policy, about which he says little these days, many of the changes in environmental policy and suggestions for welfare reform originated in that period. Then you have the shadow, as it were, of Watergate. But Watergate had less to do with the substantive policies of the administration than with the role of what I call the political side of the house.

Over his thirty years in politics, he had acquired many enemies that were not imaginary—the so-called Nixon haters. Other presidents, who had an easier style, a greater gift for political accomodation, an easier relationship with the press, might well have extricated themselves. Indeed, I believe that to be the case. Watergate may have been the final act of the Vietnam War. Those who were not angry with Nixon as a result of the Jerry Voorhis campaign, or the Helen Gahagan Douglas campaign, or Checkers—the younger people—tended to be angry about the continuation of the Vietnam War. As far as my evaluation is concerned, I always use the story about the Lincoln assassination that goes: "Aside from that unfortunate incident, Mrs. Lincoln, how was the show?"* That is my view of the Nixon presidency. Aside from that unfortunate incident, the show was a quite remarkable one.

---

* A reference to the shooting of President Lincoln as he watched a theatrical performance at Ford's Theatre in Washington, D.C.

Afterword

For the twenty years between his resignation and his death, Richard Nixon struggled assiduously against long odds—and with considerable success—to redefine his image; to repair some of the damage done to his reputation by Watergate; and to ensure that history's judgment of his presidency will center on his accomplishments in the foreign affairs field.

His books, meetings with world leaders, consultations with successors in the presidency including Bill Clinton, and carefully orchestrated schedule of public appearances and media opportunities, all contributed to the goal of putting Watergate and its ancillary events out of sight and out of mind.

The long road back had begun in the hours before his resignation, when he refused the pleas of his longtime associates, H. R. Haldeman and John Ehrlichman, for amnesty from the charges against them. Mr. Nixon's road was made smoother by the pardon issued to him by President Gerald Ford—an act undertaken to enable the new chief executive to get on with the business of government, rather than as an expression of favoritism to his immediate predecessor.

Mr. Nixon's recovery from the trauma of resignation was also aided by the love and care given him by his wife, Pat, children Julie and Tricia, and their husbands, David Eisenhower and Edward Cox. Mr. Nixon also benefitted from the concern of old friends and associates, many of whom treasured communication or contact with their former leader.

In his life after August 9, 1974—as in all the years since his decision to run for Congress in 1946—Mr. Nixon had been at the center of a singular, remarkable, political constellation, one in which his ideas, needs, ambitions, and personality have moved all other considerations into a decidedly lesser role. Along the way, he enjoyed considerable support: initially, from a group of local Orange County businessmen who helped provide the funds required to launch his political career; from his first major political loyalists, Murray Chotiner and Robert Finch; from the *Los Angeles Times*—then as now a potent force in Southern California politics; from Dwight Eisenhower, who selected him as his running mate in 1952, and stayed with him during the dark hours of the Checkers controversy; from his party—which extended its presidential nomination in 1960; from a small band of California and New York associates who refused to allow him to be counted out as a presidential hopeful following the debacle of the 1962 loss to Pat Brown; from the Republican leaders and delegates who gave him one more chance at the brass ring in Miami Beach in 1968; and most of all, from the people of America, who narrowly elected him in 1968 and who presented him with a mandate in 1972.

And it is the people—not his family, not his close friends and political associates, not his party comrades—who had the greatest stake in his presidency and who were most betrayed by his acts of wrongdoing. It was on their behalf that he had sworn on those January days in 1969 and 1973 to uphold, protect, and defend the Constitution of the United States. The judgment of history may well be that Richard Nixon succeeded in fulfilling his domestic and foreign affairs responsibilities, but that he failed to protect the Constitution against himself.

Epilogue

Richard Milhous Nixon died in New York Hospital on the evening of April 22, 1994, five days after suffering a stroke at his home in northern New Jersey.

On the very day he was stricken, Nixon, by then a widower, was still engaged in the most important work of his post-presidential life: the rehabilitation of his personal and political reputation, both of which had been so badly tarnished by the Watergate scandal, culminating in his humiliation and resignation on August 9, 1974.

Pilloried by the media, attacked by Democrats, and, most hurtfully, abandoned by all but the most fervently loyal of his fellow Republicans, and with the specter of impeachment growing inexorably, the thirty-seventh president of the United States had been forced on that hot Washington summer day to relinquish the office he had won by a miniscule margin in 1968 and by a landslide in 1972.

Nixon and his wife, Thelma Catherine, known to all as "Pat"—whose famous "cloth coat" had been instrumental in salvaging his vice presidential nomination in 1952—retreated to California. It was there that Nixon spent the early years of his retirement from the world of elective politics, writing his memoir, as well as a number of other well-received books, and planning his comeback. Later he returned to the East Coast to be near his grown daughters, Julie and Tricia, and their families.

In retirement, Nixon was able to assess the long-term consequences of his political career and the ways in which his actions—first as a congressman, then as a senator, vice president, and, finally, as president—had been instrumental in the shaping of both national and world events. That opportunity had been denied his two immediate predecessors, John Fitzgerald Kennedy and Lyndon Baines Johnson, Kennedy by virtue of his assassination and Johnson due to his death in 1973, only four years after leaving office.

In examining and evaluating the Nixon presidency nearly a decade following his death, two issues loom especially large: Nixon's conduct of foreign affairs and the Watergate affair, including the latter's causes and ramifications. One can only wonder how a leader so adept, even courageous, in dealing with foreign policy issues could have allowed himself and his administration to be embroiled in the tawdry mess of Watergate. Political analysts, historians, and journalists have attempted to answer this question in numerous books, dissertations, and considerable—and continuing—debate, resulting in much speculation but no definite conclusions.

We do know the basic facts about Watergate and have benefited from the availability of a portion of the Nixon White House audio tapes. Many key questions remain unanswered, however, due mainly to the continuing restrictions on the release of many hundreds of hours of additional tapes; the questionable and self-serving testimony offered by Watergate personalities, both before Congress and in later memoirs; and Nixon's evasiveness in his own memoir.

These facts are undisputed: In the early morning hours of June 17, 1972, a team of burglars, later traced to the White House, broke into the headquarters of the Democratic National Committee. It was their third attempt to do so, the two previous ones having failed for a variety of reasons, some of them bizarre. (Another attempt, made on May 28 by the same team that would conduct the June 17 break-in, had been successful.) Once inside the Committee headquarters, the burglers photographed documents and planted wiretaps.

Not that break-ins by operatives related to the Nixon regime were uncommon. Another one had occurred on the Labor Day weekend of the previous year at the Beverly Hills office of Dr. Lewis Fielding, the psychiatrist who had treated Dr. Daniel Ellsberg, the former government official who had given the Pentagon Papers to the *New York Times* and the *Washington Post*.

Almost thirty years since the word "Watergate" entered the public consciousness, we still do not know with certainty the level of Nixon's involvement in that felony, or whether he was even privy to the decision to mount the operation.

If Nixon did have prior knowledge of the break-in, it is difficult to understand his motivation in setting the operation in motion. By the spring of 1972, according to opinion polls and the predictions of professional politicians and objective observers, he appeared to be headed for a relatively easy reelection campaign.

After all, the Democrats did not appear to have an electable candidate. Senator Edward M. "Teddy" Kennedy, once viewed as the inevitable Democratic standard bearer, had destroyed his chance for 1972 three years earlier, on a boozy July night on Chappaquiddick Island. The other Democratic hopefuls, Senators Henry M. Jackson and George McGovern (who would win his party's nomination), while both highly regarded legislators, were not likely candidates to defeat Nixon, who, since his narrow victory in 1968, had solidified his hold on the Republican Party and gained ground with the electorate.

At any rate, once the Watergate break-in became public knowledge, Nixon mounted a cover-up of epic proportions. That act would have resulted in his being named an unindicted co-conspirator had he not been pardoned in September 1974 by his successor, Gerald R. Ford.

In trying to get at the inner Nixon, writers of a spate of articles and books published both before and after his presidency attempted to psychoanalyze him, producing "explanations" of dubious validity.

We do know, however, that Nixon was intent on winning by a huge majority in 1972 so that the notion that he could only win the presidency by a narrow margin would be laid to rest once and for all. Thus an elaborate campaign strategy built around the Committee to Reelect the President was put into motion. It was from this committee and its leadership that most of Nixon's later problems emanated.

We also know that Nixon had engaged in "dirty tricks" during his 1952 campaign for the Senate. Yet he was not alone in doing so. Indeed, the Democrats had bugged Nixon's campaign plane in 1968.

More important for Nixon was his belief that the Eastern establishment, the major print and broadcast media, and the Kennedy family were his natural enemies—the last view notwithstanding his friendship with John F. Kennedy during their years together in the Senate.

Further, in the late winter and early spring of 1972, Nixon still assumed, despite overwhelming evidence to the contrary, that Teddy Kennedy would oppose him in the fall.

Once the Watergate break-in had become public knowledge—due in great measure to the investigative work of two *Washington Post* reporters— Nixon made a series of critical mistakes, the most damaging of which was opting not to immediately acknowledge the participation of Reelection Committee personnel or to apologize for their actions, thus intentionally misleading the public.

Nixon's ineptitude and deception in attempting to bury the issue made

Watergate the defining moment of his presidency. It resonates to this day whenever his political career is discussed.

When the remainder of the Nixon tapes are eventually made public, further light may be cast on the president's role, if any, in ordering the break-in, as well as providing new, and not always flattering, insights into those with whom he conversed. A case in point is a conversation Nixon had with the Rev. Billy Graham, during one of his many visits to the White House, in which the Reverend Graham had made derogatory remarks about Jews. In 2002, with the release of the specific tape of that conversation, Reverend Graham was reminded, to his dismay and horror, of exactly what he had said. (He has since apologized for having made those remarks.) Whatever else additional tapes may reveal, they have the potential of embarrassing scores of prominent people who, in their naiveté, if not ignorance of the taping system, never considered that their words would reach beyond the president's ears.

Of the 2,800 hours of recorded conversations involving Nixon, as of March 2002, 1,779 have been made public. Yet even the release of all the remaining taped material may not provide the answer as to whether Nixon knew in advance of plans for the Watergate break-in. That is because the tape of the conversation Nixon had with H. R. Haldeman on June 20, 1972, just three days after the burglars had been arrested, contains an eighteen-and-one-half minute gap, one that resulted either from a high-level decision to destroy incriminating evidence, or due to a mistake made by the transcriber, the ever-loyal Rose Mary Woods. Whatever the cause of the gap, it may be possible through the use of new technology, unavailable at the time of the original investigation, to reconstruct the missing parts of the conversation. Those hoping either to administer the coup de grace or to exonerate Nixon could well be disappointed to learn that the gap consisted of innocuous conversation, although that would be extremely unlikely.

Although some might conclude that Watergate was a mere blip on an otherwise notable presidency, that issue threatened to overshadow Nixon's foreign policy initiatives and achievements.

Today, for example, we take for granted the U.S. relationship with the People's Republic of China. But before Nixon on February 27, 1972, became the first American president to visit that country—"Red China" in common post–World War II parlance—official contact with that communist regime was considered anathema, a sure path to political suicide.

Nixon himself had been a strong anticommunist, his early political career based largely on that issue. In Congress, he had joined the so-called China Lobby, a loose-knit but highly effective group comprising members of Congress, journalists, and academics who refused to recognize the Chinese government, supporting instead the cause of Chiang Kai-shek and his Nationalist followers. Thus Nixon possessed all the anticommunist credentials needed to convince the conservative right wing of the Republican Party that his opening to China would not result in the sellout of the Nationalist regime that had been established on the island of Taiwan.

In the years since Nixon's revolutionary visit to Beijing, China has become a major trading partner of the United States and many large American corporations have established bases of operations there. In terms of politics and international relations, the United States and China continue to argue over the fate of Taiwan. American officials worry that China may launch an attack there, while the Chinese believe that full normalization of relations cannot occur while the United States remains a strong ally of the Nationalist government.

When viewed from today's perspective, the opening to China—regarded by many historians as the major foreign policy accomplishment of the Nixon presidency—loses some of its luster. In Nixon's view, developing a relationship with the People's Republic had the potential of driving a wedge between the Chinese and Soviet communists. When he sent Secretary of State Henry A. Kissinger on a secret mission to Beijing in 1971, and then went there himself the following February, however, the president could not have predicted that the Soviet empire would collapse two decades later, a momentous happening that would render moot his essential reason for establishing U.S.–China relations.

Regarding the impact of Nixon's Middle East policy, the president could justifiably conclude that his action in resupplying Israel during the 1973 October War and his active involvement in the cease-fire negotiations between Egypt and Israel following the war's end had paved the way for President Anwar Sadat's historic visit to Jerusalem in 1977, as well as to the signing two years later of the Camp David Accords. That in the intervening years Israel and Egypt have experienced a decidedly "cold" peace does not diminish Nixon's accomplishment in bringing together those longtime enemies. Further, the treaty between Egypt and Israel has broken the ground for other Arab nations to reassess their hostile relations with the Jewish State. Thus Jordan and Israel were able to achieve peace in 1991, and the door is now somewhat open to Israel's negotiations with its Lebanese and Syrian neighbors.

While initiating the opening to China and resolving the Middle East conflict were major items of the Nixon agenda, it was the U.S. relationship with the Soviet Union that stood at the center of the president's foreign policy.

There, as with China, Nixon acted in an unexpected fashion: The man who had established his political bona fides with hard-line anticommunism in his first run for the House in 1946, printing his left-wing opponent's record on pink paper, now sought to lessen tensions between the two superpowers by pursuing and facilitating détente, as well as by seeking a reduction in nuclear arms.

At that time, Nixon's policies made much sense. The president was determined to end U.S. involvement in Vietnam—where the North Vietnamese were supplied and otherwise supported by the Soviets—while dealing with the continuing threat posed by the USSR's thermonuclear arsenal. If those goals could be accomplished, Nixon's reputation as a major statesman would be assured.

Today the efficacy of détente can be questioned. In the early 1970s, the Soviet Union was financially strained as a result of its huge defense spending. Further, its leadership was deeply troubled by people's restiveness, both internally and in the other nations of the Soviet bloc. Thus a case can be made that if Nixon had remained firm in his opposition to Soviet rule, the fall of that empire might not have been delayed for almost two decades—the Soviet Union might have imploded much earlier, enabling the United States and its NATO allies to safely reduce arms and military forces. Additionally, had the Soviet Union collapsed at that time, the Soviet incursion into Afghanistan—the ramifications of which continue to preoccupy U.S. policy makers to this day—could have been prevented.

When Nixon took his oath of office on January 20, 1969, his most urgent priority was to deal with the Vietnam situation. On that day, approximately 540,000 U.S. troops were stationed in South Vietnam. Within the next few years, Nixon greatly reduced the American military presence, favoring an air war over confrontation on the ground. At the same time, the administration conducted a series of arduous negotiations with the North Vietnamese, resulting in the cease-fire of January 1973. But Nixon left office without having fulfilled his campaign promise of implementing his plan to end the war. Nor did he achieve his goal of peace with honor.

In fairness to Nixon, it must be said that the president faced formidable obstacles in attempting to resolve the Vietnam conflict, including the intransigence of the South Vietnamese; the issue of the several hundred U.S. prisoners of war; and the disruptive, and highly effective, actions of the antiwar movement.

Whether Nixon could have salvaged South Vietnam had he remained in office for his full second term will never be known. It is difficult to know what measures he could have taken to reverse the course of the war, short of "bombing the North back into the Stone Age."

Nixon was to witness profound changes in Southeast Asia, but did not live to see President Bill Clinton's visits to both Ho Chi Minh City—the former Saigon—and Hanoi, where in recent years American companies have established an important economic presence.

In the almost twenty years between Nixon's resignation and his death, he would witness the passing parade of individuals who had played roles, either for good or for ill, in his presidency. From his vantage points, first in San Clemente and later in Hillside, New Jersey, Nixon would note the deaths of former adversaries Mao Tse-tung, Chou En-lai, Ho Chi Minh, and Leonid Brezhnev, and, in the United States, two public figures who had been instrumental in forcing his resignation, Sam Ervin, head of the Senate Watergate Committee, and John Sirica, the federal judge who had ruled that Nixon would have to surrender the White House tapes. To Nixon's sorrow, he would lose his great friend, former Attorney General John Mitchell, whose funeral procession he led, as well as his close White House associate H. R. Haldeman.

As the years passed, Nixon would also observe the success of many of his former associates in new careers, including Gerald Ford, whom Nixon had chosen to replace Vice President Spiro T. Agnew when, in October 1973, Agnew was forced to resign. Ford went on to serve out what would have been Nixon's second term, only to be defeated in the 1976 presidential election by the Democratic Party's candidate, Jimmy Carter.

Most political specialists believe that President Ford's decision to pardon his predecessor was the major reason for his failure to win election in his own right. And while Ford did lose the popular vote by a significant margin, the election could have gone his way had he won New York's electoral votes. Those who cite the Nixon pardon as having been responsible for Ford's defeat do not take into account his refusal to assist New York City in avoiding a fiscal crisis. Indeed, Ford himself has acknowledged that his refusal, rather than the pardon, had cost him the 1976 election.

In any case, Nixon may have taken some comfort in the fact that Ford and Carter would prove to be transitional presidents, that the nation could not settle for a leader not of his own stature. And Nixon must have been gratified when Ronald Reagan, whose basic political philosophy was rooted in the Republicanism Nixon had championed in his long political career, was twice elected president.

In his nearly twenty years of retirement from public service, Nixon could point with pride to the accomplishments of former associates, for instance,

Henry A. Kissinger, whom Nixon had insisted be kept on as secretary of state by President Ford. Another Nixon cabinet member, George Shultz, who replaced the ousted Alexander Haig, Jr., would serve with great distinction as secretary of state in the Reagan administration. Nixon may have been dismayed, however, at the firing of Haig, who had served as his own chief of staff, from Reagan's cabinet after less than two years of service.

And as the years passed, Nixon may have been both surprised and bemused at the paths taken by several of the major Watergate personalities: G. Gordon Liddy would become, and remains, a popular radio talk show host; Jeb Magruder went on to pastor a large church in Lexington, Kentucky; Charles Colson would found a ministry among prison inmates; and John Dean would become a best-selling author.

On the day Nixon resigned the presidency, Watergate was a huge story, its origins and ramifications not yet fully understood. Today, while many questions remain unanswered, the nation has moved on to other and, perhaps, more important scandals. Surely the Iran-contra affair of the second Reagan term, with its serious foreign policy implications, was of greater magnitude and import than the troubling, but essentially domestic, issue of Watergate.

In assessing Watergate, Nixon's inveterate critics maintain that the scandal was all but inevitable, given the political chicanery and paranoia that characterized Nixon's entire public career, earning him the sobriquet "Tricky Dick." And whatever the extent of the former president's culpability, it was his attitudes, predilections, and prejudices that set the stage for the events known throughout the world as "Watergate."

Nixon's supporters, while not necessarily subscribing to the view that Watergate was a mere "second-rate burglary," maintain that the issue could be viewed in context—that the president's major foreign policy achievements far outweighed the negatives of Watergate.

Despite Nixon's foreign policy accomplishments, however, Watergate will likely loom large for some time to come. When we interviewed Ben Bradlee—one of those most responsible, we believe, for the demise of the Nixon presidency—in his office at the *Washington Post*, he predicted (correctly, as it would come to pass) that Watergate's impact would be apparent in that the first paragraph of Nixon's obituary would mention that he was the only U.S. president forced to resign from office.

More than a decade after Nixon's death, however, while Watergate remains an indelible stain on his record, renewed attention is being paid to the former president's intellectual gifts and diplomatic skills, as well as to his perseverance in making a remarkable political comeback from his devastating defeat in the 1962 California gubernatorial election and winning the presidency six years later.

One cannot conclude a discussion of Watergate without noting its grievous toll on the Nixon family. Who can forget the expression on Pat Nixon's face as she stood at her husband's side during his farewell address on the morning of August 9, 1974?

And about twenty-five years after that terrible day for the Nixons, their daughters, Julie Nixon Eisenhower and Patricia ("Tricia") Nixon Cox, became estranged and didn't speak for five years. The cause of their dispute was whether the privately run Nixon Library should be operated by the Nixon family, Ms. Cox's view, or by a twenty-four-member board of directors, the position of both Ms. Eisenhower and the Nixon Library foundation.

In dispute also was the disposition of $20 million willed to the Nixon Library by the late president's close friend and confidant, Charles ("Bebe") Rebozo. While the Library Foundation did receive $781,000 after Rebozo's death in 1998, the remainder had been frozen and the Foundation sued to receive those funds. In April 2002, a Florida judge ordered the sisters to join the lawsuit. While Ms. Cox wanted the Nixon family to retain control of the funds so that she would be able to use them, in part to bankroll biographies favorable to the late president, Ms. Eisenhower did not. She supported the foundation's position that it should exercise control over the funds—and, by implication, over their father's legacy. The siblings have since reconciled their differences.

As to Nixon's own view, we do know that during his lifetime he moved to exert control over his presidential library, the only facility of its kind not under the jurisdiction of the federal government. In fairness to the late president, it should be said that presidential libraries by their very nature tend to extoll their subjects. In Nixon's case, however, there has been a concerted attempt to depict the events of his presidency, particularly Watergate, in a less negative, and more nuanced, manner than fact would dictate.

Ultimately, it will fall to the public to determine the true Nixon legacy. Aided by the availability of new documentation, as well as by greater candidness on the part of some of the key players (notably Henry Kissinger), the American people may at last have the factual background to make a fair assessment of the Nixon presidency.

As this process continues to unfold, one can only wonder which aspects of the late president's record will dominate the historical record. Will Watergate, the "Enemies List," Kent State, the Christmas bombing of

Hanoi, and Nixon's spiteful—and at times hateful and racist—comments revealed on the tapes gain the upper hand? Or will Nixon be remembered more for détente with the Soviet Union, the opening to China, the reduction in nuclear arms, or his political achievement of twice winning the presidency?

What is certain is that Richard Milhous Nixon will remain controversial, a figure of either adulation or scorn: a singular American politician whose name evokes conflicting emotions when one considers both his love for his nation and his flouting of the Constitution by which it is governed.

Appendix A

THE WATERGATE CRIMES ROSTER

Courtesy of the Nixon Presidential Materials Project

Nixon, Richard M.: Unindicted co-conspirator; pardoned.

Barker, Bernard L.: Pleaded guilty to conspiracy, burglary, wiretapping, and unlawful possession of intercepting devices; sentenced to serve 18 months to 6 years; served 12 months.

Chapin, Dwight L.: Convicted of lying to a grand jury; sentenced to serve 10 to 30 months; served 8 months.

Colson, Charles W.: Pleaded guilty to obstruction of justice; sentenced to serve 1 to 3 years and fined $5,000; served 7 months.

Dean, John W., III: Pleaded guilty to conspiracy to obstruct justice; sentenced to serve 1 to 4 years; served 4 months.

Ehrlichman, John D.: Convicted of conspiracy to obstruct justice, conspiracy to violate civil rights, and perjury; sentenced to serve concurrent terms of 20 months to 8 years; served 18 months.

Gonzalez, Virgilio R.: Pleaded guilty to conspiracy, burglary, wiretapping, and unlawful possession of intercepting devices; sentenced to serve 1 to 4 years; served 15 months.

Haldeman, H. R.: Convicted of conspiracy to obstruct justice and perjury; sentenced to serve 2½ to 8 years; served 18 months.

Hunt, E. Howard: Pleaded guilty to conspiracy, burglary, and wiretapping; sentenced to serve 30 months to 8 years and fined $10,000; served 33 months.

Kalmbach, Herbert W.: Pleaded guilty to violation of the Federal Corrupt Practices Act and promising federal employment as a reward for political activity; sentenced to serve 6 to 18 months and fined $10,000; served 6 months.

Kleindienst, Richard G.: Pleaded guilty of refusal to answer pertinent questions before a Senate subcommittee; sentenced to 30 days and fined $100; sentence suspended.

Krogh, Egil, Jr.: Pleaded guilty to conspiracy to violate civil rights; sentenced to serve 2 to 6 years (all but 6 months were suspended); served 4½ months.

LaRue, Frederick: Pleaded guilty to conspiracy to obstruct justice; sentenced to serve 1 to 3 years (all but 6 months were suspended); served 5½ months.

Liddy, G. Gordon: Convicted of conspiracy, conspiracy to violate civil rights, burglary, and wiretapping; sentenced to serve 6 years and 8 months to 20 years and fined $40,000; served 52 months.

Magruder, Jeb S.: Pleaded guilty to conspiracy to obstruct justice, wiretapping, and fraud; sentenced to serve 10 months to 4 years; served 7 months.

Martinez, Eugenio R.: Pleaded guilty to conspiracy, burglary, wiretapping, and unlawful possession of intercepting devices; convicted of conspiracy to violate civil rights; sentenced to serve 1 to 4 years; served 15 months.

McCord, James W., Jr.: Convicted of conspiracy, burglary, wiretapping, and unlawful possession of intercepting devices; sentenced to serve 1 to 5 years; served 4 months.

Mitchell, John N.: Convicted of conspiracy to obstruct justice and perjury; sentenced to serve 2½ to 8 years; served 19 months.

Segretti, Donald H.: Pleaded guilty to campaign violations and conspiracy; sentenced to serve 6 months; served 4½ months.

Stans, Maurice H.: Pleaded guilty to five misdemeanor violations of the Federal Elections Campaign Act; fined $5,000.

Sturgis, Frank A.: Pleaded guilty to conspiracy, burglary, wiretapping, and unlawful possession of intercepting devices; sentenced to serve 1 to 4 years; served 13 months.

Appendix B

SCHEDULE OF INTERVIEWS

Date	Interviewee	Title/Activity During Nixon Years	Venue
12/16/93	Morris J. Amitay	Congressional aide, Jewish activist	Washington, D.C.
2/15/94	Roy Ash	Chairman, Presidential Advisory Council on Executive Organization; director, Office of Management and Budget	Los Angeles, California
12/3/93	Bobby Baker	Confidant of Lyndon Johnson	Washington, D.C.
10/23/93	Bernard Barker	Participant in Fielding and Watergate break-ins	Miami, Florida
1/8/94	Yuri V. Barsukov	Watergate correspondent/*Izvestia*	Telephone
1/26/94	Richard Ben Veniste	Watergate assistant special prosecutor; chief, Watergate Task Force	Washington, D.C.
1/20/93	Richard Bergholz	Political editor, *Los Angeles Times*	Pasadena, California

Date	Interviewee	Title/Activity During Nixon Years	Venue
11/19/93	Robert Bork	Solicitor general of the United States; acting attorney general	Washington, D.C.
3/1/94	Ben Bradlee	Vice-president, executive editor, *Washington Post*	Washington, D.C.
9/22/93	Herbert Brownell	Former attorney general; Republican Party leader	New York, New York
12/29/92	Stephen Bull	Special assistant to the president	Washington, D.C.
1/21/93	Alexander P. Butterfield	Special assistant to the president	Beverly Hills, California
11/1/93	Dwight Chapin	White House appointments secretary	New York, New York
11/17/93	William Colby	Deputy director of operations; director, Central Intelligence Agency	Washington, D.C.
6/16/93	Charles Colson	Special counsel to the president	Telephone
9/29/93	Archibald Cox	Watergate special prosecutor	Cambridge, Massachusetts
10/18/93	Samuel Dash	Chief counsel and staff director, Senate Watergate Committee	Washington, D.C.
2/13/94	John Dean	Associate deputy attorney general; counsel to the president	Beverly Hills, California

Date	Interviewee	Title/Activity During Nixon Years	Venue
12/16/93	Arnaud de Borchgrave	Correspondent, *Newsweek*	Washington, D.C.
12/17/93	Bui Diem	Ambassador of the Republic of South Vietnam to the United States	Rockville, Maryland
10/22/93	John Ehrlichman	Counsel to the president; assistant to the president for domestic affairs	Atlanta, Georgia
10/27/93	Hermann Eilts	U.S. ambassador to Egypt	Boston, Massachusetts
12/3–12/15/93	Daniel S. Ellsberg	Defendant in Pentagon Papers case	Washington, D.C.
5/25/94	James Farmer	Assistant secretary, Department of Health, Education and Welfare (HEW)	Telephone
2/24/93	Mohammed Fawzi	Former minister of war, Egypt	Cairo, Egypt
1/27/94	Fred Fielding	Deputy counsel to the president	Washington, D.C.
1/20/93	Robert Finch	Secretary of Health, Education and Welfare; counselor to the president	Pasadena, California
11/22/93	Gerald R. Ford	House minority leader; vice-president; president of the United States	New York, New York
11/16/93	Leonard Garment	Special assistant to the president; acting legal counsel to the president	Washington, D.C.

Date	Interviewee	Title/Activity During Nixon Years	Venue
10/29/92	Mordechai Gazit	Director general, Israel Foreign Ministry, Prime Minister's Office	Jerusalem, Israel
1/7/94	Seymour Glanzer	Assistant U.S. attorney, Washington, D.C.; chief, Commercial Crimes Division, U.S. Attorney's Office	Telephone
11/17/93	Marshall Green	Assistant secretary of state for Far Eastern affairs	Washington, D.C.
1/25/94	Alexander M. Haig, Jr.	Military assistant, National Security Council; vice chief of staff, U.S. Army; assistant to the president and chief of staff	Washington, D.C.
1/19/93	H. R. (Harry Robbins) Haldeman	Assistant to the president; White House chief of staff	Santa Barbara, California
3/4/94	Morton Halperin	Staff member, consultant, National Security Council	Telephone
8/23/93	Robert T. Hartmann	Chief of staff to Vice-President, President Ford	Bethesda, Maryland
5/26/94	Richard Helms	Director of Central Intelligence; ambassador to Iran	Telephone
12/29/93	Walter Hickel	Secretary of the interior	Telephone
2/15/94	Lawrence Higby	Assistant to the White House chief of staff	Los Angeles, California

Date	Interviewee	Title/Activity During Nixon Years	Venue
2/23/93	Hafez Ismail	National security adviser to President Sadat	Cairo, Egypt
2/6/94	Jerry Jones	Campaign aide; director, White House Personnel Office; White House staff secretary	New York, New York
2/17/94	David Keene	Deputy assistant for national affairs; assistant for national affairs to the vice-president	Telephone
1/22/93	Herbert Klein	Director of communications for the executive branch	San Diego, California
2/11/94	Richard Kleindienst	Deputy attorney general; attorney general of the United States	Telephone
3/8/94	Philip A. Lacovara	Deputy solicitor general of the United States; special counsel, Watergate Prosecution Force	New York, New York
1/31/94	Frederick C. LaRue	White House consultant; campaign aide	Telephone
11/15/93	G. Gordon Liddy	Treasury Department aide; White House aide; general counsel, Committee and Finance Committee to Reelect the President	Fairfax, Virginia

Date	Interviewee	Title/Activity During Nixon Years	Venue
12/2/93	Winston Lord	Staff member, National Security Council; director, State Department Policy Planning Staff	Washington, D.C.
5/24/94	Jeb Stuart Magruder	Special assistant to the president; deputy director, Committee to Reelect the President (CRP)	Telephone
2/1/94	Frederic V. Malek	Director, White House Personnel Office; deputy director, Office of Management and Budget	Washington, D.C.
2/16/94	Robert Mardian	General counsel, HEW; assistant attorney general, Internal Security Division; deputy director, Committee to Reelect the President	Phoenix, Arizona
1/26/94	George McGovern	U.S. senator, D-S.Dak.; Democratic candidate for president, 1972	Washington, D.C.
12/3/93	Richard Moore	Special counsel to the president	Washington, D.C.
12/16/93	Thomas Moorer	Chief of naval operations; chairman, Joint Chiefs of Staff	Alexandria, Virginia
11/16/93	Robert C. Odle, Jr.	Director of administration, Committee to Reelect the President	Washington, D.C.
1/19/94	Terrence O'Donnell	Assistant to the White House chief of staff	Washington, D.C.
8/17/93	David Packard	Deputy secretary of defense	Palo Alto, California

Date	Interviewee	Title/Activity During Nixon Years	Venue
1/18/94	Howard Phillips	Director, Office of Economic Opportunity	Vienna, Virginia
1/12/94	Raymond Price	Special assistant to the president; special consultant to the president	New York, New York
11/17/93	Robert Reisner	White House aide; assistant to the deputy director, CRP	Washington, D.C.
2/21/94	George Romney	Secretary of Housing and Urban Development	Telephone
11/15/93	Susan Porter Rose	Appointments secretary, the first lady	Washington, D.C.
3/16/94	A. M. Rosenthal	Executive editor, *New York Times*	New York, New York
12/16/93	William Ruckelshaus	Director, Environmental Protection Agency; acting director, FBI; deputy attorney general	Washington, D.C.
2/18/94	Donald Rumsfeld	Director, Office of Economic Opportunity; . counselor to the president; director, Cost of Living Council; ambassador to NATO	Telephone
10/23/93	Kenneth Rush	U.S. ambassador to the Federal Republic of Germany; deputy defense secretary; deputy secretary of state; counselor to the president for economic affairs	Delray Beach, Florida

Date	Interviewee	Title/Activity During Nixon Years	Venue
9/20/93	William A. Rusher	Vice-president and publisher, *National Review*	New York, New York
2/2/94	Donald E. Santarelli	Associate deputy attorney general; administrator, Legal Enforcement Assistance Administration	Telephone
10/1/93	William B. Saxbe	U.S. senator, R-Ohio; attorney general of the United States	New York, New York
3/30/94	James R. Schlesinger	Staff member, Bureau of the Budget; chairman, Atomic Energy Commission; director of central intelligence; secretary of defense	Telephone
1/8/93	Donald H. Segretti	Head of "black advance"	Newport Beach, California
8/12/93	George P. Shultz	Secretary of labor; director, Office of Management and Budget; secretary of the Treasury	Palo Alto, California
1/18/93	Rocco C. Siciliano	Deputy secretary of commerce	Beverly Hills, California

Date	Interviewee	Title/Activity During Nixon Years	Venue
12/3/93	Joseph Sisco	Assistant secretary of state for Near Eastern affairs; undersecretary of state for political affairs	Washington, D.C.
3/4/94	Hugh W. Sloan, Jr.	White House assistant appointments secretary; treasurer, CRP	Telephone
3/1/94	Helmut Sonnenfeldt	Staff member, National Security Council; counselor to the State Department	Washington, D.C.
9/30/93	James D. St. Clair	Special counsel to the president	Boston, Massachusetts
2/15/94	Maurice H. Stans	Secretary of commerce; chairman, Finance Committee to Reelect the President	Pasadena, California
5/24/94	Viktor Sukhodrev	Interpreter to Leonid Brezhnev	New York, New York
2/28/94	William H. Sullivan	Deputy assistant secretary of state for Far Eastern affairs; member of Paris negotiating team; ambassador to the Phillipines	Telephone
3/10/94	Fred Dalton Thompson	Minority counsel, Senate Watergate Committee	Telephone
8/24/93	Vernon A. Walters, Jr.	Lieutenant general, U.S. Army; deputy director, Central Intelligence Agency	Washington, D.C.

Date	Interviewee	Title/Activity During Nixon Years	Venue
8/19/93	Gerald Warren	Deputy White House press secretary	Telephone
1/5/94	William Westmoreland	Chief of staff, U.S. Army	Telephone
3/4/94	Charles E. Wiggins	Member, House of Representatives, R-Calif.; member, House Judiciary Committee	Telephone
1/19/94	David Wilson	Deputy counsel to the president	Washington, D.C.
3/8/94	Bob (Robert) Woodward	Reporter, *Washington Post*	Telephone
1/20/93	James Wrightson	Editor, *Sacramento Bee*	Pasadena, California
10/30/92	Aharon Yariv	Major general, Israel Defense Forces; Chief Israeli negotiator, Cease-Fire Talks	Ramat Aviv, Israel
1/25/94	Ronald L. Ziegler	White House press secretary	Alexandria, Virginia

Appendix C

THE INTERVIEWEES: WHERE ARE THEY TODAY?

Morris J. Amitay served as executive director of the American–Israel Public Affairs Committee. He is the founder and treasurer of the Washington Political Action Committee and writes a regular column on political and foreign affairs. He currently practices law in Washington, D.C.

Roy Ash was chairman and chief executive officer of AM International, vice chairman of the Los Angeles Olympic Organizing Committee, and chairman of the Republican National Committee's advisory council on general government. He pursues business interests in Los Angeles.

Bobby Baker pursues business interests from Washington, D.C.

Bernard Barker served almost thirteen months in prison for his involvement in the Watergate and Fielding break-ins. The U.S. Court of Appeals in Washington, D.C., reversed his conviction for the Watergate break-in, citing the failure of the trial judge to tell the jury that Barker believed the break-in was legal because it had White House approval.

Yuri V. Barsukov is retired and lives in Moscow.

Richard Ben Veniste was a special counsel to the Senate Subcommittee on Governmental Operations. He is the co-author of *Stonewall: The Real Story of the Watergate Prosecution;* was chief minority counsel, Senate Whitewater Committee; and is a partner in the Washington office of Weil, Gotshal, and Magnes.

Richard Bergholz retired as a political writer for the *Los Angeles Times* and lived in Pasadena, California. He died in February 2000.

Robert Bork was Alexander M. Bickel professor of public law at Yale Law School. From 1982 to 1988 he was a judge on the U.S. Court of Appeals for the D.C. circuit. He was nominated as an associate justice of the Supreme Court but his confirmation was denied by the U.S. Senate. He is a senior fellow at the American Enterprise Institute for Public Policy Research in Washington, D.C., and professor of law at Ava Maria School of Law.

Benjamin C. Bradlee was managing editor of the *Washington Post* and served as the newspaper's vice president and executive editor from 1986 to 1991. He is now the *Post's* vice president at large. He is also the author of a memoir.

Herbert Brownell remained an elder statesman of the Republican Party. He published his memoirs and was active in the New York law firm Lord, Day, Lord, Barrett, Smith. He died on May 1, 1996.

Stephen Bull worked for Philip Morris for ten years. In 1991, he became director of government relations at the Washington, D.C.–based U.S. Olympic Committee.

Alexander P. Butterfield was president of California Life Corporation, a financial holding company, and chairman of Armstead and Alexander, a management consulting firm. He lives in Southern California.

Dwight L. Chapin was convicted on two counts of perjury and served nearly eight months in prison for lying to a grand jury about his knowledge of campaign tricks. He published a monthly magazine and worked for United Airlines.

William E. Colby was chief of the CIA's Far East Division as well as the organization's director of Central Intelligence from 1973 to 1976. He was a consultant to corporations and governments and was counsel to the Washington law firm of Donovan, Leisure, Rogovin, Huge and Schiller. He disappeared on his boat on April 27, 1996, and his body was found in the Wicomica River, Maryland, on May 6, 1996.

Charles W. Colson served seven months in prison after pleading guilty to a charge of obstructing justice in connection with disseminating derogatory information on Dr. Daniel Ellsberg. He has written several books, was the winner of the Templeton Prize, and cofounded and is the president of Prison Fellowship, an organization based in northern Virginia that helps to rehabilitate prisoners and ex-convicts.

Archibald Cox was Williston Professor of Law and Carl M. Loeb University Professor at Harvard University, where he is a professor emeritus. He teaches at the Boston University Law School and maintains an office at the Harvard Law School.

Samuel Dash has written two books and served as chairman of the American Bar Association's special committee on criminal justice. He is a professor of law and director of the Georgetown University Criminal Law and Procedure and Appellate Litigation Clinic, in Washington, D.C.

John W. Dean III pleaded guilty to a charge of obstruction of justice and served four months in prison. He is the author of *Blind Ambition* and is a financial consultant in Southern California.

Arnaud de Borchgrave was chief *Newsweek* correspondent from 1964 to 1980. From 1985 to 1991 he served as editor in chief of the *Washington Times* and *Insight* magazine. His many awards include the medal of honor of the World Business Council. He is editor at large at the *Washington Times* and at United Press International, where he was previously president and CEO.

Bui Diem served in the government of South Vietnam and was that nation's ambassador to the United States. He has taught at the Indochinese Institute at George Mason University, Fairfax, Virginia, and is the author of *In the Jaws of History*.

John D. Ehrlichman served a total of eighteen months in prison for conspiracy in the Fielding break-in, as well as for conspiracy, perjury, and obstruction of justice in the Watergate cover-up. He wrote six books, including *Witness to Power*, and served as senior vice president of Law Companies Group, in Atlanta, Georgia. He died on February 14, 1999.

Hermann F. Eilts served as ambassador to Egypt until 1979. He was Distinguished University Professor of International Relations and chairman of the departments of political science and international relations at Boston University, where he is a professor emeritus.

Daniel S. Ellsberg faced federal charges totaling a possible 115 years in prison in connection with the release of the Pentagon Papers. Since the charges against him were dismissed in 1973, he has conducted research, lectured widely, and been an activist in the antinuclear movement. He was one of the organizers of the Mobilization for Survival, and served on the strategy task force of the national nuclear freeze campaign. He has received grants from the John T. and Catherine D. MacArthur Foundation.

James Farmer was an assistant secretary of health, education and welfare under President Nixon. He remained active in the civil rights movement and was Distinguished Professor at Mary Washington College, Fredericksburg, Virginia. He died on July 9, 1999.

Mohammed Fawzi is retired and lives in a Cairo suburb. A large photograph of Abdel Gamal Nasser hangs on his study wall.

Fred F. Fielding was counsel to President Ronald Reagan from 1981 to 1986. He has served on several presidential commissions and was senior legal adviser to the Bush–Quayle campaign in 1992. He is a partner in the Washington law firm of Wiley, Rein & Fielding and served on the Bush–Cheney transition team.

Robert H. Finch has received thirteen honorary degrees; was appointed to the Presidential Clemency Board by President Gerald Ford; was cofounder and is a director of Republican Associates; serves on the boards of the American Assembly, Occidental College, and the Beverly Foundation; and received a U.S. Department of Health and Human Services commendation for leadership in the fight against AIDS. He was of counsel to the law firm Fleming, Anderson & Salisbury, with offices in Pasadena, California. He died on October 10, 1995.

Gerald R. Ford was Republican minority leader of the House of Representatives and became vice president of the United States on December 9, 1973, succeeding to the presidency on the resignation of Richard M. Nixon. He served in that office from August 9, 1974 to January 20, 1977. Since leaving the White House he has served on the boards of several corporations, has lectured in over 175 colleges and universities, and has been active in Republican politics. He is associated with the Betty Ford Center, the Gerald R. Ford Foundation, the Gerald R. Ford Library in Ann Arbor, and the Gerald R. Ford Museum in Grand Rapids, Michigan.

Leonard Garment served as assistant to President Ford, as vice chairman of the Administrative Council of the United States, as U.S. representative to the UN Commission on Human Rights, and as counselor to the U.S. delegation to the United Nations. He has played an active role in the National Endowment for the Arts and the National Endowment for the Humanities. He was managing partner in the Washington law firm Mudge, Rose, Guthrie, Alexander, and Ferdon, and has authored *In Search of Deep Throat* and *Crazy Rhythm.*

Mordechai Gazit has served as director general of Israel's foreign ministry and as that nation's ambassador to France. He has been associated with Hebrew and Tel Aviv Universities and with the American Jewish Committee's Israel office.

Seymour Glanzer has lectured at both the Georgetown University and American University law schools, and at the Catholic University of America. He is a partner in the Washington law firm of Dickstein, Shapiro & Monn.

Marshall Green was ambassador to Australia and coordinator of population affairs at the Department of State. He held the personal rank of career minister and was honorary president of the Japan America Society. He died on June 6, 1998.

Alexander M. Haig, Jr., was a candidate for the Republican Party's nomination for president in 1988. General Haig is the author of three books. He is currently an international business consultant based in Washington, D.C.

H. R. (Harry Robbins) Haldeman spent eighteen months in prison following his conviction for conspiracy, perjury, and obstruction of justice. He later served as senior vice president of the Murdock Development Company and as president of the Murdock Hotels Corp. He was the author of *The Ends of Power* and *The Haldeman Diaries,* and was a consultant to minority group businessmen. He died on November 13, 1993.

Morton H. Halperin was a senior fellow at the Brookings Institution, director of the Washington office of the American Civil Liberties Union, director of the Center for National Security Studies, and a senior associate at the Carnegie Endowment for International Peace. He has authored, coauthored, or edited more than a dozen books. He was a special assistant to the president and senior director for democracy at the National Security Council and director of the

State Department Policy Planning Staff under President Clinton. He is now a senior fellow at the Council on Foreign Relations.

Robert T. Hartmann was counselor, with cabinet rank, to President Gerald Ford. He is the author of *Palace Politics: An Inside Account of the Ford Years* and is a senior research fellow at the Hoover Institution.

Richard M. Helms was deputy director of Central Intelligence and served as CIA director from 1966 to 1973. He was U.S. ambassador to Iran and operated an international business consulting firm. He died on October 22, 2002.

Walter Hickel has been in business in Anchorage, and served as governor of Alaska from 1990 to 1994.

Lawrence M. Higby served in executive positions with Pepsi Cola, Taco Bell, and America's Pharmacy, Inc. He was the senior vice president of Times Mirror Cable TV and executive vice president for marketing at the *Los Angeles Times*. He is COO of a health care company in Southern California.

Hafez Ismail served as Egypt's ambassador to France. After retiring, he lived in Cairo. He died on January 1, 1997.

Jerry Jones served in the Ford White House. He has been active in business ventures in his native West Texas and in New York City.

David Keene served on the staff of Senator James Buckley (R-N.Y.). He worked in the presidential campaign of Ronald Reagan and was national political director for George Bush in 1980. He has played a leadership role in the American Conservative Union.

Herbert Klein wrote *Making It Perfectly Clear.* He was vice president for corporate relations of Metromedia, Inc., and since 1980 has been editor in chief and vice president of the Copley Newspapers, with offices in San Diego, California.

Richard G. Kleindienst pleaded guilty to a misdemeanor charge of refusing to testify accurately before a Senate committee and was fined $100 and given a one-month jail sentence; both were suspended. He practiced law in Prescott, Arizona. He died on February 3, 2000.

Philip A. Lacovara lectured at Georgetown and Columbia University law schools; was chairman of the board of trustees for the Washington, D.C., Public Defender Service; served as president of the Columbia University Law School Alumni Association; was vice president and senior counsel to GE; and was managing director and general counsel to Morgan Stanley and Co. He is currently a partner at Mayer Brown Rowe & Mawe in New York City.

Frederick C. LaRue served five and a half months in prison after pleading guilty to one count of obstruction of justice. He has been a businessman in Mississippi.

G. Gordon Liddy was convicted for participation in the Watergate burglary and for the break-in at the office of Dr. Lewis Fielding. He was sentenced to a six-to-twenty–year prison term, which was commuted by President Jimmy Carter in 1977 after fifty-two months of incarceration. He wrote an autobiography, *Will,* has lectured throughout the country, and is the host of a radio talk show broadcast on more than 170 stations.

Winston Lord was president of the Council on Foreign Relations and served from 1985 to 1989 as U.S. ambassador to the People's Republic of China. He was assistant secretary of state for East Asian and Pacific Affairs in the Clinton administration. He is co-chairman of the International Rescue Committee.

Jeb Stuart Magruder pleaded guilty to conspiracy to obstruct justice, wiretapping, and fraud. He served seven months in prison. He then graduated from the Princeton Theological Seminary. He was the minister of a church in Columbus, Ohio, and was pastor of the First Presbyterian Church of Lexington, Kentucky.

Frederic V. Malek was an executive with the Marriott Corporation and served as president of Northwest Airlines. He has lectured at the University of Southern California and at Harvard University's Kennedy School of Government. He was campaign manager for the Bush–Quayle ticket in 1992, and is chairman of Thayer Capital Partners, in Washington, D.C., and a member of the board of Northwest Airlines.

Robert C. Mardian was convicted of conspiracy in the Watergate cover-up. The conviction was overturned and he was not retried. He operated a construction business in Phoenix, Arizona.

George S. McGovern served in the U.S. Senate until 1981. He was a contender for the Democratic presidential nomination in 1992. He has served as chairman of Americans for Common Sense and has lectured at Northwestern University. He maintains an office in Washington, D.C.

Richard A. Moore was a founder and associate producer of the McLoughlin Group. He was U.S. ambassador to Ireland, 1989–92. He died on January 27, 1995.

Thomas H. Moorer retired as chairman of the Joint Chiefs of Staff in 1974. He directed corporations and was an adviser to the Center for Strategic and International Studies. He received the Forrestal Award and was named to the Naval Aviation Hall of Fame. He is chairman of the board emeritus of the Association of Naval Aviation. He lives in Northern Virginia.

Robert C. Odle, Jr., was acting assistant secretary and deputy assistant secretary at HUD and served as assistant secretary of the Department of Energy, where he was principal adviser to the secretary in the formulation and review of national energy policy. He is a partner in the Washington office of the law firm Weil, Gotshal & Magnes, specializing in trade practices and regulatory law.

Terrence O'Donnell was appointments secretary to President Gerald Ford. He was a member of the administrative council of the United States and is a member of the code committee of the U.S. Court of Military Appeals. He was a partner in the Washington law firm Wiliams and Connolly, and is executive vice president and general counsel of Textron, Inc.

David Packard was chairman of the presidential commission on defense management and a member of the president's council of advisers on science and technology. He was chairman of the board of the Hewlett-Packard Company, with offices in Palo Alto, California. He died on March 26, 1996.

Howard Phillips has written several books and has lectured widely throughout the United States. He is the host of a television program and since 1974 has been chairman of the Conservative Caucus. He was the Constitution Party's candidate for president in 2000.

Raymond Price is the author of *With Nixon*. He collaborated with Nixon on books, worked with the late CBS chairman William Paley, and served in the 1992 Bush campaign. He is president of the Economic Club of New York.

Robert Reisner served in the White House Personnel Office, at OMB, and at HUD. He was a lecturer at the Yale School of Organizational Management. He served in executive positions at the U.S. Postal Service and is an executive manager at PRI WEEFA, Washington, D.C.

George Romney was a candidate for the Republican presidential nomination in 1968. He was a member of the Wayne State Board of Governors from 1979 to 1984. He died on July 26, 1995.

Susan Porter Rose was appointments secretary to First Lady Betty Ford. She served as chief of staff to First Lady Barbara Bush 1981–1989 and 1989–1993, when she was also deputy assistant to the president. She lives in Northern Virginia.

A. M. Rosenthal retired from the *New York Times* in 1988 but wrote a column that appeared regularly on the Op Ed page of the *Times*. He has written two books and over one hundred articles. He has won a Pulitzer Prize, Front Page prizes, and several Overseas Press Club awards. He is now a columnist for the *New York Daily News*.

William Ruckelshaus was senior vice president for law and corporate affairs, the Weyerhauser Company, and administrator of the Environmental Protection Agency. From 1988, he served as chairman of the board and CEO of Browning-Ferris Industries, Inc., based in Houston, Texas.

Donald Rumsfeld was White House chief of staff and secretary of defense in the Ford administration. He then served as chief executive officer, president, and chairman of G. D. Searle & Co., and as chairman and chief executive officer of the General Instrument Corporation. A recipient of the Presidential Medal of Freedom in 1977, he currently serves as secretary of defense in the administration of President George W. Bush.

Kenneth Rush served as ambassador to France from 1974 to 1977. He was chairman of the President's Commission for the German–American Tricentennial and chairman of the Council of American Ambassadors.

William A. Rusher was vice president and publisher of the *National Review* from 1957 to 1988. He has written six books, has appeared on the television program *The Advocates* and written a syndicated column.

Donald E. Santarelli has served, by presidential appointment, on several boards, including the Corporation for Public Broadcasting, the Legal Services Corporation, and the Overseas Private Investment Corporation. He is chairman of the National Committee on Community Corrections and was a partner in the Washington law firm Santarelli, Smith & Carroccio. He is a member of Boll, Boyd & Lloyd.

William B. Saxbe was U.S. ambassador to India from 1975 to 1977. He practiced law in Florida.

James R. Schlesinger was assistant to the president and secretary of energy in the Ford administration. Based in Washington, D.C., he is a counselor at the Georgetown University Center for Strategic and International Studies, and a senior adviser to Lehman Brothers. He is chairman of the board of trustees of the MITRE Corporation.

Donald H. Segretti served a four-and-a-half–month prison term for distributing illegal campaign literature. He practices law in Southern California.

George P. Shultz was executive vice president and vice chairman of the Bechtel Corporation. He served as chairman of President Reagan's Economic Policy Advisory Board and secretary of state from 1982 to 1989. His nine books include *Turmoil and Triumph: My Years as Secretary of State*. He is currently distinguished fellow at the Hoover Institution and chairman of the International Council of J. P. Morgan Chase.

Rocco C. Siciliano was president and CEO of Ticor and chairman and CEO of American Health Properties. He was president of the Dwight D. Eisenhower World Affairs Institute and chairman of the Center for Governmental Studies. He lives in Southern California.

Joseph Sisco served as assistant secretary of state for international organizational affairs, assistant secretary of state for Near Eastern and South Asian affairs, and undersecretary of state for political affairs. He was president and then provost of the American University and a partner in Sisco Associates.

Hugh W. Sloan, Jr., held executive positions at the Budd Company. He is deputy chairman of the Woodbridge Foam Corporation, Troy, Michigan.

Helmut Sonnenfeldt served as a trustee of Johns Hopkins University and is a member of the executive committee of the Council on Foreign Relations. Since 1978, he has been a guest scholar at the Brookings Institution.

Maurice H. Stans was not involved in Watergate. He did, however, plead guilty to violation of laws regulating campaign contributions and paid a $5,000 fine. He served as chairman of the boards of both the Dwight D. Eisenhower World Affairs Institute and the Minority Enterprise Development Advisory Council. He retired and lived in Southern California. He died on April 14, 1998.

Viktor M. Sukhodrev was employed in the Soviet Foreign Ministry and was his country's leading English-language interpreter, serving professionally at summit meetings between seven U.S. presidents and Soviet leaders. He was special assistant to the secretary general of the United Nations and served in the UN Office of General Assembly Affairs. He retired in 2001.

William H. Sullivan was head of the Interdepartmental Task Force on Vietnam and special assistant to the secretary of state. He served as ambassador to Laos, the Philippines, and Iran and was a member of the U.S. negotiating team at the Paris peace talks on Vietnam. He was president of the American Assembly from 1979 to 1986. He is a member of the American Academy of Diplomacy.

Fred Dalton Thompson has been involved in the private practice of law and has appeared as an actor in seventeen films and the television show *Law and Order*. He was a Republican senator from Tennessee from 1994 to 2000.

Vernon A. Walters, Jr., retired as a lieutenant general of the U.S. Army. He was senior adviser to the secretary of state; ambassador at large, 1981–85; U.S.

permanent representative to the UN, 1985–89; and ambassador to the Federal Republic of Germany, 1989–91. He died on February 10, 2002.

Gerald Warren was deputy press secretary to President Gerald Ford, 1974–75. He was managing editor and then editor of the *San Diego Union*.

William Westmoreland retired as a four-star general in the U.S. Army. He initiated unsuccessful libel action against CBS over that network's coverage of a Vietnam-related story. He lives in South Carolina.

Charles E. Wiggins practiced law in Los Angeles and San Francisco following his service in the 90th to 95th Congresses as a Representative from the 25th and 39th districts of California. He was a judge of the U.S. Court of Appeals for the Ninth Circuit, in Reno, Nevada. He died on March 2, 2000.

David Wilson served on the staff of the Cost of Living Council and at the Federal Energy Office. He practices law in Washington, D.C.

Bob (Robert) Woodward won the Pulitzer Prize, with Carl Bernstein, for their reporting on Watergate. He and Mr. Bernstein coauthored *All the President's Men* and *The Final Days*. Mr. Woodward's other books include *The Brethren* (with Scott Armstrong); *Wired; Veil;* and *Shadow: Five Presidents and the Legacy of Watergate*. He is an assistant managing editor of the *Washington Post*.

James Wrightson was editorial writer and associate editor of the *Sacramento Bee*. He opened that newspaper's Los Angeles bureau. He retired in April 1885.

Aharon Yariv was a Labor Party member of the Israeli Parliament and served in two cabinet-level positions. He was the founder and director of the Jaffe Center for Strategic Studies at Tel Aviv University. He died on May 7, 1994.

Ronald L. Ziegler was president of the National Association of Truck Stop Operators and the president and CEO of the National Association of Chain Drug Stores. He was active in AIDS education and served on the national advisory board of the University of Oklahoma. He died on February 10, 2003.

Index

The Authors

Deborah Hart Strober was for many years a journalist with the *New York Jewish Week*. Her husband, Gerald S. Strober, is the author of several books, including *American Jews: Community in Crisis* and *Billy Graham: His Life and Faith*. Together they have compiled four oral histories, *"Let Us Begin Anew": An Oral History of the Kennedy Presidency; Nixon: An Oral History of His Presidency; Reagan: The Man and His Presidency;* and *The Monarchy: An Oral Biography of Elizabeth II*. The Strobers live in New York City.